ROBERT CURTHOSE
DUKE OF NORMANDY

c. 1050–1134

The career of Robert Curthose, William the Conqueror's eldest son and duke of Normandy from 1087 to 1106, has long merited detailed reappraisal.. Robert's relationship with members of his family shaped the political landscape of England and Normandy for much of the late eleventh and early twelfth centuries, and this new biography firmly locates the duke's career in the social, cultural and political context of the times.

Twice driven into exile, Robert defeated his father in battle and eventually succeeded to the duchy of Normandy, although the throne of England was seized by his brothers William Rufus and Henry. For twenty years Robert successfully defended Normandy, developing policies to counter the vastly superior English resources at the disposal of his brothers. His leading role in the success of the First Crusade (1095–99) also made him one of the most famous warriors of his age: he returned to Western Europe in 1100 a chivalric hero with a reputation that stretched from Scotland to Palestine.

William Aird's biography offers a fresh assessment of the dynamics of Norman political culture and presents a critique of medieval rulership. For much of his life, Robert's presence influenced the actions of the kings of England and even after his incarceration by Henry I (from 1106 until his death in 1134) his son William Clito (d. 1128) continued the fight. Robert Curthose is returned to centre stage in the bloody drama of the period, a drama which has been so long dominated by accounts from a royal and English perspective.

Dr WILLIAM M. AIRD is Lecturer in Medieval History, Cardiff University.

ROBERT CURTHOSE
DUKE OF NORMANDY

c. 1050–1134

William M. Aird

THE BOYDELL PRESS

First published 2008
The Boydell Press, Woodbridge
Reprinted in paperback 2011

ISBN 978 1 84383 310 9 hardback
ISBN 978 1 84383 660 5 paperback

The Boydell Press is an imprint of Boydell & Brewer Ltd
PO Box 9, Woodbridge, Suffolk IP12 3DF, UK
and of Boydell & Brewer Inc.
668 Mt Hope Avenue, Rochester, NY 14620, USA
website: www.boydellandbrewer.com

A CIP record for this book is available
from the British Library

Papers used by Boydell & Brewer Ltd are natural, recyclable products
made from wood grown in sustainable forests

Printed in Great Britain by
CPI Antony Rowe, Chippenham and Eastbourne

CONTENTS

For my mother June
and in memory of my father
William Aird (1930–2001)

ACKNOWLEDGEMENTS

The story of Robert Curthose has fascinated me since I first read of his participation in the First Crusade. It seemed odd to me that a man who had taken a leading role in the armed pilgrimage to Jerusalem should not have succeeded his father as king of England in 1087. Why was it that England never had a King Robert? Although postgraduate research at Edinburgh took me in another direction, it was always my intention to return to the subject and produce a biography of Robert of Normandy. In recent years there has been renewed interest in the sons of William the Conqueror and new biographies have appeared of William Rufus and Henry I. A biography of Robert Curthose appeared in 1920 but, largely I suspect because he never became king of England, he has since been comparatively neglected. But Robert occupied a central place in the policies of his father and brothers, and a study of his career offers the chance to examine the medieval connections between Normandy and England from the other side of La Manche.

This book has taken longer to write than I intended. The British university system continues to change and, as under-resourced expansion progresses, time for research is hemmed in closer by the demands of teaching and administration. Increasingly, the need for supportive colleagues has become apparent and I must thank mine here in the School of History and Archaeology at Cardiff University for their encouragement. For a number of years now they have heard more about Robert Curthose than I'm sure they ever thought they would need to hear. I would particularly like to thank Peter Coss, and, for their advice on aspects of the First Crusade, Peter Edbury and Helen Nicholson. Chapters from the book have been read in draft by Peter Coss, Peter Edbury and David Bates and I am especially grateful to Judith Green and Emma Mason, who read most of the book in draft and made detailed and helpful comments, which saved me from many errors. Any blunders that remain are the author's. My thanks are also due to Frances, who not only accompanied me to Apulia in search of Conversano but also read several chapters and saved me from some infelicities of expression. The first draft of the book was completed with the assistance of the Arts and Humanities Research Board's Research Leave scheme. Colleagues in the Cardiff University Arts and Humanities Library, especially Helen d'Artillac-Brill, have helped greatly in obtaining materials. Particular thanks are due to Ian Dennis for the maps. Over the years, my students have been very patient with an approach to Anglo-Norman history which focused, perhaps surprisingly for them, on the career of the Conqueror's eldest son.

ACKNOWLEDGEMENTS

Sections of this book were first presented as research papers at a number of conferences and colloquia and I would like to thank those who invited me to speak. In particular, I am grateful to Björn Weiler and colleagues from the UK, Europe and the USA involved in the British Academy funded Research Network on Political Culture. I would also like to thank colleagues and students who attend the annual University of Wales Gregynog Medieval Colloquium, which over the years has provided a welcome opportunity for me to try out some ideas. A version of Chapter 5 was presented at the 'Crusades Seminar' at the Institute for Historical Research and I would like to thank Jonathan Phillips for the invitation to speak. I would also like to thank colleagues and friends from the annual Battle and Haskins Society Conferences for discussing aspects of Robert's career with me and for generously allowing me access to their work, often in advance of publication. In particular, my thanks to Richard Sharpe, Pauline Stafford, Stephen Church, Marjorie Chibnall, Elisabeth M.C. van Houts, David Wyatt, Christopher Harper-Bill, John Gillingham, Chris Lewis, Susan B. Edgington, Graham Loud, Paul Dalton, Matthew Strickland, Ann Williams, Katherine Keats-Rohan, David Roffe, Hirokazu Tsurushima, Stephen Morillo, Bruce O'Brien, Steven Isaacs, Malcolm John Rebennack, Richard Abels, Mary Frances Giandrea and Robin Fleming. I have tried to acknowledge in the appropriate place specific thanks for references and help but I hope that anyone I have omitted will accept my apologies – it wasn't intentional.

I would also like to thank those who attended the colloquium at Tinchebray in September 2006 and politely suffered my attempts to deliver a paper en français: Judith Green, Kathleen Thompson, Richard Barton, Matthew Bennett and Hugh Doherty. My thanks are also due to Cathy Molinaro of the School of European Studies at Cardiff University for her assistance with the translation of my paper and for greatly improving my French pronunciation. The advice and assistance of Véronique Gazeau, Pierre Bauduin and their colleagues in the Centre de Recherches Archéologiques et Historiques Médiévales at the Université de Caen Basse-Normandie made my research visits to Normandy especially rewarding. I am also grateful to Heather Perry for accompanying me to obscure historical sites along the Norman frontier. At Edinburgh University I was fortunate to be taught by lecturers who have since become good friends and I would like to thank for their continuing encouragement Tony Goodman, Tom Brown and Michael Angold.

In writing about Robert's career, it has become clear how important family and friendships are. Many have been generous with their encouragement, especially during some difficult times. The following have helped perhaps more than they know: Rab Thomson, John Keenan, Charles Ogilivie, Max Johnson, Peter Fowlie, Niall Joss, Syd Reid, Brian Spencer, Neil Hanley, Kenny McNally, Stewart Normand, Donald MacFarlane, Norman MacLeod, Bill Jones, Simon Roles, Paul Herring, Dave Hounsell and Mark Sweet.

To Caroline Palmer and her colleagues at Boydell and Brewer Ltd I owe a very great debt for their patience and encouragement. As if the burden of supporting Norwich City was not enough, Caroline has had to deal with the present author's persistent prevarication.

My mother June has always encouraged me in whatever I have attempted. My sister Rachel and her family, Paul, Ben, Becky and Victoria, are also always ready with their support. It is a great sadness to me, however, that my father, Bill Aird, did not live to see the completed work. My father always had a great belief in the boundless potential of human beings. He was also rightly critical of the motives of those who desire to wield power over their fellows.

This book is dedicated in his memory.

Cardiff, 28 April 2008

ABBREVIATIONS

AA	*Albert of Aachen,* Historia Ierosolimitana. *History of the Journey to Jerusalem,* ed. and trans. Susan B. Edgington (Oxford, 2007)
Actus Pontificum	*Actus Pontificum Cenomannis in Urbe Degentium,* ed. G. Busson and A. Ledru, Société des Archives Historiques du Maine (Le Mans, 1901)
AHR	*American Historical Review*
AN	*Annales de Normandie*
Ann. Mon.	*Annales Monastici,* ed. H.R. Luard, 5 vols., Rolls Series (London, 1864–9)
ANS	*(Proceedings of the Battle Conference on) Anglo-Norman Studies*
ASC, D	*The Anglo-Saxon Chronicle, A Collaborative Edition, Volume 6, MS. D,* ed. G.P. Cubbin (Cambridge, 1996)
ASC, E	*The Anglo-Saxon Chronicle, A Collaborative Edition, Volume 7, MS. E,* ed. Susan Irvine (Cambridge, 2004)
ASE	*Anglo-Saxon England*
Bates, *Acta*	D. Bates, ed., *Regesta Regum Anglo-Normannorum. The Acta of William I (1066–1087)* (Oxford, 1998)
BIHR	*Bulletin of the Institute of Historical Research*
BSAN	*Bulletin de la Société des Antiquaires de Normandie*
CCCM	Corpus Christianorum Continuatio Mediaevalis
DNB	*Dictionary of National Biography*
EHR	*English Historical Review*
Ep.	*Epistola* (letter)
Fauroux	*Recueil des actes des ducs de Normandie (911–1066),* ed. Marie Fauroux, Mémoires de la Société des Antiquaires de Normandie, 36 (Caen, 1961)
FC	*Fulcher of Chartres, Historia Hierosolymitana,* ed. H. Hagenmeyer (Heidelberg, 1913)
GF	*Gesta Francorum et aliorum Hierosolimitanorum,* ed. Rosalind Hill (London, 1962)
GN	*Guibertus abbas S. Mariae Nogenti, Dei Gesta per Francos,* ed. R.B.C. Huygens, CCCM, 127A (Turnhout, 1996). Translation in *The Deeds of God through the Franks. A Translation of Guibert de Nogent's* Gesta Dei per Francos, trans. R. Levine (Woodbridge, 1997)

HH   *Henry of Huntingdon*, Historia Anglorum. *The History of the English People*, ed. and trans. Diana Greenway (Oxford, 1996)

HN   *Eadmeri Historia Novorum in Anglia*, ed. M. Rule, Rolls Series (London, 1884). Translation of Books I–IV in *Eadmer's History of Recent Events in England*. Historia Novorum in Anglia, trans. G. Bosanquet (London, 1964)

HSJ   *The Haskins Society Journal*

Hyde Chron.   *Liber Monasterii de Hyda*, ed. E. Edwards, Rolls Series (London, 1866)

JEH   *Journal of Ecclesiastical History*

JMH   *Journal of Medieval History*

Malaterra   *De Rebus Gestis Rogerii Calabriae et Siciliae Comitis auctore Gaufredo Malaterra*, ed. E. Pontieri, Rerum Italicarum Scriptores, 2nd ed. (Bologna, 1927–8). Translated in *The Deeds of Count Roger of Calabria and Sicily and of his Brother Duke Robert Guiscard, by Geoffrey Malaterra*, trans. K.B. Wolf (Ann Arbor, MI, 2005)

MGH   *Monumenta Germaniae Historica*, ed. G.H. Pertz et al. (Hanover, 1826–)

OV   *The Ecclesiastical History of Orderic Vitalis*, ed. and trans. Marjorie Chibnall, 6 vols. (Oxford, 1969–80)

PBA   *Proceedings of the British Academy*

PL   *Patrologiae cursus completus, series Latina*, ed. J-P. Migne, 221 vols. (Paris, 1844–64)

P&P   *Past and Present*

RC   'Gesta Tancredi in expeditione Hierosolymitana auctore Radulfo Cadomensi', in *RHC Occ.*, III, pp. 587–716. Translated in *The* Gesta Tancredi *of Ralph of Caen. A History of the Normans on the First Crusade*, trans. B.S. Bachrach and D.S. Bachrach (Aldershot, 2005)

Regesta   *Regesta Regum Anglo-Normannorum 1066–1154*, vol. i, *Regesta Willelmi Conquestoris et Willelmi Rufi, 1066–1100*, ed. H.W.C. Davis (Oxford, 1913); vol. ii, *Regesta Henrici Primi 1100–1135*, ed. C. Johnson and H.A. Cronne (Oxford, 1956)

RHC   *Recueil des historiens des croisades*, ed. Académie des Inscriptions et Belles-Lettres, 16 vols. in 17 (Paris, 1841–1906)

RHC, Occ.   *RHC historiens occidentaux*, 5 vols. (Paris, 1844–95)

RHF   *Recueil des historiens des Gaules et de la France*, ed. M Bouquet, rev. L. Delisle, 24 vols. in 25 (Paris, 1840–1904)

s.a.   *sub anno*

SHR   *Scottish Historical Review*

Swanton   *The Anglo-Saxon Chronicle*, trans. and ed. M.J. Swanton (London, 1996)

TRHS   *Transactions of the Royal Historical Society*

VCH   *Victoria County History*

WM, *GR*   *William of Malmesbury,* Gesta Regum Anglorum. *The History of the English Kings,* Vol. I, ed. and trans. R.A.B. Mynors (†), completed by R.M. Thomson and M. Winterbottom (Oxford, 1998)

WP   *The Gesta Guillelmi of William of Poitiers,* ed. and trans. R.H.C. Davis and Marjorie Chibnall (Oxford, 1998)

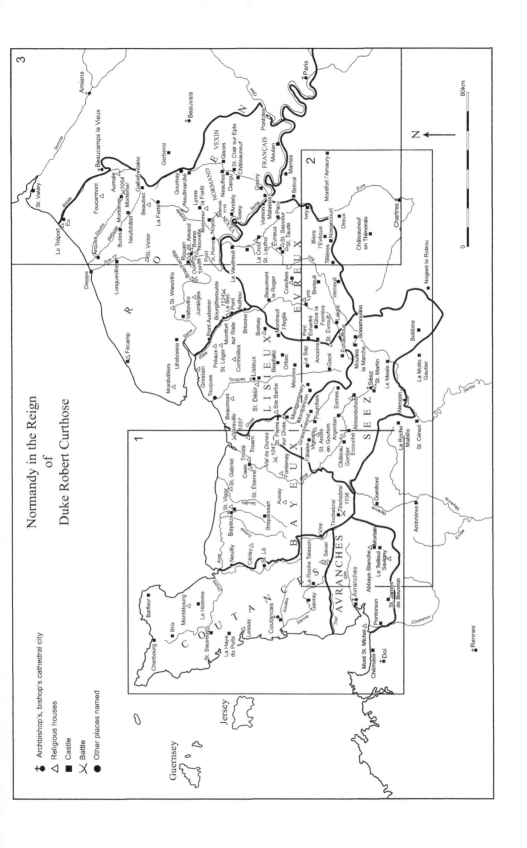

Normandy in the Reign
of
Duke Robert Curthose

† Archbishop's, bishop's cathedral city
△ Religious houses
■ Castle
✕ Battle
● Other places named

N

0   80km

3

2

1

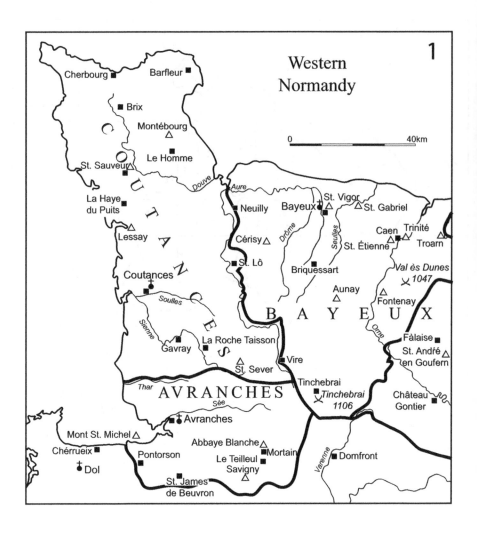

Southern Frontier

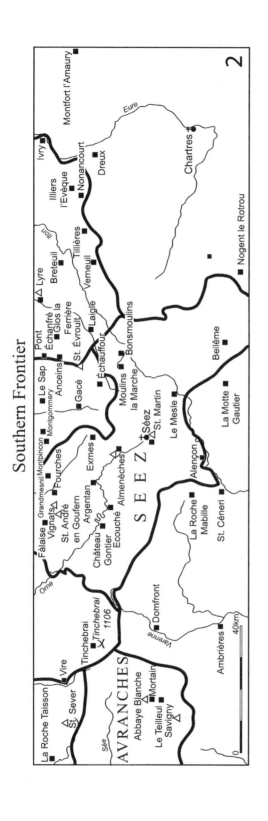

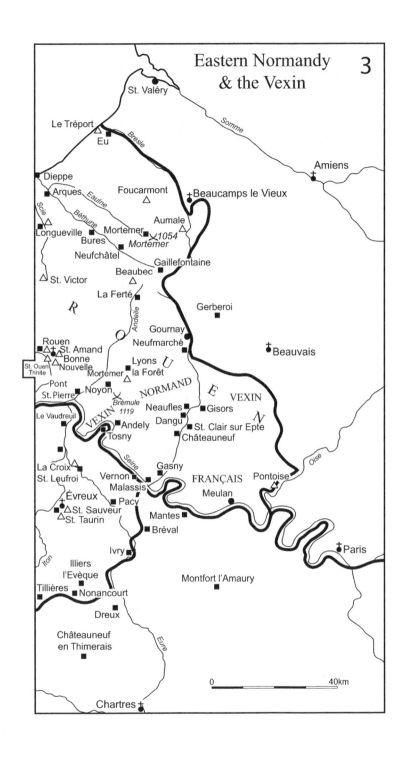

Eastern Normandy & the Vexin

3

St. Valéry

Le Tréport

Eu

Somme

Bresle

Amiens

Dieppe

Arques

Foucarmont

Beaucamps le Vieux

Eaulne

Béthune

Aumale

Longueville

Mortemer

1054

Bures

Mortemer

Scie

Neufchâtel

Gaillefontaine

St. Victor

Beaubec

La Ferté

Gerberoi

R

Andelle

O

Gournay

Neufmarché

Beauvais

Rouen

St. Amand

U

St. Ouen
Trinité

Bonne
Nouvelle

Lyons
la Forêt

E

VEXIN

Mortemer

NORMAND

Pont
St. Pierre

Noyon

*Brémule
1119*

Neaufles

Gisors

N

VEXIN

Le Vaudreuil

Dangu

St. Clair sur Epte

Andely

Châteauneuf

Tosny

Seine

Gasny

Oise

La Croix
St. Leufroi

Vernon

FRANÇAIS

Pontoise

Malassis

Évreux

Pacy

Meulan

St. Sauveur

Mantes

St. Taurin

Bréval

Iton

Ivry

Paris

Illiers
l'Evèque

Montfort l'Amaury

Tillières

Nonancourt

Dreux

Châteauneuf
en Thimerais

Eure

0   40km

Chartres

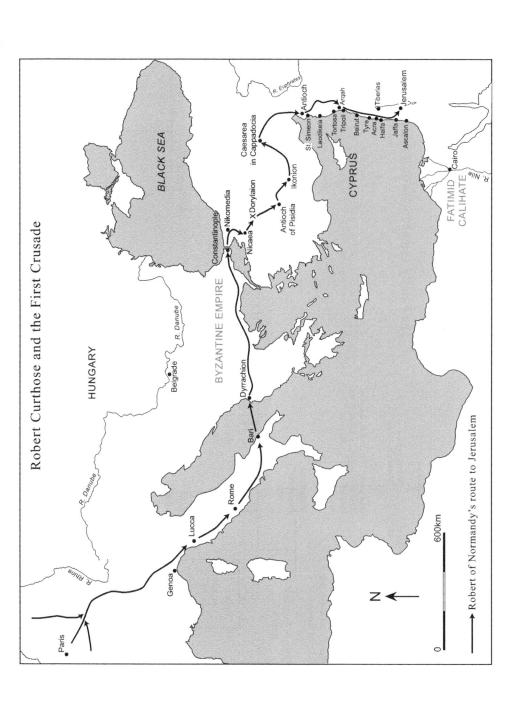

Robert Curthose and the First Crusade

HUNGARY

BYZANTINE EMPIRE

BLACK SEA

FATIMID
CALIHATE

CYPRUS

R. Rhine
R. Danube
R. Danube
R. Euphrates
R. Nile

Paris
Genoa
Lucca
Rome
Bari
Belgrade
Dyrrachion
Constantinople
Nikomedia
Nicaea
Dorylaion
Ikonion
Antioch
of Pisidia
Caesarea
in Cappadocia
Antioch
St. Simeon
Laodikeia
Tortosa
Arqah
Tripoli
Beirut
Tyre
Acra
Haifa
Jaffa
Ascalon
Tiberias
Jerusalem
Cairo

N

0   600km

Robert of Normandy's route to Jerusalem

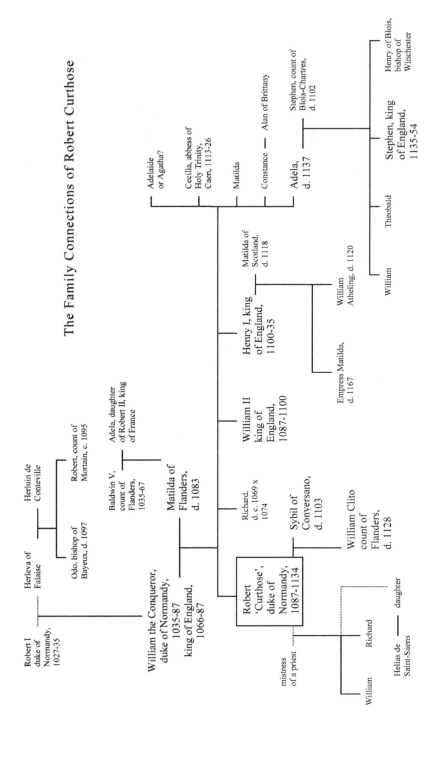

The Family Connections of Robert Curthose

INTRODUCTION

The Hero of Ascalon

A T dawn on Friday 12 August 1099 an army from Western Europe drew up its battle lines in a valley near the town of Ascalon south of Jerusalem.[1] The battle of Ascalon required another supreme effort of will and physical endurance from the Franks who had left their homes three years before.[2] In a hard fought engagement, the Egyptians were routed and forced to abandon their plans to recapture Jerusalem.

One incident at Ascalon stands out as the epitome of the courage that the Franks had shown throughout the expedition to the Holy Land. Robert, duke of Normandy, the eldest son of William the Conqueror, made a daring direct attack on the Egyptian command position. Robert, a short stocky man in his late forties, drove towards the Vizier's standard-bearer and delivered him a mortal wound. Robert's decision to target the heart of the enemy lines was risky, but the sheer audacity of the charge led to panic and began the rout of the Egyptians.

In the year 1100, there can have been few men more famous in north-western Europe than Robert of Normandy. His participation in the First Crusade had given him a leading role in the greatest chivalric adventure of his day, an achievement which overshadowed his father's victory at Hastings in 1066. However, despite the *kudos* that came with the status of a successful 'Jerusalemite', by the end of 1106 Robert was languishing in a castle gaol, a prisoner of his younger brother King Henry I of England. Henry had defeated Robert at Tinchebray in southern Normandy and the hero of Ascalon remained a prisoner for the rest of his long life. He died in Cardiff, South Wales twenty-eight years later in February 1134.

---

[1] Rosalind Hill, ed., *Gesta Francorum et aliorum Hierosolimitanorum. 'The Deeds of the Franks and the Other Pilgrims to Jerusalem'* (London, 1962), p. 95.
[2] J. France, *Victory in the East. A Military History of the First Crusade* (Cambridge, 1994), pp. 360–5.

A Medieval Life

This is a biography of Robert nicknamed 'Curthose', who ruled as duke of Normandy from 1087 until 1106.[3] He lived into his eighties and his long and eventful life offers the chance to examine one of the most dramatic periods in the history of Western Europe from a prominent individual's point of view.[4] The writing of a biography of a medieval individual might seem at the outset to be an impossible task. Roger Collins, writing about the famous Frankish emperor, noted that '[i]t is not really possible to write a biography of Charlemagne, in the sense of a work that uncovers its subject's personal hopes, fears, aims, ambitions, phobias and foibles, and tries to explain what he thought, rather than something of what he did'.[5] Medievalists excuse the limitations of their biographical studies by suggesting that no biography 'in the modern sense' can be written or they point out the impossibility of writing 'a conventional biography' about medieval people.[6] Historians and biographers writing in the medieval period tended to concentrate on the deeds of prominent members of the secular and ecclesiastical elites. This suggests that there exists consensus as to the standard form and content of a historical biography.[7]

Biography is a very popular but also maligned genre of historical writing. Many modern historians reacting against nineteenth-century studies of 'Great Men', and preoccupied by the search for the underlying structures of human societies, are suspicious of the biographical approach to the past.[8] There is a revealing passage in Jacques Le Goff's memoirs, in which Le Goff, who is closely associated with the *Annales* school's structuralist approach to the past, explains his decision to write a biography of Louis IX of France as a search for a 'globalising figure'.[9] Yet biography offers the prospect of understanding past

---

3   The nickname, *Robelinus Curta Ocrea*, which might be rendered 'Little Bobby Short-Pants', is reported by William of Malmesbury; see *William of Malmesbury*, Gesta Regum Anglorum. *The History of the English Kings*, ed. and trans. R.A.B. Mynors, R.M. Thomson and M. Winterbottom (Oxford, 1998), I, pp. 700–1. I am grateful to Stephen Church for the suggested translation of Robert's nickname.

4   For an introduction to the eleventh and twelfth centuries, see R. Bartlett, *The Making of Europe. Conquest, Colonization and Cultural Change, 950–1350* (Harmondsworth, 1993) and *idem, England under the Norman and Angevin Kings, 1075–1225* (Oxford, 2000).

5   R. Collins, *Charlemagne* (Basingstoke, 1998), viii.

6   Eileen Power, *Medieval People* (London, 1924), vii, noted that '[i]n point of fact there is often as much material for reconstructing the life of some quite ordinary person as there is for writing a history of *Robert of Normandy* or of Philippa of Hainault; and the lives of ordinary people so reconstructed are, if less spectacular, certainly not less interesting' [my italics].

7   On biography see, for example, R. Gittings, *The Nature of Biography* (Seattle, 1978); L. Edel, *Writing Lives. Principia Biographica* (New York, 1984); Ira B. Nadel, *Biography. Fiction, Fact and Form* (London, 1984); P. France and W. St Clair, eds., *Mapping Lives. The Uses of Biography* (Oxford, 2002); Catherine N. Parke, *Biography. Writing Lives* (New York and London, 2002); L.E. Ambrosius, ed., *Writing Biography. Historians and their Craft* (Lincoln, NB, 2004); N. Hamilton, *Biography. A Brief History* (Cambridge, MA, 2007).

8   Sarah Hamilton, 'Review Article: Early Medieval Rulers and their Modern Biographers', *EME*, 9 (2000), pp. 247–60.

9   See J. Le Goff, *My Quest for the Middle Ages*, trans. R. Veasey (Edinburgh, 2003), pp. 96–7; translated from J. Le Goff, *A la recherche du Moyen Age*, with the collaboration of J.-M. de Montremy

societies from the inside. Biography's popularity reflects the desire to understand some fundamental questions about the individual's place in the world
and his or her ability to influence the course of events and respond to change.
The chronology imposed on biography by the life course also highlights the
individual's relationship with longer-term changes in society: some welcomed
change and some resisted it. An appreciation is needed for the often chaotic
nature of human lives and without an acknowledgement of the effect of the
contingent, biography loses immediacy and the individuals portrayed tend to
behave like automata reacting in a predetermined manner.

The character traits of individuals are necessary agents of the historical
process. Rationality does not always guide an individual's deeds and they can
be as much the result of an emotional or instinctive reaction as of a carefully
weighed response. Therefore, in order to understand the opportunities open
to individuals in past societies, historical context is needed and some idea
of how far the subject could manoeuvre within, or was constrained by, the
conventions and mental outlook of the society into which they were born.[10]

Biographers aim to present a rounded representation of a 'living' subject,
with some indication of character and the inner life of the man or woman,
rather than merely an account of their public deeds.[11] To a degree, the quantity of source material, whether too much or too little, is always a problem
for the biographer. However much evidence survives, the historical biographer is called upon to make a selection and to understand the biases and
problems inherent in those sources. Biographers of modern subjects often
have access to vast collections of personal and private papers and, on the face
of it, this would seem to be a boon not enjoyed by those whose interests lie
in the medieval period. Yet it is recognised that these private papers, while
promising to reveal the inner thoughts and motivations of individuals, were
often consciously edited by those individuals with a view to influencing future
biographies. Even that most personal of documents, the diary or journal, was
written with one eye on the future. Other individuals destroyed personal
documents, denied access to private papers or ensured their destruction.[12]
This happened in the medieval period as well. For example, St Anselm, archbishop of Canterbury (1093–1109) forbade his companion Eadmer from
completing the *Vita* he had begun.[13]

The life-course is a process involving psychological as well as physical

---

(Paris, 2003), p. 133: 'La biographie ne m'intéresse pas en soi. Je suis ici Bourdieu, qui a parlé de
l'illusion biographique. La biographie ne me retient que si je peux – ce fut le cas pour saint Louis
– réunir autour du personnage, un dossier qui éclaire une société, une civilisation, une époque.
C'est ce que nous avons appelé, Pierre Toubert et moi, un sujet *globalisant*.'

[10] Janet L. Nelson, 'Writing Early Medieval Biography', *History Workshop Journal*, 50 (2000), pp.
129–36. Cf. W.L. Warren, 'Biography and the Medieval Historian', pp. 5–18.

[11] Nelson, 'Writing Early Medieval Biography', p. 130.

[12] R. Skidelsky, 'Only Connect: Biography and Truth', in *The Troubled Face of Biography*, ed. E. Homberger and J. Charmley (London, 1988), pp. 1–16 at 9.

[13] R.W. Southern, ed. and trans., *The Life of St Anselm Archbishop of Canterbury, by Eadmer* (Oxford,
1972), pp. 150–1.

growth.[14] This aspect of life-writing is occasionally neglected and often the subject of the biography is given a fixed character that remains unaffected by life experience. Recognition of the possibility of psychological development is not a wholly modern phenomenon, a product of the influence of developmental psychology.[15] Medieval writers also commented on changes in the behaviour of their subjects, although they found other ways of explaining them. As well as recording their *gesta* or 'deeds' of the *vita* or 'life', medieval writers explored their *conversatio* or 'life-style' in order to reveal aspects of character.[16]

Biography is never about an isolated individual; it is about men and women in society.[17] Personal identity partly depends on the role that the individual plays in groups. Identity can also be derived partly from the groups in question.[18] In any society where the exercise of power depends on human interaction, whether as individuals or groups, aspects of personality have a crucial role to play. This was recognised by one of the founders of modern sociology, Max Weber, in his study of 'charisma'.[19] Among the elite of eleventh-century society where power was exercised face-to-face, individual character traits certainly had an impact. Personal lives inevitably became politically charged, as individuals attempted to fulfil the social roles that they had chosen for themselves or which had been assigned to them. In these circumstances the public *persona* shaded into the private and it is debateable whether medieval rulers had a 'private life' at all; whether they were ever allowed to remove the mask and relax their guard away from the scrutiny of their subjects.[20]

---

[14] Nancy Partner, 'The Hidden Self: Psychoanalysis and the Textual Unconscious', in *eadem*, ed., *Writing Medieval History* (London, 2005), pp. 42–64.

[15] P. Gay, *Freud for Historians* (New York, 1985); Garthine Walker, 'Psychoanalysis and History', in *Writing History. Theory and Practice*, ed. S. Berger, H. Feldner and K. Passmore (London, 2003), pp. 141–60.

[16] Nelson, 'Writing Early Medieval Biography', pp. 130, 134; cf. J. Rubenstein, 'Biography and Autobiography in the Middle Ages', in *Writing Medieval History*, ed. Nancy Partner (London, 2005), pp. 22–41 at 27–9. Caroline W. Bynum, 'Did the 12th Century Discover the Individual?' in *eadem, Jesus as Mother. Studies in the Spirituality of the High Middle Ages* (Berkeley, CA, 1982), pp. 82–109.

[17] Cf. M. Clanchy, 'Documenting the Self: Abelard and the Individual in History', *Historical Research*, 76 (2003), pp. 293–309 at 293–9.

[18] Hamilton, 'Review article', p.248 citing A. Gurevich, *The Origins of European Individualism* (Oxford, 1995), pp.19–88.

[19] *Max Weber, On Charisma and Institution Building. Selected Papers*, ed. S.N. Eisenstadt (Chicago and London, 1968); C. Lindholm, *Charisma* (Oxford, 1990); K. Morrison, *Marx, Durkheim, Weber. Formations of Modern Social Thought* (London, 1995).

[20] Janet L. Nelson, 'The Problematic in the Private', *Social History*, 15 (1990), pp. 355–64. On the question of 'modes of characterization', see Jean Blacker, *The Faces of Time. Portrayal of the Past in Old French and Latin Historical Narrative of the Anglo-Norman* Regnum (Austin, TX, 1994), pp. 53–134.

Robert Curthose and the Historians

Although he left no private papers or personal accounts of his deeds that we know of, sources for a biography of Robert Curthose are relatively abundant.[21] Most were written in Latin, the language of the educated classes in the period. How far did this vocabulary borrowed from ancient Roman authors accurately reflect conditions in the eleventh century?[22] This has led to heated debate and some have questioned whether any Latin medieval source can accurately reflect the conditions of medieval life. But all societies make use of allusion in the form of simile and metaphor and their use does not necessarily invalidate the information conveyed. In a related point, there was a tendency for medieval writers to represent not individuals but rather 'ideal types'. Saints' 'lives' in particular were designed to show how far their subject conformed to a recognised 'saintly' stereotype, rather than accurately represent the individual. In this case the anecdote for which no precedent can be found would seem to offer some idea of the subject's personality.[23]

Similarly, medieval authors invented speeches for the people they wrote about. This was a rhetorical device, borrowed from ancient Latin writers, who employed it in order to convey aspects of character. It is unlikely that these were the actual words spoken, but these were the sort of things that an individual *might* have said.[24] However, there are cases where the writer clearly had a close relationship with his subject and may have recorded the actual words. In addition, medieval monks, who wrote many of the sources used in this study, developed mnemonic techniques to allow them to cope with memorising the liturgy and their other monastic duties.[25] For someone like St Anselm's constant companion Eadmer there was ample opportunity to record what was actually said. Even if they were heavily edited, perhaps by the speaker himself, these speeches might be closer to what was actually said than historians have generally admitted.[26]

Robert Curthose was one of the most widely travelled men of his era. During the course of his long life, he met and interacted with – however briefly – thousands of people. It is impossible to say how many lives were influenced by his existence, but of the many who knew him personally, or knew him only

---

21 Some medieval secular rulers left accounts of their own lives; Jane Martindale, 'Secular Propaganda and Aristocratic Values: The Autobiographies of Count Fulk le Réchin of Anjou and Count William of Poitou, Duke of Aquitaine', in *Writing Medieval Biography 750–1250*, ed. David Bates, Julia Crick and Sarah Hamilton (Woodbridge, 2006), pp. 143–59.

22 *The Gesta Normannorum Ducum of William of Jumièges, Orderic Vitalis and Robert of Torigni*, ed. and trans. Elisabeth M.C. van Houts, 2 vols. (Oxford, 1992, 1995), I, lvii and n. 171.

23 Rubenstein, 'Biography and Autobiography in the Middle Ages', pp. 22–4.

24 Marjorie Chibnall, *The World of Orderic Vitalis* (Oxford, 1984; reprinted Woodbridge, 1996), pp. 196–7.

25 Mary Carruthers, *The Book of Memory. A Study of Memory in Medieval Culture* (Cambridge, 1990).

26 Eadmer's *Life of St Anselm* was produced in circumstances similar to those that enabled James Boswell to write his life of Dr Johnson; cf. Edel, *Writing Lives*, pp. 42–58.

by reputation, comparatively few men and women left written records.[27] The evidence presents a life in fragments scattered in a variety of texts throughout Christendom. In many respects this situation reflects the fragmented nature of memory and the lived experience of human beings. Even when reflecting autobiographically, memories may not be entirely coherent. They have to be marshalled together and interpreted according to present need in order to convey a structured and intelligible personal history. The act of narrating thus organises these fragments of autobiography and can never produce a full and unfiltered personal history.[28]

None of those who described Robert's deeds was close to the duke. He did not have a 'court historian' and Robert is thus viewed, as it were, from afar. That said, proximity was no guarantee of faithful historical representation. William of Poitiers, who was archdeacon of Lisieux in Normandy, attempted a biography of William the Conqueror as a celebration and legitimisation of the greatest of his subject's achievements, namely the conquest of England. Poitiers seemed well placed to offer an intimate account of his subject as he had served as a soldier and later as chaplain to the Conqueror.[29] However, the *Gesta Guillelmi ducis Normannorum et Regis Anglorum* ('The Deeds of William, duke of the Normans and king of the English') is something of a disappointment for modern historians.[30] William of Poitiers produced a panegyric which peters out with a description of events at the end of the 1060s. William of Poitiers' text raises the issue of how a biographer is to deal with his living subject, an individual he knew well and admired. The tone of the *Gesta Guillelmi* suggests that it was a response to growing criticism of the king's actions.[31] Unfortunately – or perhaps 'fortunately' given the problems with the text – William of Poitiers has little to say about Robert. The violent estrangement between the Conqueror and his eldest son may have contributed to the archdeacon's abandonment of the *Gesta Guillelmi* in the late 1070s.

William of Poitiers drew on a strong tradition of historical writing in Normandy.[32] At the beginning of the eleventh-century, the ruling house of Normandy commissioned an account of its own rise to power. Dudo, a canon

---

27 Unusually, a woman writer, the Byzantine princess Anna Komnena, probably saw Duke Robert when he passed through Constantinople on his way to Jerusalem. Cf. E.R.A. Sewter, trans., *Anna Comnena, The Alexiad* (Harmondsworth, 1969).

28 B. Roberts, *Biographical Research* (Buckingham, 2002), pp. 134–49.

29 R.H.C. Davis and Marjorie Chibnall, ed. and trans., *The Gesta Guillelmi of William of Poitiers* (Oxford, 1998), xv–xix.

30 D. Bates, 'The Conqueror's Earliest Historians and the Writing of his Biography' in *Writing Medieval Biography*, ed. Bates et al., pp. 129–41.

31 Bates, 'The Conqueror's Earliest Historians', pp. 130, 132.

32 Nancy Partner, *Serious Entertainments: The Writing of History in Twelfth-century England* (Chicago, 1977); Leah Shopkow, *History and Community. Norman Historical Writing in the Eleventh and Twelfth Centuries* (Washington DC, 1997); Emily Albu, *The Normans and their Histories. Propaganda, Myth and Subversion* (Woodbridge, 2001); Elisabeth M.C. van Houts, 'Historical Writing', in *A Companion to the Anglo-Norman World*, ed. C. Harper-Bill and Elisabeth van Houts (Woodbridge, 2003), pp. 103–34; N. Webber, *The Evolution of Norman Identity, 911–1154* (Woodbridge,

of the church of Saint-Quentin in neighbouring Vermandois, an envoy to the court of Richard I (ruled 945–96), was asked to write a serial biography of the rulers of Normandy.[33] The usefulness of Dudo's *De moribus et actis primorum Normannie ducum* ('On the customs and deeds of the first rulers of Normandy'), written probably between *c.*996 and *c.*1015, has been questioned.[34] Nevertheless, Dudo's work, the first of its kind, formed the basis of a tradition of historical writing in Normandy which carried on into the twelfth century and beyond.[35]

Dudo's *De moribus* reveals a ruling house conscious of its own status and anxious to project an image of sophistication. The rulers of Normandy recognised the value of establishing and cultivating a dynastic view of the past to suit the purposes of the present. In the 1050s, at the beginning of the reign of Robert Curthose's father, a monk named William Calculus from the Benedictine abbey of Jumièges began to revise and extend Dudo's history.[36] The *Gesta Normannorum ducum* ('The Deeds of the Dukes of the Normans'), in the version as William of Jumièges first wrote it (designated 'Redaction C' by its modern editor) was finished before 1060. Later the monk added more material including an account of the conquest of England ending at around 1070.[37] An introduction to the whole work in the form of a dedicatory letter to William the Conqueror and a brief 'Epilogue' were added at the same time.[38]

There is little information on William Calculus, although he refers to being an eye-witness for events in the reign of Duke Richard III (1026–7) and this suggests that he was born *c.*1000; he died after 1070.[39] When he wrote the dedicatory letter and Epilogue to his version of the *Gesta Normannorum ducum*, William of Jumièges was confident that Robert had succeeded his father as duke of Normandy. Conscious of being removed from events across the Channel, William of Jumièges had decided to leave an account of the Conqueror as king of England 'to the men, most eminent in wisdom and eloquence who are surrounding him'.[40] It is clear, then, that Jumièges had

---

2005). Cf. Pierre Bauduin, 'Les Sources de l'histoire du duché. Publications et inventaires récents', *Tabularia 'Études'*, 3 (2003), pp. 29–55.

[33] J. Lair, ed., *De moribus et actis primorum Normanniae Ducum* (Caen, 1865). E. Christiansen, trans., *Dudo of St Quentin, History of the Normans* (Woodbridge, 1998).

[34] D. Bates, *Normandy before 1066* (London, 1982), xii–xiv. Cf. Eleanor Searle, 'Fact and Pattern in Heroic History. Dudo of St Quentin', *Viator*, 15 (1984), pp. 75–85; E. Albu Hanawalt, 'Dudo of St Quentin: the Heroic Past Imagined', *HSJ*, 6 (1994), pp. 111–18; Leah Shopkow, 'The Carolingian World of Dudo of St Quentin', *JMH*, 15 (1989), pp. 19–37.

[35] *WJ*, I, li.

[36] *WJ*, I, xxx–xxxi. William's nickname is given by Orderic Vitalis and probably refers to his duty of maintaining tables of the dates of religious festivals.

[37] *WJ*, I, liii. He may have used a 'legal exposition of the ducal claim to the English throne' as the principal source for his section on the Conquest.

[38] *WJ*, I, xx, xxxv, xlix. William of Jumièges stopped writing in the late 1050s and Bates suggests the 'idea of an author withdrawing from a subject which he was finding increasingly intolerable'; see 'The Conqueror's Earliest Historians', p. 134.

[39] *WJ*, I, xxxi.

[40] *WJ*, I, xlix–l. A reference to William of Poitiers?

conceived of his history as a *Gesta Normannorum ducum* and did not intend to include details about the kingdom of England. To that end he turned to an account of Robert Curthose.

> But since we have decided to write down the history of the peace and wars of the dukes of the Normans we shall now direct our pen to Robert, son of the king, whom at present we rejoice as duke and advocate.[41]

It is worth noting the author's determination to concentrate on a separate history of Normandy under its own duke. Indeed, throughout his text, William takes a specifically Norman and ducal point of view. This strong sense of place suggests that even after 1066, at least in William of Jumièges's mind, Normandy and England were still separate entities: there was no unified Anglo-Norman *regnum* when he stopped writing. By *c.*1070 Robert was recognised as duke of Normandy and could be seen embarking on his own distinctive rule.[42]

The *Gesta Normannorum* was extended by substantial revisions and additions made by two twelfth-century historians, Orderic Vitalis and Robert of Torigni. In addition, four anonymous redactors worked independently on versions of the text at the end of the eleventh century.[43] Orderic was also a Benedictine monk and his version of the *Gesta Normannorum* ('Redaction E') was composed between *c.*1109 and *c.*1113.[44] Later Robert of Torigni (died 23 or 24 June 1186), a monk of Le Bec and later abbot of Mont-Saint-Michel, used Orderic's work to produce a further version dated *c.*1139. This text ('Redaction F') added an account of the reign of Henry I (1100–1135).[45] Later, Robert of Torigni also produced a chronicle of his own which was based on the work of Sigebert of Gembloux.[46]

After revising the *Gesta Normannorum*, Orderic Vitalis spent almost three decades writing his *Historia ecclesiastica* ('The Ecclesiastical History'), which began as a history of his own monastery of Saint-Évroul, but became a detailed record of Norman history to the end of the 1130s. Orderic was born on 16 February 1075 at Atcham, near Shrewsbury on the Anglo-Welsh frontier. He was one of three sons of Odelerius, a cleric from Orléans in the

---

41 *WJ*, II, pp. 184–5.
42 *WJ*, I, liv and appendix.
43 *WJ*, I, lx–lxv. A monk of Saint Ouen in Rouen made some revisions concerning Robert Curthose ('Redaction α'). His work influenced two other authors ('Redactions A and B'). Redaction α appeared between 1096 and 1100. Redaction B, written 1097 x 1100 and *c.*1125, is the earliest record that before 1087 the Conqueror had entrusted Normandy to Robert in the presence of the magnates of the palace. Redaction D, produced in England, modified the passages dealing with Robert's succession: *WJ*, I, xx–xxi, lxv–lxvi. The omission of a sentence in 'Redaction D' expressing the hope that Robert might reign long as duke suggests that this version was written after 1106.
44 *WJ*, I, lxxv.
45 *WJ*, I, xxi, lxxvii–xci. Elisabeth van Houts, 'Robert of Torigni as Genealogist', in *Studies in Medieval History presented to R. Allen Brown*, ed. C. Harper-Bill, C.J. Holdsworth and Janet Nelson (Woodbridge, 1989), pp. 215–33.
46 *WJ*, I, lxxviii. L. Delisle, ed., *Chronique de Robert de Torigni*, 2 vols., Société de l'Histoire de Normandie (Rouen and Paris, 1872–3).

service of Roger II of Montgomery, a leading baron in the Conqueror's entourage. Orderic's mother was an English woman, but was never named by her son.[47] After an elementary education at Shrewsbury, Orderic was sent by his father to Saint-Évroul in southern Normandy. As a boy of ten and unable to understand the language, Orderic likened this to being sent into exile. The emotional parting from his father made a deep impression on the boy, and he carried the painful memory into old age. Saint-Évroul had been re-founded in 1050 by monks from Jumièges and its patrons included several families with landed interests in the frontier regions of the duchy.

Orderic provides the most detailed account of Duke Robert's career, but his evidence needs to be treated with care. As a historian Orderic probably learned his trade by compiling a series of annals for his abbey from 1095 onwards and producing his version of the *Gesta Normannorum ducum*.[48] However, Orderic's most famous text was his *Historia ecclesiastica*, divided into thirteen books and written between 1114 and 1141.[49] The impetus for the writing of the *Ecclesiastical History* may have been the visit of King Henry I to Saint-Évroul in 1113.[50] As well as the royal visit to his abbey, Orderic's opinion of Robert was affected by the violence he saw in the region around his abbey: violence he attributed to members of the Bellême family whom he believed Duke Robert failed to control. Generally, Orderic saw Robert's reign as duke as ineffective and he welcomed Henry I's victory in 1106, but recognised that matters were not always simple.

Orderic's work has an immediacy about it, a vividness which offers insights into the character of the individuals he describes. There are echoes of the popular *chansons de geste* in his *Ecclesiastical History*. These chivalric tales described heroic deeds of the warrior-caste and raise interesting questions about how far the knights who visited Orderic's monastery slipped into the conventions of the genre when describing campaigns in which they themselves had taken part. Many monks were from aristocratic families and shared the same values and outlook as their kinsfolk. However, it must be remembered that Orderic was a monk and his world-view was affected by his belief that the recording of historical events carried with it the obligation to point out the moral lessons of the past and the unfolding of the divine plan.[51] At one point he wrote:

---

47 Chibnall, *World of Orderic Vitalis*, pp. 3–41; WJ, I, lxvi–vii.
48 Marjorie Chibnall, ed. and trans., *The Ecclesiastical History of Orderic Vitalis*, 6 vols. (Oxford, 1969–80), I, pp. 23–9.
49 *OV*, I, pp. 29–39.
50 *OV*, I, pp. 31–2. Henry visited at Candlemas (2 February) and offered to issue a confirmation of the abbey's possessions. Marjorie Chibnall suggests that this offer prompted some historical research by the monks in order to prepare the documents necessary for the king's confirmation. Cf. *OV*, VI, pp. 174–6.
51 Chibnall, *World of Orderic Vitalis*, pp. 210–13 and *OV*, I, pp. 38–9.

I find many things in the pages of Scripture which, if subtly interpreted, seem to resemble the happenings of our own time.[52]

Orderic was critical of secular rulers and in describing events before 1100 felt less inhibited in this regard than his predecessors.[53]

The *Gesta Normannorum ducum* continued to influence historical writing in Normandy in the twelfth century, although some of the relevant texts, now in verse, were transmitted in Old French.[54] Between 1160 and 1173, Wace, a cleric from Jersey who was educated in Caen and became a canon of Bayeux cathedral, produced the *Roman de Rou*, a 'Geste des Normands' which presents a verse-history of the rulers of Normandy from Rollo (or 'Rou') to Robert Curthose.[55] Wace's text was based on a version of the *Gesta Normannorum ducum* and ended with Robert's defeat in 1106.[56] Wace stopped writing and abandoned the project to Benoît de Sainte-Maure, who produced a ponderous tome.[57] Henry I's grandson, Henry II, commissioned Wace's 'Geste' and possibly the withdrawal of patronage halted the work. Alternatively, 1106 might have seemed to mark the end of the reign of the last legitimate duke of Normandy from the line of Rollo and thus, from a Norman point of view, it was a logical place to end the text.

The value of Wace's work has been reassessed and it is now recognised that he approached the task of a historian seriously.[58] He included eye-witness and oral testimony and preserved traditions from western Normandy, especially from the area around Caen and Bayeux.[59] Of all the writers being considered here, Wace was the most sympathetic towards Duke Robert Curthose. This was not the way to please his patron and the implied criticism of Henry II's grandfather might have been too much for the Angevin king to bear.

Historians writing in England during the later eleventh and twelfth centuries also provide information on Robert Curthose. William of Malmesbury's *Gesta regum Anglorum* ('The deeds of the kings of the English') contains a character sketch of Duke Robert and devotes considerable attention to his career.[60] William was born around 1090, probably not far from the Benedictine monastery at Malmesbury which he entered during the abbacy of Godfrey of

---

52 *OV*, IV, pp. 228–9.
53 *WJ*, I, lxxv.
54 P. Damian-Grint, *The New Historians of the Twelfth-century Renaissance. Inventing Vernacular Authority* (Woodbridge, 1999).
55 G.S. Burgess, trans., *Wace, The Roman de Rou*, Société Jersiaise (St Helier, 2002).
56 Damian-Grint, *New Historians*, pp. 53–8. Wace's text was based on *WJ*, 'Redaction E'.
57 Benoît de Sainte-Maure, *Chronique des ducs de Normandie*, ed. Carin Fahlin, Bibliotheca Ekmaniania 56 and 60 (Uppsala, 1951–54). Damian-Grint, *New Historians*, pp. 58–61.
58 M. Bennett, 'Poetry as History? The *Roman de Rou* of Wace as a Source for the Norman Conquest', *ANS*, 5 (1983), pp. 21–39; Elisabeth van Houts, 'Wace as Historian', in *Family Trees and the Roots of Politics*, ed. Katherine S.B. Keats-Rohan (Woodbridge, 1997), pp. 103–32.
59 Damian-Grint, *New Historians*, p. 57; Wace stopped writing because his exemplar, 'Redaction E' of *WJ*, gave out.
60 R.A.B. Mynors, R.M. Thomson and M. Winterbottom, eds. and trans., *William of Malmesbury, Gesta Regum Anglorum. The History of the English Kings*, vol. 1 (Oxford, 1998).

Jumièges (died *c.*1106).[61] Before 1118, Henry I's queen, Matilda, visited Malmesbury and provided the spark for the *Gesta regum Anglorum*, which traced the history of England from Bede's time until his own day. The *Gesta regum* was completed around 1125–26, but revised until at least 1134.[62] William was a diligent historian and travelled widely through England and probably Normandy in search of materials. During his travels he met and exchanged stories with Eadmer of Canterbury and Orderic Vitalis. Like Orderic, William was the offspring of a Norman/English union and this, he claimed, allowed him 'to keep a middle path' when reporting the deeds of the Conqueror and his two sons (*sic*).[63] As a conscientious scholar, William was aware of the problems of writing contemporary history, but decided to trust his own judgement in order to avoid its pitfalls.[64]

Eadmer of Canterbury was born around 1060 of English parents and entered Christ Church Abbey, Canterbury, as a child oblate. When Anselm of Bec became archbishop in 1093, he made Eadmer a member of his household and the two were constantly together until Anselm's death in 1109. Archbishop Anselm's eventful career was recorded in two texts, written between 1093 and 1125; the *Vita Sancti Anselmi* ('The Life of St Anselm') and the *Historia novorum* ('The History of Recent Events').[65] Eadmer bears witness to his master's difficulties with Robert's two brothers, William Rufus and Henry I. Eadmer's English background affected his view of the past. His family, probably from the ranks of the Anglo-Saxon lesser nobility, was impoverished and reduced in status by the Conquest and this 'dominated all his thoughts and feelings: pride of race, the grievances of the conquered, and the love of Canterbury, all combined to produce a sense of indignation and nostalgia in writing of the present and the past'.[66]

By around 1130, Henry, the hereditary archdeacon of Huntingdon, had completed the first version of his *Historia Anglorum* ('The History of the English People').[67] Written at the direction of Bishop Alexander of Lincoln (1123–48), Henry's work presented a history of the English from the Roman invasions to 1129. He continued to write and revise the text until just before

---

61 R.M. Thomson, *William of Malmesbury*, revised ed. (Woodbridge, 2003), pp. 3–13 and Appendix I, pp. 199–201. R.M. Thomson, 'Malmesbury, William of (b.c.1090, d. in or after 1142)', *Oxford DNB* (Oxford, 2004).

62 Thomson, *William of Malmesbury*, pp. 3–75. WM, *GR*, I, pp. 2–13.

63 WM, *GR*, I, 'Prologue to Book III', pp. 424–5. William of Malmesbury omitted Duke Robert presumably because he never became king of England.

64 WM, *GR*, 'Prologue to Book IV', pp. 540–3.

65 Southern, *Life of St Anselm*; M. Rule, ed., *Eadmeri Historia Novorum in Anglia*, Rolls Series (London, 1884). There is a translation of the first four books of the *Historia Novorum* in G. Bosanquet, trans., *Eadmer's History of Recent Events in England. Historia Novorum in Anglia* (London, 1964). R.W. Southern, *Saint Anselm. A Portrait in a Landscape* (Cambridge, 1990), pp. 404–36.

66 Southern, *Saint Anselm*, p. 407.

67 Diana Greenway, ed. and trans., *Henry, Archdeacon of Huntingdon. Historia Anglorum. The History of the English People* (Oxford, 1996). *Eadem*, 'Henry of Huntingdon and the Manuscripts of his *Historia Anglorum*', *ANS*, 9 (1986), pp. 103–26; *eadem*, 'Authority, Convention and Observation in Henry of Huntingdon's *Historia Anglorum*', *ANS*, 18 (1995), pp. 105–21.

his death around 1157.[68] The final of six different versions of the text took the history to the accession of Henry II in 1154. Henry's *Historia* was intended to demonstrate that five invasions of Britain by the Romans, the Picts and Scots, the Angles and Saxons, the Danes and, finally, the Normans, were punishments visited by God on the island's faithless people: this was history as a moralising tract.[69] Henry's major sources were Bede's *Historia ecclesiastica* and at least two versions of the *Anglo-Saxon Chronicle*.[70] Henry presents a more even-handed account of Robert's career and it is possible to detect a note of sympathy.[71] Born around 1088, Henry was of the same generation as William of Malmesbury and Orderic Vitalis. Like them he was the son of an English-woman and a Norman clerk giving him a bipartisan view of the past. His father Nicholas was archdeacon of Huntingdon.[72] With the help of his mother Henry learnt English and his French and Latin were probably acquired in a formal education at Lincoln. There he was part of the household of Bishop Robert Bloet (died 1123). The royal court made a considerable impression on Henry and he probably got closer to the powerful secular figures of his age than did his cloistered contemporaries.[73] Henry paid attention to character, an interest probably derived from his training in the art of rhetoric. As archdeacon of Huntingdon from 1110, Henry travelled widely in the East Midlands and was active in ecclesiastical affairs there and at a national level. He was, therefore, well-placed to gather information on political events.[74] Apart from the *Historia Anglorum*, Henry's tract *De contemptu mundi* ('On Contempt for the World') provides a commentary on the 'great men' of his time.[75]

Henry of Huntingdon made use of at least two versions of the *Anglo-Saxon Chronicle*. Although focused on events in England, the *Chronicle*, written in Old English, necessarily mentions Robert. For his reign in Normandy, there is only one version of the *Chronicle*, known as the 'E' text or 'Peterborough Chronicle'.[76] It was compiled at Peterborough around 1121 with subsequent additions to 1154. As one might expect from a set of annals written by monks in Old English and describing the conquest and settlement of their country, the tone was 'pessimistic' and critical of Norman government.[77]

[68] *HH*, lxvi–lxxvii.
[69] *HH*, lxxvii–lxxxv.
[70] *HH*, lxxxv–cvii.
[71] *HH*, 'De Contemptu Mundi', pp. 604–5.
[72] *HH*, xxiii–lvii.
[73] *HH*, xxix–xl.
[74] *HH*, lii–lvi.
[75] *HH*, pp. 584–619.
[76] Susan Irvine, ed., *The Anglo-Saxon Chronicle. A Collaborative Edition, Volume 7, MS. E* (Cambridge, 2004). M. Swanton, trans. and ed., *The Anglo-Saxon Chronicle* (London, 1996). Only MS. E extends beyond 1080. The 'Worcester' MS. D, has a marked interest in Northumbrian affairs and might be associated with Archbishop Ealdred of York, but ends in 1079; see G.P. Cubbin, *The Anglo-Saxon Chronicle. A Collaborative Edition, Volume 6, MS. D* (Cambridge, 1996). A fragment of another version, known as MS. H, covers 1113 and 1114; see Irvine, *MS. E*, lxxxiv–v.
[77] Hollister, *Henry I*, pp. 6–7.

There was also a strong tradition of historical writing at Worcester Abbey and as well as a version of the *Anglo-Saxon Chronicle* (MS. D), a series of annals was compiled there by the monk John on the orders of Bishop Wulf-stan.[78] The *Worcester Chronicle* was a 'world history' and extended from the Creation to 1140. Like Henry of Huntingdon, John of Worcester made use of the *Anglo-Saxon Chronicle*, but instead of the vernacular, John wrote in Latin. For the period 1102 to 1121, John used Eadmer's *Historia novorum* as his chief source.[79] There was contact between Worcester and Canterbury, including more than one visit by Eadmer himself.[80] For the later years of the reign of Henry I, John becomes an important contemporary witness. Again, although a monk, John of Worcester had access to men at the very centre of royal government.[81]

Orderic Vitalis had visited Worcester no later than 1124 and saw John at work on a chronicle there. Orderic tells us that John was an Englishman who had entered the abbey at Worcester as a boy.[82] Given Eadmer's contact with Worcester and evidence of a close relationship between John's work and that of William of Malmesbury, it is worth pausing to emphasise the connections between these chroniclers and historians working at roughly the same time. That these historians knew each other personally or through their written work reinforces the point that we are dependent on a relatively small number of writers for our view of the period and the characterisation of Duke Robert.[83] It is tempting to imagine Orderic Vitalis swapping opinions with John and discussing his portrayal of the major figures of the day, or William of Malm-esbury's eyes lighting up as he was shown the historical materials collected at Worcester.[84]

The Old French verse text *L'Estoire des Engleis* ('The History of the English'), compiled by Geffrei Gaimar between 1136 and 1137, is to a large extent a trans-lation of the *Anglo-Saxon Chronicle*. It is the oldest surviving historical text in French. *L'Estoire* closes with the death of William Rufus in 1100 and thus fails to cover the last years of Robert's governance of Normandy. However, Gaimar claimed that he could write things about Henry I that the now lost history

---

[78] P. McGurk, ed., *The Chronicle of John of Worcester. Volume III, The Annals from 1067 to 1140 with the Gloucester Interpolations and the Continuation to 1141* (Oxford, 1998), xv. Cf. M. Brett, 'John of Worcester and his Contemporaries', in *The Writing of History in the Middle Ages. Essays presented to Richard William Southern*, ed. R.H.C. Davis and J.M. Wallace-Hadrill (Oxford, 1981), pp. 101–26; Emma Mason, *St Wulfstan of Worcester, c.1008–1095* (Oxford, 1990), pp. 217–18.

[79] Brett, 'John of Worcester', p. 111.

[80] Brett, 'John of Worcester', pp. 112–13.

[81] P. McGurk, 'Worcester, John of (fl.1095–1140)', *Oxford DNB* (Oxford, 2004).

[82] *OV*, II, pp. 186–7.

[83] R.W. Southern, 'Aspects of the European Tradition of Historical Writing, 4: The Sense of the Past', *TRHS*, 5th ser., 23 (1973), pp. 243–63.

[84] The evidence for 'an active traffic between Canterbury, Malmesbury and Worcester' and Durham is examined in Brett, 'John of Worcester'.

by a certain David had never mentioned.[85] Gaimar wrote at the request of Constance, the wife of Ralf fitz Gilbert, a nobleman living in Lincolnshire in the early twelfth century. The author was given access to materials held by several high-ranking barons including Earl Robert of Gloucester and Walter Espec.[86] The text, which is in general 'a conscientious historical narrative', was a product of the ongoing assimilation of the incoming French to the traditions of their new English home.[87] L'Estoire is a useful counterpoint to the monastic view of the reigns of William the Conqueror and William Rufus and a very different picture of the royal court emerges from Gaimar's work. Rufus's court in particular appears a vibrant, colourful arena of *bele chevalerie* ('fair chivalry'), with splendid set pieces of courtly ritual such as the dubbing of thirty young men as knights.[88]

This study uses other narrative sources from Normandy and England. Annals and narrative histories with a more local focus often have material concerning events in the wider world. Shorter tracts, written in response to particular situations, also have their uses.[89] For example, there is a short history of Normandy and England from *c.*1035 until 1106, written by an anonymous monk of Battle Abbey in Sussex.[90] This *Brevis relatio* was composed during the abbacy of Ralph of Battle (1107–24) using his testimony about the Norman Conquest and the reigns of William I and his sons.[91] Although the duke was already in captivity when the anonymous monk was writing, there is the suggestion in the text that the struggle between Robert and Henry might resume.[92]

The Norman abbey of Bec-Hellouin also had a strong historiographical tradition. A series of biographies of the abbots of Bec survives, providing another monastic view of the period, and there is additional material for the

---

85 A. Bell, ed., *Geffrei Gaimar, L' Estoire des Engleis* (Oxford, 1960), lines 6477–83. There is a translation in vol. 2 of T.D. Hardy and C.T. Martin, eds., *L'Estoire des Engles*, 2 vols., Rolls Series (London, 1888–9).

86 Bell, *L'Estoire*, lines 6430–76.

87 Hugh M. Thomas, *The English and the Normans. Ethnic Hostility, Assimilation and Identity 1066–c.1220* (Oxford, 2003), pp. 85–6. The quotation is from I. Short, 'Gaimar, Geffrei (fl.1136–1137)', *Oxford DNB* (Oxford, 2004).

88 Damian-Grint, *New Historians*, pp. 49–53. J. Gillingham, 'Kingship, Chivalry and Love. Political and Cultural Values in the Earliest History Written in French: Geoffrey Gaimar's *Estoire des Engleis*', in *Anglo-Norman Political Culture and the Twelfth-century Renaissance*, ed. C.W. Hollister (Woodbridge, 1997), pp. 33–58; reprinted in *The English in the Twelfth Century. Imperialism, National Identity and Political Values* (Woodbridge, 2000), pp. 233–58.

89 Elisabeth M.C. van Houts, *Local and Regional Chronicles*, Typologie des Sources du Moyen Âge Occidental, Fasc.74 (Turnhout, 1995).

90 Elisabeth M.C. van Houts, ed., 'The *Brevis Relatio de Guillelmo nobilissimo comite Normannorum*, Written by a Monk of Battle Abbey', in *Chronology, Conquest and Conflict in Medieval England. Camden Miscellany*, Camden Fifth Ser., 10 (Cambridge, 1997), pp. 1–48. Cf. *eadem*, ed. (and trans.), 'The *Brevis Relatio de Guillelmo nobilissimo comite Normannorum*, Written by a Monk of Battle Abbey', in *eadem*, *History and Family Traditions in England and the Continent, 1000–1200* (Aldershot, 1999), no. VII. The terminal date of 1106 should be noted here. I am very grateful to Dr van Houts for supplying me with a copy of her edition and translation of the *Brevis Relatio*.

91 *Brevis Relatio*, pp. 14–15.

92 *Brevis Relatio*, p. 20 and paragraph 15, pp. 42–4.

secular history of the duchy. Bec's influence with the ducal house also lends interest to its historiography.[93]

Another text with a local focus is the *Warenne Chronicle*, also known as the 'Hyde Chronicle' due to its association with the abbey of that name near Winchester. It provides a historical narrative from 1035 to 1120 with a particular focus on the fortunes of the Warenne family.[94] The narrative was composed in the late 1150s and the material relating to the Warennes gathered from oral accounts was attached to a historical framework provided by the work of English and Norman sources, especially that of Orderic Vitalis. Although a comparatively late source, the value of the *Warenne Chronicle* lies in its preservation of historical traditions from a family at the centre of the political stage.[95]

As well as historical narratives, there are hagiographical sources in the form of saints' lives and related material such as *miracula* ('miracle stories') or accounts of the translation of relics, which can throw sidelights on Robert's career.[96] Papal and episcopal letter collections have also been examined for references to the duke.[97] Medieval letters were 'self-conscious, quasi-public literary documents, often written with an eye to future collection and publication'. They were not, therefore, private and personal communications. The extant texts were often only part of the message conveyed as more sensitive material was delivered orally by trusted envoys.[98]

Northern France in the eleventh and twelfth centuries also produced a good many literary compositions. Although not considered strictly 'historical' sources, Latin poetry composed for the English and Norman courts reveals general aspects of the culture that produced them and throws light on specific incidents.[99]

---

[93] Translations of the lives of the abbots in Sally N. Vaughn, *The Abbey of Bec and the Anglo-Norman State, 1034–1136* (Woodbridge, 1981).

[94] E. Edwards, ed., 'Chronica monasterii de Hida iuxta Wintoniam', in *idem*, ed., *Liber Monasterii de Hyda*, Rolls Series (1866), Appendix A, pp. 283–321. Elisabeth van Houts, 'The Warenne View of the Past 1066–1203', *ANS*, 26 (2004), pp. 103–21.

[95] On dating and authorship, see van Houts, 'Warenne View of the Past', pp. 110–14.

[96] E.g. 'Vita beati Simonis Comitis Crespeiensis auctore synchrono', in *PL*, 156, pp. 1211–24 and M. l'Abbé Sauvage, 'Des Miracles advenus en L'Église de Fécamp', in *Mélanges Documents publiés et annotés par MM. L'Abbé Blanquart, F. Bouquet, Ch. Bréard, Le Cte A. de Circourt, L. Régnier, L'Abbé Sauvage*, 2nd ser. (Rouen, 1893), pp. 7–49; Elisabeth M.C. van Houts, 'Historiography and Hagiography at Saint-Wandrille: the *Inventio et Miracula sancti Vulfranni*', *ANS*, 12 (1990), pp. 233–51.

[97] E.g. F.S. Schmitt, ed., *Sancti Anselmi Cantuariensis archiepiscopi Opera Omnia*, 6 vols. (Stuttgart-Bad Canstatt, 1963–68); W. Fröhlich, trans., *The Letters of Saint Anselm of Canterbury*, 3 vols., Cistercian Publications (Kalamazoo, MI, 1990, 1993 and 1994).

[98] G. Constable, *Letters and Letter Collections*, Typologie des Sources du Moyen Age Occidental, Fasc.17 (Turnhout, 1976), p. 11; P. Chaplais, *English Diplomatic Practice in the Middle Ages* (London, 2003).

[99] F.J.E. Raby, *A History of Secular Latin Poetry in the Middle Ages*, 2nd ed., 2 vols. (Oxford, 1957); A.G. Rigg, *A History of Anglo-Latin Literature 1066–1422* (Cambridge, 1992). For example, Monika Otter, 'Baudri of Bourgueil, "To Countess Adela"', *Journal of Medieval Latin*, 11 (2001), pp. 60–141.

As duke of Normandy, Robert had dealings with the principalities that bordered the duchy. Fragments of his life were recorded in the chronicles and histories of Anjou and Maine, as well as in those of his mother's homeland.[100] For a brief period, Robert's son William Clito was count of Flanders and the circumstances of his rise to power were outlined in a remarkable, detailed account of the political struggles that followed the murder of his predecessor, Charles the Good.[101]

Robert Curthose was also a great traveller. In his youth he spent two periods in exile away from Normandy and in one of these he may have journeyed as far as Italy. In addition, his participation in the First Crusade brought him to the attention of writers far beyond Normandy and England.[102] Although there were several eye-witness accounts of the expedition, none was by someone close to Robert and, as a consequence, his contribution to the success of the Crusade has been underplayed.[103] On his return from the Holy Land, Robert met and married Sibyl the daughter of Count Geoffrey of Conversano, the Norman lord of Brindisi in Apulia. Thus Robert's career also forms part of the history of the Norman settlement in Southern Italy and Sicily, as well as that of the establishment of Latin principalities in the Holy Land. The geographical range of Robert's life was, therefore, far more extensive than that of his father or brother and at various points in his career he was to be found in Perthshire in Scotland, Apulia in Southern Italy and Jerusalem in the Holy Land. Not only does this suggest an appetite for adventure, it also hints at a robust constitution able to deal with the hardships of very long distance travel and warfare.

Documentary Sources

Until recently medieval historians used documentary sources as a kind of 'factual brake' on the wilder excesses of the narrative materials. Charters or documents produced to record transfers of land or other forms of property, and writs – brief written orders to officials – seemed to be more prosaic, more matters of fact than of opinion. Although more will be said later about the problems associated with relying on the 'objectivity' of these documents with

---

100 For example, for Anjou, L. Halphen and R. Poupardin, *Chroniques des comtes d'Anjou et des seigneurs d'Amboise* (Paris, 1913); for Maine, L'Abbé G. Busson and L' Abbé A. Ledru, *Archives Historiques du Maine II. Actus pontificum cenomannis in urbe degentium*, Société des Archives Historiques du Maine (Le Mans, 1902). I am particularly grateful to Dr Richard Barton for helping me to access a copy of the latter text.

101 H. Pirenne, ed., *Histoire du Meutre de Charles le Bon, comte de Flandre (1127–1128) par Galbert de Bruges* (Paris, 1891); J.B. Ross, trans., *Galbert of Bruges, The Murder of Charles the Good, Count of Flanders*, revised ed. (New York, 1967).

102 The narrative sources for Robert and the First Crusade are surveyed in more detail in the chapter on Robert as crusader.

103 Susan Edgington, 'The First Crusade: Reviewing the Evidence', in *The First Crusade. Origins and Impact*, ed. J. Phillips (Manchester, 1997), pp. 55–77.

regard to Duke Robert's reign, it might be noted here that there have been significant changes in the way that historians now approach these texts. Each of these seemingly objective documents carries with it a potentially contentious narrative. Each text needs to be analysed carefully and its purpose, audience and context fully explored.[104]

Charters were in particular contexts and they reflect, more or less explicitly, the tensions, disputes and resolutions of the moment, together with the self image and aspirations, not only of those in whose name the document–was issued, but also of its recipients and those writing it down. For example, a document issued in the name of the duke of Normandy might not, in fact, reflect the ducal conception of power. Many documents were drawn up by recipients and the representation of power and lordship may therefore be that as understood by the recipient rather than the ruler. A related point is that if the documents are being drawn up by recipients, does this mean that the issuing authority has no need of a chancery? This becomes significant if the historian assumes that the operation of a centrally directed writing office or chancery is a marker of increasingly advanced and administrative royal government.

Of particular interest to historians are the lists of the names of those who witnessed the transactions recorded by the documents. It was assumed that the number and frequency of attestations reflected political influence. However, the nature of the transaction being recorded and the conventions of the document issued affected the recording of witnesses. For example, writs, which are usually brief instructions to named individuals, typically have few attestations. Accidents of archival survival can also influence the texts. Many charters are only known from copies of their texts made in later cartularies where witness lists are sometimes omitted.[105] Sometimes the scribe ended the witness clause with the vague *et multis aliis* ('and [witnessed] by many others'). Can we be sure that only the fringe players in the scene were omitted or included in this formula?

Similarly, documents known as *pancartes* were produced. These amalgamated the texts of all available relevant documents into one comprehensive statement about the possession of rights and properties of a particular ecclesiastical institution. The editing of the original documents for the purposes

---

[104] D. Bates, 'The Prosopographical Study of Anglo-Norman Royal Charters', in *Family Trees and the Roots of Politics*, ed. Katherine S.B. Keats-Rohan (Woodbridge, 1997), pp. 89–102; *idem*, 'Charters and Historians of Britain and Ireland: Problems and Possibilities', in *Charters and Charter Scholarship in Britain and Ireland*, ed. Marie Therese Flanagan and Judith A. Green (London, 2005), pp. 1–14 at 10: '… a narrative and a context lies behind each and every document'. Cf. Marjorie Chibnall, 'Charter and Chronicle: The Use of Archive Sources by Norman Historians', in *Church and Government in the Middle Ages*, ed. C.N.L. Brooke, D.E. Luscombe, G.H. Martin and Dorothy M. Owen (Cambridge, 1976), pp. 1–17. I am grateful to Marjorie Chibnall for supplying a copy of her article.

[105] G. Declercq, 'Originals and Cartularies: The Organization of Archival Memory (Ninth–Eleventh Centuries)', in *Charters and the Use of the Written Word in Medieval Society*, ed. K. Heidecker (Turnhout, 2000), pp. 147–70.

of the *pancarte* might also skew the conclusions. Thus interpretations based on the statistical analysis of witness lists have the potential to mislead.[106]

There is also the issue of forgery.[107] Even at their most complete, charters and related documents are selective accounts of the events they record. In addition, it was sometimes deemed necessary to confect charters to provide written support for claims to land and other forms of property and rights. When the original grant was made it may not have been usual for documents to be issued, or the destruction of an archive might have led to an active scribal campaign of replacement. Later, the contents and even the form of forged materials were incorporated into genuine documents thus making it difficult for historians to use the records with complete confidence.[108]

Finally, the historian rarely approaches documentary evidence with a completely open mind. The form in which the material is presented also implies its particular historical significance. For example, at the beginning of the twentieth century it was decided to calendar all the known charters of the Norman and Angevin kings of England in a series of *Regesta*.[109] The calendared arrangement obscured the archival context of the documents concerned and the important fact that many of the charters were drawn up by the recipients. So, what looks at first glance to be a record of the efficiency of royal government masks the role of monastic and episcopal chanceries in the process. Similarly, these documents survive from a period before the systematic enrolment of copies of charters issued by the royal chancery. For this reason the original *Regesta* series did not represent the archival and administrative practice of the Norman kings so much as the efficiency of late Victorian and Edwardian scholarship.[110]

There are relatively few surviving charters issued in the name of Robert Curthose and, although some recent discoveries have been added, the corpus

---

106 Bates, 'The Prosopographical Study of Anglo-Norman Royal Charters', pp. 89–92. Cf. the approach of C.W. Hollister, 'Magnates and "Curiales" in Early Norman England', *Viator*, 4 (1973), pp. 115–22; reprinted in *idem, Monarchy, Magnates and Institutions in the Anglo-Norman World* (London and Ronceverte, 1986), pp. 97–115; *idem*, 'Courtly Culture and Courtly Style in the Anglo-Norman World', *Albion*, 20 (1988), pp. 1–18; Stephanie L. Mooers, '"Backers and Stabbers": Problems of Loyalty in Robert Curthose's Entourage', *Journal of British Studies*, 21 (1981), pp. 1–17.

107 Marjorie Chibnall, 'Forgery in Narrative Charters', *Fälschungen im Mittelalter, Teil IV, Diplomatische Fälschungen (II), MGH Scriptores*, 33, iv (Hanover, 1988), pp. 331–46. I am grateful to Dr Chibnall for supplying me with a copy of this article.

108 D. Bates, 'The Forged Charters of William the Conqueror and Bishop William of St Calais', in *Anglo-Norman Durham 1093–1193*, ed. D. Rollason, Margaret Harvey and M. Prestwich (Woodbridge, 1994), pp. 111–24.

109 H.W.C. Davis, ed., *Regesta Regum Anglo-Normannorum 1066–1154*, vol. I, *Regesta Willelmi Conquestoris et Willelmi Rufi, 1066–1100* (Oxford, 1913); vol. II, *Regesta Henrici Primi 1100–1135*, ed. C. Johnson and H.A. Cronne (Oxford, 1956).

110 D. Bates, ed., *Regesta Regum Anglo-Normannorum. The Acta of William I (1066–1087)* (Oxford, 1998), 'Introduction', pp. 1–109. These issues have been addressed by Professor David Bates in his new edition of *The Acta of William I* and by Professor Richard Sharpe and his team editing the acts of William Rufus and Henry I. I would like to express my thanks to Professor Sharpe for making the database of these *acta* available to me.

is still less than fifty documents. It has been assumed that there should be more. Although there may be many reasons for this perceived dearth of ducal *acta*, historians have invariably seen the lack of documents as indicative of the political instability of Robert's regime. The presumed historical context for these documents has influenced their interpretation and, in a circular argument, reinforced the negative characterisation of the duke's reign.[111]

The reigns of Robert's brothers, William Rufus and Henry in England, saw an increase in the volume of governmental records. Henry I's reign, in particular, has been characterised as beginning 'administrative kingship' in England.[112] From the nineteenth century, if not before, historians evaluated medieval monarchs in terms of their advancement or retardation of the development of the institutions of the modern state. Thus Henry I, although the figurehead of an oppressive regime, is given a positive role in the constitutional development of English government. The credit for the administrative achievements of those who were appointed by him is aggregated to the monarch and we are left with the dual image of a man who, on the one hand, was a ruthless and sometimes brutal warrior-king and, on the other, an advocate of rational government. The contrasting roles are not wholly incompatible, but this is not the place to debate the extent of the king's personal contribution to the rise of administrative kingship. However, it was the struggle against Duke Robert and his son that prompted both William Rufus and Henry I to demand greater and greater supplies of cash from their subjects. This demand for the funds to pay the mercenaries who fought in Normandy was the impetus that drove the more ingenious of the king's ministers to milk the English kingdom's cash-cow.[113]

Administrative documents of the kind found in England, such as the financial records of the Exchequer, descriptions of the king's household, and extensive legal compilations, do not exist for Normandy in this period.[114] However, Robert faced the same problems of government as his father and brothers, albeit on a smaller scale, and one would expect similar documents to have been generated. The lack of such documents reinforced Haskins's view of the anarchic state of the duchy under Robert. However, two men closely associated with royal government in England found a refuge at Robert's court. Two bishops of Durham, William of Saint-Calais and the notorious Ranulf Flambard, fled to Normandy when they fell foul of incoming regimes.[115]

---

[111] V.K. Dibble, 'Four Types of Inference from Documents to Events', *History and Theory*, 3 (1963), pp. 203–21.

[112] C.W. Hollister and J.W. Baldwin, 'The Rise of Administrative Kingship: Henry I and Philip Augustus', *AHR*, 83 (1978), pp. 867–905; reprinted Hollister, *Monarchy, Magnates and Institutions*, pp. 223–45.

[113] WM, *GR*, I, pp. 558–9.

[114] Hollister, *Henry I*, pp. 24–9; cf. Green, *Henry I*, pp. 12–13.

[115] C.H. Haskins, *Norman Institutions* (New York, 1918). Cf. V. Moss, 'Normandy and England: the pipe Roll Evidence', in *England and Normandy in the Middle Ages*, ed. D. Bates and Anne Curry (London, 1994), pp. 185–95.

Reading this Biography

This biography follows the chronology of Robert's life. Thematic approaches to biography have many advantages but tend to give a misleading impression of the development of the individual's life-course. It is not possible to neatly compartmentalise the many facets of life. If Robert's relationship with the Norman Church is examined in isolation from, say, his dealings with the Norman aristocracy, connections between the two areas might be obscured. Perhaps more importantly, we lose sight of the duke having to cope with more than one issue at a time.[116] The tendency is to organise the examination of the reigns of medieval kings as if they were modern governmental regimes with an assessment of various 'policies'. It is not impossible that some medieval monarchs attempted to deal with the various demands imposed upon them in such a systematic and consistent way, but it is surely more likely that they had to respond to ever-changing situations and that it was not always possible to complete one task before having to deal with another crisis. In fact, the demands on an individual often run concurrently and this materially affects how they are met. This biography therefore is organised as a chronological narrative and attempts to remain focused on Robert as much as possible. Wherever possible, contextual material is introduced as the narrative demands, but the reader is always returned to the narrative at a chronologically appropriate point.

It is important to give the impression of a life unfolding with all the contingencies that that involves. The ability to cope with the unforeseen is, surely, one of many markers of personality. Similarly, the ability to anticipate and exploit future opportunities marks the nature of an individual's response to lived experience. For many reading this biography, Duke Robert's story will be familiar and judgements will already have been formed about his career and character. In order to understand the trajectory of Robert's career, it is necessary to try to forget what we know of what happened to him. For him, as he lived, the future was unwritten and still had possibilities.[117] For us, with the knowledge of hindsight, there is the very real danger of constructing a path of inevitability for this medieval duke. Medieval and modern historians looked at the end of Robert's career and constructed their account in an attempt to explain his eventual fate. Orderic Vitalis, William of Malmesbury and their fellows, Charles Homer Haskins, Charles W. David and others, all attribute Robert's demise to the personal character faults of their subject. It is instruc-

---

116 Cf. W.L. Warren, *Henry II* (London, 1973), 'Preface' [no pagination].
117 Cf. J-P. Sartre, *Words*, trans. Irene Clephane (Harmondsworth, 1967), pp. 125–6 at 125: 'you cannot help assessing his [the biographical subject's] behaviour in the light of results which he could not foresee and of information which he did not possess, or attributing a particular solemnity to events whose effects marked him later, but which he lived through casually'. Original, J-P. Sartre, *Les Mots* (Paris, 1964), pp. 165–7 at 166.

tive to note that William of Jumièges, writing before the later troubles of the duke's career unfolded, could write that 'Robert afterwards succeeded to his parents' duchy, performing his father's office, *long may he do so*.'[118] For William of Jumièges, then, there was no reason that Robert should not reign as successfully as his father had done.

Historiographical Note

The last biography of Robert Curthose in English was written by Charles W. David and published in 1920.[119] David was a student of the influential American medievalist Charles Homer Haskins and shared his mentor's generally unfavourable opinion of Duke Robert.[120] At the end of the nineteenth century Gaston Le Hardy attempted to portray Robert in a more positive light, but his sketch of the duke is contentious.[121] Until recently, Robert Curthose has been a largely peripheral figure in histories of the period and in the biographies of members of his immediate family.[122] However, in 1999 Judith Green published a study of the duke's career which suggested that a reassessment of the evidence might lead to a more positive view of Robert and his reign.[123] This biography is intended as a contribution to this on-going reassessment of Robert Curthose. It is also a call for further research on aspects of the development of Normandy during the period that the history of the duchy was intimately bound to that of England. In addition, by examining the history of England from the perspective of Normandy, it may allow a more balanced view of both.

---

118 *WJ*, II, pp. 130–1.
119 C.W. David, *Robert Curthose, Duke of Normandy* (Cambridge, MA, 1920).
120 *Charles Wendell David. Scholar, Teacher, Librarian* (Philadelphia, PA, 1965). I am grateful to Adrian Gill for drawing my attention to this *festschrift* for C.W. David.
121 G. Le Hardy, 'Le dernier des ducs normands: étude de critique historique sur Robert Courte-Heuse', *Bulletin de la Société des Antiquaires de Normandie*, 10 (1882), pp. 3–184.
122 There have been a number of studies of aspects of Robert's career; e.g. G. Paris, 'Robert Courte-Heuse à la première croisade', *Comptes-rendus des séances de l'Académie des inscriptions et belles-lettres*, 34 (1890), pp. 207–12; Stephanie L. Mooers, '"Backers and Stabbers": Problems of Loyalty in Robert Curthose's Entourage', *Journal of British Studies*, 21 (1981), pp. 1–17; W.M. Aird, 'Frustrated Masculinity: The Relationship between William the Conqueror and his Eldest Son', in Dawn M. Hadley, ed., *Masculinity in Medieval Europe* (Harlow, 1999), pp. 39–55. Kathleen Thompson, 'Robert [called Robert Curthose], Duke of Normandy (b. in or after 1050, d. 1134), Prince and Crusader', *Oxford DNB* (Oxford, 2004). I am grateful to Kathleen Thompson for allowing me to consult her article in advance of publication.
123 Judith A. Green, 'Robert Curthose Reassessed', *ANS*, 22 (1999), pp. 95–116.

CHAPTER ONE

CHILDHOOD

I shall say something briefly about the … character of his parents, so that the reader may know from what root came the qualities that later shone forth in the child.[1]

IN the early 1050s, two of the most powerful rulers of mid-eleventh-century north-western Europe met in the small county of Ponthieu, which lay between their two principalities, to conclude the marriage alliance which probably quite soon afterwards produced Robert 'Curthose', the subject of this biography. Count Baldwin V of Flanders brought his daughter Matilda, a 'very beautiful and noble girl of royal stock', to meet William, ruler of Normandy, who was accompanied by his mother, Herleva, and step-father, Herluin de Conteville.[2] Matilda was probably in her mid to late teens, and her husband, William, was slightly older, perhaps twenty-one or twenty-two years of age.[3] There is no evidence, however, that he was any more sexually experienced than his partner, as the contemporary sources record no premarital liaisons. Indeed, by the early twelfth century, stories were circulating that such was William's 'respect for chastity, especially in early manhood, that public gossip told of his impotence'.[4]

There is no reliable evidence as to any early affective bond between Robert's parents, although one version of the story of their courtship claimed that initially Matilda had rejected William's advances because she refused to marry a bastard. Determined to win her affection or at least her consent to marriage the duke made his way to Bruges and broke into her residence where he beat and kicked her. Not surprisingly Matilda took to her bed to recover, but she was apparently impressed or intimidated enough by this display to declare that

---

[1] *The Life of St Anselm, Archbishop of Canterbury, by Eadmer*, ed. and trans. R.W. Southern (Oxford, 1962), p. 3.
[2] *WP*, pp. 32–3; cf. *WJ*, II, pp. 128–9, places this meeting at Eu.
[3] Douglas, *William the Conqueror*, p. 392; Baldwin V's marriage to Adela of France was not consummated until 1031 and even if Matilda was the eldest child of this union, then she may have been sixteen or seventeen at most by 1049. Adela was still a very young child when she was given in marriage: *WJ*, II, pp. 52–3.
[4] WM, *GR*, I, pp. 500–1. I am grateful to Klaus van Eickel for pointing out this reference.

she would marry no-one else.[5] From Ponthieu, the wedding party proceeded to Eu and, after making various gifts, Count Baldwin formally handed over his daughter to her new husband and the nuptials were celebrated. William and his mother then conducted Matilda to the ducal capital at Rouen, 'with the greatest ceremony and honour'.[6] Robert's maternal lineage was illustrious for there was royal blood in Matilda's veins. Her mother, Adela, was the daughter of King Robert II 'the Pious' of France. Robert's maternal grandfather, Count Baldwin V, was recognised as a man of noble stock and considerable political influence. Even kings acknowledged Baldwin's influence and he had often challenged the Holy Roman Emperor in major wars, concluding them to his own advantage.[7] Clearly, given the doubts concerning the lineage of William's own mother, and the illegitimate nature of her union with his father Robert in the eyes of the Norman court, the match enhanced William's status among the political elite after a decade or more during which his very survival had sometimes been in doubt.[8]

The marriage has been seen as a reflection of the growth of William of Normandy's power in the 1040s.[9] Equally, it enhanced his security through an alliance with his influential neighbour. The marriage was also significant for Robert's father in terms of marking his transition into adulthood. According to the normative values of eleventh-century society a *iuvenis* ('youth') only acquired full adult status when he established for himself an independent household with a suitable wife, and, in due course, the generation of children.[10] It was in the interests not only of the secular lord, but also of his retinue, that he should establish a court from which he could disburse *largesse*. Although marriage by no means always precluded other sexual relationships, the establishment of a stable familial unit was the necessary foundation for long-term dynastic ambition.[11]

The period in a nobleman's life characterised as 'youth' (*iuventus*) was seen as a disruptive influence in society, a time when young men were likely to act rashly, whether by rushing recklessly into battle, or indulging in illicit sexual liaisons, which might prove something of an embarrassment in later life.[12] William's supporters among the Norman aristocracy were anxious for him

---

5 'Chronicle of Tours' in *RHF*, xi, p. 348, cited by Douglas, *William the Conqueror*, p. 79, n. 1.
6 *WJ*, II, pp. 128–31; the translation downplays the sense of jubilation suggested by *tripudium*, a word originally associated with religious dance.
7 *WP*, pp. 30–3.
8 *WJ*, II, pp. 96–7. See also, Elisabeth M.C. van Houts, 'The Origins of Herleva, Mother of William the Conqueror', *EHR*, 101 (1986), pp. 399–404. D.R. Bates, 'The Conqueror's Adolescence', *ANS*, 25 (2002), pp. 1–18.
9 Bates, *William the Conqueror*, pp. 44–5; cf. Crouch, *The Normans*, pp. 71–2.
10 W.M. Aird, 'Frustrated Masculinity: The Relationship between William the Conqueror and his Eldest Son', in Dawn M. Hadley, ed., *Masculinity in Medieval Europe* (London, 1999), pp. 39–55.
11 Bates, 'The Conqueror's Adolescence', pp. 4–5.
12 *WP*, pp. 30–31, stresses that Duke William, by contrast, acted in his youth as 'a man of *the greatest* moderation' [my italics]. G. Duby, 'Youth in Aristocratic Society. Northwestern France in the Twelfth Century', in *idem*, *The Chivalrous Society* (London, 1977), pp. 112–22.

to establish a stable household, a more permanent symbol of dynastic intent, with which they could associate their own ambitions for the future.[13]

The marriage was equally advantageous for Matilda's father. To begin with, it normalised relations with the Norman court. In the early 1030s Robert I of Normandy had been responsible for thwarting Baldwin's attempt to seize power from his own father Baldwin IV.[14] It was also an important alliance in the context of the count of Flanders's wider territorial ambitions, especially with regard to his relationship with the German empire. Despite earlier cordial relations, Baldwin V's policy to expand his influence eastwards brought him into conflict with his German overlord Henry III. To bolster his position, Baldwin V actively sought allies in the 1040s and early 1050s, making use of marriage alliances such as that between his daughter and William to extend his own lordship.[15]

Yet, the negotiators for the marriage between Robert's parents had taken a risk, for although clearly beneficial to both parties the projected union was rumoured to be incestuous and therefore open to condemnation by the ecclesiastical authorities.[16] At the Council of Reims in October 1049, called principally to deal with the problem of simony, Leo IX, an early reforming pope, forbade the projected marriage. Although the reason for the prohibition is not stated explicitly in the report of the council, doubt about the blood relationship between William and Matilda was reason enough for the papal intervention.[17] At this time, the Church condemned marital unions between partners related 'in the seventh degree', which, in effect, meant that individuals were barred from marrying their sixth-cousins.[18] Given the relatively small number of suitable marriage partners allowed by this ruling, this was a considerable problem for the eleventh-century nobility. However, consanguinity could also be deployed by them as an excuse to annul unions which had proved unfruitful or otherwise unsatisfactory.[19]

---

[13] *WJ*, II, pp. 128–9.

[14] *WJ*, II, pp. 52–3 and 53, n. 3.

[15] Nicholas, *Medieval Flanders*, pp. 48–51.

[16] Constance B. Bouchard, 'Consanguinity and Noble Marriages in the Tenth and Eleventh Centuries', *Speculum*, 56 (1981), pp. 268–87.

[17] Dom J. Hourlier, ed., 'Anselme de Saint-Remy, *Histoire de la Dédicae de Saint-Remy*', in *Contribution a l'année Saint Benoît (480–1980). La Champagne Bénédictine*, Travaux de l'Académie de Reims, 160 (Reims, 1981), pp. 179–297 at 252–3. I am grateful to Chris Dennis for drawing my attention to this document. Robert's parents were related in the fifth degree according to the relationship between William and Matilda elucidated by Henri Prentout, in 'Études sur quelques points de l'histoire de Guillaume le Conquérant. II. Le mariage de Guillaume', *Mémoires de l'Académie Nationale de Caen*, 6 (1931), p. 24. I am grateful to David Bates for drawing my attention to Prentout's work mentioned in his review of H.E.J. Cowdrey, *Lanfranc: Scholar, Monk, Archibishop* (Oxford, 2003), in *EHR*, 120 (2005), pp. 433–5 at 434, n. 1.

[18] J. Goody, *The Development of the Family and Marriage in Europe* (Cambridge, 1983), pp. 134–46, 272–7; cf. J.A. Brundage, *Law, Sex and Christian Society in Medieval Europe* (Chicago and London, 1987). I am grateful to Peter Coss for this reference.

[19] C.N.L. Brooke, *The Medieval Idea of Marriage* (Oxford, 1989), pp. 134–6. This prohibition may have provided an incentive for the preservation of genealogical material among the aristocracy of the period.

Despite the papal condemnation, Robert's parents went ahead with the union. Although the growing sacramentalisation of marriage by the Church in this period meant that the approval of the ecclesiastical authorities was becoming increasingly desirable, such politically motivated alliances were too important in the ambitions of the secular aristocracy to be left wholly at the mercy of the papacy. The marriage took place but not without some opposition from within the Norman Church.[20] The marriage between William and Matilda of Flanders has been assigned to the period between its condemnation at the Council of Reims in October 1049 and the first recorded appearance of Matilda as countess in charters issued to the abbey of Saint-Wandrille in Normandy in 1051.[21] If, therefore, William and Matilda consummated their union in 1050 or 1051, it is likely that their eldest child, Robert, was born between 1050 and 1053.[22] Given that the marriage was finally only sanctioned by Pope Nicholas II in 1059, Robert was, for the first few years of his life, the son of an illicit union. Like his father, although for different reasons, Robert was illegitimate. Perhaps it was this ecclesiastical censure, rather than any indifference attributed to the authors of our sources, that worked against the recording of Robert's birth, for the baby was a living embodiment of the couple's defiance of the Church's wishes. Whether this illegitimacy was the subject of the gossip of Norman courtiers is not recorded, but it is the sort of social stigma that might have adhered to Robert from his earliest years.[23]

Brothers and Sisters

The marriage of Robert's parents proved fruitful and the dynastic ambitions of the rulers of Flanders and Normandy were soon realised in the birth of a son. For Baldwin V of Flanders, the infant Robert represented his hopes for the long-term success of his policy of *rapprochement* with his powerful neighbours. For William of Normandy the birth of a healthy son bolstered the chances of his lineage dominating Normandy for at least another generation. The medieval sources are almost silent about Robert's early years and this has led historians to pass over discussions of the childhood and early education of

---

20 WM, *GR*, I, pp. 494–5, claimed that Archbishop Mauger of Rouen's opposition to the marriage cost him his archdiocese.

21 *Fauroux*, nos. 124, 126. *WJ*, II, p. 129, n. 5; the negotiations may have been opened in May 1048, when Duke William and Count Baldwin both attested a royal charter at Senlis (*Fauroux*, no. 114); cf. Bates, 'The Conqueror's Adolescence', p. 15. Among the subscriptions to these charters are *Signum + Roberti iuvenis comitis* (no. 124) and *Signum Roberti + iunioris comitis* (no. 126). These subscriptions which suggest that the infant Robert was present may have been added later; see *Fauroux*, pp. 294, 296.

22 Cf. David, *Robert Curthose*, p. 5 and n. 10.

23 None of the later sources, otherwise assiduous in pointing out Robert's failings, make any capital out of the circumstances of his birth. Once the union had been sanctioned by the papacy, any children already born were legitimised. I am grateful to Emma Mason for discussing with me the possibility of court gossip and the circumstances of Robert's birth.

members of the Norman aristocracy.[24] It is possible to draw on comparative material to give an impression of Robert's childhood experience.

The name 'Robert' was chosen for William and Matilda's eldest son. For the medieval aristocracy names were redolent with genealogical references and conjured up significant memories of key figures in the history of the dynasty.[25] In naming their children, individuals made deliberate genealogical references, perhaps recalling figures from the family's very earliest days.[26] For example, Robert's father was named after his great-great grandfather, William 'Longsword', the son of Rollo, founder of the duchy of Normandy.[27] According to Dudo of Saint-Quentin, Rollo took the name Robert on his conversion to Christianity.[28] So, in naming their child 'Robert', William and Matilda were alluding to the history of their families and conjuring up a series of role models for the child.[29] Similarly, when in due course Robert named his only legitimate son 'William', he was following established practice, linking his son to his family's glorious past and expressing hopes for an illustrious future for the boy.[30]

Robert's name was that of his paternal grandfather and may reveal William of Normandy's wish to commemorate the father he had lost in early child-hood.[31] But the name was also significant in Matilda's family history, for not only was her own grandfather Robert 'the Pious', the Capetian king, but the

---

[24] Exceptions are F. Barlow, *William Rufus* (London, 1983), pp. 8–28; R.V. Turner, 'The Children of Anglo-Norman Royalty and their Upbringing', *Medieval Prosopography*, 11 (1990), pp. 17–52; Judith Green, *The Aristocracy of Norman England* (Cambridge, 1997), chapter 10 'Kinship, Marriage and Family', pp. 329–60, and Emma Mason, *William II. Rufus, the Red King* (Stroud, 2005), pp. 33–5. Pauline Stafford, 'Review article: Parents and Children in the Early Middle Ages', *EME*, 10 (2001), pp. 257–71, and Barbara Hanawalt, 'Medievalists and the Study of Childhood', *Speculum*, 77 (2002), pp. 440–60.

[25] Patricia Skinner, 'Gender and Memory in Medieval Italy', in Elisabeth van Houts, ed., *Medieval Memories. Men, Women and the Past, 700–1300* (Harlow, 2001), pp. 36–52 at 46–7. Cf. Elisabeth van Houts, *Memory and Gender in Medieval Europe, 900–1200* (London, 1999). See R. Bartlett, *England under the Norman and Angevin Kings, 1075–1225* (Oxford, 2000), pp. 538–41.

[26] See Janet Nelson, 'Writing Early Medieval Biography', *History Workshop Journal*, 50 (2000), pp. 129–36 at 131.

[27] WM, *GR*, I, pp. 426–7. William Rufus was also nicknamed 'Longsword' like his great-great-great grandfather: Herman, 'De Miraculis Sancti Eadmundi', in *Memorials of St Edmunds Abbey*, ed. T. Arnold, 3 vols., Rolls Series (London, 1890–6), I, pp. 77, 145. I am very grateful to Emma Mason for supplying this reference.

[28] *Dudo of St Quentin. History of the Normans*, trans. E. Christiansen (Woodbridge, 1998), p. 50. Rollo took the name of his baptismal sponsor, Robert, duke of the Franks.

[29] The naming of children after godparents was also significant as it alluded to the wider kin group into which the infant had been symbolically admitted: B. Jussen, *Spiritual Kinship as Social Practice. Godparenthood and Adoption in the Early Middle Ages*, trans. Pamela Selwyn (Cranbury, NJ, and London, 2000).

[30] WM, *GR*, I, pp. 704–5: 'the son born to him by his wife … was called William for the good omen of his grandfather's name, and encouraged great worth in the future'.

[31] WM, *GR*, I, pp. 504–7; the Conqueror ordered his father's remains to be brought back to Normandy from Nicaea, but when news of William's death came, the bones were reburied in Apulia. Duke William's half brother, the son of Herleva and Herluin de Conteville was also named Robert: B. Golding, 'Robert of Mortain', *ANS*, 13 (1991), pp. 119–44. On the importance of remembering the deeds of one's ancestors, see *Carmen de Hastingæ Proelio*, pp. 20–1.

younger of her two brothers also carried the name.[32] In this case, then, the infant Robert had homonymous ancestors with rather different reputations. On the maternal side Robert 'the Pious', King of France but, in stark contrast, on his father's side, Robert 'the Devil', a man who had died on returning from a pilgrimage to Jerusalem, undertaken, it was rumoured in expiation of the sin of fratricide.[33]

It is not known where Robert was born, but, the palace at Rouen is as likely as any other location.[34] In spite of the ecclesiastical censure of his parents' marriage, it was important that Robert receive baptism, for, in an era of high infant mortality, it was essential to bring the newborn as quickly as possible into the Church. If the child died in infancy, but was baptized, it was thought that its soul would enter heaven, but if un-baptized it might be consigned to Limbo. In an emergency, it was possible for lay people to perform the baptism but, increasingly and especially in an age of reform, members of the clergy claimed a monopoly on the rite. The baptism began with exorcisms and then the godparents, acting on behalf of the infant, made a brief profession of faith. The sources are silent on Robert's baptism and there is no way of knowing who acted as his godparents or whether either of his uncles named Robert stood as sponsor to the child. Perhaps the silence of the sources reflects a certain unease with Robert's status as an illegitimate child, although nothing is known about the baptism of his siblings either. Nevertheless, the baptism would have been among the earliest of Robert's public appearances and it marked a crucial first stage in the creation of his social identity, not only within Norman society, but also as a *fidelis*, a son of the Church.[35]

The physical appearance of Robert's parents excited comment from contemporaries. William of Jumièges, who probably saw Matilda in person, described her as 'a very beautiful and noble girl of royal stock'.[36] For William of Malmesbury, writing after her death, Matilda was 'a model of wisdom and an exemplar of modesty without parallel in our time'.[37] For medieval writers, beauty and nobility were intimately linked, the inner quality manifesting itself

---

32 Matilda's brother Robert married Gertrude of Saxony, the widow of Count Floris I of Frisia in 1063: C. Verlinden, *Robert I le Frison* (Antwerp and Paris, 1935); F-L. Ganshof, *La Flandre sous les premiers comtes* (Brussels, 1943), pp. 47–50 and Nicholas, *Flanders*, pp. 56–57.

33 *WJ*, II, pp. 78–85. On the rumours of Robert's part in the poisoning of his brother, Duke Richard III, see WM, *GR*, I, pp. 308–9.

34 D. Bates, 'Rouen from 900–1204: From Scandinavian Settlement to Angevin "Capital"', in J. Stratford, ed., *Medieval Art, Architecture and Archaeology at Rouen*, British Archaeological Association Conference Transactions (1993), pp. 1–11.

35 On the ceremony itself, see B. Hamilton, *Religion in the Medieval West* (London, 1986), p. 112, and N. Orme, *Medieval Children* (New Haven and London, 2001), pp. 21–35 and (on names), pp. 35–43. On the wider significance, W. Ullmann, *The Individual and Society in the Middle Ages* (London, 1967), pp. 7–9.

36 *WJ*, II, pp. 128–9.

37 WM, *GR*, I, pp. 436–7. Cf. Wace, *The Roman de Rou*, trans. G.S. Burgess (St Helier, 2002), line 4502, pp. 198–9: Matilda was 'mult bele e gente'.

in outward appearance.[38] In 1961 excavation of Matilda's tomb in the choir of the L'Abbaye-aux-Dames (or La Trinité), in Caen, and an examination of the bones purported to be the duchess's revealed that Duke William's wife was petite, less than 1.5m tall.[39] It is very unlikely, however, that these bones can be positively identified as those of Matilda, given the disruptions of the religious wars of the sixteenth century. Without more secure analysis, the origins of Robert's diminutive stature, which later provided an opportunity for his father to heap ridicule upon him, cannot be traced with confidence to his mother's genes.[40]

Robert's father, on the other hand, was, by all accounts, a powerfully built man. His medieval biographer describes him newly armed as a knight in glowing terms.

> It was a sight both delightful and redoubtable to see him hold the reins, girded honourably with his sword, his shield shining, formidable with his helmet and javelin. For as he stood out in beauty when wearing the garments of a prince and at peace, so also the adornments which are put on against the enemy suited him perfectly. From this time a virile spirit and valour shone brilliantly and clearly in him.[41]

Matilda and her husband were a handsome couple, their innate nobility apparent to all. Descriptions of William in later life are less flattering however. According to William of Malmesbury,

> He was of a proper height, immensely stout, with a ferocious expression and a high bald forehead; his arms exceedingly strong, so that it was often a remarkable sight to see no one able to draw his bow, which he himself, while spurring his horse to a gallop, could bend with a taught bowstring. He had great dignity both seated and standing, although his prominent corpulence gave him an un-shapely and un-kingly figure.[42]

Despite remaining a powerful man, William tended towards the obese as he aged, a trait that Malmesbury obviously considered unbecoming in an anointed ruler. Malmesbury could not resist recording an anecdote about the Conqueror's obesity in which he was the butt of a joke made by the French king, Philip I. After falling out with Philip, King William remained indoors. Philip provokingly remarked that 'The King of England lies in Rouen, keeping his bed like a woman who has just had her baby.' Malmesbury explained that Philip was 'joking at his [William's] corpulence, which he had reduced by

---

38 M. Camille, 'The Image and the Self: Unwriting Late Medieval Bodies', in Sarah Kay and Miri Rubin, eds., *Framing Medieval Bodies* (Manchester, 1994), pp. 62–99.

39 Douglas, *William the Conqueror*, p. 370; cf. M. de Boüard, *Guillaume le Conquérant* (Paris, 1984), p. 173.

40 I am grateful to David Bates for pointing out that these earlier speculations about Matilda's stature are 'nonsensical': personal communication, 18 October 2005.

41 *WP*, pp. 8–9.

42 WM, *GR*, I, pp. 508–9.

a drug'. From his father, then, Robert seems to have inherited a powerful build, but one that was prone to run to fat.[43] Combined with his diminutive stature, Robert's physique may have been startling, perhaps even unsettling and ominous to contemporaries conditioned to relate outward appearance to inner nobility and fitness to rule.

William and Matilda's marriage proved fruitful and eventually Robert was to have three brothers and as many as five or possibly six sisters. Robert may have had his parents to himself for two or three years before a brother, Richard, and perhaps one or more of his sisters appeared. The third son, William, was born in, or just before, 1060, and the last, Henry, in 1068, or 1069.[44] Orderic Vitalis noted five daughters: Adelaide, Constance, Cecilia, Adela, and Agatha.[45] When she was a child, Cecilia was offered to the abbey of La Sainte-Trinité (Holy Trinity) in Caen, becoming a nun in 1075 and, eventually, abbess.[46] Adelaide, too, 'vowed herself to God'.[47] Agatha, according to Orderic, was betrothed to Earl Harold of Wessex, and was then sent to marry King *Amfurcius* of Galicia, but died *en route* to the wedding.[48] Constance married Alan Fergant, count of Brittany in 1086, but had no children. By contrast, Adela married Count Stephen of Blois and was mother to the future king of England, Stephen.[49] This then was a large family, not uncommon in eleventh-century Normandy, and, although the survival of so many children seemed to bode well for William and Matilda's dynastic ambitions, it also held out the potential for fault lines to develop within the family's relationships. In particular, those children 'born in the purple' after their parents were crowned, namely Henry and Adela, seem to have had an enhanced sense of self-worth.

---

[43] WM, *GR*, I, pp. 510–11.

[44] WM, *GR*, I, pp. 576–7; when William Rufus died in August 1100, he was at least forty. For the year of Henry's birth, usually given as 1068/9, see Hollister, *Henry I*, pp. 30–1, and Green, *Henry I*, p. 20.

[45] *OV*, II, pp. 104–5, 224–5. WM, *GR*, I, pp. 504–5, names Cecilia, abbess of Caen who was still living when he wrote; Constance, who married Alan Fergant count of Brittany, but was poisoned by her subjects; Adela who married Stephen of Blois and had just taken the veil at Marcigny when Malmesbury was writing. There may have been a sixth daughter, Matilda, mentioned in *Domesday Book*, I, fol. 49. Cf. Douglas, *William the Conqueror*, pp. 394–5.

[46] *OV*, III, pp. 8–11 and n. 5. Cecilia's entry into La Sainte-Trinité was commemorated in a poem by Fulcoius of Beauvais; see Elisabeth van Houts, trans. and ed., *The Normans in Europe* (Manchester, 2000), no. 39, pp. 132–3.

[47] *OV*, III, pp. 114–15, Adelaide 'made a pious end under the protection of Roger of Beaumont'.

[48] *OV*, III, pp. 114–15.

[49] *OV*, III, pp. 116–17. Kimberly A. Lo Prete, 'Adela of Blois: Familial Alliances and Female Lordship', in *Aristocratic Women in Medieval France*, ed. T. Evergates (Philadelphia, PA, 1999), pp. 7–43, 180–200; *eadem*, 'Adela of Blois as Mother and Countess', in *Medieval Mothering*, ed. J.C. Parsons and Bonnie Wheeler (New York, 1996), pp. 313–33; *eadem*, 'Adela of Blois and Ivo of Chartres', *ANS*, 14 (1992), pp. 131–52, and *eadem*, 'The Anglo-Norman Card of Adela of Blois', *Albion*, 22 (1990), pp. 569–89. See now, Kimberley A. Lo Prete, *Adela of Blois. Countess and Lord (c.1067–1137)* (Dublin, 2007). I am grateful to Dr Lo Prete for providing me with copies of these articles and materials from her biography of Countess Adela in advance of publication.

Emotion and the Medieval Family

Medieval family life has only fairly recently received detailed investigation.[50] Although the evidence tends to be fragmentary and concentrates upon the upper echelons of medieval society, it is now recognised that historians can arrive at some arresting conclusions concerning the relationships and roles which shaped and articulated medieval family life. These conclusions challenge stereotypes made popular by earlier writers, whose descriptions of the medieval aristocratic family combined memories of and assumptions about the practices of the nineteenth and early twentieth centuries, rather than those of the eleventh and twelfth, with attempts to make use of Freudian psychology in the reading of medieval texts.[51] Thus medieval aristocratic parents were represented as displaying minimal 'psychological investment' or 'emotional capital' in their children and having an insignificant role in the education and social development of their offspring, especially as they were predisposed to committing their children into the care of wet-nurses, tutors and other guardians.[52]

A more nuanced reconstruction of medieval family life draws on medieval evidence of the normative roles and relationships in operation. Descriptions of medieval family life carried with them the writers' own experience and expectations of suitable parental behaviour, but it is possible to examine contemporary sources in the light of these normative codes in order to illuminate more fully medieval family life.[53] An understanding of how the medieval aristocratic family functioned is all the more crucial given the fact that the institution was at the heart of medieval social and political structures. It was the arena where individuals first learned the rules of social interaction and its influence reached out into the ecclesiastical, cultural and economic spheres.[54]

Medieval family relationships were as susceptible to the vagaries of emotion

---

[50] Janet L. Nelson, 'Family, Gender and Sexuality in the Middle Ages', in M. Bentley, ed., *Companion to Historiography* (London, 1997), pp. 153–76; Cathy Jorgensen Itnyre, *Medieval Family Roles* (New York and London, 1996); Clarissa W. Atkinson, *The Oldest Vocation. Christian Motherhood in the Middle Ages* (Ithaca, NY, 1991); J.C. Parsons and Bonnie Wheeler, eds., *Medieval Mothering* (New York and London, 1996). As yet there is little on the family role of medieval fathers, but see Cathy J. Itnyre, 'The Emotional Universe of Medieval Icelandic Fathers and Sons', in *eadem*, ed., *Medieval Family Roles*, pp. 173–96.

[51] Nancy F. Partner, 'The Family Romance of Guibert of Nogent: His story/Her story', in Parsons and Wheeler, eds., *Medieval Mothering*, pp. 359–79.

[52] P. Ariès, *L'enfant à la vie famille sous l'ancien régime* (Paris, 1960), trans. R. Baldick, *Centuries of Childhood: a Social History of Family Life* (London, 1962); L. Stone, *The Family, Sex and Marriage in England 1500–1800* (London, 1977; abridged and revised 1979). Cf. Turner, 'The Children of Anglo-Norman Royalty', pp. 17–44.

[53] E.g. *OV*, VI, pp. 552–5, where Orderic describes his own tearful parting from his father at the age of ten when he was sent to Saint-Évroul. It is possible that this coloured his view of the proper relationship between Robert and Duke William.

[54] Nelson, 'Family', pp. 154–5.

as those in any other human society. The study of emotion in past societies has encouraged medievalists to re-examine assumptions about the nature
and representation of affective bonds within the medieval family. Whether
or not it is accepted that there are certain 'basic emotions' which all human
beings share as part of their genetic make-up, there is some agreement that
the modes of the expression of emotion vary from one human society to
another.[55] The expression of emotion is culturally specific and, as such, can
be located historically. Thus sensitised, medievalists have begun to explore the
ways in which medieval people expressed and communicated their emotional
responses to one another, their social situation, and their environment.[56]

The expression of emotion by medieval people, rather than representing
an uncontrolled response to a particular situation, has been seen, instead,
as a carefully choreographed and structured form of communication used
to transmit complex ideas relating to the exercise of social and political
power.[57] Although there is the danger of over-interpreting our sources and
reading each instance of social interaction as symbolic communication and
unfolding according to the rules of elaborate ritual, this methodology does
at least offer the opportunity to reconstruct aspects of the personal lives of
medieval people, previously ignored or dismissed as being irrecoverable from
the sources.[58] As long as the conclusions are grounded in close reading of the
sources, it might even be possible to discuss the personalities of medieval
people as they were understood by their contemporaries. Character develops
through the life-course and, in a similar fashion, family relationships evolve as
members of the family mature, review and modify their expectations of their
place within the family, or leave it altogether.[59] With these points in mind, it is
possible to examine the family created by Robert's parents. It is important to
gain some sense of the early relationship between Robert and his mother and
father given the dramatic fashion in which it was to unfold in later years.

Medieval writers recognised that parental affection was not evenly distrib-

55 D. Evans, *Emotion. A Very Short Introduction* (Oxford, 2001). See also, W.M. Reddy, *The Navigation of Feeling. A Framework for the History of Emotions* (Cambridge, 2001); S. Williams, *Emotion
and Social Theory* (London, 2001); R. MacMullen, *Feelings in History, Ancient and Modern* (New
Haven, CT, 2003); D.M. Gross, *The Secret History of Emotion. From Aristotle's Rhetoric to Modern
Brain Science* (Chicago, 2006).

56 P.N. Stearns and Carol Z. Stearns, 'Emotionology: Clarifying the History of Emotions and
Emotional Standards', *AHR*, 90 (1985), pp. 813–36. See also 'The History of the Emotions: a
Debate', *EME*, 10 (2) (2001), pp. 225–56; cf. Barbara Rosenwein, 'Writing without Fear about
Early Medieval Emotions', *ibid.*, pp. 229–34; S. Airlie, 'The History of Emotions and Emotional
History', *ibid.*, pp. 235–41.

57 Cf. Barbara Rosenwein, ed., *Anger's Past. The Social Uses of an Emotion in the Middle Ages* (Ithaca,
NY, and London, 1998). J.E.A. Jolliffe drew attention to the structured use of 'ira et malevolentia'
by the Angevin kings in 1955: *Angevin Kingship*, 2nd ed. (London, 1963), esp. pp. 87–109.

58 For a *caveat* see P. Buc, *The Dangers of Ritual. Between Early Medieval Texts and Social Scientific
Theory* (Princeton, NJ, and London, 2001); cf. Stuart Airlie's comments on the work of Gerd
Althof, *Spielregeln der Politik im Mittelalter* (Darmstadt, 1997) in 'The History of Emotions and
Emotional History', p. 237.

59 Cf. Stafford, 'Parents and Children', p. 269.

uted and that mothers and fathers had favourites among their offspring.[60] Given that each partner brought to an aristocratic marriage dynastic ambitions of their own, any favouritism might have serious political consequences. Such fault lines were most obvious when a nobleman contracted a second marriage and the new wife sought to ensure that her own children displaced those of the earlier union.[61] The figure of the 'wicked stepmother' is common enough in the medieval sources. Even in marriages such as that of William and Matilda, generally viewed as co-operative, the partners might have differing views as to the suitability of their children for the roles mapped out for them.

Family Affections

There is compelling evidence to suggest that Matilda's favourite son was her first born, Robert, whereas her husband, William, came to look upon his namesake as a man in his own image. During a turbulent period in the late 1070s, Matilda took her eldest son's part in his violent quarrel with her husband. She declared the depth of her feelings for Robert to her husband:

> O my lord, do not wonder that I love my first-born child with tender affection. By the power of the most high, if my son Robert were dead and buried seven feet deep in the earth, hid from the eyes of the living, and I could bring him back to life with my own blood, I would shed my life blood for him and suffer more anguish for his sake than, weak woman that I am, I dare to promise.[62]

Similarly, after the death of Richard probably around 1069, we are told that the Conqueror favoured William Rufus and Henry over and above Robert, deliberating playing them off against his wife's favourite. William of Malmesbury portrays Rufus as his father's loyal son, 'always obedient, displaying himself in battle before his eyes, and walking by his side in peacetime'.[63] At one point Rufus was willing to put himself in physical danger in defence of his father.[64] Malmesbury also suggested that the Conqueror had some insight into his youngest son's temperament, although the anecdote in which the Conqueror consoled Henry by predicting his eventual coronation has a mythical ring to it.[65]

---

60 The Empress Matilda favoured William, her youngest child by Geoffrey, Count of Anjou; Marjorie Chibnall, 'The Empress Matilda and her Sons', in Parsons and Wheeler, eds., *Medieval Mothering*, pp. 279–94, at 283. In medieval Icelandic society, fathers preferred those sons who most resembled them: see Cathy Itnyre, 'Emotional Universe', p. 180.

61 E.g. Sikelgaita of Salerno, the second wife of Robert *Guiscard* the Norman ruler of Apulia, worked for her son Roger Borsa against Bohemond, Guiscard's son by his first marriage: see Patricia Skinner, *Women in Medieval Italian Society* (Harlow, 2001), pp. 134–6.

62 *OV*, III, pp. 102–5.

63 WM, *GR*, I, pp. 542–3.

64 *ASC*, E, *s.a.* 1079, p. 92; Swanton, p. 214.

65 WM, *GR*, I, pp. 710–11.

Far from being emotionally detached, Robert's parents were deeply concerned with the welfare of their children, even to the point of taking opposing sides in familial disputes. Given this high level of involvement, it is likely that they also took an active interest in their children's education. The evidence is fragmentary, but in conjunction with contemporary descriptions of the education of other aristocratic children, it is possible to give some impression of Robert's early years.

During his first two years of life, a period known as *infantia* ('infancy'), Robert probably spent much of his time with his mother and perhaps a wet-nurse.[66] It is unlikely that he was absent from the ducal court and probably never strayed far from his mother's side. From an early age, he was present when his parents confirmed donations to churches and, although probably largely unaware of proceedings, his presence represented the future security of the gift.[67]

Medieval writers assigned mothers a principal role in rearing children under seven.[68] So, from Matilda Robert learned to speak the Norman variety of the French vernacular, or perhaps even some early form of Flemish. She may even have imposed discipline on her young children, resorting to corporal punishment, like her contemporary, Queen Margaret of Scotland.[69] As he grew, Robert absorbed the social and cultural traditions of the Normans and, from his mother, those of their Flemish neighbours. Others might also have influenced the infant, perhaps the wet nurse, other servants or his grandmothers, Herleva and Adela, when they were at court.[70] As he grew up, therefore, Robert had access, largely through the women of the family, to the dynastic traditions of the Norman, Flemish and Capetian ruling houses.[71]

Robert's Education

As well as this kind of informal socialisation, the higher nobility in eleventh-century Northern France took care to provide a more structured education for their children when they reached the age of seven. There has been reluctance to imagine that William the Conqueror had any accomplishments other than those of a man of action.[72] Despite evidence to the contrary, older and more negative views on the literacy of the laity in the High Middle Ages continue

---

66 Monica H. Green, *The Trotula* (Philadelphia, PA, 2002), pp. 83–5; cf. Shahar, *Childhood*, p. 23 ('infantia') and 53–76 ('Nursing').
67 Mason, *William II*, p. 33.
68 Shahar, *Childhood*, p. 209
69 See Huneycutt, *Matilda*, p. 166.
70 Herleva's husband, Herluin de Conteville, witnessed, alongside Robert, the charter for the priory of Saint-Martin-du-Bosc, between 1059 and 1066: *Fauroux*, no. 218, pp. 409–15. In 1065, Countess Adela of Flanders contracted a *conventio* with Abbess Elisabeth of Montivilliers, which mentions among others, her grandson Robert: *Fauroux*, no. 226, pp. 434–5.
71 Van Houts, *Memory and Gender*, pp. 65–92.
72 Douglas, *William*, p. 37; cf. Barlow, *Rufus*, p. 20; David Bates, 'Conqueror's Adolescence', p. 16 and

to hold sway.[73] It is argued that there was an antipathy towards education from members of the knightly class, who held the accomplishments of clerks in low regard.[74]

The problem stems partly from a rather narrow interpretation of what literacy involved in this period, and partly from an outmoded and rigid conceptual division between warriors and, for want of a better expression, 'thinkers'. As studies of William Rufus and Henry I have shown, a cultured court at the centre of literary and artistic patronage and an active and successful military entourage might well comprise the same personnel.[75]

Literacy can be viewed in functional terms as the ability to read and to write, especially in Latin, or it can be interpreted as a cultural predisposition, or mentality.[76] Similarly, the inability to read and write, in any language, does not necessarily exclude people from access to written materials. The information or the messages in written texts can be transmitted orally or visually. If the ideas thus transmitted are accepted by those who read, hear or see them, the formally literate and the functionally illiterate together might be part of a single 'textual community'.[77] Perhaps the most extensive expression of this idea was the textual community called 'Christendom', whose members, the powerful and the powerless, the literate and the illiterate, identified with each other through a common acceptance, in theory at least, of the Word of God as transmitted through the Scriptures. In the eleventh century, the Norman ducal court recognised and nurtured literary pursuits, and it is reasonable to suppose that its elite would ensure that such ideas were transmitted to the younger generation.

As a child, Robert's father was provided with a *pedagogus* or *nutricius*. The *pedagogus* was associated with the role of a schoolmaster, which suggests that, like many of the sons and daughters of the ruling families of the French principalities, William was given at least a basic literate education. This may have involved the rudiments of Latin.[78] Similarly, there is evidence that Robert's maternal grandparents provided a formal education for their children. Matilda's Capetian grandfather, Robert 'the Pious', was a well-educated man and it is likely that his daughter, Adela, carried positive ideas about education to Flanders.[79]

n. 102, has a more positive and persuasive view, noting that William continued to have a tutor well into adolescence.

73　V.H. Galbraith, 'The Literacy of the Medieval English Kings', *PBA*, 21 (1935), pp. 201–38.

74　Galbraith, 'Literacy', p. 201; cf. G. Duby, 'The Culture of the Knightly Class. Audience and Patronage', in R.L. Benson and G. Constable, eds., *Renaissance and Renewal in the Twelfth Century* (Oxford, 1982), pp. 248–62.

75　Barlow, *Rufus*, pp. 99–155; Green, *Henry I*, pp. 284–306.

76　C.F. Briggs, 'Literacy, Reading, and Writing in the Medieval West', *JMH*, 26 (2000), pp. 397–420. Cf. M.B. Parkes, 'The Literacy of the Laity', in *idem*, *Scribes, Scripts and Readers. Studies in the Communication, Presentation and Dissemination of Medieval Texts* (London, 1991), pp. 275–97.

77　On this, see B. Stock, *The Implications of Literacy. Written Language and Models of Interpretation in the Eleventh and Twelfth Centuries* (Princeton, NJ, 1983).

78　*WJ*, II, pp. 80–1.

79　J.T. Rosenthal, 'The Education of the Early Capetians', *Traditio*, 25 (1969), pp. 366–76 at 370–1.

The counts of Flanders were also seen by contemporaries as well educated and receptive to the work of scholars. For example, Matilda's brother, Robert 'the Frisian', was recognised as a 'literate man' by Pope Gregory VII in a letter of 1083.[80] Given that aristocratic women were also provided with an education, it seems unlikely that Matilda was less educated than her brother when she departed for Normandy. Orderic Vitalis, whose informants had been close to Matilda herself, noted that, among other virtues, she was endowed with 'learning'.[81] Although Matilda may have been more accomplished than her husband, whose other concerns would undoubtedly have curtailed his opportunities for study, the point to be made is that both Robert's parents were favourably disposed to providing their children with an education, which was as much literary as practical.

The Norman court was a centre of literary patronage in the eleventh century. From the reign of Richard I (942–96), Normandy's rulers commissioned, or had dedicated to them, histories of their dynasty. The Norman ruling house commissioned a dynastic history from Dudo of Saint-Quentin.[82] Accomplished theologians and monastic reformers, such as William of Volpiano, Anselm and Lanfranc of Bec, were also at work in monastic houses under ducal patronage.[83] In addition, Latin poetry, addressed to members of Robert's immediate family, was composed.[84] Picking up the work of Dudo, William of Jumièges began his *Gesta Normannorum ducum* in the early 1050s, later dedicating it to the Conqueror. William of Jumièges noted the 'illustrious men excellently versed and learned in letters' who surrounded the king and his family at court and this statement should not simply be dismissed as meaningless flattery.[85] If the surviving examples of the eleventh-century visual arts are also considered, Robert and his brothers and sisters had access to vibrant and stimulating cultural resources. The picture that emerges is of a family at the centre of a court providing patronage for a variety of eleventh-century cultural activities. The Norman court offered an environment where education in dynastic history, in the essential points of the Christian faith, and in the stories of the classical world could proceed as much by absorption and 'passive literacy' as by active tuition.[86]

---

80 Cowdrey, *Register*, 9.35, pp. 435–9 at 439; J.W. Thompson, *The Literacy of the Laity in the Middle Ages* (Berkeley, CA, 1939; reprinted New York, 1963), p. 141.

81 *OV*, II, pp. 224–5: 'litterarum scientia'.

82 J. Lair, ed., *De moribus et actis primorum Normannie ducum*, Mémoires de la Société des Antiquaires de Normandie (Caen, 1865); cf. *Dudo of St Quentin. History of the Normans*, trans. E. Christiansen (Woodbridge, 1998).

83 Bates, *Normandy before 1066*, pp. 189–235.

84 Elisabeth van Houts, 'Latin Poetry and the Anglo-Norman Court 1066–1135: the *Carmen de Hastingæ proelio*', *JMH*, 15 (1989), pp. 39–62.

85 *WJ*, I, pp. 4–5: 'preclari uiri litterarum pericia admodum eruditi'.

86 Thompson, *Literacy of the Laity*, chapters VI and VII, pp. 123–95. For a broader survey, see J. Bumke, *Courtly Culture. Literature and Society in the High Middle Ages* (Woodstock, NY, 2000). The term 'passive literacy' refers to the idea that written texts can be accessed, even by the formally illiterate, through oral recitation, or performance. Similarly, stories as texts can be transmitted in

Like his father, Robert was assigned tutors who took over his education when he was about seven years of age. It was thought that this age marked the beginning of discretion.[87] Robert's tutors appeared alongside him witnessing documents issued, or confirmed, by the Conqueror. For example, in 1066, just as he was about to depart for the invasion of England, William, along with his eldest son, confirmed lands to Marmoutier Abbey. Among the witnesses was a certain 'Ilgerius, pedagogue of Robert, son of the count'.[88] By 1066 Robert was perhaps fourteen or fifteen years old, indeed the charter referred to him as 'now being of age', yet he was still accompanied by his pedagogue.[89] In an earlier document for the abbey of Saint-Ouen, Rouen, Ilger appears as 'Hilgerius magister pueri', which seems to confirm his position.[90] This also suggests that the titles *magister pueri* and *pedagogus* were interchangeable.[91] Two other individuals were associated with Robert's early education, namely 'Raherius consiliarius infantis' and 'Tetboldus gramaticus'.[92] However, the young Robert's most secure association is with this man Hilger.

In a dramatic account of the beginnings of a rift between Robert and his father, Orderic has the young man refer to his education. After being harangued by his father, Robert rounded on William and exclaimed, 'My lord king, I did not come here to listen to a lecture, for I have had more than enough of these from my schoolmasters.'[93] Whether or not this is an accurate account of the quarrel, or wholly an invention of Orderic, it confirms that contemporaries thought that Robert had been educated, but just what did Robert learn from Hilger and the others, and how was that knowledge conveyed?

Orderic's passage makes reference to the *lectio*, a method of teaching common in the schools of the eleventh and twelfth centuries, whereby the master would take selected passages from approved texts and slowly explain them for his audience. The involvement of the pupil was minimal, the aim being to transmit the approved corpus of knowledge without question. During the twelfth century a more inquisitive method was developed,

---

visual imagery, the premise which underlies the sculptural and artistic decoration of medieval churches. See Stock, *Implications of Literacy*, pp. 13–18.

[87] Shahar, *Childhood*, p. 24.

[88] *Fauroux*, no. 228, pp. 437–8.

[89] *Fauroux*, no. 228, pp. 437–8: 'auctoramento Roberti filii sui faceret confirmari, quia scilicet majoris jam ille etatis'.

[90] *Fauroux*, nos. 204 and 204 *bis.*, pp. 390–2. David, *Curthose*, p. 6 and n. 15 suggested that this might be the same *Hilgerius* who attested a charter of the Conqueror issued at Le Vaudreuil in April 1067. There is, however, no confirmation of this; see Bates, *Acta*, no. 251, pp. 759–62.

[91] Bates, 'Conqueror's Adolescence', p. 16 and n. 102, drew attention to 'signum + Vuillelmi magistri comitis' ('the sign of William master of the count') in two grants dating from the late 1030s or early 1040s; *Fauroux*, nos. 100, pp. 256–7 and 103, pp. 260–2. Barlow, *Rufus*, p. 19, sees a distinction between the *tutor*, a governor or master, and the *pædogogus* or tutor who was socially inferior.

[92] *Cartulaire de l'abbaye de la Sainte-Trinité du Mont de Rouen*, ed. A. Deville (Paris, 1840), no. 60. David, *Curthose*, p. 6 and n. 13. Raherius 'counsellor (adviser) of the child' and Tetbold 'the scholar of grammar'; see Latham, *sv.* 'gramma', p. 214. Engeran, the tutor of Philip I of France, appears in the sources as 'pædagogus, regis custos' and 'magister regis'; see J.T. Rosenthal, 'Education of the Early Capetians', p. 372.

[93] *OV*, III, pp. 100–1.

involving students interrogating discordant or contradictory texts using the tools of logic.[94] Robert may have received the sort of literary education that his brother Henry, or near contemporaries, such as Peter Abelard, experienced, or, perhaps merely elementary instruction in Latin.[95] There are, unfortunately, no surviving indications as to how apt a pupil Robert was. Whether Hilger was involved in Robert's education in letters or concentrated on guiding the boy through the more practical accomplishments of the warrior and courtier is unclear.

A near contemporary of Robert – he was born perhaps ten years later – Guibert, abbot of Nogent not far from Laon, left an account of his own early education by a tutor appointed by his widowed mother. Until the schoolmaster was engaged, Guibert was taught at first by his mother, and he 'had learned the shapes of the letters, but hardly yet to join them into syllables'.[96] Guibert remembered his tutor as a poor grammarian, 'utterly unskilled in prose and verse composition'. To compensate for his own shortcomings, Guibert's schoolmaster imposed an iron discipline on the boy and overworked him to the point of apathy. Under this regime, the boy was not allowed to play with other children, and would often receive floggings, which he naturally considered unjust.[97] Medieval teachers were often depicted carrying a rod or switch, with which literally to beat knowledge into their pupils, but there is nothing to suggest that Robert suffered the same sort of unforgiving regime. St Anselm of Canterbury, who was himself close to the Norman court, railed against such brutality in the education of children in the monastery, suggesting that better results might be obtained through 'fatherly sympathy and gentleness'.[98] Although Guibert's mother intended for him to enter the monastic life, his education at home gives some insight into how the eleventh-century French aristocracy provided for their children.

Robert's parents provided for an early education in the rudiments of the Christian faith.[99] Detailed study of the Scriptures tended to be reserved for boys in monastic education, although children were also instructed in the *Psalter*, and their religious education may even have been a special preserve of their mother. According to the 'Life of Queen Margaret of Scotland',

[94] For this scholastic method, see Abelard in his *Historia Calamitatum* ('History of my Misfortunes'); see *The Letters of Abelard and Heloise*, trans. Betty Radice (Harmondsworth, 1974), pp. 57–106.

[95] For Henry's education see WM, *GR*, I, pp. 708–11. On the curriculum, see Shahar, *Childhood*, pp. 177–8; M.T. Clanchy, *Abelard. A Medieval Life* (Oxford, 1997), p. 82 and see p. 59 where Clanchy draws attention to a letter from Abelard which refers to St Jerome's recommendation that children should be taught using toy letters made of ivory. Nicholas Orme, *From Childhood to Chivalry. The Education of the English Kings and Aristocracy 1066–1530* (London, 1984), p. 18 and n. 92, interpreted Hilger's role as pedagogue in terms of 'knightly master' and suggested that Hilger was therefore 'probably a knight'.

[96] J.F. Benton, *Self and Society in Medieval France* (New York, 1970; revised ed. Toronto, 1984), p. 45.

[97] Benton, *Self and Society*, pp. 47–8.

[98] *Life of St Anselm*, p. 38, cited in Clanchy, *Abelard*, p. 59.

[99] WP, pp. 82–3; OV, II, pp. 224–5, noted that Matilda's most praiseworthy personal trait was 'firma fides et studiosus amor Christi' ('a strong faith and fervent love of Christ').

written for Robert Curthose's god-daughter, Edith-Matilda, Margaret 'taught them [her children] about Christ and faith in Christ, using words suitable to their age and understanding'.[100] In addition, communion, however infrequent, and attendance at great religious ceremonies, such as the dedication of churches, exposed Robert to the intense, if conventional, piety attributed to both his parents. Very often such ceremonies were the occasion for making or confirming grants of resources to religious houses. Although written documents were nearly always issued on such occasions to record the endowment, other methods of fixing the event in the memory were also employed. Robert's father had witnessed the grant of an estate to the abbey of St Peter at Préaux. So that William would remember the transaction, his father instructed him to place the record of the donation on the altar of the church, and then he, and other youngsters among the witnesses, were struck, 'ob causam memorie', so that they would remember the cuff around the ear and bear witness to the event in the future.[101]

Robert's formal education was probably shared, at least in its basics, by his brothers and sisters.[102] For example, Cecilia, admittedly given as a child oblate, was taught the *trivium*, Latin grammar, rhetoric and logic, by the Fleming Arnulf of Chocques, whom William and Matilda had recruited as schoolmaster and chaplain to the nuns of La Sainte-Trinité in Caen.[103] It is often claimed that medieval families tended to earmark certain of their sons and daughters for a career in the Church, and that the early education of these aristocratic children was geared towards preparing them for this. Certainly, some, like Orderic Vitalis, were given to monasteries as child oblates, or promised to the monastic life on the understanding that they would enter it at some future date. However, given the uncertainty of the survival of medieval children, families needed to keep their options open. Occasionally, it was necessary to recall a man from the cloister to take over as lord of the family lands. Conversely, some eleventh-century knights decided to renounce the world and enter the religious life, many after making an agreement with their wives and family. Some, who were found to be inadequate in their roles as secular lords, or, who were, like Richard III of Normandy's son Nicholas, an obstacle to ambitious relatives, were also packed off to monasteries.[104]

Modern historians seem reluctant to accept that the parents of the early medieval nobility recognised the efficacy of a literary education for members of their family who were destined for secular positions of power. Nevertheless, William of Malmesbury tells us that Robert's brother, Henry, who had received a 'princely education', 'served his apprenticeship to learning in the

---

100   Huneycutt, *Matilda of Scotland*, p. 166.
101   *Fauroux*, no. 89, pp. 230–1; cf. Van Houts, *Normans*, no. 19, pp. 76–7, and Emily Z. Tabuteau, *Transfers of Property in Eleventh-Century Norman Law* (Chapel Hill and London, 1988), p. 149.
102   There is no information on the education of Richard. For William Rufus, Barlow, *Rufus*, pp. 21–4; cf. Mason, *William II*, p. 32.
103   David, *Curthose*, p. 219 and n. 15.
104   *WJ*, II, pp. 46–7.

grammar school, and with such eagerness did he absorb the honeyed sweets of books that in later life war's alarms and the thronging cares of peace were alike unable to dislodge them from his noble heart'. Malmesbury also wrote that Henry was wont to repeat in his father's hearing the proverb 'rex illiteratus asinus coronatus' ('an illiterate king [is] a crowned ass').[105] This has been taken as a slight against the Conqueror's own education but, equally, it might be read as Henry attempting to ingratiate himself with his father, by pointing out that he had the qualities considered necessary for a ruler by his parents.

Robert's education should not, therefore, be taken as a sign that his parents had any special reason for thinking he was more suited to the contemplative rather than the active life. It is rather that, like his brothers and sisters, he was given a literate education because it was felt that it was appropriate for the sons and daughters of the nobility. Rulers such as William of Normandy and his contemporaries recognised the practical value of education. Education was also a distinction of status, another marker of difference between the nobility and the rest.[106] It therefore seems unlikely that the sons of obscure knights from Brittany or the Beauvaisis received a scholarly education while the children of the most powerful ruling dynasties of Northern France did not.[107]

William and Matilda prepared their eldest son to participate in the duties associated with lordship over Normandy. By the time that Robert reached adolescence, he was considered the successor to his father's duchy. However, just as he was being groomed for this role, Robert's expectations of power were frustrated, by the very man he was expected to emulate: his father.

---

[105] WM, *GR*, I, pp. 708–11; cf. Galbraith, 'Literacy', pp. 212–13, where attention is drawn to John of Salisbury's explanation of the origins of this proverb. See also Barlow, *Rufus*, p. 20, and Hollister, *Henry I*, pp. 33–7, where it is pointed out that Henry's soubriquet *Beauclerc* cannot be found earlier than the late fourteenth century.

[106] Rosenthal, 'Education of the Early Capetians', pp. 374–5.

[107] The reference is to Abelard, born in 1079 at Le Pallet near Nantes, and Guibert, born around 1064 in the Beauvaisis.

CHAPTER TWO

THE DUTIFUL SON

A S Robert grew into boyhood, his father's power within Normandy was
consolidated. In 1054 and 1057 William successfully defended his duchy
against attacks by Henry I of France and Count Geoffrey of Anjou. Their
enmity was largely a response to William's growing influence but, in 1060,
both died, leaving problems for their successors and opportunities for their
neighbours. By the end of his first decade, Robert was already a key figure
in his father's plans to extend Norman influence. This chapter deals with
Robert's betrothal to Margaret, heiress to the county of Maine. It also considers
Robert's military training and the acquisition of skills that were considered
essential not only for his career as a great chivalric hero, but also in creating
and maintaining his social identity.

Margaret of Maine

William wished, as a wise conqueror and dutiful parent, to make the best provision
for the future of his children. For that reason he had Herbert's sister brought from
the Germanic lands by his generosity, at great expense, and destined her to marry
his son, so that through her he and his offspring could, by that same right which
could not be overthrown or weakened by any contention, possess the inheritance of
Herbert as brother-in-law and grandchildren.[1]

The betrothal to Margaret of Maine initiated Robert into his father's ambitions for the extension of Norman lordship and influence. Although no more
than about ten or eleven, Robert found himself committed to a marriage with
a girl barely older. Margaret, 'far more beautiful than any pearl' – a pun on the
Latin *margarita*, 'a pearl' – was the daughter of Count Hugh IV of Maine and
his wife, Bertha. Count Hugh had died in 1051, leaving Margaret's brother,
Herbert II 'Bacon', as his heir; after the death of Herbert in 1062, William
invaded Maine.[2]

---

[1] *WP*, pp. 62–3.
[2] R. Latouche, *Histoire du Comté du Maine pendant le Xe et le XIe siècle* (Paris, 1910), p. 29 and
Appendix III, pp. 113–15. R. Barton, *Lordship in the County of Maine, c.890–1160* (Woodbridge,

The county of Maine lies to the south of Normandy and in the eleventh century it was caught between two more dominant powers: Anjou and Normandy. It was also under pressure from the Bellême family who were intent on carving out an independent lordship by annexing lands in northern Maine and southern Normandy. At the time of Count Hugh's death, the Angevin count, Geoffey Martel, asserted his lordship and in the 1050s consolidated his hold over Maine by capturing Le Mans. Geoffrey was the inveterate opponent of William and resistant to any interference in the region. To that end he had fostered links with the Bellême clan, encouraging their encroachments into southern Normandy at Alençon and in the bishopric of Sées.[3]

Before 9 March 1062, Count Herbert came to an arrangement with William of Normandy which provided the latter with a pretext for becoming more directly involved in Maine. However, the principal source for these events is the duke's partisan William of Poitiers. Duke William's biographer felt the need to preface his account of the invasion of Maine by saying that:

> We know that the tongues of men are more apt to speak at length of evil than of good, often out of envy, at other times because of some other depravity. For sometimes even the finest deeds are, by evil distortion, turned into the opposite. So it often happens that the virtuous acts of kings, dukes, or other great persons, when they are not truly reported, are condemned in a later age by good men; while wrongs, which should on no account be imitated are held up as examples of usurpations and other wicked deeds. Wherefore we think it worthwhile to hand down to posterity the exact truth of how this William – whose memory we wish to preserve in writing, and whom we wish to seem in no way displeasing, in everything pleasing to all men both present and future – was able to gain possession of the principality of Maine in the same way as the English realm, not just by force but also by the laws of justice.[4]

No precise date is given, but Herbert came to Normandy before 14 November 1060, when Geoffrey Martel died. Not surprisingly, the Norman source portrays Angevin lordship in Maine as oppressive and Herbert's submission to Robert's father as voluntary and part of a search for protection.[5] William

---

2004); Bruno Lemesle, *La société aristocratique dans le Haut-Maine (XIe–XIIe siècles)* (Rennes, 1999); I should like to thank Richard Barton for bringing Lemesle's work to my attention.

3   J. Boussard, 'La seigneurie de Bellême aux Xe et XIe siècles', *Mélanges Louis Halphen* (Paris, 1951), pp. 43–54; G.H. White, 'The First House of Bellême', *TRHS*, 22 (1940), pp. 67–99, and Kathleen Thompson, 'Family and Influence to the South of Normandy in the Eleventh Century', *JMH*, 11 (1985), pp. 215–26.

4   *WP*, pp. 56–9. Cf. D. Bates, 'Writing a New Biography of William the Conqueror', pp. 15–16, and *idem*, 'The Conqueror's Earliest Historians', pp. 133–5.

5   *WP*, pp. 58–61. Herbert was still on good terms with Geoffrey Martel as late as 31 July 1056; see *WP*, p. 58, n. 1. *OV*, II, pp. 116–17, added that Herbert was advised by his mother Bertha, daughter of Stephen, count of Blois, to commend himself to William. *WP*'s account was a positive reconstruction and ordering of the past using the rituals of seeking protection and performing homage as instruments of legitimisation. See P. Buc, 'Political Rituals and Political Imagination in the Medieval West from the Fourth Century to the Eleventh', in *The Medieval World*, ed. P. Linehan and Janet L. Nelson (London, 2001), pp. 189–213.

of Normandy, offering good lordship, was the antithesis to Geoffrey's tyrant. Herbert performed homage to William, then acknowledged that he would hold his lands from him 'as a knight (or vassal) from his lord'.[6] William of Poitiers is careful to underline the justice of Duke William's cause on a number of levels. He strengthened his case by stating that Herbert designated William his heir, if he should die childless, and, in order to make that eventuality less likely, the count agreed to marry one of the duke's daughters.[7]

William of Poitiers' account does seem a little too neat in providing a justification for William's invasion of Maine supposedly soon after Hugh of Maine's demise in 1062.[8] Perhaps William had in fact moved more swiftly after the deaths in 1060 of those most likely to oppose him. Geoffrey of Anjou's death precipitated a succession struggle between his nephews Geoffrey the Bearded and Fulk le Rechin. By a fortuitous coincidence, Henry I's death left his young son Philip I in the hands of his guardian, Duke William's father-in-law, Baldwin V of Flanders.[9] Even the troublesome Bellêmes had been brought to heel by the time William launched his attack.[10]

In case Herbert's death should appear to have weakened the justification for Norman claims to intervene in Maine, Poitiers added the proposed marriage between Margaret, Herbert's sister, and an unnamed son of Duke William, whom Orderic identifies as Robert.[11] Margaret was brought to Normandy, but because Robert was still too young to consummate the marriage, she was committed to the care of 'noble matrons and wise men'.[12] At this period, it was thought that only when children reached the age of seven could they express their own will adequately and might they be betrothed. Whether Robert and Margaret exchanged rings or signified the arrangement with a ritual kiss, or whether they even actually met each other at this stage, is not known.[13] This was essentially an arrangement made on their behalf to further the dynastic ambitions of an older generation and the sentiments of the betrothed were of secondary importance. The iniquities of the betrothal of children were recognised and, as the Church gradually came to influence the conduct of marriage, this practice was no longer considered binding from the latter half of the twelfth century.[14]

---

6   *WP*, pp. 58–9.
7   *WP*, pp. 58–9. The daughter is not named.
8   Bates, *Normandy before 1066*, pp. 81–2, and cf. *idem*, *William the Conqueror*, p. 51.
9   *WP*, pp. 56–7. Geoffrey Martel died 14 November 1060. Henry I of France died 4 August 1060.
10 Bates, *Normandy before 1066*, pp. 79–80.
11 *WP*, pp. 62–5, and *OV*, II, pp. 116–17. The editors of the *Gesta Guillelmi* suggested that Robert was not named by William of Poitiers possibly because when he was writing (c.1073–77) Robert was in rebellion; *WP*, pp. 62–3, n. 3.
12 *WP*, pp. 62–3; Margaret was nearly marriageable (*prope nubilem*). Girls as young as twelve might be considered marriageable; see Shahar, *Childhood*, p. 224. *OV*, II, pp. 118–19 and n. 6, names Stigand of Mézidon, a ducal steward (*dapifer*) from at least 1061, as one of her guardians.
13 See Brundage, *Law, Sex and Christian Society*, pp. 33–4 and 497–8; cf. M.P. Foley, 'Betrothals: Their Past, Present and Future', *Studia Liturgica*, 33.1 (2003), pp. 37–61, esp. 39–45.
14 Shahar, *Childhood*, p. 24.

However, Margaret died before the wedding could take place. William of Poitiers presented the tragedy as the fulfilment of Margaret's wish to dedicate herself to Christ.[15] His portrayal of Margaret's piety is worth quoting:

> This noble virgin whose name was Margaret was far more beautiful than any pearl. But not long before the day when she should have been joined to her mortal spouse, the Son of the Virgin, Spouse of Virgins and King of Heaven, took her from men; the pious girl was so inflamed by His saving fire and so desired Him that she devoted herself to prayer, abstinence, mercy, humility, and indeed to all good works, vehemently wishing never to know any marriage except to Him. She was buried in the monastery of Fécamp which, along with other churches, grieved greatly (as far as religious faith allows) that she for whom it tenderly desired a long life had been snatched away by premature death. Her soul, indeed, was prudently watchful, awaiting with lighted lamp the coming of Christ, and she had begun to cherish and honour churches. The hair shirt, which she had resolved to wear secretly to tame her flesh, showed after her death how intent her mind had been on things eternal.[16]

There is no reason to doubt the sincerity of Margaret's intense piety, and the display of asceticism described by Poitiers may have been an attempt to avoid marriage. There would have been few avenues of resistance open to a young girl exiled in a foreign land and forced into an arranged marriage, but Margaret seems to have succeeded in thwarting Duke William's plans for her, albeit at the cost of her own life.[17] If the girl herself was too young to respond to anti-Norman sentiment, perhaps the 'noble matrons and wise men' into whose care she was given influenced her, or perhaps other interests were determined to thwart William's plans. Duke William may have thought better of the marriage once Le Mans had fallen, as the marriage of his eldest son was a diplomatic advantage to keep in reserve as long as possible. There is no way of knowing what Robert's views on the marriage were, but it is probably safe to assume that, at this stage, he would have followed his parents' wishes. Margaret was buried at the abbey of Fécamp, where her tomb may have become the focus of a cult.[18]

There is the possibility that William had in fact invaded Maine and forced Count Herbert to come to terms. In this case, Poitiers' account looks like an attempt to whitewash an act of aggression and might explain violent opposition in Maine to Norman lordship. Whether the nominal overlord of Maine,

---

15 I am grateful to Emma Mason for the suggestion that William of Poitiers' account may reflect the promotion of her cult at the abbey of Fécamp.

16 *WP*, pp. 62–5. This passage contains a number of motifs often found in narratives of medieval saints' lives.

17 There are parallels here with the fate of Robert's own sister Agatha; *OV*, III, pp. 114–15 and n. 1. See also Christina of Markyate's resistance to an arranged marriage in C.H. Talbot, ed. and trans., *The Life of Christina of Markyate, a Twelfth-century Recluse* (Oxford, 1959). Cf. T. Head, 'The Marriages of Christina of Markyate', *Viator*, 21 (1990), pp. 75–101.

18 M. l'Abbé Sauvage, 'Des Miracles advenus en L'Église de Fécamp', in *Mélanges, Documents*, 2e série, Société de l'Histoire de Normandie (Rouen, 1893), pp. 9–49. I owe to Emma Mason the suggestion that Margaret's guardians influenced the girl and that her tomb may have been the focus of a cult.

Geoffrey le Barbu ('the Bearded') of Anjou, was able to resist is open to question. William's campaign isolated Le Mans by ravaging the county and picking off major castles one by one. As a successor to Count Herbert II, the Manceaux had chosen Walter III of Mantes, Count of the Vexin, who had a claim through his wife Biota, daughter of Count Herbert I 'Wake Dog'. Despite this resistance, Duke William was successful and before the end of 1063 he had entered Le Mans in a triumphal *adventus*, a ritual that signified the recognition of his lordship by the bishop and people of the city.[19] Walter and his wife were sent as captives to Falaise, where they both died.[20] Finally, William captured the castle of Geoffrey of Mayenne, one of the most powerful lords in Maine.[21]

It is unclear exactly when Margaret died, but William of Poitiers places her death after the fall of Le Mans. When it is added to those of Walter of Mantes and his wife, it is understandable why the Conqueror's biographer felt it necessary to offer his own version of the Norman conquest of Maine.

Although William had been successful in Maine, he was prepared to allow his young son to acknowledge Angevin claims to lordship. So, at the age of eleven or so, Robert occupied centre stage in a ceremony that regularised the relationship between Anjou, Normandy and Maine.[22] Shortly afterwards Geoffrey of Anjou's brother Fulk rebelled against him.[23] It is significant that Geoffrey met William and Robert at Alençon, which was on Norman soil. Usually a lord would summon his vassal to come to him as a sign of where the power lay in their relationship. However, Geoffrey's problems with his brother may have forced him to come to Alençon in order to acknowledge Duke William's claims in Maine. By having Robert perform the act of homage, William also avoided the potential difficulty of becoming another man's vassal. Although Robert was recognised as the heir to Herbert's fief, it was clear that as he was still a boy, any effective control in Maine belonged to his father.

This was Robert's first personal experience of the performance of homage, a demonstrative act, which was one of the fundamental bonds between indi-

---

19 WP, pp. 60–3.
20 WP, pp. 60–1. OV, II, pp. 118–19, n. 2 and pp. 312–13; writing in the mid-1120s reported a rumour that Walter and Biota, who died at Falaise, were poisoned by their enemies. Cf. David, *Curthose*, p. 8; Douglas, *William the Conqueror*, p. 410, and Bates, *William the Conqueror*, p. 52.
21 WP, pp. 64–9. Note WP's vague chronology of Geoffrey's resistance, pp. 64–5, n. 3; cf. Bates, *William the Conqueror*, p. 53. On Mayenne as a stronghold, see WP, pp. 64–7. The detail in WP's account suggests that he may have been present at the siege. Annie Renoux, 'Château et pouvoir dans le comté du Maine: Mayenne du dernier tiers du IXe au début du XIIe siècle (c.870–1120)', *Château Gaillard*, 20 (2002), pp. 235–45, and R. Early, 'Le Château de Mayenne: les temoins archéologiques de l'évolution d'un centre de pouvoir entre le Xe et le XIIe siècle', *Château Gaillard*, 20 (2002), pp. 247–62.
22 OV, II, pp. 304–5. The ceremony is not dated but it would fit the circumstances after the fall of Le Mans in 1063. OV, II, pp. 304–5, n. 3, implies that Margaret was still alive at this point.
23 O. Guillot, *Le Comte d'Anjou et son entourage au XIe siècle*, 2 vols. (Paris, 1972), I, pp. 102–11 at 105–6.

viduals in eleventh-century society.[24] Descriptions of acts of homage are comparatively rare, but one survives from early twelfth-century Flanders. In the town of Bruges, between 7 and 10 April 1127, the men of Flanders performed homage to their new count, William Clito, who, incidentally, was Robert's son and heir. The ceremony is described in detail by Galbert of Bruges, who produced a dramatic account of the murder of William's immediate predecessor, Count Charles 'the Good'. The ritual proceeded in the following way: first, Count William asked each noble whether he was willing to become his man. The noble replied, 'I so wish' and clasped his hands together. The count then enclosed the noble's hands with his own and 'they were bound together by a kiss'. The kiss was usually on the mouth and was a sign of trust. This, then, was an act of homage. It was followed by the pledge of faith, or fealty, by the vassal:

> I promise on my faith that I will henceforth be faithful to Count William and that I will maintain my homage toward him completely against everyone, in good faith and without guile.

To make the oath more binding and more solemn, it was sworn on the relics of the saints. This brought the supernatural power of God, working through the saints, into the act and promised divine retribution if the oath should be discarded.[25] On the face of it, the ceremony seems to represent the voluntary submission of one man to another and the creation of a hierarchical bond. There was a degree of reciprocity, however, as the vassal had a right to expect his lord to fulfil his side of the bargain, that is granting the vassal some gift in return and offering protection and support in the future.[26]

Although there may have been variations between the ceremony described by Galbert of Bruges in Flanders in the late 1120s and that performed by Robert on the borders of Normandy in the early 1060s, it is likely that the essence of the bond remained constant. Robert would have seen the act performed at the Norman court, but this was his personal initiation into the idea of accepting a man other than his father as his lord. It was also Robert's introduction to the formation of meaningful social bonds beyond those of the family. The ceremony at Alençon broadened his social and political horizons at a stroke and, perhaps for the first time, focused the boy's attention on the future role his parents had mapped out for him. Robert's personal horizons had been extended, but his father, who witnessed the ceremony, relied on the fact that Robert would always acknowledge his filial duty above any

---

24 J. Le Goff, 'The Symbolic Ritual of Vassalage', in *idem, Time, Work and Culture in the Middle Ages*, trans. A. Goldhammer (Chicago, 1980), pp. 237–87.

25 *Galbert of Bruges, The Murder of Charles the Good*, trans. and ed. J.B. Ross (New York, 1959; reprinted 1982), pp. 206–7. Le Goff, 'The Symbolic Ritual of Vassalage', pp. 237–87 at 250–3. Cf. Constance Brittain Bouchard, *Strong of Body, Brave and Noble. Chivalry and Society in Medieval France* (Ithaca, NY, and London, 1998), pp. 43–6.

26 For the oath of fidelity, see *The Letters and Poems of Fulbert of Chartres*, ed. and trans. F. Behrends (Oxford, 1976), no. 51, pp. 91–3.

other obligations, so that his control over Maine might be maintained. On the other hand, Robert, young as he was, now had lordship, albeit it nominal, over a substantial fief and the acquisition of Maine and his betrothal held out the prospect of a secure and independent future. We can only speculate on what effect these events had on Robert's own self-esteem as he approached his teenage years.

The strength of Norman control in Maine during William of Normandy's lifetime should not be overestimated. There was no wholesale Norman settlement of the county and few, if any, of the local castellan families were displaced.[27] The duke received the fealty of members of the aristocracy of Maine, Le Mans was occupied by a Norman garrison and, in 1065, a Norman was installed as bishop, but the realities of Norman rule did not, however, extend much beyond these measures. The campaign of 1063, far from imposing secure Norman control in Maine, merely extended the range of problems with which William and his successors would have to deal.

Robert's title may have been an empty one, but it does appear to have been used. In a document issued before 1066, Robert appears as 'comes Cenomannis' or 'Count of the men of Maine'.[28] It is not recorded whether Robert actually took part in the campaign which presented him with his first title, or whether he joined his father's triumphal entry into Le Mans. It seems unlikely that the boy would have been put in harm's way, especially given the plans Duke William had for him to marry Margaret, but he may have been needed as a visible claimant to Maine. He was the acknowledged heir to Normandy itself for, in a record of a donation made to the abbey of Saint-Ouen at Rouen by a certain Estigandus, perhaps William's steward Stigand de Mézidon, who had had custody of Margaret, Robert was recorded as giving his consent as he had been chosen to rule the principality (*regnum*) after his father's death.[29]

From Boy to Youth

Before the Norman invasion of England in September 1066, Robert was educated at his father's court in the roles he was expected to fulfil. Robert's socialisation involved learning the skills that would ensure his acceptance and effective functioning among Normandy's ruling class. The advantages he possessed as the son of the ruler were crucial, but if he was to have any independent influence at some stage in the future, he had to assimilate the

---

[27] Bates, *William the Conqueror*, p. 53.

[28] *Fauroux*, no. 224, pp. 426–32.

[29] *Fauroux*, no. 158, pp. 343–4, an edition of Archives Seine-Maritime, 14 H 744. Robert is styled *Rodberti, eorum filii, quem elegerant ad gubernandum regnum post suum obitum*. The date of 29 June 1063 suggests that the prospect of the campaign prompted Duke William to make provision for the succession to Normandy.

norms of behaviour and fulfil the expectations of those who counted among Normandy's political elite.

Robert was developing his aristocratic masculine identity through learning to behave in a manly fashion. One of the roles he was expected to perform was that of a soldier. Eleventh-century noblemen identified themselves closely with the figure of the mounted warrior, the *miles* or knight. The aristocracy's social position derived from their noble status, but presenting and conducting themselves as mounted warriors gave them the opportunity to display their distinctiveness, whether that was at court or on the battlefield.[30] Robert's induction into the social idioms of the Norman nobility formed an important element of his personal identity.

By the time Robert became Count Geoffrey of Anjou's vassal, he had already begun his military training at his father's court. From an early age children imitated their elders and played with toy horses, fighting mock-battles with wooden swords and miniature lances or taking it in turn to build and defend castles made out of sticks or sand.[31] Robert's father may have taken a hand in educating his sons but it is more likely that they were handed over to a trusted member of the ducal entourage. One of those designated *consiliarius* or *pedagogus* may have trained Robert. The usual practice was for the sons of the nobility to be sent away from their family to be socialised at the court of their father's lord, who might be the duke himself. This practice appealed especially to the lower echelons of the nobility as it offered their offspring the chance of associating with a great lord and, as a member of his household, sharing in some of the *kudos* generated by his social standing. However, it is unlikely that William would have let his eldest son far out of his sight, especially after Robert had been designated heir to Normandy and the County of Maine.

Given the necessity of acquiring equestrian skills, it is certain that Robert had already learnt to ride by the time he began his military training and his later prowess in mounted warfare suggests that he displayed an early natural aptitude as a horseman. Only through disciplined practice could he learn how to control his horse while handling the weapons and armour characteristic of the Norman mounted warrior, namely the sword, shield, lance, hauberk and helmet, which we see depicted so vividly in the Bayeux Tapestry.[32]

An essential element in Robert's military training would have been learning how to manoeuvre his horse and fight in co-operation with other mounted

---

[30] D. Crouch, *The Birth of the Nobility. Constructing Aristocracy in England and France 900–1300* (Harlow, 2005).

[31] Bartlett, *England under the Norman and Angevin Kings*, p. 238 and n. 120; Gerald of Wales tells us that when his brothers built sand castles he built sand cathedrals thus indicating a future career in the church; see Giraldus Cambrensis, 'De rebus a se gestis', in *Giraldus Cambrensis, Opera*, ed. J.S. Brewer, J.F. Dimock and G.F. Warner, 8 vols., Rolls Series (London, 1861–91), I, pp. 3–122 at 21, trans. H.E. Butler, *The Autobiography of Gerald of Wales* (London, 1937; reprinted Woodbridge, 2005), p. 35. See also R. Bartlett, *Gerald of Wales. A Voice of the Middle Ages* (Stroud, 2006).

[32] E.g. Musset, *Bayeux Tapestry*, scenes 48, 51–2. See I. Peirce, 'The Knight, his Arms and Armour in the Eleventh and Twelfth Centuries', in *The Ideals and Practice of Medieval Knighthood I*, ed. C. Harper-Bill and Ruth Harvey (Woodbridge, 1986), pp. 152–64.

warriors. On the battlefield knights were organised into small groups known as 'constabularies' or *conrois*. These, rather than the lone knight, were the effective fighting formations of the eleventh century.[33] The members of each *conroi* learned to fight as a unit and their sense of teamwork was crucial, not only for the success of their lord, but also for their own survival in the midst of the noise and chaos of medieval battle. The emphasis was on loyalty to one's comrade, for a knight's survival might depend as much on his sense of duty as his fighting effectiveness. Robert was trained in the company of other boys his own age and many of them would in time become members of his retinue. Although they were taught to co-operate, there was still room for competitiveness among Robert's peer group. His position as the duke's eldest son would have made him attractive as a potential lord, a source of future patronage and *largesse*. A few years later Robert's younger brother, William Rufus, 'passed his youth in knightly exercises, riding and shooting, competing with his elders in courtesy, with his contemporaries in courtly duties'. In addition, Rufus was always striving to get noticed by his father in battle.[34]

Military training was hazardous and adolescents lost their lives in accidents associated with their martial apprenticeship. For example, two sons of the family of Giroie were killed in just such a fashion. Arnold of Giroie died after being thrown against rocks in a wrestling match and his younger brother, Hugh, was struck and killed during javelin practice.[35]

As well as formal, organised training in chivalric skills, the favourite pastime of the medieval nobility also honed equestrian and martial skills. Robert's father was particularly fond of hunting – as his creation of the New Forest in Hampshire attests – and this characteristically aristocratic activity offered his sons the chance to ride and shoot with purpose in pursuit of a living and unpredictable prey.[36] But the hunt could be dangerous, indeed fatal, as the deaths of Robert's brothers, Richard and William Rufus, demonstrate. According to Orderic, Richard

> had gone hunting in the New Forest, near Winchester; and whilst he was galloping in pursuit of a wild beast he had been badly crushed between a strong hazel branch and the pommel of his saddle, and mortally injured.[37]

The death of William Rufus while hunting in the New Forest on Thursday 2 August 1100, is more suspicious. He was killed by an arrow fired by Walter

---

33 See Peirce, 'The Knight, his Arms and Armour', p. 162; see S. Morillo, 'Introduction' in *idem*, ed., *The Battle of Hastings* (Woodbridge, 1996), pp. xi–xxxii at xxiii–xxx and the comment at xxii.

34 WM, *GR*, I, pp. 542–3.

35 *OV*, II, pp. 24–5 [Arnold]; III, pp. 114–15 [Hugh]; cf. Chibnall, *World of Orderic Vitalis*, pp. 132–3.

36 Bartlett, *England under the Norman and Angevin Kings*, pp. 238–4, 670–4.

37 *OV*, III, pp. 114–15; Richard's death occurred before he was made a knight. WM, *GR*, I, pp. 502–5, claimed that Richard's death occurred due to his being enveloped in a poisonous miasma; Mason, *William II*, pp. 37–8; Barlow, *Rufus*, p. 13, n. 37 suggested that Richard's death should be assigned to the years c.1069 x 1074.

Tirel, a member of his retinue, and within days Rufus's brother Henry had seized the throne of England.[38] Despite the dangers of the hunt and military training, Robert successfully negotiated the rigours of his apprenticeship and became, by all accounts, a formidable warrior. In one of several character sketches, he appears as 'very courageous in battle, a powerful and sure archer'.[39]

As Robert trained for a military career, he associated with his father's veteran companions in arms. From these men Robert learned not only the practicalities of wielding the arms and armour of his day, but also aspects of the ethos associated with the eleventh-century knight.[40] Robert had to learn chivalric conduct and this was as much about behaviour off the battlefield as the display of valour on it. It was essential that Robert behaved *viriliter*, 'in a manly fashion', in order to gain acceptance in this important masculine milieu. Notions of honour and shame informed the ethos of the nobility as well as being essential components of chivalric identity. Robert learned that he would risk his personal honour if he ignored any of the 'rules of the game'. For example, one of the Conqueror's men was deprived of the belt of knighthood for his shameful conduct in the killing of King Harold at the battle of Hastings:

[o]ne of the knights hacked at his thigh with a sword as he lay on the ground; for which he was branded with disgrace by William for a dastardly and shameful act (*rem ignauam et pudendam*) and was degraded from his knighthood (literally, 'driven from the *militia*').[41]

A knight was expected to behave with honour even in the heat of battle. Robert fully absorbed this code of behaviour, conducting himself according to its precepts on and off the battlefield.

Military training was about learning to co-operate effectively with other warriors and, from the start, this sense of group identity was inculcated in the trainees. Communal activities such as eating and sleeping and the experience of shared risks and triumphs provided the occasions for a sense of camaraderie to develop.[42] The individual was imbued with a sense of honour and a fear of shame. The approbation or condemnation of the warrior group to which he belonged moulded the young knight's behaviour. These chivalric *mores* were demonstrated by Robert's elders and young trainees were expected to imitate them. There may also have been a more theoretical side to the lessons learnt by the young Robert, for there is evidence that the work

---

[38] Mason, *William II*, pp. 222–8.

[39] *OV*, II, pp. 356–7.

[40] M. Bennett, 'Military Masculinity in England and Northern France c.1050–1225', in Hadley, ed., *Masculinity in Medieval Europe*, pp. 71–88.

[41] WM, *GR*, I, pp. 456–57; cf. M. Strickland, *War and Chivalry. The Conduct and Perception of War in England and Normandy, 1066–1217* (Cambridge, 1996), pp. 4, 37 and 154. Emma Mason discusses this episode in *The House of Godwine*, p. 173.

[42] Bennett, 'Military Masculinity', pp. 73–4.

of Vegetius, a late Roman military theorist, was known in eleventh-century Normandy. There are passages in the *Gesta Guillelmi* which echo Vegetius's *De re militari*.[43] Vegetius taught that battles were risky ventures and to be avoided unless one was absolutely sure of victory. It was far better to ravage an enemy's territories and, by practising a kind of economic warfare, reduce his capacity to continue the fight. However, such a pragmatic approach to warfare was unlikely to provide many opportunities for the kind of heroic act young knights wanted to be remembered for.

Role Models

The struggles of Robert's father to hold on to Normandy in the 1040s and extend his power in the 1050s provided ample opportunity for the performance and memorialisation of deeds of martial valour. Stories of these campaigns were related at the communal meals shared with Robert and the other boys. A series of legends gathered around the Conqueror and found their way into William of Poitiers' work.[44] The Norman court was the focus for considerable literary activity and people and events from recent history were compared with the heroes of the ancient world. William of Poitiers compared the Conqueror with Caesar and found the Roman wanting.[45] The court and military expeditions of the ninth-century Frankish emperor Charlemagne also provided tales of chivalric heroism. The earliest manuscript of the epic poem *The Song of Roland* survives from an Anglo-Norman milieu.[46] *The Song of Roland* tells, in epic verse, of the defeat of Charlemagne's rearguard at the Pyrenean pass of Roncesvaux. The heavily outnumbered Christians were slaughtered, but the focus is on the heroic death of Charlemagne's nephew Roland. Although the story refers to the late eighth century, the poem is suffused with the knightly ethos of Robert's day.

The eleventh century also saw a great geographical expansion in the activities of knights from Normandy as they embarked on campaigns in Southern Italy, Spain and even the British Isles.[47] As contacts beyond Normandy multiplied, visitors and envoys brought news from all over Christendom. Returning pilgrims described the wonders of Byzantium, or the Holy Land. Robert's own

---

[43] WP, p. 190. *Vegetius: Epitome of Military Science*, trans. N.P. Milner, 2nd revised ed. (Liverpool, 1996). J. Gillingham, 'William the Bastard at War', in *Studies in Medieval History presented to R. Allen Brown*, ed. C. Harper-Bill, C.J. Holdsworth and Janet L. Nelson (Woodbridge, 1989), pp. 141–58, reprinted in M. Strickland, ed., *Anglo-Norman Warfare* (Woodbridge, 1992), pp. 143–60.

[44] E.g. WP, pp. 112–13, pp. 116–17.

[45] WP, pp. 168–77.

[46] The text in Oxford, Bodleian Library, MS Digby 23, executed in the twelfth century, probably between 1130 and 1160, is in Anglo-Norman French; *The Song of Roland*, trans. G. Burgess (Harmondsworth, 1990), p. 7, and D.D.R. Owen, *The Legend of Roland. A Pageant of the Middle Ages* (London, 1973).

[47] R. Bartlett, *The Making of Europe. Conquest, Colonization and Cultural Change, 950–1350* (Harmondsworth, 1993), esp. pp. 24–59.

grandfather had died on a pilgrimage to Jerusalem and stories circulated of his exploits in the East. As Robert I approached Constantinople, he

> ordered his mule to be shod with gold, instead of the iron horseshoes it had used up till then, and that none of his men should dare to pick up the golden horseshoes when the same mule cast them from its hoofs, so that the Greeks, who had formerly been used to call the French greedy for gold, should not be able to find an opportunity to accuse them of avarice.[48]

Similarly, Normans had begun to settle in Southern Italy, and, at about the time Robert was doing homage to Geoffrey of Anjou, they were invading Muslim Sicily.[49]

Orderic Vitalis, with his monastery's contacts in every theatre of Norman activity, reveals just how many tales of valour made their way back to Normandy.[50] These tales instilled in Robert and the other young boys at court a love for adventure and a respect for martial prowess. Orderic described the court of one of the Conqueror's companions-at-arms, Hugh of Avranches, later earl of Chester. Hugh's household was especially dissolute, a reflection of the indulgences of the earl himself. Into this arena came Gerold of Avranches, a clerk intent on improving the morals of the young men there:

> To great lords, simple knights, and *noble boys* alike he gave salutary counsel; and he made a great collection of tales of the combats of holy knights, drawn from the Old Testament and more recent records of Christian achievements, *for them to imitate*. He told them vivid stories of the conflicts of Demetrius and George, of Theodore and Sebastian, of the Theban legion and Maurice its leader, and of Eustace, supreme commander of the army and his companions, who won the crown of martyrdom in heaven.[51]

Whereas the knights of Hugh of Avranches found inspiration in the legends of the martial saints, or stories from the ancient world, others undoubtedly found their heroes closer to home.

---

[48] WJ, II, pp. 82–3; see Elisabeth van Houts, 'Normandy and Byzantium in the Eleventh Century', *Byzantion*, 55 (1985), pp. 544–59, and J. Shepard, 'Byzantine Diplomacy, A.D. 800–1205: Means and Ends', in *Byzantine Diplomacy*, ed. J. Shepard and S. Franklin (Aldershot, 1992), pp. 41–71. There are other stories about Duke Robert in the *Brevis relatio*, pp. 1–2, and Wace's *Roman de Rou*, iii, lines 2987–3240, pp. 124–7.

[49] See *De rebus gestis Rogerii Calabriae et Siciliae Comitis auctore Gaufredo Malaterra*, ed. E. Pontieri, Rerum Italicarum Scriptores, 2nd ed. (Bologna, 1927–8); *The Deeds of Count Roger of Calabria and Sicily and of his brother Duke Robert Guiscard, by Geoffrey Malaterra*, trans. K.B. Wolf (Ann Arbor, MI, 2005). Cf. Loud, *Age of Robert Guiscard*, pp. 146–85.

[50] Chibnall, *World of Orderic Vitalis*, pp. 202, 210–13 and chapter 7 'The World Outside', pp. 146–66.

[51] OV, III, pp. 216–17 (my emphasis). The saints mentioned are associated with the Byzantine Empire and the stories may have been brought back by Normans from adventures in the eastern Mediterranean. Relics of St George were brought back from the First Crusade by Count Robert of Flanders: see J. Riley-Smith, *The First Crusaders, 1095–1131* (Cambridge, 1997), pp. 151–2. It was reported that St George fought alongside the Normans during their campaigns in Sicily: Pontieri, *Malaterra*, p. 44 (trans. Wolf, 2.33, p. 110).

As Robert grew up he could not fail to hear tales about his father's successes, for by the early 1070s William was being portrayed as a paragon among knights. It may have been William's early achievements and the stories that were already gathering around his campaigns that prompted William of Jumièges to begin his *Gesta Normannorum ducum*.[52] Similarly, William of Poitiers' *Gesta Guillelmi* gives a flavour of the reputation that Robert's father had acquired. Here, William of Poitiers, who had served in the Norman army before becoming a cleric, describes the Conqueror's first appearance as a knight:

> The news of this spread fear throughout France. Gaul had not another man who was reputed to be such a knight at arms. It was a sight both delightful and redoubtable to see him hold the reins, girded honourably with his sword, his shield shining, formidable with his helmet and javelin. For as he stood out in beauty when wearing the garments of a prince and at peace, so also the adornments which are put on against the enemy suited him perfectly. From this time a virile spirit and valour shone brilliantly and clearly in him.[53]

For Robert and his brothers, their father was an accessible, if perhaps rather daunting, masculine role model.

This period in Robert's life also saw the beginning of personal friendships which developed into more formal social bonds as he matured. Although there are few indications of close companions among his contemporaries at court, those who are later found in his retinue may already have begun to gather around him in the hope of benefiting from an association with the recognised heir to Normandy.[54] Robert was the most prominent in a cohort of adolescents who were trained together. They looked to their elders for models of behaviour, but like any group they had a sense of being different. As they matured this sense of difference was shown in new fashions in dress and hairstyles, or in novel and unexpected ways of behaving at social functions. Such markers of generational difference drew criticism from their elders which found a voice in disapproving passages in contemporary histories.[55]

The Making of a Knight

Under heaven there was no better lord.
He was duke of Normandy.
Over the Normans he had lordship
Much good and many deeds of valour,

---

[52] *WJ*, I, xxxii–l.
[53] *WP*, pp. 6–9.
[54] *OV*, II, pp. 358–9 and III, pp. 100–3.
[55] This is developed further below, Chapter 3, pp. 69–71.

> Much marvellous service and much beautiful chivalry,
> This duke of Normandy performed.[56]

For Robert and his fellows, the ritual known as *adoubement* (dubbing) marked the public recognition of military proficiency.[57] The occasion for the ceremony might be prearranged or the individual might win his belt of knighthood in recognition of some act of valour, perhaps while serving as a squire on campaign. There has been much debate over the nature and evolution of this key element in the making of a medieval knight. A particular point at issue concerns the degree to which the Church had influenced what was, in essence, a purely secular rite. By the thirteenth century there were elaborate dubbing ceremonies, conducted according to a well-developed liturgy, but the eleventh-century evidence is both rare and more prosaic. This raises the question of whether such an act was routinely recorded by contemporaries. Perhaps it was so common an occurrence that it was only when the context of the dubbing was worthy of notice that the making of a knight was mentioned at all.[58]

In the eleventh century, the essence of the dubbing ceremony was the granting of weapons to the new knight. This was usually done by the lord in whose court the young man had trained and it marked the creation of a significant social bond between the two men. The origins of this granting of arms – the literal meaning of *adouber* ('to dub') was to equip a man with weapons – have been traced to the practices of early Germanic warbands, where it marked the association of an individual with a particular war-chief. The Church gradually insinuated elements of the liturgy into the ceremony but the process remained at its core essentially secular throughout the Middle Ages. The delivery of arms became associated with a young man's coming of age, when he was recognised as capable of holding land and bearing arms to defend it. The belting to knighthood also had connotations of status, partly derived from personal ancestry, but also from association with the social standing of the lord making the grant. Youths knighted by a particular lord were drawn into his retinue, associated with that lord's honour and dignity, and placed under an obligation to emulate his exploits. This explains why the sons of lesser nobles were sent away to be educated in the courts of greater lords. If the young man was thought worthy of receiving his arms, this 'associative honour' would necessarily enhance his status and, if he performed as

---

56 *Gaimar*, lines 5738–44, p. 182: Suz ciel n'aveit meillur barun,/ Celui fud duc de Normendie,/ Sur Normanz ot la seignurie;/ Maine bunté e maint barnage/ E maint estrange vassalage/ Fist icest duc de Normendie/ E mainte bele chevalerie.

57 On the ceremony of dubbing, see J. Flori, *L'Essor de la Chevalerie, XIe–XIIe siècles* (Geneva, 1986), pp. 64–82; P.R. Coss, *The Knight in Medieval England* (Stroud, 1993), pp. 52–3; M. Strickland, *War and Chivalry. The Conduct and Perception of War in England and Normandy, 1066–1217* (Cambridge, 1996), pp. 17, 25, 57, 74; Bartlett, *England under the Norman and Angevin Kings*, pp. 233–5, and Dominique Barthélemy, 'Modern Mythologies of Medieval Chivalry', in *The Medieval World*, ed. Janet L. Nelson and P. Linehan (London, 2001), pp. 214–28.

58 I am grateful to Peter Coss for discussing this point with me.

his lord hoped, then the knight's own valour would, at the same time, enhance the reputation of his lord.

A particular feature of knighting ceremonies was that a whole cohort of knights might be dubbed together. At the Pentecost Feast in 1099 – the first to be held in the king's magnificent new hall at Westminster – William Rufus presided over the knighting of perhaps as many as three hundred young men in a splendid ceremony.[59] The ceremony was almost undermined by a protest by a certain Giffard the Poitevin who wanted thirty of his own young followers knighted and objected to being kept waiting for a month by the king. The protest took the form of Giffard cutting short the fashionably long hair of his followers. The king could not miss the protestors but saw it as a joke and an example of courtly behaviour rather than an insult. More than three hundred others at court also had their hair cut.[60]

Another bond was forged between the young men who had trained and undergone the ceremony at the same time. There was clearly a sense of group solidarity among Giffard's men as they protested. These young men and others like them had lived together, perhaps for some years, in the household of a great lord, and had developed ties with that lord akin to fosterage.[61] The ritual of dubbing thus made these social ties visible to all, to participants as much as onlookers. Given the importance of this moment in a young noble-man's life, it is surprising that none of the sources for Robert's life, records his *adoubement*.

It is inconceivable that Robert was never knighted, and it seems strange that contemporaries failed to record the knighting of the duke's, subsequently the king's, eldest son. It was an event of great importance, not only to Robert himself, but also to his companions and, indeed, to the entire Norman polity, which had been required to recognise him as heir to Normandy and Maine. However, contemporary historians were members of a clerical and monastic caste predisposed to be critical of the ranks of chivalry, and they preferred to focus attention on occasions when the Church played a significant role. The eleventh century saw a concerted effort by the ecclesiastical hierarchy to exert some control over the activities of the *milites*, the knights. From expedients such as the introduction of the Peace and Truce of God, to attempts to channel the energies of the knights towards goals approved by the papacy, there were attempts to give the military caste of society a more honourable and, above all, Christian function.[62]

---

[59] *Gaimar*, lines 5972–6103, pp. 189–93, trans. Hardy and Martin, lines 5978–6109; *ASC*, E, *s.a.* 1099, p. 109; Swanton, pp. 234–5; cf. J. Gillingham, 'Kingship, Chivalry and Love. Political and Cultural Values in the Earliest History Written in French: Geoffrey Gaimar's *Estoire des Engleis*', in *idem*, *English in the Twelfth Century*, pp. 233–58 at 237–9; Mason, *William II*, pp. 204–5.

[60] *Gaimar*, lines 6076–103, pp. 192–3, trans. Hardy and Martin, II, lines 6082–110, pp. 192–3.

[61] Keen, *Chivalry*, p. 69.

[62] T. Head and R. Landes, eds., *The Peace of God. Social Violence and Religious Response in France around the Year 1000* (Ithaca and London, 1992).

By the time that the major sources for Robert's life were being written, he had already been defeated and incarcerated by his youngest brother. In these circumstances, William of Malmesbury and Orderic Vitalis may have felt less inclined to celebrate Robert's chivalric initiation. Members of Robert's immediate family were dubbed and this gives some idea of how his own initiation might have been conducted. Robert's father may have received his belt of knighthood in the early 1040s and he may have been thought a little young to be receiving his weapons.[63] Later, it was suggested that William was 'knighted' by the French king, Henry I, 'as soon as he was old enough'.[64] As the relationship between the king and duke was at its closest during the 1040s and especially in the successful campaign of 1046–7 against the rebels, perhaps William was knighted in around 1043, when he was around sixteen. The association with his royal patron helped the young man strengthen his position within Normandy.

There are also descriptions for the knighting of two of Robert's three brothers. Richard was killed in a hunting accident at some time between 1069 and 1074. He was born around 1055 and 'had not yet received the belt of knighthood' when he died.[65] If he was to have been knighted at around the age of sixteen had he lived, this suggests that his death was nearer 1069 than 1074.

Archbishop Lanfranc of Canterbury educated William Rufus and 'made him a knight'.[66] If William was knighted at around the same age as his father, the ceremony may have taken place around 1076 or 1077 just at the time that the relationship between Robert and his father was becoming strained.

As for Robert's youngest brother, sources agree that Henry was knighted by his father at Westminster at Pentecost (24 May) 1086.[67] The Feast of Pentecost was one of the great occasions in the medieval liturgical calendar and by the end of the eleventh century its associations with the spiritual transformation of the individual were being embraced by the chivalric class.[68] Orderic reported that when Henry had attained the strength of a young man, Archbishop Lanfranc

> presented him for knighthood for the defence of the kingdom, invested him with the hauberk, placed the helmet on his head and girded him with the belt of knighthood in the name of the Lord as a king's son born in the purple.[69]

---

63 WP, pp. 6–11; Bates, 'The Conqueror's Adolescence', p. 4, suggests that William came of age around 1042 and notes that William of Poitiers 'very obviously believed that he began to rule when he was knighted'.

64 WM, GR, I, pp. 426–7.

65 OV, III, pp. 114–15.

66 WM, GR, I, pp. 542–3; cf. H.E.J. Cowdrey, Lanfranc, Scholar, Monk and Archbishop (Oxford, 2003), pp. 186 and 217–19; Barlow, Rufus, p. 22.

67 ASC, E, s.a. 1085 [1086], p. 94; Swanton, pp. 216–17. Cf. WM, GR, I, pp. 710–1.

68 The Holy Spirit descended on the Apostles at Pentecost: Acts 2: 1–4.

69 OV, IV, pp. 120–1.

Here, the knighting of Henry marks the transition from childhood to youth. Lanfranc may have played a part in the ceremony and the description of the archbishop arming Henry is reminiscent of a scene in the Bayeux Tapestry where Duke William 'gave arms to Harold' and is shown placing a helmet on the earl's head.[70]

Orderic may have assumed that the archbishop had a role in Henry's dubbing ceremony, but the passage, especially with the emphasis on Henry's status as a king's son 'born in the purple' seems like a piece of special pleading.[71] The reputation of William the Conqueror had suffered by the time Orderic was writing.[72] Perhaps Orderic felt it more appropriate that Henry, as defender of the kingdom and patron of the Church – especially the abbey of Saint-Évroul – should have Lanfranc as his sponsor at this crucial moment in his personal development. For a monastic audience Lanfranc, as archbishop, abbot, and as hero of the reformed church, brought more positive associative honour to Henry than the tainted figure of the Conqueror.

The medieval sources do not say when Robert was knighted. If it was at around the same age as his brother Henry, it may have been in the mid to late 1060s when he was about sixteen. There were great occasions in the 1060s when it might have also been thought appropriate to mark a significant transition in the young man's status. Robert's betrothal to Margaret of Maine before 1062 was just such an occasion, but it is unlikely that a boy of barely eleven would have been considered worthy, or indeed capable, of bearing arms. Again, Robert's homage to Geoffrey of Anjou a year or so later was an equally propitious moment for his dubbing, perhaps from his new lord. Again, Robert may have been too young despite the fact that there is some evidence to suggest that his father had already designated him heir to Normandy.[73]

A clue as to when Robert was knighted may be found by looking at the careers of those who trained with him at his father's court.[74] In 1073, during a campaign in Maine, one of Robert's companions, Robert of Bellême, was knighted by King William.[75] The occasion for Robert of Bellême's knighting was, therefore, his participation in warfare, perhaps for the first time.[76] Orderic does not say why Bellême was deemed worthy, but it was perhaps in recognition of some act of valour and possibly part of a strategy to keep the Bellême clan sweet, given the proximity of their lands and the danger of them joining the revolt. Others may have been dubbed along with Robert of Bellême in

---

70 Musset, *Bayeux Tapestry*, scene 21.
71 Hollister, *Henry I*, pp. 36–7, and Green, *Henry I*, p. 23.
72 *OV*, II, pp. 232–3.
73 *Fauroux*, no. 158.
74 Barlow, *Rufus*, p. 25.
75 *OV*, II, pp. 306–7.
76 Robert of Bellême, born around 1057, may have been as young as sixteen on this campaign. See Kathleen Thompson, 'Robert of Bellême Reconsidered', *ANS*, 13 (1990), pp. 263–86.

1073, and King William's eldest son may have been among them.[77] It seems unlikely, however, that Orderic would omit the knighting of the king's son but record that of his monastery's inveterate enemy. Although the idea that Robert received the belt of knighthood from his father on campaign in 1073 is an attractive thesis, there is no confirmation in the contemporary sources. It also seems rather too late in the day for by 1073 Robert was over twenty years old. However, it may be that he was given this honour at the same time as he was made heir to the duchy in 1066.

This omission in the medieval sources of when Robert received his belt of knighthood is puzzling. Later writers accepted that Robert was a knight and the very model of chivalry. A brief statement by William of Malmesbury provides a clue to when Robert was knighted.

> Robert, son of William I king of England, had been born in Normandy and *was already a young man of established prowess when his father came to England*, although he was small in stature and pot-bellied.[78]

If Malmesbury is correct then Robert had had some experience of warfare *before* 1066 and had proved himself worthy of being belted to knighthood.

During the preparations for the invasion of England in 1066, William again confirmed Robert as heir to the duchy of Normandy. Given the unpredictability of the campaign ahead, this was a prudent precaution and it suggests that his father saw Robert as someone around whom effective loyalties could form.[79] Two English sources add the detail that King Philip of France, as overlord, agreed to Duke William's designation of his eldest son as his heir.[80] Additional credence is given to Robert's status by the fact that, in a document dated to 1066 and issued at Rouen just as he was about to depart for England, Duke William confirmed the possessions which the abbey of Marmoutier held in Normandy. As an additional guarantee William had his eldest son add his consent and here Robert is described as having reached his majority.[81] Therefore, in 1066 Robert, aged fourteen or fifteen, was considered able to give independent assent to his father's provision for Marmoutier. Although it does not necessarily follow that he was old enough to bear arms and receive the belt of knighthood, the recognition that he had reached his majority is suggestive and a ceremony with the king of France present was an entirely fitting occasion at which to be knighted.

In 1066, Robert was effectively elevated to the ducal throne by his father and this occasion was appropriate for the recognition of the designated heir

---

[77] Barlow, *Rufus*, p. 25.

[78] WM, *GR*, I, pp. 700–1 (my emphasis).

[79] *OV*, II, pp. 356–7; III, pp. 98–99; IV, pp. 92–3.

[80] *ASC*, D, *s.a.* 1079, p. 88; Swanton, pp. 213–14, and *JW*, III, *s.a.* 1077, pp. 30–1.

[81] *Fauroux*, no. 228, pp. 437–8; cf. *Fauroux*, p. 438, 'auctoramento Roberti filii sui faceret confirmari, quia scilicet majoris iam ille esset'. Douglas, *William the Conqueror*, p. 185 and n. 3; cf. Bates, *Normandy before 1066*, p. 60 and n. 36, dates Philip I's confirmation of William's designation of Robert as heir to 1060–3.

as a warrior. Robert may have been dubbed by his father's overlord, Philip of France, and this, in turn, adds significance to Philip's later support for him. The ceremony in 1066 created a bond between Philip and Robert that endured and went beyond that between an overlord and the eldest son of a vassal. Perhaps the most straightforward reason for the omission of any record of Robert's knighting was that such essentially secular ceremonies were rarely recorded by ecclesiastical writers unless they were part of some unusual or magnificent occasion, and we should not, therefore, infer anything sinister from their silence.

The year 1066 was a momentous one, not only for the duke and duchy of Normandy, but also for young Robert. He had been recognised by his father and the members of the Norman polity as the heir to the duchy, perhaps also receiving the belt of knighthood from the king of France. While his father was on campaign in England, Robert was associated with his mother in the government of the duchy. On Christmas Day, 1066, Robert's father was crowned king of England, thus realising the ambition of acquiring a kingdom shared by many who had been belted to knighthood in the eleventh century. For a boy of fifteen, his father's success must have fuelled expectations of a glorious career, basking in the afterglow of William the Conqueror's triumphs. Writing in the late 1130s, Geoffrey Gaimar noted that 'He who in this life does good, ever are his children more honoured.'[82] As Robert awaited the return to Normandy of the new king of England in the early months of 1067, he anticipated trying to emulate his father's glorious achievements knowing that his future was secure.

---

[82] *Gaimar*, lines 6051–2, p. 192: 'Ki en sa vie fait bunté,/ Si eir en sunt [mielz] honuré.'

CHAPTER THREE

THE KING'S SON

IN March 1067, William, Duke of Normandy and, since Christmas Day 1066, King of England, returned to Normandy and was greeted by a triumphal *adventus*:

> It was a time of winter, and of the austere Lenten penances.[1] Nevertheless everywhere celebrations were held as if it were a time of high festival. The sun seemed to shine with the clear brightness of summer, far more strongly than usual at this season. The inhabitants of humble or remote places flocked to the towns or anywhere else where there was a chance of seeing the king. When he entered his metropolitan city of Rouen old men, boys, matrons and all the citizens came out to see him; they shouted out to welcome his return, so that you could have thought the whole city was cheering, as did Rome formerly when it joyfully applauded Pompey. Communities of monks and clerks vied with each other as to who could show the greatest deference at the arrival of their beloved protector. Nothing which ought to have been done in celebration of such honour was left undone. Furthermore, if anything new could be devised, it was added.[2]

The Conqueror's family had remained in Normandy during the arduous campaign in England. Robert's mother Matilda, operating with the help of a council of advisers, had ensured that Normandy's government continued smoothly.[3] Whether Robert had a direct role in the government of Normandy during his father's absence is not known, but as the recognised heir to the duchy he was kept at his mother's side for safety in the anxious months between William's departure in September 1066 and the triumphal return of March 1067. Matilda was ruling as much on behalf of her son as her absent husband. Mother and eldest son working together strengthened the bond between them, which was to serve Robert so well a decade later.

The new king brought home lavish gifts for the churches of Normandy and William of Poitiers noted in particular the needlework and the gold thread

---

1 Ash Wednesday was 21 February in 1067 and Easter Sunday, 8 April. Was this a criticism that such celebrations were held at such a significant moment in the liturgical year?
2 *WP*, pp. 174–7. Cf. *OV*, II, pp. 196–9.
3 *WP*, pp. 178–9. On Matilda's role in government, see D. Bates, 'The Origins of the Justiciarship', *ANS*, 4 (1982), pp. 1–12 and 167–71 at 6.

for which the English were famous.[4] In addition, Robert's father brought over a number of high-ranking Englishmen including Archbishop Stigand of Canterbury and three leading earls, Edwin, Morcar and Waltheof.[5] Also among them was Edgar Ætheling, a member of the West Saxon royal family who had briefly been regarded as a candidate for the English throne. It may have been at this point that Robert and Edgar first struck up a friendship that was to continue for many years.[6]

Easter was celebrated at Fécamp Abbey and there the Norman court assembled curious to see the 'longhaired sons of the Northern lands, whose beauty the most handsome youths of long-haired Gaul might have envied; nor did they yield anything to the beauty of girls'. In addition, the visitors were fascinated by the 'splendid garments, interwoven and encrusted with gold' worn by William and his entourage.[7] The king, perhaps mindful of observing religious propriety on such an occasion, forced the crowds of soldiers and people to leave their revelries and go to church. It was usual for rulers at this time to make use of the great religious feast days to highlight or reinforce their worldly office.[8] The Easter service, which normally involved a suitably impressive gathering of the court, was augmented and presented as a ceremony of thanksgiving for the victory in England.[9]

Among those at court were distinguished visitors from outside Normandy, including Raoul, Count of Crépy and Valois, a relative of William's wife, Matilda. Raoul's son, Simon, had been sent to William's court to be educated.[10] Those who witnessed this magnificent celebration

4   WP, pp. 176–7. P.H. Sawyer, 'The Wealth of England in the Eleventh Century', TRHS, 5th ser., 15 (1965), pp. 145–64. P. Bouet, B. Levy and F. Neveux, eds., The Bayeux Tapestry: Embroidering the Facts of History (Caen, 2004).

5   OV, II, pp. 196–7; WP, pp. 176–7. See D.M. Dumville, 'Anglo-Saxon Books: Treasure in Norman Hands?' ANS, 16 (1994), pp. 83–99.

6   ASC, E, s.a. 1066, p. 87; Swanton, p. 199. N. Hooper, 'Edgar the Aetheling: Anglo-Saxon Prince, Rebel and Crusader', ASE, 14 (1985), pp. 197–214.

7   WP, pp. 178–9; OV, II, pp. 198–9. Bates, Acta, no. 142, pp. 472–3, confirmation of an agreement between Fécamp and Roger de Montgomery, possibly granted at this Easter meeting, witnessed, inter alios, by 'Roberti consulis'. Annie Renoux, Fécamp: Du palais ducal au palais de Dieu (Paris, 1991); eadem, '"Palatium" et "castrum" en France du Nord (fin IXe – début XIIIe siècle)', in The Seigneurial Residence in Western Europe AD c. 800–1600, ed. G. Meirion-Jones, E. Impey and M. Jones, British Archaeological Reports, International Series, 1088 (Oxford, 2002), pp. 15–25.

8   M. Biddle, 'Seasonal Festivals and Residence: Winchester, Westminster and Gloucester in the Tenth to Twelfth Centuries', ANS, 7 (1986), pp. 51–68; M. Hare, 'Kings, Crowns and Festivals: the Origins of Gloucester as a Royal Ceremonial Centre', Transactions of the Bristol and Gloucestershire Archaeological Society, 115 (1997), pp. 41–78; cf. S.D. Church, 'Some Aspects of the Royal Itinerary in the Twelfth Century', in Thirteenth Century England, 11 (2007), pp. 31–45. I am grateful to Stephen Church for providing me with a copy of his article.

9   WP, pp. 178–9; cf. WJ, II, pp. 172–3.

10 WP, pp. 178–9 and n. 5. 'Vita Beati Simonis comitis Crespeiensis auctore synchrono', in PL, 156, cols. 1211–24. Partial translation in Elisabeth van Houts, Normans in Europe, no. 56, pp. 197–9. See also, H.E.J. Cowdrey, 'Count Simon of Crépy's Monastic Conversion', in Papauté monachisme et théories politiques. 1: Le pouvoir et l'institution ecclésiale. Études d'histoire médiévale offertes à Michel Pacaut (Lyons, 1994), pp. 253–66, reprinted in idem, The Crusades and Latin Monasticism,

marvelled at the vessels of gold and silver, of whose number and beauty incredible things could truthfully be told. At a great banquet they drank only from such goblets or from horns of wild oxen decorated with the same metal at both ends. Indeed, they noted many such things, fitting the magnificence of a king, which they praised on their return home because of their novelty. But they recognised that far more distinguished and memorable than these things was the splendour of the king himself.[11]

The lustre of the occasion and the assertion that Robert's father looked the part served to underline the fact that the Conqueror was a worthy king, although not from royal stock. The new king's son, Robert, accompanied his father during his time in Normandy, no doubt basking in the reflected glory of his father's achievement, but perhaps also regretting that he had been unable to participate in the campaign himself, or rather, that he had been prevented from participating.

Another grand occasion that year was the dedication of the abbey church of Jumièges on 1 July 1067.[12] Such ceremonies were an opportunity for the king to endow Normandy's churches with estates and other valuables seized in England.[13] Some of this wealth rewarded the composers of a number of Latin panegyrics that celebrated the new king's return. Certainly, William of Poitiers was not alone in portraying the full magnificence of William's royal *persona*, which had so impressed the foreign dignitaries.[14]

The victory in England transformed William's personal status. By association, the prestige of members of his family was similarly augmented. Robert was now a king's son, doubtless with raised expectations of his own that he too might one day wear a crown. In the later months of 1067, Robert's relationship with his father seems to have been strengthened for when the situation in England began to deteriorate in December William once again affirmed Robert's place in his plans.

William of Jumièges indicated Robert's status when he stated that the Conqueror appointed his son as ruler in the duchy before he returned to England at the beginning of December 1067.[15] Robert had the *dominium*, the 'lordship', of the duchy of Normandy and had been given governmental responsibility as his father's successor in Normandy. William's confidence in the young man's abilities was probably bolstered by the knowledge that his son would be guided by a council of magnates of the kind that had aided Matilda

11th–12th Centuries (Aldershot, 1999), no. XI. Matilda of Flanders was related to Simon of the Vexin through her mother Adela, daughter of King Robert the Pious. Elisabeth van Houts, 'The Norman Conquest through European Eyes', *EHR*, 110 (1995), pp. 832–53.

11 *WP*, pp. 178–81.

12 *WJ*, II, pp. 172–3; *OV*, II, pp. 198–9. David Bates provides a post-Conquest outline itinerary for the Conqueror: *Acta*, pp. 76–84.

13 E.g. Bates, *Acta*, no.159, pp. 525–6; a grant of Hayling Island (Hants) to Jumièges.

14 *WP*, pp. 180–1; Van Houts, 'Latin Poetry', pp. 40–2.

15 *WJ*, II, pp. 178–9.

during the autumn and winter of 1066/67.[16] With competent advisers at hand there was probably little for Robert to do; according to William of Jumièges, the young man had assumed responsibility for Normandy, and father and son together ruled England, Normandy, and Maine as a family concern.

Robert's designation as ruler of Normandy also solved the problem of whether William, as king, was obliged to do homage to Philip I of France.[17] As duke of Normandy, William was Philip's vassal, but medieval kings saw the performance of homage to another king as compromising their royal dignity. Given that kingship was seen as an office deriving ultimately from a personal relationship with God, any intermediate worldly tie necessarily weakened that bond. As Robert had already done homage to Philip I for Normandy prior to the Conquest, here was a convenient way of allowing William to escape any personal subordination to the king of France. After 1066, William rarely used the title *comes* or 'count', normally preferring to have himself referred to as *rex Anglorum* and *princeps* in his documents for Continental beneficiaries. This has been linked to the increasing tendency to use the title *comes* for his sons.[18] Robert appears as *comes* in thirty-one documents, but also as *consul* in a Fécamp document and once as *regis primogenitus* ('first born of the king').[19] As many of these documents were drawn up by the beneficiaries, descriptions of Robert's status were disseminated beyond the court itself and into the regions of Normandy and England.

The territories William ruled were thought of as separate entities, forming an agglomeration of lands united under his lordship. The Conqueror's biographer had an imperial model in mind when he described William's status after 1066. In making comparisons with Caesar, William of Poitiers was drawing attention to the fact that, albeit on a smaller scale, the Conqueror now had a kind of imperial dominion ruling England as king, but also holding sway over the nominal ruler of Normandy and Maine, his son Robert.[20]

In spring 1068, William summoned his wife to England and, on Whit

---

16 *OV*, II, pp. 208–9. R.H.C. Davis, 'William of Jumièges, Robert Curthose and the Norman Succession', *EHR*, 95 (1980), pp. 597–606 and, now, G. Garnett, *Conquered England. Kingship, Succession and Tenure 1066–1166* (Oxford, 2007), pp. 156–64.

17 C.W. Hollister, 'Normandy, France and the Anglo-Norman *regnum*', *Speculum*, 51 (1976), pp. 202–42, reprinted in *idem, Monarchy, Magnates and Institutions*, pp. 17–57.

18 Hollister, 'Normandy, France and the Anglo-Norman *regnum*', p. 22 and n. 24. See Bates, *Acta*, pp. 85–96.

19 Bates, *Acta*, pp. 94–5.

20 *WP*, pp. 172–5. Cf. Van Houts, 'Latin Poetry' pp. 41–2. B.S. Bachrach argues that references to classical models indicate self-perceptions of the early medieval nobility: *Fulk Nerra, the neo-Roman Consul, 987–1040. A Political Biography of the Angevin Count* (Berkeley, CA, 1993), xii–xiv. On Robert ruling in Normandy and Maine, see Bates, *Acta*, p. 95: e.g. 'regnante Philippo in Francia, Guilielmo regum nobilissimo apud Anglos, Rotberto filio eius principante apud Normannos et Cenomannos' ('with Philip ruling in France, the most noble of kings William [ruling] among the English, Robert his son ruling the Normans and the men of Maine'). References to Robert exercising power in Normandy all date to either before 1069, or after 1080. Cf. Garnett, *Conquered England*, p. 160.

Sunday (11 May), Matilda was anointed queen consort in Westminster Abbey.[21] Again, an important feast in the liturgical calendar enhanced the symbolic power of the queen's elevation and transformation. Matilda was probably already pregnant with her youngest son Henry when she was crowned by Ealdred, Archbishop of York.[22] Matilda's elevation also enhanced Robert's status and increased the effectiveness of her support for him.[23] According to Orderic, Matilda was accompanied on her journey to England by Bishop Guy of Amiens, 'who had already celebrated the battle between Harold and William in verse'. This poem was the *Carmen de Hastingæ Proelio* ('The Song of the Battle of Hastings').[24] Matilda's coronation would certainly have been a fitting occasion for the bishop to present his work.

Given that Robert was left in charge of Normandy, it is unlikely that he attended his mother's coronation. In a charter issued at Whitsun 1068, King William and Queen Matilda were accompanied only by their son Richard, which suggests that Robert was otherwise occupied in Normandy.[25] For the young man, now being addressed as 'Consul' or 'Count' of the Normans, the glorious conquest of 1066 had brought tangible rewards and persuaded him of his own central role in his father's plans. That William and Matilda were willing to commit the duchy to their eldest son also indicates that hitherto, there had been no sign of instability or weakness in Robert's behaviour to suggest that he was unworthy of such trust.

Robert, 'Count of the Normans'

The Conqueror had returned to England at the end of 1067 to deal with an early challenge to his rule from Count Eustace II of Boulogne in Kent.[26] Further revolts by increasing numbers of disaffected Englishmen followed in 1068 and William was forced to deal with localised uprisings in the south-west of England and the west Midlands. The situation deteriorated to the point that Matilda was sent back to Normandy for safety and 'so that she might give up her time to religious devotions in peace, away from the English tumults, and together with the boy (*puer*) Robert could keep the duchy secure'.[27] Robert

---

21 *ASC*, D, *s.a.* 1067 (for 1068), p. 83; Swanton, p. 202; cf. *JW*, III, *s.a.* 1068, pp. 6–7. Laura L. Gathagan, 'The Trappings of Power: the Coronation of Mathilda of Flanders', *HSJ*, 13 (1999), pp. 21–39.

22 *OV*, II, pp. 214–15.

23 Pauline Stafford, *Queens, Concubines and Dowagers. The King's Wife in the Early Middle Ages* (Leicester, 1998), pp. 127–34.

24 *OV*, II, pp. 214–15; cf. van Houts, 'Latin Poetry' pp. 39–40; F. Barlow, ed. and trans., *The* Carmen de Hastingæ Proelio *of Guy Bishop of Amiens* (Oxford, 1999).

25 Bates, *Acta*, no. 181, pp. 594–601. Bates, *Acta*, no. 286, pp. 863–5, a grant to Wells cathedral also issued at Whitsun 1068 and witnessed by Richard 'the king's son'.

26 *WJ*, II, pp. 176–9; *WP*, pp. 182–5. See Heather J. Tanner, *Families, Friends and Allies. Boulogne and Politics in Northern France and England, c.879–1160* (Leiden, 2004), pp. 101–2.

27 *OV*, II, pp. 222–3.

assisted his mother in the campaign of prayers and almsgiving designed to ensure the Conqueror's victory.[28]

As well as the rebellions in England, the king also faced a challenge to another part of his 'empire'.[29] In 1069 a revolt led to the collapse of Norman rule in Maine and perhaps helps to account for the ruthlessness with which William dealt with the rebels in England. There is no suggestion that Robert had any direct authority in the county, so it is difficult to judge whether his actions precipitated the revolt. It was surely a case of opportunism on the part of the Manceaux. The political situation in eleventh-century Maine has been reassessed in recent years and it has been suggested that comital authority in the county, whether native or external, was much weaker than hitherto acknowledged. Rather than think of a strong, centralised comital administration, which the Normans sporadically took control of, we should view the county as comprising a series of localised lordships not always predisposed to acknowledge the overlordship of an individual calling himself the Count of Maine. This suggests that Norman 'rule' in Maine was never wholly secure in this period.[30]

Between the end of 1068 and the middle of 1071, the situation in England prevented Robert's father from immediately re-establishing his lordship in Maine.[31] Even if Robert had wanted to invade Maine, it is unlikely that his father would have been able to spare the men and resources necessary. The attention of the chroniclers focused on his father's struggles at this time and there are few notices of Robert's activities.[32]

There are, however, occasional glimpses of Robert in the sources. In 1070, he was consulted about the proposed appointment of Lanfranc, abbot of the ducal foundation at Saint-Étienne in Caen, to the archbishopric of Canterbury. Lanfranc was reluctant to accept the post and consulted his friend and former abbot, Herluin, at the Norman monastery of Bec-Hellouin. Herluin ordered his protégé to go to the queen and her son the prince, who were co-operating in the government of the duchy. Lanfranc had been closely connected with the ducal house for some time and it is likely that he would have sought the

---

28 *OV*, II, pp. 224–5.
29 *Actus Pontificum Cenomannis in Urbe Degentium*, ed. G. Busson and A. Ledru, Société des Archives Historiques du Maine (Le Mans, 1901), pp. 377–9; see R. Latouche, 'Essai de critique sur la continuation des *Actus Pontificum Cenomannis in urbe degentium*', *Le Moyen Age*, 11 (1907), pp. 225–75, and now Magarete Weidemann, *Geschichte des Bistums Le Mans von der Spätantike bis zur Karolingerzeit: Actus Pontificum Cenomannis in Urbe Degentium und Gesta Aldrici*, 3 vols. (Mainz, 2002). Douglas, *William the Conqueror*, pp. 223–4; Bates, *William the Conqueror*, p. 109; Lemesle, *Haut-Maine*, p. 35.
30 R.E. Barton, 'Lordship in Maine: Transformation, Service and Anger', *ANS*, 17 (1995), pp. 41–63, and *idem*, *Lordship in the County of Maine, c.890–1160* (Woodbridge, 2004).
31 *ASC*, D, *s.aa.* 1067–1072, pp. 81–5; Swanton, pp. 202–4, 206, 208. *ASC*, E, *s.aa.* 1068–1071, pp. 87–90; Swanton, pp. 202–3, 205, 207–8.
32 Both William of Poitiers and William of Jumièges stopped writing around this time. *OV*, II, pp. 184–5, 258–61, noted that unspecified unfavourable circumstances forced William of Poitiers to abandon his work. William of Jumièges finished writing in 1070: *WJ*, I, xxxiv.

advice and encouragement of Matilda and her son.[33] The abbot of Caen was obliged to obtain the approval of the rulers of the duchy before transferring from Caen to Canterbury.[34] However, Lanfranc's most recent biographer noted that the two major influences on the decision to accept Canterbury were Herluin and Pope Alexander II.[35]

Mother and Son

In 1067, Robert mourned the death of his maternal grandfather, Count Baldwin V of Flanders. Queen Matilda's elder brother, Baldwin VI (1067–1070) succeeded, but when he died, the younger brother, Robert 'the Frisian', challenged for the county. In 1070, he deposed his young nephew Arnulf III, who was supported by his mother, Richildis. The worsening situation in Flanders presented a severe problem for Robert of Normandy and his mother. It was perhaps at the request of Queen Matilda and her son that the Conqueror's close friend, William fitz Osbern, was despatched to Normandy. He was to act as guardian for Mathilda's nephew, Arnulf, probably in tandem with King Philip of France.[36] However, Robert 'the Frisian' defeated Richildis's party and William fitz Osbern was killed at the battle of Cassel on 20 or 22 February 1071.[37]

At around the same time, Robert's brother, Richard, was killed in a hunting accident in the New Forest. Unlike Robert, Richard, who remains a rather shadowy member of the family, had accompanied his parents to England and is found attesting documents issued there in 1068 and 1069.[38] The Conqueror had great hopes for Richard, who was elegant and ambitious, but as there are very few details about Richard it is difficult to characterise his relationship with Robert.[39] His premature death did, however, warrant a tribute from Godfrey of Cambrai, prior of Winchester, who lamented the unfulfilled promise of this chivalrous youth.[40] If Richard was buried at Winchester, which, given his

---

[33] Chibnall, *OV*, II, pp. 252–3, n. 2. The *Vita Lanfranci*, compiled between 1136 and 1150, also mentions that the queen and her son 'prayed that Lanfranc would accept': 'The Life of Lanfranc' in Sally N. Vaughn, *The Abbey of Bec and the Anglo-Norman State 1034–1136* (Woodbridge, 1981), p. 96.

[34] In 1093, Robert was instrumental in Anselm of Bec's transfer to Canterbury: see below, Chapter 4, pp. 147–8.

[35] *Lanfranc*, pp. 78–9, 85–6. Lanfranc's letter to Alexander highlighted the role of the papal legation of 1070 in his decision: *Letters of Lanfranc*, no. 1, pp. 30–1. Cf. A.J. Macdonald, *Lanfranc. A Study of his Life, Work and Writing*, 2nd ed. (London, 1944), p. 65. Margaret Gibson, *Lanfranc of Bec* (Oxford, 1978), does not mention Robert's role.

[36] *ASC*, E, *s.a.* 1070, p. 89; Swanton, p. 207.

[37] *OV*, II, pp. 280–1. Nicholas, *Medieval Flanders*, p. 52. Karen S. Nicholas, 'Countesses as Rulers in Flanders', in *Aristocratic Women in Medieval France*, ed. T. Evergates (Philadelphia, PA, 1999), pp. 111–37 at 115–17.

[38] Bates, *Acta*, p. 94 and nos. 181, 251, 254 and 286.

[39] WM, *GR*, I, pp. 502–5; *OV*, III, pp. 114–15.

[40] Godfrey, Prior of Winchester's (d.1107) tribute to Richard in T. Wright, ed., *The Anglo-Latin Satirical Poets and Epigrammatists of the Twelfth Century*, Rolls Series (London, 1872), II, p. 152. On

in the New Forest, is likely, Godfrey may have tried to benefit his church by encouraging a tomb cult.[41]

Robert's father returned to Normandy at the end of 1071. Orderic suggests that peace there had been disturbed in his absence, implying that Robert and Matilda's rule had faltered, but this may be an exaggeration generated by hindsight. In an attempt to restore order William convened a great council of the nobles of Normandy and Maine. Given Robert's importance in dealings with Maine, it is likely that he was involved in the assembly. The fact that the Manceaux were called to the council suggests that it was to prepare the way for an intervention in that county and that the disturbances were on Normandy's southern frontier.[42]

Robert was probably also present at an ecclesiastical council at Rouen in 1072.[43] It was important for Robert to attend in order to learn his supervisory role as duke and advocate of the Norman Church. The canons of the council dealt primarily with liturgical matters and clerical discipline.[44]

It is not known whether Robert accompanied his father on an expedition to Scotland in the summer of 1072, but the campaign resulted in a meeting between William and the Scots king Malcolm (Maelcoluim) III at Abernethy in Perthshire.[45] According to the *Anglo-Saxon Chronicle*, the two kings made peace and Malcolm became William's man and handed over hostages including his son Duncan.[46] Whether this entailed anything more than a personal recognition of William's overlordship is a hotly debated topic of Anglo-Scottish history.[47] By the beginning of November, the Conqueror was in Durham where he paid his respects at the tomb of the great Northumbrian saint, Cuthbert.[48] If Robert accompanied his father on this expedition and met Malcolm III, that might explain why the Scots king was later willing to make peace with Robert, who was acting on his father's behalf in 1080.[49]

Godfrey, see WM, *GR*, I, pp. 794–5 and II, p. 395; A.G. Rigg, *A History of Anglo-Latin Literature, 1066–1422* (Cambridge, 1992), pp. 17–20.

[41] My thanks to Emma Mason for suggesting a nascent cult at Richard's tomb.

[42] *OV*, II, pp. 284–5. On the chronology of these years, see Bates, *Acta*, pp. 79–80.

[43] *OV*, II, pp. 284–93. Raymonde Foreville, 'The Synod of the Province of Rouen in the Eleventh and Twelfth Centuries', in *Church and Government in the Middle Ages. Essays presented to C.R. Cheney on his 70th Birthday*, ed. C.N.L. Brooke, D.E. Luscombe, G.H. Martin and Dorothy Owen (Cambridge, 1976), pp. 19–39 at 30.

[44] *WJ*, II, pp. 184–5: '… dirigere stilo decreuimus ad Rodbertum eiusdem regis filium, quo in presentiarum duce et aduocato gaudemus'. On lay advocacy, see Bates, *Normandy before 1066*, pp. 121–2; J. Yver, 'Autour de l'absence d'avouerie en Normandie', *BSAN*, 53 (1957 for 1955–6), pp. 188–283.

[45] *JW*, III, *s.a.* 1072, pp. 20–1, dates the expedition after the Assumption of St Mary [15 August].

[46] *ASC*, D, *s.a.* 1073 [1072], p. 85; Swanton, p. 208. Cf. *ASC*, E, *s.a.* 1072, p. 90.

[47] A.A.M. Duncan, *The Kingship of the Scots, 842–1292* (Edinburgh, 2002), pp. 45, 48.

[48] Symeon, *Libellus de exordio*, pp. 196–7 and n. 72; cf. H.H.E. Craster, 'The Red Book of Durham', *EHR*, 40 (1925), pp. 504–35 at 528; cf. W.M. Aird, *St Cuthbert and the Normans. The Church of Durham, 1071–1153* (Woodbridge, 1998), pp. 85–9.

[49] *Historia Ecclesie Abbendonensis. The History of the Church of Abingdon*, ed. and trans. J. Hudson (Oxford, 2002), II, pp. 14–15; Duncan, *Kingship of the Scots*, pp. 45–6.

'Most noble Count of Maine'

Before the end of March 1073, the Conqueror felt confident enough in the security of England that he was able to address the problem of Maine. Drawing on the resources of his new kingdom, William invaded with a large army to enforce recognition of his son's lordship in Maine. He quickly captured several castles en route to Le Mans. After the fields and vineyards around the city were devastated, Le Mans surrendered swiftly and William was spared the inconveniences of a protracted siege.[50] The citizens met William at a peace conference outside Le Mans, at which the king swore oaths to uphold the ancient customs and laws of their city and in return 'the citizens surrendered themselves and all their possessions into his power and authority'.[51]

It is not clear whether Robert played any part in the expedition to Le Mans, although he would have been keen to demonstrate his abilities on a military campaign. His father may still have viewed him as too precious an asset to expose to the dangers of warfare, but it was politically important for him to be present. It was, after all, through him that William justified his intervention in Maine and there are signs that the campaign of 1073 resulted in recognition of Robert's lordship in Le Mans. A confirmation for the abbey of Saint-Vincent at Le Mans refers to the 'year in which Robert, son of William, king of the English, recovered the county of the men of Maine'.[52] Although this document may simply be recording the recognition that his title was restored by his father's actions, it suggests that Robert actively took part in the recovery of the county. A picture gradually emerges of Robert exercising lordship in Le Mans. He was also referred to as the 'count of Maine' ('Rotbertus comes Cenomannensis') in a document issued for Bayeux cathedral in 1074. It seems probable that Robert, described as the 'most noble count of Maine', was indeed given some independent experience of ruling the county. Another charter was issued, in August 1076, 'with Robert, son of the king of the English, governing the city of the men of Maine (Le Mans)'.[53] If Robert had indeed some experience of the political situation in Maine it may explain his willingness to cultivate Robert de Bellême as a companion. The Montgomery-Bellême family was one of the dominant forces on the southern frontiers of Normandy. It is also noticeable that Robert had connections with members of other families in the region, such as the Grandmesnils.

There was a further recognition of Robert's status as his father's heir in

---

[50] *Actus Pontificum*, pp. 380–1; OV, II, pp. 306–7.
[51] *Actus Pontificum*, p. 381.
[52] Bates, *Acta*, no. 173, and p. 95.
[53] Bates, *Acta*, no. 27 (Bayeux) and cf. Bates, *Acta*, no. 172 (Le Mans), where Robert is 'comes Cenomannensis nobilissimus'; *Cartulaire de Saint-Vincent*, I, no. 589: '... Robertoque, Willelmi regis Anglorum filio, Cenomannicam urbem gubernante'. Cf. Garnett, *Conquered England*, pp. 161–2, who sees Robert's titles as no more than claims.

Normandy when the Conqueror fell seriously ill at Bonneville-sur-Touques.[54] This illness may have been connected with the recent campaign in Maine. William issued a charter confirming a grant to the abbey of Saint-Pierre-de-la-Couture at Solesmes. The charter was dated at Bonneville-sur-Touques on 30 March 1073 when the Conqueror is described as 'holding the city of the principality of the men of Maine'.[55] Medieval kings enduring bouts of serious illness often made arrangements for the succession in the event of their deaths. Robert and his father had just collaborated in the successful expedition to restore Norman lordship at Le Mans and it would be natural for the king to summon his nobles and, in a public ceremony, have them renew their homage and oath of fealty to his son. Not only was this an opportunity to reaffirm the succession, it was also a public acknowledgement of Robert's role in the expedition to Le Mans.[56] It was important to reinvigorate social bonds by periodically restaging the rituals that had created them. Thus, in his early twenties, Count Robert was recognised as lord of Maine, although whether this was anything more than a title and a claim is doubtful. In addition, he had been assured on more than one occasion of the succession to Normandy. Moreover, there had been many witnesses to his father's promises: by the mid-1070s, Robert's future seemed assured.

Generations

From the mid-1070s William the Conqueror began to experience challenges, not so much from external enemies as from members of his own family and from among the ranks of the Norman aristocracy. The knighting of Roger of Montgomery's son on the 1073 expedition to Maine was emblematic of a new generation emerging. These young men, the 'sons of the conquerors', had benefited from their fathers' achievements in 1066, but they shared attitudes and values with each other which distinguished them from their elders. In this instance, 'generation' refers not so much to a group of men of about the same age, as to one whose members share a certain mentality. In this respect, the contingents that had accompanied Robert's father on the invasion of England in 1066 comprised men of various ages, but they were bound together by their shared experience of the traumas and triumph of that campaign. That said, the events of 1066 would have been experienced in very different ways by veteran campaigners and those, like Robert de Beaumont, facing their first battles.

---

54 *OV*, II, pp. 356–7; cf. *OV*, III, pp. 112–13.
55 Bates, *Acta*, no. 275: 'apud Bonam villam, qui Willermus Cenomannensis civitatis tunc principatum tenebat'. Cf. Garnett, *Conquered England*, p. 161.
56 Cf. H. Fichtenau, *Living in the Tenth Century. Mentalities and Social Orders*, trans. P.J. Geary (Chicago, 1991), p. 37.

Similarly, men who were too young, or too old, to fight in 1066 and the women left behind, had a very different view of events. Although they celebrated the Conqueror's triumphant return in 1067 and benefited materially from the spoils of war brought back by their relatives, there was a certain sense of alienation. For some who remained in Normandy, the Conqueror's campaigns in England destabilised family life. Wives unable to join their husbands across the Channel threatened to marry other men if they were left alone much longer.[57]

What stories of derring-do could those left behind contribute when the Hastings veterans began their reminiscences? Such differences in life experience, especially among the members of a social elite for whom warfare was such a large component of their self-identity, bred divisions. These and other less dramatic distinctions between men of diverse ages, such as the adoption of new fashions in speech, dress or social mores, had the potential to act as catalysts of social change and conflict.[58]

In 1075, King William and his entourage celebrated Easter at Fécamp, and probably Robert was present, especially as it was something of a family occasion with the consecration of Robert's sister, Cecilia, as a nun.[59] Although she had been given to her mother's foundation of La Trinité in Caen when that church was dedicated in June 1066, the ceremony conducted by Archbishop John of Rouen in 1075 probably marked her adult profession as a nun.[60] Cecilia later became abbess of La Trinité, and Robert seems to have remained close to her.[61] Cecilia's career was not untypical of aristocratic women in this period, whose pious vocations were accepted or even encouraged by their relatives. The size of William and Matilda's family allowed them to free one of their daughters from the prospect of a diplomatic marriage, although Queen Matilda might also have had one eye on the management of her foundation at Caen.

Towards the end of 1075 Robert's father faced a serious challenge to his rule in England. For writers looking back on the Conqueror's reign from the twelfth century, this marked a downturn in the great man's fortunes. Ralph, earl of Norfolk and Suffolk, Roger, earl of Hereford, and Waltheof, earl of Northumbria, conspired together to bring an end to the king's reign. Earl Roger was the son of the Conqueror's close friend, William fitz Obern, who had been killed in 1071. Earl Ralph de Gael was a Breton and William fitz Osbern's son-in-law. As the one Englishman, Waltheof seems out of place in the conspiracy, but he was married to Judith, the Conqueror's niece.[62]

William remained in Normandy during the crisis, leaving his deputies to

57   *OV*, II, pp. 218–21.
58   D. Herlihy, 'The Generation in Medieval History', *Viator*, 5 (1974), pp. 347–64.
59   *OV*, III, pp. 8–9; Bates, *Acta*, p. 80.
60   *OV*, III, pp. 8–9 and n. 5; *Fauroux*, no. 231; J. Walmsley, 'The Early Abbesses, Nuns and Female Tenants of the Abbey of Holy Trinity, Caen', *JEH*, 48 (1997), pp. 425–44.
61   Cecilia died 13 July 1127: *OV*, III, pp. 10–11, n. 1.
62   *OV*, II, pp. 310–21; cf. F.S. Scott, 'Earl Waltheof of Northumbria', *Archaeologia Aeliana*, 4th ser., 30

deal with the rebels, who were either captured or driven into exile. Although the king had survived, the execution of Earl Waltheof, the only one of the three conspirators to lose his life, was seen as especially shocking and unjust. By the time he came to write his account, Orderic had visited the Fenland abbey of Crowland in England and had seen for himself the growing cult of Waltheof, which centred on the miraculously preserved body of the earl with its severed head that had reattached itself after the execution. Given Orderic's English origins and affinity with the community at Crowland, it is hardly surprising that he saw the execution of Waltheof as a stain on the Conqueror's reputation. Orderic suggested that the severe problems faced by King William in the last years of his reign could be explained by his unjust execution of Waltheof. William never again enjoyed lasting peace and perhaps the greatest challenge the king faced in these years was the rebellion of his eldest son.[63]

Laigle

In the mid-1070s, Robert's relationship with his father began to fall apart. The hostility was enacted in full view of leading members of the Norman political community. Orderic again provides the most detailed account and, although he was writing some fifty years after the events, his vivid narrative was informed by someone very close to events. This was Samson, a monk in Orderic's abbey of Saint-Évroul. He was a Breton and one of Queen Mathilda's messengers. When the Conqueror discovered that Matilda had been corresponding with her son against his wishes, he exploded with rage and threatened to have Samson arrested and blinded. Friends of the queen warned him and he fled to the abbey of Saint-Évroul.[64]

Messengers were more than just carriers of letters. Often the written letter would carry only part of the message and it was left to the messenger to convey orally the most sensitive points of the communication. Messengers were among the most trusted of medieval retainers.[65] Moreover, in order to represent accurately the wishes of their lord or lady they had to possess retentive memories as well as shrewdness and eloquence.[66] By the time that Orderic had joined Saint-Évroul, in 1085, Samson's story had doubtless grown in the telling, but the queen's messenger gave him the perspective of a court insider and a man caught in the middle.

There was no hint of tension between Robert and his father until around 1077. The plot against the king exposed in 1075, and a failed campaign in Brittany, in the following year, may have made the king more alive to poten-

---

(1952), pp. 149–213; Douglas, *William the Conqueror*, pp. 231–3; Bates, *William the Conqueror*, pp. 180–1.

63 *OV*, II, pp. 350–1.
64 *OV*, III, pp. 104–5.
65 P. Chaplais, *English Diplomatic Practice in the Middle Ages* (London, 2003), pp. 133–55 at 144.
66 *OV*, III, p. 104, n. 1.

tial shortcomings in his son, or perhaps made William suspicious of his son's intentions and reluctant to entrust his territories to anyone but himself. The campaign in Brittany was conducted in pursuit of the rebel Ralph de Gael. Outside the castle of Dol, in the autumn of 1076, the Conqueror was defeated by Ralph's French allies and William was forced into a humiliating retreat.[67] A truce with Philip I of France was negotiated in 1077, but there was no disguising the fact that William had suffered a major setback which undermined his reputation for invincibility. From Robert's perspective, his father was yesterday's man and on a downward path. It was time for new blood to take over and reinvigorate the regime.[68]

After the death of Margaret of Maine, Robert 'was moved by youthful ambition and the fatal advice of his comrades to ask for Maine and Normandy as honours that were rightly his'.[69] William refused the request and tried to persuade his son to be patient, but this was not what Robert wanted to hear and, when nothing was conceded, he took offence. This led to quarrels, violence and eventually exile for the heir to Normandy. Orderic's purpose in writing history was to provide examples of the rewards of right behaviour and the consequences of sin. Therefore his account is heavily editorialised and his reporting of the facts reflects these concerns.[70]

Late in 1077 or early 1078, Robert and his father clashed as the result of an incident at Laigle in south-eastern Normandy, not far from Saint-Évroul. The Conqueror led an expedition into the Corbonnais, attempting a show of strength to discourage raiding across that part of Normandy's frontier.[71] Orderic knew the area well and had access to local tradition, as well as Samson's memories.[72] At the time, Robert's younger brothers, William Rufus (aged around eighteen) and Henry (about nine or ten), were favoured by their father and thought themselves the equals of their brother.[73] They resented Robert's claims for the whole inheritance and were appalled that he was surrounded by 'a swarm of obsequious sycophants' and considered himself the equal of their father.[74] This was about hierarchy: the father's position chal-

67 JW, III, s.a. 1075, pp. 28–9; ASC, D, p. 88; Swanton, pp. 212–13; ASC, E, p. 91, Swanton, pp. 212–13; OV, II, pp. 350–3.
68 Orderic's narrative forms the basis for what follows, but his chronology is a little confused; OV, II, pp. 356–61; III, pp. 96–7. Cf. WM, GR, I, pp. 700–1.
69 OV, II, pp. 356–7.
70 R.D. Ray, 'Orderic Vitalis and his Readers', Studia Monastica, 14 (1972), pp. 17–33; Chibnall, World of Orderic Vitalis, pp. 181–203, and Jean Blacker, The Faces of Time. Portrayal of the Past in Old French and Latin Historical Narrative of the Anglo-Norman Regnum (Austin, TX, 1994), pp. 66–77.
71 The Corbannais was the district around Mortagne and part of the County of the Perche: D. Power, The Norman Frontier in the Twelfth and Early Thirteenth Centuries (Cambridge, 2004), pp. 116, 117.
72 OV, II, pp. 356–7; cf. Kathleen Thompson, Power and Border Lordship in Medieval France. The County of the Perche, 1000–1226 (Woodbridge, 2002), pp. 40–5; eadem, 'The Lords of Laigle: Ambition and Insecurity on the Borders of Normandy', ANS, 18 (1996), pp. 177–99.
73 WM, GR, I, pp. 710–11, 712–13 and 542–3; Malmesbury suggests that the three brothers quarrelled during their years at their father's court. William Rufus remained wary of Henry, who trusted neither of his elder brothers.
74 OV, II, pp. 358–9; Bates, William the Conqueror, p. 185.

lenged by the eldest son; the eldest son in turn denied recognition of his status by younger brothers. Their behaviour thus had significance beyond the pranks of annoying siblings. William and Henry

> came to the town of Laigle, where Robert had taken up residence in the house of Roger Cauchois, and began to play dice in the upper gallery, as knights do.[75] They made a great noise about it and soon began to pour 'water' down on Robert and his sycophants underneath. Then Ivo and Aubrey of Grandmesnil said to Robert, 'Why do you put up with such insults? Just look at the way your brothers have climbed up above your head and are defiling you and us with filth to your shame. Don't you see what this means? Even a blind man could. Unless you punish this insult without delay it will be all over with you: you will never be able to hold up your head again.' Hearing these words he leaped to his feet in a towering rage, and dashed to the upper room to take his brothers unawares.[76]

The noise of Robert dealing with his brothers brought the king to the house and his 'royal authority' brought an end to the quarrel.[77] The next night, however, Robert, in a manoeuvre, either daring or foolhardy, made an attempt to seize the citadel at Rouen, but he was thwarted by the king's butler, Roger d'Ivry. When the matter was reported, the king became angry and ordered the arrest of all Robert's supporters. Only a few were captured and the rest fled into exile.

The level of circumstantial detail in Orderic's account suggests that this was a well-known story at the time that he was writing. Laigle was near Saint-Évroul. Ivo and Aubrey of Grandmesnil were members of a family of major benefactors of the house.[78] Robert's attack on Rouen may suggest that his rebellion had been planned before the expedition to Laigle. He had become increasingly frustrated and alienated by his father's treatment, and the fight at Laigle was probably the final act in a protracted drama, rather than a simple emotional outburst. At Laigle Robert's personal honour as well as his social position was under threat.

Robert's Sense of Honour

In this society a nobleman's sense of honour was a key component of his social identity. At Laigle Robert's younger brothers were, in the act of urinating on him, demonstrating their contempt for his honour and challenging his posi-

---

[75] Dicing and gambling were condemned by the Church for associations with the prohibited practice of prognostication: Bartlett, *England*, p. 237; Rhiannon Purdie, 'Dice-games and the Blasphemy of Prediction', in *Medieval Futures: Attitudes to the Future in the Middle Ages*, ed. J.A. Burrow and I.P. Wei (Woodbridge, 2000), pp. 167–84.

[76] *OV*, II, pp. 356–9.

[77] *OV*, II, pp. 358–9; the language at this point suggests legal disputes ('iurgia') settled by royal authority ('regali auctoritate').

[78] Chibnall, *World of Orderic Vitalis*, pp. 22–3.

tion as their father's heir. More than that, they were calling into question his right to be treated as a social superior. The insult also had the potential to affect Robert's relationship with his own followers. As members of his retinue they shared in the insult and had a responsibility to help him restore his and their position.[79] Here, Orderic may have misrepresented, perhaps wilfully, the nature of Robert's relationship with these 'sycophants' in order to reinforce his condemnation of the young man's subsequent actions. Orderic knew what would eventually happen to Robert and his narrative is structured with this fate in mind. The incident also needs to be seen in the context of the Conqueror's court. The court was an arena where individuals and groups competed for the king's attention in the hope of reaping the rewards of his patronage.[80]

The court was not a homogeneous social grouping. It was an ever-changing organism and those attending varied from assembly to assembly. When it came together, at the great liturgical festivals for example, the court was composed of several sub-groups, each with its own internal structures and social dynamic.[81] The queen had her own household and its members assisted her when she was called to govern Normandy. As he matured, Robert, too, gathered around him other youths of similar age, anxious to become members of the entourage of the future duke of Normandy, and, possibly, king of England. It is, however, debatable whether Robert could freely choose the members of his own retinue. It was difficult to turn away the sons of his father's magnates or even *their* sons, if they indicated a desire to join him. On the other hand, there is no evidence that William attempted to manage his son's retinue by assigning certain trusted individuals to keep an eye on things.[82] It seems that the Conqueror's preferred method of managing his son's retinue was to keep him short of cash.

The members of the group around Robert had their own ambitions, but to guarantee their positions in the future, they had come to identify their own interests with those of the heir to Normandy and Maine. Robert's retinue developed its own internal hierarchy, character and sense of group identity; therefore an insult against their leader was an insult shared by the group. The actions of William Rufus and Henry at Laigle were a deliberate under-mining of the social position of a significant section of the Conqueror's court. Robert and his retinue had a keen sense of the level of respect to which they were entitled. Their consciousness of their own worth was a manifestation of their sense of collective honour. The difficulty was that other members of

79 OV, II, pp. 358–9.
80 There has, as yet, been no systematic treatment of the Conqueror's court and its social, political, and artistic culture; but cf. Green, *Henry I*, pp. 284–306.
81 T. Reuter, 'Assembly Politics in Western Europe from the Eighth Century to the Twelfth', in P. Linehan and Janet L. Nelson, eds., *The Medieval World* (London, 2001), pp. 432–50, and G. Koziol, 'Political Culture', in M. Bull, ed., *France in the Central Middle Ages* (Oxford, 2002), pp. 43–76.
82 Henry II assigned William Marshall the task of keeping the Young King's entourage in order: W.L. Warren, *Henry II* (London, 1973), pp. 581–2. My thanks to Professor Matthew Strickland for discussing this point with me.

the Conqueror's court did not share this view. Honour was not only a quality internalised by individuals, but also an attribute of identity that had to be negotiated with others.[83]

The contours of Robert's relationship with his father also had a bearing on his violent reaction to the incident at Laigle. Among the aristocracy of north-western Europe, the relationship between a father and his sons was crucial in determining the success or failure of dynastic ambition. From the eleventh century, aristocratic families favoured a method of passing on land and property from generation to generation via the eldest son rather than distributing resources among all surviving family members. The advantage of this system, known as primogeniture, was that the family's lands remained intact, rather than being divided among siblings until, eventually, they became economically unviable. Primogeniture allowed dynasties to endure as long as there was an heir. The corollary of this system was that younger siblings were assigned a diminished role in the family's affairs. Primogeniture was by no means in universal use at the end of the eleventh century, but the advantages of the system were becoming clearer to the nobility. That said, much depended on the number of sons in a given family and whether they were strong enough to push their claims for a share of the inheritance. As in the case of Queen Matilda's natal family, an elder brother or his line might be displaced by a more ambitious younger brother.[84]

Whatever system or *ad hoc* process was employed, the longevity of the father was an obstacle. Occasionally ageing fathers relinquished political control of their lordship in favour of their son. For example, in the late 1030s, Count Fulk Nerra turned over the governance of Anjou to his son Geoffrey Martel. Although he telescopes a dispute which lasted eighteen months into a few days, William of Malmesbury's account of Fulk and Geoffrey demonstrated that turning over power to a son prematurely might have disastrous results.[85]

Before about 1076, the Conqueror had acknowledged Robert as his heir on two or three occasions. In so doing, William also assigned a provisional future role for his other sons and daughters as subordinates to their eldest brother. It seems reasonable to assume that when the other Norman nobles were called upon to acknowledge Robert's status, his younger brothers would also have done so. However, until Robert had the resources to wield power in his own name and at his own volition, his recognition as his father's heir was little more than a frustrating promise of future power. Given that Robert had

83 F.H. Stewart, *Honor* (Chicago, 1994). I am grateful to Richard Barton for this reference.
84 See above, p. 66.
85 WM, *GR*, I, pp. 436–9. Bachrach, *Fulk Nerra*, pp. 234–6. Jessica Hemming, '*Sellam Gestare*: Saddle-Bearing Punishments and the Case of Rhiannon', *Viator*, 28 (1997), pp. 45–64; cf. M. Strickland, 'Réconcilation ou humiliation? La suppression de la rébellion aristocratique dans les royaumes anglo-normand et angevin', in Catherine Bougy and Sophie Poirey, eds., *Images de la contestation du pouvoir dans le monde normand (Xe–XVIIIe siècle)* (Caen, 2007), pp. 65–78. I am grateful to Professor Strickland for supplying me with a copy of his paper.

been recognised formally as the heir to Normandy and Maine, his behaviour at court and his exercise of such responsibilities as his father allowed him would have been scrutinised minutely, not only by those in power, but also by those who considered that their future social position depended on Robert's effectiveness.

This pattern was reproduced in other noble families and the pressures of the social expectations under which Robert laboured would have been well-understood by his companions. Robert needed to show that he was deserving of the status designated to him by his father. Such a demonstration of worth entailed looking and behaving like a fully fledged member of the Norman ruling class. It was, however, an expensive business as many of the social markers of high nobility – good food, opulent and fashionable dress, participation in hunting and the distribution of *largesse* – required ready cash, or at least the resources to generate it.[86] Robert had to compete with the extravagance of aristocratic courts such as that of Hugh of Avranches, earl of Chester, described by Orderic.[87]

The ability to afford a suitable lifestyle was not the end of the story, for Robert had to look the part. He had to behave in a manner which lent credibility to his claims to social pre-eminence. Impressive social display was an integral part of Robert's public and private *persona*. What Robert was doing by spending large amounts of cash, or giving elaborate gifts to members of his retinue, was converting economic capital into 'symbolic capital', which he hoped would bring social and political pre-eminence. Orderic's later condemnation of Robert's wastefulness misrepresented as a character fault his attempts to answer the pressures that came with maintaining his position at court. Orderic also had the parable of the prodigal son in mind when he wrote about Robert's excesses, and some modern historians have also disapproved, commenting, for example, that Robert should have marshalled his assets more carefully. But, then, this is to misunderstand the mentality that informed noble behaviour.[88]

Robert Curthose's Body

In the preamble to the incident at Laigle, Orderic gave a brief sketch of Robert:

> He was talkative and extravagant, reckless, very courageous in battle, a powerful and sure archer with a clear and cheerful voice and a fluent tongue. Round faced,

---

86 Crouch, *Image of the Aristocracy*, pp. 247–51; Françoise Piponnier and Perrine Mane, *Dress in the Middle Ages* (New Haven and London, 1997), pp. 55–76; J. Bumke, 'Material Culture and Social Style' and 'Courtly Feasts', in *idem, Courtly Culture*, pp. 103–202, 203–73.

87 *OV*, III, pp. 216–17. For some, the extravagances of the court were a spur to religious conversion. The knight Herluin must have cut a sorry figure eating bread and water at sumptuous banquets: 'Life of Herluin', in Vaughn, *Abbey of Bec*, pp. 67–86 at 70.

88 P. Burke, *History and Social Theory* (Oxford, 1992), pp. 67–9.

short and stout, he was commonly nick-named 'fat legs' (*Gambaron*) and 'curt hose' (*brevis ocrea*).[89]

This description gives us elements of what has become the archetype of the medieval aristocratic youth.[90] Robert was extravagant and reckless, but these were characteristics valued by the nobility if not by sententious monks. Despite the disapproving tone, Orderic concedes that Robert was also an accomplished warrior. Thus Robert possessed the attributes deemed essential for a successful courtier. As well as courage in battle and prowess with the bow, Robert was an engaging speaker, 'with a clear, cheerful voice and a fluent tongue'; for eleventh-century courtiers this facility of easy and engaging speech was essential.[91] Certainly, the speeches attributed to Robert by Orderic demonstrate an ability to argue his case with his father. Even allowing for the possibility that it is not Robert's but Orderic's voice we hear in these exchanges, we can be sure that the audience would have understood these speeches as the sort of thing that Robert would have said. But, given the source of the information, namely Samson the queen's messenger, Orderic's reportage might be more accurate than historians usually allow. Messengers were known for their retentive memories and monks developed mnemonic techniques that enabled them to recall scriptural and liturgical works in detail.[92] But there is one element in descriptions of Robert which suggests that he may have been an easy target for those who wished to undermine his position at court.

Orderic and William of Malmesbury assure us that Robert acquired a series of nicknames. This, in itself, was not unusual for the period and his brothers William and Henry were also given nicknames.[93] Unfortunately for Robert, his nickname referred specifically to his small stature. Robert is described as short and pot-bellied, so there seems little possibility that the nickname 'Curthose' was given ironically in order to emphasis that he was, in fact, a tall man. Possibly the nickname was not meant to have any detrimental impact on Robert's social standing and, among an elite dominated by warriors, it might be imagined that genial banter would bestow such nicknames on companions at arms.[94] Although perhaps crude or obscene, the nicknames were, at least, a demonstration that the individual had been recognised by the group.

---

[89] *OV*, II, pp. 356–7; WM, *GR*, I, pp. 700–3; Malmesbury gives the nickname as 'Robelinus Curta Ocrea', which might be rendered 'Little Bobby Short-Pants'. Malmesbury explains that the nickname was given because of his small size but 'in other respects there was nothing to criticize, for he was neither unattractive in feature nor unready in speech, not feeble in courage nor weak in counsel'.

[90] Duby, 'Youth in Aristocratic Society', pp. 112–22.

[91] C.S. Jaeger, *The Origins of Courtliness. Civilising Trends and the Formation of Courtly Ideals, 939–1210* (Philadelphia, PA, 1985), pp. 19–48.

[92] See above, Introduction, p. 00.

[93] WM, *GR*, I, pp. 700–1. William was known as 'Rufus' ('the Red') and 'Longsword'; Mason, *William II*, pp. 9–10. Henry I was nick-named 'Beauclerc', 'Stag's Foot' and, less positively, 'Godric': Green, *Henry I*, pp. 23, 307 and 61.

[94] However, nicknames could be given with the intention of ridicule: Henry I and his wife Matilda were called 'Godric and Godgifu' by members of the Norman nobility: WM, *GR*, I, pp. 716–17.

However, as we are specifically told that William jeered at his son in public, driving him away, Robert's nickname may have been coined by his father in order to ridicule him.[95] It is surely one thing to be given a nickname by one's companions-in-arms, but when it is an often repeated insult by one's father, it is likely to acquire an edge.

Physical attributes, especially appearance, were understood by medieval people to reflect inner qualities.[96] Thus a king should look like a king and his authority should be represented by his physical attributes and bodily comportment. Kings became angry and exacted cruel punishment if they felt that their regal image was being ridiculed and undermined.[97] It is also significant, then, that the Conqueror in the hearing of the courtiers debased his son's social identity, perhaps hoping to make it easier to exclude him from his plans. Robert may have been slow to react to insult, as Ivo and Aubrey de Grandmesnil's prompting suggests, but there is no reason to doubt that his sense of self-worth was as well-honed as that of his father and brothers.

Absalom and Polynices

In the summer of 1077 Robert attended, with his parents and his brother William, the dedication of a number of important Norman churches. The consecration of Bayeux cathedral took place on 14 July and on 13 September Robert attended the re-dedication of his father's own abbey of Saint-Étienne in Caen.[98] Although the mere attendance at these ceremonies tells us nothing about the health of the relationship between the two men, it suggests that the break might be dated to the last months of 1077 or early 1078.

Orderic's narrative has a dramatic quality transmitted through long passages of direct speech that could be represented as a play complete with stage-directions.[99] Robert's followers, 'factious young knights', pointed out that he was impoverished and incited him to claim a share of England, or

<hr />

Malmesbury tells us that Henry took these names as an insult and while pretending to laugh, he made a note of the jokers so that later he could exact his revenge.

95 WM, GR, I, pp. 700–1.

96 Caroline Walker Bynum, 'Why All the Fuss about the Body? A Medievalist's Perspective', *Critical Inquiry*, 22 (1995), pp. 27–31.

97 OV, VI, pp. 352–5; Henry I ordered the blinding of Luke of La Barre 'for his scurrilous songs' ('pro derisoriis cantionibus').

98 OV, III, pp. 10–13; L. Musset, ed., *Les actes de Guillaume le Conquérant et de la reine Mathilde pour les abbayes Caennaises*, Mémoires de la Société des Antiquaires de Normandie, 37 (Caen, 1967), pp. 14–15, 58. Bates, *Acta*, p. 80. Bates, *William the Conqueror*, p. 185, suggests, with reference to the disaster at Dol in 1076, that these dedications were timed to 'propitiate God's anger after a military defeat'.

99 OV, II, pp. 356–61; III, pp. 96–117. Medieval historians sometimes claimed that they tried to recover, as far as possible, the words that were actually spoken. E.g. WP, pp. 122–3, assured his audience that: 'We wish to bring the tenor [*compertam sententiam*] of the duke's own words (which we have diligently sought out) rather than our own composition to the notice of many, because we desire him to have the widest possible esteem and praise for ever.'

at least ask for the duchy of Normandy again.[100] They argued that Robert was denied the material resources appropriate to his social standing: once again, it was a matter of honour.

> It is a great dishonour to you and injury to us and many others that you should be deprived of royal wealth in this way. Why do you tolerate it? A man deserves to have wealth if he knows how to distribute it generously to all petitioners.[101]

Robert's followers felt the insult as much as their lord and alleged that the Conqueror was deliberately denying his son the resources to set up his own court. Robert must have had some financial resources to distribute in order to build up the following mentioned by Orderic, but the demands of his retinue soon exhausted his coffers. From William's point of view this parsimony was perhaps his most effective method of controlling access to his son, or at least influencing the membership of his son's retinue.

Robert's father employed restricted access to wealth as a regulatory mechanism designed to mould the opinions and behaviour of the next generation of the political elite. It was a key element in the Conqueror's attempt to manage his family and ensure the future of his dynasty. It was important for Robert to listen to the counsel of more than one group at court and it was perhaps the Conqueror's intention to broaden his son's contacts.[102] But for Robert and his followers, this was an intolerable restriction on the young man's ability to fulfil his social role as the king's heir.[103] In other words, without the resources he demanded, Robert was in danger of suffering a loss of honour and descending into social invisibility. At each public recognition of his status and especially after the rich spoils of the Conquest were paraded through Normandy, Robert felt his embarrassment more acutely. His dilemma was essentially the result of a conflict of loyalties between obeying his father or responding to the demands of his retinue. In addition, William Rufus and Henry were competing perhaps more and more successfully with Robert for their father's attention. Robert's hopes for social independence, as his advisers pointed out, were thwarted by his father and there was little alternative but to confront him. It was a formidable task as William carried the weight not only of a father's authority, but also that of a king. If it was the Conqueror's intention to manage Robert and his retinue by starving them of resources, then this policy backfired dramatically.

Orderic's account reflected early twelfth-century views on the proper relationship between father and son. These behavioural norms were informed by scriptural models and the customs and expectations of Norman society. In addition, Orderic had from the age of ten been educated in the monastic life

---

[100] Robert of Torigny suggested that Robert also wanted to rule in Maine: *WJ*, II, pp. 202–3.
[101] *OV*, III, pp. 96–7.
[102] G. Althoff, *Family, Friends and Followers. Political and Social Bonds in Early Medieval Europe* (Cambridge, 2004), p. 10.
[103] *OV*, III, pp. 96–9.

and trained to respect the authority of the abbot, the 'father' of his monks.[104] Furthermore, the quarrel between Robert and William brought back painful childhood memories. After his account of the dispute between Robert and William, Orderic inserted an autobiographical passage that forty-two years had passed since his father 'sent [him] into exile for love of his Creator' and that '[t]hese things are often in my mind'.[105] Orderic's critical opinion of Robert was the result of the application of contemporary norms, monastic moralising and, perhaps, personal regret at a curtailed relationship with his own father.[106]

During the exchanges between Robert and his father allusions were made to figures from the Old Testament and from classical antiquity.[107] William accused Robert of behaving like Absalom, who rebelled against his father King David, or Rehoboam, son of Solomon who rejected the Lord and the advice of his elders.[108] The story of David and Absalom could be read as a criticism of the father as well as of the son, so perhaps Orderic's account was more neutral than has been assumed.[109]

Robert likened himself to the Greek tragic hero, Polynices, son of Oedipus. Robert and William would probably have been familiar with the stories of these men and may even have used such allusions in their exchanges.[110] However, it is more likely that the choice of allusion says more about Orderic's – or Samson's – narrative technique than the actual content of the angry exchanges between father and son.

The origin of Robert's dissatisfaction with life at court lay in the complaints made by his retinue. Responding to them, Robert asked his father for Normandy and pointed out that he had been given the duchy before the invasion of England. William replied that he held Normandy by hereditary right and that as long as he lived he would not relax his grip on it. Robert then asked how he was to provide for his dependants, but his father's reply offered no direct answer: 'Show me the obedience due to me in all things, and take a wise share in the government of all my dominions *as a son with his father*.'[111]

---

104 The prologue to the *Rule of Saint Benedict* opens 'Hearken, *my son*, to the precepts of the master and incline the ear of thy heart; freely accept and faithfully fulfil the instructions of *a loving father* ...': *The Rule of St Benedict*, trans. Justin McCann (London, 1976) (my emphasis). Cf. *The Monastic Constitutions of Lanfranc*, ed. and trans. D. Knowles and C.N.L. Brooke (Oxford, 2002), pp. 4–5 *et passim*.

105 *OV*, III, pp. 150–1.

106 On Orderic's father, Odelerius of Orleans, see Chibnall, *World of Orderic Vitalis*, pp. 7–11.

107 Orderic's account is the basis of what follows.

108 Absalom: 2 Sam. 12:7–12; 13:1–29; 14; 15–18. King David's grief was intense at the death of his son: 2 Sam. 18:33–19:8. Rehoboam: 1 Kings 14:25–8 and 2 Chron. 12:5.

109 S.L. McKenzie, *King David. A Biography* (Oxford, 2000), pp. 34–5. David exiled Absalom from Jerusalem for three years; was this Orderic's reference to Robert's first exile from c.1077/8 to 1080?

110 Statius, *Thebaid, Books 1–7*, and *Thebaid, Books 8–12. Achilleid*, both ed. and trans. D.R. Shackleton Bailey (Cambridge, MA, 2003). The *Thebaid* was known at the Norman court in the Conqueror's reign; cf. *WP*, pp. 136–7.

111 *OV*, III, pp. 98–9 (my emphasis).

This last comment raises interesting questions as to what sort of relationship was envisaged. What was this 'share in the government'? Did it involve any possibility of independent rule? It seems that Robert was offered joint rule with his father, but obviously this was not a partnership of equals for the phrase 'as a son with his father' implies the son's subordinate role obeying the dictates of the *paterfamilias*. Robert's reaction was to reject the status of a mercenary in his father's service. Although this exchange draws heavily on passages from the Gospels, it does seem to encapsulate Robert's dilemma.

> I am not prepared to be your hireling (*mercennarius*) forever. I want at last to have property of my own, so that I can give proper wages to my dependents. I ask you therefore to grant me legal control of the duchy, so that, just as you rule over the kingdom of England, I, under you, may rule over the duchy of Normandy.[112]

Robert was asking for the promises of control in Normandy to be made good, but he also envisaged ruling the duchy independently under the lordship of his father, again giving us the idea of the Norman lands run as a kind of family concern.

At this point in his dealings with his son, the king raised the spectre of Absalom. He pointed out that Robert's demands were premature and that he should be patient, for he would receive what he desired in due course 'if you continue to deserve it'. He also advised him not to listen to his young companions who were leading him astray. Robert should remember the grisly fate that befell Absalom and his advisers Achitophel and Amasa. Similarly, Rehoboam also paid the price for discounting the counsel of wise men such as Benaiah. It was foolish, then, to follow the bad counsel of young men and Robert would be better asking the assistance of the venerable archbishops William of Rouen and Lanfranc of Canterbury. But Robert had had enough of his father's pontificating: 'My lord king, I did not come here to listen to a lecture, for I have more than enough of these from my schoolmasters and am surfeited with them.' He then asked for the 'honour' that was due to him and repeated that he would 'no longer fight for anyone in Normandy with the hopeless status of a hired dependent.'[113]

William's patience was exhausted by his son's intransigence and he angrily repeated his determination to hold on to his native Normandy and not allow his son a share of England, quoting the biblical aphorism that 'every kingdom divided against itself is brought to desolation'. The Conqueror argued that he alone had been given the English throne and had been crowned by the vicars of Christ and it was a responsibility that was not his to give away. For Robert, this was the last straw, and he stormed out of his father's court and

---

112   *OV*, III, pp. 98–9 and 98, n. 2: 'behind the language of the gospel is the complaint of a man treated as a landless knight'.
113   *OV*, III, pp. 98–101.

left Normandy. His parting shot was to liken himself to the Theban Polynices, one of the heroes of Statius's epic the *Thebaid*.[114]

The *Thebaid* was known in Normandy and it is not wholly impossible that Robert did represent himself as a latter-day Polynices. However, the choice of the *Thebaid* suggests that Orderic structured his account of the Norman ruling house as a tragedy comparable with that which befell the house of Oedipus.[115] There has been a tendency to see Orderic's criticism directed solely at Robert, but the thing to note is that Statius's *Thebaid* was a criticism of the *whole* house of Thebes/Normandy, father, mother and sons together.

An obvious feature of the exchanges between Robert and his father is that they were conducted in anger. William of Malmesbury reported that

> When filled with the hot blood of youth, he [Robert] was encouraged by foolish companions to hope that he could secure Normandy from his father during his lifetime. When his father refused, driving the young man away with jeers in that terrific voice of his, Robert went off in a passion, and harried his own country with frequent attacks. At first his father merely laughed. 'By God's resurrection!' he used to say, 'He'll be a hero, will our little Robby Curthose!'[116]

Both father and son lost control of their emotions and righteous anger descended into uncontrolled wrath. Situations like this were likely to lead to emotional outbursts, which, in turn, could lead to violence. It was essential for kings and other rulers to govern their emotions as an essential prerequisite for governing others.[117] The dispute, as reported by Orderic, therefore portrays both father and son as losing control, guilty of descending into animal and therefore sinful rage.[118]

It was usual in these tense situations for the political community to try to seek a reconciliation between the parties in dispute, but matters were allowed to escalate until Robert was forced into exile.[119] Orderic presents Robert's banishment as the result of a decision made in anger and William of Malmesbury implied that Robert was driven out by his father.[120] If William was determined

---

114 *OV*, III, pp. 100–1; Luke, 11:17. Polynices and his brother Eteocles were the sons of Oedipus, born of his incestuous union with his mother Jocasta. Eteocles and Polynices agreed that one of them should rule Thebes, while the other went into exile for a year before they exchanged roles. When Polynices claimed his place as king of Thebes, his brother refused to give way. A bloody fraternal war ensued at the end of which Thebes fell to Theseus of Athens.

115 While Orderic structured his account using these models, it does not necessarily mean that what he has to say was 'fictionalised'. Medieval writers sought authority in the past and used models that they considered most apt for the events described.

116 WM, *GR*, I, pp. 700–1. *WJ*, II, pp. 184–91, refers to William's voice as 'rasping' ('voce rauca').

117 G. Althoff, '*Ira Regis*: Prolegomena to a History of Royal Anger', in Rosenwein, ed., *Anger's Past*, pp. 59–74; Barbara Rosenwein, 'Controlling Paradigms', in *Anger's Past*, pp. 233–47.

118 Bates, *William*, p. 187: 'It is hard to avoid the conclusion that Robert had come to hate his father.'

119 E.g. G. Koziol, *Begging Pardon and Favour. Ritual and Political Order in Early Medieval France* (Ithaca, NY, 1992).

120 *OV*, III, pp. 100–1; WM, *GR*, I, pp. 700–1; *JW*, III, *s.a.* 1077, pp. 30–1, reports that Robert went to France after he had not been allowed to take possession of Normandy.

come what may to exclude his eldest son from government, this would explain why there is no trace at this stage of attempts to effect a reconciliation. There is, however, no indication in the sources as to what prompted the Conqueror's loss of faith in the abilities of his eldest son, unless the destabilising activities of Robert's retinue threatened to undermine his rule in increasingly difficult times.

Exile

When Robert went into voluntary exile he sought aid from his overlord, King Philip I of France, and his mother's relatives.[121] Orderic's chronology is confused but it is possible to reconstruct the broad sequence of events from other sources. Robert went into exile at the end of 1077 or early in 1078 and Orderic tells us that he wandered in foreign lands 'for about five years'. However, as he was back in his father's court by the summer of 1080, this figure probably refers to a second period of exile lasting from around the beginning of 1084 until after his father's death in September 1087.

Robert was accompanied by members of his retinue, perhaps the same men who had precipitated the crisis: Robert de Bellême, William of Breteuil, Ivo and Aubrey de Grandmesnil, Roger, son of Richard of Bienfaite, Joel, son of Alfred the Giant, Robert of Mowbray, William of Moulins-la-Marche and William of Rupierre, together with many others 'of noble birth and knightly prowess, men of diabolical pride and ferocity, terrible to their neighbours, always far too ready to plunge into acts of lawlessness'. Robert's band of exiles included the sons of the Conquest generation. They were men also seeking independence from their fathers and seeing their best chances of success lying in their loyalty to Robert. Despite Orderic's characterisation of them, Robert's companions were demonstrating not only their loyalty to their lord, but also their confidence in his leadership.[122]

Robert first took refuge with his mother's brother, Robert the Frisian, and Archbishop Odo of Trèves.[123] This indicates that Robert's flight was perhaps not as headlong as Orderic suggests.[124] Robert was successful in finding help

---

121 WM, *GR*, I, pp. 542–3; Malmesbury refers to Robert's abdication (*abdicationem*) as a result of which Rufus's hopes for the succession rose. Elisabeth M.C. van Houts, 'L'exil dans l'espace anglo-normand', in P. Bouet and Véronique Gazeau, eds., *La Normandie et l'Angleterre au Moyen Âge* (Caen, 2003), pp. 117–27; Laura Napran, 'Exile in Context', in Laura Napran and Elisabeth van Houts, eds., *Exile in the Middles Ages* (Turnhout, 2004), pp. 1–9.

122 *OV*, III, pp. 100–3. Kathleen Thompson, 'Robert of Bellême', p. 268. Bellême's support for Robert was due to a 'youthful aberration' rather than a sense of loyalty. Orderic had very little time for Robert de Bellême: Kathleen Thompson, 'Orderic Vitalis and Robert of Bellême', *JMH*, 20 (1994), pp. 133–41.

123 *OV*, III, pp. 102–3. *ASC*, D, *s.a.* 1079, p. 88; Swanton, p. 213. *JW*, III, *s.a.* 1077, pp. 30–1, has Robert going to Philip of France first.

124 *OV*, III, pp. 102–3: Robert toured Lotharingia, Germany, Aquitaine and Gascony in search of patronage, and when he had exhausted the generosity of those sympathetic to his plight he was forced to run up debts with foreign usurers. This itinerary probably refers to the second exile.

and later rewarded his benefactors.[125] His mother also sent aid, precipitating a quarrel with her husband.

Matilda's dispute with William provides an insight into their relationship as well as a commentary on the power of queens and their place in family politics. Matilda proved capable of ruling Normandy in her husband's absence. Her reliance on a council of barons does not necessarily detract from her power, as William also drew support and advice from the leading magnates of the duchy. A considerable degree of political power was wielded by aristocratic women in this period.[126] Matilda sent her son large sums of silver, gold and other valuables without her husband's knowledge.[127] Orderic reported that Matilda's motivation was simply 'a mother's affection for her son', perhaps informed by memories of how her elder brother's family had been displaced in Flanders by a younger brother.[128] It may also have been a reaction to the developing bonds between William Rufus and his father. However, the involvement of Robert the Frisian suggests that Matilda may have put Flemish interests above those of her Norman husband.

When he found out what she was doing, William angrily ordered her to desist, but she defied him. Her willingness to incur the king's anger suggests that she was confident in her own strength at court and that she felt that her husband's treatment of their son was unnecessarily harsh.[129] There were angry exchanges between husband and wife and, in exasperation, William trotted out an old saying: 'A faithless woman (ship)wrecks things for her husband.'[130] Matilda then gave a compelling expression of motherly affection:

> O my lord, do not wonder that I love my first-born child with tender affection. By the power of the most high, if my son Robert were dead and buried seven feet deep in the earth hid from the eyes of the living, and I could bring him back to life with my own blood, I would shed my blood for him and suffer more anguish for his sake than, weak woman that I am, I dare to promise. How do you imagine that I can find any joy in possessing great wealth if I allow my son to be burdened by dire poverty? May I never be guilty of such hardness of heart; all your power gives you no right to demand this of me.[131]

Matilda demonstrated that strong affective bonds had a significant role in the family politics of the medieval nobility.

---

[125] *OV*, III, pp. 102–3. In 1100 Robert gave Theobald Pain custody of the castle of Gisors on the Vexin frontier 'because he had once given him shelter': *OV*, V, pp. 308–9.

[126] Laura L. Gathagan, 'Embodying Power: Gender and Authority in the Queenship of Mathilda of Flanders', unpublished Ph.D. dissertation, City University of New York, 2002. I am very grateful to Dr Gathagan for allowing me to consult her thesis.

[127] *WM, GR*, I, pp. 500–1. Malmesbury suggests that the queen provided a troop of soldiers for Robert using revenues from the royal estates.

[128] *OV*, III, pp. 102–3.

[129] Gathagan, 'Embodying Power', pp. 67–8.

[130] *OV*, III, p. 103 and n. 4: 'Naufragium rerum est mulier malefida marito'. Chibnall was unable to identify this aphorism; her translation is 'A faithless wife brings ruin to the state'.

[131] *OV*, III, pp. 102–5.

At Matilda's words, William 'grew pale with anger and, bursting with rage, he commanded one of the queen's messengers named Samson, a Breton, to be arrested and then blinded'.[132] William had lost control over himself and the members of his household. By extension this threatened his authority in the kingdom. His rage against Samson suggests that the Breton had been entrusted with conveying the queen's gold to Robert, or perhaps he was just the nearest scapegoat. Given that Samson was on the receiving end of the king's 'terrible voice' it seems likely that, even years later, he would remember the details of the quarrel that put his sight in jeopardy.[133]

Matilda also expressed concern for her son by consulting a hermit living in Germany, who was famous for prophecy. She asked him what would happen to her son and husband. The hermit had a vision in which he was taken by a spirit guide to a meadow of grass and flowers in which a fierce horse was feeding. A great herd of cattle, anxious to graze, was driven back by the horse. A 'wanton cow' took charge of the meadow and allowed all the other cattle to enter the field, eat the meadow's grass and flowers and then defile it with their dung. The hermit admitted that he had been appalled at the sight and asked his guide for an interpretation of the vision. The meadow was Normandy, the grass was the duchy's population and the flowers 'the churches where pure companies of monks and clerks and nuns dwell'. The horse represented King William who protected these clerks and monks. The herd of cattle standing around the field were Normandy's enemies, the French, Bretons, Flemings and Angevins, envious of the duchy's wealth and ready to seize what they could. The hermit then predicted disaster.

> But later when, since he is human, he [the king] comes to die, Robert his son will succeed him in the duchy of Normandy. Whereupon his enemies from all sides will compass it about and invade the honourable and wealthy land deprived of its guardian, strip it of its beauty and riches and, disregarding this foolish ruler, trample all Normandy contemptuously underfoot. He, like the wanton cow, will give himself up to lust and indolence, and will be the first to plunder the wealth of the church to distribute it amongst his base panders and other lechers. To such men will he lay open his duchy and from them will he take counsel on his needs.[134]

The hermit described Robert's regime as one governed by catamites and effeminates, abounding in vice and wretchedness. Robert was portrayed as 'foolish and idle', a weak duke enjoying 'no more than an empty title, and a swarm of nobodies will dominate both him and the captive duchy, bringing ruin to many'.[135]

Orderic, writing this section of his *Historia* between 1127 and 1130, knew what happened after William's death in 1087. His report of the hermit's vision

---

132 *OV*, III, pp. 104–5.
133 WM, *GR*, I, pp. 700–1: 'terrisonae uocis'.
134 *OV*, III, pp. 106–7.
135 *OV*, III, pp. 104–7.

allowed him to give free rein to criticisms of Robert. The gendered language of the piece undermined Robert's authority by feminising both him and his retinue. Had Orderic faithfully reported Matilda's consultation with the holy man, or did he insert a fictitious passage in order to underline the consequences of Robert's rebellion? Matilda would hardly have appreciated the gloomy predictions for her favourite son and it could have been little comfort to know that the hermit had predicted that she would never live to see this dreadful outcome.

Gerberoy, January 1079

As a wronged vassal, Robert sought assistance from his lord and kinsman King Philip I of France and his mother's relatives.[136] Philip sent Robert to the castle of Gerberoy in the Beauvaisis near the River Epte, which marked the frontier in the Vexin between the lordship of the king of France and lands in eastern Normandy subject to the Norman king-duke.[137] Helias, the *vidame* of the castle there, welcomed Robert and allowed him to recruit mercenaries with which he launched a series of raids against the Norman frontier.[138] Robert allied with Hugh of Châteauneuf, who placed a number of fortresses at his disposal.[139] Hugh's support for Robert was probably due to the fact that he was the brother-in-law of Robert de Bellême. Orderic also noted that Ralph of Conches was another who had joined the rebels.[140] These recruits to Robert's cause were members of frontier families, who may have seen this as an opportunity to counteract the growing influence of the Norman king-duke in the area and further their own interests. In response, King William had confiscated their estates and used the proceeds to pay the mercenaries fighting against them.[141]

The warfare in these border regions was particularly vicious and this may have been because both sides employed a great many mercenaries.[142]

---

[136] Robert was related to Philip through his grandmother, Adela of France, and as duke of Normandy he was the king's vassal.

[137] Judith A. Green, 'Lords of the Norman Vexin', in *War and Government in the Middle Ages. Essays in honour of J.O. Prestwich*, ed. John Gillingham and J.C. Holt (Woodbridge, 1984), pp. 46–63; Power, *The Norman Frontier*, pp. 85, 162.

[138] A *vidame* was the vassal of a bishop holding his lands as his representative and defender in temporal matters. On *milites gregarii*, see Strickland, *War and Chivalry*, pp. 81, 288; Marjorie Chibnall, 'Mercenaries and the *familia Regis* under Henry I', *History*, 62 (1977), pp. 15–23, reprinted in Strickland, ed., *Anglo-Norman Warfare*, pp. 84–92. Mercenaries were known for engaging in a particularly brutal form of warfare.

[139] *OV*, II, pp. 358–9: Châteauneuf, Rémalard and Sorel.

[140] Ralph of Conches was the son of Roger de Tosny: L. Musset, 'Aux origines d'une classe dirigeante: les Tosny, grands barons normands du Xe au XIIe siècles', *Francia*, 5 (1978), pp. 45–80.

[141] *OV*, II, pp. 358–9.

[142] See, for a slightly later period, Steven Isaac, 'The Problem with Mercenaries', in *The Circle of War in the Middle Ages. Essays on Medieval Military and Naval History*, ed. D.J. Kagay and L.J.A. Villalon (Woodbridge, 1999), pp. 101–10.

William strengthened the garrisons of his border castles in an attempt to prevent Robert's attacks. In addition, he used his wealth to enlist allies. For example, William recruited Rotrou, count of Mortagne, another of these frontiersmen, who had been attacking the lands of the church of Chartres.[143] William redirected Rotrou to an attack on the castle of Rémalard and during this siege Aymer of Villerai, another who had sided with Robert, was captured and killed. His body, 'slung like a slaughtered sow across a horse', was taken to Earl Roger of Montgomery, against whom he had fought for many years. On seeing the fate of his father, his son Gouffier made his peace with William. The treatment of Aymer's body suggests that warfare between knights in this period could be less than 'civilised' and Aymer was clearly being used as an example to encourage Robert's supporters to defect.[144]

In the winter of 1078/9, Robert's father besieged the stronghold of Gerberoy for about three weeks.[145] The fact that it was a winter campaign suggests that William saw Robert as a serious threat to his authority. A charter was dated: 'at the siege of Gerberoy conducted by the aforementioned kings, Philip king of the French and William, king of the English, in the year of the Incarnation of the Word, 1079'.[146] This suggests that Robert's lord, Philip of France, had come to terms with William, possibly because Robert's activities threatened to destabilise both sides of the frontier. Philip, as much as William, was concerned not to lose all influence in the region and so joined with his rival to bring an end to Robert's plundering. On the other hand, Philip may have appeared at the siege to mediate a truce between Robert and his father, rather than actively to support William's military activity. As it was, the siege ended badly for the Norman king.

In January 1079, Robert met his father in a battle outside the fortress of Gerberoy. During the engagement, King William was unhorsed and wounded by his son.[147] There, in a scene reminiscent of the *chansons de geste*, Robert was about to strike when his father called out. 'As soon as Robert recognized William's voice, he quickly dismounted and ordered his father to remount his horse and in this way allowed him to leave.'[148] Robert's decision to strike directly at the leader of an enemy force was a risky tactic, but if successful could turn the battle at a stroke. It was a sign of his personal bravery, but perhaps also a lack of caution.[149] This incident may be read as a chivalrous act on Robert's part, a sign of a lack of ruthlessness, or a recognition of the magnitude of the sin of patricide. On the other hand, it was also a striking

143   *OV*, II, pp. 360–1; Thompson, *Power and Border Lordship*, pp. 40–1.
144   *OV*, II, pp. 360–61.
145   *OV*, III, pp. 108–9; WM, *GR*, I, pp. 476–7; JW, III, *s.a.* 1079, pp. 30–3.
146   Prou, *Recueil*, no. XCIV, pp. 242–5.
147   *ASC*, D, *s.a.* 1079, p. 88; *ASC*, E, *s.a.* 1079, p. 92; Swanton, p. 214 and n. 7.
148   JW, III, *s.a.* 1079, pp. 30–3.
149   Robert's brave gambit may have been repeated in later campaigns; cf. J. France, *Victory in the East. A Military History of the First Crusade* (Cambridge, 1994), p. 279.

victory for Robert and a humiliating moment for the Conqueror, not only because he had suffered defeat at his son's hands, but also because many of his men had been captured and some, including his son William, had been wounded.[150] For Orderic, the success of the rebellious son was too much to bear and he could not bring himself to report it. In Orderic's moral universe it was important that those who flouted God's law should not be seen to prosper, besides there was something fundamentally unnatural about the victory of a son over his father, something that shook Orderic's sense of justice and the right order of things.[151]

This was a major defeat for the Conqueror, made worse, perhaps, by the fact that it was at the hands of his rebellious eldest son. The defeat at Gerberoy, following that at Dol, compromised the Conqueror's image as an invincible warrior. Despite the understanding reached by the kings of France and England at Gerberoy, Robert may have continued to plunder in the frontier region for much of 1079. However, perhaps by Easter 1080, and certainly by May of that year, father and son had been reconciled.[152] It was in the king's interests to reach an agreement as Robert had provided a focus for rebellion among members of the Norman aristocracy and his activities also gave William's enemies a chance to weaken his position on Normandy's frontiers. Robert's decision to go into exile and to strike back at his father was a tactic often used by disaffected members of noble and royal houses in the period.[153] The idea was to make things so difficult that the ruler was forced to accede to demands previously rejected. Robert's conduct of operations was of sufficient concern for members of the highest echelon of William's magnates to meet together and discuss how best to resolve the dispute between father and son.[154]

Robert's entourage included sons of the Norman aristocracy, and this threatened the dynastic ambitions of their fathers. As a result, these Norman magnates mediated between father and son. Violent disputes among the early medieval nobility were usually settled through a process of mediation and reconciliation.[155] The intercessors had to be of sufficient social standing to

---

150 *JW*, III, *s.a.* 1079, pp. 32–3.
151 *ASC*, D, *s.a.* 1079, pp. 88–9; Swanton, p. 214; the author of the Worcester (D) version of the *Anglo-Saxon Chronicle* also had difficulty reporting the event: 'We do not want, though, to write more of the harm which he [did] his father …'. Is it significant that half a leaf of the manuscript has been cut away at this point?
152 Easter was 12 April.
153 E.g. the attacks of the Godwine family after their expulsion from Edward the Confessor's court in 1051: Emma Mason, *The House of Godwine. The History of a Dynasty* (London, 2004), pp. 49–77.
154 *OV*, III, pp. 110–11.
155 G. Althoff, 'Satisfaction: Peculiarities of the Amicable Settlement of Conflicts in the Middle Ages', in B. Jussen, ed., *Ordering Medieval Society. Perspectives on Intellectual and Practical Modes of Shaping Social Relations* (Philadelphia, PA, 2001), pp. 270–84. For the debate on interpreting 'ritualised' behaviour, see Buc, *The Dangers of Ritual*, and G. Koziol's robust response in 'The Dangers of Polemic: Is ritual still an interesting topic of historical study?' *EME*, 11:4 (2002), pp. 367–88.

mediate between the two parties and restore order. In theory, they would broker a deal in private and agree terms before the reconciliation was made public in some demonstration that the dispute was over. This public act involved a dramatic ritual that showed everyone that both sides accepted the terms.

A group of magnates, led by Roger of Montgomery, earl of Shrewsbury, Hugh, earl of Chester, Hugh of Gournay, Hugh of Grandmesnil, Roger de Beaumont and his sons, Robert and Henry, met to discuss how they might end the war. These nobles, many of whom had sons in Robert's retinue, then approached the king and pointed out that Robert had been led astray 'by the evil counsel of degenerate youths'. This was an odd assertion given the place of their sons in Robert's entourage. They claimed that Robert repented his errors, but dared not approach the king in person. Begging William for mercy, they asked him 'as a dutiful father' to pardon Robert. According to the conventions of begging pardon from a ruler, the petitioners had to approach the king in a properly respectful manner.[156] They also reminded William of his obligations as a father: 'Correct your child when he errs, welcome him when he returns, mercifully spare him when he repents.' The nobles also asked for mercy for their sons and relatives.

The approach was met with an angry response from the king:

> He has stirred up civil dissent against me, lured away my young knights, whom I have educated and invested with arms, and supported Hugh of Châteauneuf and other foreign enemies against me. Which of my ancestors from the time of Rollo ever had to endure such hostility from any child as I do?[157]

William accused Robert of trying to take Normandy and Maine from him, as well as inciting foreign enemies. The Conqueror ended by pointing out that, according to the Law of Moses, his son deserved death in the manner of Absalom.[158]

The king's harsh words perhaps reflected the pain of his humiliation at Gerberoy and the seriousness of the threat posed by Robert. They were also obviously the opening shots in the negotiations designed to bring about reconciliation. The Norman nobles met repeatedly with William and 'endeavoured by fair speech and pleading to soften his harshness'.[159] The mediators were joined by the queen, the king of France and members of the ecclesiastical hierarchy. The seriousness of the problem brought representations from the papacy as well as the intercession of Simon of Crépy, a nobleman who had given up his worldly office to live as a hermit. He had been brought up at William's court and was well-known to the Conqueror. His status as a

---

[156] *OV*, III, pp. 110–11. Orderic's account employs this language of submission and entreaty.
[157] *OV*, III, pp. 110–13.
[158] Exodus 21:15. Cf. 2 Sam. 18:9–33: Absalom was found hanging, caught in the branches of a tree.
[159] *OV*, III, pp. 112–13.

holy man undoubtedly lent weight to his opinions. Simon's involvement in the negotiations offers a clue as to when the dispute between father and son was resolved. The hermit was present at Compiègne at the translation of the Holy Shroud to the golden reliquary which Queen Matilda had given to the church of Saint-Corneille. Further evidence, in the form of a charter by Philip I, reported that this translation took place on the fourth Sunday of Lent, so Simon of Crépy probably made his way to Normandy at the end of March 1080.[160]

Eventually, William, displaying the essential quality of *clementia*, relented and allowed himself to be persuaded by the mediators that his son should be permitted to return to Normandy. If these negotiations took place during Lent 1080, then the Easter festival itself would have been a suitable occasion for the reconciliation to be made public, in a ceremony utilising the powerful religious symbolism of the Easter Mass. It was also the occasion for a further promise by William of the inheritance of the duchy of Normandy, 'as he had once before granted it to him [Robert] when he [William] lay sick at Bonneville'.[161] William may have disinherited his son, or at least confiscated his lands as those of an exile, so this re-confirmation of his claim to Normandy was essential for the reconciliation.

Robert's actions during his exile had proved very effective and he should be seen in a stronger position in 1079 or 1080 than historians have admitted. Orderic suggested that Robert had been aimlessly wandering, but, on the contrary, he struck at a particularly vulnerable part of his father's duchy. Whether Robert thought of this strategy himself or was advised by his Flemish relatives, or by King Philip, it is clear that he was successful in his attempt to regain his position in Normandy.[162] He was certainly not returning 'cap-in-hand' to his father and there is no record of any sort of public humiliation or submission.[163] That Robert should have been willing to launch a war against his father suggests that his reasons for leaving Normandy were deeply felt. It may be that the sources misrepresent his grievance. If Robert actually had been ruling in Normandy and Maine and then, during the period of crisis after 1075, his father had decided to resume direct control, his son may have felt that he had been dispossessed. In that case, likening Robert to an exile, whose lands would have been confiscated, seems an apt description of his situation.

---

160 'Life of St Simon of the Vexin', c. 14, in Elisabeth van Houts, *Normans in Europe*, p. 199. Cf. David, *Curthose*, p. 29 and n. 52 for references. Matilda paid for Simon's tomb.

161 *OV*, III, pp. 112–13 and cf. *OV*, II, pp. 356–7.

162 It was not unusual for exiles to return to the duchy; see Emily Zack Tabuteau, 'Punishments in Eleventh-century Normandy', in W.C. Brown and P. Górecki, eds., *Conflict in Medieval Europe. Changing Perspectives on Society and Culture* (London, 2003), pp. 131–49 at 145–6.

163 Robert's absence for a period of three years seems to match the term for 'lesser outlawry' discussed in Elisabeth van Houts, 'The Vocabulary of Exile and Outlawry in the North Sea Area around the First Millennium', in Napran and van Houts, eds., *Exile in the Middle Ages*, pp. 13–28.

Reconciliation and Responsibility

At Easter, 1080, Robert appeared at his father's court to witness a charter for La Trinité-du-Mont in Rouen.[164] A letter to Robert from Gregory VII expressed his joy that the dispute had been resolved. The pope warned Robert to behave correctly in the future:

> Therefore you should take care, beloved son, we urge you that you may not henceforth agree to the counsels of wicked men by which you may offend your father and sadden your mother. Let divine precepts and admonitions be indelibly engraven upon you: 'Honour your father and mother, that you may be long-lived upon the earth', and this: 'He who shall speak evil of father or mother, let him die the death.' If, then, in return for honour of father and mother a longer life is ascribed you may very well see. For if divine scripture thunders forth death for speaking evil things, it proclaims a more certain death for doing evil things. What, then, remains if you wish to live as a member of Christ and to walk honestly in this world? By virtue of our office we charge you that you wholly banish the counsels of wicked men and in all things agree to the will of your father.[165]

As well as confirming details provided by the narrative sources, Gregory's letter suggests that the dispute had been settled recently. Robert remained with his father in Normandy through the summer of 1080 and as part of their new working relationship William was prepared to give him some responsibility.[166]

In the autumn of 1080 Robert undertook an important and dangerous mission to Scotland to confront King Malcolm III, who had invaded the northeast of England in the previous year.[167] The region had also been destabilised by the murder of Walcher, bishop of Durham and earl of Northumbria, who had been caught up in a local feud.[168] Earlier in 1080, Robert's uncle Odo of Bayeux had led a punitive expedition, which had plundered Durham and devastated the surrounding area.[169] Robert and his father had returned from Normandy in the autumn of 1080 and the expeditionary force was prepared.

---

164 Bates, *Acta*, no. 235, pp. 728–29; this memorandum notes that the case was heard 'in the presence of King William and Queen Matilda and their sons Robert and William'.

165 H.E.J. Cowdrey, *The Register of Pope Gregory VII, 1073–1085* (Oxford, 2002), 7.27, pp. 358–9. Matilda had written to the pope about the reconciliation of her husband and son. Gregory replied to Matilda and wrote to William reminding him of the duties of kingship; see *Register*, 7. 25 (to William, 8 May 1080) and 7. 26 (to Matilda, 8 May 1080), pp. 356–8. See also H.E.J. Cowdrey, *Pope Gregory VII, 1073–1085* (Oxford, 1998), pp. 462–3, 467, 646.

166 Bates, *Acta*, pp. 80–1 and nos. 236 (Rouen, abbey of La Trinité-du-Mont), 246 (Rouen, abbey of Saint-Ouen), 257 (priory of Saint-Gabriel confirmed to the abbey of Fécamp).

167 *ASC*, E, *s.a.*1079, p. 92; Swanton, pp. 213–14, says that Malcolm invaded between the two feasts of St Mary, that is between the Assumption (15 August) and the Nativity (8 September) of St Mary.

168 Aird, *St Cuthbert and the Normans*, pp. 95–101.

169 Symeon, 'Historia Regum', II, pp. 210–11; Symeon, *Libellus*, pp. 218–21.

Robert made his way into Scotland meeting Malcolm at Egglesbreth (Falkirk in Stirlingshire).[170]

As in 1072, the Scots king negotiated with the Normans rather than attempt battle. Among those in Robert's army was Abbot Adelelm of Abingdon, and his abbey's chronicle gives a few details of the expedition.

> [King William] ordered them to offer peace or armed conflict – peace if obedience were promised him, otherwise conflict. King Malcolm came into Lothian with his men and chose to make an agreement rather than fight. Accordingly he gave hostages that the principality of Scotland would be subject to the kingdom of England. Following this agreement, the king's son joyfully (*hilaris*) marched back with his army to his father by whom he was rewarded in recompense for his achievements, as were his companions, as befitted their rank.[171]

Robert had been entrusted with an important mission and as his father's representative he was given the task of re-establishing peace between Scotland and England. His success earned him and his men their rewards.

Robert also stood as godfather to Malcolm's daughter Edith.[172] Entering into a bond of spiritual kinship such as this was a recognised method of sealing diplomatic arrangements and Robert's sponsorship of Edith strengthened the agreement with her father.[173] Later, Robert demonstrated that he took this bond as Edith's godfather seriously.[174]

Returning south, Robert oversaw the construction of a 'New Castle' on the north bank of the River Tyne. Despite the re-establishment of the relationship with Malcolm of Scotland and this attempt to protect an important river crossing, the author of the Durham *Historia regum*, noted that this expedition had 'achieved nothing.' Certainly, after the devastation of the previous year, the local chronicler might have expected a more robust response from the king's son, but this seems an unreasonable assessment of Robert's achievements in the summer of 1080. After all, Robert had succeeded in moving

---

170   *Egglesbreth*: 'the speckled church'.

171   *Historia ecclesie Abbendonensis*, pp. 14–15. Duncan, *Kingship of the Scots*, pp. 45–6.

172   J.H. Lynch, *Christianizing Kinship. Ritual Sponsorship in Anglo-Saxon England* (Ithaca, NY, 1998), pp. 205–28, and, for an earlier period, see B. Jussen, *Spiritual Kinship as Social Practice. Godparenthood and Adoption in the Early Middle Ages*, trans. Pamela Selwyn (Newark, NJ, 2000). On this specific incident, see Mason, *William II*, pp. 113–14 and n. 82; Lois L. Huneycutt, *Matilda of Scotland: A Study in Medieval Queenship* (Woodbridge, 2003), p. 10 and n. 5.

173   *Letters and Charters of Gilbert Foliot*, ed. A. Morey and C.N.L. Brooke (Cambridge, 1967), no. 26, pp. 60–6. A letter from the 1140s of Gilbert Foliot, abbot of Gloucester, reported that Robert's mother had stood as Edith's godmother at around the same time. Apparently, the little girl grabbed the queen's veil while she was bending over her, and pulled it over her own head, a sign that she would one day become a queen. Emma Mason points out that this was a reworking of an anecdote from a *Life of St Edith*. The tale was passed down from the girl, who took the name Matilda to her own daughter, the Empress Matilda, from whom it reached Abbot Gilbert; cf. Elisabeth van Houts, *Memory and Gender in Medieval Europe*, pp. 73, 170 n. 14.

174   See below, pp. 215–17.

Norman influence further north after normalising relationships with Scotland, and had provided the Tyne with a castle.[175]

Despite the report of Robert's joyful return to his father and the rewards he received for his efforts, it is difficult to judge whether he had fully recovered his father's trust. Reports of the king's humiliation of his son at court suggest that there was an underlying antipathy towards him: William 'had from time to time cursed his presumptuous son and wished him many and various misfortunes'. Robert's exile had also allowed others, including his younger brothers, to get closer to the king.[176] The term *Königsnähe* ('nearness to the king') has been borrowed from German scholarship to convey the idea that it was crucial for those with political ambition in this society to maintain as close a relationship as possible with the king and others at the centre of power.[177] Often this meant that courtiers had to remain in the physical presence of the powerful, share their confidences and, when asked, proffer their advice. Personal networks were established and these might be the basis of future political action. Although Robert had persuaded many to support him in exile, he had also strained or severed many links that might have been useful to him in the future. Political and social relationships needed careful maintenance and cultivation, which required considerable personal effort. Robert had also acquired a reputation as a rebellious son, and reputations are notoriously hard to modify once in circulation.[178] How far could someone who had discarded the bonds of family and lordship so publicly be trusted to rule adequately in the future? During the late 1070s, Robert had distanced himself from the court and, in so doing, he inadvertently made it much harder for himself to lay the important foundations for the day when he would succeed his father. Robert also cleared a path for his younger brothers and it was during this period that William Rufus and Henry were to be found constantly in their father's company.[179] Rufus 'was always obedient (to his father), displaying himself in battle before his eyes, and walking by his side in peacetime. Thus his hopes began to rise and he began to covet the succession.' Indeed, this devotion had put Rufus in danger outside the castle of Gerberoy.[180]

Robert remained in England through the winter of 1080/1 but before the end of 1081, the situation in Maine demanded the attention of father

---

175 Symeon, 'Historia Regum', II, p. 211.
176 *OV*, III, pp. 114–15.
177 E.g. Janet L. Nelson, *Charles the Bald* (London, 1992), pp. 56, 70–1, and S. MacLean, *Kingship and Politics in the Late Ninth Century. Charles the Fat and the End of the Carolingian Empire* (Cambridge, 2003). I am grateful to Dr Sarah Hamilton for drawing my attention to this work.
178 Thelma Fenster and D.L. Smail, eds., *Fama. The Politics of Talk and Reputation in Medieval Europe* (Ithaca, NY, 2003).
179 *OV*, III, pp. 114–15.
180 WM, *GR*, I, pp. 542–3.

and son.[181] In 1076 or 1077, while the Conqueror had been preoccupied with other matters, the ruler of Anjou, Count Fulk le Réchin, had attempted to undermine support for Norman overlordship in Maine.[182] The target of Fulk's campaigns was John of La Flèche, who had been sympathetic to Norman interests. William was able to reinforce La Flèche, and Fulk, wounded in the siege, was forced to withdraw and agree to a truce at a place called 'castellum Vallium'. This truce lasted until 1081.[183] In that year, Fulk renewed his attack, this time in alliance with Count Hoël of Brittany. La Flèche was captured and burnt, forcing William to recruit a great army of English and Normans to confront Fulk. William marched through Maine and the armies were drawn up and ready to fight, when an unnamed cardinal priest and a party of monks intervened in the interests of peace. William's barons, William of Évreux and Roger of Montgomery, also involved themselves in the mediation and eventually an agreement was reached at Blanchelande or La Bruyère. Fulk recognised the rights of the Conqueror's son in Maine and Robert, in turn, performed an act of homage to Fulk 'as a vassal to his lord'. There followed a general amnesty and, finally, an exchange of hostages to guarantee the agreement.[184] So, once again, Robert's status as nominal ruler in Maine had been acknowledged.

There is no indication whether or not Robert was given any real responsibility in Maine in the years after the agreement at Blanchelande. The death of Arnold, the bishop of Le Mans, on 29 November 1081 brought about a dispute over the right to appoint to the see, with Fulk of Anjou opposing the Norman's candidate Hoël and delaying his consecration until 21 April 1085. The weakness of central authority in Maine was exposed once again soon after (in either 1083 or 1084) when rebels led by the *vicomte* Hubert used the castle of Sainte-Suzanne as a stronghold from which to defy Norman authority. Again, it is not possible to say whether Robert was involved in Norman interventions in Maine between 1081 and 1083, but he does appear in a number of charters from these years, which suggests that he was keeping close to the king and queen, in both Normandy and England, perhaps trying to repair the damage done by his recent estrangement.[185]

---

181 Bates, *Acta*, p. 81. The king spent Christmas at Gloucester and was in London in February 1081. Whitsun at Winchester was followed by a journey into Wales. William crossed to Normandy in the autumn of 1081.

182 *OV*, II, pp. 308–9; Douglas, *William the Conqueror*, pp. 242–3; Bates, *William the Conqueror*, pp. 189–90.

183 *Cartulaire de Saint-Vincent*, no. 99, a document issued by the abbey of Saint-Vincent at Le Mans and witnessed by Abbot William. The abbot may have had a hand in negotiating the truce and he was appointed to the see of Durham by King William, 5 November 1080, and consecrated 3 January 1081, probably in recognition of his service of Norman interests in Maine: see David, *Curthose*, pp. 32–3 and n. 74.

184 *OV*, II, pp. 310–11.

185 Bates, *Acta*, p. 81 and, for 1082, nos. 59 (Caen, abbey of La Trinité), 60 (Caen, abbey of La Trinité), 158 (Grestain, abbey of Notre-Dame), 253 (Saint-Calais, abbey). No. 253 was issued at Downton in Wiltshire late in 1082. For 1083, see nos. 230 (Rouen, cathedral and see, April 1083),

Final Estrangement

After 9 January 1084, the date of his last appearance in a charter in company with his father, Robert left the court. This may have been connected with the loss of his most influential supporter.[186] Queen Matilda's death, on 2 November 1083, left Robert to face his father alone and their relationship had deteriorated once again:

> The peace between the king and his son which had taken so long to achieve was soon clouded. The stubborn young man contemptuously refused to follow or obey his father; the quick-tempered king continually poured abuse and reproach on him in public for his failings.[187]

Orderic certainly associated Matilda's death with 'storms of troubles' facing her husband.[188] It is unlikely that his brothers would have supported him, given Rufus and Henry's closeness to the king and their realisation that Robert's loss was their gain. There is also evidence to suggest that Henry was already being groomed for an important role by his father.[189] Robert may have obtained some sisterly advice from Cecilia, a nun at La Trinité at Caen, when they interred their mother in the choir of the abbey church there.[190] Possibly Archbishop Lanfranc was no longer able to mediate between father and son, and another potential supporter, Robert's uncle, Bishop Odo of Bayeux, had been removed from the court and imprisoned by William in 1082.[191] There may have been some support for Robert from Odo's brother, Count Robert of Mortain, and it is a pity that not more is known about the relationship between Robert and his uncles.[192] Without clear support at court, Robert may have feared a similar fate to that of Odo or felt that, in spite of his father's repeated promises of the duchy of Normandy, nothing was to be gained until William died. The public humiliation he suffered through his father's rebukes made Robert's position at court intolerable, especially if he was as isolated as has been suggested. The

---

279 (Tours, abbey of Saint-Julien, 25 December 1082 x 2 November 1083; 'certainly the summer or autumn of 1083').

[186] Bates, *Acta*, no. 252, pp. 763–4, dated 9 January 1084. *OV*, IV, pp. 80–1, says that Robert had taken offence at some trivial cause and had gone to the court of Philip I of France.

[187] *OV*, III, pp. 112–13.

[188] *OV*, IV, pp. 46–7.

[189] WM, *GR*, I, pp. 542–3; *OV*, III, pp. 114–15. His brothers were loyal to their father, although perhaps not to each other. Green, *Henry I*, p. 23. I am grateful to Professor Green for this reference.

[190] *OV*, IV, pp. 44–7.

[191] WM, *GR*, I, pp. 504–5; D.R. Bates, 'The Character and Career of Odo Bishop of Bayeux', *Speculum*, l (1975), pp. 1–20.

[192] Bates, *Acta*, p. 95, notes that 'three out of the five occasions on which Robert received one of his most prestigious titles (*comes Normannorum*) occur in diplomas confirming grants by his uncle count Robert of Mortain'. *Acta*, nos. 158, 204 and 205. See J.-L. Kupper, 'L'oncle maternel et le neveu dans la société du Moyen Age', *Académie royale de Belgique. Bulletin de la classe des lettres et des sciences morales et politiques*, ser.6, 15:7–12 (2004), pp. 247–62.

heir to Normandy can have had little alternative but to go into exile once again.

Robert probably never saw his father alive again. There is no evidence that he was in Normandy or England from January 1084 until after the Conqueror's death in September 1087. Robert did not attempt another series of campaigns against his father's lands on the scale of the first exile. Perhaps support had dwindled away since the late 1070s, as the fathers of Robert's former companions had spent considerable effort ensuring that their sons were reintegrated into Norman society. Taking only a few men with him this time, Robert spent almost five years in exile.[193] Perhaps travels through Lotharingia, Germany, Aquitaine and Gascony should be assigned to this second period of exile. William of Malmesbury, always willing to record a good story, tells us that Robert made his way to Northern Italy in the hope of marrying Countess Matilda of Tuscany, a formidable woman.[194] The marriage was designed to raise forces to help in his war with his father, but there is no corroborating evidence to suggest that Robert visited the countess's court.[195] Failing in Italy, Robert once again sought Philip of France's assistance. It has been suggested that Robert may have entered the tournament circuit in Northern France. This is certainly an attractive idea, and the fighting and social display associated with the tournament would certainly have allowed him to enjoy himself while retaining a sense of self-worth in exile.[196]

Robert found the opportunity during his exile to father illegitimate children. When Robert was raiding Normandy's frontier with a 'great band of robbers', he fell in love with the beautiful mistress of an old priest.[197] Years later a woman appeared at Robert's court with two grown-up sons. She 'reminded him of many familiar proofs of their close intimacy in his youth' and claimed that he was the father of her two boys, Richard and William.[198] The few details provided by Orderic cannot firmly assign Robert's liaison with this woman to one or the other period of exile as for both there is evidence to suggest that he was operating near Normandy's frontier.[199]

The woman probably appeared after Robert had succeeded his father in

---

[193] OV, III, pp. 102–3. Orderic's chronology is suspect.

[194] WM, GR, I, pp. 502–3.

[195] There is no mention of Robert in the sources for Countess Matilda's reign; see, for example, Donizone, *Vita Mathildis Comitissae*, ed. L. Bethmann, *MGH Scriptores* 12 (Hanover, 1856), pp. 348–409, and *Die Urkunden und Briefe der Markgräfin Mathilde von Tuszien*, ed. Elke Goez and Werner Goez, *MGH Diplomata Laienfürsten* 2 (Hanover, 1998). Nora Duff, *Matilda of Tuscany. La Gran Donna d'Italia* (London, 1909), pp. 187–8, accepts that in spring 1087 Robert visited Matilda at Lucca, but his proposal of marriage was rejected. Cf. Patricia Skinner, *Women in Medieval Italian Society, 500–1200* (Harlow, 2001), pp. 136–41.

[196] D. Crouch, *Tournament* (London, 2005), p. 7 and n. 18 referring to D. Crouch, *The Normans. The History of a Dynasty* (London, 2002), pp. 207–12.

[197] OV, V, pp. 282–3.

[198] OV, V, pp. 282–3, does not identify these 'familiar proofs'.

[199] WJ, II, pp. 202–3.

1087, perhaps confident that the new duke, now with access to the resources of Normandy, would be able to provide for her boys. As Richard's death occurred in the New Forest in May 1100, the woman appeared at Robert's court before his departure on Crusade in 1096. If her sons were born around 1080, this would just about allow sufficient time for them to grow to adulthood, sixteen or so, before they were presented to their father. They might equally have been a few years younger when their uncle William acknowledged them in 1096 and admitted them to his retinue.[200]

When he was confronted with the boys, Robert denied paternity, but the woman proved her claims by undergoing the ordeal of hot iron. The ordeal invoked God's direct judgement in the matter and it was especially useful in cases, such as this, where it might be difficult to find witnesses. Specific rituals were developed to ensure the successful outcome of the procedure. The ordeal iron was blessed by the officiating priest a number of times before it was heated in the fire. The hot iron was then carried by the person undergoing the ordeal for a set distance, measured by a certain number of paces, or marked by a line. Afterwards, the hand was bound and in three days – three being a particularly significant liturgical number – the wound was inspected. If the burn was healing without complications, then it was judged that the petitioner had proved her veracity.[201] In the case of the woman who claimed to be the mother of Robert's bastards, Orderic tells us that she suffered no burns at all.[202] The outcome of the ordeal needed interpretation and the subjectivity of the decision meant that there was always room for either dispute or compromise. Orderic's point about the absence of any residual scarring is significant, therefore, because it meant that there was no room for debate: the woman had proved her case. The sources give us no clues as to why Robert felt the need to deny paternity, but, if the woman had appeared in his court shortly after his succession to Normandy, he may have felt that the appearance of two sons might have complicated his own plans for the duchy. Alternatively, Robert's advisers might have suggested the ordeal in order to discourage freeloaders who might have come to the court hoping to take advantage of the new duke's good nature. As Robert also acknowledged an illegitimate daughter, he may have had more than one liaison as she is not mentioned in the same account.[203]

Robert was living at Abbeville in the neighbouring county of Ponthieu

---

[200] *OV*, V, pp. 282–3. Richard's death was reported as occurring as the result of a hunting accident in the New Forest in Hampshire at Rogationtide (7–9 May), 1100. Robert's other illegitimate son, William made a career in the Crusader states, where he is found, *c.* 1108; see *Albert of Aachen, Historia Ierosolimitana. History of the Journey to Jerusalem*, ed. and trans. Susan B. Edgington (Oxford, 2007), pp. 760–1, 814–15.

[201] Bartlett, *England under the Norman and Angevin Kings*, pp. 180–1 and *idem, Trial by Fire and Water. The Medieval Judicial Ordeal* (Oxford, 1986), pp. 14–23 at 20.

[202] *OV*, V, pp. 282–3.

[203] *OV*, IV, pp. 182–3.

when messengers from Rouen brought news that ended his period of exile. Aubrey de Coucy came to the exiled prince and reported that, very early in the morning of Thursday 9 September, Robert's father had died.[204] Robert was then invited to return as duke of Normandy.

[204]   *OV*, III, pp. 112–13.

CHAPTER FOUR

THE DUKE OF NORMANDY, 1087–1096

ROBERT's father died at the priory of Saint-Gervase in Rouen soon after dawn on Thursday 9 September 1087.[1] In late July of that year, William had launched an attack on Mantes but during the fighting had been severely injured. The dying man had been taken back to the priory of Saint-Gervase in Rouen. It is not known whether Robert knew of his father's injuries, or whether he would have returned to Rouen if he had.[2] Now in his mid-thirties, Robert was living at Abbeville in Ponthieu, 'accompanied by young men like himself, sons of Norman magnates, who seemingly followed him as their future lord but in reality were drawn towards him by their greed for new acquisitions and from that place laid waste the duchy of Normandy, especially the border area with raids and robbery'.[3] Robert had re-established contact with his lord, Philip of France, who encouraged his operations in the Vexin.[4]

Succession

The Conqueror's intentions for the succession to Normandy and England have been the cause of considerable debate.[5] The Conquest of England certainly changed the context of the succession, but perhaps it should not be assumed that the kingdom of England was the overriding priority in the

---

[1] *WJ*, II, pp. 202–3; *ASC*, E, *s.a.* 1086 [1087], pp. 95–9; Swanton, pp. 217–22; *JW*, III, *s.a.* 1087, pp. 46–7; *OV*, IV, pp. 100–1; Bates, *William the Conqueror*, p. 204.

[2] *OV*, IV, pp. 78–9; cf. WM, *GR*, I, pp. 510–11; *WJ*, II, pp. 194–5.

[3] *WJ*, II, pp. 202–3.

[4] *WJ*, II, pp. 194–5; cf. WM, *GR*, I, pp. 510–11.

[5] *WJ*, II, pp. 194–5. Cf. J. Le Patourel, *Normandy and England, 1066–1144*, Stenton Lecture 1970 (Reading, 1971), reprinted in *idem*, *Feudal Empires Norman and Plantagenet* (London, 1984), no. VII; *idem*, 'The Norman Succession, 996–1135', *EHR*, 86 (1971), pp. 225–50; R.H.C. Davis, 'William of Jumièges, Robert Curthose and the Norman Succession', *EHR*, 95 (1980), pp. 597–606; G. Garnett, 'Ducal Succession in Early Normandy', in *Law and Government in Medieval England*, ed. G. Garnett and J. Hudson (Cambridge, 1994), pp. 80–110; H.E.J. Cowdrey, 'Death-bed Testaments', in *MGH Scriptores*, 33, iv (1988), pp. 703–24; Barbara English, 'William the Conqueror and the Anglo-Norman Succession', *Historical Research*, 64 (1991), pp. 221–36, and now G. Garnett, *Conquered England. Kingship, Succession and Tenure 1066–1166* (Oxford, 2007), pp. 136–261 at 156–87.

minds of all those who witnessed the death of King William. Robert had twice been prepared to leave his father's court and launch a series of campaigns in order to gain possession of Normandy and Maine. For him and many of the Norman magnates Robert's claims to the duchy were irrefutable. By contrast, neither Robert, nor either of his brothers, had a secure claim to England.

The two detailed accounts of the Conqueror's death both have their problems. The first, by a monk of Saint-Étienne, Caen, was based on ninth-century accounts of the death of the Carolingian emperor, Louis the Pious, together with passages concerning Charlemagne.[6] Although this text, *De obitu Willelmi* ('About the Death of William'), is more useful than some have suggested, the second account, written decades later by Orderic Vitalis, provides the most detailed narrative of the Conqueror's last days.[7] The key point was that, despite their quarrels, William could not prevent Robert's succession to Normandy; England, however, was another matter.[8]

The conquest of England had brought the Normans unprecedented access to land and resources.[9] For the '1066 generation' the acquisitions in England eclipsed the material, but not necessarily the emotional, value of their patrimonial lands in Normandy. Usually the Normans passed on their patrimonial lands to their eldest sons and shared the lands they had acquired among their other heirs. That said, there was still no well-established 'law of succession' in eleventh-century Normandy and much still needed to be done if a designated heir was to secure his inheritance.[10] The unusual situation created by the Conquest complicated matters and the scale of the lands acquired in England called into question whether the Normans would always follow custom. Sentimental attachment to the patrimony was weighed against the attractions of the often more substantial and lucrative English estates, but not every Norman lord found England irresistible.

Orderic's account of the king's death is something of a literary set-piece. It was important in this period for the terminally ill to make peace with God and die a good death.[11] William delivered a death-bed résumé of his career, including an acknowledgement that he had won the crown of England by divine grace and not by hereditary right. Particularly emphasised is the king's treatment of the Church, his appointment of worthy churchmen and his support for monks and nuns. Here, Orderic was as much providing a template for good government as he was giving a pen-portrait of the Conqueror and

---

6   English, 'Anglo-Norman Succession', pp. 222–7; cf. Garnett, *Conquered England*, pp. 167–9.
7   'De Obitu Willelmi', in *WJ*, II, pp. 184–91. The 'De Obitu' was probably written in the 1090s. Orderic had access to eye-witness accounts: his diocesan, Bishop Gilbert of Lisieux (1077–1101), had been at William's bedside at Saint-Gervase (*OV*, IV, pp. 80–1). Anselm, then abbot of Bec, and Abbot Mainer of Saint-Évroul were at the funeral in Caen (*OV*, IV, pp. 104–5).
8   English, 'Anglo-Norman Succession', p. 222.
9   *OV*, II, pp. 266–7.
10 Garnett, *Conquered England*, pp. 165–77.
11 Bartlett, *England under the Norman and Angevin Kings*, pp. 591–93. D. Crouch, 'The Culture of Death in the Anglo-Norman World', in *Anglo-Norman Political Culture and the Twelfth-Century Renaissance*, ed. C. Warren Hollister (Woodbridge, 1997), pp. 157–80.

his achievements.[12] William then set out his wishes for his duchy and the kingdom of England.

> I invested my son Robert with the duchy of Normandy before I fought against Harold on the heath of Senlac; because he is my first-born son and has received the homage of almost all the barons of the country the honour then granted cannot be taken from him. Yet I know for certain that any province subjected to his rule will be most wretched. He is a proud and foolish fellow, doomed to suffer prolonged and grim misfortune. I name no man as my heir to the kingdom of England; instead I entrust it to the eternal Creator to whom I belong and in whose hands are all things.[13]

William felt obliged to honour the repeated designations of Robert as his heir to Normandy, but no-one was named as his successor to England.

On hearing his father's plans, Henry the youngest son tearfully asked what he would be given and his father promised him five thousand pounds of silver.[14] At this point, the king predicted great things for his youngest son and, in so doing, contradicted himself by assigning England to William Rufus, betraying Orderic's perspective as someone writing during Henry's reign. 'Be satisfied, my son, and take comfort in the Lord. Patiently allow your elder brothers to take precedence over you. Robert will have Normandy and William England. But you in your own time will have all the dominions that I have acquired and be greater than your brothers in wealth and power.'[15] Later, Henry was to claim his mother's lands in England.

The Conqueror gave William Rufus a letter for Archbishop Lanfranc, presumably asking him to ensure that the favoured son secured the throne of England. This was the pay-off for Rufus's loyalty to his father, especially during the final ten years of troubles with Robert. On reaching the Channel, Rufus heard of his father's death, but continued on to England. Henry, on the other hand, hurried to count up his money. Just before his last breath, the king was persuaded to release all the prisoners he held. He agreed, but excepted his brother Odo until the special pleading of the nobles gathered around his death-bed prevailed.[16] The opinions of powerful men who surrounded the king had to be taken into account and a dying man was certainly in no position to resist.

It is unlikely that Robert was wholly unaware of his father's condition. One source suggests that Robert refused to attend his father and apologise for his behaviour.[17] At the Conqueror's death, panic gripped Rouen; the noblemen

---

12 *OV*, IV, pp. 80–95.
13 *OV*, IV, pp. 92–3.
14 *OV*, IV, pp. 94–5.
15 *OV*, IV, pp. 96–7.
16 'De Obitu Willelmi', pp. 186–7; *OV*, IV, pp. 96–7. Later Robert freed and knighted Ulf, son of Harold Godwineson, and Duncan, son of Malcolm III, king of Scots.
17 'De Obitu Willelmi', pp. 186–7.

attending him rode off at speed to protect their properties, while the king's servants stripped his body and plundered his possessions.

> The physicians and others present, who had watched the king as he slept all night without a sigh or groan, and now realized that he had died without warning, were utterly dumbfounded and almost out of their minds. But the wealthier among them quickly mounted horses and rode off as fast as they could to protect their properties. The lesser attendants, seeing that their superiors had absconded, seized the arms, vessels, clothing, linen and all the royal furnishings, and hurried away leaving the king's body almost naked on the floor of the house. Behold, I beg you all, of what earthly loyalty is made. Each one of them, like a bird of prey, seized what he could of the royal trappings and made off at once with the booty. So when the just ruler fell lawlessness broke loose, and first showed itself in the plunder of him who had been the avenger of plunder.[18]

This dramatic scene at the king's death, especially the lack of respect shown his body, was a chance for the monastic author to reflect on the vanity of worldly glory.[19] Whenever there was doubt over the succession, the death of a ruler marked a crisis and the actions of the Norman barons are understandable in this context.[20] That said, monastic writers like Orderic undoubtedly enjoyed the opportunity to moralise on the fragility of earthly power.

The leading clergy of Rouen solemnly processed to Saint-Gervase and Archbishop William ordered that the king's body be taken to Caen for burial in the abbey of Saint-Étienne, which the Conqueror himself had founded. As none of the king's family was initially present, the funeral was arranged by Herluin, 'a certain country knight'.[21] If Herluin's participation was meant as a barbed comment by Orderic, then the description of the funeral proper certainly undermined the solemnity of the occasion. Abbot Gilbert of Saint-Étienne met the corpse as it arrived in the ducal abbey, but a fire broke out and caused panic in Caen. Bishop Gilbert of Évreux preached a sermon, extolling the Conqueror's achievements before an assembly of dignitaries gathered in the abbey, including the king's youngest son, Henry, and the recently released Odo of Bayeux.[22] At this point the funeral was disrupted when a local man claimed the land upon which the abbey had been built.[23] A deal was hastily made, but that was not the end of the trouble, for the Conqueror's corpse had swollen and was now too large for the coffin. When someone tried to stuff it in, the innards burst out releasing the stench of death. Despite flooding the abbey church with clouds of incense, the priests, overcome by the noxious odour of the Conqueror's putrefying corpse, were forced to hurry proceed-

---

18 *OV*, IV, pp. 100–3.
19 See above, Chapter 3, pp. 60–2.
20 *OV*, IV, pp. 112–13.
21 *OV*, IV, pp. 100–1. Cf. WM, *GR*, I, pp. 512–13.
22 *OV*, IV, pp. 104–5.
23 Musset, *Abbayes caennaises*, pp. 45–6; *OV*, IV, p. 106, n. 1.

ings along. 'How vain is the glory of the flesh', Orderic noted as he concluded his account.[24]

Orderic and Duke Robert

The most detailed account of Robert's independent rule of Normandy comes from the eighth book of Orderic Vitalis's *Ecclesiastical History*.[25] Writing in the mid-1130s, Orderic always had in mind the eventual defeat of Duke Robert in 1106.[26] Orderic's account of these years seems at first reading to offer damning testimony to Robert's incompetence.

> All men knew that Duke Robert was weak and indolent; therefore trouble-makers despised him and stirred up loathsome factions when and where they chose. For although the duke was bold and daring, praiseworthy for his knightly prowess and eloquent in speech, he exercised no discipline over either himself or his men. He was prodigal in distributing his bounty and lavish in his promises, but so thoughtless and inconstant that they were utterly unreliable. Being merciful to suppliants he was too weak and pliable to pass judgement on wrongdoers; unable to pursue any plan consistently he was far too affable and obliging in all his relationships, and so he earned the contempt of corrupt and foolish men. Since he was short in stature and stout he was nicknamed Curthose by his father. Through his wish to please all men he either gave or promised or granted whatever anyone asked. He diminished his inheritance daily by his foolish prodigality, giving away to everyone whatever was sought; and as he impoverished himself he strengthened the hands of others against him.[27]

Here was a brave man but a prodigal and ineffectual ruler, unable to control unruly barons and presiding over the ruin of Normandy. This historical *persona* created for Robert by Orderic has proved enduring and few have seriously questioned it.[28]

Throughout Book VIII Orderic asserts that during Robert's reign all Normandy experienced violent disruption.[29] However, when individual episodes are explored in detail, a rather different picture with a more assertive and effective duke emerges. Thankfully Orderic was too honest an historian – or too poor a polemicist – to omit all that was relevant from the episodes

---

[24] *OV*, IV, pp. 108–9.

[25] *OV*, IV, pp. 110–341.

[26] *OV*, IV, xix–xxv; Book VIII was composed between 1133 and 1135/6 with some additions from 1137/8.

[27] *OV*, IV, pp. 114–15.

[28] The exceptions are Gaston Le Hardy, 'Le dernier des ducs normands. Étude de critique historique sur Robert Courte-Heuse', *BSAN*, 10 (Caen, 1882), and, more successfully, Judith Green, 'Robert Curthose Reassessed', *ANS*, 22 (1999), pp. 95–116.

[29] E.g. *OV*, IV, pp. 150–1, 162–3, 198–9, 212–13, 220–1, 226–7, 228–9. *OV*, IV, pp. 146–7, suggests that not only were crimes of arson, rapine and murder committed daily, but 'sodomy walked abroad unpunished' and 'acts of adultery openly defiled the marriage bed'; this is apocalyptic language rather than sober political commentary.

he was describing. He preserved detail which suggests that Robert responded to challenges to his authority not only with decisiveness and alacrity, but also with great success. There is a consistency in Robert's recorded actions that suggests that he and his counsellors had formulated a policy for dealing with the turbulent barons of Normandy. However, he was also able to deal flexibly with the unexpected and, in many instances, revealed a sensibly pragmatic assessment of the difficulties of ruling Normandy without the support provided by the huge resources of England.[30]

Monastic chroniclers dealt in moral absolutes and for them the subtleties and compromises necessary to retain power in medieval secular government signified weakness in the ruler's character which manifested itself in the dissolute state of the principality he ruled.[31]

Orderic and his fellow historians judged Robert's government knowing that he was defeated by his brother. However, if the events of 1106 and Orderic's mantra of widespread destruction are set aside, it is possible to get a clearer view of Duke Robert in action during the first decade of his rule in Normandy. Although he was writing decades later, Orderic often had access to eye-witnesses of the events he was recording. Many of his sources had direct links with the monastery at Saint-Évroul, which may explain why he was reluctant to omit their testimony even when it compromised his bleak summary of the duke's reign.

The contradictions and inconsistencies in Orderic's account begin with his assertion that Robert was weak and indolent. The duke spent two periods in exile in single-minded pursuit of the goal of ruling Normandy independently of his father. If Robert was as dedicated to indolence and luxury as Orderic suggested, surely the option of biding his time in comfort would have been more to his taste.[32] Even if the policy of confronting his father and demanding the duchy was misguided, Robert demonstrated dogged determination and considerable energy in pursuing it.

Taking Control

On receiving the news of his father's death, Robert rode to Rouen, taking control of the city and the rest of the duchy. Whether Robert expressed any emotion at the news of his father's death was not recorded.[33] Certainly, he did not neglect prayers for his father's soul when he confirmed gifts the

---

[30] According to Orderic, England provided Robert's father with £1161 10s 1½d each day, although the figure was probably exaggerated; OV, II, pp. 266–7 and n. 7.

[31] Cf. M.T. Clanchy, 'Did Henry III have a Policy?' History, 53 (1968), pp. 203–16. D. Carr, 'Place and Time: On the Interplay of Historical Points of View', History and Theory, 40 (2001), pp. 153–67.

[32] Participation in the Crusade from 1096 to 1100 also suggests anything but indolence.

[33] WJ, II, pp. 202–5. Aubrey de Coucy's family castle was not far from Abbeville: Barlow, William Rufus, p. 50, n. 203. David, Curthose, p. 42 speculated that Robert welcomed news of the death of his father.

Conqueror had made to religious institutions. For example, Robert confirmed a manor, which his father had granted to the abbey of Saint-Étienne of Caen during his final illness, 'for the salvation of his [i.e. his father's] soul and mine, those of my brothers and all our predecessors'.[34] Robert was also obliged to distribute treasure from Rouen to monasteries, churches and the poor in fulfilment of his father's wishes and, again, for the salvation of his father's soul.[35] William Rufus provided gold, silver and gems to Otto the goldsmith, who was instructed to build the Conqueror a suitably magnificent tomb.[36]

Robert had been recognised as his father's successor to Normandy on several occasions and, at each confirmation, the Norman magnates had sworn oaths to acknowledge his succession. Exile had not invalidated his claim to the duchy and in September 1087 neither William Rufus nor Henry was in a position strong enough to resist their brother. Nevertheless, Robert had been absent from Normandy since January 1084 and he needed to win support quickly. The pragmatic, but strictly short-term solution was to reward his followers with payments from the treasury at Rouen. He was obliged to reward those members of his retinue who had stayed with him in exile and he also had mercenaries to pay. If, as is more than likely, Robert marked his arrival in Normandy with a lavish gathering of the ducal court, the celebrations would also have been costly. Robert also had obligations deriving from the terms of his father's will.[37]

As the incoming duke, especially one forced to reintroduce himself and impress his subjects, this was no time for Robert to stint on providing feasts or distributing favours. Feasting was a crucial element in expressions of medieval lordship and the conviviality of eating and drinking together provided the opportunity for a ruler to build or cement relationships.[38] Robert could not afford to ignore the chance to display this essential element of lordship in the first few weeks after obtaining power in Normandy. Medieval lords had to work hard to build loyalties and a sense of cohesion among followers whose ties were to their lord and not necessarily to each other. There was also something to celebrate: after years of frustrated ambition, Robert was now undisputed ruler of Normandy.

---

[34] Haskins, *Norman Institutions*, pp. 66–70 and Appendix E 'Unpublished Charters of Robert Curthose', no. 1, p. 285; cf. J-M. Bouvris, 'Une version inédite de la confirmation par le duc Robert Courte-Heuse d'une donation faite en 1087 par Guillaume le Conquérant à l'abbaye de Saint-Etienne de Caen', *Revue de l'Avranchin et du pays de Granville*, 64 , no. 331 (1987), pp. 82–5. For matters relating to Robert's charters, I am most grateful for the assistance offered by Pierre Bauduin, Véronique Gazeau, and their colleagues at the University of Caen engaged on the project to collect and edit the duke's *acta*. The texts of many of the *acta* in question have been edited by the ARTEM project (University of Nancy). See also Green, 'Robert Curthose Reassessed', p. 102 and nn. 27, 28, 29.

[35] *JW*, III, *s.a.*1087, pp. 46–9.

[36] *OV*, IV, pp. 110–11.

[37] Haskins, *Norman Institutions*, Appendix E, no. 1, p. 285; in the confirmation to Saint-Etienne in Caen, Robert retained the proceeds from tolls.

[38] Althoff, *Family, Friends and Followers*, pp. 152–9.

As a consequence of his various obligations and the appearance at his court of men eager to take advantage of the new regime, the duke's disposable treasure seems soon to have been exhausted.[39] Robert did not have access to the vast wealth of England and his control of ducal estates in Normandy rested on his ability to convince the Norman barons of his authority. On the Conqueror's death many of them had withdrawn from Rouen to their own estates and the garrisons loyal to Robert's father had been expelled from their castles. The Conqueror's unprecedented access to the resources of England meant that his authority in Normandy reached an intensity probably unmatched in the history of the duchy. Cut off from those resources, Robert had to try to reconstitute earlier patterns of ducal authority, which relied on the identification and harnessing of the mutual interests of the Norman duke and his aristocracy. The exceptional circumstances of his father's reign as king *and* duke have been underestimated in assessments of the effectiveness of Robert's tenure of Normandy.

The change of any regime marks a period of crisis and passes the advantage to those whose political support is crucial to the success of the incoming ruler. Orderic referred to a 'great change' taking place in Normandy and cold fear gripping the 'unarmed people' as the unbridled ambition of the powerful became clear.[40] The Norman barons used this transitional period to push their own claims and reinforce their own positions in the localities. Although some of those who had driven out the royal garrisons had been Robert's allies during his rebellions against his father, they now expected reward for their earlier support. It is in this context that Robert's rule should be assessed. It was natural and expected that Robert should meet their wishes. Robert may have had a certain sympathy for those who were claiming lands and castles withheld from them by the Conqueror. After all, Robert himself had spent years trying to win possession of Normandy from his father. The new duke gave the castle of Ivry to William of Breteuil, and that of Brionne to Roger de Beaumont as compensation for being displaced as castellan of Ivry.[41] In 1087, the barons of Normandy saw the chance to reassert themselves and took it.

Robert's expenses meant that he needed cash and in a hurry. Once the treasury at Rouen had been exhausted he was forced to look to other sources to meet the initial costs of his regime. There was someone close at hand, who had recently acquired a huge sum of money. Robert's brother Henry had been bequeathed five thousand pounds of silver by his father. Although this sum of money seems poor compensation for being excluded from ruling England or Normandy, the ready cash put Henry in a strong bargaining position with his impecunious brother. Perhaps the Conqueror realised that the money would be of more use to Henry in the coming struggles than the greater prizes whose

---

39 *OV*, IV, pp. 118–19.
40 *OV*, IV, pp. 112–13.
41 *OV*, IV, pp. 114–15. Robert of Torigny in *WJ*, II, pp. 226–7, suggested that Robert of Meulan, son of Roger de Beaumont, was castellan of Ivry while he was *vicomte* there.

value would only be realised after they had been secured. Certainly, Henry's anxiety to have the money quickly paid over before his brother arrived in Rouen suggests that he, too, realised the huge advantage he was being given and explains the care with which he had the cash weighed and counted.

Henry's resources gave him an advantage in 1087 and when Robert asked him for a loan, he drove a hard bargain. At first Henry refused but then Robert offered to sell him land, which was exactly what Henry wanted. A formal bargain was struck: Henry gave Robert three thousand pounds of silver and received 'the whole of the Cotentin, which is a third part of Normandy'. The region included Avranches, Coutances, the fee of Hugh of Avranches, earl of Chester, and the monastery of Mont-Saint-Michel.[42] Wace wrote that Robert secured a loan from Henry using the Cotentin, but on the understanding that his brother should make no permanent claim. In addition, Henry asked whether Richard de Redvers could enter his service. Richard was upset by this request as he did not want to leave the duke for Henry.[43] Richard clearly felt uneasy about serving another, but he later became one of Henry's most loyal supporters.[44]

Robert could not know that by ceding western Normandy to his brother he was creating a problem for himself in the future. It is difficult to see what else he could have done in order to bolster his regime in its first crucial months. Despite their earlier antagonism, he had, as yet, no reason to question his younger brother's loyalty and Robert perhaps envisaged the pair of them ruling Normandy together.[45] Certainly, in 1088, Henry witnessed his brother's charters for the abbeys of Jumièges and Fécamp.[46] Robert's provision for his youngest brother can be seen as a generous act designed to promote family harmony and a practical solution to establishing his authority in the far west of his duchy while he concentrated on securing Rouen.[47] This policy of installing brothers in certain areas of the duchy was not new. In 1026, Robert's grandfather and namesake had been given Falaise and the Hiémois by his father Richard II, while his brother Richard III became duke.[48] Although this sharing of power had proved unworkable in the late 1020s, Robert's policy

---

[42] *OV*, IV, pp. 118–21; *WJ*, II, pp. 204–5 and n. 4. See Hollister, *Henry I*, pp. 51–5, and Green, *Henry I*, p. 25.

[43] Wace, *Roman de Rou*, lines 9375–420, pp. 296–9. Richard was from Reviers, Calvados, arr. Caen, cant. Creully, and after the accession of Henry I in 1100, he acquired Plympton in Devon. His son, Baldwin, was made earl of Devon; R. Bearman, ed., *Charters of the Redvers Family and the Earldom of Devon, 1090–1217*, Devon and Cornwall Record Society, 37 (1994), pp. 2–11.

[44] Wace, *Roman de Rou*, lines 9409–12, pp. 298–9. Cf. *OV*, IV, pp. 220–1.

[45] *The Cartulary of the Abbey of Mont-Saint-Michel*, ed. Katherine S.B. Keats-Rohan (Donington, 2006), no. 69, pp. 147–8. In this grant to the abbey of Mont-Saint-Michel made in 1088, Robert specified that it was made 'for my soul, the souls of my father and mother, and of all my ancestors … and for the soul of my brother Henry'; William Rufus was not mentioned.

[46] Haskins, *Norman Institutions*, Appendix E, nos. 6 (Jumièges: 30 March 1088) and 4 (Fécamp: 7 July 1088).

[47] Henry may have understood the 'sale' of the Cotentin differently and perhaps expected autonomy.

[48] *WJ*, II, pp. 40–1.

with regard to the Cotentin should not be dismissed too readily as ill-considered. Robert may also have counted on the support of Bishop Geoffrey of Coutances to rein in the excesses of his brother.[49]

Among those who appeared at Robert's court at the end of 1087 was his uncle, Bishop Odo of Bayeux. The dying King William had reluctantly released Odo from prison and presumably Odo had regained his Norman lands with his nephew's agreement and in return for recognising Robert as duke.[50] It is likely that he put himself forward as Robert's chief counsellor.[51] The duke and his uncle may have found common cause during the Conqueror's lifetime. Odo's imprisonment in 1082 and Robert's second quarrel with his father may also have been connected.[52] The bishop's support in the Bessin was crucial, especially in the light of Henry's acquisition of the Cotentin. However, like so many of the Norman elite, Odo also had estates in England and he needed to re-establish contact with his other nephew, William Rufus. To that end he was probably at Canterbury just before Christmas 1087.[53] There is no reason to suppose that Norman ecclesiastical and secular magnates could not pass freely between the lands ruled by the brothers, as the two new regimes were being established. In these crucial first months neither ruler could afford to alienate powerful men.

While Robert was consolidating his takeover in the duchy, William Rufus had been crowned king of England at Westminster on Sunday 26 September 1087. Rufus, too, took a leading churchman, Archbishop Lanfranc, as his counsellor and it was through the latter's influence that the new king's assumption of power proceeded smoothly in the first few months. William of Saint-Calais, bishop of Durham, also threw in his lot with Rufus and the new king followed his counsel closely. One distinct advantage that Rufus had over his elder brother was the overflowing treasury at Winchester. The *Anglo-Saxon Chronicle* noted that

> it was impossible for any man to say how much was gathered there in gold, and in silver, and in vessels and in purple cloth and in gems and in many other precious things which are difficult to recount.[54]

Although Rufus, following his father's will, was obliged to distribute a huge sum from the treasury to the churches of England, it was still less than the

---

[49] J. Le Patourel, 'Geoffrey of Montbray, Bishop of Coutances, 1049–93', *EHR*, 59 (1944), pp. 129–61.

[50] WM, *GR*, I, pp. 544–5, suggests that Odo confirmed Robert in the duchy; cf. Bates, 'Character of Odo', pp. 1–20 at 15–16.

[51] *OV*, IV, pp. 114–15. For Odo giving Robert advice, see *OV*, IV, pp. 150–5. Cf. J. Hudson, 'Henry I and Counsel', in *The Medieval State. Essays presented to James Campbell*, ed. J.R. Maddicott and D.M. Palliser (London, 2000), pp. 109–26.

[52] Bates, 'Character of Odo', pp. 16–17.

[53] Mason, *William II*, p. 54 and n. 51.

[54] *ASC*, E, *s.a.* 1086 [1087], p. 98; Swanton, p. 222. *JW*, III, *s.a.* 1087, pp. 46–7; Mason, *William II*, pp. 49–50.

income from only one year's geld.[55] As for Robert, this disbursement of vast sums of money was an essential component of Rufus's strategy for establishing his credentials as ruler.

1088: The Barons' Dilemma

The establishment of separate regimes in Normandy and England was a problem for those barons with interests on both sides of the Channel.[56] The leading men of both principalities met together during the first few months of Robert and William's rule to discuss the situation.[57] Some sensed that their power and wealth had declined and identified the cause as the problem of trying to serve two masters:

> How can we provide adequate service to two lords who are so different and who live so far apart? If we serve Robert duke of Normandy, as we ought, we will offend his brother William, who will then strip us of great revenues and mighty honours in England. Again, if we obey King William dutifully, Duke Robert will confiscate our inherited estates in Normandy.[58]

Orderic then depicted the magnates citing examples from the Bible and classical literature of the perils of divided rule. In each case the resulting civil war caused not only thousands of deaths, but also the kingdoms concerned fell prey to foreign powers.

Odo of Bayeux took a leading role in persuading the magnates to depose Rufus and support Robert. Odo's support for Robert was the result of finding that Rufus had entrusted Bishop William of Durham with running his administration. Odo realised that he would not be able to recover the sort of influence he thought he had held at the English court before 1082. He argued that the throne of England belonged to Robert, who, according to William of Malmesbury, 'was of a milder disposition and by a long period of activity had corrected the follies of his youth'.[59] William Rufus, by contrast, had been brought up to expect luxury and 'his wild temperament so visible in the expression on his face would prompt him to try everything contrary to divine and human law'.[60] Referring to his own situation but also hinting at the fate of others close to the Conqueror, Odo noted that those who had

---

55 For the calculations, see Barlow, *William Rufus*, p. 64.
56 *OV*, IV, pp. 120–35; *ASC*, E, *s.a.* 1087 [1088], pp. 99–101; Swanton, pp. 222–5; WM, *GR*, I, pp. 544–9; JW, III, *s.a.* 1088, pp. 48–57; Symeon, 'Historia Regum', *s.a.* 1088, pp. 214–17.
57 *OV*, IV, pp. 120–5. This may have been at William Rufus's first Christmas court; Mason, *William II*, p. 55.
58 *OV*, IV, pp. 122–3.
59 WM, *GR*, I, pp. 544–5; *ASC*, E, *s.a.* 1087 [1088], p. 99; Swanton, p. 222. Cf. Bates, 'Character of Odo', pp. 17–18.
60 WM, *GR*, I, pp. 544–5.

been made captive by the father would gain nothing if they were executed by the son.

Without assigning Odo such a prominent role, Orderic echoed aspects of Malmesbury's account and provided the outcome of the disaffected magnates' deliberations. They were to form a sworn association against the king.[61]

> Let us form an inviolable league; since King William is the younger of the two and very obstinate and we are under no obligation to him he must be deposed or slain. Then let us make Duke Robert ruler over England and Normandy to preserve the union of the two realms, for he is older by birth and of a more tractable character, and we have already sworn fealty to him during the lifetime of the father of both men.[62]

These magnates had already committed themselves to Robert the elder brother, a reference to the oaths they had taken to recognise Robert as duke. They also argued that they owed nothing to the more intractable Rufus. There is no suggestion that Robert was a party to these deliberations.

Those implicated in the conspiracy were Odo of Bayeux, Earl Roger of Montgomery, Bishop Geoffrey of Coutances and his nephew Earl Robert of Northumbria, Eustace of Boulogne, and many others.[63] After Christmas 1087 Robert of Normandy was informed of the plot on his behalf. Orderic's contempt for the conspirators and their lord was clear. Robert was 'thoughtless and improvident' and 'he was delighted by their empty promises and undertook to give them his full support in their enterprise, and swift and effective aid in carrying out this shameless crime'.[64] The impetus for the plan came from these disaffected magnates rather than from the duke himself and there is no clear indication that, in the first months of his reign, he had any desire to seize England. Robert had repeatedly sought to rule Normandy and Maine and this may well have been the sum of his ambition. After all, Normandy was his by right and his attachment to England, a country he had visited only a few times, may not have been that of his brothers. On the other hand, if presented with the opportunity, he would have found it difficult to resist the invitation to rule England, especially if those making the offer included some of those who had been prominent at his father's court.

The *Anglo-Saxon Chronicle* provides the most detailed narrative for the

---

[61] Bishop William of Durham claimed that he had not sworn any oaths against the king: see *De iniusta Vexatione*, in R.C. van Caenegem, ed., *English Lawsuits from William I to Richard I. Vol. I. William I to Stephen*, Selden Society, 106 (London, 1990), pp. 93, 101. Richard Sharpe, '1088 – William II and the Rebels', *ANS*, 24 (2004), pp. 139–57, suggested that these oaths were perhaps oaths of fealty taken from some of the conspirators 'on behalf of the king's brother, Duke Robert'. Bloch, *Feudal Society*, I, p. 147: 'homage could not be offered or accepted by proxy'. Alternatively, the oaths can be interpreted as creating an essential bond between the conspirators; cf. Althoff, *Family, Friends and Followers*, pp. 90–101.

[62] *OV*, IV, pp. 122–5. Orderic's ambivalence towards Odo is seen in an earlier passage, which praises the bishop's generosity to the Church: *OV*, IV, pp. 114–19.

[63] WM, *GR*, I, pp. 544–5; *OV*, IV, pp. 124–5.

[64] *OV*, IV, pp. 124–5.

events of 1088, although this can be supplemented with other material.[65] A list of the conspirators suggests that the rebellion was widespread and involved many of the most prominent of the Norman nobility. As well as Odo of Bayeux, his brother Robert of Mortain was named.[66] In the West Country, Bishop Geoffrey of Coutances, his nephew Robert de Mowbray and Robert fitz Baldwin rose against the king. From the Welsh March, Osbern, son of Richard Scrop, his son-in-law Bernard of Neufmarché, Roger de Lassy and Ralf de Mortemer together with the men of the earl of Shrewsbury invaded the diocese of Worcester. In the East Midlands and East Anglia, Hugh of Grandmesnil, sheriff of Leicester, and Roger Bigod are cited as opposing the king, while in the North, Bishop William of Durham was suspected of supporting the rebels. However, the epicentre of the revolt was in the South East, in Kent and Sussex, where Odo, Eustace III of Boulogne, and Robert de Bellême were operating. Roger of Montgomery, earl of Shrewsbury, was then at his castle in Arundel and if he did not actively oppose the king, he did not actively aid him either.[67] The fact that Earl Roger's sons, Robert de Bellême, Hugh de Montgomery and Roger of Poitou, were named among the rebels explains his inertia.[68] Gilbert of Tonbridge, William, Count of Eu, and Robert of Rhuddlan are also named as defying the king.

The rebellion broke out at Easter 1088.[69] The rebels were all well-known to each other and would have had ample opportunity to discuss opposition to the king, even amid the Christmas festivities of 1087 and during a subsequent journey to Yorkshire in the early months of 1088.[70] The sources suggest that Odo of Bayeux was the leader of the rebellion and his thwarted ambition after years of captivity would explain his opposition to Rufus. The aim of the other rebels may have been to confirm their influence in the regions because Rufus's accession threatened the position of all of the Conqueror's magnates. The events of 1088 were driven not by Duke Robert's ambition, but by the concerns of powerful noblemen, looking after their own interests.

The first sign of trouble was the absence of many of the rebels from the king's Easter court.[71] In the next fortnight, the various regional uprisings broke out. Bishop Geoffrey and his nephew attacked Bristol and Bath, while William of Eu attacked the royal estate at Berkeley in Gloucestershire.[72] Worcestershire was ravaged by the men of Hereford, Shropshire and the Welsh March, but their attack on Worcester itself was beaten off by forces organised by Bishop

---

65 Recent analysis of the rebellion of 1088 reconciles a chronological problem in the narratives by suggesting a modification to a date in one of the sources. The revised chronology of the rebellion is followed here: see Sharpe, '1088', pp. 145–6.
66 ASC, E, s.a. 1087 [1088], p. 99; Swanton, pp. 222–3. Cf. JW, III, s.a. 1088, pp. 48–9.
67 OV, IV, pp. 124–5.
68 Sharpe, '1088', pp. 142–3.
69 ASC, E, s.a. 1087 [1088], p. 99; Swanton, p. 223. Easter 1088 was 16 April.
70 Sharpe, '1088', pp. 139–40 and 140, n. 7.
71 Usually the Easter court was held at Winchester.
72 ASC, E, s.a. 1087 [1088], p. 99; Swanton, p. 223.

Wulfstan.[73] Roger Bigod at Norwich plundered the surrounding territory and Hugh of Grandmesnil 'did not improve anything, neither in Leicestershire nor in Northampton'.[74] Towards the end of April, Rufus called an assembly to raise forces and defend his kingship. The king 'promised them (English men) the best law that ever there was in this land; and forbade every unjust tax, and granted men their woods and coursing'.[75] It was at this point that Bishop William of Saint-Calais deserted the king, leaving the court for Durham.[76] Rufus concentrated his attack on the conspirators in the South East, targeting the ring-leader Odo of Bayeux.[77] Tonbridge was captured and then the king pursued his uncles Odo of Bayeux and Robert of Mortain to Pevensey.

Meanwhile, Duke Robert had managed to gather troops and sent a contingent over to join the rebels.[78] William of Malmesbury suggested that Henry, probably as a precaution, be sent to Brittany by Robert, while the latter awaited a favourable wind to cross to England. Robert spent £3,000 on troops, all the money that he had only recently acquired from his youngest brother.[79] A source from the abbey of Fécamp suggests that Robert tried to control the Channel by recruiting 'pirates' to harass English shipping and to allow a Norman invasion fleet unhindered passage.[80] The ducal expeditionary force was intercepted at sea by English ships.[81] It was probably this setback that delayed Robert's departure from Normandy until it was too late. The surrender of the garrison at Pevensey may be associated with the defeat of Robert's fleet.[82]

Odo left Pevensey promising Rufus that he would also leave England, but not before securing the surrender of Rochester. The bishop was sent on ahead to make good his promise but, as he approached Rochester, the garrison rode out and liberated Odo from the king's escort. The bishop joined Eustace of Boulogne and the 'three sons of Earl Roger [of Montgomery] and all the best-born men who were in this land or in Normandy'.[83] William Rufus

---

73 Emma Mason, *St Wulfstan of Worcester, c.1008–1095* (Oxford, 1990), pp. 142–5.
74 *ASC*, E, *s.a.* 1087 [1088], p. 99; Swanton, p. 223.
75 *ASC*, E, *s.a.* 1087 [1088], p. 99; Swanton, p. 223.
76 The bishop was disseised on 12 May 1088: Sharpe, '1088', pp. 145–6. His defection is puzzling given Odo's resentment of his influence with Rufus. Perhaps he simply backed what he thought would be the winning side.
77 *ASC*, E, *s.a.* 1087 [1088], p. 99; Swanton, p. 223.
78 Wace, *Roman de Rou*, lines 9375–420, 9421–48, pp. 296–9, suggests that Robert was anxious to cross to England to challenge his brother for the throne. However, Wace is mistaken to then suggest that Robert actually invaded and that as a result of the peace made Rufus was to give Robert £5000 annually. It looks as though Wace has confused 1088 with the invasion of 1101.
79 WM, *GR*, I, pp. 710–11. Cf. *OV*, IV, pp. 94–5, 118–21. Wace, *Roman de Rou*, lines 9155–6, pp. 292–3. Malmesbury (*ibid.*) suggests that when peace was made between Rufus and Robert, Henry overlooked this. Henry garrisoned Rouen on Robert's behalf.
80 L'Abbé Sauvage, 'Des miracles advenus en l'église de Fécamp', in *Mélanges, Documents*, 2nd series, Société de l'Histoire de Normandie (Rouen, 1893), pp. 9–49 at 29.
81 WM, *GR*, I, pp. 548–9.
82 *ASC*, E, *s.a.* 1087 [1088], p. 100; Swanton, p. 224.
83 *ASC*, E, *s.a.* 1087 [1088], p. 100; Swanton, p. 224; WM, *GR*, I, pp. 546–7. The three sons of Earl Roger were Robert de Bellême, Hugh and Roger.

summoned as many men as he could, especially from the English, and then blockaded Rochester, damaging the cathedral priory in the process. According to Orderic, the rebels in Rochester waited 'in vain for help from Duke Robert, who was delayed through his inertia and love of ease'.[84]

Orderic's comment seems a harsh judgement and one wonders what resources Robert still had at his disposal given that he had already despatched a force which had been destroyed by Rufus's ships and his allies had been outfought by the young king. Nevertheless, there is evidence which indicates that as late as the first week in July Robert still intended to invade. In a grant to the abbey of Fécamp, Robert referred to 7 July 1088 as 'when I ought to have crossed to England'.[85]

The end of the siege of Rochester was reported laconically by the *Anglo-Saxon Chronicle*: 'A great company then came to him [William Rufus], French and English, and he went to Rochester and besieged the castle, until they who were in it made peace and gave up the castle.'[86] Orderic provided more detail saying that Odo was accompanied by five hundred knights and the besieged were well-equipped. Rufus built two siege towers, which prevented the garrison leaving the castle to gather provisions or plunder the surrounding countryside. Odo's plan was to wait for Duke Robert's forces to arrive, for despite the strength of his garrison he dared not take on the king in battle. Earl Roger 'of the Mercians' assisted the king in the siege, but covertly tried to help his son in Rochester castle and Orderic suggests that Earl Roger was not the only magnate acting in this duplicitous manner.[87] As the king pointed out, the problem for the earl and others who questioned Rufus's designation by the Conqueror as his heir was that they also owed their position to the same man's judgement: 'The same man who made me king chose you as magnates.'[88]

Orderic thought that all the bishops of England and all the English supported the king, although his view of what constituted 'Englishness' has to be questioned in the light of his naming Hugh of Avranches, earl of Chester, Robert de Mowbray, earl of Northumbria, William de Warenne and Robert fitz Hamon among the king's supporters.[89] The situation inside Rochester castle deteriorated as the garrison was struck by pestilence. Dense swarms of

84 *OV*, IV, pp. 126–7.
85 Haskins, *Norman Institutions*, Appendix E 'Unpublished Charters of Robert Curthose' no. 4 (c), p. 289. For discussion of this document, see Sharpe, '1088', p. 147.
86 *ASC*, E, *s.a.* 1087 [1088], p. 100; Swanton, p. 224; WM, *GR*, I, pp. 548–9.
87 *OV*, IV, pp. 126–9.
88 WM, *GR*, I, pp. 546–7.
89 A point made by Sharpe, '1088', p. 143. On this issue of Norman and English identities, see Judith A. Green, 'Unity and Disunity in the Anglo-Norman State', *Historical Research*, 62 (1989), pp. 114–34; D. Crouch, 'Normans and Anglo-Normans: A Divided Aristocracy?' in D. Bates and Anne Curry, eds., *England and Normandy in the Middle Ages* (London, 1994), pp. 51–67; Hugh M. Thomas, *The English and the Normans. Ethnic Hostility, Assimilation, and Identity 1066–c.1220* (Oxford, 2003).

flies filled the eyes and nostrils of the besieged, contaminating their food and drink and eventually forcing Odo and his men to seek terms of surrender.

The negotiations for the surrender of Rochester followed a familiar pattern. Through intermediaries the rebels asked to keep their fiefs, lands and all the property they had previously held and in return they offered to serve Rufus faithfully as their rightful lord in the future. Perhaps as the opening salvo in the bargaining process, the king angrily rejected the request and threatened to hang the traitors on gibbets or execute them in other ways. The rebels had to act in the manner of repentant sinners in order to placate their justifiably aggrieved lord. According to Orderic, it was Rufus's own allies who 'approached him with a humble petition, and tried to appease him with earnest prayers and soft words'. Orderic reported that these intercessors addressed the king in the following manner:

> 'Praise be to God who always helps those who put their trust in him and gives good fathers a worthy offspring to succeed them. Surely these presumptuous youths and blindly ambitious old men have now fully learnt the lesson that the royal might has not yet faltered in this island. Those who swooped down on us from Normandy like hawks on their prey, imagining that the royal stock was weakened in England, have now discovered with God's aid that young William is no less powerful than old William. Now on the point of defeat they yield to your forces; they are worn out and throw themselves as suppliants on your mercy. We who have stood beside you no less than your father in grave perils, now approach you humbly and plead the cause of our fellow countrymen. It is most proper that, just as you should by your graciousness spare them now that they are humbled and penitent. Temper your royal vigour with mercy (*clementia*) and let the victory proclaim the triumph of your might.'

As Orderic warmed to his theme, the intercessors are depicted reminding Rufus of models of mercy in Holy Scripture and in the 'Book of the wonders of the world'.[90] The language is that of supplication, of the kind used when asking for divine forgiveness.[91] Earl Roger of Montgomery was prominent among the intercessors, as the presence of his sons in Rochester was an incentive for him to help end the siege peacefully.

Rufus was reluctant to allow the traitors to go free: 'He who spares traitors and robbers, oppressors and accursed men, destroys the peace and security of the innocent and sows the seeds of endless massacres and troubles for good, defenceless people.'[92] In his turn, Rufus cited examples of Old Testament kings executing rebels. This brought further pleading by the intercessors, especially for Odo of Bayeux, the king's uncle and a consecrated bishop, Eustace of Boulogne and Robert de Bellême. The intercessors reminded Rufus that each

---

[90] *OV*, IV, pp. 128–31 and 130, n. 3 for the *libellus de mirabilibus mundi*.
[91] Koziol, *Begging Pardon and Favor*, pp. 177–213.
[92] *OV*, IV, pp. 130–1.

of these men had at one time found favour with his father. Finally the king was swayed by the argument that:

'[t]he man who does an injury today may perhaps serve as a friend in the future. Among these men are many distinguished knights, ready to offer their service to you, and you ought not, great king, to underrate its worth. Now that you have defeated them by your strength, resources and great courage, win their hearts by your generosity and compassion.'[93]

Rufus finally allowed the petition and guaranteed the besieged life and limb and a safe conduct. As described by Orderic, this was the Norman aristocracy drawing together to protect its own members from the wrath of the king. However, there is some indication that Rufus insisted that his erstwhile enemies should suffer some indignities.

Although Odo and his allies were permitted to leave Rochester with some honour, bearing their arms and riding their horses, Rufus refused the bishop's request that trumpets heralding their departure should not be sounded 'as is customary when an enemy is defeated and a stronghold taken by force'. As the garrison made its way out, they were jeered by the English, who demanded that the traitors be hanged. Orderic ends his account by pointing out that Odo and his supporters lost their lands in England and left its shores for good.[94] Thus before Duke Robert could bring over his invasion force, the garrison of Rochester surrendered in early July 1088. It is likely that Robert overestimated the ability of the garrison of Rochester to withstand his brother's siege, but his failure to bring help allowed them to surrender without compromising their honour by failing to do their duty. Garrisons under siege were allowed to appeal to their lord for assistance and, if this aid was not forthcoming, they could negotiate terms for surrender and not risk charges of disloyalty.[95]

By the end of July it was clear that Robert was not going to displace his brother in England and so the Norman barons on both sides of the Channel were forced to decide where their loyalties lay. In order to keep their lands in England, they had to do homage to the new king and, for the time being at least, serve two masters hoping that their relationship could be restored. Robert's youngest brother also seems to have accepted the situation. After witnessing Robert's charter to Fécamp, Henry crossed to England in July 1088 to make his peace with Rufus. Orderic reports that the king 'received him kindly as a brother should and fraternally granted his petition', probably a reference to Henry's request for his mother's lands in England. Despite Orderic's account, Rufus granted the lands in question to his follower Robert fitz Hamo, leaving Henry to return angrily to Normandy.[96]

In the autumn, Rufus dealt with the most prominent rebels. Bishop

---

93 *OV*, IV, pp. 132–3.
94 *OV*, IV, pp. 134–5.
95 Strickland, *War and Chivalry*, pp. 212–18, 224–9.
96 *OV*, IV, pp. 148–9.

William of Durham was put on trial at Old Sarum and was forced into exile in Normandy.[97] In general, though, Rufus treated the rebels leniently, realising that some owed him no obligations and therefore could not be treated as disloyal vassals. This attitude was also informed by the need to normalise relations with major landholding families. The most prominent among Robert's supporters, Odo of Bayeux, Eustace of Boulogne, and Robert de Bellême, were allowed to return to Normandy, although all lost their English lands. A series of charters issued during these crucial months of 1088 and analysed by Richard Sharpe suggests that Rufus was indeed lenient with the majority of the rebels.[98] Roger of Poitou was able to transfer his allegiance to Rufus and recovered his English estates. Others pardoned or restored to favour were Bishop Geoffrey of Coutances and his nephew, Robert, Roger Bigod, the Grandmesnils and Gilbert fitz Richard of Tonbridge. Robert of Mortain was also pardoned, perhaps as early as at the siege of Pevensey, and seems to have returned to Normandy where he died on 8 December 1090.[99]

The duke's absence from the campaign in England may have contributed to the failure of the rebellion against Rufus, as not only was he acknowledged as an accomplished soldier but his presence would have bolstered morale and reminded the Norman barons of their obligations to him. Crossing the Channel would also have been a demonstration of his commitment to the scheme. In his absence, the leader of the revolt was Odo of Bayeux, a man whose reputation had been tarnished by his imprisonment by the Conqueror. Before heaping criticism on Robert for the failure of the revolt in his name, certain points might be considered. Rufus was a crowned king and the symbolic power of royal anointing should not be forgotten. It is to be doubted whether Robert could have sanctioned regicide or even his brother's deposition, even if he had gained the upper hand. Robert had barely had time to settle in at Rouen before his uncle was involving him in a major military undertaking. It is unlikely that Robert would have had time to gather any of the ducal revenues before he was required to raise troops and a fleet to support the rebels. There is no suggestion that he was present when the plot against his brother was first mooted. The war of succession in 1088 was more about setting the parameters of the relationship between the brothers and allowing the Norman baronage to find ways of accommodating themselves to the changed political circumstances. All parties were searching for the legitimacy of their positions, a legitimacy thrown into doubt by the death of the Conqueror. As the events of 1088 show, the strength of Robert's claim to Normandy was accepted more readily than was his brother William's right to England.

There is a tendency to overestimate the power of the Norman kings and,

---

[97] R.C. van Caenegem, ed., *English Lawsuits*, no. 134, pp. 90–106; cf. H.S. Offler, 'The tractate *De iniusta vexacione Willelmi episcopi primi*', *EHR*, 66 (1951), pp. 321–41, reprinted in *idem, North of the Tees. Studies in Medieval British History*, ed. A.J. Piper and A.I. Doyle (Aldershot, 1996), VI.

[98] Sharpe, '1088', pp. 155–7.

[99] J. Le Patourel, 'Geoffrey of Montbray, Bishop of Coutances, 1049–93', *EHR*, 59 (1944), pp. 129–61; B. Golding, 'Robert of Mortain', *ANS*, 13 (1991), pp. 119–44.

although Rufus cornered his main enemies at Rochester, there were many in his own ranks who had an ambivalent attitude towards him. If the war was begun by the Norman nobility, it was also ended by them. Rufus as much as Robert needed the co-operation of the major landholders of England if he was to survive the crucial first year or so. Similarly, the barons needed to get the measure of the new king and find out how far they could push their own interests. There may also be something in Orderic's comment that Rufus 'shrewdly spared the older barons, although the conspiracy had temporarily weakened their allegiance to him, out of love for his father whom they had served long and faithfully, and through respect for their grey hairs. *In any case he knew that disease and speedy death would soon put an end to their activities.*'[100]

Robert, Bishop Odo and Ducal Government

In the aftermath of events in England, Robert's brother Henry was arrested.[101] After the defeat at Rochester, Henry's attempts to secure estates in England from Rufus, seemed a sign of double-dealing. Orderic makes it clear that there were certain forms of expected behaviour associated with the relationship between brothers. When Henry visited Rufus's court, the king received him 'kindly as a brother should'.[102] The politics of the next two decades were to be dominated by the interaction between these brothers and the social and cultural constructions of the fraternal relationship informed and constrained their behaviour towards one another. This raises the question whether political expediency justified ignoring these expected patterns of behaviour, or whether affective bonds influenced a ruler's actions. Robert was reluctant to accept that his brothers did not share his belief in the importance of the fraternal bond. This is not to say that on occasion Robert did not resent his brothers' behaviour, but that this was the result of his sense of how they *should* behave towards him.[103]

Henry returned from England with one of the duke's chief supporters, Robert de Bellême, who had also been reconciled with Rufus though the efforts of his father Earl Roger and others.[104] Bellême had consistently supported Robert during his struggles with the Conqueror and the duke may have been angered at the prospect of losing his support, which had implications for the security of Normandy's southern frontier. For his part, Robert de Bellême may have reached an accommodation with Rufus, simply to escape England and further punishment. Messengers from England put a negative interpretation

---

100 *OV*, IV, pp. 134–5 (my emphasis).
101 WM, *GR*, I, pp. 710–11.
102 *OV*, IV, pp. 148–9.
103 Hollister, *Henry I*, pp. 48–9.
104 *OV*, IV, pp. 148–9.

on the accommodation made between Henry, Robert de Bellême and Rufus, and it was suggested that they had sworn an oath to oppose Duke Robert.[105] After consulting his uncle Odo, Robert arrested them when they returned in the autumn of 1088.[106]

Robert de Bellême's imprisonment brought his father, Earl Roger, back to Normandy. Roger then fortified all his castles against the duke, threatening the southern frontier.[107] Robert had thus alienated two of the major Norman landholders. This episode has usually been interpreted as demonstrating Robert's ineptitude as duke as well as the malign influence of Odo of Bayeux, but there were, however, good reasons for the duke to ensure the loyalty of these two.[108] Henry controlled the Cotentin and Robert de Bellême's family was dominant in the south of the duchy. The duke was acting resolutely to make clear the consequences for his vassals if they compromised their loyalty to him. Henry and Robert de Bellême soon found out for themselves the difficulties of trying to serve two masters.

Orderic ascribed the arrest of Henry and Robert de Bellême to the influence that Bishop Odo had over his nephew Duke Robert. He suggested that Robert feared Odo but not to the extent that he was incapable of rejecting some of his counsel.[109] During his father's absences in England, Robert had been associated in the government of Normandy with his mother and a group of advisers, but he had little or no experience of ruling in his own right.

Until recently, studies of medieval lordship and government focused largely on the evolution of administrative institutions which were the precursors of the bureaucratic machinery of the modern state.[110] However, the more personal aspects of medieval lordship have been receiving greater attention.[111] In more recent studies of social and political power in the eleventh and twelfth centuries concepts such as status, honour and fidelity play a greater role than the ability to govern through supposedly more developed and impersonal administrative institutions.[112] Although it is not possible here to provide a detailed account of ducal government, it is worth outlining its structure and indicating the duke's place within it. What was Robert expected to do as duke of Normandy? How much control could he expect – or want – to have over what was done in his name?

---

105   *OV*, IV, pp. 148–9, calls the messengers 'maliuoli discordiæ satores', literally 'malevolent sowers of discord'.
106   *OV*, IV, pp. 148–9. WM, *GR*, I, pp. 712–13; *WJ*, II, pp. 204–5.
107   *OV*, IV, pp. 148–9.
108   David, *Curthose*, pp. 52–3; Hollister, *Henry I*, pp. 64–6; Green, *Henry I*, pp. 28–9.
109   *OV*, IV, pp. 148–9.
110   E.g. Haskins, *Norman Institutions* and, especially, C.W. Hollister and J.W. Baldwin, 'The Rise of Administrative Kingship: Henry I and Philip Augustus', *AHR*, 83 (1978), pp. 867–905.
111   E.g. T.N. Bisson, 'Medieval Lordship', *Speculum*, 70 (1995), pp. 743–59, and the essays in *idem*, ed., *Cultures of Power. Lordship, Status, and Process in Twelfth-century Europe* (Philadelphia, 1995).
112   The development of 'impersonal administrative institutions' is perhaps something of a mirage. Even the most bureaucratic of governments rely on the smooth operation of personal relationships. Personal favours and/or obligations regularly circumvent regulatory mechanisms and procedures in any organisation.

According to Orderic, Bishop Odo attended the duke at Rouen and instructed him in how best to perform his duties.[113] It was a function of the clerical as well as the secular elite to provide counsel for the prince. Odo's advice reflects an ideal of rulership which recurs in Orderic's *Historia* and the other narratives of the period. Robert was advised to be kindly or severe as occasion demanded. The advice turned into criticism as Odo pointed out that Robert was deaf to the cries of monks and widows suffering as outlaws and other evil-doers pillaged the duchy. Orderic depicted Odo providing Robert with a series of role models to imitate, from King David, Alexander the Great and Caesar to the duke's own Norman predecessors, including his father.[114] Odo ended his speech to general applause by urging his nephew to

> 'Reflect carefully on all that I have said; and stand up worthily as a good prince should for the peace of holy Mother Church and for the defence of the poor and helpless; put down all opponents with resolution.'[115]

The protection of the Church and the weak in society was the primary duty of those who wielded public power.

The personality of the prince was crucial in this world of face-to-face politics and the histories of this period provide many examples of the strengths and defects of character exhibited by those in power. In this context, Orderic's accusation that Duke Robert was given to idleness has a significance for the portrayal of his role as duke.[116] However, when necessity drove, Robert was capable of decisive and swift action, especially when what was required was leadership in war.

Political power in this period rested as much on personal charisma as on the willingness of the other members of the social elite to recognise the legitimacy of claims to that power. The position of the ruler was not only created, but also periodically reinforced through a series of rituals of recognition.[117] It took a great deal of work to win over and retain the loyalty of the various interest groups at court and the accusation was that Robert was not adept at this aspect of lordship. William of Malmesbury's character sketch of the duke suggests that Robert preferred the more straightforward problems of the battlefield. He had no patience for the subtleties of the court:

> He was, then, a man with no memory for the wrongs done to him, and forgave offences beyond what was right; to all who came to him he gave the answer they desired rather than send them away disappointed, and anything that he could not give he promised. By this gentleness of character, a man who ought to have been

---

[113] *OV*, IV, pp. 150–5.
[114] *OV*, IV, pp. 150–1.
[115] *OV*, IV, pp. 152–3.
[116] E.g. *OV*, IV, pp. 150–1; cf. WM, *GR*, I, pp. 705–5.
[117] C. Lindholm, *Charisma* (Oxford, 1990).

praised for it, and to have won the affection of his subjects, goaded the Normans into such contempt that they thought him of no account at all.[118]

For Malmesbury, Robert displayed admirable qualities, but they were inappropriate for an effective ruler. Perhaps Robert's generosity was a reaction to the notorious parsimony of his father.[119]

The economic basis of ducal power rested on the exploitation of estates scattered throughout Normandy. The extent of the ducal lands fluctuated as alienations were made or estates were acquired as the result of forfeitures and the other benefits of lordship.[120] Resources were also collected in the form of taxes and tolls.[121] These revenues were gathered in the regions of Normandy by *vicomtes*, who were also responsible for enforcing other ducal rights.[122] Other household officials are found in the documents produced in the duke's name.[123] The relatively small number of ducal *acta* surviving for Robert's reign has been taken as a sign of the inefficiency of his administration.[124] However, the *acta* show no signs of a regime in terminal decline: they deal with the same sorts of transactions as those of his father and brothers. When historians examined them with assumptions in mind about Robert's political and administrative ineffectiveness a circular argument developed. Approaching the corpus of surviving documents with the narrative of ducal failure in mind, historians found what they expected to find. There were few documents issued in Robert's name because his government was weak and inefficient; a sign of the weakness of ducal government under Robert was the small corpus of *acta*.[125] Those who sought Robert's confirmation of grants obviously felt that it was worthwhile doing so and perhaps historians should investigate other hypotheses for the pattern of survival of his *acta*.

Justice, especially in those cases involving the social and political elite, was dispensed in the ducal court, but probably in an informal and *ad hoc* manner. The idea of bringing the dispute before the duke was to reach a settlement between the parties, rather than submit to his will. The duke was expected to maintain peace and protect the rights of his subjects, especially those of the Church and nobility, without whose support a regime was unlikely to survive. Disputes, which were often violent, were a feature of eleventh-century Normandy and can be found in the reigns of Robert's father and

---

118 WM, *GR*, I, pp. 704–5. The similarities between Malmesbury's account and Orderic's criticisms perhaps suggest that Henry I's propaganda lies behind their portraits of Robert.
119 E.g. the portrait of the Conqueror in *ASC*, E, *s.a.* 1086 [1087], pp. 95–9; Swanton, pp. 217–22.
120 E.g. the forfeitures of estates by those exiled from the duchy: see E. Johnson, 'The Process of Norman Exile into Southern Italy', in Napran and van Houts, eds., *Exile in the Middle Ages*, pp. 29–38.
121 Bates, *Normandy before 1066*, pp. 147–88.
122 M. Hagger, 'The Norman Vicomte, c. 1035–1135: What did he do?', *ANS*, 29 (2006), pp. 65–83.
123 Bates, *Normandy before 1066*, pp. 161–2.
124 Haskins, *Norman Institutions*, pp. 62–84.
125 V.K. Dibble, 'Four Types of Inference from Documents to Events', *History and Theory*, 3 (1963), pp. 203–21 at 210–13.

grandfather. However, the level of this violence should not be exaggerated.[126] Unlike his father, Robert had the disadvantage of limited opportunities to turn the violence outwards beyond the frontiers of the duchy. But the most significant difference was that Robert did not have access to the resources of England with which to bolster his position within the duchy. English cash was the key to control of the duchy of Normandy after 1066.

Securing Maine

Robert claimed the lordship of Maine as well as Normandy and he asserted his rights in the county soon after his return to Rouen.[127] Orderic presented Bishop Odo's advice on ducal government as the prelude to an expedition to Maine and the southern frontier of Normandy.[128] Robert was urged to march to Le Mans and summon the magnates of Maine to acknowledge his lordship. The duke's forces were then to besiege any castle whose lord defied him. Bishop Odo then advised Robert to attack Roger of Montgomery and secure the Bellême castles. Here Orderic betrayed his own antipathy to Robert de Bellême's family and this coloured his opinion of the success of the ducal campaign.[129]

Robert summoned an army and in August 1088 marched to Maine where he was received joyously by the clergy and citizens of Le Mans. The fact that Robert was able to assemble an army so soon after the setback in England suggests that his authority was not as precarious as Orderic makes out. Orderic's information for this campaign was probably provided by a fellow monk, Arnold, who returned the body of Osmund of Gasprée, one of the casualties of this expedition, to Saint-Évroul for burial.[130]

The ducal forces were led by Odo, Count William of Évreux, Ralph of Conches and his nephew William of Breteuil. Joined by contingents from Maine, they laid siege to the castle of Ballon whose lord, Pain of Mondoubleau, had defied Robert. After the garrison of Ballon made peace with the duke, his army laid siege to the castle of Saint-Céneri, which was held by Robert Quarrel. The castle was taken when its food supplies were exhausted. According to Orderic, the duke was so angry that he had Robert Quarrel blinded.[131] 'Many others too who had contumaciously resisted the duke of

---

126 M. Bennett, 'Violence in Eleventh-century Normandy: Feud, Warfare and Politics', in G. Halsall, ed., *Violence and Society in the Early Medieval West* (Woodbridge, 1998), pp. 126–40.

127 Robert was styled 'dux Normannorum et princeps Cenomannorum' in the charter of confirmation issued to Saint-Étienne issued shortly after his return to Normandy in September 1087: Haskins, *Norman Institutions*, Appendix E, no. 1, p. 285.

128 *OV*, IV, pp. 150–63.

129 *OV*, IV, pp. 152–3; cf. Thompson, 'Orderic Vitalis and Robert of Bellême'.

130 *OV*, IV, pp. 154–5.

131 Emily Zack Tabuteau, 'Punishments in Eleventh-century Normandy', in W.C. Brown and P. Górecki, eds., *Conflict in Medieval Europe. Changing Perspectives on Society and Culture* (London, 2003), pp. 131–49 at 138.

Normandy at Saint-Céneri were mutilated by sentence of the duke's court.' Not only was this brutal treatment of rebels reminiscent of his father's campaigns in the region, it was the result of a decision of Robert's court ('ex sentencia curiæ'). Robert's personal authority was supported by the usual institutions, and decisions made in his name were implemented.[132]

When Robert's father had campaigned in the region around 1050, he had demonstrated similarly brutal treatment of the garrison at Alençon.[133] Robert's action at Saint-Céneri was interpreted in the same way by Orderic who noted that the castellans of Alençon and Bellême were unnerved by the fate of Robert Quarrel and were ready to surrender to the duke.

After the successful siege of Saint-Céneri, a delegation of the Manceaux led by Geoffrey of Mayenne approached Robert on behalf of Robert Giroie who claimed the castle.[134] The duke agreed to hand over the castle to Giroie who offered his service and fealty.[135] The campaign had thus been particularly successful: Robert had asserted his lordship in Maine and had reduced two castles. In the process he had dented the prestige of the Montgomery-Bellême family and established a loyal vassal in the region. The duke's success was sufficient to bring Roger of Montgomery to the bargaining table. Earl Roger asked for peace and the release of his son, Robert de Bellême. With his mission accomplished, the duke was disposed to mercy and freed his friend. This last act prompted Orderic to put a negative slant on the campaign and he suggested that just at the point when the Montgomery-Bellême castles were about to surrender, the duke's natural idleness induced him to withdraw and disband his army.[136] It is surely more plausible to suggest that Robert believed he had achieved the aims of his campaign and when Roger of Montgomery's envoys appeared offering peace he seized the opportunity to restore this relationship with this powerful frontier lord. Robert de Bellême had been the duke's supporter in the struggles against King William and their former camaraderie probably played a part in the settlement. Orderic, however, could not agree with Duke Robert's policy towards the Montgomery-Bellême family.[137]

132   *OV*, IV, pp. 154–5. Haskins, *Norman Institutions*, p. 77, noted that this was one of the very few references to Robert's *curia*, implying that it was the exception rather than the rule.
133   *WJ*, II, pp. 124–5.
134   For the Giroie and Saint-Céneri, see *OV*, II, pp. 28–9, 80–3; III, pp. 134–5.
135   J.-M. Maillefer, 'Une famille aristocratique aux confins de la Normandie: Les Géré au XIe siècle', in *Autour du pouvoir ducal normand Xe–XIIe siècles*, ed. L. Musset, J.-M. Bouvris and J.-M. Maillefer (Caen, 1985), pp. 175–206 at 196.
136   *OV*, IV, pp. 156–9.
137   *OV*, IV, pp. 158–61. Thompson, *Power and Border Lordship*, pp. 28–53, and *eadem*, 'Robert de Bellême', p. 270.

William Rufus and Normandy, 1089

The events of 1088 prompted William Rufus to carry the fight into Normandy.[138] Orderic portrayed an assembly at Winchester where Rufus gave his reasons for attacking his brother: Robert had incited his men to rebel and had conspired to deprive him of his kingdom and life. Orderic then introduced a motif that was to be used again and again to justify opposition to Robert: 'the holy Church in Normandy has sent a cry of distress to me because, lacking a just defender and patron, its daily lot is mourning and weeping, for it is surrounded by enemies like a lamb among wolves'.[139] Rufus suggested to his men that it was their duty to defend the monasteries that their fathers had founded in Normandy. He promised good lordship in the duchy: 'I will bring help to the Church of God, protect helpless widows and orphans, and punish thieves and murderers with the sword of justice'.[140] Rufus's barons approved the scheme and, at some point after Easter 1089, Rufus began to subvert Robert's rule in Normandy. William of Malmesbury suggested that Rufus was motivated by resentment and simply wanted 'to avenge his wrongs and inflict disgrace on his brother'.[141]

Rufus's strategy set a pattern for the future as he relied upon the lure of cash to undermine the personal bonds between Robert and his vassals. His subversion began with those of Robert's men holding lands north and east of the Seine in the area most accessible to England, along the frontier with the County of Ponthieu and the lands of the French king. Rufus first secured a valuable harbour by an agreement with the garrison of Saint-Valéry on the Somme.[142] Stephen of Aumâle was the first to take the king's money and with it he fortified his castle at Aumâle against Robert.[143] Gerard de Gournay also joined Rufus, handing over his castles at Gournay, Gaillefontaine and La Ferté-en-Bray, while trying to persuade his neighbours to follow his example.[144]

> Then Robert, count of Eu, and Walter Giffard and Ralph of Mortemer and almost all the lords between the Seine and the sea joined the English and received large

---

[138] OV, IV, pp. 178–81; cf. WM, GR, I, pp. 548–9.

[139] OV, IV, pp. 178–9.

[140] OV, IV, pp. 180–1. The assembly at Winchester is associated by Orderic with the elevation of William (I) de Warenne to the earldom of Surrey, which is problematic if Rufus's assembly was in 1089. Between Christmas 1087 and the end of March 1088, William de Warenne was given his earldom and his death followed on 24 June 1088: C.P. Lewis, 'Warenne, William (I) de, First Earl of Surrey (d.1088)', Oxford DNB.

[141] WM, GR, I, pp. 548–9.

[142] ASC, E, s.a. 1090, p. 101; Swanton, p. 225; cf. JW, III, s.a. 1090, pp. 56–7; WM, GR, I, pp. 548–9.

[143] OV, IV, pp. 182–3 and n. 2. Stephen was related to Duke Robert. He was the son of Eudo of Champagne, the third husband of the Conqueror's sister, Adelaide: OV, II, p. 264, n. 3.

[144] OV, IV, pp. 182–3; Gerard de Gournay married Edeva de Warenne, daughter of William I de Warenne and Gundreda: see Power, Norman Frontier, pp. 190, 233, 355, 368–9, 504.

sums of money from the king's resources to provide arms and men for the defence of their homes.[145]

These men all had landed interests in the vulnerable frontier area between the Seine and the sea, but their decision to support Rufus may also have been the result of ties of kinship and local rivalries. Stephen of Aumâle's wife was Hadvisa, daughter of Ralph de Mortemer and Gerard de Gournay's aunt was the wife of Walter II Giffard. There were also connections by marriage between the Giffards and the counts of Eu.[146] These families also had interests of their own in the region best served by allying with Rufus against the duke.[147] William of Malmesbury noted that Normandy suffered a long civil war, in which first one side then the other was successful, 'each party being roused to fury by the nobles, men of no worth at all and loyal to neither side'.[148]

From these bases, Robert's enemies plundered the surrounding region. The duke's positive and effective reaction to this threat during the summer of 1089 contradicts allegations that he was unable to respond to critical situations. First, Robert sought the help of his overlord, King Philip I of France, whose co-operation was vital if these frontier lords were to be controlled. William of Malmesbury interpreted the duke's action as a sign that he lacked any spirit to resist his brother. Malmesbury gave a very unflattering portrait of Philip, who was easily bought off by Rufus:

> Lazy as he was, and belching up his daily potations, the king was preparing with many a glutton's hiccough to take the field, when his lavish promises of help were forestalled by the coin of the English king. This melted him; he unbuckled his belt, and returned to the pleasures of the table.[149]

Duke Robert's lord was a much vilified figure at the end of the eleventh century. In particular, Philip I's amorous adventures scandalised the Church and resulted in his excommunication.[150] Far from being the result of a lack of spirit, Robert was taking reasonable steps to counter the actions of men destabilising a frontier in which the king as much as the duke of Normandy had interests.

As early as 24 April 1089, Robert was at Vernon on an expedition into France. There he confirmed a grant made to the cathedral of Bayeux.[151] With

---

145 *OV*, IV, pp. 182–3.
146 *WJ*, II, pp. 268–71.
147 Power, *Norman Frontier*, pp. 368–9.
148 WM, *GR*, I, pp. 548–9.
149 WM, *GR*, I, pp. 548–9.
150 WM, *GR*, I, pp. 596–7; *OV*, IV, pp. 260–5. Cf. G. Duby, *The Knight, the Lady and the Priest. The Making of Modern Marriage in Medieval France*, trans. Barbara Bray (London, 1984), pp. 3–21.
151 V. Bourienne, *Antiquus cartularius ecclesiæ Baiocensis ou Livre Noir*, Société de l'Histoire de Normandie, 2 vols. (Rouen, 1907–8), I, pp. 6–8; Haskins, *Norman Institutions*, no. 1, p. 66; *Regesta*, I, no. 308. A confirmation by Robert, duke of Normandy and count of Maine to St Mary of Bayeux, dated 'octavo kalendas maii, dum esset idem Robertus comes apud Vernonem

Robert at Vernon were Archbishop William of Rouen, the recently exiled
Bishop William of Durham, Abbot Gilbert of Saint-Étienne, Caen, as well as
a number of laymen, many of whom had connections with the duke or his
supporters: Roger of Ivri, *pincerna* or butler,[152] Engelramm fitz Ilbert,[153] and
William Bertrannus or Bertram,[154] Richard de Redvers,[155] Ranulf the *vicomte*
and his son Ranulf,[156] Hugo fitz Baldric,[157] Aigellus of the Cotentin may be
Nigellus or Niellus, son of Nigellus (II), *vicomte* of the Cotentin.[158] The list of
witnesses at Vernon is similar to that to another document of the same period
recording Duke Robert's consent to his uncle Odo's plan to restore the abbey
of Saint-Vigor, Bayeux.[159] The witnesses included Bishop Gilbert of Évreux,
Bishop William of Durham, Bishop Odo, Count William of Évreux,[160] Count
Robert of Meulan,[161] William de Breteuil,[162] Hugo de Vernon,[163] Richard de
Courcy,[164] *Engleramm fitz Ilbert*, William Crispin,[165] Robert de Montfort,[166]

... iturus in expeditionem in Franciam' ('the eighth of the kalends of May, while the same Robert
    was at Vernon ... about to go on campaign in France').

152   Roger of Ivry, from Ivry-la-Bataille, Eure, arr. Évreux, cant. Saint-André; L.C. Loyd, *The Origins of
    Some Anglo-Norman Families*, ed. C.T. Clay and D.C. Douglas, Harleian Society, 103 (1951), p. 52.
    Roger was a tenant of Hugh of Grandmesnil in England and married Hugh's daughter Adelina.
    Hugh's sons, Ivo and Aubrey supported Duke Robert during the quarrels with his father.

153   An Ingelran fitz Ilbert and his wife made a grant to the abbey of Saint-Étienne, Caen, between
    1079 and 1087: Musset, *Abbayes caennaises*, no. 18, p. 121 = Bates, *Acta*, no. 48; cf. *Fauroux*, no.
    197. Ingelran may have been the uncle of Ilbert de Lacy: see W.E. Wightman, *The Lacy Family in
    England and Normandy 1066–1194* (Oxford, 1966), pp. 26–45, 48–52, 55–8, and Sanders, *Baro-
    nies*, p. 138.

154   The Bertram family were lords of Bricquebec, Calvados; see *Fauroux*, no. 205, a confirmation
    witnessed by Duke Robert as a boy.

155   According to Wace, *Roman de Rou*, lines 9409–12, Richard de Redvers and his fief had been
    transferred from the duke to his brother Henry when the latter purchased the Cotentin.

156   He may be the son of Ranulf *vicomte* of Bayeux and nephew of Hugh of Avranches, earl of
    Chester: Musset, *Abbayes caennaises*, no. 18, p. 121 = Bates, *Acta*, no. 48, a record of grants to
    the abbey of Saint-Étienne, Caen, also witnessed by Duke Robert, dated 1079 x 1082 or 1079 x
    1087.

157   Hugh was a Domesday tenant-in-chief in Yorkshire and Lincolnshire and sheriff of York until
    c.1080. He lost his lands after he supported the rebellion against Rufus in 1088; *EYC*, ix, pp.
    72–3.

158   Bates, *Acta*, nos. 197, 214.

159   *Regesta*, I, no. 310. Names in italics also witnessed the document issued at Vernon.

160   William, count of Évreux (died 18 April 1118), later opposed Henry I, see *OV*, VI, pp. 34, 40, 65,
    146–8, 180, 188, 204; cf. P. Bauduin, *La première Normandie (Xe–XIe siècles). Sur les frontières de
    la haute Normandie: identité et construction d'une principauté* (Caen, 2004), pp. 333–7.

161   Robert I, count of Meulan (d.1118), was the son of Roger de Beaumont. Cf. Crouch, *The Beau-
    mont Twins*, pp. 3–4, 16.

162   William de Breteuil, who died 12 January 1103 at Bec, was the son of the Conqueror's close friend
    William fitz Osbern. The disputed succession to William's lands posed severe problems for Duke
    Robert, see *OV*, IV, pp. 198–202, 288–92.

163   Vernon, Eu, arr. Évreux.

164   Richard de Courcy was named as one of those who ravaged the lands of the abbey of Holy
    Trinity, Caen: Haskins, *Norman Institutions*, pp. 63–4. His son Robert married the daughter of
    Hugh of Grandmesnil. Richard de Courcy and Hugh opposed Robert de Bellême: *OV*, IV, pp.
    230–1 and n. 9.

165   William Crispin opposed Robert of Meulan's proposal to take the abbey of Bec into his own
    domain: 'On the Liberty of the Abbey of Bec', in Vaughn, *Abbey of Bec*, p. 135.

166   Robert de Montfort succeeded his father Hugh II c.1088. He was banished by Henry I in 1107

William the monk of Arques,[167] Serlo of Maton,[168] William de Molendinis,[169] and *William Bertram*. Many of these men had been Robert's supporters during his quarrels with his father, or had opposed Rufus the previous summer. Others were associated with Calvados and the Bessin in central Normandy, a region where Duke Robert perhaps could count on more support. Also noticeable are the family connections among those attending the duke. It may be that here were Robert's main supporters in 1089, but witness lists rarely if ever give explicit indications of the political relationships of those present and without corroboration can be misleading.[170]

As well as leading an army against the defectors, Robert tried other ways of strengthening the ducal presence in the Seine-Maritime region. By marrying his illegitimate daughter to Helias, son of Lambert of Saint-Saëns, he shrewdly recruited a man who remained loyal throughout his reign. As Robert's wife's marriage portion, Helias was given the castles of Arques and Bures and the surrounding region, 'so that Helias would resist his enemies and defend the county of Le Talou'.[171] Arques was a formidable fortress that had resisted the attempts of Robert's father to take it in the early 1050s. It was important that he had a trusted man in this strategically important region and Helias's unwavering loyalty demonstrated that, on this occasion, Robert was a shrewd judge of character.[172]

Around Easter 1089, Robert released his brother Henry from prison, perhaps reasoning that he needed all the help he could get against Rufus. However, Henry's imprisonment cannot have improved his opinion of Robert, but his resentment was hidden until he found an opportunity to repay his brother in kind.[173]

In the late summer or early autumn of 1089, Robert carried the fight against Rufus's supporters. The duke enlisted the support of his lord the king of France, following his father's example when facing similar difficulties in the duchy.[174] Philip I and Robert besieged Gerard de Gournay's castle of La Ferté-en-Bray. In return for his help, Robert granted Philip the castle of Gisors on the River Epte, which belonged to the cathedral of Rouen. This

---

and took service with Bohemond of Taranto in Apulia: *OV*, VI, pp. 100–1, and Green, *Henry I*, p. 100. His Suffolk lands passed to his sister Adelina who was married to Simon de Moulins, son of William de Moulins (see below).

167 William *monachus* is assumed to be the William monk of Arques noticed here.

168 Serlo de Maton may be Serlo de Mateom, from Mathieu, Calvados, arr. Caen, cant. Douvres: Loyd, *Origins*, p. 62.

169 William de Molendinis or Moulins-la-Marche (died 1100), married Duda, the daughter of Waleran of Meulan (d.1068): see Emily Zack Tabuteau, 'The Family of Moulins-la-Marche', *Medieval Prosopography*, 13.1 (1992), pp. 29–65.

170 Cf., however, Stephanie Mooers Christelow, '"Backers and Stabbers": Problems of Loyalty in Robert Curthose's Entourage', *Journal of British Studies*, 21 (1981), pp. 1–17.

171 *OV*, IV, pp. 182–3; this daughter was *de pelice* ('by a concubine').

172 *WP*, pp. 38–43; cf. *WJ*, II, pp. 102–5; cf. Power, *Norman Frontier*, p. 369.

173 *OV*, IV, pp. 164–5; cf. WM, *GR*, I, pp. 712–13.

174 *WP*, pp. 10–11.

brought protests from Archbishop William of Rouen.[175] In addition, before September, Robert mounted a successful siege of the castle of Eu.[176] By the end of the year, therefore, Robert had success against his brother's allies and had proved capable of organising and leading an army effectively. Robert's response to the machinations of his brother William not only demonstrated the duke's ability to muster an army and use it successfully, but also his diplomatic skills in recruiting aid from Philip I and securing the services of Helias of Saint-Saëns. Robert's problems were by no means at an end, for despite his successful campaign of the previous year there were rumours that Maine was on the verge of revolt. Once again, Robert's diplomatic skills were to be called into action.

Robert, Fulk of Anjou, and the Men of Maine, 1089–90

Robert's problems with Maine resurfaced when he was occupied with the defections among the nobles of Upper Normandy. Not only did Robert face his brother's machinations, he also fell seriously ill, although there are no details as to the nature of the ailment.[177] This was the first mention of Robert suffering any bodily infirmity. His general health seems to have been good and his constitution robust enough to cope with the extreme physical difficulties of the later expedition to Jerusalem. The fact that he lived into his early eighties also suggests that the duke was blessed with good health.[178]

When the men of Maine learned of Robert's difficulties in Normandy, they decided to throw off his lordship. Robert could not intervene in person and so sent envoys to Count Fulk of Anjou, his lord for Maine, asking him to come to Rouen. When Fulk arrived, he found Robert recovering and they began to negotiate the terms of their peace and friendship.[179]

Fulk agreed to subdue the Manceaux on Robert's behalf and act in all things as his ally, if the duke would arrange for him to marry Bertrade, the daughter of Simon de Montfort. Bertrade was in the care of her uncle, Count

---

[175] 'Notitia excommunicationis latæ in Guillelmum I Rotomagensem archiepiscopum ab Urbano II papa', originating at Fécamp, in *Gallia Christiana*, XI, Instrumenta, cols. 18–19.

[176] *Regesta*, I, no. 310 is dated 'anno ab Incarnatione Domini millesimo octogesimo nono, indictione duodecima, *secundo anno principatus Roberti Guillelmi regis filii ac Normanniae comitis dum idem Robertus esset ad obsidionem Auci ea die qua idem castrum sibi redditum est'* ('in the second year of the princely rule of Robert, son of King William and count of Normandy, while the same Robert was at the siege of Eu, and on the day when the said fortification surrendered to him'). Neither William of Malmesbury nor Orderic mentions this triumph for the duke. *ASC*, E, *s.a.* 1090, p. 101; Swanton, p. 225.

[177] *OV*, IV, pp. 184–5.

[178] It is possible that Robert's frequent bouts of inactivity reported by Orderic and others may have had their origins in a recurrent and debilitating medical condition. However, it seems more likely that Orderic's preoccupation with the duke's idleness has more to do with his generally negative opinion of Robert.

[179] *OV*, IV, pp. 184–5.

William of Évreux, and his wife Helwise. Robert passed on Fulk's request to William, who consulted his friends and carefully weighed the implications of such an alliance. Count William attended the ducal court and made it known that he felt that it was inappropriate for the twice-married Fulk to ask for the hand of the young virgin. William then complained that the girl was being used simply to advance the duke's own interests in Maine. The count of Évreux would not agree to the marriage unless Robert offered him adequate compensation. Count William wanted the lands of his uncle Ralph Tête d'Âne ('Ass-head'), and the restoration of Le Pont-Saint-Pierre and other properties to his nephew William of Breteuil.[180] William of Évreux stated that he could produce credible witnesses that Robert's father had unjustly appropriated Ralph Tête d'Âne's properties.[181] Robert, in turn, consulted his closest advisers, who were named here as Edgar the Ætheling, Robert de Bellême and William of Arques, a monk of Molesme.[182] Robert decided to agree to Count William's requests, deciding that the only property he was unable to hand over was Écouché, held by Gerard de Gournay.[183] This gave Count William and his kinsman a further reason to support the duke against an ally of William Rufus. Orderic rather disapprovingly noted that the overjoyed Fulk married the girl as his third wife, 'although the two former wives were still living'.[184] For his part, Fulk managed to contain matters in Maine for at least a year.

After detailing Robert's diplomatic success, Orderic launched into an extraordinary diatribe against sartorial fashions and outrageous styles of *coiffure* at the courts of the nobility. Count Fulk was partly to blame because to accommodate the bunions on his feet he had shoes made with long toes. The count's adapted footwear set a fashion and cobblers produced 'shoes like scorpions' tails which are commonly called pulley-shoes, and almost all, rich and poor alike, now demand shoes of this kind'. Orderic described the indecent hairstyles adopted by members of the court. 'Our wanton youth is sunk in effeminacy', he wailed, 'and courtiers fawning, seek the favours of women with every kind of lewdness'. Orderic associated decent behaviour with the days of Pope Gregory VII and William the Conqueror, but it is not clear whether his criticisms were levelled at the courts of Robert and William Rufus, or at practices prevalent when he was writing in the 1130s.[185]

In 1090, despite Robert's Angevin pact, Norman garrisons were driven

---

180 *OV*, IV, pp. 184–5; Count William wanted Bavent, Noyon-sur-Andelle, Gacé, Gravençon, Écouché. Ralph 'Ass-head' was so called 'in jest because of his huge head and shaggy hair'. For the relationship between William of Évreux and William of Breteuil, see *OV*, IV, p. 184, n. 2.

181 *OV*, II, pp. 118–21.

182 Hooper, 'Edgar the Ætheling', pp. 206–7.

183 *OV*, IV, pp. 186–7.

184 *OV*, IV, pp. 186–7 and n. 3 for Fulk's marriages.

185 *OV*, IV, pp. 186–93. Pauline Stafford, 'The Meanings of Hair in the Anglo-Norman World: Masculinity, Reform, and National Identity', in Mathilde van Dijk and Renée Nip, *Saints, Scholars, and Politicians. Gender as a Tool in Medieval Studies. Festschrift in honour of Anneke Mulder-Bakker on the occasion of her sixty fifth birthday*, Medieval Church Studies, 15 (Turnhout, 2005), pp. 153–71. I am grateful to Pauline Stafford for supplying me with a copy of her paper.

from castles in Maine and a new count was invited to take control. Messengers were sent to Italy to the sons of Azzo, marquess of Liguria, who had married the sister of Count Hugh IV of Maine.[186] The younger brother, Hugh of Este, claimed Maine and he was welcomed there by Geoffrey of Mayenne, Helias of La Flèche and other citizens and castellans. Bishop Hoël of Le Mans remained loyal to Robert of Normandy and excommunicated the rebels. He was eventually seized by Helias of La Flèche and imprisoned until Hugh was allowed to enter Le Mans. The capture of their bishop provoked a strong reaction from the clergy who demonstrated their opposition by removing holy images from public display, humiliating the relics of the saints, blocking the doors to churches with thorns and, after ceasing all services, going into institutional mourning.[187]

Support soon ebbed away from Hugh and Helias of La Flèche released the bishop, who took his case to Duke Robert. According to a Le Mans source, Robert was enjoying a rest and he was in no mood to launch another expedition. The bishop was instructed not to concede patronage and returned to Le Mans.[188] There he found Hugh, who demanded that the bishop receive the temporalities of his office from his hands. Bishop Hoël refused and after the clergy were stirred up against him he fled for safety to England and Rufus's court.[189] He may have accompanied the king to Normandy in January 1091 and in the spring he was reconciled with Hugh and his enemies in Maine.[190]

Meanwhile, the rebels had decided that Hugh was 'foolish, cowardly and idle, and had no idea how to hold the reins of high office'. Helias of La Flèche counselled Hugh to leave Maine, and his reference to the reconciliation of the sons of King William suggests that this was after February 1091. Hugh offered to sell the comital title and Helias put forward his claim. Hugh was paid off with ten thousand Manceaux shillings and, in July 1092, Helias assumed control, gaining the recognition of Bishop Hoël and Count Fulk.[191]

Duke Robert has been criticised for failing to respond more effectively to Helias's assumption of the comital office in Le Mans.[192] However, the political situation in Maine was much more fragmented than historians have allowed. The counts based in Le Mans did not hold sway over a unified polity, and the power of the many castellan families meant that imposing the sort of centralised authority envisaged by some modern historians was beyond even figures like Robert's father. The assumption has also been that Robert was idle

186 OV, IV, pp. 192–8.
187 For similar reactions, see Koziol, *Begging Pardon*, pp. 144 and 221–23, 263. Cf. P.J. Geary, 'The Humiliation of Saints', in *Living with the Dead in the Middle Ages* (Ithaca, 1994), pp. 95–115.
188 *Actus Pontificum*, pp. 385–6.
189 *Actus Pontificum*, pp. 387–90.
190 *Actus Pontificum*, pp. 391–2.
191 OV, IV, pp. 194–5, 196–9. R. Barton, 'Henry I, Count Helias of Maine, and the Battle of Tinchebray', in D.F. Fleming and Janet M. Pope, eds., *Henry I and the Anglo-Norman World. Studies in memory of C. Warren Hollister, The Haskins Society Journal Special Volume 17, 2006* (Woodbridge, 2007), pp. 63–90.
192 David, *Curthose*, p. 74.

at the time that the crisis of 1090–1091 erupted, but he had been active, first defending his own duchy against the machinations of his brothers, and then, as will be seen, spending the latter half of 1091 aiding Rufus in an expedition to Scotland. A combined force led by Robert and William Rufus might have had the sort of success that the duke achieved in 1088, but the king was unwilling to commit himself.

Duke Robert had been unable to intervene more directly in the affairs of Maine because he was forced to deal with Norman barons who continued to press their claims to properties lost during the Conqueror's reign. Robert was the unwilling heir to problems created by the policies of his father and he had to tread a careful path in order not to alienate other sections of the Norman baronage.

The Arrogance of Robert of Meulan

Between September 1088 and September 1089, Robert became entangled in a dispute over the castle of Ivry.[193] At the beginning of his reign the duke had restored the castle to William of Breteuil, whose family had lost control of Ivry during the reign of Robert's grandfather.[194] However, the castellan, Ascelin Goel, surrendered Ivry to Robert hoping to be granted possession. William of Breteuil was anxious to keep the castle and paid the duke 50,000 *livres*. Robert decided in favour of William of Breteuil and returned Ivry to him, whereupon Ascelin Goel was driven out. In the subsequent fighting, Amaury de Montfort was killed by William of Breteuil's men.[195] Amaury's death brought his brother Richard into alliance with Ascelin Goel and probably in February 1091 William of Breteuil was defeated and captured by his enemies. After Lent a truce was arranged by a group of frontier lords and William was ransomed. As part of the treaty Breteuil married his daughter Isabel to Ascelin, who was also given the castle of Ivry.[196]

Orderic associates the struggles at Ivry with a violent dispute between Gilbert de Laigle and Robert de Bellême in the winter of 1089/90. Duke Robert had given Gilbert the castle of Exmes as reward for military service in a move to counter Bellême ambitions. It provoked Robert de Bellême and he besieged the castle in the first week of January 1090.[197] Gilbert de Laigle and his nephew successfully resisted until the following year when Gilbert was killed by men loyal to Geoffrey, count of Mortagne. The incident was unfortunate not least because Count Geoffrey was also opposed to Bellême

---

193   *OV*, IV, pp. 198–203. This is another chapter of Book VIII which begins with a notice of widespread destruction in Normandy. Cf. J. Yver, 'Les châteaux-forts en Normandie jusqu'au milieu du XIIe siècle', *BSAN*, 53 (1955–6), pp. 28–115 at 66–9.
194   *OV*, IV, pp. 114–15; 198–9 and n. 4.
195   *OV*, IV, pp. 198–201.
196   *OV*, IV, pp. 202–3; *WJ*, II, pp. 228–9.
197   *OV*, IV, pp. 200–1.

ambitions in the Corbonnais. Peace was made through a marriage alliance between Geoffrey's daughter Juliana and Gilbert's nephew and namesake. The detail in Orderic's account was a result of his abbey's close interest in the affairs of the region.[198]

Orderic's account of Robert's reign leaves the impression that the duke was a man careless of his own honour and unwilling to confront threats to his authority. However, the same author's work provides evidence that Robert was ready to confront even the most powerful and bend them to his will. His treatment of Robert, count of Meulan is a case in point.

In 1090, the count, son of the Conqueror's old companion-in-arms, Roger de Beaumont, came to Duke Robert in Rouen.[199] He had been at William Rufus's court and was evidently confident of the king's support. Meulan insolently demanded the castle at Ivry. Duke Robert pointed out that Ivry had been fairly exchanged for Brionne by Meulan's father. At this Count Robert refused to accept the exchange and swore by Saint-Nicaise that unless the duke restored Ivry, he would regret it.[200] Understandably, the duke became angry and ordered the imprisonment of Robert de Meulan. In addition, Robert son of Baldwin de Meules was given custody of Brionne.[201] However, there was more to this incident than Orderic reported.

A tract *De libertate Beccensis monasterii* ('On the Liberty of the Monastery of Bec') produced after 1136 suggests that Duke Robert's anger against Robert of Meulan was connected with the latter's attempt to gain control of the abbey of Bec, which lies near Brionne in the valley of the Risle.[202] Robert of Meulan sent messengers to Abbot Anselm and offered to add to the monastery's possessions if it passed into his ownership. The monks of Bec sent to the duke and made him aware of the count of Meulan's approach. Robert exploded in anger:

'By God's miracles (*per mirabilia dei*), what does this mean? What sort of madness is this I hear? Does the count of Meulan want to snatch my abbey from me? Does this traitor wish to take from me by stealth the one thing I love beyond all else? By God's miracles, he won't enjoy the gift I made him for long!'[203]

When William Crispin, William of Breteuil and Roger de Bienfaîte heard of Robert of Meulan's plan, they threatened to remove their patronage from the

---

198 *OV*, IV, pp. 200–3; Gilbert de Laigle's body was buried at Saint-Sulpice-sur-Risle by Bishop Gilbert of Évreux and Abbot Serlo of Saint-Évroul.

199 Sally N. Vaughn, *Anselm of Bec and Robert of Meulan. The Innocence of the Dove and the Wisdom of the Serpent* (Berkeley, CA, 1987), pp. 96–102.

200 St Nicasius was a fifth-century martyred bishop of Reims.

201 *OV*, IV, pp. 204–5.

202 'De libertate Beccensis Monasterii', in J. Mabillon, ed., *Annales Ordinis Sancti Benedicti* (Paris, 1745), V, pp. 601–5; the tract is translated in Sally N. Vaughn, *The Abbey of Bec and the Anglo-Norman State, 1034–1136* (Woodbridge, 1981), pp. 134–43. The references here are to Vaughn's translation.

203 'De libertate', p. 135.

monks of Bec and censured the duke for allowing Brionne, 'the key to his province', to pass from ducal control.[204]

A few days later, Count Robert arrived at Bec in person throwing the monks into a panic until Anselm intervened. Anselm pointed out that Meulan's plan would not succeed because the duke had no intention of relinquishing his protection of Bec. The castle of Brionne was also in Duke Robert's gift and it might be taken back at any moment. Anselm advised the count of Meulan to hear the duke's decision for himself. The monks of Bec made sure that they reached the ducal court before the count of Meulan and, forewarned, the duke teased Robert of Meulan, asking how things stood between him and Bec. The count dissembled and Duke Robert challenged him, barely able to speak for rage:

> 'You lie in your teeth! By God's miracles you are utterly deceived if you expect me to be so stupid. Why would I want to give you my abbey?'

Shortly afterwards, the duke removed Brionne from Meulan's custody, giving it to Roger de Bienfaîte.[205]

This episode has been explored in terms of the personal confrontation between Robert of Meulan and Abbot Anselm and as an example of the principle of ecclesiastical liberty being maintained against an acquisitive lord.[206] But it also presents the duke's response to a direct challenge to his authority by one of the duchy's most powerful families. It is useful as a guide to the etiquette of the court and the necessity for courtiers to play their part according to 'the rules of the game'. The first thing to draw attention to is the fact that, for the author of the *De libertate Beccensis*, the ducal court was the place to settle the dispute between the monks and Robert of Meulan. Both parties looked to Robert for a judgement.[207]

Robert of Meulan's behaviour was a challenge to ducal authority and Duke Robert could not afford to let it go, even if it inevitably meant taking on Roger de Beaumont, one of his father's leading barons. By 1090, Roger was an elderly man, but he was forced to draw on all of his experience to mend the rift with the duke and rescue his son.[208] Roger's attempts to secure the release of his son provide an illuminating picture of the ducal court and of the techniques employed to mollify an offended lord.

At first Roger de Beaumont affected disinterest in his son's folly and for a number of days 'concealed his mental distress under a cheerful face.'[209] Under the gaze of his fellow courtiers, it was important for Roger not to betray

---

[204] 'De libertate', p. 136.
[205] 'De libertate', pp. 136–7; cf. *OV*, IV, pp. 204–5, 210–11. Roger de Bienfaîte and Robert, son of Baldwin, were both descendants of Gilbert, lord of Brionne: Vaughn, *Abbey of Bec*, p. 162, n. 15.
[206] Vaughn, *Anselm of Bec and Robert of Meulan*, pp. 106–16.
[207] A number of documents for Bec, issued in Robert's name, confirmed or witnessed by him, may belong to this period: Haskins, *Norman Institutions*, p. 68, nos. 6–12.
[208] *WP*, pp. 178–9.
[209] *OV*, IV, pp. 204–5.

his hand too quickly. When the duke's temper had cooled, Roger prepared the ground by sending gifts before appearing before him and greeting him respectfully. Roger thanked the duke for punishing his son's pride 'with a severity becoming in a prince' and said that he would have done so himself if the feebleness of old age had not prevented him. He admitted that his son had often ignored his advice and he certainly 'needed a lesson in how to speak to his lords and seniors'.[210] Even if Roger's words were Orderic's, this suggests that clashes between father and son were not restricted to the ducal/royal family.

Gradually Roger placated Duke Robert and gained his trust. Roger reminded the duke that as one of his father's closest and most loyal counsellors he was worthy of respect: 'God forbid that now I am grey with age, I should try my hand at deceits, which hitherto I have loathed and have utterly shunned from my earliest years.'[211] Robert responded positively and explained that he had not imprisoned Roger's son out of contempt for the old man, 'but because of his foolish pride and rash presumption with which he made threatening and importunate demands of me'. Robert thus drew an explicit contrast between the respectful behaviour of the father and the insulting *hauteur* of the son. Roger promised that if his son were to be freed he would render the duke faithful service. Duke Robert was sufficiently mollified to allow Robert de Meulan to leave the court in the custody of his father.

Robert had demonstrated that his authority as duke was not to be challenged. Roger de Beaumont had to work hard and patiently to release his son. Not long after the reconciliation the duke agreed to return Brionne, but the castellan, Robert de Meules, was reluctant to turn it over to the Beaumonts. Instead his claim to the castle was asserted and Robert was forced to attack a stronghold that his father had subdued only after a protracted siege. Encouraged by Roger, Robert led the assault during Pentecost in June 1090. The decisive factor was the use of incendiary arrows which, in the dry summer heat, set fire to the wooden shingles on the roof of the great hall. The defenders had no option but to throw themselves on the duke's mercy. Even Orderic's generally disapproving attitude to Robert's actions could not stifle his admiration:

> So between the ninth hour and sunset Duke Robert captured Brionne, which his father William, even with the help of Henry, King of France, had scarcely been able to subdue in three years, when Guy son of Reginald the Burgundian made it his centre of resistance after the battle of Val-ès-Dunes.[212]

The duke restored Brionne to Roger de Beaumont and compensated Robert de Meules by granting him his ancestral fief. Robert de Meules had allies within the ducal retinue and they worked on his behalf and, just as Roger de

210 *OV*, IV, pp. 204–5.
211 *OV*, IV, pp. 206–7.
212 *OV*, IV, pp. 210–11.

Beaumont had done, reminded Duke Robert of the Conqueror's affection for the family.

The dispute over the castles of Ivry and Brionne tested Duke Robert's resolve against some of the greatest barons of his duchy. He had shown himself ready and able to defend his honour and authority. In military affairs, Robert had shown himself to be superior to his father, even in the estimation of one of his harshest critics. To cap it all, he had even managed to bring about a reconciliation of the parties concerned. Robert has been criticised for allowing former ducal castles to pass into the hands of the nobility, but in most cases the nobles concerned had long-standing claims. Robert did not have the resources of his father and had less opportunity to ignore the demands of those on whom he relied for recognition. Despite his success in the affair of Brionne, a few months later Robert almost lost control of his capital, Rouen, partly because of his brother William's machinations.

Conan's Leap, November 1090

Rufus undermined Robert's control of Rouen by exploiting already existing rivalries among the city's merchants.[213] In November 1090, conflict broke out between the pro-ducal Calloenses, the smaller faction, and the Pilatenses who had accepted Rufus's bribes.[214] The anti-ducal faction was led by Conan, son of Gilbertus Pilatus, whom Orderic described as the wealthiest man in the city, and one who maintained a retinue of men-at-arms. Conan's wealth allowed him to oppose the duke openly and he agreed to turn the city and the duke over to the king. Conan met opposition in Rouen but, fuelled by Rufus's bribes, he was a serious threat to Robert's regime. The loss of the seat of ducal dynasty would have been a severe blow to Robert's prestige as well as denying access to the economic resources of the city and its port.[215] Conan and his co-conspirators enlisted the support of the king's men, who were based at Gournay.[216]

Robert called upon the assistance of William of Évreux, Robert de Bellême, William of Breteuil, Gilbert de Laigle and other loyal vassals.[217] Robert also made a *foedus amiciciæ* ('treaty of friendship') with his brother Henry, who was to take a leading role in the defence of Rouen. Since his release, Henry

213 OV, IV, pp. 220–9. Cf. C. Warren Hollister, 'The Rouen Riot and Conan's Leap', *Peritia*, 10 (1996), pp. 341–50, and Green, *Henry I*, pp. 29–31, 314–15. S.D. White, 'The Politics of Anger', in Rosenwein, *Anger's Past*, pp. 127–52 at 141.
214 Haskins, *Norman Institutions*, pp. 91–2; cf. *Regesta*, II, no. 1002.
215 D. Bates, 'Rouen from 900–1204: From Scandinavian Settlement to Angevin "Capital"', in J. Stratford, ed., *Medieval Art, Architecture and Archaeology at Rouen* (British Archaeological Association Conference Transactions, 1993), pp. 1–11; B. Gauthiez, 'Paris, un Rouen capétien? (Développements comparés de Rouen et Paris sous les règnes de Henri II et Philippe Auguste)', *ANS*, 16 (1993), pp. 117–36.
216 WM, *GR*, I, pp. 712–13; some of Rufus's troops were already in the city.
217 OV, IV, pp. 220–3: 'amicos in quibus confidebat'.

had unsuccessfully sought favour from William Rufus and, after growing tired of the king's empty promises, returned to Normandy. William of Malmesbury suggests that by occupying Avranches Henry managed to force Robert to come to terms. The fact that Robert had to negotiate a formal pact suggests that neither brother fully trusted the other without it.

On 3 November 1090, Gilbert de Laigle entered Rouen from the south as Reginald of Warenne and three hundred men attacked the western, Cauchoise, gate.[218] The whole city was thrown into confusion and from the castle Robert, Henry and a troop of soldiers attacked the rebels. The duke was in the thick of the fighting, demonstrating his personal bravery and his abilities as a leader in a crisis. However, his supporters feared that he might be wounded or suffer an ignoble death in the chaos.[219] Taking their advice, he withdrew into the suburb of Malpalu where he was welcomed by loyal citizens. It was because Robert was in danger of being killed in the confused street fighting that his supporters urged him to retire to a place of safety. There was little point in fighting for the duke if he was to fall ignobly in the first skirmishes. At no stage do the sources suggest that Robert's personal bravery was in doubt.[220] Robert then took a boat across the Seine to Émendreville to join his counsellor William of Arques, monk of Molesme. Together they awaited the outcome in the priory of Notre-Dame-du-Pré.[221]

Led by Gilbert de Laigle and Henry, the citizens loyal to the duke defeated the revolt.[222] Conan and many others were captured and the king's men fled. With his allies securely in control, Robert returned to the city to deal with the rebels. The duke was inclined to treat them leniently and exhibit *clemencia*, a key quality of rulership. However, the barons, perhaps with a view to putting the upstart burgesses in their place, insisted on harsher punishments.[223] William of Breteuil reaped his reward for supporting the duke by

---

[218] Kathleen Thompson, 'The Lords of Laigle: Ambition and Insecurity on the Borders of Normandy', *ANS*, 18 (1995), pp. 177–99. Reginald/Rainald de Warenne was the younger son of William I de Warenne, and inherited the possessions of his mother Gundreda in Flanders. He also supported Robert against Henry I in 1105. C.P. Lewis, 'Warenne, William (I) de, First Earl of Surrey (d.1088)', *Oxford DNB*. For the topography of Rouen, see B. Gauthiez, 'Hypothèses sur la fortification de Rouen au onzième siècle. Le donjon, la tour de Richard II et l'enceinte de Guillaume,' *ANS*, 14 (1992), pp. 61–76 at 74.

[219] *OV*, IV, pp. 222–3.

[220] *OV*, IV, pp. 224–5. Cf. Hollister, 'Rouen Riot', p. 345; Barlow, *William Rufus*, p. 275.

[221] William the monk witnessed two charters of Duke Robert, *Regesta*, I, nos. 308, 310, and was one of Robert's close counsellors ('precipui ducis consilarii') in *OV*, IV, pp. 186–7. Robert rewarded the monks of Notre-Dame, a priory of Bec, by confirming gifts made by his parents to the church of Émendreville and adding the tithe of the hay in his park at Rouen; cf. Haskins, *Norman Institutions*, no. 7, p. 68; *Regesta*, I, no. 327. The charter was issued after the reconciliation between Robert and William Rufus as it allows either of them to elevate the priory into an independent abbey, if they so wished, without opposition from the monks. Hollister ('Conan's Leap', p. 346, n. 17) amends the date of Robert's charter to the monks of Notre-Dame to 6 February 1091, rather than 1092.

[222] *OV*, IV, pp. 224–5.

[223] *OV*, IV, pp. 226–7 and n. 1. Cf. WM, *GR*, I, pp. 710–11. This may be a case of applying different rules to the burgess class; J. Gillingham, '1066 and the Introduction of Chivalry into England', in

holding William, son of Ansgar, one of the richest men in city, for a ransom of £3000.[224] The men of Bellême and Laigle also carried off numbers of citizens in chains, stripping them of all their possessions 'as if they had been foreign enemies'.[225] But most shocking was the fate of the ringleader Conan.

Robert was content to imprison Conan in fetters, but Henry planned a more sadistic end for the rebel.[226] He led him to the top of the tower at Rouen, from where they could see the whole of the city and its surrounding region. Henry addressed his prisoner sardonically:

'Admire, Conan, the beauty of the country you tried to conquer. Away to the south there is a beautiful hunting region, wooded and well-stocked with beasts of the chase. See how the river Seine, full of fish, laps the walls of Rouen and daily brings in ships laden with merchandise of many kinds. On the other side, see the fair and populous city, with its ramparts and churches, and town buildings, which has rightly dominated the whole of Normandy from the earliest days.'[227]

Trembling, Conan admitted his guilt and pleaded for mercy, promising faithful service. He offered all the gold and silver he could find as a ransom, but Henry swore on the soul of his mother that traitors should not be allowed to live.

Then Conan, groaning aloud, cried in a loud voice, 'For the love of God, allow me to confess my sins.' But Henry, stern avenger of his brother's wrong, trembled with rage and, scorning the wretch's prayers, thrust him violently with both hands, hurling him down from the window of the tower. Shattered by this frightful fall, he was dead before he reached the ground. His body was then tied to a horse's tail and dragged shamefully through all the streets of Rouen as a warning to traitors.[228]

When Orderic was writing, in the mid-1130s, the place was still known as 'Conan's Leap'. The account suggests that Henry lost control and there is certainly the implication that Henry took a sadistic pleasure in defenestrating Conan. It might also have been an instance of Henry building up his own reputation as a man to be feared. William of Malmesbury wrote that Henry caught Conan off guard and that the act was much more malicious and less orderly and judicial than Orderic suggests.[229]

The *post mortem* treatment of the traitor's body was the humiliation of an enemy's corpse and an horrific warning to others. Henry had not granted Conan a 'good death' even though the man had pleaded to be allowed to confess his sins. The practice of *damnatio memoriæ*, inherited from the clas-

---

G. Garnett and J. Hudson, eds., *Law and Government in Medieval England and Normandy. Essays in honour of Sir James Holt* (Cambridge, 1994), pp. 31–55.

224   *OV*, IV, pp. 226–7; cf. Hollister, 'Conan's Leap', p. 349, n. 28.

225   Orderic's comment about the treatment of foreign prisoners is worth noting, as it suggests that 'chivalric' behaviour towards captives might only apply to fellow countrymen.

226   WM, *GR*, I, pp. 712–13.

227   *OV*, IV, pp. 224–5. Translation adapted.

228   *OV*, IV, pp. 226–7.

229   WM, *GR*, I, pp. 712–13.

sical world, denied individuals memorialisation. It might also extend to a ban on prayers designed to help the soul towards salvation.

Henry justified his treatment of Conan by protesting that it was a fitting punishment for a man 'who has done homage on oath'. There is a whiff of hypocrisy here given his policy of oscillating his fidelity between his brothers, 'supporting or opposing either as they happened to deserve'.[230] In the end, this brutal act may have alienated his brother, for Malmesbury tells us that Robert drove Henry out of Rouen and forced him to retire to the Cotentin. Malmesbury saw Robert's decision to expel Henry as due to the duke's 'inconstant temper', but it is more likely that he considered that his brother's action had overstepped the bounds of what was acceptable and threatened his policy of bringing about the necessary reconciliation in Rouen.[231]

Orderic rounded off his account of the revolt at Rouen not by celebrating Duke Robert's victory but by launching instead into a comparison of Normandy and Babylon. The duchy which had once conquered England was now torn apart by evil and violence. Normandy was plagued by the four passions of fear and greed, sorrow and joy.[232]

'In war she rode armed as knight': Women and Violence in the County of Évreux

William Rufus had gained little from his vast outlay of bribes and the English bore the huge cost of his policies in the autumn of 1090.[233] Nevertheless, there was another opportunity for Rufus to exploit divisions between Robert's vassals almost as soon as the upheavals at Rouen had ended. A constant threat was that essentially local disputes between members of the Norman nobility could escalate through Rufus's intervention. For a noble disappointed with his treatment at the ducal court the king was able to offer his encouragement and, more often than not, his gold. The struggles between the Conqueror's sons strained notions of honour and fidelity among the Norman nobility.

In the county of Évreux, a violent dispute broke out between Count William and Ralph of Tosny (Conches).[234] Isabel of Conches made some abusive comments about Helwise, wife of the count of Évreux, who persuaded her husband to defend her honour.[235] The incident gave the monk Orderic a chance to indulge in some misogynist invective about the dangers of women dominating their husbands. Of the two women, Orderic preferred Isabel of Conches, who was generous, daring and had a good sense of humour. Helwise,

---

230 WM, *GR*, I, pp. 710–11 and cf. 714–15; 'he was faithful and helpful to each [brother] in turn'.
231 WM, *GR*, I, pp. 710–11.
232 *OV*, IV, pp. 226–9.
233 *ASC*, E, *s.a.* 1090, p. 101; Swanton, p. 225.
234 William and Ralph were both related to the ducal house: see the table in Green, 'Robert Curthose Reassessed', pp. 96–7.
235 *OV*, IV, pp. 212–13: 'pro quibusdam contumeliosis uerbis irata est'.

on the other hand, although clever and persuasive, was also cruel and avaricious.[236] Isabel rode to war armed as a knight and she was as courageous as the warlike heroine Camilla in Virgil's *Aeneid*.[237]

After his lands had been plundered by the men of Évreux, Ralph of Conches complained to his lord Duke Robert of the injuries being done. The duke would not intervene, so Ralph sent envoys to Rufus and promised to become his man. Rufus was delighted with the offer and sent Stephen of Aumâle, Gerard de Gournay and others to his assistance. No reason is given for Robert's reluctance to support Ralph and it may simply be that Ralph saw his best interests as being served by renouncing his fidelity to his lord.

Orderic's chronology of the struggle is difficult to disentangle and he may have telescoped events that actually unfolded in a more sporadic manner and over a longer period. The quarrel between Count William and Ralph of Conches may have begun before the reconciliation between Duke Robert and Rufus in February 1091, when, Orderic tells us, Ralph of Tosny's lands passed into the king's hands.[238] In November 1091, William of Évreux and his nephews, William of Breteuil and Richard de Montfort, besieged Conches. Richard was struck down in the act of seizing the possessions of the monastery of Saint-Pierre-de-Conches and died the same day. He was mourned by both sides as he was related to Isabel of Conches as well as to Count William.[239] After a second engagement during which Ralph of Conches captured William of Breteuil, peace was made. William of Breteuil gave his uncle £3000 in ransom and made Ralph's son, Roger, his heir. William of Évreux also appointed his nephew Roger his heir to the comital office.[240]

Defusing the Tensions:
the Siege of Courcy, January 1091

It was Duke Robert's failure to deal with Robert de Bellême that earned him the most opprobrium from Orderic. Nevertheless there is evidence that the duke was capable of managing the lord of Bellême and to a degree defusing the tension his actions created. Operating from the fortified town of Fourches, Robert de Bellême built Château Gontier from which he tried to bring the region of Houlme under his control. Bellême's activities brought organised resistance by local magnates led by Hugh of Grandmesnil and Richard de Courcy, whose families were allied through the marriage of Richard's son

---

[236] *OV*, IV, pp. 212–13. Cf. Marjorie Chibnall, 'Women in Orderic Vitalis', *HSJ*, 2 (1990), pp. 105–21; Jean A. Truax, 'Anglo-Norman Women at War: Valiant Soldiers, Prudent Strategists or Charismatic Leaders?' in Kagay, *The Circle of War*, pp. 111–25.

[237] *OV*, IV, pp. 214–15.

[238] *OV*, IV, pp. 214–15, nn. 4, 6.

[239] *OV*, IV, pp. 216–17.

[240] *OV*, IV, pp. 218–19, n. 5. Roger de Conches died soon after.

Robert to Hugh's daughter Rohais.[241] Hugh rallied his wider family against Bellême, who also brought in his brothers Roger and Arnulf for support.[242]

The effective opposition to Robert de Bellême forced him to ask the duke for assistance. In January 1091, Duke Robert besieged Courcy 'but he spared his native barons and did not press the besieged closely'. Both sides took prisoners and ransomed them and the elderly Hugh of Grandmesnil, although fighting himself, sent messengers to Duke Robert reminding him of the service he had done his father and asking why he was being attacked. Hugh publicly acknowledged Duke Robert as his lord and offered him 200 *livres* to withdraw just for a day so that his men could attack Bellême's forces. Hugh pointed out that his men were reluctant to attack the ducal army and that Bellême was relying on this fact to keep the besieged in check. Hugh's strategy, reminiscent of Roger de Beaumont's, worked and the duke turned a blind eye while supplies of arms and food were brought into the castle.

Duke Robert was in a difficult position because both parties in the conflict acknowledged his lordship. His solution was to negotiate with both sides and try to minimise the effects of the fighting. His policy did not meet with Orderic's approval, but it helped to defuse the situation. Attempts were also made by Bishop Gerard of Sées to end the conflict, but he died on 23 January. In the end the siege of Courcy fizzled out when news arrived that William Rufus had landed in Normandy.[243]

Rufus in Normandy, January to August 1091

Although Rufus had bribed some of the nobles of Upper Normandy to desert Duke Robert, and struggles for local supremacy disrupted other areas, Robert had responded successfully and managed to retain significant support. By the end of 1090, Rufus's fiscal exactions in England were leading to hardship so he decided to increase the pressure on his brother. At the end of January 1091, Rufus landed in Normandy, when his brother was besieging Courcy. Orderic suggests that almost all the great barons of Normandy abandoned Robert and flocked to Rufus, 'offering him gifts in the hope of receiving greater ones'.[244] Rufus's presence at Eu encouraged men from Brittany, France and Flanders to pay court and offer their services as mercenaries in the future, but rather than augment the ranks of his forces, they returned home, declaring that he was a prince beyond compare.[245] There is no record of any fighting and it is possible that before the king could organise a campaign, Duke Robert enlisted

---

241 *OV*, IV, pp. 228–31; cf. M. Hagger, 'Kinship and Identity in Eleventh-century Normandy: the Case of Hugh de Grandmesnil, c. 1040–1098', *JMH*, 32 (2006), pp. 212–30 at 226.
242 *OV*, IV, pp. 230–1.
243 *OV*, IV, pp. 234–5.
244 *OV*, IV, pp. 236–37. Rufus was in Dover on 27 January 1091: *Regesta*, I, no. 315. *ASC*, E, *s.a.* 1091 [1090], p. 101; Swanton, p. 226. Cf. *JW*, III, *s.a.* 1091, pp. 56–9.
245 *OV*, IV, pp. 236–7 and n. 3. For the recruitment of mercenaries, see Mason, *William II*, p. 87.

the help of Philip of France.[246] Faced with the prospect of his brother's forces being supported by the French, Rufus agreed to Philip's mediation and the brothers met in peace.[247]

In February 1091 a formal agreement between Robert and his brother was reached at Rouen.[248] Perhaps as compensation, or as a sweetener, Rufus made substantial but unspecified gifts to his brother. In return Robert agreed to hand over the county of Eu, which Count William surrendered with his castles, Aumâle, the lands of Gerard de Gournay and those of Ralph of Conches. In addition, the abbey of Fécamp and the abbey of Mont-Saint-Michel, together with Cherbourg, passed into Rufus's hands. The cession of the abbey of Mont-Saint-Michel and Cherbourg, at either end of the Cotentin peninsula, may have been an attempt to challenge Henry's influence in the area. Robert also promised to leave the king's men in possession of their castles in Normandy.[249]

For his part Rufus would return their English lands to Robert's adherents. The only one of Robert's supporters who seems to have suffered was Edgar the Ætheling, who was deprived of the 'honour' the duke had given him and expelled from Normandy. Edgar made his way to Scotland and the court of his sister Queen Margaret and her husband Malcolm III.[250]

Rufus promised to grant Robert land in England, perhaps to balance the lands the king held in his brother's *regnum*, and assist him in the imposition of his lordship over any castles still resisting him in Normandy and in Maine. Finally, the king and the duke each made the other the heir to his lands, should they die without legitimate offspring. This is perhaps the most significant point in the agreement. For perhaps the first time, Robert had a recognised and unequivocal claim to the English throne.[251] The agreement was ratified by the oaths of twelve barons from each side, who were to act as

---

246 WM, *GR*, I, pp. 548–9; Malmesbury suggests that peace was organised in advance of the king's arrival in Normandy.

247 *WJ*, II, pp. 206–7; *OV*, IV, pp. 236–7. A Durham source noted that Bishop William of Durham was restored to Rufus's favour by assisting the king's men when they were besieged and on the point of being captured. It is possible that Bishop William acted as intermediary in the negotiations between the brothers. See *Symeon of Durham*, Libellus de Exordio atque procursu istius, hoc est Dunhelmensis Ecclesie. *Tract on the Origins and Progress of this the Church of Durham*, ed. and trans. D. Rollason (Oxford, 2000), pp. 242–3, and H.S. Offler, 'William of St Calais, First Norman Bishop of Durham', *TAASDN*, 10 (1950), pp. 258–79 at 273.

248 *OV*, IV, pp. 236; *WJ*, II, pp. 204–6, where Robert of Torigny says that the peace was concluded at Caen through the agency of Philip of France. It may have then been ratified at Rouen by the brothers. On the treaties of Rouen and Winchester (Alton, 1101), see N. Strevett, 'The Anglo-Norman Aristocracy under Divided Lordship: a Social and Political Study', unpublished Ph.D. dissertation, University of Glasgow, 2005, pp. 182–209. I am very grateful to Neil Strevett for allowing me to consult his doctoral dissertation.

249 Judith A. Green, 'Fécamp et les rois anglo-normands', *Tabularia 'Études'*, 2 (2002), pp. 9–18.

250 *ASC*, E, *s.a.* 1091, p. 102; Swanton, p. 226; *JW*, III, *s.a.* 1091, pp. 58–9. There is no indication as to what constituted Edgar's 'honour' in Normandy: Hooper, 'Edgar the Ætheling', p. 207.

251 *ASC*, E, *s.a.* 1091, p. 102; Swanton, p. 226; *JW*, III, *s.a.* 1091, pp. 58–9; WM, *GR*, I, pp. 548–51; *WJ*, II, pp. 206–7; *OV*, IV, pp. 236–7. On Robert's claim, see J.C. Holt, 'Politics and Property in Early Medieval England', *P&P*, 57 (1972), pp. 3–52; 65 (1974), pp. 130–2. Reprinted in *idem*, *Colonial England*, pp. 113–59, at Appendix 2, pp. 149–51.

a tribunal in the event of complaints from either of the parties.[252] To a large extent this was a recognition of the stalemate in Normandy, but with the concessions to Robert's supporters and the king's undertaking to assist his brother in imposing his lordship in the duchy and in Maine this pact was hardly the humiliation for Robert that some supposed.[253]

There are signs that the brothers were co-operating after peace was made. Two documents in the name of Robert and his brother William referring to an exchange of land between a certain William de Tournebu and Abbot Gilbert of Saint-Étienne at Caen have been assigned to this period.[254] The fact that the abbot secured confirmation of the exchange from both parties may indicate a recognition that the brothers were exercising a sort of condominium in Normandy. These documents have been associated with an investigation into the ducal customs of Normandy that was conducted through an inquest held on 18 July 1091. The results of this inquest, known as the *Consuetudines et Iusticie*, may indeed have been drawn up in this year and the political context might indeed have prompted the inquiry. However, it has been suggested that this inquest might be assigned to the summer of 1096 in advance of William Rufus's assumption of sole responsibility for the governance of Normandy.[255]

Conspicuously absent from the agreement was Henry. Robert and William excluded him from inheritance in England and Normandy, although the fact that neither of the elder brothers had a legitimate son may have been some encouragement for him. The sources associate a rebellion by Henry with the terms of this treaty. Robert of Torigny stated that Robert and Rufus deliberately joined forces against Henry, rather than giving him the honourable life befitting the son of a king.[256] Following the terms of their pact, Robert and William collected an army and marched towards the county of Maine.[257] However, Henry had begun to make trouble in western Normandy, raising a force of Bretons and Normans and fortifying Coutances and Avranches, from which to make attacks on the king's lands.[258]

---

252 *ASC*, E, *s.a.* 1091, p. 102; Swanton, p. 226; *JW*, III, *s.a.* 1091, pp. 58–9. E.J. King, 'Dispute Settlement in Anglo-Norman England', *ANS*, 14 (1992), pp. 115–30, and D. Crouch, 'A Norman *conventio* and Bonds of Lordship in the Middle Ages', in G. Garnett and J. Hudson, eds., *Law and Government in Medieval England and Normandy. Essays in honour of Sir James Holt* (Cambridge, 1994), pp. 299–324.

253 *WJ*, II, pp. 206–7; in the 1140s, Robert of Torigny saw the pact as 'shameful and injurious' for Robert, while acknowledging that the situation had arisen due to the infidelity of duke's men.

254 D. Bates, 'Four Recently Discovered Norman Charters', *AN*, 45 (1995), pp. 35–48 at 39–40.

255 Haskins, 'The Norman *Consuetudines et Iusticie* of William the Conqueror', in *idem, Norman Institutions*, Appendix D, pp. 277–84. Haskins, *Norman Institutions*, p. 278, dated the inquest to 18 July 1091 'as the only year in the July of which these princes were in Normandy and in friendly relations'.

256 *WJ*, II, pp. 204–7.

257 *WM*, *GR*, I, pp. 550–1. Malmesbury suggests that Rufus's arrival in Normandy in 1091 was connected with the proposed expedition to Maine.

258 *JW*, III, *s.a.* 1091, pp. 58–9; *OV*, IV, pp. 250–1.

It is possible that Henry's occupation of western Normandy had led to ravaging in the Cotentin and the neighbouring Bessin.[259] Henry is specifically named as one of those who abstracted property from the nuns of La Sainte-Trinité in Caen. A list detailing the despoliation of the estates of the convent has been cited as evidence of Robert's failure to ensure good government in the duchy. It has been pointed out that many of those named as attacking the convent's property were related to the original donors. The seizures may represent a change of mind by the donors' relatives. The scale of the depredations may also have been exaggerated, as the convent's building programme between c. 1090 and c. 1120 does not suggest that it was struggling for funds. In short, the evidence from Caen has been used to reinforce a negative estimation of Robert's regime, rather than explored in its own context.[260]

The first test of his elder brothers' alliance was, therefore, the elimination of the threat posed by Henry. The army intended for Maine thus diverted towards the base of the Cotentin peninsula. Henry gathered troops from Brittany as well as Normandy and fortified Coutances, Avranches and other castles ready for his brothers' attack. However, his allies, including Earl Hugh of Chester, decided that their best interests lay in capitulating to the king. Henry retreated to the island monastery of Mont-Saint-Michel and for the whole of Lent (26 February to 12 April), 1091, he was besieged by Robert and William. Wace, who preserved many traditions from western Normandy, recorded that Rufus blockaded Henry from Avranches, while Robert was a few kilometres away at Genêts opposite the island.[261]

There were frequent skirmishes between knights of the opposing sides and Rufus was almost killed during one of these engagements. He was unhorsed by one of Henry's knights and had to shout out that he was the king to stop the knight striking him. So impressed was Rufus by his opponent that he recruited him.[262] As the siege progressed, Henry and his men began to run short of water and asked for a truce in order to collect supplies. Rufus was reluctant to allow the request, reasoning that this would only prolong the siege, but Robert was inclined to be lenient and sent his younger brother a barrel of wine. He granted the truce so that Henry's men could secure a supply of water. This was the last straw for the king and he threatened to abandon the siege. Robert justified his actions by replying memorably, 'Good

---

259 WM, *GR*, I, pp. 712–13. *OV*, IV, pp. 220–1, prefaces the account of the Rouen revolt by describing Henry's energetic government of the Cotentin: 'Eodem tempore Constantinienses Henricus clito strenue regebat.' However, 'strenue' simply means that Henry was very active: it does not indicate whether his rule was effective.

260 *Charters and Custumals of the Abbey of Holy Trinity, Caen. Part 2. The French Estates*, ed. J. Walmsley, Records of Social and Economic History, n.s., 22 (Oxford, 1994), pp. 125–8 (text) and 10–12 (commentary). Cf. Haskins, *Norman Institutions*, pp. 63–4; Green, 'Robert Curthose Reassessed', p. 115.

261 *OV*, IV, pp. 250–1; Wace, *Roman de Rou*, lines 9531–72, pp. 300–1.

262 WM, *GR*, I, pp. 550–1; cf. Wace, *Roman de Rou*, lines 9531–72, pp. 300–1. The episode bears a striking resemblance to the incident at Gerberoi when Robert unhorsed his father and was about to strike him when the Conqueror called out.

heavens, should I leave our brother to die of thirst? And where shall we look for another if we lose this one?'[263] While this seems an act of folly on Robert's part, it demonstrates not only his commitment to the bonds of family, but also his inclination to chivalrous behaviour. Again, in a difficult situation, Robert seems to have adopted the policy already employed at the siege of Courcy.[264] Rightly or wrongly, he felt that, having come to an arrangement with Rufus, he might effect a reconciliation with Henry.

For historians, both medieval and modern, expecting a certain ruthlessness in their rulers, Robert's action seems ill-judged, but by the standards of chivalric society it was reasonable to allow Henry the supplies he needed. It was unusual, although not entirely unheard of, for members of the Norman nobility to procure the deaths of other nobles, but it was far more likely that aristocratic opponents would be allowed to survive and then be ransomed. Sieges were also governed by this code of behaviour and the besiegers were under certain obligations with regard to their treatment of the besieged.[265] Robert was responding to an expectation among the knightly class, an expectation of behaviour doubtless heightened because it involved his own brother. To understand Robert's actions, it is necessary to set aside crude pragmatism and to look at the siege in terms of a breakdown of the bonds of lordship between the duke and his brother. If the aim was to re-establish a working relationship with Henry, then Robert's display of that greatness of spirit, *franchise* or *mansuetudo*, expected of a knight, served to convince the younger man that there was the possibility of a restored relationship. Robert's action appears weak but was, in fact, a demonstration of good lordship, a fact Henry understood better than his brother William. Henry shrewdly played on Robert's chivalric sensibilities. Rufus's comment was that this was a 'pretty way to wage war, giving your enemies access to water! How are we to beat them, if we let them have all the meat and drink they need?' Here, William Rufus's impatience got the better of his chivalric sensibilities. However, William of Malmesbury reported that Robert's 'courteous reply deservedly became famous'.[266]

The end of the siege of Mont-Saint-Michel is variously reported in the sources. Orderic tells us that Henry managed to negotiate an honourable surrender and was allowed to leave with his baggage. He then passed through Brittany and into France.[267] Eventually Henry found a refuge at the castle of Domfront on Normandy's southern frontier.[268] According to Orderic, the peace

---

263   WM, *GR*, I, pp. 552–3. Malmesbury juxtaposed this incident with that of Rufus's unhorsing, in order to demonstrate the courtly attributes of the brothers, namely *magnanimitas* ('generosity of spirit') and *mansuetudo* ('clemency'), both of which were expected of rulers.

264   *OV*, IV, pp. 232–3.

265   Strickland, *War and Chivalry*, pp. 204–29, especially at 210–11.

266   WM, *GR*, I, pp. 552–3.

267   *OV*, IV, pp. 250–3.

268   *JW*, III, pp. 58–9; *WJ*, II, pp. 206–7; WM, *GR*, I, pp. 552–3. Wace, who seems to have confused his account, suggested that Robert managed to reconcile his brothers before they left Avranches, and allowed Henry to retain the Cotentin until he had repaid the loan: Wace, *Roman de Rou*, lines 9573–618, pp. 302–3.

established by Robert and William ensured stability in Normandy for two years.

After their victory at Mont-Saint-Michel, Robert and William Rufus did not go on to recover Maine. Instead, in June 1091, Robert attended an ecclesiastical synod at Rouen. Orderic provided a detailed account of the election of Serlo, abbot of Saint-Évroul, as bishop of Sées. Duke Robert was also called upon to give his assent to the election of Roger of Le Sap, Serlo's successor at Saint-Évroul. Abbot Roger was invested with the temporalities of the abbacy by the duke in a ceremony of lay investiture which, as Orderic pointed out, was customary at that time. Writing about the investiture of the abbot of his own monastery at the hands of a duke he generally criticised, Orderic clearly felt constrained to explain the anomaly to his audience who, in the aftermath of the Investiture Contest, might have found the detail disturbing.[269] Again, there was no suggestion that Robert was derelict in his conduct of ecclesiastical matters in the summer of 1091. Indeed, Robert sent letters to the bishop of Lisieux instructing him to bless Roger as abbot. It is worth noting that this detailed account of ecclesiastical affairs comes from Orderic, who repeatedly suggests that during Robert's reign the Norman Church was without effective protection.[270]

Scotland, 1091

In May 1091, Edgar the Ætheling's brother-in-law, Maelcoluim (Malcolm) III of Scotland, invaded the North of England.[271] At the end of July or early August, Robert accompanied his brother to England. According to William of Malmesbury there were problems in Wales in addition to the threat from Scotland. Rufus led an expedition against the Welsh, but achieved little success and it is not unlikely that Robert accompanied his brother.[272] In August, they advanced against the king of Scots, but a few days before Michaelmas, 29 September, the fleet supporting the army was wrecked. Many of the cavalry perished from cold and hunger. However, the brothers continued to Durham and, on 14 November, restored Bishop William to his see.[273] They then pushed on and met Malcolm in Lothian, perhaps near Edinburgh.[274]

---

269 *OV*, IV, pp. 252–3. Raymonde Foreville, 'The Synod of the Province of Rouen in the Eleventh and Twelfth Centuries', trans. G. Martin, in *Church and Government in the Middle Ages. Essays presented to C.R. Cheney on his 70th birthday*, ed. C.N.L. Brooke, D.E. Luscombe, G.H. Martin and Dorothy Owen (Cambridge, 1976), pp. 19–39 at 31.

270 *OV*, IV, pp. 254–5 and n. 6.

271 *ASC*, E, *s.a.* 1091, p. 102; Swanton, p. 226; Symeon, 'Historia Regum', *s.a.* 1091, p. 218; *JW*, III, *s.a.* 1091, pp. 58–9.

272 WM, *GR*, I, pp. 552–3. Malmesbury is alone in suggesting that Rufus was accompanied by *both* Robert and Henry.

273 Symeon, *Libellus de exordio*, pp. 242–3; 'De iniusta vexatione', p. 105; Symeon, 'Historia Regum', p. 218. For discussion of this date see David, *Curthose*, Appendix B, pp. 215–16.

274 Symeon, 'Historia Regum', p. 218. Cf. *OV*, IV, pp. 268–9; the meeting took place on the banks of the 'Scotte Watra' (River Forth). For the 1080 meeting, see Symeon, 'Historia Regum', p. 211.

Once again, Robert's diplomatic skills were called upon and he acted as an intermediary between the Scots and English kings. His friendship with Edgar the Ætheling, the fact that Robert had already met Malcolm in the autumn of 1080, and he was godfather to Malcolm's daughter Edith, made him an ideal mediator. Robert went to Malcolm's camp where he was warmly greeted and entertained for three days.[275] Orderic described Malcolm leading Robert up a mountain and showing him two great armies waiting for the Normans. The Scot acknowledged that he had been given Lothian by Edward the Confessor when he married Margaret, that the Conqueror had confirmed his possession, and that he had given his fealty to Robert. The duke then explained that conditions had changed and that the Conqueror's arrangements had been disrupted. He then asked Malcolm to meet Rufus, pointing out that he would be kind and generous. He was more powerful and wealthier and his kingdom was closer than Robert's duchy. Malcolm was persuaded and made peace with Rufus.[276]

Robert and Edgar Ætheling were reunited and they used their respective influence to bring about a settlement.[277] The terms of the agreement were that the Scots king would obey William Rufus as he had Rufus's father. In return, Rufus would return twelve townships which Malcolm had possessed in England during the Conqueror's reign, and pay the Scots king a symbolic annual subsidy of twelve golden marks.[278] The difficulty of the task facing Robert and Edgar was hinted at by William of Malmesbury: the agreement between Rufus and Malcolm was doomed because the two did not like each other.[279] Robert also used the occasion to reconcile Edgar and Rufus, further demonstrating his preference for, and skill in bringing about, negotiated settlements.[280]

Robert and William returned through Mercia to Wessex, but just before Christmas they quarrelled over the king's failure to implement their treaty regarding Normandy and England, perhaps a reference to the failure to press Robert's claims in Maine. Accompanied by Edgar Ætheling, Robert crossed from the Isle of Wight to Normandy on 23 December 1091. Robert had proved indispensable to his brother in Scotland but he was frustrated at Rufus's inertia with regard to Maine.[281]

---

275 *OV*, IV, pp. 268–9.
276 *OV*, IV, pp. 268–71. Orderic's account is flawed in a number of ways: Malcolm did not marry Margaret until around 1068 and there is no suggestion that Lothian was ceded to the Scots by Edward the Confessor.
277 Hooper, 'Edgar the Ætheling', p. 207.
278 *ASC*, E, *s.a.* 1091, p. 102; Swanton, pp. 225–7; *JW*, III, *s.a.* 1091, pp. 60–1. Cf. Duncan, *Kingship of the Scots*, pp. 46–9, who suggests the properties housed Malcolm on his visits to the English court.
279 *WM*, *GR*, I, pp. 552–3.
280 Symeon, 'Historia Regum', p. 218.
281 *ASC*, E, *s.a.* 1091, pp. 102–3; Swanton, p. 227.

Normandy, 1092–1095

In comparison with the beginning of Robert's reign, the sources record fewer incidents for the three or four years after his return to Normandy at Christmas 1091. This suggests that, with the agreement of February 1091 in place and, more importantly, without Rufus's direct interference in the affairs of the duchy, Robert enjoyed a period of relative peace. Certainly, Rufus was otherwise occupied in 1092, extending his dominion into Cumbria, driving out the native ruler, Dolfin, fortifying the castle at Carlisle, and settling English peasants in the area.[282] However, there were a number of unresolved issues involving sections of the Norman baronage and the duke's youngest brother.

Robert returned to his duchy to discover that Henry had occupied Domfront and was waging war on Robert de Bellême.[283] There is some confusion in the sources as to Henry's fate after the siege of the Mont-Saint-Michel. Orderic wrote that Henry was badly treated by his brothers: 'Because he was the youngest he was not treated as a brother by his brothers, but rather as a stranger, so that he was forced to seek the support of strangers, namely the French and the Bretons, and for five years had been wearied by constant changes of fortune.'[284] Henry was in exile in France when messengers from the inhabitants of Domfront invited him to help them stem the excesses of Robert de Bellême. Orderic names a certain Harcherius receiving Henry with honour and installing him as lord of the town.[285] At some stage after his brothers returned to England in late July or early August 1091, Henry recovered control of the Cotentin. Rufus had apparently consented to this and Henry had been assisted by Richard de Redvers, Roger de Mandeville and Earl Hugh of Chester, the latter having been rewarded with the grant of Saint-James-le-Beuvron.[286]

The great scandal of 1092 was the marriage of Philip I of France to Bertrade, countess of Anjou.[287] In Normandy, the feud between Ascelin Goel and William of Breteuil flared up again. While Robert and his brother William were in England, William of Breteuil attacked the castle of Ivry but encountered stiff resistance from Goel and his men. Eventually, William de Breteuil offered subsidies to Philip of France and Robert of Normandy if they would help him defeat his enemies.[288]

---

[282] ASC, E, s.a. 1092, p. 103; Swanton, p. 227; cf. W.E. Kapelle, *The Norman Conquest of the North. the Region and its Transformation, 1000–1135* (London, 1979), pp. 151–2; Mason, *William II*, pp. 98–102.

[283] OV, IV, pp. 256–7.

[284] OV, IV, pp. 256–7.

[285] OV, IV, p. 258, n. 1; cf. Green, *Henry I*, p. 32. Orderic may have had a good source for the events at Domfront: OV, IV, pp. 258–61.

[286] WJ, II, pp. 206–9.

[287] OV, IV, pp. 260–5. Orderic wrongly accused Odo of Bayeux of conducting the marriage ceremony.

[288] OV, IV, pp. 288–9.

During Lent 1092, Robert, Philip and Robert de Bellême, who had a grudge of his own against Goel, besieged Bréval. Bellême was noted as a builder of siege engines and brought his expertise to the assault.[289] Eventually, Ascelin Goel recognised that he could not withstand the siege and sought terms from William of Breteuil and the price of peace was the restoration of the castle of Ivry. Everyone except Robert de Bellême rejoiced at the settlement; Bellême had been excluded from the negotiations for fear that he would scupper them.[290] He withdrew his forces and attacked the castle at Saint-Céneri, which had been lost to Robert Giroie in 1088.[291] Giroie's garrison were unprepared for an attack, thinking that Bellême forces were still with the ducal army. Both sides then proceeded to raid each other's territory. The duke's brother Henry also joined in, operating from Domfront. At the beginning of July 1092 Henry and Robert Giroie were co-operating against Bellême when rumours that Giroie was dead caused the garrison of his castle to panic leaving it open for Bellême to sack. The monks of Saint-Martin of Sées joined in the plundering and made off with the arm of Saint Cenéri.[292]

In 1093 Robert Giroie built a castle above Montaigu from which he attacked Robert de Bellême.[293] Duke Robert was asked for help by Robert de Bellême and was persuaded to bring the 'army of Normandy' to attack Montaigu. The fact that the duke could summon the *exercitus Normanniæ* also questions Orderic's assertion that Robert lacked authority. However, the lords of Maine made an appeal to the duke on Giroie's behalf and, in keeping with his policy of favouring reconciliation, Robert agreed to a settlement. The castle of Montaigu was demolished and in return Giroie was pardoned and his whole inheritance was restored.[294] Once again, Duke Robert had ensured that Robert de Bellême was not able to eliminate an important rival. So consistently did Robert maintain a balance in the region that it looks like deliberate policy expertly handled.

Robert and Anselm of Bec, 1093

During Lent 1093 Robert's brother William fell dangerously ill and was taken to Gloucester for medical care. Thinking that he was at death's door, the king vowed to change his life for the better. He promised never to sell or tax churches; he would annul unjust laws and establish just ones. As a sign of this personal reformation, he appointed Anselm, the abbot of Bec

---

289   *OV*, IV, pp. 288–91.
290   *OV*, IV, pp. 290–3.
291   See above, pp. 121–2.
292   *OV*, IV, pp. 294–5.
293   *OV*, II, pp. 26–9.
294   *OV*, IV, pp. 294–7; the men of Saint-Évroul were ordered to help Robert de Bellême pull down the castle of Montaigu.

to the archbishopric of Canterbury, vacant since 1089.[295] As the abbot of a Norman monastery, Anselm's translation to Canterbury needed Duke Robert's approval. In June or July 1093, Robert wrote to Anselm, informing him that he had received Rufus's envoys. Robert did not want to refuse his brother's petition although he recognised what a loss Anselm would be to Normandy. Robert had earlier supported Anselm in the struggles against the ambition of Robert de Meulan and the two seem to have been on good terms.[296] Anselm himself may have contacted the duke, expressing his reluctance to accept the post, as Robert's letter continues,

> I admonish your love not to fear to accept the archbishopric of Canterbury, since I truly believe you to be worthy of such an honour. I inform you that I not only concede this but, since I know your life and character, I even desire it above everything else.[297]

Robert's willingness to co-operate with his brother on the appointment to Canterbury was another sign of his determination to preserve the terms of their agreement of 1091. Anselm's appointment to Canterbury also demonstrated that as far as the king of England and one of the leading churchmen of the duchy were concerned, there were no questions about Robert's authority as duke.

'Bad faith': 1093–4

In August 1093, Malcolm, king of Scots, attempted to see Rufus in Gloucester to discuss the arrangements brokered by Duke Robert two years earlier. The leading men at the king's court wanted to restore peace between Malcolm and Rufus, but the meeting on St Bartholomew's day (24 August) proved fruitless. One of the bones of contention was Rufus's attempt to have Malcolm 'do right' at his court 'in accordance with the judgement of his barons'. Malcolm refused and would only 'do right' on the frontier between their countries 'and in accordance with the judgement of the chief men of both realms'.[298] Rufus was trying to demonstrate Malcolm's subordinate position in their relationship by having him answer charges at his court and only according to the judgement of his men. Malcolm viewed the relationship as more equal, as suggested by his insistence on a meeting on the Anglo-Scottish frontier. The reference to

---

295 JW, III, s.a. 1093, pp. 64–5. Lent was between 2 March and 16 April 1093; *The Life of St Anselm, archbishop of Canterbury by Eadmer*, ed. and trans. R.W. Southern (Oxford, 1972), pp. 64–5. Eadmer, *HN*, pp. 31–8.
296 See above, pp. 131–2.
297 Fröhlich, *Letters of Anselm*, II, no. 153.
298 Symeon, 'Historia Regum', pp. 220–1; *ASC*, E, s.a. 1093, p. 103; Swanton, pp. 227–8; JW, III, s.a. 1093, pp. 64–5; cf. *OV*, IV, pp. 270–1. Mason, *William II*, pp. 112, 257, n. 76, where it is pointed out that 'in curia sua rectitudinem ei faceret' has been misconstrued in JW as 'he wanted to force Malcolm to do homage to him at his court.'

the judgement of men of the English king and men of the Scots king suggests that the agreement of 1091 had involved the same sort of mechanism of guarantee as that between Robert and Rufus earlier that year.

Malcolm left Gloucester without seeing Rufus. On St Brice's day (13 November) Malcolm and his eldest son Edward were killed by knights of Robert de Mowbray, earl of Northumbria. Malcolm's death and the struggles for the Scottish throne allowed Rufus to intervene by backing his own candidates.[299]

The collapse of the agreement between William Rufus and Malcolm III of Scotland parallels the breakdown in the relationship with Robert at the end of the same year. The duke sent envoys to Rufus's Christmas court at Gloucester to demand that the English king fulfil his part of the agreement made in February 1091. If he failed to honour these arrangements, Robert would renounce the peace they had made, accusing his brother of perjury and faithlessness. If he wished to clear himself of these charges Rufus might return to the place where the pact was made and there exonerate himself.[300] Robert was summoning his brother to Normandy to answer charges of bad faith: what is surprising is that Rufus answered the summons.

Around the third week of March 1094, Rufus crossed to Normandy to meet his brother and resolve the difficulties between them.[301] It is not clear whether Rufus was really prepared to argue his case – although this should not be discounted – or whether he intended to embark on a military conquest of Normandy. The king had certainly gathered substantial sums of money for the expedition although a contribution offered by the new archbishop of Canterbury was rejected as being too paltry.[302] Rufus needed great sums of cash to subvert Robert's adherents as he had done before, and to pay for mercenaries. But it is also certain that Robert was better prepared for his arrival than he had been in 1091.[303]

Once Rufus was in Normandy, negotiations took place between the brothers, but they achieved nothing. Later it was decided to invoke the judgement of the twenty-four barons who had agreed to guarantee the 1091 peace. The two sides met at the Campus Martius, which, if Rufus was returning to the place where the original agreement was made, may have been just outside Rouen. Rufus was answering charges at his brother's court and the duke's complaint was upheld, for

---

[299] *ASC*, E, *s.a.* 1093, pp. 103–4; Swanton, pp. 227–8; WM, *GR*, I, pp. 552–5; JW, III, *s.a.* 1093, pp. 66–7; *OV*, IV, pp. 270–5 gives a confused summary of Scottish history from 1093 to the early 1130s.

[300] *ASC*, E, *s.a.* 1094, p. 104; Swanton, pp. 228–9; JW, III, *s.a.* 1094, pp. 68–9.

[301] *ASC*, E, *s.a.* 1094, p. 104; Swanton, p. 229; JW, III, *s.a.* 1094, pp. 70–1. Mason, *William II*, pp. 134–5.

[302] Eadmer, *Life of Anselm*, p. 67; *HN*, pp. 43–4.

[303] A point uncharacteristically admitted by David, *Curthose*, p. 85.

... those who confirmed on oath the peace between them (Rufus and Robert), put all the blame on the king. But he would neither accept the blame nor implement the agreement. Thereupon they departed angry and un-reconciled.[304]

Duke Robert was vindicated, but his faith in the agreed procedures was misplaced. Rufus retired to Eu and began to gather mercenaries and use the wealth he had brought over from England to buy allies among the Norman barons. In the first engagement of these renewed hostilities, Rufus's men stormed the castle of Bures. Some of the duke's garrison were sent to captivity in England, others were held in the duchy.[305]

Robert once again called for the assistance of Philip I of France and they had considerable success. Invading Normandy, Philip besieged and took the castle at Argentan in just a single day. Without bloodshed, he captured the entire garrison and held them all until ransoms had been paid and then, according to John of Worcester, returned to France. The *Anglo-Saxon Chronicle* on the other hand suggests that Philip remained in Normandy to assist Robert.[306] Duke Robert was equally successful and besieged the castle at Houlme until its castellan, William Peverel, and his eight hundred men surrendered.[307] These operations may be connected with the death of Earl Roger of Montgomery on 27 July 1094, and a struggle between his heirs for control of the Montgomery-Bellême lands. One of Earl Roger's sons, Roger of Poitou, was at Argentan and the swift surrender to King Philip may have been connected with the inheritance.

Rufus's response was to send to England for reinforcements, although, when the twenty thousand foot soldiers arrived at Hastings, the king's minister, Ranulf Flambard, relieved them of the cash they had brought and shipped it off to his master.[308] In the meantime, Robert and his ally were advancing on Eu when Rufus managed to defuse the situation, perhaps by buying Philip off once again.[309] It was in Philip of France's interests that neither brother should emerge victorious, for a destabilised Normandy relieved the pressure on his own kingdom. He had made gains, such as the castle of Gisors, from his alliance with Robert and recognised that if William secured control of the duchy, the resources he could bring from England would make him a far more threatening neighbour.

[304] *JW*, III, *s.a.* 1094, pp. 70–1. Freeman, *Rufus*, I, p. 251, suggested that the 'Campus Martius' was the Champs de Mars and lay outside the east gate of Rouen. Cf. Barlow, *Rufus*, p. 281, n. 77; Mason, *William II*, pp. 134–5.
[305] *ASC*, E, *s.a.* 1094, pp. 104–5; Swanton, p. 229; cf. *JW*, III, *s.a.* pp.70–1; Symeon, 'Historia Regum', pp. 223–4.
[306] *JW*, III, *s.a.* 1094, pp. 70–3.
[307] *JW*, III, *s.a.* 1094, pp. 72–3. Barlow, *Rufus*, p. 333, n. 293 identifies Le Houlme with Briouze.
[308] *JW*, III, *s.a.* 1094, pp. 72–3.
[309] *ASC*, E, *s.a.* 1094, pp. 104–5; Swanton, p. 229. The army got as far as Longueville (Seine-Maritime) before Philip withdrew.

Although Robert's army turned back from attacking Eu, he managed to threaten his brother's position sufficiently for the king to summon Henry to his aid. Henry, at Domfront, provided a welcome second front for Rufus in the war against Robert. The duke's control of central Normandy was so complete, however, that Henry and his ally Earl Hugh of Chester were forced to travel by sea to meet Rufus in England. Although the king remained in the duchy to the end of 1094, he achieved very little for his vast outlay of treasure. In addition, the Welsh had attacked the Marcher lands and Rufus's ally in Scotland, Duncan, had been killed by a faction opposed to the English alliance. Therefore, with troubles mounting on all sides, Rufus finally admitted that, for the time being, he could not pursue the struggle, and on 29 December he returned to Dover.[310]

Once again, Robert had engineered a successful resistance against his brothers, employing a strategy that his father may well have recommended. Robert's reliance on Philip I repeated a pattern established early in his father's reign of calling on the help of the Capetians. Philip's support for the duke had also been consistent throughout, beginning with his assistance during the quarrels between Robert and his father at the end of the 1070s. Robert's calls on Philip have been seen as a desperate measure to avert the collapse of his regime, yet the strategy could also be represented as a sensible and legitimate response to the problem of dealing with an opponent with far greater resources than his own. Duke Robert retained his authority in Normandy and he was ready to defend his duchy if the need arose. If he had to acknowledge his brothers' interests in their homeland, Robert also managed successfully to contain their ambitions. This was no small achievement given the vastly superior resources available to William Rufus.

Rufus's problems in 1095, which included a rebellion by the earl of Northumbria and William of Eu, meant that he could not afford to return to Normandy. Instead, he turned to Henry and provided him with funds to harass Robert until he could continue the war in person. The *Anglo-Saxon Chronicle* noted that Henry remained in England until the spring of 1095, 'and then, in loyalty to the king against their brother Earl Robert, went across the sea to Normandy with great treasures and frequently warred against the earl and did him great harm in both lands and in men'.[311] Robert de Mowbray's revolt began soon after Easter. In addition, the Welsh attacked the castle of Montgomery, killing Earl Hugh's garrison. Rufus retaliated with an expedition after Michaelmas (29 September).

Although he had been under severe pressure from his brothers and from the defection of some of his vassals in Upper Normandy, Robert had retained his duchy. Indeed, Robert had displayed tenaciousness worthy of his father and there were many Norman barons still content to follow their duke, rather

310 *ASC*, E, *s.a.* 1094, pp. 104–5; Swanton, pp. 229–30.
311 *ASC*, E, *s.a.* 1094, pp. 104–5; Swanton, pp. 229–30.

than accept the king of England's gold. In the closing weeks of 1095, however, Robert received news from a papal council which seemed to offer him the chance to dedicate his undoubted military skill to the service of God and to achieve a victory comparable to that of his father's conquest of England.

CHAPTER FIVE

MILES CHRISTI:
THE SOLDIER OF CHRIST, 1095–1099

The Councils of Clermont and Rouen,
November 1095 to February 1096

IN the autumn of 1095, Pope Urban II toured France, promoting church reform. At the close of a council held at Clermont in the Auvergne, the pope delivered a sermon which inspired thousands of Western Christians to undertake an arduous pilgrimage. Although Urban's exact words are a matter of debate, it was understood as a call to liberate the churches of the East and, in particular, the holy city of Jerusalem.[1]

After Clermont, Urban continued his tour of France and although he did not enter Normandy, he was at Le Mans in February and at Tours in March 1096. The message concerning Urban's call to arms was brought back to Normandy by those who had attended the council at Clermont including Odo, bishop of Bayeux, Gilbert, bishop of Évreux, and Serlo, bishop of Sées, together with the envoys of their episcopal colleagues.[2] Less formally, but perhaps more effectively, rumours of a great stirring among the people undoubtedly made their way into the duchy.[3] In February 1096, a provincial council was held at Rouen, but although there was no direct mention of the proposed expedition to the

---

[1] *OV,* V, pp. 14–17; WM, *GR,* I, pp. 592–607; cf. J. Riley-Smith, *The First Crusade and the Idea of Crusading* (London, 1993), pp. 13–30. N. Housely, *Contesting the Crusades* (Oxford, 2006), pp. 24–47. There are several modern narratives of the First Crusade; see F. Duncalf, 'The First Crusade: Clermont to Constantinople', Sir Steven Runciman, 'The First Crusade: Constantinople to Antioch', and *idem,* 'The First Crusade: Antioch to Ascalon', in *A History of the Crusades, Volume I. The First Hundred Years,* ed. M.W. Baldwin (Madison, Milwaukee and London, 1969), pp. 253–79, pp. 280–304 and pp. 308–41 respectively. Cf. J. France, *Victory in the East. A Military History of the First Crusade* (Cambridge, 1994); T. Asbridge, *The First Crusade. A New History* (London, 2004); J. France, 'The Normans and Crusading', in R. Abels and B.S. Bachrach, eds., *The Normans and their Adversaries at War. Essays in memory of C. Warren Hollister* (Woodbridge, 2001), pp. 87–101.

[2] *OV,* V, pp. 18–19; the Norman bishops carried back synodal letters (*sinodales epistolas*) from the pope.

[3] *OV,* V, pp. 18–19; Orderic may have gleaned his information either from Serlo, who had been abbot of Saint-Évroul, or Bishop Gilbert, who was one of those who dedicated the abbey church of Saint-Évroul in November 1099.

East the council dealt with matters germane to Urban's reform programme and the decrees issued at Clermont, stopping short of a call to arms.[4]

The canons issued at Rouen prepared the way for the armed pilgrimage to the East. Part of the papal scheme was to ensure that Christian society cleansed itself of abuses that might impair the path to salvation. It was imperative to bring peace to Western Europe and allow its knights to re-direct their energies to the service of the Church. To this end the Council of Rouen re-imposed the Peace of God, which was to be strictly observed.[5] The canons guaranteed the safety of all churches, monks, clergy, pilgrims, merchants and agricultural workers. The form of an oath, sworn on relics, to uphold the Truce of God was also given, and all men over the age of twelve were to swear on pain of excommunication. The canons of the Council of Rouen aimed at establishing peace in Normandy, the essential precondition for allowing a Norman contingent to join the great expedition to the East.

Orderic followed his account of the canons of the Council of Rouen by affirming that they were ineffective in Normandy because there was great unrest at the time. He claimed that the 'whole country was devastated by fire and plunder, which drove many of the inhabitants into exile and left whole parishes destroyed and churches abandoned as the priests fled'.[6] Orderic was exaggerating once again and it is no surprise to find that his characterisation of the state of Normandy in 1096 was followed by a digression concerning the fact that the Normans were an unruly race in need of a firm ruler. The point of Orderic's rhetoric was to explain why Duke Robert decided to make the journey to Jerusalem:

> Finally, Duke Robert, distressed by the sight of such misery and fearing still worse to come since almost everyone had abandoned him, resolved on the advice of certain men of religion to hand over the administration of his duchy to his brother and, himself taking the cross, to go on pilgrimage to Jerusalem to make amends to God for his sins.[7]

Orderic's description of the problems Robert faced in 1096 has been influential, but it does less than justice to both the duke's ability to counter the threat posed by his brothers and his motivation for taking the cross.

Although the sources for the history of the First Crusade are relatively abundant, none of them was written by one of Duke Robert's followers. Nowhere are we given Robert's point of view and as a result historians have tended to underestimate the duke's role in the Crusade. However, there is a case to be made for Robert as one of the key figures in the expedition. As one

---

4   *The Councils of Urban II, i. Decreta Claromontensia*, ed. R. Sommerville, Annuarium Historiæ Conciliorum, Suppl., 1 (Amsterdam, 1972); *OV*, V, pp. 20–5, for the canons of the council of Rouen. Cf. Foreville, 'The Synod of the Province of Rouen', p. 31.
5   *OV*, V, pp. 20–1. H.E.J. Cowdrey, 'The Peace and Truce of God in the Eleventh Century', *P&P*, 46 (1970), pp. 42–67.
6   *OV*, V, pp. 24–5.
7   *OV*, V, pp. 26–7.

of the *principes* or 'leading men', Robert had a crucial role to play, not only in military affairs, but also in ensuring that the divisions between the various contingents did not lead to the dissolution of the expedition. In addition, members of his entourage were instrumental in establishing the Latin Church in the Holy Land.

There are several accounts of the First Crusade, including three principal eye-witness narratives: the *Gesta Francorum et aliorum Hierosolimitanorum* ('The Deeds of the Franks and the other Jerusalem-farers'), whose author remains anonymous, and the *Histories* by Raymond d'Aguilers and Fulcher of Chartres.[8] In addition, there are narratives by Albert of Aachen, Robert the Monk of Reims, and Ralph of Caen.[9] All of these accounts were composed within ten to fifteen years of the events they describe and, although they represent different viewpoints, they all tell the story of the Crusade in the light of the eventual victory of the expedition. It is possible that the ideology of the Crusade only gradually began to gain coherence as the expedition unfolded and that the meaning of the expedition only became fully intelligible once Jerusalem had fallen. In other words the production of narratives provided a shape and a focus for an interpretation of the meaning of what had happened.[10]

The main accounts of the crusade were, therefore, written from different perspectives. For example, the author of the *Gesta Francorum* was in the company of the southern Italian Norman, Bohemond of Taranto, but he finished the journey to Jerusalem with the southern French contingents of

---

8   *Gesta Francorum et aliorum Hierosolimitanorum*, ed. Rosalind Hill (London, 1962); *Le 'Liber' de Raymond d'Aguilers*, ed. J.H. and L. Laurita Hill (Paris, 1969); *Raymond d'Aguilers. Historia Francorum qui ceperunt Iherusalem*, trans. J.H. Hill and Laurita L. Hill (Philadelphia, PA, 1968). (The translation is referred to in the following pages.) *Fulcheri Carnotensis Historia Hierosolymita (1095–1127)*, ed. H. Hagenmeyer (Heidelberg, 1913), trans. Martha E. McGinty in *The First Crusade. The Chronicle of Fulcher of Chartres and Other Source Materials*, ed. E. Peters (Philadelphia, PA, 1971), pp. 23–90, and Frances R. Ryan, trans., *Fulcher of Chartres. A History of the Expedition to Jerusalem, 1095–1127* (Knoxville, TN, 1969). Raymond of Aguilers, writing at the beginning of the twelfth century, was chaplain to Raymond of Toulouse and presents a distinct Provençal viewpoint. A fourth 'eye-witness' account by Peter Tudebode was based so heavily on the *Gesta Francorum* that, although the author did participate in the expedition, his testimony is of limited independent value: *Petrus Tudebodus, Historia de Hierosolymitana Itinere*, ed. J.H. and Laurita L. Hill (Paris, 1977), and trans. J.H. and Laurita L. Hill, *Peter Tudebode. Historia de Hierosolymitana Itinere* (Philadelphia, PA, 1974), and see Susan Edgington, 'The First Crusade: Reviewing the Evidence', in *The First Crusade. Origins and Impact*, ed. J. Phillips (Manchester, 1997), pp. 55–77 at 56.

9   *Albert of Aachen*, Historia Ierosolimitana. *History of the Journey to Jerusalem*, ed. and trans. Susan B. Edgington (Oxford, 2007). I am very grateful to Dr Edgington for allowing me to make use of sections of her translation in advance of publication. *The* Historia Vie Hierosolimitane *of Gilo of Paris*, ed. C.W. Grocock and J.E. Siberry (Oxford, 1997); 'Roberti Monachi Historia Iherosolimitana', *RHC Occ.*, III, pp. 717–882; *Robert the Monk's History of the First Crusade. Historia Iherosolimitana*, trans. Carole Sweetenham (Aldershot, 2005); 'Gesta Tancredi in expeditione Hierosolymitana auctore Radulfo Cadomensi', in *RHC Occ.*, III, pp. 587–716; *The Gesta Tancredi of Ralph of Caen. A History of the Normans on the First Crusade*, trans. B.S. Bachrach and D.S. Bachrach (Aldershot, 2005). I am grateful to Professors Bernard S. and David S. Bachrach for supplying a pre-publication copy of their translation of Ralph of Caen's work.

10 J. Riley Smith, *The First Crusade and the Idea of Crusading* (London, 1993), pp. 91–119.

Raymond of St Gilles, count of Toulouse.[11] The cleric Fulcher of Chartres had been at the Council of Clermont and began the journey in the entourage of Duke Robert's brother-in-law, Count Stephen of Blois, before joining that of Baldwin of Boulogne.[12] Historians have also made use of letters from participants on the crusade, including those from Stephen of Blois to Robert's sister, Adela.[13] The surviving charters involving the crusaders and their families have also been examined, particularly for evidence of the motivations of the participants and their expectations of returning.[14]

There are also several narratives composed in the West which drew not only on these eye-witness histories, particularly the *Gesta Francorum*, but also on the memories of returning crusaders.[15] Two of the longest of these secondary histories were produced by William of Malmesbury and Orderic Vitalis, our most detailed sources for the career of Duke Robert.[16] Although derivative, these accounts allow us to view Robert's participation in the Crusade in the context of his career as duke of Normandy. Orderic and Malmesbury also utilised oral accounts from returned Crusaders, but both historians were aware that the memories of campaign veterans might be embellished. These Anglo-Norman historians concentrated on the chivalric aspects of the Crusade, perhaps, especially in Malmesbury's case, reflecting the interests of a courtly audience.

There are also several sources extant from the Byzantine Empire and the Crusaders' opponents.[17] The narratives of the First Crusade generated other works, which enhanced the elements of chivalric romance in the tale. For example there was an vernacular epic poem, the *Chanson d'Antioche* in existence by the late twelfth century.[18]

---

[11] Edgington, 'Reviewing the Evidence', pp. 55–6. R. Yewdale, *Bohemond I Prince of Antioch* (Princeton, 1917); J.H. Hill, *Raymond IV of Saint-Gilles 1041 or 1042–1105* (Syracuse, 1962).

[12] *Fulcheri Carnotensis Historia Hierosolymita (1095–1127)*, ed. H. Hagenmeyer (Heidelberg, 1913).

[13] H. Hagenmeyer, *Die Kreuzzugsbriefe aus den Jahren 1088–1100* (Innsbruck, 1901), no. IV, pp. 48–56, 138–40 (text), 217–38; no. X, pp. 75–7, 149–52 (text), 275–94. There are translations of these letters in D.C. Munro, *Letters of the Crusaders* (Philadelphia, PA, 1896), six of which are reprinted by Peters, *First Crusade*, pp. 222–33.

[14] M. Bull, *Knightly Piety and the Lay Response to the First Crusade. The Limousin and Gascony (c.970–c.1130)* (Oxford, 1993), and J. Riley-Smith, *The First Crusaders, 1095–1131* (Cambridge, 1997).

[15] Among those who drew on the *Gesta Francorum* were Abbot Guibert of Nogent in *Guibertus abbas S. Mariae Nogenti, Dei Gesta per Francos*, ed. R.B.C. Huygens, CCCM, 127A (Turnhout, 1996), trans. in R. Levine, *The Deeds of God through the Franks. A Translation of Guibert de Nogent's* Gesta Dei per Francos (Woodbridge, 1997); 'Baldrici episcopi Dolensis Historia Jerosolymitana', in *RHC Occ.*, IV, pp. 1–111; and Sweetenham, *Robert the Monk's History of the First Crusade*.

[16] *OV*, V, pp. 4–303. Orderic drew heavily on the work of his friend Baldric of Bourgueil; *OV*, V, pp. 188–9; cf. *OV*, V, xiii–xix. William of Malmesbury used Fulcher of Chartres as his base text and also drew on the *Gesta Francorum*: WM, *GR*, I, pp. 592–665; cf. R. Thomson, 'William as Historian of Crusade', in idem, *William of Malmesbury*, revised ed. (Woodbridge, 2003), pp. 178–88.

[17] E.g. Anna Comnena, *The Alexiad*, trans. E.R.A. Sewter (Harmondsworth, 1969); F. Gabrieli, *Arab Historians of the Crusades*, trans. E.J. Costello (London, 1969). See the discussion by Edgington, 'Reviewing the Evidence', pp. 73–4.

[18] *La Chanson d'Antioche*, ed. S. Duparc-Quioc, 2 vols. (Paris, 1976–8). Also useful is *William of Tyre, A History of the Deeds Done Beyond the Sea*, trans. E.A. Babcock and A.C. Krey, 2 vols. (New York,

Taking the Cross, February to July 1096

The sources do not say precisely when Robert decided to make a vow to join the expedition to Jerusalem. According to Orderic he was advised by 'certain men of religion' to take the cross. These may have included his uncle Bishop Odo of Bayeux, Gilbert, bishop of Évreux, and Serlo, bishop of Sées, and the other prelates who had attended the Council of Clermont. Bishop Odo was prominent among the duke's counsellors and his opinion would necessarily carry great weight. Although William of Malmesbury does not elaborate on Robert's reasons for taking the cross, he stated that he was 'longing to attempt this expedition'.[19]

Archbishop William 'Bona Anima' who convened the synod of Rouen had also made the pilgrimage to Jerusalem in 1058 with the abbot of Saint-Évroul.[20] Thus there were men with experience of the journey to the Holy Land close at hand to advise and encourage Robert. Archbishop William had also been abbot of Saint-Étienne, Caen, so the story of his pilgrimage to Jerusalem is likely to have been well-known to Robert.[21] In addition, the duke may have received word of the expedition from his cousin, Robert count of Flanders, because soon after Clermont Urban addressed a letter to the people of Flanders.[22] Neither Orderic nor William of Malmesbury explicitly mentions any ritual or ceremony connected with taking the cross but the Council of Rouen would have been a suitably impressive occasion to make the commitment. Alternatively, Robert may have taken the cross at the abbey of Mont-Saint-Michel, asking the saint for protection. On his return to the duchy Robert made a pilgrimage to Mont-Saint-Michel perhaps indicating a return to the place of his vow. Again, given the association of the Normans with the cult of St Michael, this would have been a suitable occasion for Robert to make his vow and accept the status of a pilgrim.[23] Indeed, there was a recog-

1943). For William of Tyre, see P.W. Edbury and J.G. Rowe, *William of Tyre. Historian of the Latin East* (Cambridge, 1988).

19 *OV*, V, pp. 26–7; cf. WM, *GR*, pp. 612–13. M. Markowski, '*Crucesignatus*: Its Origins and Early Usage', *JMH*, 10 (1984), pp. 157–65, and Riley-Smith, *The First Crusade and the Idea of Crusading*, pp. 24–6.

20 *OV*, II, pp. 68–9. This is probably the same pilgrimage made by Gundulf, later bishop of Rochester; see *The Life of Gundulf Bishop of Rochester*, ed. R. Thomson, Toronto Medieval Latin Texts (Toronto, 1977), p. 27.

21 For a short biography of Archbishop William, see G.H. Williams, *The Norman Anonymous of 1100 A.D.* (Cambridge, MA, 1951), pp. 102–25; P. Bouet and Monique Dosdat, 'Les évêques normands de 985 à 1150', in P. Bouet and F. Neveux, eds., *Les évêques normands du XIe siècle* (Caen, 1995), pp. 19–37 at 20–1; D.S. Spear, 'William Bona Anima, Abbot of St Stephen's Caen (1070–79)', *HSJ*, 1 (1989), pp. 51–60, and *idem*, *The Personnel of the Norman Cathedrals during the Ducal Period, 911–1204* (London, 2006), p. 197.

22 Hagenmeyer, *Kreuzzugsbriefe*, pp. 45–6, 136–7 (text), 209–13; translated in A.C. Krey, *The First Crusade: The Accounts of Eye-Witnesses and Participants* (Princeton, PA, 1921), pp. 42–3, and Peters, *First Crusade*, pp. 15–16.

23 *OV*, V, pp. 300–1. For the origins of the cult of St Michael in Normandy, see P. Bouet, 'La *Revelatio ecclesiae sancti Michaelis* et son auteur', *Tabularia 'Études'*, no. 4 (2004), pp. 105–19.

nised pilgrim route from Mont-Saint-Michel to Jerusalem via the shrine of St Michael at Monte Gargano in south-eastern Italy.[24]

Perhaps as early as February or March 1096, Robert resolved to take the cross, 'to go on pilgrimage to Jerusalem to make amends to God for his sins'.[25] Robert had, therefore, accepted the status of a pilgrim and the goal of his penitential journey was Jerusalem; to mark his changed status he attached the symbol of the cross to his clothing.[26] Normally pilgrimage involved a kind of social exile and for a knight this meant a visible loss of status in that he had to lay aside his weapons, the signifiers of his social function.[27] The crusade therefore offered warriors like Duke Robert the chance to take on the status of a pilgrim without losing the social markers of knighthood.

Robert's reasons for vowing to make the journey to Jerusalem were more complex than those described by Orderic. It was not simply a case of the duke trying to escape from difficulties at home. Robert's position in Normandy was not as weak as Orderic would have had his audience believe. The monk of Saint-Évroul's comments present a crude attempt to question the sincerity of Robert's pious desire to take the cross and may have more to do with the aftermath of 1106 than the situation in 1096.

First, Robert's personal piety and his desire to visit the Holy Sepulchre should not be dismissed. In promoting the idea of an expedition to Jerusalem to aid the Christians in the East, Urban managed to tap into ideas already strong among the knightly classes of Western Europe.[28] The papal reform movement, which had gathered pace during the pontificate of Gregory VII (1073–85), envisaged a place for the knights as defenders of the Church. From the mid-1070s, Gregory had promoted the notion of the *milites sancti Petri* ('soldiers of St Peter'), putting the military skills of the chivalric class at the service of the papacy.[29] Combined with the growth of the eleventh-century peace movement, these ideas provided knights with an ideological defence of their vocation.[30] These aspects of papal policy held out the prospect of salvation through the practice of arms. When Pope Urban combined these ideas with well-established notions of the spiritual benefits of penitential pilgrimage and Christian reconquest, the knights and other groups in Western society responded in their thousands.[31]

---

[24] J. C. Arnold, 'Arcadia becomes Jerusalem: Angelic Caverns and Shrine Conversion at Monte Gargano', *Speculum*, 75 (2000), pp. 567–88 at 583.

[25] *OV*, V, pp. 26–7; cf. *WJ*, II, pp. 210–11.

[26] Riley-Smith, *First Crusaders*, pp. 69–70. J.A. Brundage, '*Cruce Signari*: The Rite for Taking the Cross in England', *Traditio*, 22 (1966), pp. 289–310.

[27] For pilgrimage and exile, see Eadmer, *Life of St Anselm*, p. 97.

[28] Cf. Bull, *Knightly Piety and the Lay Response to the First Crusade*, pp. 250–81.

[29] H.E.J. Cowdrey, 'Pope Gregory VII's "Crusading" Plan of 1074', in *Outremer*, ed. B.Z. Kedar, H.E. Mayer and R.C. Smail (Jerusalem, 1982), pp. 27–40.

[30] Cowdrey, 'The Peace and Truce of God in the Eleventh Century', pp. 42–67.

[31] J. Flori, 'Ideology and Motivations in the First Crusade', in Helen J. Nicholson, ed., *The Crusades* (Basingstoke, 2005), pp. 15–36.

Robert was a man of more than conventional piety. He shared the religious sensibilities of his class, but it was recognised, even by his critics, that his devotions went beyond the merely formulaic.[32] Like many Normans, Robert seems to have had a special attachment to the cult of the warrior-saint Michael, as the pilgrimage he made to Mont-Saint-Michel on his return to Normandy in 1100 demonstrated.[33] By invoking the name of Jerusalem, Pope Urban simplified his message and provided a readily identifiable and powerful goal. The city occupied a central place in the medieval Christian's world view, being literally the centre of the world and linking the heavenly and earthly realms. In a description of the Holy Places of Jerusalem found in manuscripts with the *Gesta Francorum*, the 'navel of the world' is located precisely 'thirteen feet west of Mount Calvary'.[34]

The geography of the Holy Land was infused with spiritual associations and acted as a powerful attraction for Western Christians.[35] From the early eleventh century there had been increasing numbers of pilgrimages from Normandy to the Holy Land, so the crusaders of 1096 were following well-worn paths.[36] Among those Norman pilgrims was Robert's own grandfather Duke Robert I. In 1034, Robert I had departed for the Holy Land leaving his eight-year-old son William as the heir to Normandy.[37] Robert died while returning from Jerusalem, but the memory of his expedition was kept alive by William the Conqueror, who, it was said, attempted to repatriate his father's remains from their resting place in the Byzantine Empire. Sharing the same name as his grandfather was a reminder of this pilgrimage and it may have played a role in making Robert receptive to Urban's call in 1096.[38] Perhaps

[32] Ralph of Caen described Robert's piety and generosity as marvellous (*mirabiles*), but this proved a handicap as he treated all men, good and bad, equally; *RC*, p. 616, trans. Bachrach and Bachrach, p. 37. A context for Robert's religious sensibilities is given in C. Harper-Bill, 'The Piety of the Anglo-Norman Knightly Class', *ANS*, 2 (1980), pp. 63–77, 173–6.

[33] *OV*, V, pp. 300–1; cf. *OV*, III, pp. 216–17, where the chaplain of Earl Hugh of Chester regaled his court with stories of the Byzantine warrior saints Demetrius, George, Theodore and Sebastian. It is possible that this anecdote is evidence of the importation of their legends in the wake of the Crusade.

[34] *GF*, p. 98: 'A monte Caluariae sunt XIII pedes usque ad medium mundum contra occidentem.' D.F. Callahan, 'Jerusalem in the Monastic Imaginations of the Early Eleventh Century', *HSJ*, 6 (1994), pp. 119–27; B. Hamilton, 'The Impact of Crusader Jerusalem on Western Christendom', *Catholic Historical Review*, 80 (1994), pp. 695–713; Riley-Smith, *The First Crusade*, p. 21, describes the attitude of eleventh-century Christians to Jerusalem and the Holy Land as 'obsessive'. For the impact of the Crusade, see A. Grabois, 'The Description of Jerusalem by William of Malmesbury: a Mirror of the Holy Land's Place in the Anglo-Norman Mind', *ANS*, 13 (1991), pp. 145–56.

[35] R. Simek, *Heaven and Earth in the Middle Ages*, trans. Angela Hall (Woodbridge, 1996), pp. 73–81.

[36] L. Musset, 'Recherches sur les pèlerins et les pèlerinages en Normandie jusqu'à la première Croisade', *AN*, 12 (1962), pp. 127–50; Riley-Smith, *The First Crusaders*, pp. 27–32.

[37] WM, *GR*, I, pp. 308–9, reported a 'very doubtful story' that Robert's pilgrimage was the result of guilt at his complicity in the poisoning of his brother Duke Richard III.

[38] *WJ*, II, pp. 78–91, 84–5, 94–5, and Elisabeth M.C. van Houts, 'Normandy and Byzantium in the Eleventh Century', *Byzantion*, 55 (1985), pp. 544–59. Duke Robert I died, reputedly as the result of poison, on 2 July 1035 and was buried in the Church of St Mary at Nicaea: *WJ*, II, pp. 84–5. Just before his own death, William the Conqueror sent envoys to retrieve his father's remains. The

Robert felt that the possession of Jerusalem by infidels was a stain on his grandfather's memory, or he merely felt a curiosity to visit the places associated with his pilgrimage. Robert's journey to Jerusalem was an act of family commemoration as well as an expression of personal piety.

The Church considered any act of violence a sin, even if it was committed in a righteous cause. Robert's father and his companions on the campaigns in 1066 and the years following were obliged to make amends for the violent acts they had committed.[39] Robert, too, had engaged in acts of violence and, if he harboured any feelings of guilt about his conduct, especially his behaviour towards his father, then the pilgrimage to Jerusalem offered him the chance to expiate his sins. Urban II had granted an indulgence at Clermont, which characterised the expedition to Jerusalem as a penitential act so arduous that it would counterbalance all their sins.[40] Orderic offered his interpretation of what Pope Urban had promised:

> The provident pope urged all capable of bearing adequate arms to march to war against the enemies of God; and by the will of God he absolved all penitents from their sins from the moment they took the cross of Christ, and with fatherly consideration excused them from any obligation to fast or mortify the flesh in other ways. Like a wise and kind physician, he fully realized that those who set out on the pilgrimage would suffer from every kind of danger at almost all times, and would daily be tormented by changes of fortune, both good and evil, through which the ardent servants of Christ would be cleansed from all the guilt of their sins.[41]

The pope thus offered Robert and his companions a release from the consequences of their sins.

Robert had travelled widely during his two exiles from his father's court and, although there is no evidence that he got as far as the Holy Land, it appears that Robert was not averse to travelling long distances. He possessed a spirit of adventure, not to mention a practical hardiness that enabled him to cope with the difficulties of travel. For a man such as Robert, who had embraced the chivalric ethos portrayed in the *chansons de geste* of the period, the chance to fight the infidel on behalf of his fellow Christians was a powerful spur to join the expedition. The Crusade offered Robert the chance to win renown and to fight in a cause that surpassed even that of his father's conquest of England. The desire to emulate or, better yet, to surpass the achievements of earlier generations was also a powerful motivation for these knights. Both Guibert of

---

body had reached Apulia when news reached the envoys that the Conqueror had died, and so Duke Robert I's body was reburied in Southern Italy; see WM, *GR*, I, pp. 308–9 and 504–7.

39 H.E.J. Cowdrey, 'Bishop Ermenfrid of Sion and the Penitential Ordinance Following the Battle of Hastings', *JEH*, 20 (1969), pp. 225–42.

40 Riley-Smith, *The First Crusade*, pp. 27–9, and J. Muldoon, 'Crusading and Canon Law', in Nicholson, *The Crusades*, pp. 37–57 at 44.

41 *OV*, V, pp. 16–19.

Nogent and Ralph of Caen reported that Robert gained courage at the battle of Dorylaeum in July 1097 by recalling 'his noble lineage'.[42]

The expedition to Jerusalem was an arduous undertaking at the best of times. Combined with the dangers of an extended military campaign, the journey was no 'easy option' for Robert. Only in the sense that he could forget about the more mundane aspects of governing Normandy could Robert's participation on the Crusade have been, as Orderic suggested, a welcome escape from difficulties at home.

Robert was his family's representative on the great expedition and in his hands was the honour of the Norman ruling dynasty. There was a tradition of pilgrimage sponsored by the ducal house, and the dynastic memories of Robert's family also predisposed him to answer Urban's call. The financial and administrative arrangements he made with William Rufus involved his brother in the venture. Throughout Western Christendom similar arrangements were made within families of every social degree in the hope that the efforts of the individual might benefit the group as a whole.[43] From what we know of the chivalric spirit of William Rufus, the king may have been tempted to join the expedition himself, but there were other considerations which prevented his participation. The attempt on his life during the rebellion of Earl Robert de Mowbray focused Rufus's attention on the internal security of his kingdom. He also had ambitions to extend his influence in Wales and Scotland, which took precedence over any other venture, no matter how glorious. Rufus also had his duties as king to consider. In addition, the prospect of gaining control of Normandy peacefully was another incentive to remain at home.[44] Perhaps more surprising is that the youngest brother Henry did not join Robert, but his ambitions undoubtedly lay closer to home. There was always the fear that he would lose what he had in Normandy with Rufus in charge. It had been Duke Robert, after all, who had tempered the king's anger towards Henry during the siege of Mont-Saint-Michel.[45]

Before Robert could embark on the pilgrimage, he needed to raise funds and also bring an end to his dispute with his brother the king.[46] Pope Urban sent a legate to bring about reconciliation between the brothers. At Easter (13 April) 1096, Abbot Gerento of Saint-Bénigne of Dijon visited the king in England and, before the end of May, he was with Duke Robert in Normandy. The account of the papal mission comes from the *Chronicon* of his companion Hugh of Flavigny.[47]

[42] *GN*, pp. 153–4, trans. Levine, pp. 65–6; *RC*, p. 622, trans. Bachrach and Bachrach, p. 46.

[43] On this theme, see Riley-Smith, *The First Crusaders*, pp. 7–22.

[44] William II's latest biographer, Emma Mason, has pointed out that none of the sources mention the king's attitude to the Crusade. It seems hard to believe that he was indifferent to the expedition. I am grateful to Dr Mason for her helpful comments to me on this matter.

[45] Green, *Henry I*, pp. 35–6.

[46] K. Leyser, 'Money and Supplies on the First Crusade', in *idem, Communications and Power in Medieval Europe. The Gregorian Revolution and Beyond*, ed. T. Reuter (London and Rio Grande, 1994), pp. 77–95.

[47] Hugh of Flavigny, 'Chronicon', ed. G.H. Pertz, in *MGH, Scriptores*, VIII, pp. 280–503 at 474–5.

On 24 May, at Bayeux, Robert confirmed the gift of his uncle, Bishop Odo, of the priory of Saint-Vigor to Abbot Gerento and it was, perhaps, during this period that Robert began to finalise arrangements for the transference of Normandy to his brother the king.[48] If part of Gerento's mission was to preach the Crusade in England and Normandy, he seems to have had more success in the duchy. As has been said, Rufus's troubles of 1095 probably precluded any thought of the king leaving for Palestine, but there is evidence that some from England answered the papal summons.[49]

The peace concluded between Robert and his brother provided the duke with the necessary funds. Robert pledged Normandy to his brother for 10,000 silver marks.[50] The sources differ on the duration of the arrangement with variations between a fixed term of three or five years or the indefinite 'until the duke's return'.[51] The raising of the money for the loan provoked an outcry among Rufus's subjects.[52] If Robert's intentions were communicated to his brother at Easter, then Rufus raised the sum inside six months because the cash was shipped to Normandy in September. The *Worcester Chronicle* recorded that 'bishops, abbots, abbesses broke up their gold and silver ornaments, earls, barons, sheriffs despoiled their knights and villeins and gave the king a large sum of gold and silver'.[53] It has been estimated that the lump sum paid to Robert was less than a quarter of the annual revenue for England; nevertheless, the sources are clear that this added burden was resented.[54]

There were advantages for Rufus in the agreement, not the least of which was possession of the duchy, a crucial advantage in the event of Robert's death in the East. When William acquired Normandy, his younger brother Henry made peace with him and was granted the whole of the Cotentin and the Bessin, with the exception of Bayeux and Caen, which was more than Robert had allowed him in 1088.[55] The guarantor of the agreement was the Church,

---

[48] For the grant of Saint-Vigor, see Haskins, *Norman Institutions*, p. 66, no. 3 (= *Regesta*, I, no. 376), and cf. Haskins, *Norman Institutions*, Appendix E, no. 2, p. 285, which records an exchange between the abbey of Saint-Étienne, Caen, and Saint-Bénigne, Dijon. Bates, 'Odo of Bayeux', pp. 19–20.

[49] C.J. Tyerman, *England and the Crusades 1095–1588* (Chicago and London, 1988), pp. 8–21.

[50] WM, *GR*, I, pp. 562–3. The 'Annals of Winchester' (*Ann. Mon.*, II, p. 38) gave the sum as 6,666 marks. David, *Curthose*, Appendix D, pp. 221–9, which includes references to the more modest arrangements made by Robert's companions.

[51] *OV*, V, pp. 26–7, puts the term of the loan at five years; Robert of Torigny, *WJ*, II, pp. 210–11, notes that Normandy was to be held in pledge as long as Robert was away and would be returned if the money was repaid. Hugh of Flavigny, 'Chronicon', p. 475, and Eadmer, *HN*, p. 75, put the term of the loan at three years. For similar arrangements, and that of 1096, see Tabuteau, *Transfers of Property*, pp. 80–7 especially at 86–7.

[52] *HN*, pp. 74–5. A.V. Murray, 'Money and Logistics in the Forces of the First Crusade: Coinage, Bullion, Service and Supply, 1096–99', in *Logistics of Warfare in the Age of the Crusades*, ed. J.H. Pryor (London, 2006), pp. 229–49. I am grateful to Peter Edbury for bringing this article to my attention.

[53] *JW*, III, *sa.* 1096, pp. 84–5; *HN*, pp. 74–5; WM, *GR*, I, pp. 562–3.

[54] Barlow, *Rufus*, p. 363.

[55] *WJ*, II, pp. 210–13.

which took responsibility for the protection of pilgrims' lands and families.[56] It was essential to reassure those who were embarking on the expedition to Jerusalem that their family and possessions would be safe on their return.[57] In September 1096, Rufus met Robert at Rouen, accepted the duchy and paid over the cash.[58]

In preparation for the handover of authority in Normandy, representatives of the king and the duke convened an inquest at Caen in the summer of 1096.[59] The resulting written record, known as the *Consuetudines et Iustice*, presents a series of statements about the rights of the duke especially in matters of law enforcement and keeping the peace. The document does not present a comprehensive survey of ducal rights but rather the 'most essential'. It is noticeable that many of the clauses concern the safety of the individual attending the court or joining the ducal army, which was, in effect, the court on campaign.[60] There were also injunctions against the building of unauthorised fortifications, such as palisades and ditches, and no-one was permitted to deny the duke any castle if he wanted to take it into his own hands.[61] The monopoly of the ducal mints at Rouen and Bayeux was upheld and merchants received assurances of safety.[62] Charles H. Haskins drew attention to the clauses against the building of fortifications and the right of the duke to garrison any he chose. These clauses and the right of demanding hostages to ensure the good behaviour of the barons were seen as indicating those precepts 'most persistently violated during the preceding anarchy'.[63] In keeping with his negative opinion of Duke Robert, Haskins believed that the *Consuetudines* 'point to the usual evils of a weak rule in this period.'[64]

Since the work of Haskins in 1918 the inquest that produced the *Consuetudines et Iusticie* has been dated to 18 July 1091. Haskins argued that 'it must be assigned to 1091 as the only year in the July of which these princes [Duke Robert and King William] were in Normandy and in friendly relations'.[65] However, there was no need for either man to be in Normandy at the time the inquest was held as the information was gathered 'through their bishops and barons' ('per episcopos et barones suos'). Negotiations between the brothers had been conducted before through intermediaries and the inquest did not need the presence of the duke or the king. Haskins' date for the document has been influential, but it is based on assumption.

---

56 I.S. Robinson, *The Papacy, 1073–1198* (Cambridge, 1990), pp. 339–40.
57 *OV*, V, pp. 10–11. It is unlikely that King Philip I of France stood as a guarantor for the agreement as he was under a sentence of excommunication for his refusal to dismiss Bertrade of Montfort.
58 *OV*, V, pp. 32–3; cf. 228–29; *JW*, III, *sa.* 1096, pp. 84–5 and n. 5.
59 Haskins, 'The Norman *Consuetudines et Iusticie* of William the Conqueror', in *Norman Institutions*, Appendix D, pp. 277–84.
60 E.g. 'Consuetudines', cc. 1, 2, 3, 8.
61 'Consuetudines', c. 4.
62 'Consuetudines', cc. 11, 13.
63 Haskins, *Norman Institutions*, p. 278.
64 Haskins, *Norman Institutions*, p. 65.
65 Haskins, *Norman Institutions*, p. 278.

Perhaps the inquest was part of the preliminaries to the transfer of the duchy into the king's hands in September 1096. The *Consuetudines* do not necessarily provide evidence that Duke Robert's reign had been anarchic; after all, these were the rights and customs that, according to the inquest, obtained under the Conqueror, whose rule in the duchy was seen by Haskins as strong and secure. Robert had been recognised as his father's successor as duke for perhaps twenty years before he took over. It is probable that he had been instructed thoroughly in the rights of the duke in his own principality. The inquest was taken with someone perhaps not so conversant with ducal rights in mind and as necessary preparation for assuming responsibility for the duchy.

The clauses about fortifications, the duke's right to garrison castles or take hostages, guarantees of safe conduct to and from the court and army, and those referring to land disputes, all seen as the 'most essential', seem to suggest a list of guide-lines for the incoming William Rufus. Robert had retained a great many supporters in Normandy during the years of struggle with Rufus and not all of them would accompany him to the Holy Land. Finally, the clause relating specifically to the safety of pilgrims in the duchy, although applicable at any time, had a special relevance for the circumstances of 1096.[66]

Departure, September 1096

Robert left Normandy for the Holy Land in late September or early October 1096.[67] Attempts have been made to provide a list of the duke's companions but the majority are beyond the reach of the available source materials.[68] The fact that Robert financed many of his men may have contributed to the comparative dearth of charter evidence, which survives from Normandy, explicitly recording fund-raising for the Crusade.[69] The terms of some char-

---

[66] 'Consuetudines', c. 12. It is hoped that these tentative comments will prompt further discussion of this important document and its significance. The document was dated to 1096 by H. Böhmer, *Kirche und Staat in England und in der Normandie im XI. und XII. Jahrhundert* (Leipzig, 1899), p. 34, n. 2. Haskins made no further comment on Böhmer's suggestion other than to point out that he had mistaken the month as June and overlooked the fact that in 1096 William Rufus did not cross to Normandy until September.

[67] *FC*, p. 159 and n. 21, says Robert left in September then corrected this to October; Peters, *The First Crusade*, p. 36. *OV*, V, pp. 32–3 and WM, *GR*, I, pp. 612–13; both say September. For matters of chronology, see H. Hagenmeyer, *Chronologie de la Première Croisade, 1094–1100* (Paris, 1902; reprinted Hildesheim and New York, 1973).

[68] David, 'Robert's Companions on the Crusade', in *Curthose*, Appendix D, pp. 221–9. Cf. Riley-Smith, *The First Crusaders*, Appendix I, 'Preliminary List of Crusaders', pp. 196–238. For this approach, see A.V. Murray, 'Prosopography', in Nicholson, *The Crusades*, pp. 109–29.

[69] There are references in several charters from the abbeys of Troarn and Fécamp to individuals who were about to go, or had already gone, to Jerusalem: Tabuteau, *Transfers of Property*, pp. 70–1, 76 (Troarn); 81 (Fécamp).

ters recording grants to ecclesiastical institutions in Normandy or England may disguise loans made to individual crusaders or the sale of properties.[70]

Robert's entourage was impressive.[71] Odo of Bayeux and Gilbert of Évreux had been at the Council of Clermont and Urban's preaching may have been their motivation for taking the cross. Odo's opposition to Rufus in 1088 made it difficult for him to remain in a Normandy controlled by the king. According to Orderic, the enmity between Odo and his nephew William was so great that no mediators were able to bring about reconciliation.[72] Robert's chaplain, Arnulf of Chocques, also accompanied his lord, together with at least two other priests from the duchy.[73] Arnulf had been tutor to the nuns at La Trinité in Caen and had educated Robert's sister Cecilia.[74] Also accompanying Robert for the first part of his journey was the historian Fulcher of Chartres, whose account is the nearest we have to an insider's view of the ducal expedition.[75]

Among Robert's companions were old friends such as Ivo and Aubrey of Grandmesnil, as well as men who had opposed the duke. Stephen, count of Aumâle, had gone over to Rufus in 1089, but his involvement in the rebellion of Robert de Mowbray in 1095 had made his absence from Normandy advisable.[76] Similarly, the presence of Gerard de Gournay and Walter of Saint-Valéry suggests that an accommodation had been reached between old enemies. If the 1096 agreement between Robert and Rufus was modelled on the terms of 1091 then there would have been an amnesty for the supporters of each brother.[77]

There were also individuals from neighbouring principalities, such as Duke Alan Fergant, Ralph de Gael, his son Alan, and others from Brittany.[78] There

---

70 G. Constable, 'Medieval Charters as a Source for the History of the Crusades', in P.W. Edbury, ed., *Crusade and Settlement* (Cardiff, 1985), pp. 73–89. I am grateful to Peter Edbury for discussing this point with me.

71 Although there is not space here, it would be useful to examine Robert's entourage more fully; cf. A.V. Murray, 'The Army of Godfrey of Bouillon, 1096–1099: Structure and Dynamics of a Contingent on the First Crusade', *Revue belge de philologie et d'histoire*, 70 (1992), pp. 301–29.

72 *OV*, V, pp. 208–9; Bates, 'Odo of Bayeux', p. 20.

73 Philip *clericus*, son of Roger of Montgomery, who may or may not have been in clerical orders, and Robert of Rouen. *OV*, III, pp. 140–1 has Philip *grammaticus*. In the aftermath of the rebellion against Rufus in 1095 Philip was imprisoned: *JW*, III, *s.a.* 1096, pp. 82–3. Philip therefore had good reason to leave the duchy.

74 David, 'Arnulf of Chocques, Chaplain of Robert Curthose', *Curthose*, Appendix C, pp. 217–20; Haskins, *Norman Institutions*, pp. 74–5; Raymonde Foreville, 'Un chef de la première croisade: Arnoul Malecouronne', *Bulletin philologique et historique du comité des travaux historiques et scientifiques* (1953–4), pp. 377–90, and Cristina Dondi, *The Liturgy of the Canons Regular of the Holy Sepulchre of Jerusalem. A Study and a Catalogue of the Manuscript Sources* (Turnhout, 2004), pp. 49–57.

75 *FC*, pp. 162–3; Peters, *The First Crusade*, p. 23; D.C. Munro, 'A Crusader', *Speculum*, 7 (1932), pp. 321–35.

76 *JW*, III, *s.a.* 1095, pp. 76–7.

77 *OV*, V, pp. 34–5. *AA*, pp. 98–9 for Gerard de Gournay at the siege of Nicaea. It would be useful to explore the motives of Robert's companions for joining the expedition.

78 *OV*, V, pp. 58–9. Duke Alan, Ralph de Gael and his son Alan are all reported at the siege of Nicaea.

were men from Maine, Artois and the county of the Perche.[79] Eustace III, count of Boulogne, may also have accompanied Robert.[80]

Robert's troops joined forces with those of his brother-in-law, Count Stephen of Blois, and his cousin Robert, count of Flanders.[81] Although the sources are not explicit on how the contingents were organised, it is likely that the knightly elements of the army were composed of a number of small, tightly knit groups of comrades-in-arms. The members of these groups needed to have trust in each other's abilities, given that, in the confusion of battle, their very lives might depend on their comrades. Robert's personal entourage, gathered around the standard carried by Pagan Peverel, included men he had already campaigned with, either in his struggles with his father or in the sieges and skirmishes which he had conducted as duke.[82] Robert had demonstrated his ability to conduct sieges effectively as well as to lead troops fearlessly in open warfare. When he thought it necessary, Robert could be as ruthless as his brothers, but he had also proved that he could be a chivalrous commander. The expedition to the Holy Land was to test whether the lessons that Robert and his comrades had learned in Northern France and Britain would be applicable against non-Western opponents.[83]

Although Rufus handed over the subsidy in September 1096, Robert's preparations had been under way since the spring. The logistical problems of organising a medieval army were considerable and it says something of Robert's abilities as a commander that his forces were ready to leave Normandy before the end of 1096.[84] As well as the fighting men, the armies that left for the Holy Land contained many non-combatants. These consisted of the many 'support' troops necessary, as well as hundreds, if not thousands, of ill-equipped poor and hangers-on using the army as a shield to undertake the pilgrimage, or

---

79 From Maine, e.g. *Cartulaire de Saint-Vincent*, nos. 317 (Guy de Sarcé), no. 460 (Hamo 'de Huna' or La Hune); David, *Curthose*, Appendix D, had his doubts about these two, but Riley-Smith, *First Crusaders*, Appendix I, p. 210, considered their participation verified. Helias of La Flèche also wanted to join the expedition, but was prevented by Rufus's decision not to grant him peace; *OV*, V, pp. 228–33, and Barton, 'Henry I, Count Helias and Tinchebray', p. 71. Hugh of Saint-Pol in Artois: *OV*, V, pp. 34–5. Rotrou of Mortagne, son of Count Geoffrey of the Perche: *OV*, V, pp. 34–5, and Thompson, *Border Lordship*, pp. 50–3.

80 *ASC*, E, *s.a.* 1096, p. 107; Swanton, p. 232; *HH*, pp. 422–3. Tanner, *Families, Friends and Allies*, pp. 135–8.

81 J.A. Brundage, 'An Errant Crusader: Stephen of Blois', *Traditio*, 16 (1960), pp. 380–95; M.M. Knappen, 'Robert II of Flanders in the First Crusade', in L.J. Paetow, ed., *The Crusades and Other Historical Essays presented to Dana C. Munro by his former students* (New York, 1928), pp. 79–100.

82 Susan B. Edgington, 'Pagan Peverel: An Anglo-Norman Crusader', in Edbury, *Crusade and Settlement*, pp. 93–7.

83 J. France, 'Crusading Warfare', in Nicholson, *The Crusades*, pp. 58–80. R.C. Smail, *Crusading Warfare, 1097–1193*, 2nd ed. (Cambridge, 1997), but see, J. France, *Western Warfare in the Age of the Crusades, 1000–1300* (London, 1999), and for the First Crusade itself, *idem, Victory in the East*.

84 On the logistics of the Crusade, see J.H. Pryor, 'Introduction: Modelling Bohemond's March to Thessalonike', in *idem, Logistics of Warfare*, pp. 1–24; B.S. Bachrach, 'Crusader Logistics: From Victory at Nicaea to Resupply at Dorylaion', in Pryor, *Logistics of Warfare*, pp. 43–62.

simply as a source of income.[85] Feeding such numbers on the march was to prove a problem for the leaders of the Western armies, but even the departure and first stages of the journey for Robert's contingent involved the organisation of food and supplies. The fact that Robert was able to lead his army out of Normandy in good time to join the expedition gives the lie to the characterisation of the duke as incapable of motivating himself and others. Even if the actual organisation was left to others, does that not say something about skilful delegation, an important aspect of leadership?

Robert's departure was attended by a great outpouring of emotion, as Fulcher of Chartres describes:

> Oh how much grief there was! How many sighs! How much sorrow! How much weeping among loved ones when the husband left his wife so dear to him, as well as his children, father and mother, brothers and grandparents, and possessions however great! But however so many tears those remaining shed for those going, these were not swayed by such tears from leaving all that they possessed; without doubt believing that they would receive a hundredfold what the Lord promised to those loving him. Then the wife reckoned the time of her husband's return, because if God permitted him to live, he would come home to her. He commended her to the Lord, kissed her and promised as she wept that he would return. She, fearing that she would never see him again, not able to hold up, fell senseless to the ground; mourning her living beloved as though he were dead. He, having compassion it seems neither for the weeping of his wife, nor feeling pain for the grief of any friends, and yet having it, for he secretly suffered severely, unchanging, went away with a determined mind.[86]

Fulcher's account gives an all too rare insight into the mentality of the departing medieval soldier and the great emotional cost of the First Crusade.[87] We can only guess at the levels of anxiety felt by combatants as they left their homes, and the apprehension of their loved ones as they watched husbands, fathers, sons, and brothers marching off to an uncertain fate. The emphasis laid on the changed spiritual status of the Crusader, perhaps marked by the wearing of the cross or the carrying of a pilgrim's staff and scrip, heightened the emotion of departure.

For those travelling in a spirit of pilgrimage, there were mixed emotions at participating in a military exercise. Warriors were often spiritually prepared for battle in this period. Combatants and their weapons were blessed before battle, their sword blades carried religious inscriptions and the pommels

---

[85] W. Porges, 'The Clergy, the Poor and the Non-combatants on the First Crusade', *Speculum*, 21 (1946), pp. 1–23.

[86] FC, pp. 162–3; Peters, *First Crusade*, pp. 35–6. J. Riley-Smith, 'The State of Mind of Crusaders to the East', in *idem*, ed., *Oxford History of the Crusades* (Oxford, 1997), pp. 66–90.

[87] Emily Albu, 'Probing the Passions of a Norman on Crusade: the *Gesta Francorum et aliorum Hierosolimitanorum*', *ANS*, 27 (2005), pp. 1–15.

contained fragments of saints' relics. The wearing of the cross acted as a protective talisman, as well as signalling membership of Christ's militia.[88]

The Journey to Constantinople,
October 1096 to May 1097

Robert's route to the Holy Land initially lay over the Alps, through Italy and across the Adriatic to the Byzantine Empire.[89] Robert may have acted as a guide for his contingent, given the possibility that he had visited the court of Countess Matilda of Tuscany during one of his periods of exile.[90] Robert gleaned details and advice about the journey to the Holy Land from other Norman pilgrims, as well as from the stories told about his grandfather's expedition.[91]

Fulcher of Chartres, travelling in Robert's entourage, reported that towards the end of October the duke met Pope Urban II at Lucca in Italy.[92] Robert and Stephen of Blois conferred with the pontiff and received his blessing.[93] According to one source, Robert's chaplain Arnulf and Alexander, chaplain of Stephen of Blois, were made ancillary legates by the pope.[94]

From Lucca Robert pushed on to Rome, which was occupied at the time by Urban II's rival, the antipope Clement III. According to Fulcher of Chartres, Robert and his entourage were harassed by Clement's men during their visit to St Peter's. The crusaders passed up the chance to assist some of Urban's allies who were besieged in a tower, deciding that their priority was to continue their march towards Jerusalem. It was at this point that the first desertions from the army occurred.[95]

The route south took Robert to the great Benedictine abbey of Montecassino, where the Normans received the monks' blessing.[96] Given the attachment of many Normans to the cult of St Michael, members of Robert's army may have made a detour to the saint's shrine on Monte Gargano, before moving

---

[88] For all these matters, see Strickland, 'A Christian Chivalry? War, Piety and Sacrilege', in *War and Chivalry*, pp. 55–97, esp. at 55–68.

[89] Hugh of Flavigny's *Chronicon*, p. 475; the march was via Pontarlier, where Abbot Gerento and Hugh of Flavigny left the expedition. The army then crossed the Alps by the Great St Bernard pass to Aosta, thence across the valley of the River Po to Lucca. Cf. David, *Curthose*, p. 96.

[90] See above, Chapter 3, pp. 000.

[91] *OV*, V, pp. 34–5, cf. *Baldric of Dol*, in *RHC, Occ.*, p. 20.

[92] *OV*, V, pp. 210–11 says that Robert and his uncle Odo met the pope at Rome.

[93] *FC*, p. 164; Peters, *First Crusade*, p. 38. For the men of Lucca, see Hagenmeyer, *Kreuzzugsbriefe*, pp. 165–7, trans. Peters, *op. cit.*, pp. 232–3.

[94] Dondi, *Liturgy of the Holy Sepulchre*, p. 52 and n. 59.

[95] *FC*, pp. 164–6; Peters, *First Crusade*, p. 38. Cf. WM, *GR*, I, pp. 612–21: a pilgrim's guide to Rome and its shrines.

[96] Petrus Diaconus, 'Chronica Monasterii Casinensis', in *MGH, Scriptores*, vii, p. 765.

south to Bari.[97] There, Robert and his men visited the shrine of St Nicholas and prayed for further help on their journey.[98] These visits to saints' shrines highlight the penitential and pilgrimage aspects of the journey.

It is not clear whether arrangements had already been made to hire ships to cross the Adriatic, but it seems that Robert was advised not to make a winter crossing.[99] Robert and Stephen of Blois spent the winter in Calabria, as the guests of Count Roger Borsa, who 'welcomed the duke of Normandy with his companions as his natural lord and provided liberally for all his needs'.[100] The fact that Count Roger welcomed Robert as his 'natural lord' is an interesting commentary on how Orderic thought the southern Italian Normans viewed the land of their origin. Orderic recorded the continued contacts between Normandy and the Normans of Italy and Sicily.[101]

In the winter of 1096/7, Robert of Flanders decided to risk crossing the Adriatic and found ships with the help of Count Roger.[102] The problems encountered in securing supplies over the winter and the fear that their leaders had deserted them, forced some in the army to abandon their attempt to reach Jerusalem. Fulcher of Chartres reported that many sold their weapons and, in the guise of pilgrims, returned home.[103]

It is not known how Robert of Normandy spent the winter, but perhaps he looked for his grandfather's final resting place or joined his uncle, Bishop Odo, in visiting Roger of Sicily in Palermo. While there Odo fell ill and died in February 1097 despite the best attention of his companion Gilbert, bishop of Évreux.[104] Odo, who must have been in his late sixties at least, was buried in the cathedral at Palermo and Roger of Sicily provided a monument for the grave.[105] Robert had not only lost a close relative, but also a trusted and experienced counsellor. Robert's chaplain, Arnulf of Chocques, was left Odo's moveable wealth.[106]

---

[97] Around the year 1000 the first Normans in Southern Italy had arrived as pilgrims visiting Monte Gargano; see *Storia de'Normanni di Amato di Montecassino*, 1.17, ed. V. de Bartholomeis, Fonti per la storia d'Italia (Rome, 1935), pp. 21–2.

[98] *OV*, IV, pp. 54–75, an account of the translation of the relics of St Nicholas from Myra to Bari in 1087. For the cult of St Nicholas in Normandy, see Chibnall, *World of Orderic*, pp. 106–7.

[99] In 1093, Roger Borsa had married Alaine, a daughter of the count of Flanders, and it is likely that he arranged transport for the Normans and Flemings: Malaterra, *De Rebus Gestis*, pp. 98–9; Wolf, *The Deeds of Count Roger*, p. 198.

[100] *OV*, V, pp. 34–5.

[101] Cf. E. Johnson, 'The Process of Norman Exile into Southern Italy', in Napran and van Houts, eds., *Exile in the Middle Ages*, pp. 29–38.

[102] *FC*, pp. 167–8; Knappen, 'Robert of Flanders', pp. 86–7.

[103] *FC*, p. 168; Peters, *First Crusade*, p. 39.

[104] *OV*, IV, pp. 118–19.

[105] *OV*, V, pp. 208–11. Cf. Bates, 'Odo of Bayeux', p. 20. It is not clear whether Gilbert continued his pilgrimage or returned to Normandy immediately after the burial of Odo: see Bouet and Dosdat, 'Les évêques normands de 985 a 1150', p. 29. Dondi, *The Liturgy of the Holy Sepulchre*, p. 52 and n. 61, citing Bouet and Dosdat's article, p. 29, suggests that 'Gilbert, bishop of Évreux, after presiding at the funeral went back to Normandy.' From 13 to 15 November 1099, Gilbert took part in the dedication of the abbey church of Saint-Évroul: *OV*, V, pp. 262–7.

[106] *GN*, pp. 290–1, trans. Levine, pp. 135–6.

In March 1097, Robert gathered his forces at the Apulian port of Brindisi, which was then in the hands of the Norman count of Conversano.[107] It was there that Robert struck up a relationship with the Count of Conversano's daughter, Sibyl. Despite planning to set sail on the propitious day of Easter Sunday (5 April), the departure was marred by the wreck of one of the ships and the loss of four hundred men and women, together with horses, mules and baggage.[108] The discovery that the bodies of some of the drowned were marked on the shoulders with the sign of the cross could not reassure those who took this as an ill-omen and, fearing to cross the sea, they abandoned the army. The rest put their faith in God and set sail for Byzantium.[109]

The fleet landed near the city of Durazzo (Dyrrachium) in modern Albania.[110] From the coast, the army made its way along the Via Egnatia, encountering some difficulties crossing a swollen river.[111] The incident enabled some knights to demonstrate their bravery by riding into the torrent to pull their companions from the flood.[112] Earlier contingents of crusaders had clashed with Byzantine troops as they foraged for food, but Robert's army seems to have been disciplined and that ensured that supplies were made readily available. Finally, after about a month on the road, Robert and his companions reached the imperial city of Constantinople about the middle of May 1097.

The city of Constantinople was astonishing for many of these pilgrim-warriors from Northern Europe. It was, however, well known to the Normans. By the time that Robert reached the Byzantine capital, some of his fellow countrymen had been in imperial service for several decades.[113] In addition, the southern Italian Normans had fought a series of campaigns against the Byzantine Emperor, Alexios I Komnenos. Naturally, the emperor was wary of these men whose relatives had waged war on Byzantium for decades.[114]

For the northerners, however, the city was stunning. Fulcher of Chartres was obviously impressed:

> Oh what an excellent and beautiful city! How many monasteries, and how many palaces there are in it, of wonderful work, skilfully fashioned! How many marvellous works are to be seen in the streets and districts of the town! It is a great nuisance to recite what an opulence of all kinds of goods are found there; of gold, of silver, of

---

107   For the crusaders' use of Southern Italian ports, see G. Loud, 'Norman Italy and the Holy Land', in *The Horns of Hattin*, ed. B.Z. Kedar (Jerusalem, 1992), pp. 49–62 at 53.
108   *FC*, pp. 168–71; Peters, *First Crusade*, p. 39.
109   *FC*, pp. 172–5; Peters, *First Crusade*, pp. 39–40.
110   *FC*, pp. 172–5; Peters, *First Crusade*, p. 40.
111   For the route and conditions on the march, see Pryor, 'Introduction: Modelling Bohemond's March', in *idem, Logistics of Warfare*, pp. 1–24. I am grateful to Peter Edbury for pointing out that Robert's contingent followed the route taken by Bohemond.
112   *FC*, pp. 172–5; Peters, *First Crusade*, pp. 40–1, giving the itinerary.
113   J. Shepard, 'The Uses of the Franks in Eleventh-century Byzantium', *ANS*, 15 (1993), pp. 275–305.
114   W.B. McQueen, 'Relations between the Normans and Byzantium, 1071–1112', *Byzantion*, 56 (1986), pp. 427–76; Loud, *Age of Robert Guiscard*, pp. 209–23.

many kinds of mantles and of holy relics. In every season, merchants, in frequent sailings, bring to that place everything that man might need. Almost twenty thousand eunuchs, I judge, are kept there all the time.[115]

William of Malmesbury included a long digression in his account of the Crusade on the history of Constantinople, its emperors and the relics found there.[116]

Robert and Stephen of Blois were taken to meet the emperor, who entertained them amid an impressive display of Byzantine court ceremonial.[117] Stephen described the occasion in a letter sent back to Robert's sister, Adela.[118] The memory of Robert's grandfather's visit to Constantinople may have been rekindled by this meeting.[119] Robert's grandfather had recognised that the gifts offered by the emperor were designed to put him in the emperor's debt and that they were intended to intimidate as well as impress. According to an interpolation in the *Gesta Normannorum ducum*, produced between 1097 and 1100, Duke Robert I countered Byzantine stereotypes of greedy westerners by having his mule shod with gold and forbidding his men from picking up any of the golden shoes that were shed. The gesture had the required effect and the Byzantines wondered at the westerners' disregard for wealth. Robert also defied the convention that all should stand in the emperor's presence, by sitting next to him 'without being asked to do so'. There was then a contest of wills, with the emperor attempting to put Robert and his men in his debt, by offering him food for as long as he was in Constantinople and then gold, precious clothes and vessels. Robert refused all these, and the emperor, taking this as a gesture of contempt, forbade the Normans access to all markets so that they would be forced to accept his generosity. When even firewood for cooking was refused, Robert ordered his men to use the shells of almonds and walnuts, at which point the emperor relented.[120] If such stories were circulating in Normandy before Robert Curthose left on the Crusade, he carried with him some idea of what to expect at Constantinople.[121]

The attitude of the Byzantine emperor towards the crusaders in 1096–7 has been the subject of discussion.[122] In particular, attention has focused on the

115   *FC*, pp. 175–7; Peters, *First Crusade*, p. 41.
116   WM, *GR*, I, pp. 622–7.
117   H. Maguire, ed., *Byzantine Court Culture from 829 to 1204* (Washington DC, 1997). I am grateful to my colleague Shaun Tougher for this reference.
118   Hagenmeyer, *Kreuzzugsbriefe*, no. IV, pp. 138–40.
119   Elisabeth van Houts, 'Normandy and Byzantium', *Byzantion*, 55 (1985), pp. 544–59. Dr van Houts is sceptical about the visit as it is not recorded in other eleventh-century sources, but cf. J. Shepard, 'Byzantine Diplomacy, A.D. 800–1205: Means and Ends', in *Byzantine Diplomacy*, ed. J. Shepard and S. Franklin (Aldershot, 1992), pp. 41–71 at 54–5.
120   *WJ*, II, pp. 82–5.
121   M. Angold, 'Knowledge of Byzantine History in the West: the Norman Historians (Eleventh and Twelfth Centuries)', *ANS*, 25 (2003), pp. 19–33 at 28–9. The story may, conversely, have been prompted by Robert Curthose's visit.
122   E.g. J. Shepard, 'Cross-purposes: Alexius Comnenus and the First Crusade', in Phillips, *The First Crusade*, pp. 107–29.

oaths of allegiance that he required from the leaders before they left Constantinople. The large numbers of warriors and non-combatants had been a considerable problem for Alexios and he was concerned to ensure that once they had crossed the Bosphorus they would not cause further disruption.[123] His first concern was to protect the Empire from the possible consequences of the crusaders' action in the region, especially with an eye to dealing with his neighbours once the westerners had departed. The crusaders posed a threat but also offered the chance to restore Byzantine possessions in Asia Minor. The task for Alexios was, therefore, to defuse the danger and turn the crusade to Byzantine advantage.[124]

Alexios's solution was to employ traditional diplomatic methods. First, he assigned troops to escort the contingents through the Balkan territories to curtail their destructive foraging. Secondly, he overawed them with displays of wealth and, if necessary, military might. Last, he attempted to bind them to him with 'the customary oath of the Latins'.[125]

The terms of the oath seem to have been that the crusaders undertook to restore any former Byzantine possessions that they liberated along their route to Jerusalem and accept the superior status of the emperor. Alexios entertained his guests in style, doubtless to make them more receptive to his terms, but this was also part of the process of establishing the parameters of the relationship. The problem was that each side understood the relationship on its own terms. For the westerners the bond between lord and vassal implied mutual obligations, whereas Alexios seems to have regarded the crusaders taking an oath to serve him as recognition of their subservience to himself as the leader of Christendom. The crusaders, as well as having confidence in their military superiority to the Byzantines, also understood their own expedition as a pilgrimage and that their ultimate obligation was to God and to no earthly power. To the Byzantines, the armies assembling at Constantinople looked like any other mercenary company in the employ of the Oikoumene, a term meaning, roughly, 'civilisation' and synonymous with the Byzantine Empire.[126]

Although there was some resistance to swearing the oath to Alexios, Robert of Normandy accepted the necessity of doing so in order to ensure Byzantine assistance on the expedition.[127] He and his brother-in-law, Stephen of Blois, were richly rewarded by the emperor.[128] Robert was not alone in taking the oath and only Raymond of Toulouse refused and had to be placated with a

---

[123] J. Harris, *Byzantium and the Crusades* (London, 2003), pp. 53–71.
[124] Harris, *Byzantium and the Crusades*, pp. 56–8.
[125] *Alexiad*, pp. 315, 319, 323. J.H. Pryor, 'The Oaths of the Leaders of the First Crusade to the Emperor Alexius I Comnenus: Fealty, Homage – Pistis, Douleia', *Parergon*, n.s., 2 (1984), pp. 111–32.
[126] Harris, *Byzantium and the Crusades*, pp. 60–3 and 13 (Oikoumene).
[127] *FC*, p. 178; Peters, *First Crusade*, pp. 41–2. WM, *GR*, I, pp. 628–9, describes Robert and Stephen prostrating themselves before the Emperor and performing homage.
[128] Stephen of Blois' letter: Hagenmeyer, *Kreuzzugsbriefe*, no. IV, p. 138.

modified version of the pledge.[129] There was also a feeling that the emperor's gifts were hollow as they were inevitably returned to him as currency in the markets of Constantinople. It was clearly necessary for the crusaders to come to an arrangement with the Byzantine emperor, otherwise the expedition was in danger of stalling or dissipating at Constantinople. However, the ambiguities of the relationship and mutual misunderstandings were to lead to problems and distrust.

The Road to Antioch, May to October, 1097

More gifts and necessary supplies came from the emperor and then, at the end of May, Robert's troops were transported across the Bosphorus into Asia Minor.[130] The northern Normans advanced to join the other contingents, who had been besieging the city of Nicaea since 14 May. Nicaea was another site of memory for Robert as the place where his grandfather had died.[131]

When Robert and Stephen arrived at Nicaea in the first week of June, a major battle had already been fought against the Seljuq Turks on 16 May.[132] Robert was assigned a position outside the southern walls of the city, between the armies of Robert of Flanders and Raymond of Toulouse.[133] The sources do not single out Robert for special mention during the siege, which lasted until the surrender of Nicaea to Byzantine representatives on 19 June 1097, but Albert of Aachen gave one of Robert's men a key role in the assault on the town.[134] Emperor Alexios had advanced to Pelekanum to be in a position to reclaim Nicaea and the leaders of the crusade met him there, receiving gifts for their services.[135] Emperor Alexios's daughter, Anna, suggests that her father ensured that the crusaders were reminded of their oaths to him.[136]

After allowing the Byzantine forces to occupy Nicaea, the Crusade leaders were anxious to push on towards Jerusalem. Within a week, some were on the march, but for those who had arrived late at the siege it seemed best to recuperate for a little longer before pushing on.[137] Robert and his men followed the main body of the army after observing the important formalities of an

---

129   *GF*, p. 13; *Raymond d'Aguilers*, trans. Hill and Hill, pp. 23–4.
130   *FC*, p. 179; Peters, *First Crusade*, p. 42. Cf. 'Letter of Stephen of Blois to Adela', in Hagenmeyer, *Kreuzzugsbriefe*, no. IV, pp. 138–9.
131   *WJ*, II, pp. 80–5.
132   *GF*, p. 15. Cf. *OV*, V, pp. 54–5. For the siege of Nicaea, see France, *Victory in the East*, pp. 157–69. Hagenmeyer, *Chronologie*, p. 75, dates the arrival to 3 June 1097.
133   *GF*, p. 16. *AA*, pp. 96–7 describes Robert as 'most warlike in military weapons and well endowed with property'.
134   *AA*, pp. 118–19.
135   Hagenmeyer, *Kreuzzugsbriefe*, pp. 140, 145. Stephen of Blois' letter home once again describes the meeting at Pelekanum in terms sympathetic to Alexios.
136   *Alexiad*, p. 340.
137   The contingents began leaving from 26 June: Hagenmeyer, *Chronologie*, p. 83.

imperial leave-taking.[138] Robert caught up with the rest of the Crusaders and the whole army resumed the march across Anatolia.[139] The army was divided in two, with the southern Italian Normans under Bohemond and Tancred, together with the northern French under Duke Robert, Robert of Flanders and Stephen of Blois, advancing before the other contingents.[140]

On the evening of 30 June 1097, as they were crossing the 'plain of Dorylaeum', the Normans spotted Turkish forces nearby.[141] The next morning they were attacked by forces commanded by Sultan Kilij Arslan, the Seljuk leader, who had earlier failed to drive off the crusaders besieging Nicaea.[142] The Turks attacked relentlessly and the situation became desperate. Fulcher of Chartres described the terror among the crusaders,

> All of us, huddled together like sheep in a fold, trembling and terrified, were fenced in by the enemy on all sides, so that we could not turn in any direction. It was evident that this had happened to us because of our sins. For dissipation had polluted certain ones and avarice or some other iniquity had corrupted others. There was a vast cry smiting the heavens, of men and women and little children, and also of the heathens who rushed in upon us. No hope of life remained.[143]

Some accounts give prominence to the efforts of Bohemond to rally the forces, while messengers were sent to the rest of the army for help.[144] This emphasis on the lord of Taranto is in large measure due to the influence of the *Gesta Francorum*, written by one of Bohemond's followers.[145] Other accounts give an interesting variation on the *Gesta*'s description of the roles of Robert of Normandy and Bohemond.

According to Guibert of Nogent, Robert fought heroically, spurred on by thoughts of his noble ancestry and remembering his father's military reputation. It is interesting that Guibert suggested that Robert was motivated by his

---

138   *FC*, p. 189; Peters, *First Crusade*, p. 45. On the importance of leave-taking and the bonds of lordship as Robert and his men understood them, see S.D.B. Brown, 'Leave-taking: Lordship and Mobility in England and Normandy in the Twelfth Century', *History*, 79 (1994), pp. 199–215.

139   On the route, see Runciman, 'The First Crusade: Constantinople to Antioch', in Baldwin, *History of the Crusades*, I, p. 292.

140   *GF*, pp. 18–21; *OV*, V, pp. 58–9, drawing on Baldric of Dol, provides a list of those prominent in this group: Hugh of Saint-Pol, Gerard de Gournay, Walter of Saint-Valéry and his son Bernard, William, son of Ralph II the vicomte of Bayeux, William of Ferrières, Hervey son of Dodeman, Conan, son of Count Geoffrey, Ralph de Gael and his son Alan, Rihou of Lohéac and Alan the steward of Dol. The Bretons probably owe their place in Orderic's *Historia* to Baldric's narrative. It was important that the names of these men were memorialised because they participated in the famous battle at Dorylaeum.

141   *Alexiad*, p. 341.

142   France, *Victory in the East*, pp. 169–84.

143   *FC*, pp. 190–8; Peters, *First Crusade*, pp. 45–8.

144   *GF*, pp. 18–19; *OV*, V, pp. 60–3; *RC*, pp. 620–9, trans. Bachrach and Bachrach, pp. 44–56.

145   *GF*, pp. 18–21. Cf. *OV*, V, pp. 58–61. C. Morris, 'The *Gesta Francorum* as Narrative History', *Reading Medieval Studies*, 19 (1993), pp. 55–71; K.B. Wolf, 'Crusade and Narrative: Bohemond and the *Gesta Francorum*', *JMH*, 17 (1991), pp. 207–16. J. France, 'The Use of the Anonymous *Gesta Francorum* in the Early Twelfth-century Sources for the First Crusade', in A.V. Murray, ed., *From Clermont to Jerusalem. The Crusades and Crusader Societies 1095–1500* (Turnhout, 1998), pp. 29–39.

father's example and concern for the honour of his dynasty, and for many, especially in the ranks of the knights who joined the expedition to Jerusalem, it was an opportunity to enhance reputations. These men were fighting not only for themselves, but also for their families and noble dynasties.[146]

Although surrounded by the Seljuks, Robert and Bohemond managed to rally their troops until relief came from the second contingent of the army. Ralph of Caen, writing some twenty years later and who claimed to have gleaned his information from Bohemond, Tancred, and other eye-witnesses, also provides a detailed account of the battle.[147] He repeats some of Guibert's observations about what drove Robert to his heroic acts, but, contrary to what one might expect, Ralph assigned more prominence to Robert of Normandy than to Bohemond. The Normans were falling back under pressure of the Seljuk attack when Robert found the courage to rally his comrades.

> There, at last, one who was of the royal blood of William recalled to himself his lineage and the fact that he was a fighter. He uncovered his head and shouted 'Normandy!' and then caught the attention of his colleague Bohemond who had followed him in flight with the following words: 'Ho! Bohemond, why are we fleeing? Apulia is far away, Otranto is far away. Hope for the borders of any Latin land is far from us. We should make our stand here for we will have either the glorious punishment of the defeated or the victor's crown. I say that both of these chances are glorious, but the first is even more blessed than the latter because it will make us blessed that much more quickly. Therefore, go forward my young men, let us die and charge them under arms.' After being admonished in this way, the remainder of the young men joined themselves to the leaders more prepared to die than to flee.[148]

Although Ralph of Caen, as his name suggests, may have been predisposed to highlight the efforts of his duke, his account is primarily focused on the southern Italian Normans, Bohemond and his nephew Tancred.[149] Therefore, Ralph's willingness to assign such a significant role to Robert suggests that others underestimated the duke of Normandy's inspirational leadership at a crucial moment.[150] Albert of Aachen also noted that Bohemond was perturbed by the Turkish assault and that his resolve weakened before the arrival of the other leaders.[151]

Ralph of Caen confirms details given by Fulcher and the author of the

---

146   *GN*, pp. 153–4, trans. Levine, pp. 65–6.
147   For the date of composition, *Ralph of Caen*, trans. Bachrach and Bachrach, pp. 3–4.
148   *RC*, p. 622, trans. Bachrach and Bachrach, p. 46.
149   *RC*, trans. Bachrach and Bachrach, pp. 1–2. Ralph's preface is addressed to Arnulf of Chocques, Robert's chaplain, who became Patriarch of Jerusalem. They maintained their relationship until Arnulf's death in 1118. Ralph may have been from an influential Norman family, given the fact that he was educated by Arnulf of Chocques, who was also tutor to William the Conqueror's daughter, Cecilia. For Tancred's career, see R.L. Nicholson, *Tancred. A Study of his Career and Work in Relation to the First Crusade and the Establishment of the Latin States in Syria and Palestine* (Chicago, 1940).
150   Cf. the Conqueror's rallying of his men at Hastings, when the young men in his army panicked: *WP*, pp. 128–31.
151   *AA*, pp. 128–37 at 130–1.

Gesta Francorum; they were both at the battle and there seems no reason to discount his additional information about Robert of Normandy's prominent role in rallying the crusaders. All of these accounts, even those of the eye-witnesses, were written after the event with the benefit of hindsight. Memories organised and made sense of what were often chaotic experiences. The sequence of battle was given a logic that was perhaps harder to see at the time. Nevertheless, these authors, if they were not eye-witnesses themselves, had access to those who were and their accounts should be taken seriously. At the least, it demonstrates that Ralph thought Robert capable of such heroics.[152]

The victory at Dorylaeum was Robert's first taste of battle on the campaign and he performed exceptionally under difficult conditions. He showed impressive qualities of leadership, keeping his men in disciplined formation during the confusion of the battle, as well as displaying great personal bravery. Nevertheless, such was the reputation of Bohemond that the duke of Normandy's role in the battle has been underestimated.[153]

The Siege of Antioch, October 1097 to June 1098

The rest of the journey to Antioch through a land 'that was deserted, water-less and uninhabitable' was arduous but, after their triumph at Dorylaeum, the crusaders enjoyed a relatively peaceful passage.[154] Robert's troops formed the vanguard of the army and attacked the defenders of the Iron Bridge over the river Orontes on the road to Antioch. After hard fighting, Robert and his men were joined by the other contingents and gradually won the day.[155] On 20 October 1097, the crusaders camped a few miles from Antioch. The author of the *Gesta Francorum* provided a description of the magnificent city. It was one of the great cities of the medieval world and certainly impressed the Norman from Southern Italy:

> The city of Antioch is a very fine and distinguished place. Within its walls are four great mountains which are exceedingly high. The citadel, a wonderful building which is exceedingly strong, stands on the highest of them. Down below lies the city, which is impressive and well-planned, adorned with all kinds of splendid buildings, for there are many churches, and three hundred and sixty monasteries. Its patriarch is metropolitan over a hundred and fifty-three bishops ... Everything about this city is beautiful.[156]

The siege of the city began the next day and, after debates on strategy among the leaders, who seem to have acted in a council of equals, it was decided

---

152 For a detailed account of the battle, see France, *Victory in the East*, pp. 169–72, 174–85.
153 Cf. David, *Curthose*, pp. 103–4. France, *Victory in the East*, p. 183, accepts Robert's role.
154 *GF*, p. 23. For the journey, see Runciman in *History of the Crusades*, I, pp. 294–98. It was at this point that Fulcher of Chartres ceased to be an eye-witness for the actions of the main army.
155 *AA*, pp. 190–3; *GF*, p. 28. France, *Victory in the East*, pp. 206–8.
156 *GF*, pp. 76–7; cf. WM, *GR*, I, pp. 630–3. Cf. France, *Victory in the East*, pp. 222–5.

to attempt a close blockade.[157] This was no easy task given the long circuit of walls protecting the city on three sides and the mountains to the east.[158] Robert, together with Robert of Flanders and Stephen of Blois, positioned their men to the north-west of the city, but it was recognised that it would be difficult if not impossible to take the city by direct assault.[159] Robert played a full part in operations during the early part of the siege. The author of the *Gesta Francorum* described an abundance of provisions, but with so large an army conditions began to deteriorate towards Christmas. In a letter to his wife from Antioch, Stephen of Blois described the hardships of the winter, particularly the difficulties of finding food, and his view is supported by the *Gesta Francorum*.[160]

The *principes* of the Crusade managed to work in harmony during the siege and this allowed them to invest the city more closely towards Christmas 1097, by building a siege castle called 'Malregard' and the 'Bridge of Boats'. The latter was designed to open the route to the port of St Symeon from where the army hoped for supplies.[161] At some point during the winter, Robert relocated to the town of Latakia (Laodicea), which lay on the Syrian coast, some eighty kilometres south of Antioch.[162]

Robert's withdrawal from Antioch has been the source of some criticism for the duke.[163] Latakia was one of the main channels of supply to the crusaders at Antioch and it seems to have fallen to an English fleet as early as August 1097.[164] The port was well stocked with supplies from Cyprus, then in Byzantine hands, and it was possibly a fleet despatched from the island and manned by Englishmen in Byzantine service that captured Latakia.[165] If this was the case, then it is conceivable, as Ralph of Caen suggests, that these Englishmen would have appealed for assistance from the duke of Normandy, the son of the conqueror of England.[166]

Robert's presence in Latakia was, therefore, a necessary aspect of the strategy for capturing the city of Antioch. Ensuring that supplies went forward to the siege army was Robert's task and he saw to it that generous provisions from

---

[157] For the siege, see France, *Victory in the East*, pp. 197–269.

[158] France, *Victory in the East*, pp. 221–4.

[159] *AA*, pp. 200–1.

[160] Hagenmeyer, *Kreuzzugsbriefe*, pp. 149–52; *GF*, p. 30.

[161] *GF*, p. 30; *AA*, pp. 204–5.

[162] Hagenmeyer, *Chronologie*, p. 114, suggests the middle of December 1097.

[163] David, *Curthose*, p. 105.

[164] *RC*, p. 649, trans. Bachrach and Bachrach, p. 84. For detailed discussions of the evidence, see David, *Curthose*, Appendix E, 'Latakia and the First Crusade', pp. 230–44, and France, *Victory in the East*, pp. 213–19.

[165] France, *Victory in the East*, pp. 215–16; cf. J. Shepherd, 'The English in Byzantium', *Traditio*, 29 (1973), pp. 52–93. It is not possible to accept Orderic's statement that the English fleet was led by Robert's close friend, Edgar Ætheling. At this period he was aiding his nephew, Edgar son of Malcolm III, in his bid for the Scots throne. Cf. Hooper, 'Edgar the Ætheling', pp. 208–10.

[166] *RC*, p. 649, trans. Bachrach and Bachrach, p. 84. Ralph associates Robert's move to Latakia with Stephen of Blois' withdrawal from the siege. Cf. *OV*, V, pp. 270–3.

Cyprus reached Antioch.[167] Life in Latakia must have been more comfortable than outside the walls of Antioch and there is the possibility that Robert was tempted to remain there beyond his commission, but this seems out of character given his conduct for the rest of the expedition. It would have been foolhardy not to make use of the respite and indeed Ralph of Caen noted that Robert took full advantage of the circumstances for a period of rest and recuperation. He goes on to note that it took three summonses and the threat of anathema to recall Robert to Antioch.[168] This reluctance to return seems out of character in a man who until then had shown himself willing to lead the attack. Perhaps Robert did not grasp the urgency of the summons from his fellow leaders. The threat to excommunicate him would have compelled the pious duke to return to the city and he was certainly there by the beginning of February 1098.[169]

The siege of Antioch had continued through the winter, which, in terms of the weather, Stephen of Blois found similar to conditions back home.[170] There had been some high profile desertions; those of William the Carpenter, lord of Melun, and Peter the Hermit were especially shocking. They were brought back by Tancred, and William spent a night of contrition prostrate on the floor of Bohemond's tent 'like a piece of rubbish'. In February, the Emperor's envoy Taticius also left the camp.[171] This may have been as a result of the machinations of Bohemond of Taranto, who at some stage during the siege decided to acquire Antioch for himself.

It was also during February that the crusaders defeated a Turkish relieving force under Ridwan of Aleppo. The 'Lake Battle' took place on Tuesday 9 February and, on this occasion, Robert was left with Bishop Adhémar to continue the siege while the others fought the battle under Bohemond's command.[172]

The siege dragged on until the night of 2 June 1098, when Bohemond managed to negotiate access to the city with a custodian of one of the towers. One source suggests that Robert and the count of Flanders were party to the negotiations, but there was perhaps some confusion between the hatching of the plan and its execution, when all the leaders were let in on the arrangements.[173] By the end of the next day, and after a bloody fight, the crusaders were in control of the city, except for the citadel. Just before the city fell, Stephen of Blois left the army and headed back towards Constantinople, despite the

---

167   RC, p. 649, trans. Bachrach and Bachrach, p. 84.
168   RC, p. 649, trans. Bachrach and Bachrach, p. 84.
169   Cf. GF, pp. 93–4; Robert and others were reluctant to answer Godfrey of Bouillon's summons to Ascalon before they had definite proof of the arrival of an Egyptian army.
170   Hagenmeyer, Kreuzzugsbriefe, p. 150: 'nam hiems apud eos Occidentali nostrae similis est'.
171   GF, pp. 33–4 (William the Carpenter and Peter the Hermit); 34–5 (Taticius).
172   GF, pp. 35–8; Raymond of Aguilers, trans. Hill and Hill, p. 40; Tudebode, ed. Hill and Hill, p. 43; OV, V, pp. 76–81. Cf. France, Victory in the East, pp. 245–51.
173   GF, pp. 44–6. Robert is named in a letter from the city of Lucca: Hagenmeyer, Kreuzzugsbriefe, pp. 165–7, trans. Peters, First Crusade, pp. 232–3. Cf. OV, V, pp. 90–1.

fact that he had already told his wife that he had been made leader of the expedition. The opprobrium he encountered as a result of what was seen as his desertion was a source of great shame when he returned to his wife.[174]

Stephen was not the only one to leave Antioch. A few days later, as a Turkish force under Kerbogha, amir of Mosul, began to besiege the crusaders now inside the city walls, the Normans William of Grandmesnil and his brothers Ivo and Aubrey fled to the port of St Symeon and sailed to Tarsus to join Stephen. Their flight was explained as the result of fear heightened by the storming of the city. This may have been especially disappointing for Robert as Ivo and Aubrey had been his companions for at least twenty years. Each notice of desertion from the army underlines the courage and determination of those who remained.[175]

The siege was pressed closely by the Turks and the situation deteriorated, made worse by spiralling inflation in the price of food. The *Gesta Francorum* describes the pitiful condition of the crusaders,

> Our men ate the flesh of horses and asses and sold it to one another; a hen cost fifteen shillings, an egg two, and a walnut a penny. All things were very dear. So terrible was the famine that men boiled and ate the leaves of figs, vines, thistles and all kinds of trees. Others stewed the dried skins of horses, camels, asses, oxen or buffaloes, which they ate. These and many other troubles and anxieties, which I cannot describe, we suffered for the Name of Christ and to set free the road to the Holy Sepulchre.[176]

The deterioration of conditions inside the city and the desertions prompted the *principes* to swear an oath to remain with the army.

According to the *Gesta Francorum* a certain priest claimed that he had experienced a vision of Christ, who told him that within the space of five days divine help would arrive. The bishop of Le Puy made the priest swear on the Gospels and a crucifix to the truth of his story and this prompted the leaders to swear an oath 'that none of them, while he lived would flee, either from fear of death or from hope of life'. Robert took the oath after Bohemond and Raymond of Toulouse.[177]

As the morale of the crusaders trapped inside Antioch reached its nadir, a Provençal pilgrim named Peter Bartholomew reported that he had experienced a vision of St Andrew. The Apostle revealed the resting place of the Holy Lance, which had pierced Christ's side as he was hanging on the cross. After a

---

[174] Brundage, 'An Errant Crusader', pp. 388–90, suggests that Stephen's actions might not have been those of a coward. *GF*, p. 63, suggests that he fell ill, but that his departure was shameful nonetheless.

[175] *GF*, pp. 56–7; *OV*, V, pp. 96–9. *RC*, p. 662, trans. Bachrach and Bachrach, p. 101. For Ivo and Aubrey as companions of the duke, see *OV*, II, pp. 358–9.

[176] *GF*, p. 62. Murray, 'Money and Logistics', pp. 245–6. I am grateful to Peter Edbury for drawing my attention to the monetary aspects of this passage.

[177] *GF*, pp. 58–9.

second visitation by the saint, Peter revealed his encounter to the crusaders.[178] The discovery of the Holy Lance was a morale booster for many in the army, although there were some who suspected that it was a fabrication. Fortified by this relic and realising that in the absence of outside help the alternative was slow starvation, the crusade leaders decided to attack the besiegers.

On 28 June 1098, after an attempt at a negotiated settlement had failed, the leaders discussed their options and at this point Robert of Normandy may have suggested a tactic he had used to good effect against his father at Gerberoy in January 1079. Robert had broken that siege by leading a frontal assault on his father's troops, striking directly at the Conqueror himself.[179] The scheme was risky but held out the prospect of spectacular victory. In preparation for the battle, the other leaders decided once again to appoint Bohemond as sole commander.

The troops were prepared spiritually for battle by the clergy, who imposed a three-day fast, a series of liturgical processions and celebrations of the mass.[180] The army was led out of the city by the bishops, priests, monks and clerks dressed in their vestments, carrying crosses and reciting prayers. They formed up in six divisions with Robert of Normandy in the third.[181] The ensuing battle was hard fought and at one stage Robert of Normandy, together with Godfrey of Bouillon, was forced to improvise a seventh division to counter a manoeuvre by the Turks. Gradually, the crusaders began to win the day and, according to the *Gesta Francorum*, the Turks were driven off with the help of a countless host of men on white horses led by Saints George, Mercurius and Demetrius.[182]

Jerusalem, July 1098 to July 1099

After the victory over Kerbogha, the crusade leaders met in council to decide when to resume their journey to Jerusalem. They sent one of the leading men of the expedition, Hugh of Vermandois, to inform the Emperor Alexius of the capture of Antioch. As the *Gesta Francorum* tersely expresses it, 'Iuit, nec postea rediit' ('he went; he never came back').[183] In view of the summer heat and the difficulty of finding enough water, food and fodder, the march was delayed until November. The leaders and their men dispersed. It is possible that Robert returned to Latakia and spent the summer recuperating there.

---

178 *GF*, pp. 59–60. Cf. C. Morris, 'Policy and Visions: The Case of the Holy Lance at Antioch', in Gillingham and Prestwich, eds., *War and Government*, pp. 33–45.
179 *JW*, III, *s.a.* 1079, pp. 30–3; see above, pp. 86–90.
180 *GF*, pp. 67–8.
181 *Raymond of Aguilers*, trans. Hill and Hill, p. 63, claimed to have carried the Holy Lance as standard bearer for Bishop Adhémar.
182 *GF*, pp. 68–71. France, *Victory in the East*, pp. 279–96.
183 *GF*, p. 72. *AA*, pp. 340–3; Hugh's companion Baldwin, count of Hainault was ambushed en route. This may have prompted Hugh's desertion.

The death of the papal legate Bishop Adhémar on the feast of St Peter's Chains (1 August) was reported in a letter to Pope Urban II dated 11 September 1098, and Robert may have been present at the discussions which drafted an appeal for the pope to join the crusade.[184]

Robert reappeared at Antioch in good time for the resumption of the march to Jerusalem. Over the summer, divisions had opened up between Bohemond and Count Raymond of Toulouse over the possession of Antioch. The issue was whether Bohemond might be allowed to keep the city in contravention of the oath of the crusaders to return former Byzantine territory to the emperor. The bishops tried to mediate and enlisted Robert, Godfrey of Bouillon, Robert of Flanders and the other leaders in trying to bring about a reconciliation. Robert may have taken the lead as he had considerable experience of bringing seemingly irreconcilable enemies together. Later in his narrative the author of the *Gesta Francorum* refers to Robert mediating between Raymond and Bohemond.[185] Raymond of Toulouse agreed to be bound by the decision of the arbiters 'saving the faith which I owe to the emperor'.[186] Bohemond agreed and he and Raymond swore to abide by the decision. Bohemond and Raymond put their hands in those of the bishops and swore that the journey would not be interrupted by them.[187] At the end of November, the crusaders, including Bohemond, attacked Ma'arra (Ma'arrat-an-Numan).[188] The siege lasted until 11 December and the city was occupied by the crusaders for a month, but disputes over the distribution of the spoils reopened the rift between Bohemond and Raymond.[189]

Despite the best efforts of Robert and his colleagues, Bohemond failed to reach an agreement with Count Raymond. As a result, he left the army and returned to Antioch. Raymond met with the other leaders at Rugia, but was as intransigent as his adversary. In the end Raymond offered the others money as an incentive to resume the march under his leadership. Robert was offered 10,000 *solidi*, possibly an indication of the relative size of his army. Only Godfrey was offered the same amount.[190] In one final attempt at mediation, Robert and the others returned to Antioch.

According to the *Gesta Francorum*, whose author had by now joined his army, Raymond, who had remained at Ma'arra, set out barefoot on 13 January 1099 for Kafartab. His penitential act was prompted by the realisation that he might be the reason that the others were delayed from reaching Jerusalem.[191] Duke Robert, anxious to continue the journey, joined him there in a last

184 *GF*, p. 74. Hagenmeyer, *Kreuzzugsbriefe*, p. 161. For Adhémar, see J.A. Brundage, 'Adhémar of Puy: the Bishop and his Critics', *Speculum*, 34 (1959), pp. 201–12.
185 *GF*, p. 81.
186 *GF*, p. 76 and n. 1, where Rosalind Hill points out that the author of the *Gesta* shifted his allegiance from Bohemond.
187 *GF*, p. 76.
188 France, *Victory in the East*, pp. 310–16.
189 *Raymond d'Aguilers*, trans. Hill and Hill, p. 80.
190 On the 'money fiefs' offered by Raymond, see France, *Victory in the East*, pp. 129–30, 315.
191 *GF*, p. 81.

attempt to mediate. Then, together with Tancred, Robert led the vanguard as his forces and those of Raymond of Toulouse advanced south by way of Shaizar and Kephalia to Arqa ('Akkar), which was reached on 14 February. As they advanced they made agreements with the governors of other cities along their route. At Arqa, Robert and Raymond were joined in the siege by the other leaders who had left Bohemond at Latakia.[192]

Easter (10 April) was celebrated at the siege of Arqa and the crusaders were re-provisioned by sea. During the siege of Arqa the northern Normans also incurred the anger of the southern French. According to Raymond of Aguilers there was hostility because Robert's chaplain, Arnulf of Chocques, was seen as the leader of those who had doubted the authenticity of the Holy Lance. There is no indication as to whether Robert shared his chaplain's doubts, but when it came to suggestions that the matter should be settled by an ordeal, the duke supported Arnulf.[193] Finally, the patience of the leaders in conducting the siege was exhausted. A peace agreement was made with the ruler of Tripoli and it was decided that the march to Jerusalem should be resumed now that the spring harvest was being gathered.[194]

The crusaders left Arqa and reached Tripoli on Friday 13 May, where they managed to purchase horses, asses and provisions.[195] The march continued until, on Tuesday 6 June 1099, the pilgrim-warriors reached Jerusalem. At once the contingents took up their positions around the holy city. Robert and his Normans stationed themselves near the church of St Stephen along the north-west wall of the city. The site may have been chosen by Robert in recognition of the patron of his father's monastic foundation in Caen. But it is more likely that, as it was also opposite the Damascus Gate, Robert had chosen the most promising site for an assault on the city.[196] We are not told how Robert reacted to seeing the Holy City, but for a pious man, this must have been a deeply moving experience. The *Gesta Francorum* reported that there was great joy at the sight of the Holy City. It is not difficult to believe that after so arduous a journey many of those who had set out from Western Europe three years before would have been reduced to tears.[197] While Robert was encamped outside Jerusalem, a certain Norman named Hugh Bunel appeared.[198]

Hugh Bunel fled Normandy during the reign of Robert's father, after

[192] *GF*, pp. 81–5.
[193] *Raymond of Aguilers*, ed. Hill and Hill, pp. 93–103; *RC*, pp. 682–3, trans. Bachrach and Bachrach, pp. 126–7. Cf. Morris, 'Policy and Visions', p. 43.
[194] *GF*, p. 85.
[195] *GF*, pp. 85–6.
[196] *GF*, p. 87; *AA*, pp. 404–5. J. Prawer, 'The Jerusalem the Crusaders Captured: Contribution to the Medieval Topography of the City', in Edbury, ed., *Crusade and Settlement*, pp. 1–16. I am grateful to Peter Edbury for this reference.
[197] *OV*, V, pp. 156–7. For the city at this time, see A.J. Boas, *Jerusalem at the Time of the Crusades* (London, 2001).
[198] *OV*, V, pp. 156–9. Although the story has elements of the *chansons de geste*, it held great interest for Orderic involving as it does the murderer of Mabel of Bellême: see *OV*, III, pp. 134–7.

beheading Mabel de Bellême. The murder had been provoked by a dispute with the Montgomery-Bellême clan over the seizure of Hugh's patrimony. After the killing, Hugh and his brothers, Ralph, Richard and Joscelin, first fled to Apulia and then to Sicily. William the Conqueror and Mabel's children sent assassins after him, forcing him to move on from place to place. Hugh briefly spent time in Byzantine service but, still in fear of the Conqueror's agents, he decided to leave Christendom. For twenty years he had lived among Muslims and had studied their customs and language. Hugh was thus a valuable recruit to Duke Robert's contingent and provided the skills of a translator as well as local knowledge for the final assault.[199]

During the siege Robert led foraging expeditions for wood to build siege engines and towers.[200] Orderic Vitalis, writing about the siege of Bréval, Normandy, in 1092, suggested that Robert de Bellême's skill in constructing siege engines helped the Christians capture Jerusalem. Robert de Bellême did not join the expedition, but it may be that Orderic was referring to men who had been in Bellême's service, or perhaps his brother, Philip of Montgomery. It is not impossible that Duke Robert directed the construction of engines that his ally had used in Normandy.[201]

During the siege, the clergy imposed three-day fasts and led liturgical processions around the walls to bolster the morale of the crusaders.[202] Finally, at dawn on 15 July 1099, the final assault on Jerusalem began. Robert and Tancred took charge of the mangonels, which bombarded the walls and allowed the siege towers to be wheeled into position.[203] At around nine in the morning, the crusaders managed to gain access to the top of the walls and then the city's gates. By the end of the day the Holy City was in Christian hands, but there had been a terrible slaughter of the inhabitants.[204]

The *Gesta Francorum* describes how the leaders ordered the removal of the corpses, which were beginning to decompose in the summer heat. Surviving Saracens were detailed to carry the dead outside the city walls and cremate them. Once the corpses and the debris from the assault had been cleared, the crusaders had a chance to visit the holy places.[205] For the pilgrims who had fought their way from Western Europe, Jerusalem and its surroundings offered topographical testimony to the course of Christ's life. For example, the crusaders could visit Golgotha:

---

[199] *OV*, V, pp. 156–9.
[200] *AA*, pp. 406–7; cf. *RC*, pp. 689–90, trans. Bachrach and Bachrach, pp. 136–7.
[201] *OV*, IV, pp. 288–9 and n. 7.
[202] *AA*, pp. 412–13. As well as having its spiritual benefits, the fast would have eased pressure on food supplies.
[203] *RC*, pp. 692–3, trans. Bachrach and Bachrach, pp. 140–1.
[204] *GF*, pp. 90–2. On the slaughter, see B.Z. Kedar, 'The Jerusalem Massacre of July 1099 in the Western Historiography of the Crusades', *Crusades*, 3 (2004), pp. 15–76. I am grateful to Peter Edbury for drawing my attention to this article.
[205] *GF*, p. 92.

where Christ the son of God was crucified, and where the first Adam was buried, and where Abraham offered his sacrifice to God. From thence, a stone's throw to the west, is the place where Joseph of Arimathea buried the body of the Lord Jesus, and on this site is a church, beautifully built by Constantine the king. From Mount Calvary the navel of the world lies thirteen feet to the west. If you turn north you will find the prison where Christ was imprisoned, and if south, near the Sepulchre, there lies the Latin monastery built in honour of St Mary the Virgin, whose house stood there.[206]

The *Gesta Francorum* describes the crusaders 'rejoicing and weeping from excess of gladness [coming] to worship at the Sepulchre of our Saviour Jesus, and there they fulfilled their vows to him'.[207] It goes on to say that the next morning they massacred the Saracens, men and women, who had taken refuge on the roof of the Temple of Solomon.[208] It is this juxtaposition of religious fervour and murderous brutality that shocks modern sensibilities.[209] There is no record of Duke Robert's reaction to the carnage, but he was almost certainly one of those 'rejoicing and weeping' who fulfilled their vows at the Holy Sepulchre.

King of Jerusalem?

About a week or so after the capture of Jerusalem, the *principes* met to appoint the secular and ecclesiastical rulers of the city. The *Gesta Francorum* simply recorded that Duke Godfrey was chosen as ruler of the city 'so that he might fight against the pagans and protect the Christians'.[210] Perhaps as a measure of Robert's prestige his chaplain Arnulf of Chocques was elected Patriarch of Jerusalem on the Feast of St Peter's Chains (1 August).[211]

Apart from Robert's military contributions and his ability to mediate successfully between rival leaders, the appointment of Arnulf indicates that the duke's influence was also stronger in other areas than has been admitted. In particular, the Latin Church in the Holy Land owed much to members of Robert's contingent.

After the death of the papal legate Bishop Adhémar of Le Puy on 1 August 1098, Arnulf assumed Adhémar's role as the spiritual leader of the Crusade. Admittedly, this is according to his ex-pupil Ralph of Caen, but the statement

---

[206] *GF*, pp. 98–103 at 98–9.
[207] For a detailed examination of the Holy Sepulchre, see M. Biddle, *The Tomb of Christ* (Stroud, 1999).
[208] *GF*, p. 92.
[209] Although, unfortunately, there are obvious modern parallels.
[210] J. Riley-Smith, 'The Title of Godfrey of Bouillon', *BIHR*, 52 (1979), pp. 83–6; J. France, 'The Election and Title of Godfrey de Bouillon', *Canadian Journal of History*, 18 (1983), pp. 321–9; A.V. Murray, 'The Title of Godfrey of Bouillon as Ruler of Jerusalem', *Collegium Medievale: Interdisciplinary Journal of Medieval Research*, 3 (1990), pp. 163–78.
[211] *GF*, pp. 92–3; *AA*, pp. 450–5. Dondi, *The Liturgy of the Holy Sepulchre*, pp. 53–4.

should not wholly be discounted.[212] It is likely, however, that Arnulf's authority was not recognised in the army of Raymond of Toulouse, not least because of the controversy over the Holy Lance. When asked why he was sceptical, Arnulf said that it was because Adhémar had been. On hearing this, a certain priest claimed to have seen the bishop in the company of St Nicholas. Adhémar's hair and beard on the right side of his head had been singed due to his scepticism about the authenticity of the Lance. Later, Arnulf changed his mind and offered to do public penance to make amends.[213] Arnulf arranged an ordeal by fire on Good Friday 1099 for Peter Bartholomew to prove himself.[214] A little later Arnulf's election as Patriarch was challenged by Daimbert, archbishop of Pisa, and he was deposed once his patron returned to Normandy. Arnulf's reputation for philandering doubtless counted against him, but Raymond d'Aguilers was hardly an impartial witness. Arnulf recovered his position in 1112.[215]

There are other indications of Robert of Normandy's influence on the Latin Church in the Holy Land. Together they lend credence to the idea that Robert may seriously have been considered as a candidate to rule there. For example, the first Latin bishop appointed during the Crusade was Robert of Rouen given custody of the church and cult centre of St George at Lydda near Ramla.[216] In addition, a study of the liturgical practices of the Church of the Holy Sepulchre at Jerusalem suggested that Arnulf 'was one of the most influential characters in the shaping of the ecclesiastical structure of the Latin East'.[217] There were also significant links between elements of the liturgical use of the Holy Sepulchre and that of the cathedral churches of Évreux, Sées, and Bayeux in Normandy.[218] As the liturgy of the Holy Sepulchre was subsequently employed in the other churches of the Patriarchate, this represents a significant contribution to the organisation of the Latin Church in the Holy Land. The conclusions drawn from this material are necessarily tentative, especially as the liturgical practices may have been transmitted via the Norman churches of Southern Italy, but they do at least suggest that Robert's crusade left a more influential ecclesiastical legacy in the Holy Land than has been identified hitherto.

This evidence suggests that Robert of Normandy was a prominent member of the council of leaders. Paradoxically, his willingness to co-operate with the

---

212 *RC*, p. 673, trans. Bachrach and Bachrach, pp. 113–14. See Riley-Smith, *The First Crusade*, p. 80 and n. 160.

213 *Raymond d'Aguilers*, trans. Hill and Hill, pp. 96–9.

214 *Raymond d'Aguilers*, trans. Hill and Hill, pp. 100–3; B. Hamilton, *The Latin Church in the Crusader States. The Secular Church* (London, 1980), p. 13.

215 *Raymond d'Aguilers*, trans. Hill and Hill, p. 131; *AA*, pp. 496–7; *GN*, p. 292. J.G. Rowe, 'Paschal II and the Relation between the Spiritual and Temporal Powers in the Kingdom of Jerusalem', *Speculum*, 32 (1957), pp. 470–501.

216 *GF*, p. 87; *AA*, pp. 396–7 and n. 67. Hamilton, *Latin Church*, pp. 11–12; cf. Riley-Smith, *The First Crusade*, pp. 80, 122.

217 Dondi, *Liturgy of the Holy Sepulchre of Jerusalem*, p. 49.

218 Dondi, *Liturgy of the Holy Sepulchre of Jerusalem*, pp. 44–57 and at 57.

others in pursuit of the communal goal of the crusaders probably meant that he made less of an impact in some of the chronicles. For the most part, there is a lack of controversy surrounding his conduct on the expedition, in stark contrast especially with Bohemond and Raymond.

By the third decade of the twelfth century it was thought that Robert had been offered the crown of the kingdom of Jerusalem. The story is reported first by William of Malmesbury, then Henry of Huntingdon and the Crusade chronicler Peter Tudebode.[219] In itself the story is not wholly implausible given Robert's influence on the Crusade and the fact that Peter Tudebode actually went on the expedition.[220] Indeed, some chroniclers reported that another leader had been offered the crown of Jerusalem before Godfrey, but they named Raymond of Toulouse rather than Robert.[221]

The story told by Malmesbury may have been generated in the aftermath of the duke's defeat in 1106 as a way of explaining why God had punished this hero with the loss of his duchy. Malmesbury reported that Robert:

> brought a lasting stain upon his noble reputation by refusing the kingdom when it was offered to him by common consent as a king's son, not from any consideration of modesty, it is supposed, but through fear of its insoluble difficulties. However, when he returned home, expecting to be free to devote himself to pleasure and delight, God visited him for this fault, as I suppose, who shows His anger everywhere in mercy, and darkened all his pleasures with most bitter pains.[222]

Clearly this associated Robert's refusal of the crown of Jerusalem with his subsequent defeat in Normandy. Later, the link was made explicit when Roger of Wendover, writing in the thirteenth century, described Robert's defeat at Tinchebray as God's revenge. Wendover also elaborated the story of the election by suggesting that the leaders of the Crusade left the decision as to who should rule in Jerusalem to God. They each held a candle and waited for the Almighty to indicate the chosen by lighting the relevant candle. When the decision fell on Robert he blew out his candle saying that he hoped for a more noble kingship in England when he returned home.[223] By the time that Wendover was writing the accretion of legendary material around the duke was well under way. That said, it is not wholly implausible that the other leaders of the Crusade saw in Robert a compromise candidate able to unite the factions that had developed during the expedition.[224]

[219] WM, *GR*, I, pp. 702–3; *HH*, pp. 442–3 and n. 114.
[220] France, *Victory in the East*, pp. 378–9 and n. 15.
[221] AA, pp. 444–7; *Raymond d'Aguilers*, trans. Hill and Hill, p. 129; FC, pp. 307–9.
[222] WM, *GR*, I, pp. 702–3.
[223] *Matthaei Parisiensis Monachi Sancti Albani, Historia Anglorum*, ed. F. Madden, 3 vols., RS (London, 1866–69), I, pp. 149–50, 205.
[224] Cf. *OV*, V, pp. 174–5.

The Hero of Ascalon, August 1099

The crusaders had little time to enjoy their victory at Jerusalem, for the Fatimid ruler of Egypt had despatched an army under his Vizier, al-Afdal, to raise the siege.[225] He and his army had arrived too late to prevent the fall of the Holy City, but they were determined to meet the crusaders in battle. The site of the last major battle on the First Crusade was the town of Ascalon lying to the south-west of Jerusalem. Godfrey summoned the leaders to prepare for battle, but Robert and Count Raymond of Toulouse preferred to wait until the necessity to fight was confirmed.[226] On 9 August Godfrey and Robert of Flanders set out from Jerusalem and met Eustace of Boulogne and Tancred at Ramla. An envoy was sent to Duke Robert and Raymond of Toulouse and they responded immediately, meeting the others at Ibelin on 11 August. The battle was fought the next day and the crusaders won a great victory.

Robert and his men formed the centre division along with Robert of Flanders and Tancred. In an act of heroism typical of his military prowess, Robert charged at the heart of the Egyptian camp, capturing the Vizier's banner and his tent. It was a feat that contemporaries viewed as worthy of extensive praise. The *Gesta Francorum* recorded Robert rushing straight at the amir's (*sic*) standard-bearer and seizing the silver pole which was topped with a 'golden apple'.[227] Robert the Monk's description was the most detailed as well as the most widely distributed version of the duke's heroic act:

> The Count of Normandy, a soldier without fear, was the first to join battle along with his column, aiming for the part where he could see the banner of the emir (which they call 'standard'). He slashed a path through the squadrons with his sword creating carnage; when he reached the standard-bearer he knocked him to the ground at the emir's feet and took the standard. The emir was lucky to escape.[228]

By the mid-twelfth century, Robert's chivalric deed was deemed worthy of depiction in a medallion of stained glass at the French royal abbey of Saint-Denis outside Paris.[229] As well as being an act worthy of a chivalric hero, Robert's attack on the very centre of the Egyptian forces was also an effective and shocking, if risky, battle tactic. Robert may have employed this manoeuvre recalling its effectiveness in the attack on his father at Gerberoy in 1079. That

---

225 France, *Victory in the East*, pp. 360–5.

226 *GF*, pp. 93–4; *AA*, pp. 454–67.

227 *GF*, p. 95.

228 *Robert the Monk*, pp. 875–6, trans. Sweetenham, p. 208; *GN*, p. 297, trans. Levine, p. 139; *AA*, pp. 468–9; cf. *OV*, V, pp. 180–3 says that Robert killed the amir himself.

229 See David, *Curthose*, frontispiece. The abbey church was dedicated 11 June 1144. For political reasons the Capetian kings of France had reason to promote the reputation of Duke Robert. Elizabeth A.R. Brown and M.W. Cothren, 'The Twelfth-century Crusading Window of the Abbey of Saint-Denis: *Praeteritarum Enim Recordatio Futurorum est Exhibitio*', *Journal of the Warburg and Courtauld Institute*, 49 (1986), pp. 1–40.

charge had been launched against the king's person and the command centre of the Conqueror's army in the hope of throwing the enemy into confusion. Similarly, at Ascalon Robert struck at the very heart of the enemy lines and 'when the pagans saw this, they began to flee at once'.[230]

After the battle, Robert bought the standard for 20 silver marks from the soldier who had taken it from the battlefield. He then presented it to Patriarch Arnulf as a memorial of the battle in the Church of the Holy Sepulchre.[231] The crusaders took great quantities of booty from the defeated Egyptian army and began to make their way back to Jerusalem. Raymond of Toulouse was offered the city of Ascalon by its inhabitants, but Godfrey refused to allow him to establish his lordship there.[232] Such was the anger between Godfrey and the count of Toulouse that Robert of Normandy, Robert of Flanders and the other *principes* were forced to act as mediators. They recommended that Raymond be allowed to hold the city subject to Godfrey's authority. Godfrey refused to allow this and Raymond left the army in exasperation. The other leaders refused to help Godfrey besiege Ascalon and departed 'exhausted and angry'. As a consequence of this dispute, Ascalon remained in Muslim hands until 1153: '[i]f the king had been guided by true love and had loved his neighbour as himself, according to God's law, he would have been able to win the hostile stronghold on that day and so opened up to the Christians a free passage to Egypt'.[233] Raymond and Godfrey's rivalry continued at Arsuf until they were once again 'brought back into agreement'.[234]

Part of the criticism of Godfrey reflects the realisation that he needed as many to stay in the Holy Land as possible if the Frankish possessions were to survive. After the battle of Ascalon, and probably before the end of August 1099, many began to think of returning home. Among these was Robert of Normandy, who, together with Robert of Flanders and Raymond of Toulouse, completed his pilgrimage by immersing himself in the River Jordan and gathering palms in Jericho.[235]

As they made their way north they passed crowds of pilgrims taking advantage of the success of the Crusade to visit Jerusalem. At Latakia, they found that Bohemond had laid siege to the Byzantine garrison there. It seems that when Robert had left the city to rejoin the siege of Antioch at the beginning of 1098, the citizens had expelled the remaining westerners in favour of re-establishing contacts with the Byzantine emperor. Robert's procurement of supplies for the siege of Antioch may have imposed severe burdens on the citizens of Latakia, and prompted this reaction. Robert had been in charge of Latakia for perhaps as little as two months, but he may have considered the town as in his lordship. Guibert of Nogent wrote that:

230 *GF*, p. 95; *OV*, V, pp. 182–3.
231 *GN*, p. 299, trans. Levine, p. 140; *GF*, p. 97.
232 *AA*, pp. 470–1.
233 *OV*, V, pp. 186–7.
234 *AA*, pp. 472–3.
235 *FC*, p. 319, trans. Peters, *First Crusade*, pp. 82–3.

Robert, the Count of Normandy, held Latakia first, but when the city's inhabitants could no longer bear the taxes levied by this prodigal man, they drove the guards from the citadel, freed themselves from his authority, and, out of hatred for him, abjured the use of the coinage of Rouen.[236]

Whether Robert was prodigal during his time at Latakia or whether Guibert was repeating a common *topos* about the duke is not clear. The comment, if accurate at all, may be related to Robert's need to send supplies on to Antioch. The use of the coin of Rouen is interesting and suggests that Robert was well supplied with cash.[237]

On hearing of the Byzantine presence, Bohemond had advanced on the city. At the approach of the crusaders the citizens of Latakia sent envoys asking them for help. Robert and his allies thus demanded that Bohemond retire or prepare for war. The prince of Antioch consulted his men and withdrew his troops. In gratitude the citizens of Latakia arranged for passage for the crusaders to Constantinople.[238]

Robert and his companions probably left the Holy Land in September or October 1099 and made their way to Constantinople.[239] Alexios's welcome was effusive and Robert and his men were showered with gifts. The emperor offered them great rewards if they would enter his service, but the duke of Normandy and the count of Flanders decided to return home and crossed to Apulia.[240] Robert of Normandy remained there for the winter, but Robert of Flanders pushed on and arrived home in the early spring of 1100. Robert decided that he needed to recuperate fully before making the journey back to Normandy and he also had thoughts of crowning a glorious period in his career by winning the hand of a southern Italian heiress.

Robert of Normandy and the First Crusade

Robert's participation in the armed pilgrimage to Jerusalem was a personal triumph. He had demonstrated courage of the highest order as well as the ability to command forces successfully in the most adverse of circumstances. He had also proved that he was determined that the expedition as a whole should reach its goal and had worked for the unity of the Christian army. Together with his cousin, the count of Flanders, Robert had mediated between bitter rivals on several occasions to ensure that the Crusade's cohesion and momentum was not dissipated. Yet evaluations of Robert's contribution to the

---

236 *GN*, p. 336, trans. Levine, p. 159.
237 On the money supply for the Crusade, see Murray, 'Money and Logistics', pp. 229–49.
238 *AA*, pp. 476–85; cf. *OV*, V, pp. 274–7. The citizens of Latakia advised the crusaders to return all their conquests to the Byzantine emperor. A letter from the crusaders to the pope dated at Latakia credits the archbishop of Pisa with making peace between Bohemond and the other crusaders: Hagenmeyer, *Kreuzzugsbriefe*, pp. 167–74, trans. Peters, *First Crusade*, pp. 234–7 at 237.
239 *AA*, pp. 484–5.
240 *OV*, V, pp. 276–7; *FC*, pp. 319–20.

Crusade only reluctantly acknowledge the importance of the role he played. The negative influence of perceptions of Robert's pre-Crusade reputation and the need to explain his fate six years after his return to Normandy coloured the opinions of medieval historians and their modern successors.[241]

Abbot Guibert of Nogent recognised Robert's pre-Crusade *fama*, or reputation, as well as the cleansing effect that the fulfilment of his vows had achieved:

> It would hardly be right to remain silent about Robert, Count of Normandy, whose bodily indulgences, weakness of will, prodigality with money, gourmandising, indolence, and lechery were expiated by the perseverance and heroism that he vigorously displayed in the army of the Lord. His inborn compassion was naturally so great that he did not permit vengeance to be taken against those who had plotted to betray him and had been sentenced to death, and if something did happen to them, he wept for their misfortune. He was bold in battle, although adeptness at foul trickery, with which we know many men befouled themselves, should not be praised, unless provoked by unspeakable acts. For these and for similar things he should now be forgiven, since God has punished him in this world, where he now languishes in jail, deprived of all his honours.[242]

The last sentence demonstrates that Guibert was writing after 1106 in the knowledge of Robert's fate. He probably also exaggerated Robert's faults to heighten the significance of the cleansing effect of the Crusade. But, rather than experiencing a personal transformation as a result of undergoing the rigours of the expedition to Jerusalem, Robert had demonstrated that the traits of leadership he had shown in Normandy were eminently suited to the task of ensuring that the armed pilgrimage reached its goal. What was needed was an effective combination of piety, military skill and, above all, the ability to mediate between individuals who threatened to tear the enterprise apart. In this sense, ruling Normandy between 1087 and 1096 was good training. It might be going too far to suggest that without Robert of Normandy's presence, the First Crusade would have foundered, but it certainly needed his spirit of compromise and dogged determination. Guibert of Nogent was not alone in thinking that after his exploits in Palestine Robert did not deserve his fate.

---

[241] E.g. David, *Curthose*, pp. 118–19.
[242] *GN*, pp. 132–3, trans. Levine, p. 54.

CHAPTER SIX

THE RETURNING HERO, 1100–1106

An Italian Heiress

DUKE ROBERT wintered in Apulia as a guest of Count Geoffrey of Conversano, Count Roger I of Sicily and Roger Borsa, duke of Apulia.[1] Robert's hosts celebrated his achievements on the Crusade and were doubtless regaled with the duke's exploits, which had done so much to enhance his reputation.

Robert's health may have suffered on the Crusade and he may have taken advantage of the medical expertise of the Southern Italians, as well as the milder winter climate, to recuperate. In the nineteenth century it was suggested that Robert was wounded at the fall of Jerusalem and sought treatment at Salerno. He was advised that the wound needed to be drained and only his wife was prepared to suck out the poison. Robert recovered and, so it was said, was given a set of medical precepts to aid his recovery. This medical treatise was known as the *Regimen Sanitatis Salernitanum*. The story is not implausible, and it may be one of the many legends that became associated with the duke.[2]

However, the negotiations to marry Sibyl, the daughter of Geoffrey of Conversano, were probably the major reason for Robert remaining in Apulia. Geoffrey was a nephew of Robert Guiscard, late duke of Apulia.[3] It was perhaps during the winter of 1096–7, while waiting to cross the Adriatic, that Robert first saw Sibyl and began the marriage negotiations. Orderic reported that Robert 'fell in love' with Sibyl. 'She was truly good in character,' Orderic

---

[1] *OV*, V, pp. 278–81.

[2] For the medical expertise of the region, see Patricia Skinner, *Health and Medicine in Early Medieval Southern Italy. The Medieval Mediterranean, II* (Leiden, 1997). Kate Norgate, 'Robert, Duke of Normandy (1054?–1134)', *DNB* (1896), pp. 1235–44 at 1239.

[3] Loud, *The Age of Robert Guiscard*, p. 247. For Geoffrey of Conversano's involvement in revolts against Robert Guiscard, see *Malaterra*, pp. 48, 77, 87, trans. Wolf, pp. 116–17, 164, 180. See Loud, *Age of Robert Guiscard*, pp. 220, 235, 237–8, 241–3. For Geoffrey's career, W. Jahn, *Untersuchungen zur normannischer Herrschaft in Süditalien (1040–1100)* (Frankfurt-am-Main and New York, 1989). I am very grateful to Graham Loud for his advice on the material about Geoffrey of Conversano.

wrote, 'endowed with many virtues and lovable to all who knew her.'[4] Order-ic's praise for Sibyl's virtues is worth noting: it was not simply his standard description of a female aristocrat.[5]

No details of the marriage negotiations survive, but Robert secured gold, silver and precious objects from his father-in-law, 'which [Robert] providently intended to hand over to his creditor in order to recover his duchy in peace'.[6] Uncharacteristically, then, Orderic attributed to Robert the foresight to secure the resources to repay the debt to William Rufus.

Robert's marriage to Sibyl altered the dynamic in the relationship with his brothers. Although Robert had been betrothed and had at least one pre-marital liaison, there is no evidence that the Conqueror, or indeed Robert himself, intended to negotiate a marriage before 1100. Robert's parents contracted marriages for their daughters, but it is noticeable that, with the exception of the Maine betrothal, their sons remained bachelors into their thirties and beyond. In 1100 Robert was approaching fifty and William Rufus, at forty, also showed no signs of marrying, although, in his case, this might have been explained by his ambivalent sexuality.[7] The most prolific sexual adventurer of the three was Henry, who in addition to making a political marriage in 1100 at the age of around thirty-two, was an enthusiastic adulterer and father of more than twenty known bastards, many of whom he employed to consoli-date his political position.[8]

By marrying in 1100, Robert signalled his dynastic ambitions. He had managed to secure an heiress of considerable wealth and expected to be able to reclaim his duchy from his brother without any difficulty. It is possible, though unlikely, that the seeming reluctance of the sons of William the Conqueror to marry before 1100 may have been the result of a deliberate policy to ensure that the succession to their respective lordships would pass peacefully from brother to brother, rather than from father to son which would exclude siblings from power.[9] The experience of the Crusade and the growing realisation that he was approaching the final stage of his life, focused Robert's mind and prompted him to provide for the ducal succession. The redemption of his vow at Jerusalem marked a new beginning for Robert cleansed of the sins of his youth. Certainly, twelfth-century commentators detected a change in his character and Guibert of Nogent thought that the Crusade had expi-ated earlier sins.[10]

News of Robert's exploits in the Holy Land had reached Normandy long before the duke himself appeared in the autumn of 1100. Stories of Robert's

---

4   *OV*, V, pp. 278–9.
5   Chibnall, 'Women in Orderic Vitalis', pp. 105–21.
6   *OV*, V, pp. 280–1.
7   Mason, *William II*, p. 126.
8   Kathleen Thompson, 'Affairs of State: The Illegitimate Children of Henry I', *JMH*, 29 (2003), pp. 129–51.
9   Cf. Duncan, *Kingship of the Scots*, p. 59.
10 See above, Chapter 5, p. 190.

heroism heightened the sense of excitement at his anticipated return.[11] The Normans hoped that Robert would lighten the burdens imposed on the duchy during William Rufus's rule.[12] It is tempting to believe that news of Robert's success on the Crusade and his marriage to Sibyl of Conversano influenced the events of August 1100 and presented him with a new set of problems on his return.

Deaths in the Family, 1100

While Robert was away, two members of his immediate family died in England. About Rogation time (7 to 9 May) 1100, Robert's illegitimate son Richard was killed.[13] Orderic wrote that Rufus's knights were in the New Forest stalking deer when someone accidentally killed Richard with an arrow.[14] The culprit fled the scene and took refuge in the priory of St Pancras at Lewes in Sussex. By taking monastic vows 'he expiated by penance the crime of homicide' and avoided the anger of Richard's companions. Richard had been too young to join his father on the Crusade in 1096, but had made a favourable impression at Rufus's court and, according to Orderic, was predicted a bright future.[15] William of Malmesbury suggested that Richard met his death hanging from a tree, after riding his horse under a low branch. The mode of Richard's death resembled that of the Old Testament figure Absalom.[16] There is no way of knowing whether this is coincidence or a comment on the young man's character.[17]

At the beginning of August 1100, Robert's brother William was also killed while hunting in the New Forest.[18] Whereas Richard was something of a novice, his uncle had some thirty years of hunting experience. Medieval descriptions of Rufus's death do not characterise the king's death as anything other than an accident. It was interpreted as a just punishment for his oppression of the Church and his debauched personal life.[19] Both Orderic and Malmesbury connected the death with William the Conqueror's creation of the New Forest, which involved the destruction of sixty parishes and the forced removal of the

---

[11] *OV*, V, pp. 280–1.

[12] Barlow, *Rufus*, pp. 337–407; Mason, *William II*, pp. 170–202. Haskins, *Norman Institutions*, pp. 78–84.

[13] 'Rogation' days were periods of fasting and prayer for the coming harvest.

[14] *OV*, V, pp. 282–3; cf. *JW*, III, *s.a.* 1100, pp. 92–3. *OV*, pp. 284–5, connects the Conqueror's establishment of the New Forest and the deaths.

[15] *OV*, V, pp. 282–3.

[16] 2 Samuel 18:9–10.

[17] WM, *GR*, I, pp. 504–5. *OV*, V, pp. 282–3; Robert's other illegitimate son, William, set out for Jerusalem after the defeat of his father at Tinchebray in 1106. He was distinguished for his military prowess and became lord of Tortosa; *AA*, pp. 760–1, 814–15. He may have been killed in the East as nothing more is heard of him after 1110; see *OV*, V, p. 283, n. 6.

[18] *OV*, V, pp. 284–5.

[19] *OV*, V, pp. 284–91; *JW*, III, *s.a.* 1100, pp. 92–3; *ASC*, E, *s.a.* 1100, pp. 109–10; Swanton, pp. 235–6.

peasantry.[20] John of Worcester also linked Richard's death with the making of the New Forest, for on the very spot where Richard died a church was demolished to make way for the king's hunting park.[21]

The account of William Rufus's death strongly resembled Orderic's report of the demise of the king's nephew Richard. The man who fired the fatal arrow, Walter Tirel, fled the scene for the Continent, from where 'he laughed in safety at the threats and curses of those who wished to harm him'.[22] However, the timing of Rufus's death and his brother Henry's response raise doubts as to whether it was indeed an accident. Within three days, Henry had been crowned and secured possession of the treasury at Winchester. It was opportunism on Henry's part of the highest order, but his decisive action need not imply that he was forewarned of his brother's demise. Nevertheless, the circumstantial evidence raised questions about Henry's involvement.[23]

Nonetheless, Robert's delayed return from the Holy Land allowed news of his exploits and, more importantly for his brothers, of his survival and marriage, to reach Normandy and England. Reports of the Crusade inspired others to make the journey. For example, Count William VII of Poitou made plans to pledge Aquitaine to Rufus to fund a pilgrimage to Jerusalem. Orderic linked this with Rufus's intention to deny Robert access to Normandy on his return.[24] Those crusaders who had returned with Robert of Flanders also brought news of Robert of Normandy. Souvenirs of the campaign and relics brought from the Holy Land or Constantinople added to the growing excitement at the expected return of the hero.[25] When the news of the duke's wedding to Sibyl of Conversano reached Henry his prospects for ruling any part of his father's domains must have seemed remote, especially as Rufus and Robert had named each other as heir to their respective lands. If Henry was to act, then the summer of 1100 represented one of the last opportunities to do so. In the later twelfth century, William of Tyre noted that Henry spread rumours that Robert would never return.[26] Henry had already shown himself ruthless enough to be capable of fratricide. On the other hand, regicide was a crime of a different magnitude.[27]

There is no doubt that the medieval hunt could be dangerous, but it also offered the possibility of isolating and disposing of an enemy. It was one of the few occasions when a lord was likely to be alone or accompanied by only

20 OV, V, pp. 284–5; WM, GR, I, pp. 504–5.
21 JW, III, s.a. 1100, pp. 92–3.
22 OV, V, pp. 292–3. Cf. Eadmer, HN, pp. 120–1.
23 Mason, William II, pp. 215–31.
24 OV, V, pp. 280–81. The count was also William IX of Aquitaine and had been an ally of Rufus in 1098. Cf. WM, GR, I, pp. 576–7. B.S. Bachrach, 'William Rufus' Plan for the Invasion of Aquitaine', in The Normans and their Adversaries, pp. 31–63.
25 Elisabeth van Houts, Memory and Gender in Medieval Europe, pp. 93–120.
26 William of Tyre, Chronicon, ed. R.B.C. Huygens, 1 vol. in 2, CCCM, 63/63A (Turnhout, 1986), Book IX, trans. E.A. Babcock and A.C. Krey, A History of Deeds Done Beyond the Sea by William Archbishop of Tyre, 2 vols. (New York, 1943, 1976), I, p. 398; Green Henry I, p. 43, n. 5.
27 For a discussion, see Green, Henry I, pp. 38–41.

a few retainers. Aelred of Rievaulx, writing in the mid-twelfth century, related a story about Rufus's contemporary King Malcolm III of Scotland. Aelred's source was his friend, Malcolm's son, King David I (1124–1153). According to David, Malcolm heard of a conspiracy to assassinate him led by one of the leading men of his court. Malcolm used the hunt as a suitable occasion to confront the traitor. He offered the assassin his chance, but the traitor fell at the king's feet and begged forgiveness.[28] The hunt was thus recognised as a dangerous time for a lord.

Rufus's death allowed Henry to seize the throne and he was crowned at Westminster on Sunday 5 August 1100, by Bishop Maurice of London.[29] William of Malmesbury explained that things had happened so quickly 'for fear that the nobles might repent of his election, shaken by the rumour that Robert duke of Normandy was on his way from Apulia and would at any moment be upon them.'[30]

The death of a king was a moment of crisis for members of the ruling aristocracy and many at Rufus's court made for their estates to prepare for the disorders they believed would follow. Some remained in Winchester, however, and some of the barons spoke in favour of Robert's claims. William of Breteuil reminded Henry that he should remember the fealty promised to Robert.[31]

> For he is the eldest son of King William and both you and I, my lord Henry, have done homage to him, which constrains us to be faithful to him in everything whether he is present or not. He has toiled for years in the service of God, and now God restores to him without the strife of battle both his own duchy, which he left as a pilgrim for Christ's sake, and his father's crown.[32]

If Orderic's account represents contemporary opinion, there was a sense that Robert was owed loyalty, not least because of his exploits on the Crusade. It was also a recognition of the agreement between Rufus and Robert to recognise each other as heir. There was also self-interest here as Henry's action threatened to undermine many dynastic arrangements made within baronial families by laying aside recognised practice.

Breteuil's speech provoked a quarrel, and supporters of both sides squared up to each other. Henry drew his sword and made it clear that he would not allow any obstacle to his seizure of his father's regalia. Henry characterised

---

[28] Aelred of Rievaulx, 'The Geneaology of the Kings of the English', §23, in *Aelred of Rievaulx: The Historical Works*, trans. Jane P. Freeland, ed. Marsha L. Dutton (Kalamazoo, MI, 2005), pp. 117–18. I am grateful to Steven Biddlecombe for bringing this episode to my attention.

[29] *OV*, V, pp. 294–5, says Archbishop Anselm of Canterbury was in exile and, erroneously, that Archbishop Thomas of York had recently died. Thomas was at Ripon when Henry was crowned and reached London too late for the ceremony: *Hugh the Chantor, The History of the Church of York, 1066–1127*, trans. C. Johnson (London, 1961), p. 10. Cf. *JW*, III, *s.a.* 1100, pp. 94–5; ASC, E, *s.a.* 1100, p. 110; Swanton, p. 236. Cf. Green, *Henry I*, pp. 43–4.

[30] WM, *GR*, I, pp. 714–15.

[31] William de Breteuil was the son of William fitz Osbern, the Conqueror's closest companion. He died on 12 January 1103 at Bec: *OV*, II, pp. 282–3; VI, pp. 40–1.

[32] *OV*, V, pp. 290–1.

his brother as an 'extraneus' (a 'stranger' or a 'foreigner') and this perhaps suggests that Robert was identified strongly with Normandy, whereas Henry's Englishness was a recurrent theme.[33] Henry had the advantage, however, as the heir on the spot and decisive action could always overcome reasoned argument and set aside claims, however legal.[34] Before there was bloodshed, Henry de Beaumont, earl of Warwick, and others intervened to defuse the situation, but Henry still took the throne.[35] In the face of baronial acceptance of his brother, there was little Robert could do personally to defend his interests as he was still several weeks away from Normandy.

By the time that Robert reached home, his brother was king of England. Among the measures Henry took to reinforce his hold on England was his marriage to Robert's god-daughter, Edith/Matilda of Scotland on the Feast of St Martin (11 November) 1100.[36] This marriage to the king of Scotland's daughter and has been interpreted as Henry's attempt to enlist the prestige of the Old English royal lineage in order to strengthen his hold on the throne.[37]

There is a suggestion that, far from being an advantage to Henry's new regime, his marriage to Matilda might actually have undermined his image. William of Malmesbury wrote that Henry took great exception to the mocking of his English connections by Robert's supporters, when he and his wife were nicknamed Godric and Godgifu. Henry bore the insults and even laughed himself, but he was biding his time, bearing the idiocy of his detractors in feigned forbearance, until he could exact revenge. This suggests that sections of the Norman nobility remembered Matilda's Old English roots and, with political gain in mind, mocked her accordingly. After all the crack about Godric and Godgifu was not meant as a compliment.[38]

More crucial was Matilda's status as the daughter of a king and the fact that she was close at hand and available.[39] The marriage brought Henry a princess of the reigning Scots royal house, not of a defeated and, to all intents and purposes, defunct dynasty. Matilda's brother, Edgar of Scotland (1097–1107), owed his throne to Henry's brother William and the new king seems to have been reinforcing this relationship between the Scots and English crowns. The alliance had the added advantage of superseding Robert's relationship of spiritual kinship with Matilda and potentially displacing the duke as the Scots king's ally.

---

33 *OV*, V, pp. 290–3.
34 *OV*, V, pp. 290–1. Green, *Henry I*, pp. 42–3; Garnett, *Conquered England*, pp. 138, 204.
35 WM, *GR*, I, pp. 714–15. *OV*, V, pp. 290–1.
36 *ASC*, E, *s.a.* 1100, p. 110; Swanton, p. 236; cf. *JW*, III, *s.a.* 1100, pp. 96–7.
37 WM, *GR*, I, pp. 716–17. Hollister, *Henry I*, p. 126; Green, *Henry I*, pp. 53–5.
38 WM, *GR*, I, pp. 716–17. The ethnic specificity of the insult suggests that it was not Matilda's Scots background that was the key to the mockery. Of course, on hearing these insults, Henry may have embraced the 'English' identity even more in order to make a point. Cf. Hollister, *Henry I*, p. 132 and Green, *Henry I*, p. 61.
39 *OV*, V, pp. 298–9, stated that Henry married in order to avoid 'wallowing in lasciviousness like any horse or mule which is without the use of reason'.

Nevertheless, Henry's marriage, like Robert's to Sibyl, was also a dynastic statement of intent. He was determined to keep the English throne and pass it on to any children he might have with Matilda. The marriage further weakened the chances of Robert or his heirs gaining access to the English crown. It also held up the potential moral dilemma of going to war with Henry, not only his own brother, but his god-daughter's husband.

The Crusader's Return

In late August or early September 1100, Robert reached Normandy.[40] He was greeted with enthusiasm by all except those who supported Henry.[41] Since 1096, Henry had held the Cotentin as well as the fortified town of Domfront on Normandy's southern frontier.[42] This had given Henry control of much of Western Normandy and threatened to undermine the re-establishment of Robert's authority.

Robert, like many of his fellow crusaders, made a high profile return to the West. Together with stories of his military prowess, news of his beautiful Apulian bride circulated and it is possible to imagine the excitement that his long anticipated reappearance generated. Robert's honour and prestige had been enhanced, an important factor in this society driven by the charisma of the individual.[43] The duke's successful redemption of his vows stands in sharp contrast with those who failed to complete the pilgrimage. They faced public criticism and papal censure. Such was the fate of Robert's brother-in-law, Count Stephen of Blois.[44]

Where Robert won glory, Stephen was burdened with opprobrium, not least from his wife Adela. Stephen is described as 'an object of contempt to almost everyone' and he was continually criticised because he had fled from Antioch 'deserting his comrades who were sharing in the agonies of Christ'.[45] Pope Urban II had pronounced a sentence of excommunication on those who had not fulfilled their vows.[46] As if that were not enough, Stephen's wife nagged him even 'between conjugal caresses' to make amends for his cowardice by returning to Jerusalem. It was a matter of family as well as individual honour and Adela could not tolerate the shame attached to her husband's reputation.[47] Stephen joined the Crusade of 1101 and died in the Holy Land.[48]

There has been comparatively little written on the return of the First

---

40 *ASC*, E, *s.a.* 1100, p. 110; Swanton, p. 236; *JW*, III, *s.a.* 1100, pp. 96–7; *HH*, pp. 448–9; *OV*, V, pp. 300–1.

41 *ASC*, E, *s.a.* 1100, p. 110; Swanton, p. 236.

42 *WJ*, II, pp. 210–13.

43 *OV*, V, pp. 268–9.

44 WM, *GR*, I, pp. 634–5.

45 *OV*, V, pp. 324–5.

46 Hagenmeyer, *Kreuzzugsbriefe*, no. XIX, pp. 174–5.

47 *OV*, V, pp. 324–5.

48 *AA*, pp. 644–5. Brundage, 'An Errant Crusader', pp. 391–5.

Crusaders and the effect that expedition had on their subsequent careers. However, Jonathan Riley-Smith has described the return of crusaders such as Count Rotrou of Mortagne, one of Robert's companions. He writes of the man experiencing the 'disorientation, the exhaustion and starvation, the disease and the sickening cruelty, the loss of pack animals and horses and therefore of rank, the stories of apparitions and ghostly armies, the penitential liturgies and hysterical religiosity, the discovery of relics and the euphoria of the final miraculous and bloody triumph at Jerusalem'.[49] We can only imagine the psychological effects of the experience on those returning from the East. The Crusade was in every sense a physical and mental ordeal, even for those inured to a life of campaigning and fortified by a resilient spirituality. Unfortunately there are few indications of Robert of Normandy's personal reaction to what he had seen and done.[50]

The duke's mental horizons had been greatly expanded and he had travelled to the very centre of the known world, passing through many of the greatest cities of his own day. The journey had been gruelling and Orderic, in a rare moment of sympathy for the duke, suggested that Robert had been exhausted by the exertions of his long pilgrimage. Later Wace also wrote that people detected a change in Robert's demeanour since his return from the Holy Land: he seemed less prudent in conduct.[51] If Robert's deeply felt piety had been reinforced by the pilgrimage to Jerusalem, it is possible that he experienced on his return a certain *contemptus mundi*, or a kind of disillusionment with worldly affairs, something medieval monastic and clerical writers promoted.[52] Indeed, some returning crusaders found refuge in monasteries, which offered medical care as well as spiritual comfort. Pilgrimage was an ideal preparation for this kind of withdrawal from the world.[53] More positively, the duke like many others, may have felt that he had atoned for the sins of his youth by undergoing the Crusade as a penitential act.[54]

Robert had performed acts of uncommon bravery that were noticed and celebrated even by his harshest critics. William of Malmesbury reported a variation on the story of Robert's heroism at the end of the Crusade. The action was relocated from Ascalon to Antioch and 'Corbaguath' (Kergbogha, ruler of Mosul) rather than al-Afdal was the object of Robert's attack. Robert achieved a great reputation as a warrior 'particularly in the fighting at Antioch, where he adorned the victory with a brilliant exploit'. The story relates to the battle fought at the end of June 1098. The crusaders had put Corbaguath's men to flight, but he rallied them and began to drive the crusaders back.

---

49 Riley-Smith, *The First Crusaders*, pp. 144–68 at 144–5.
50 W.M. Aird, 'Le retour du Croisé: Robert Courteheuse, Duc de Normandie, et les conséquences de la Première Croisade' (forthcoming).
51 *OV*, V, pp. 304–5; Wace, *Roman de Rou*, lines 10923–30, pp. 328–9.
52 E.g. 'De Contemptu Mundi', in *HH*, pp. 584–619.
53 Riley-Smith, *The First Crusaders*, pp. 144–68.
54 *GN*, pp. 132–3, trans. Levine, p. 54.

At that point the duke of Normandy and Philip the Clerk, son of Roger of Mont-gomery, and Warin of Taney, a castle in Maine, shouted mutual encouragement at one another – for they were retiring in pretended flight – turned their horses, made each for his adversary, and overthrew him. Corbaguath recognized the duke, but took his measure by his size alone, and in any case thought it inglorious to run away; he paid for this rash encounter by immediate death, for he was killed at once. The Turks were already voicing yells of triumph, but when they saw him fall, deprived of their new-found hope they fled a second time.[55]

Robert shared the glory with Philip of Montgomery and Warin of Taney, but it was the duke whose exploits took centre stage. The story was taken up in later vernacular traditions.[56]

The prestige of returning crusaders was attached to the relics and other souvenirs they brought back. These were often presented to local churches and the donor's exploits memorialised. On his return, Robert visited his sister Cecilia, who was later to become abbess of their mother's foundation of La Trinité in Caen.[57] According to Wace, who although writing his account in the 1160s preserved earlier traditions from Caen, the duke presented his sister with a banner captured at Antioch. Wace tells us that Robert 'received great renown and great honour; and many people spoke of him (*e mult en parlerent plusor*)'.[58]

There was enthusiasm for the returning crusader. Stories circulated and there were visual reminders of these exploits. His fellow crusaders also had their own stories of Robert's prowess, adding to the reputation of their lord. This renown reached beyond the frontiers of Normandy.[59] So Robert returned home with his reputation enhanced as the veteran of a successful expedition to liberate Jerusalem. It was an achievement to rival if not eclipse that of his father's seizure of the English throne.

Robert 'the Jerusalemite' made his way into his duchy without opposi-tion.[60] His return to Rouen may have been marked by a ritual *adventus*.[61] It

---

55 WM, *GR*, I, pp. 702–3. Kerbogha survived the encounter.
56 Cf. Wace, *Roman de Rou*, lines 9685–98, pp. 304–5.
57 J. Walmsley, 'The Early Abbesses, Nuns and Female Tenants of the Abbey of Holy Trinity, Caen', *JEH*, 48 (1997), pp. 425–44.
58 Wace, *Roman de Rou*, lines 9691–9698, pp. 304–5. Wace's personal connections with Caen give this account some weight. See Musset, *Les Abbayes caennaises*, p. 14, n. 8.
59 In addition to the celebration of Robert in the windows of Saint-Denis, there are references to other relics and souvenirs in Normandy and Britain. A topaz among the possessions of Canterbury cathedral was said to have been brought back by Robert: *Materials for the History of Thomas Becket, Archbishop of Canterbury*, ed. J.C. Robertson, 7 vols., Rolls Series (London, 1875–85), I, pp. 482–4. A suit of Turkish armour given to St Andrews by King Alexander I (d.1124) may also be connected with Robert: A.A.M. Duncan, 'The Foundation of St Andrews Cathedral Priory, 1140', *SHR*, 84 (2005), pp. 1–37 at 7 and n. 27. My thanks to Matthew Strickland for drawing my attention to this article. See also Nicholas Paul, 'Crusade and Family Memory before 1225', unpublished Cambridge Ph.D. dissertation, 2005, pp. 108–12. I am very grateful to Dr Paul for allowing me to consult the relevant material from his dissertation.
60 *Suger, Vie de Louis VI le Gros*, ed. H. Waquet (Paris, 1929), p. 246, trans. R. Cusimano and J. Moor-head, *The Deeds of Louis the Fat* (Washington DC, 1992), p. 140.
61 *OV*, V, pp. 300–1.

may have been as magnificent as his father's triumphant return from England in 1067, but the sources do not provide any details.[62] Soon after, Robert made a pilgrimage with Sibyl to Mont-Saint-Michel, where they gave thanks for his safe return. This was an ostensibly pious act but it had heavy political overtones, designed to underline his status as a successful pilgrim and to smooth his resumption of authority in the duchy.[63] It was a potentially provocative act, as Mont-Saint-Michel lay within his brother's sphere of influence.[64] The pilgrimage was a conscious reclamation of his ducal authority in the west of his duchy.

Robert's father had been adept at making such political statements clothed in, but not concealed by, the guise of pilgrimage. For example, in 1072, the Conqueror had made a 'pilgrimage' to St Cuthbert's shrine at Durham, during an expedition to Scotland.[65] The king's presence at the shrine of the region's most powerful saint was designed to win recognition for his regime. At the beginning of the 1080s, William visited St David's in south-west Wales in a show of force presented as a pious journey.[66] The pilgrimage offered the chance to penetrate hostile territory, protected by the status of a pilgrim, and advance the recognition of personal authority.

According to Orderic, Robert and Sibyl had refrained from consummating their marriage until after their pilgrimage to Mont-Saint-Michel:

> There he gave thanks to God for his safe return from his long pilgrimage, and afterwards consummated his marriage with the daughter of Geoffrey of Conversano. Next year she bore him a son, and Archbishop William baptized the child, giving him his own name.[67]

Until he had completed his pilgrimage, Robert was bound by the vows he had made, vows which presumably included abstinence from sexual intercourse. Given his experiences on crusade, it is not difficult to imagine Robert's heightened sense of religious propriety. To a medieval audience, the birth was a sign of divine favour that Robert enjoyed at that moment. It may also have

---

62 There is a noticeable reticence in the major sources to celebrate Robert's achievement, probably a result of the events of September 1106.

63 Devotions and ceremonial were essential elements in the presentation of ducal authority, not some 'optional extras'; *pace* David, *Curthose*, p. 124.

64 *OV*, V, pp. 300–1.

65 H.H.E. Craster, 'The Red Book of Durham', *EHR*, 40 (1925), pp. 504–32 at 528; cf. Symeon, *Libellus de Exordio*, pp. 196–7. Aird, *St Cuthbert*, pp. 87–8.

66 *ASC*, E, *s.a.* 1081, p. 92; Swanton, p. 214. *Brut y Tywysogyon or The Chronicle of the Princes, Peniarth MS 20 Version*, ed. T. Jones (Cardiff, 1952), *s.a.* 1079–81, p. 17; *Brut y Tywysogyon or The Chronicle of the Princes, Red Book of Hergest Version*, ed. T. Jones (Cardiff, 1955), *s.a.* 1081, p. 31.

67 *OV*, V, pp. 300–1. On 25 October 1102, Sibyl gave birth to a son, William: see C. Warren Hollister, 'William Clito', *Oxford DNB* (Oxford, 2004). The monks at Mont-Saint-Michel remembered both Robert (11 February) and his wife Sibyl (18 March) in their Martyrology-Necrology: *Cartulary of Mont-Saint-Michel*, p. 250.

been during this visit to Lower Normandy that Robert presented his sister with the Saracen banner captured in the East.

Robert recovered his duchy without opposition and his visits to Mont-Saint-Michel and Caen, as well as his reception in Rouen, demonstrated his repossession of the whole duchy.[68] In the autumn of 1100, Henry, with problems of his own in England, was in no position to offer resistance to his brother.

Robert brought peace for, on news of Rufus's death reaching Normandy, a number of barons began private wars. William of Évreux and his ally Ralph of Conches invaded the Beaumont lands and seized property from Robert of Meulan. They were taking revenge for injuries done to them during Rufus's reign. William of Évreux and his half-brother were also partisans of the duke and this disturbance may have been the beginning of the struggle between the rival supporters of Robert and Henry.[69] Old scores lay behind the warfare, but Orderic attributed it to the loss of the king's firm hand in the duchy. The violence also probably had more to do with the uncertainties of the English succession than opposition to the return of the duke.[70] Orderic also reprised an earlier theme, describing Robert's rule in the duchy as ineffectual. This had more to do with his justification of the events of 1106 than the situation in Normandy at Robert's return.

The death of William Rufus had released Robert from his obligation to redeem the duchy. Sibyl's dowry and other lavish gifts, if not the proceeds from his involvement in the Crusade, provided Robert with sufficient funds to repay the loan he had secured from his brother.[71] Henry had no claim on the money, nor could he challenge Robert's resumption of office. Released from his financial obligations, Robert was in the happy position of having funds sufficient to recover the duchy.

It is difficult to say how long it took Robert to acquaint himself with what had happened in Normandy since his departure in 1096. The prestige of the Crusade has to be weighed against Robert's lack of contact with the Norman aristocracy for four years. Eleventh-century politics depended on face-to-face encounters and the ability of individuals to read the intentions of others. The Crusade created a divide between those who went and those who stayed at home. Those who accompanied Robert to Jerusalem shared memories of hardships and triumphs, but the crusaders were at a disadvantage when they

---

68 *OV*, V, pp. 300–1. Orderic noted that Robert held the duchy for 'about eight years in name only'. It is puzzling that Orderic should have suggested that Robert's reign ended in 1108. This may be connected with the death of Philip I of France on 29 July that year and his son Louis VI's demand for homage from Henry for Normandy: see Hollister, *Henry I*, pp. 222–3; Green, *Henry I*, pp. 118–20. Cf. Wace, *Roman de Rou*, lines 10320–322, pp. 316–17.

69 *OV*, V, pp. 300–1.

70 Vaughn, *Anselm of Bec and Robert of Meulan*, p. 225, suggests that Robert of Meulan was attempting to secure the allegiance of certain Norman barons at this time.

71 *OV*, V, pp. 278–81.

came home, and had to ensure that they learned about realignments that had taken place among the aristocracy of Normandy and England.

Helias of La Flèche and Maine

Among the first decisions Robert had to take on his return to Normandy was whether or not to lead an army to the assistance of the garrison of Le Mans. While Robert had been in the Holy Land, Rufus had attempted to deal with resistance to Norman lordship in Maine and, despite the king's best efforts, there was still considerable opposition. Helias of La Flèche, Count of Maine, had adopted the language and symbolic paraphernalia of the Crusade to defend his lands against Rufus. The king had refused to guarantee the security of Helias's lands when the count announced that he had taken the cross and wanted to join Robert's expedition in 1096.[72]

On news of Rufus's death, Helias marched to Le Mans, where he was welcomed by the citizens. In concert with Count Fulk of Anjou, Helias began a siege of the citadel of Le Mans. The Norman garrison under Aymer of Moira and Walter, son of Ansger of Rouen, was well supplied with food and arms for a long siege.[73] The problem for the garrison was that, with the death of Rufus, it was not certain for whom the citadel was being defended. With Helias and Fulk holding the town and the Norman garrison the citadel, the siege was conducted in a restrained manner, with regular meetings and both sides swapping threats and jokes. Helias wore a white tunic, the badge and guarantee of his safe passage, as he was shuttling back and forth between the besiegers and the besieged.[74] The dilemma for the Norman garrison was who to recognise as their new lord, Robert or Henry. Perhaps realising the difficult position of the besieged, Helias and Fulk agreed a truce to allow the garrison to seek help from each of the brothers.[75]

Messengers went first to Robert, but he was 'exhausted by the fatigues of his long pilgrimage and more anxious to enjoy the peace of his couch than the toils of war'. Robert explained:

> I am worn out by my years of toil and the duchy of Normandy is sufficient for me. Besides the magnates of England are inviting me to cross the sea as soon as possible, because they are ready to receive me as king.[76]

Robert's inability to lead an army to relieve Le Mans opened the way for his brother. The messengers then visited Henry but were no more successful in

---

72 *OV*, V, pp. 230–1. For an account of Helias's struggles against the king, see *OV*, V, pp. 232–51; Barlow, *Rufus*, pp. 367–8, 381–8, 390–2, 402–6; Mason, *William II*, pp. 199–201.
73 *OV*, V, pp. 302–3 and p. 302, n. 1. On the conduct of the siege, see Strickland, *War and Chivalry*, pp. 137–8.
74 *OV*, V, pp. 302–3
75 *OV*, V, pp. 302–5.
76 *OV*, V, pp. 304–5.

securing assistance. However, Henry's reasons for refusing to come to the aid of the Normans at Le Mans demonstrate Orderic's tendency to favour Henry over his brother. The king was unable to render assistance because he was 'fully occupied with the affairs of his kingdom across the sea [and] prudently decided to concentrate on what was lawfully his than burden himself out of pride with heavy and unnecessary undertakings abroad'.[77] Orderic juxtaposes Robert's inertia against Henry's purposeful activity, but the end result was the same. Orderic admitted that Robert had been exhausted by the exertions of the Crusade and suggested that he thought that he would be offered the English crown. In Orderic's view, even if Robert should ride to Le Mans, it would be an act of pride and embroil the Normans in an unnecessary under-taking. The fact that the messengers went first to Robert suggests that the commanders of the garrison believed that Robert had the prior claim on their loyalties.

As neither Robert nor Henry appeared, the garrison had fulfilled their obligations and could surrender with honour. Helias was asked to put on the white tunic, which had earned him the nickname of 'candidus bacularis' (or 'the white bachelor-knight'), and receive the surrender of the citadel.[78] Towards the end of October 1100, the Normans marched out of the city with all their weapons and possessions. They were treated as 'faithful friends rather than defeated enemies'.[79] Nevertheless, Helias still had to provide an armed escort to protect the garrison from the anger of the citizens of Le Mans, whose homes the Normans had burnt the previous year. Helias was to play a part in the subsequent struggles between Robert and Henry.[80]

The surrender of Le Mans has been seen as marking the end of 'Norman domination' in Maine.[81] However, recent studies of the nature of lordship in the county suggest that the strength of the Norman presence in Maine may have been overestimated. The decentralised nature of lordship in the region made it very difficult for any party, including the nominal counts of Maine, to 'dominate' in any meaningful way. Despite the best efforts of William the Conqueror, Duke Robert and William Rufus, the county of Maine remained a source of disturbance for their neighbours to the north, a weakness repeat-edly exploited by the counts of Anjou. Helias and Fulk's success at Le Mans in 1100 was not the end of the story.

---

[77] OV, V, pp. 304–5.
[78] OV, V, pp. 304–5 and n. 1; Chibnall translated 'candidus bacularis' as 'white bachelor', but it might be a reference to Helias's pilgrim status and the 'baculus peregrinationis', or 'pilgrim staff'.
[79] OV, V, pp. 306–7; *Actus Pontificum*, p. 404.
[80] Barton, 'Helias I, Count Helias of Maine, and the Battle of Tinchebray', pp. 63–90.
[81] David, *Curthose*, p. 126.

The Invasion of England, 1101

One of the reasons Robert gave for his inability to support the Normans at Le Mans was that he had been invited to become king of England.[82] In 1100, Robert's prestige was high and there were barons in England willing to support him. The most prominent of these were Robert de Bellême and his brothers Roger the Poitevin and Arnulf of Montgomery, William de Warenne, earl of Surrey, Walter Giffard, Ivo of Grandmesnil and Robert son of Ilbert (de Lacy).[83] In order to reinforce his relationship with these men and others, Robert had made a number of concessions. He gave Robert de Bellême power over the bishopric of Sées, the castle at Argentan and the forest of Gouffern.[84] To Theobald Pain he granted the castle at Gisors in the Vexin 'because he had once given him shelter' during his exile.[85]

Orderic suggested that Robert made lavish gifts from his private property and made promises he could never keep if he became king. Orderic then launched into a personal attack, claiming that Robert kept the company of courtesans and jesters and wasted his resources in entertaining them:

> He often lacked bread in spite of the wealth of his extensive duchy and, being without clothing, lay in bed until the sixth hour, not daring to go to church to hear the divine office because he had nothing to wear. The whores and rogues who always surrounded him because they knew his weakness often pilfered his breeches and boots and other garments with impunity. He was a perfect example of the saying of a certain sage, 'They drift abroad who waste their goods at home.'[86]

The inconsistency in Orderic's representation of Duke Robert is never more apparent than here. Although clearly associated with events in 1101, Orderic seemed to be referring to Robert's pre-Crusade *persona*. It is hard to believe that so soon after his triumphant return to Normandy with his new wife, Robert would have been reduced to penury. What makes Orderic's invective implausible is that within a few weeks, this 'indigent duke' had successfully invaded England.

Orderic's reconstruction of events suggests that there were Norman magnates who had little respect for the duke and preferred to side with Henry. They offered the king the duchy and sent messenger after messenger

---

82   *OV*, V, pp. 304–5. On the 1101 invasion, see Edward A. Freeman, *The Reign of William Rufus*, 2 vols. (Oxford, 1882), II, pp. 392–415; David, *Curthose*, p. 137; C. Warren Hollister, 'The Anglo-Norman Civil War: 1101', *EHR*, 88 (1973), pp. 315–34, reprinted in *idem, Monarchy, Magnates and Institutions in the Anglo-Norman World* (London, 1986), pp. 77–96; *idem, Henry I*, pp. 103–48, and N. Strevett, 'The Anglo-Norman Civil War of 1101 Reconsidered', *ANS*, 26 (2004), pp. 159–75.

83   *OV*, V, pp. 308–9 and n. 1, where the accuracy of Orderic's list of disloyal barons is questioned.

84   Robert de Bellême's claims on the bishopric of Sées were of long standing: *OV*, IV, pp. 296–7.

85   *OV*, V, pp. 308–9 and n. 3; cf. pp. 216–17. Theobald Payn de Neaufle was the son of Hugh, from Neaufles-Saint-Martin (Eure), near Gisors, where his family were castellans.

86   *OV*, V, pp. 308–9 and n. 4.

inviting him to accept it. The disloyalty of the barons exasperated Orderic: 'So both peoples were corrupted by the climate of perfidy and plotted deeds of treachery to harm their lords.'[87] The tendency to challenge authority was one of Orderic's major criticisms of the Normans and the factions coalescing around Robert and Henry gave him ample opportunity to pursue his theme.

Ranulf Flambard, bishop of Durham, was singled out as the root cause of the dissension. Flambard's treachery was contrasted with the loyalty of Archbishop Anselm and that of all the bishops, abbots, consecrated clergy and 'all the English' to Henry. Flambard had acted as Rufus's chief agent and on the death of his master he was imprisoned in the Tower of London. After a dramatic escape, Flambard made his way to Normandy, where he was given refuge by Robert. Orderic clearly had little time for Bishop Ranulf, whose mother, he alleged, was a witch.[88]

Flambard used his privileged position to prompt Robert into action. Orderic may have been right to see Flambard as Robert's chief counsellor at this time as he had accumulated intimate knowledge of the workings of royal government in England. Robert's motives for invading England are not clear in the sources, but Robert of Torigny wrote that the duke was indignant at the news of Henry's coronation.[89] Orderic suggested that Flambard urged the duke to engage in a trial of strength with his brother. William of Malmesbury indicated that Robert clearly meant to seize the kingdom and that when Flambard arrived the duke was 'panting with eagerness for the fray'.[90]

Henry clearly feared his brother's reaction to his seizure of the throne. He had written to Anselm of Canterbury shortly after Rufus's death, explaining why he had not waited to be crowned by the archbishop. He also advised him to avoid Normandy on his way back to England, as he did not want to give Robert the chance to make his case.[91] In addition, at Dover on 10 March 1101, Henry concluded a treaty with Count Robert of Flanders.[92] It was designed to isolate Robert of Normandy and prevent Flanders allying with the duke. The treaty envisaged the possibility of Philip of France invading England on behalf of his vassal the duke of Normandy.[93] The terms of the treaty had to accommodate the count of Flanders' obligations to Philip of France and reflected the complexities of the situation. The defence of England is given

---

[87] *OV*, V, pp. 310–11.

[88] *OV*, V, pp. 312–13; WM, *GR*, I, pp. 714–15; Symeon, 'Historia Regum Anglorum', pp. 232–3.

[89] *WJ*, II, pp. 218–19.

[90] *OV*, V, pp. 312–15; WM, *GR*, I, pp. 716–17. *JW*, III, *s.a.* 1101, pp. 96–7.

[91] Anselm, *Ep.* 212, Schmitt, *Anselmi Opera Omnia*, IV, p. 109, trans. Fröhlich, *Letters*, pp. 162–4.

[92] *Diplomatic Documents Preserved in the Public Record Office*, I, *1101–1272*, ed. P. Chaplais (London, 1964), no. 1, pp. 1–4; there is a translation by Elisabeth M.C. van Houts, 'The Anglo-Flemish Treaty of 1101', *ANS*, 21 (1998), pp. 167–74; P. Chaplais, *English Diplomatic Practice in the Middle Ages* (London, 2003), pp. 42–3. For the wider context, R. Nip, 'The Political Relations between England and Flanders (1066–1128)', *ANS*, 21 (1998), pp. 145–67; Green, *Henry I*, pp. 61–3.

[93] Van Houts, 'The Anglo-Flemish Treaty', c. 1, p. 170.

priority but, ominously, the treaty also makes provision for the count of Flanders to aid the king in Normandy and Maine.[94]

Robert recruited some powerful support of his own. In February 1101, Archbishop Anselm received a letter from Pope Paschal II. The letter congratulated Anselm on his return from exile and encouraged him to implement recent papal decrees in England. Paschal also informed the archbishop that he had received a complaint from Robert that Henry had broken his oath to his brother in taking England. The king had also 'invaded' Robert's duchy, which was presumably a reference to those castles held by his men. Robert had reminded Paschal of his service in the Holy Land, which the pope acknowledged:

> And you know that we owe this same duke assistance in respect of the labours which he carried out for the liberation of the Church in Asia. Therefore we wish that if peace has not yet been agreed between them to your satisfaction, it should be agreed upon through the intervention of your messengers.[95]

The correspondence suggests shrewd diplomatic activity by Robert and it won him papal support in his dispute with Henry. It is also the first reference to Robert cashing in on his 'crusade dividend'. Anselm was also a beneficiary here as it gave him leverage with the king should he prove resistant to church reform.

In addition to the pope, Robert contacted Philip I of France. He had relied on him in his dealings with Rufus and together they had successfully countered his attempt to conquer Normandy before 1096. The Anglo-Flemish treaty of 1101 certainly envisaged Philip invading England and this implies that Robert had already contacted his ally. Philip's reputation also suffered at the hands of Orderic and William of Malmesbury and he should perhaps be given more credit for the revival of Capetian fortunes than he is usually accorded.[96] Robert had successfully prepared the ground for taking action against his brother in 1101.

Orderic's concise account of Robert's invasion of England in the summer of 1101 tends to lessen its significance. Within a few months of returning to Normandy, Robert had managed to assemble a large force of cavalry, archers and infantry at Tréport.[97] Orderic was aware that comparisons could be made with the invasion of 1066, but he was reluctant to acknowledge that Robert's successful landing bore any relation to that of his father. It was not the courage that the Normans had shown in 1066 that brought Robert to Portsmouth on 20 July 1101 but, rather, the result of the machinations of traitors. In fact, Henry, who had been waiting for his brother's forces to land at Pevensey, had been comprehensively outmanoeuvred. The king had sent ships sent into

---

94 Van Houts, 'The Anglo-Flemish Treaty', cc. 10, 11, p. 171.
95 Anselm, *Ep.* 213, Schmitt, *Anselmi Opera*, IV, pp. 110–11; Fröhlich, *Letters*, pp. 164–6.
96 Cf. A. Fliche, *Le règne de Philippe Ier, roi de France (1060–1108)* (Paris, 1912).
97 *JW*, III, *s.a.* 1100, pp. 96–7. Eadmer, *HN*, p. 127.

the Channel to intercept the Norman invasion force, but some of the sailors defected and guided the duke into the Solent.[98]

Robert approached Winchester escorted by magnates who had done homage to him long before. The duke was about to capture Winchester but, on being informed that Queen Matilda, his god-daughter and sister-in-law, was heavily pregnant, he withdrew, thinking it dishonourable to attack a woman in her condition.[99] Robert's decision not to press home his advantage at Winchester has been criticised. However, to be caught besieging the town by Henry's approaching army would have put Robert at a disadvantage and in a position reminiscent of that of the Crusaders at Antioch. The duke's chivalrous act in sparing the pregnant Matilda the ordeal of siege warfare was militarily pragmatic.[100]

Some of Henry's supporters defected to the duke once he was on English soil: Robert de Bellême and William, earl of Surrey, were named as defectors.[101] Despite periods of tension between them, Bellême had been Robert's supporter for many years, but it is unclear why William de Warenne decided to abandon Henry. As in 1087, the rivalry between the brothers was an ideal opportunity for ambitious barons to secure their own interests. Some threatened to desert the king, or made unreasonable demands which, when refused, acted as a justification for deserting their lord.[102] The Norman baronage, whether based in England or Normandy, emerges with little honour from these accounts. Only Robert of Meulan, Richard de Redvers, and the English remained loyal to Henry. William of Malmesbury described the king instructing the English levies in battle techniques to counter his brother's cavalry.[103]

Orderic gives prominence to Robert of Meulan, who advised the king to give his supporters whatever they wanted if by losing a little the king might keep the kingdom. There is some irony in the fact that he put the following words into Robert of Meulan's mouth:

> There is no doubt that anyone who chooses to desert his lord in an hour of deadly danger and seek another lord for greed of gain, or insists on payment for the military service that he ought to offer freely to his king for the defence of the realm, and attempts to deprive him of his own demesnes will be judged a traitor by a just and equitable judgement, and will rightly be deprived of his inheritance and forced to flee the country.[104]

---

98   *OV*, V, pp. 314–15. Cf. *ASC*, E, *s.a.* 1100, p. 111; Swanton, pp. 236–7. *JW*, III, *s.a.* 1100, pp. 98–9, where the landing is dated to 'about the Feast of St Peter Ad Vincula' (1 August).

99   Wace, *Roman de Rou*, lines 10337–40, pp. 316–17. If Matilda's first child, a girl, was born in February 1102, then in July/August she was near the beginning of her term rather than at the end; Marjorie Chibnall, *The Empress Matilda. Queen Consort, Queen Mother and Lady of the English* (Oxford, 1991), p. 9.

100   Wace, *Roman de Rou*, lines 10335–40, pp. 316–17. Green, *Henry I*, p. 64; Hollister, *Henry I*, p. 139.

101   *OV*, V, pp. 314–15; WM, *GR*, I, pp. 704–5.

102   *OV*, V, pp. 314–15. *Hyde Chron.*, pp. 305–6.

103   WM, *GR*, I, pp. 7161–7.

104   *OV*, V, pp. 316–17.

This was an encapsulation of the behaviour of the Norman barons for much of the period between 1087 and 1106. Henry took the count of Meulan's advice and won over many with promises and gifts.

Once established at Alton near Winchester, Robert challenged his brother to battle unless the latter renounced the crown. His father had done much the same thing in 1066, when he challenged Harold to single combat in an effort to spare the bloodshed of others. However, whether this was a conscious imitation of his father is unclear.[105] This offer of trial by battle began the negotiation between the brothers. They moved towards a settlement through a process that unfolded in a pattern that both sides understood and followed. Messengers arrived from Henry to ask Robert why he had entered England with an army. Robert replied that he had entered the kingdom of his father with his magnates and demanded the 'right due to me as the eldest son'. According to Orderic, the envoys 'twisted words and sowed seeds of discord' because they saw advantages in keeping the dispute going. The king realised that something was going wrong with the negotiation through intermediaries; he was in the weaker position and needed to ensure that the situation was defused. It was decided that only in face to face meetings could the brothers be sure of what was being said.

When they met, it may have been the first time that the brothers had seen each other since 1096. Robert was acutely aware of the obligations that family ties imposed and when he met Henry, 'feelings of brotherly love surged up in both'.[106] It was expected that the fraternal bond would enable Robert and Henry to reconcile their differences. Henry may have agreed to dispense with the usual methods for resolving conflict because he was confident that he could manipulate his brother's good will, by playing on Robert's sense of family, sentiment heightened by his experiences on the Crusade. Orderic's reference to the 'feelings of brotherly love', may not, therefore, be entirely fanciful and the public demonstration of emotion at the moment of reconciliation would have been entirely appropriate. Encircled by the Norman and English armies, Robert and Henry 'openly and honestly voiced what they had in their hearts'. Eventually, Robert and Henry embraced, exchanged the kiss of peace and were reconciled, 'without a mediator'.[107]

Orderic is the only source to suggest that the brothers' agreement was unmediated. William of Malmesbury, John of Worcester and the *Anglo-Saxon Chronicle* all suggest that leading counsellors or the chief men acted as intercessors.[108] Eadmer attributed the reconciliation to the intervention of Archbishop Anselm. Wace named Robert de Bellême, William of Mortain and Robert fitz Hamon as three of the negotiators. All were men of the first rank in the Norman aristocracy. The fact that two of the three, Robert de Bellême

---

[105] *OV*, V, pp. 314–15. Cf. *WP*, pp. 120–3.
[106] *OV*, V, pp. 318–19: 'et conuenientes fraterni amoris dulcedo ambos impleuit'.
[107] *OV*, V, pp. 318–19.
[108] WM, *GR*, I, pp. 716–19; *JW*, III, *s.a.* 1101, pp. 98–9; *ASC*, E, *s.a.* 1101, p. 111; Swanton, p. 237.

and William of Mortain, were supporters of the duke suggests the strength of his position and Henry's reliance on their intervention.[109]

The treaty of Winchester defused the situation and prevented war between the brothers. Robert renounced his claim to the kingdom of England in favour of his brother, and 'out of respect for his royal status' released him from the homage he had previously done to him. These two concessions were linked, for Henry could not continue to hold England if he was still bound by homage to his brother. For his part, Henry promised to pay Robert the sum of £3000 sterling every year and relinquished the Cotentin and everything in Normandy except for Domfront, which the king retained in order to keep his pledge to the townsmen never to allow it to pass to another.

In the absence of mediators, the brothers confirmed their undertakings and decided that they would help each other 'as brothers should' in an effort to recover all their father's domains and punish those who had fomented discord. Henry agreed to restore the English honours of the duke's supporters and Robert reciprocated in kind restoring their Norman lands to the royalists. Only Eustace of Boulogne was named specifically in the treaty.[110] The *Anglo-Saxon Chronicle* added a clause reminiscent of the earlier agreement between Robert and William Rufus: 'whichever of the brothers survived the other should be heir to all of England and Normandy, unless the deceased had an heir in lawful wedlock'. The treaty was ratified by twelve men from either side. As a *coda* to his account of the agreement, Orderic describes the programme of church building that marked Henry's peaceful reign in England.[111]

Robert's decision to agree the treaty with his brother rather than offer battle has astonished some commentators.[112] Yet it seems entirely in keeping with the duke's attitude to disputes with his brothers. He found it difficult to set aside the fact that William and Henry were family and he seems to have displayed a particular abhorrence of warfare that divided the Norman baronage. On a practical level, Robert also became less confident of over-whelming support among the barons.

Wace's account of the negotiations at Alton perhaps preserves other aspects of Robert's thinking.[113] Negotiators approached the duke and urged him to make peace. They pointed out that 'a brother should not do this to his brother or make so many men fight each other; on both sides there were sons and fathers and on both sides nephews and brothers'. In addition, Robert was reminded of his experiences on the Crusade:

---

[109] Eadmer, *HN*, pp. 127–8; Wace, *Roman de Rou*, lines 10397–472, pp. 318–21.

[110] *JW*, III, *s.a.* 1101, pp. 98–9, has 3000 marks, or 2000 silver pounds, as the king's annual payment to Robert. On Eustace, see Tanner, *Families, Friends and Allies*, p. 145.

[111] *ASC*, E, *s.a.* 1101, p. 111; Swanton, p. 237. Cf. *OV*, V, pp. 318–21.

[112] E.g. David, *Curthose*, p. 133; Hollister, *Henry I*, pp. 139–48, but cf. Green, *Henry I*, p. 65.

[113] A *caveat* must be borne in mind when using Wace, in that he was writing a vernacular verse-history and may have constructed his narrative according to the conventions of that genre. Damian-Grint, *New Historians of the Twelfth-century Renaissance*, pp. 181–207.

'My lord', they said, 'have mercy, in God's name! You who have been to the Holy Sepulchre should instruct us all, teach us and educate us. A battle is greatly to be feared. One cannot bring forces together in the way you and the king have done without there being a large number of men. You could lose such good friends that you would never again know joy. Moreover, a man who from the start expects to win and is ready for action can end up departing wretchedly and doing so in great shame. Make peace and, if you are reconciled, be friends as you should be.'[114]

There are a number of considerations here, not the last of which is the desire among the barons to avoid internecine conflict. It was not in their interests to have a decisive battle as prolonged fraternal rivalry was to their advantage. The reference to Robert's crusading experience may preserve further evidence of the expedition's effects on his psyche. Battle was a risky venture at the best of times and even those most confident of victory could through some accident end up shamed and defeated, if not dead. Robert's willingness to avoid battle might not fit modern conceptions of an unremittingly bellicose Middle Ages, but his policy of negotiation rather than bloodshed, especially when matters involved his brothers, seems consistent.

Archbishop Anselm may also have influenced the terms of this settlement. One of the key functions of the medieval bishop was to promote peace. The archbishop may also have introduced the precepts of canon law into the negotiations and particularly notions of sacral kingship.[115] Robert faced the difficulty of Henry's status as an anointed king. Robert faced ecclesiastical censure if he was instrumental in his brother's deposition. This may lay behind the suggestion that Anselm threatened Robert with excommunication, a matter he did not take lightly, according to Eadmer.[116]

Robert's faith in his brother's integrity was misplaced. Henry had achieved his immediate objective of holding on to the English throne and defusing his brother's successful invasion. The terms of agreement with Robert of Flanders suggest that he intended to invade Normandy and, if this is the case, it is doubtful that the king ever intended to honour the terms of 1101. Nevertheless, the treaty was ratified with oaths at Winchester on the anniversary of Rufus's death.[117] Robert remained in England with his brother for another two months or so. He was at Windsor early in September and confirmed a grant of his brothers William and Henry to the bishop of Bath.[118] This might be seen as an attempt to put the idea of condominium that lay behind the treaty of Winchester into practice. The duke returned to Normandy after Michaelmas,

---

114 Wace, *Roman de Rou*, lines 10425–40, pp. 318–19.
115 Strevett, 'The Anglo-Norman Aristocracy', pp. 182–209.
116 Eadmer, *HN*, pp. 127–8. On episcopal peace-making, see P. Dalton, 'Churchmen and the Promotion of Peace in King Stephen's Reign', *Viator*, 31 (2000), pp. 79–119, and C.J. Holdsworth, 'Peace-making in the Twelfth Century', *ANS*, 19 (1997), pp. 1–17.
117 MS. Cotton Caligula A viii, fol. 41; Hollister, 'Anglo-Norman Civil War', p. 334. MS. Cotton Caligula A viii, preserves fragments of a version of the Durham 'Historia Regum'.
118 D. Bates, 'A Neglected English Charter of Robert Curthose, Duke of Normandy', *BIHR*, 59 (1986), pp. 122–4.

'laden with royal gifts' and accompanied by William de Warenne. The *Anglo-Saxon Chronicle* suggests that Robert's men caused damage as they moved around Henry's realm.[119]

Robert's successful invasion of England in 1101 contradicts his image as a indecisive and inactive prince. Perhaps the Crusade had given him the confidence and experience to organise and lead troops on campaign, but that is to underestimate his energy and ability before 1096. Certainly, he had outmanoeuvred his brother's forces guarding England's south coast, and his advance towards Winchester threatened one of England's most important royal centres. It is not clear whether Robert would have been able to depose his brother even if with a majority of the Norman baronage in his camp. They had brought the two sides together and had, in effect, exercised what they considered to be their right to influence the choice of who should rule. Of the two brothers, Henry was probably the more relieved. Robert had acknowledged his brother's right to the English throne and had given him the respite to secure his position.

The Boy Bishops of Lisieux

Robert's first year back in Normandy had been dramatic but any support he had managed to generate from the Church was threatened by a scandal concerning the appointment of a successor to Bishop Gilbert of Lisieux.[120] One of those who accompanied Robert back to Normandy after the treaty of Winchester was Ranulf Flambard, bishop of Durham. His brother, Fulcher, was consecrated as bishop of Lisieux by Archbishop William of Rouen in June 1102. Orderic was scathing about Fulcher's unsuitability for the office: 'He was almost illiterate and had been picked out of the court for the bishopric by his brother's influence.'[121] Flambard had exploited his influence with Duke Robert to promote his brother, but Fulcher died in January 1103. Flambard was determined to retain Lisieux and tried to secure the see for his son Thomas, who was 'a mere boy' of about twelve. If Thomas died, his even younger brother was to succeed. Ranulf ruled the bishopric on behalf of his son for about three years.[122]

Eventually the episode came to the attention of the zealous Bishop Ivo of Chartres, who wrote to the Norman bishops and Pope Paschal II denouncing the situation. Bishop Ivo alleged that Robert had invested the boy with the

---

[119] *OV*, V, pp. 320–1; *ASC*, E, *s.a.* 1101, p. 111; Swanton, p. 237. MS. Cotton Caligula A viii, fol. 41, places his departure on 1 November 1101; Hollister, 'Anglo-Norman Civil War', p. 334.

[120] *OV*, V, pp. 320–1. Gilbert Maminot, physician and chaplain to William the Conqueror, was bishop from 1078 and died in August 1101. See Spear, *Personnel of the Norman Cathedrals*, p. 170 and n. 2.

[121] *OV*, V, pp. 322–3. Spear, *Personnel of the Norman Cathedrals*, p. 170.

[122] *OV*, V, pp. 322–3 and n. 3.

pastoral staff.[123] This lay investiture of a Norman bishop would have been frowned on by the pope even if the prelate concerned had been of suitably canonical age. Pressure from the pope prompted Robert to force Flambard and his sons from Lisieux and call for a canonical election. The cathedral chapter elected William, archdeacon of Évreux, and Flambard retaliated by trying to install one of his own clerks, William of Pacy. Orderic alleged that William of Pacy paid a great deal of money to the duke for the see and was later condemned both at Rouen and in Rome.[124] Archdeacon William could not obtain consecration because the archbishop of Rouen was under suspension, so Ivo of Chartres recommended that he seek help in Rome. Meanwhile, William of Pacy was forced to admit at an archiepiscopal inquiry at Rouen that he had no legitimate claim to the see of Lisieux.

Largely through Ivo of Chartres' efforts the scandal put the duke in a bad light and in 1105, when the issue came to a head, he needed the Church's assistance. Pope Paschal wrote to Robert complaining of his treatment of the Norman Church.[125] The duke had treated the Church as a slave girl rather than as the spouse of Christ. Robert seems to have tried to defend his actions, but although he had served the papacy in the Holy Land, he could not disguise the fact that his proprietary attitude to the Norman Church was from another era.

Sibyl of Conversano, 1102–3

Robert returned to Normandy in the autumn of 1101 having reached a political accommodation with his brother. The separation of Normandy and England had been re-established and the duke had the king's oath to respect the terms of the treaty. As long as the brothers remained at peace, there was no conflict of interest for the Norman baronage. However, the long-term success of the arrangement depended on the sincerity of all parties.

Robert's marriage to Sibyl of Conversano produced a son, born on 25 October 1102. According to Orderic, the infant was named William after the archbishop of Rouen, who baptised him.[126] William of Malmesbury preferred the idea that the boy was 'called William for the good omen of his grandfather's name'.[127] The birth of William 'Clito' was probably seen by Henry as a threat to his own dynastic ambitions, especially as his own

---

[123] PL, clxii, Ep. 157, pp. 162–3. Ivo also wrote to Archbishop William of Rouen and Robert of Meulan about the case; Ep. 149, 153, 154, op. cit., pp. 154–5, 157–8. T.A. Archer, 'Ranulf Flambard and his Sons', EHR, 2 (1887), pp. 103–112 at 108. In 1103 Pope Paschal II came to France and celebrated Easter at Chartres. The Lisieux case may have been discussed on that occasion. Robert's sister, Countess Adela of Blois, gave financial support for the papal visit and earned an apostolic blessing: OV, VI, pp. 42–3.

[124] OV, V, pp. 322–3 and n. 4.

[125] L. Delisle, 'Une lettre de Paschal II à Robert Courte-Heuse, duc de Normandie', Bibliothèque de l'École des Chartes, 71 (1910), pp. 465–6. Cf. David, Curthose, p. 154, n. 72.

[126] OV, V, pp. 278–9.

[127] WM, GR, I, pp. 704–5.

first legitimate child was a daughter, Matilda, born in February 1102.[128] But Robert's joy at the birth of his son was soon soured by the death of Sibyl on 18 March 1103.[129]

In recording the death of Duchess Sibyl, Orderic also noted the deaths of several Norman magnates, including William of Breteuil, Ralph of Conches and Walter Giffard. The body of Walter Giffard was returned to Normandy and buried at the church of St Mary at Longueville-sur-Scie, the *caput* of the family's Norman lands.[130] Walter Giffard's widow, Agnes, was the sister of Anselm of Ribemont the deceased crusader.[131] Agnes was a capable woman and administered her husband's estates until her son, Walter, attained his majority. This widow 'burning with a woman's lust' had, however, developed an infatuation for Duke Robert and had 'bound him to herself in the artful snares of illicit passion'.[132]

It is not clear whether Agnes and Robert were having an affair within months of his return from the Holy Land, or if she desired him from afar. The infatuation may have pre-dated Robert's departure for the Crusade, but his triumphant return would have been reason enough for her to pursue him. Nobles often maintained affective extra-marital relationships, possibly as a method of fulfilling emotional needs lacking in formal relationships which were frequently the product of diplomatic negotiation rather than mutual affection. Where love did blossom between husband and wife, it was commented on as though such a prodigy was worthy of note.

Agnes promised Robert her support and that of her powerful kinsfolk, if he would agree to marry her on the death of his wife and let her rule Normandy. Subsequently, Orderic goes on, Sibyl was poisoned and died in Lent 1103; her death occasioned general mourning.[133] In one version of William of Malmesbury's *Gesta Regum*, Sibyl's death was ascribed to the advice of Robert's 'mistress', although a later version of the text recorded 'mid-wife' rather than 'mistress'.[134]

It is not wholly implausible that Robert and Agnes were lovers, or that she was piqued by the arrival of the Italian woman, but it is perhaps stretching a point to say that William of Malmesbury was covering up an unsavoury side to the duke's character.[135] Malmesbury loved a good story even when he said, as he often did, that there was no truth to it.[136]

128 'Annals of Winchester', in *Ann. Mon.* II, p. 43.
129 *OV*, VI, pp. 38–9 and nn. 3, 4.
130 *OV*, VI, pp. 36–7.
131 *GF*, p. 85; *OV*, V, pp. 150–1. Anselm died at the siege of Arqa in April 1099. Cf. Anselm's letters to Manasses, archbishop of Rheims: Hagenmeyer, *Kreuzzugsbriefe*, nos. VIII, XV, pp. 144–6, 156–60.
132 *OV*, VI, pp. 38–9.
133 *OV*, VI, pp. 38–9. Lent began on 11 February in 1103.
134 WM, *GR*, I, pp. 704–5; II, p. 352.
135 WM, *GR*, II, p. 352.
136 Cf. Malmesbury's account of William the Conqueror's affair with a priest's daughter; *GR*, I, pp. 500–3.

The duchess's funeral was conducted by Archbishop William and she was buried in a place of honour in the nave of Rouen cathedral. The grave was covered by a polished slab of white stone into which was carved an epitaph.[137] Sibyl made a favourable impression on her Norman subjects, if her epitaph is anything to go by. When Robert was absent from Normandy, 'she managed the private and public affairs of the duchy better than the duke would have done, had he been present'.[138] Despite the removal of Agnes's rival, Duke Robert was unable to marry her because war flared up in the duchy, and she longed 'in vain to climb into the prince's bed'.[139]

Orderic's story of Agnes de Ribemont has elements of the myths that grew up around Robert after the Crusade.[140] He returned to Normandy a hero and he may, indeed, have been especially attractive to the recently widowed Agnes, but to say that Robert would allow himself to be seduced and then watch as she poisoned his wife seems less plausible. Orderic's story was intended as another indictment of Robert's character. The medieval Church in general, and monks in particular, had an ambivalent attitude towards women, and the danger represented by their sexual machinations was both a source of fascination and repulsion. For Orderic, the fact that Robert was weak enough to succumb to Agnes's charms was another sign of his unsuitability to rule.[141]

The fact that as recently as 25 October 1102 Sibyl had given birth provided William of Malmesbury with an alternative account of her demise. Although he does not name Sibyl, Malmesbury wrote that she had been misinformed by a midwife, 'who had told her when she was in childbed to restrain the superabundant flow of milk by the very tight lacing of her breasts'. Complications related to the birth of William Clito may have led to Sibyl's death. If it was a fatal puerperal infection, it is possible to understand how that might have been construed as the effect of poison administered by a rival for the duke's affections.[142]

Robert's reaction to Sibyl's death does not survive, although the sources agree that there was general mourning at her passing. The death of a spouse was an opportunity for medieval historians to indicate affective bonds between husband and wife. For example, Robert's father 'showed by many days of the deepest mourning how much he missed the love of her whom he had lost. Indeed from that time forward, if we believe what we are told, he abandoned pleasure of every kind.'[143] The Conqueror gave his wife a splendid funeral, and perhaps Sibyl's burial was attended with a similar expression of regret at

---

137 *OV*, VI, pp. 38–9.
138 *WJ*, II, pp. 222–3.
139 *OV*, VI, pp. 40–1.
140 Robert of Torigny, *WJ*, II, pp. 224–25, suggested that Sibyl was pursued by a cabal of jealous noblewomen, which may be connected with the story of Agnes de Ribemont.
141 Chibnall, 'Women in Orderic Vitalis', pp. 105–21.
142 WM, *GR*, I, pp. 704–5. For medieval medical opinion on complications associated with childbirth, see *The Trotula. An English Translation of the Medieval Compendium of Women's Medicine*, ed. and trans. Monica H. Green (Philadelphia, PA, 2001), p. 93.
143 WM, *GR*, I, pp. 502–3.

her passing. William of Malmesbury suggested that Robert's consolation was his young son.[144]

Despite the story of Agnes de Ribemont, there is no evidence that Robert had any other sexual liaisons after his return from Jerusalem. If his experiences on the Crusade had affected him profoundly, then he may have seen his wife's death as a warning to live a more pious life. Now in his fifties, and with a legitimate male heir, Robert did not have the inclination to seek out another wife, however politically expedient that may have been.

Humiliation, 1103

Sibyl's death was a blow to Robert, not least because she and her brother, William of Conversano, had assisted him in the government of Normandy. There are hints, however, that the Southern Italians were seen as a threat by the Norman baronage. They were, after all, wealthy interlopers and had the potential to monopolise the duke's attention. Access to any ruler was a jealously guarded privilege and perceived loss of influence provoked many reactions against princely favourites, especially if they were foreigners. There are few details of a reaction against these newcomers until Henry I's campaigns in Normandy a few years later and even then the criticism is directed at the Italian Normans by a royalist adherent.[145]

Around the time of Sibyl's death, Robert was approached by Earl William de Warenne, who asked for his intercession with Henry I.[146] Soon after the settlement at Winchester, the king had begun to take action against those he considered a threat in England. The following year Henry moved against several barons, including Ivo of Grandmesnil, Robert de Bellême and his brothers, and William de Warenne. Although he was one of the most powerful Norman barons, Earl William seems to have lost his lands without a formal trial. It is possible that Henry bore several grudges against Warenne which, when added to the events of 1101, sealed his fate. Earl William may have been a rival for Matilda's hand and, according to Wace, he had made jokes at Henry's expense which he had borne until such time that he could exact revenge. Warenne used to mock Henry's love of hunting by nicknaming him 'Stag's Foot' and suggesting that he could look at the tracks made by a deer and determine how many antlers it had. Unable to do anything about it at the time because Warenne was a favourite of William II, he nurtured his resentment until he could take revenge.[147]

Faced with this petition from a man who held land in Upper Normandy,

144 WM, *GR*, I, pp. 704–5.
145 *OV*, VI, pp. 62–3.
146 William de Warenne witnesses one of Robert's charters in Normandy: Haskins, *Norman Institutions*, Appendix E, no. 3, pp. 286–7; *Regesta*, II, no. 621, pp. 27–8.
147 *OV*, IV, pp. 272–3; Wace, *Roman de Rou*, lines 10513–74, pp. 320–3.

Robert felt obliged to act.[148] Wace suggested that the hatred between Henry and William de Warenne was feigned and that the latter was sent to Normandy to entrap Robert.[149] Robert crossed to Southampton with a dozen knights, and an unknown number of men-at-arms and squires. His retinue was not large enough to constitute an effective invasion force and it is unlikely that Robert expected any trouble, since, as far as he knew, the agreement of 1101 was still in place. However, on landing in England, the duke provoked his brother's anger, as Henry saw his brother's unannounced arrival as an invasion.[150]

Robert was met by members of his brother's household who explained that he had crossed England's frontiers unasked and that if he did not accept better counsel, he would be held and not allowed to return to Normandy.[151] Orderic represented the king's anger as a response to invasion. Robert had not formally asked permission to enter England. Evidently Robert had wrongly assumed that the agreement they had reached in 1101 allowed him to dispense with the usual diplomatic procedures. He might be the king's brother, but he was being treated like a potential enemy.

Among the king's messengers was Robert of Meulan, who had advised the king not to capture and thereby shame his brother. Meulan offered to engineer Robert's renunciation of the annual subsidy negotiated at Alton in 1101, and he may have been rewarded by Henry with the earldom of Leicester.[152] Robert of Meulan met the duke near Southampton and reminded him that he had renounced his claims on England. Meulan warned that Robert was in grave danger of imprisonment. Robert had, perhaps naively, trusted his brother's goodwill, but now Henry had him at his mercy. Wace, true to the genre in which he was writing, provided a moment of drama as the duke realised for the first time that his brother despised him.[153]

His first thought was to take a boat for his duchy, but he realised that it might be seen as cowardice and, in any case, the wind was against him. On the advice of Meulan, Robert looked for help from the queen. Although she had recently given birth, Matilda received her god-father with honour, reassured him and offered her protection. The queen's role in this episode is plausible as she was the ideal intermediary between the brothers. Her inter-

---

148 The *caput* of Warenne estates in Normandy was at Bellencombre: Loyd, *Origins*, pp. 111–12.

149 Wace, *Roman de Rou*, lines 10555–62. C. Warren Hollister, 'The Taming of a Turbulent Earl: Henry I and William of Warenne', *Réflexions Historiques*, 3 (1976), pp. 83–91, reprinted *idem*, *Monarchy, Magnates and Institutions*, pp. 137–44; Green, *Henry I*, pp. 76–7

150 *OV*, VI, pp. 12–15; *ASC*, E, *s.a.* 1103, p. 112; Swanton, p. 238; *JW*, III, *s.a.* 1103, pp. 104–5; Wace, *Roman de Rou*, lines 10653–706, pp. 322–5; *HH*, pp. 450–3.

151 *OV*, VI, pp. 14–15. Here *inconsultus* relates to Robert entering England without formally seeking the king's position, rather than simply signifying an unconsidered act.

152 Wace, *Roman de Rou*, lines 10575–662, pp. 322–3. Vaughn, *Anselm and Robert of Meulan*, p. 252. For the earldom of Leicester, see D. Crouch, 'Robert de Beaumont, Count of Meulan and Leicester: His Lands, his Acts, and his Self-Image', in Fleming and Pope, eds., *Henry I and the Anglo-Norman World*, pp. 91–116 at 94.

153 Wace, *Roman de Rou*, lines 10629–34, pp. 322–3.

vention mollified her husband's anger and Robert felt safe enough to visit Henry's court.[154]

Although Robert was given an honourable escort, he was apprehensive and forced to disguise his fear by appearing cheerful. Henry was equally careful to conceal his anger, and with forced *bonhomie* the brothers attempted to defuse the situation by acting out the roles of polite courtiers.[155] This dissimulation of emotion was essential if the potentially damaging situation was to be resolved. The descriptions of the meeting between the brothers reveal once again carefully choreographed diplomacy.

Henry laid a series of charges against his brother. He alleged that Robert had breached the terms of the 1101 agreement by failing to pursue known traitors. The duke had welcomed Robert de Bellême back to Normandy after he and his brothers had been expelled from England. Bellême had not only secured Argentan, the bishopric of Sées and the forest of Gouffern, also he had acquired influence over the strategically placed county of Ponthieu. Bellême was married to Agnes, daughter of Guy of Ponthieu. When Count Guy died, Bellême secured the county for his son William Talvas.[156]

Arraigned before Henry's court, Robert was obliged to admit his fault and, with suitable humility, he promised to make amends. In addition, the queen intervened and persuaded Robert to renounce the annual subsidy. It may be that the queen's intercession enabled Robert to emerge from the episode with some semblance of dignity, having been reduced to the status of the humble and contrite petitioner confessing his faults and promising redress to a more powerful man. It was unlikely that he ever would have received the pension in any case.[157]

Wace presented the conversation between the brothers as an exercise in courtly behaviour. Robert assured his brother that he had not come to claim any of his lands or revenues. The duke emphasised that it was important to maintain their fraternal bond and acknowledged that, other than seniority of birth, he had no privilege over Henry. He conceded that the 'dignity of the crown' gave Henry a distinct advantage. At the queen's request, he had conceded the annual payment and asked Henry not to seek anything else from him. Henry replied that his brother had 'spoken in true courtly fashion'.[158]

Having achieved his aims, Henry reassured Robert by confirming that their friendship had been restored. Finally, he renewed the treaty of Winchester and restored the earldom of Surrey to William de Warenne. Warenne served the

---

[154] Wace, *Roman de Rou*, lines 10653–66, pp. 322–3. Matilda gave birth to William Ætheling at some point between June and August 1103: Green, *Henry I*, p. 75.
[155] *OV*, VI, pp. 14–15.
[156] *OV*, VI, pp. 14–15 and n. 3.
[157] *WJ*, II, pp. 220–1.
[158] Wace, *Roman de Rou*, lines 10671–706, pp. 324–5. Cf. WM, *GR*, I, pp. 718–19. Robert agreed to Matilda's request 'for she was his god-daughter'.

king faithfully for thirty-three years and 'he prospered as one of the king's closest friends and counsellors'.[159]

The reference to friendship being restored between the brothers reflects the importance of this concept in the ordering of political relationships in medieval society, even those between members of the same family. The bond of friendship was not so much one based on mutual affection as one reflecting a series of rights and obligations. The friendship between Robert and his brother had been ruptured because Henry had believed that the duke had failed to fulfil his obligations. It is possible to see here the importance of demonstrative behaviour in political relationships. Robert was forced to admit his breaking of the bonds of friendship, and had to attempt to restore them by assuming the role of a suitably humble and contrite petitioner. With the aid of intercessors of suitable status, Robert promised to redress all wrongs. The price of Henry's agreement was £3000 of silver *per annum*.[160]

Robert had been at his brother's mercy and had been forced to relinquish an annual subsidy that would have considerably helped his government. Henry's actions had exploited Robert's trust to weaken the duke's position. When Robert returned to Normandy he was despised by his men even more than before, as such was the importance of honour that Robert could hardly have returned from England with his reputation enhanced. Wace's account hit the mark when he described Robert returning to his own land 'very upset and considering himself a fool for making such a foolish journey and releasing the king from all the money he owed him'.[161] Orderic does not say whether the duke returned angry from his experiences, merely that he had gained nothing from the journey except 'fear, toil, and shame'.[162]

The result of this humiliating episode was a moment of realisation for Robert: he, at last, understood that his brother was without honour and could no longer be trusted. For a man who valued the bonds of family and chivalric honour, this realisation was profoundly disillusioning. If Robert had anticipated that his exploits in the Holy Land had earned him peace in Normandy, his brother's behaviour in 1103 would surely have dispelled that hope.

Robert de Bellême, 1102–3

Robert's duchy became a refuge for those barons driven out of England by Henry. One such was Robert de Bellême, an individual for whom Orderic had nothing but contempt.[163] A damning accusation made against Duke Robert in

159 OV, VI, pp. 14–15.
160 G. Althoff, 'Friendship and Political Order', in *Friendship in Medieval Europe*, ed. J. Haseldine (Stroud, 1999), pp. 91–105.
161 Wace, *Roman de Rou*, lines 10663–726, pp. 324–5.
162 OV, VI, pp. 16–17.
163 OV, VI, pp. 20–37. See C. Warren Hollister, 'The Campaign of 1102 against Robert of Bellême', in *Studies in Medieval History presented to R. Allen Brown*, ed. C. Harper-Bill, C.J. Holdsworth and

the twelfth-century sources was that he was unable to prevent the duchy slipping into political disorder. This was explicitly associated with the arrival of Robert de Bellême, his brothers and their followers.[164] The duke's relationship with the Bellême-Montgomery family dominates the narratives concerning his rule in the duchy of Normandy after his return from the Crusade. Before 1096, the duke had been reasonably successful in containing the ambition of perhaps his most powerful vassal. Ties of friendship were the basis of their relationship, but Bellême's acquisition of Ponthieu obliged the duke to keep him close to the ducal court.[165]

Orderic suggested that Robert de Bellême's return to Normandy in 1102 was greeted with universal opposition, but that nothing was achieved because there was no-one capable enough of leading the campaign against the rebel, a clear slight against Duke Robert's abilities.[166] Henry sent envoys to his brother informing him of his action against Robert de Bellême and reminding him that under the terms of their treaty 'they should join forces to punish the man who had turned traitor to either of them'. In fulfilment of his obligations, Robert besieged the castle at Vignats. There were elements in the ducal army who opposed the campaign against Bellême and they set fire to their own tents and fled from the scene. The episode is used by Orderic as another example of the duke's ineptitude. Following the failed siege, Bellême's men ravaged the Hiémois, despite the best efforts of Robert of Grandmesnil and his brothers-in-law Hugh of Montpinçon and Robert de Courcy to resist.[167]

Orderic suggested that, in fact, the barons of Normandy had bound themselves together by oaths in a sworn association.[168] These sworn associations were contracted, often by large groups, for specific purposes. There is no indication that the sworn association against Robert de Bellême was the result of an intiative by Duke Robert, although, in effect, it worked to his benefit.[169]

Dissension within the Bellême-Montgomery clan also worked to their enemies' advantage. Robert de Bellême alone enjoyed possession of the family's lands in Normandy, thereby excluding his brothers, who had shared his fate as a result of Henry I's policies in England. Arnulf of Montgomery defected to the duke and handed over the castle of Almenèches. Orderic's monastery of Saint-Évroul was directly affected by this warfare, centred on the ecclesiastical province of Sées. Given the violence in the vicinity of his own monastery,

---

Janet L. Nelson (Woodbridge, 1989), pp. 193–202; Marjorie Chibnall, 'Robert of Bellême and the Castle Tickhill', in *Droit Privé et Institutions Régionales. Études historioques offertes à Jean Yver*, ed. R. Carabie, A. Guillot and L. Musset (Paris, 1976), pp. 151–6.

164 *OV*, VI, pp. 32–3. Orderic again provides the most detailed account of these years. Book XI of his *Historia* was written probably in 1136 and 1137, although passages written during Henry I's reign may have been incorporated; *OV*, VI, xviii.

165 Strevett, 'The Anglo-Norman Aristocracy', pp. 146–63.

166 *OV*, VI, pp. 32–3. Cf. WM, *GR*, I, pp. 718–19.

167 *OV*, VI, pp. 22–5.

168 On the *coniuratio*, see Althoff, 'Friendship and Political Order', p. 93.

169 *OV*, VI, pp. 32–3.

Orderic exaggerated the degree to which the rest of the duchy was disturbed by war in the years after Duke Robert's return from Jerusalem.

Arnulf of Montgomery's defection brought other men to the duke's side.[170] The defection of his brother was a severe blow to Robert de Bellême and provoked such anxiety that he had no faith in any of those who still adhered to him.[171] In June 1103 Duke Robert's allies gathered in the nunnery of Almenèches, stabling their horses in consecrated buildings. Orderic derived his detailed account of these events from Emma, the abbess of the nunnery, who was Robert de Bellême's sister.[172] Robert de Bellême's reaction was to attack his sister's convent and burn it to the ground. He captured Oliver de Fresnay and many others, imprisoning some for a long time, while others were put to death or mutilated. This provoked a reaction from Duke Robert and he summoned 'the army of Normandy' commanded by Roger de Lacy.[173] The duke rode to the castle of Exmes in the company of many powerful barons all of whom had opposed Bellême in the past: Count William of Évreux, Count Rotrou of Mortagne, Gilbert de Laigle, Robert Giroie of Saint-Céneri, Burchard his steward and Hugh of Nonant.[174]

The duke's attempt to deal with Robert de Bellême at Exmes resulted in defeat. Robert's brother-in-law, William of Conversano, and many others were captured. It seems that Bellême surprised the duke and attacked his troops when they were on a causeway and possibly unable to manoeuvre as they would have wished. In what is perhaps an oblique reference to the Crusade, Orderic noted how the defeated Normans, 'after triumphantly conquering foreign peoples in barbarous regions', felt an acute sense of humiliation at the hands of one of their own. Bellême's victory directly affected Orderic's monastery and he saw this as bringing savage warfare to the region. Without support, Duke Robert could do little to curb Bellême's activities. Exmes and Château-Gontier and a number of other castles fell into Bellême's hands.[175]

Bellême's activities eventually forced Robert to make peace unilaterally and thereby break the agreement with his brother Henry.[176] An agreement was reached in the summer of 1104 by which Robert confirmed Bellême's patrimonial lordships. In response, Henry I sent men into Normandy and, together with disaffected ducal barons, they set about raiding and burning.[177] Orderic's estimation of Duke Robert's attempts to control Robert de Bellême was coloured by both his own abbey's proximity to the centre of Bellême's activities and by his partisanship towards Henry I. On neither account was he

---

170 *OV*, VI, pp. 32–5.
171 *OV*, VI, pp. 34–5.
172 *OV*, VI, pp. 36–7 and n. 3. Abbess Emma and three nuns fled to Saint-Évroul, taking refuge in the chapel for six months before returning to rebuild their convent.
173 Roger de Lacy had been expelled from England in 1095; *OV*, IV, pp. 284–5.
174 *OV*, VI, pp. 34–5.
175 *OV*, VI, pp. 34–5.
176 *OV*, VI, pp. 46–7.
177 *ASC*, E, *s.a.* 1104, p. 113; Swanton, p. 239.

liable to give a measured report of Duke Robert's difficulties. By contrast, the *Anglo-Saxon Chronicle* reported that those men who joined Henry betrayed their lord, earl (i.e. Duke) Robert.[178]

As a consequence of Robert de Bellême's dominance in the diocese of Sées, Bishop Serlo and Ralph, abbot of Saint-Martin at Sées, abandoned their charges and made for England. Orderic tried to excuse their actions as a reaction to tyranny, but he could not disguise the fact that, rather than stay in Normandy and defend the interests of their churches, Serlo and Ralph defected to Henry.[179] Once again, Orderic's attitude here can be explained as an expression of sympathy for men who had close connections with his own abbey. Serlo of Orgères had been abbot of Saint-Évroul and Ralph d'Escures was a close friend of Orderic's master John of Rheims.[180] Given these circumstances, it is hardly surprising that Orderic's reports of the disturbances in the diocese of Sées display a bias against the duke and Robert de Bellême.

Rather than representing incipient anarchy in the duchy, Robert de Bellême's actions can be seen as typical of a baron determined to secure his patrimony. Given the fact that he had been driven from England, it became imperative for Robert de Bellême to secure his lands in Normandy. Whether he intended to or not, Henry I had fomented unrest in Normandy by expelling the Montgomery-Bellême clan from his kingdom.

Breteuil and Évreux

On 12 January 1103, William of Breteuil, son of the Conqueror's close friend, William fitz Osbern, died at the abbey of Bec. He had no legitimate heirs with his wife, Adeline of Montfort, and there followed a contest for the inheritance between his nephew William of Gael and a kinsman Reginald of Grancey. A third claimant, an illegitimate son, Eustace, was recognised because the Normans 'chose to be ruled by a fellow countryman who was a bastard rather than by a legitimate Breton or Burgundian'.[181] This passage suggests not only that the vassals of a lordship had a decisive say in the transmission of title, but also that there was a sense that it was inappropriate for outsiders to rule in Normandy.

The death of William de Gael left the field to Reginald and Eustace. For Henry I, the dispute was another opportunity to foment problems for his brother and the king declared his support for Eustace by marrying him to one of his illegitimate daughters, Juliana. Henry may have developed the policy of using his illegitimate daughters to construct a network of alliances after

---

178 *ASC*, E, *s.a.* 1104, p. 113; Swanton, p. 239.
179 *OV*, VI, pp. 46–7.
180 *OV*, VI, p. 46, n. 4. Serlo had been appointed with Duke Robert's approval: see *OV*, IV, pp. 252–3, 296–9. Ralph became archbishop of Canterbury: *OV*, VI, pp. 48–9.
181 *OV*, VI, pp. 40–41.

noting how successful Robert had been in recruiting Helias of Saint-Saëns. Henry also married another daughter to Rotrou of Mortagne, presumably to detach him from the duke.[182] Eustace also had the support of William Alis and Ralph *Rufus* of Pont-Échanfray and a certain Theobald.[183] Again it is worth noting that Orderic's institutional sympathies were naturally aligned with Eustace's party, given that Ralph the Red was a benefactor of Saint-Évroul and had been granted confraternity with the monks there.[184] Against them were Reginald's supporters, Count William of Évreux, Ralph of Conches, Ascelin Goel and Amaury de Montfort. Perhaps unsurprisingly, the actions of these men against Eustace's allies were condemned by Orderic.

The contested succession brought war to the Évrecin. The struggle for the Breteuil inheritance allowed Henry I to destabilise one of the important regions of Normandy and then represent himself as the restorer of order. The king sent Robert of Meulan 'to put down the civil disturbances in Normandy'. Further, Henry ordered his brother and the other leading men of Normandy to cease their operations against Eustace or risk his royal enmity.[185]

Henry was presuming to interfere in the government of his brother's duchy and his royal commands were construed as high-handed. Nevertheless, they had the desired effect and many who had opposed Eustace now either withdrew or changed sides. Reginald and Goel, however, continued their efforts with a brutality which suggests that any notions of 'chivalrous' warfare were abandoned. Eventually Reginald was driven out of Normandy and incarcerated by his brother.[186]

Peace was restored by Robert of Meulan, who used the betrothal of his infant daughter to Amaury, nephew of William, count of Évreux, as the focal point around which to bring the various enemies together. The count of Meulan felt obliged to take matters into his own hands after the capture by Goel of John, son of Stephen of Meulan, a wealthy burgess.[187]

Orderic gives us few indications as to Duke Robert's role in these proceedings and his narrative suggests that the border barons were left to their own devices to resolve disputes. In Orderic's view, Robert's lack of intervention was a measure of his ineffectiveness as duke, although he might have been fully occupied by Robert de Bellême. It must always be remembered, however, that Orderic constructed his account with an eye on the events of 1106. Border lordships were notoriously difficult to control and even under Robert's father

---

[182] *OV*, VI, pp. 40–1 and n. 11. Rotrou's wife was Henry's illegitimate daughter Matilda. Thompson, 'Affairs of State', pp. 129–51, and *eadem*, 'From the Thames to Tinchebray', pp. 24–5.

[183] *OV*, VI, pp. 40–1. Orderic is again well-informed about events because Ralph 'the Red' was a benefactor of Saint-Évroul: *OV*, VI, pp. 40–1, n. 9.

[184] *OV*, VI, p. 41, n. 9.

[185] *OV*, VI, pp. 44–5.

[186] *OV*, VI, pp. 44–5.

[187] *OV*, VI, pp. 44–7.

the marcher barons enjoyed a degree of freedom that recognised their quasi-independence.[188]

Endgame

Henry I's intervention in Robert's duchy indicated to some of the duke's vassals not only the king's determination to undermine his brother's authority, but also the advantages to be gained through careful management of loyalties. The dispute between the brothers handed power over to the barons of Normandy and England. Orderic remains the main source for the king's campaigns and, generally, he was a partisan of the king. The verse-historian Wace, writing in the reign of Henry II (1154–89), provides some balance and he has more sympathy for the duke.[189]

The political calculations of the Norman barons dominate the period between 1100 and 1106. Their priority was to retain land and political influence, and personal loyalties were weighed against those goals. Henry had several advantages over his brother, including his status as king and the economic resources of England. Henry was also less concerned about the propriety of subverting lord-vassal bonds in order to detach his brother's supporters: if there is one motif that encapsulates Henry's policy, it is a line from Wace's *Roman de Rou*: 'Li reis se fia es deniers' ('The King put his faith in money').

The first to defect to Henry, perhaps as early as 1102, was Ralph III of Tosny (Conches), who crossed to England after the death of his father. The king granted him his father's estates and Ralph was allowed to marry Adeliza, daughter of Earl Waltheof and the king's kinswoman, Judith.[190] Other 'prudent magnates' followed Ralph's example, and in Orderic's representation of their motives, they did so out of a sense of duty to the Church and those suffering in the duchy. The theme of the suffering of the Church in Normandy became the lynchpin of Henry's defence of his treatment of his brother. Naked political self-interest was clothed in the rhetoric of defending the Church. In Orderic's view, Robert was a 'foolish' (or 'weakminded') lord. Robert's foolishness was contrasted with the wisdom displayed by the barons who defected.[191] Using the language of supplication, Orderic has these traitors approach the king 'imploring him with tears to succour the suffering church of God and the unhappy land'. The king was repeatedly petitioned by men of all ranks to visit his 'paternal inheritance', a province without a governor, and 'take up the rod

---

188 David, *Curthose*, p. 148.
189 Elisabeth M.C. van Houts, 'Wace as Historian', in *Family Trees and the Roots of Politics*, ed. Katherine S.B. Keats-Rohan (Woodbridge, 1997), pp. 103–32, reprinted in *The History of the Norman People. Wace's Roman de Rou*, trans. G.S. Burgess (Woodbridge, 2004), xxxv–lxii.
190 *OV*, VI, pp. 54–55.
191 *OV*, VI, pp. 54–5.

of justice to defend the land against sacrilegious brigands'.[192] Robert's right to Normandy had been established and Henry had no valid claim to the duchy.

Henry crossed to Normandy in August 1104, visiting his stronghold at Domfront and other castles he controlled.[193] He made his tour in royal fashion and was fêted wherever he went. Orderic conveys the idea of a legitimate ruler making a royal progress through his domain. Orderic listed those who welcomed the king with their vassals and now stood ready to fight with him: Robert, count of Meulan, Richard, earl of Chester (a boy of about ten), Stephen, count of Aumâle, Henry of Eu, Rotrou of Mortagne, Eustace of Breteuil, Ralph of Conches, Robert fitz Hamon, Robert de Montfort and Ralph de Mortemer. They each had their own motives for supporting the king, but all held lands in England and some, like Rotrou and Eustace, were bound to Henry through marriage alliances or through rivalry with Robert de Bellême. Orderic is the only source to mention Henry's visit in 1104, but one of his charters may have been issued in the autumn of that year at Lyons-la-Forêt.[194]

Henry imperiously summoned his brother to a conference and when Robert arrived with his followers, he was accused of breaking the treaty contracted in England. He had made peace with Robert de Bellême and confirmed the rebel's patrimonial lands 'contrary to right and ordinance.' The king continued: Robert was

> sunk in lethargy and had abandoned all Normandy to thieves and robbers and other evil doers, and had fecklessly left it to the mercy of the shameless scoundrels by whom he was dominated; that he was a mere figurehead in the seat of prince and pastor, for he did not use the office of governor to provide for the Church of God and the helpless people, but abandoned them to their unprincipled persecutors like sheep left behind to be devoured by wolves.

The duke was on trial before his brother's court and, according to Orderic, the charges brought against him could not be denied on the oaths of his equally guilty retinue. The legalistic tone continued and the king observed that the duke was foolish and friendless 'because he did not value the company of good men or the counsel of wise ones, but unhappily chose companions of the opposite sort, thereby harming himself and many others'.[195] Robert was ensnared by the complexities of the king's charges and, after taking counsel with his men, had no other choice but to seek the friendship of his brother. Robert was evidently caught off guard and he and his advisers could not match Henry's machinations. The price of a settlement on this occasion was the transfer of Robert's lordship over William, count of Évreux. Orderic represented the duke as fearful of either losing his duchy as the result of

---

192 *OV*, VI, pp. 56–7.
193 *OV*, VI, pp. 56–7. Green, *Henry I*, pp. 80–1.
194 *OV*, VI, pp. 56–7 and n. 1. Cf. Hollister, *Henry I*, p. 184.
195 *OV*, VI, pp. 56–9.

forfeiture after a public trial, or in a war against his brother which he could not possibly win.[196]

To an extent, Count William of Évreux's reaction to his transfer from the duke to Henry sums up the situation facing all those Norman barons who held land in England as well as in Normandy. Évreux was one of the most powerful of the Norman barons and the loss of his support was a blow to Robert.[197] Orderic portrays Count William as a man of honour and has him make a declaration before the assembly.

> I served your father faithfully all my life, never once compromising my oath to him in any way; likewise I have kept faith with his heir up to now and am resolved to do so always with all the power I have. But since, as God himself says in the Gospel and I have often heard from men of learning, it is impossible to serve in tranquillity two masters who disagree with each other, I elect to place myself under the rule of one, for fear of being unable to satisfy either if I am involved in double loyalty. I love the king and the duke; but I shall do homage to one of them and him I will serve as my lawful lord.

The count's statement, we are told, was applauded by all.[198] To symbolise the transfer of lordship, the duke placed William's hand in that of the king and peace was made between the brothers. Henry returned to England before the winter.

Robert's reaction to Henry's intervention in 1104 suggests that he was still willing to reach a compromise with his brother. Nowhere in Orderic's account is there evidence of Robert responding to this invasion of his duchy in the same way that Henry reacted to Robert's unannounced appearance in England the year before. Despite the representation of the meeting as a judicial process, it was nothing more than a kangaroo court with the duke trapped and left with little option but to make his concession. On the other hand, Évreux emerged honourably from the episode. He had reluctantly agreed to break the bonds with his duke and had even won approbation as he deserted his lord. If Robert had been humiliated in 1103, he had soon forgotten that Henry had little respect for his status.

Orderic's account consistently presents the king riding to the rescue of the Normans whose country was in turmoil and unprotected by an idle, foolish lord. William of Malmesbury, however, seems to suggest that Henry knew that by answering the call of the Normans to invade the duchy he was acting against justice:

> Henry, subscribing to Caesar's opinion: 'If you must break the law, break it in the interest of your fellow citizens; in every other case you should mind your duty', took his forces across to Normandy more than once to rescue justice in its extremity,

---

[196] *OV*, VI, pp. 58–9.
[197] Hollister, *Henry I*, p. 175.
[198] *OV*, VI, pp. 58–9.

and so strong was he in the end that he subdued the whole country except Rouen, Falaise and Caen.[199]

Needless to say, Henry's departure heralded the return of warfare in the duchy. Bandits disrupted the peace settled by the king and the nobility. Robert de Bellême and Count William of Mortain were named as the chief culprits. William of Mortain was the son of Robert, the Conqueror's half-brother. Count William left England in 1104 after being denied his uncle Odo's earldom of Kent. William of Malmesbury presents the story of William of Mortain's disaffection from Henry in dramatic terms. William had envied Henry's success from boyhood and when the king temporised over his request for the earldom of Kent, William vowed never to wear a cloak until he was given his uncle Odo's estates. Henry then demanded, through due process of law, the return of unnamed properties. William left the king's court in a rage and vented his spleen with attacks on the lands of the king's supporter Richard of Chester in the Cotentin.[200]

Orderic described this warfare as scarring the whole province, with peasants fleeing to France and suffering hardships in exile. The Normans who had once conquered the English and the Apulians now suffered in exile while the orchards of their homeland were overgrown with weeds.[201] Here was an allusion to the vision of the German hermit, who had predicted that the meadows of Normandy would be destroyed as a result of Duke Robert's misrule.[202]

Orderic paints a bleak picture of Normandy under Duke Robert, but he was writing to justify subsequent events. The actions of Robert de Bellême, Count William of Mortain and others loyal to the duke could be seen as designed to defend his interests against those who had deserted their natural lord in favour of a foreign interloper. By contrast, Wace's account presents Robert making a more robust response to his brother. Once he realised that Henry had no intention of honouring their agreement, he demanded the return of the Cotentin and Domfront. Henry refused to restore their English lands to Robert's supporters and they encouraged him to attack the king's men in the duchy. In effect, Robert was retaliating in kind, perhaps provoking Henry to intervene on behalf of his men in the way that the duke had done on behalf of his in 1103. Robert responded to his brother's complaints by pointing out that the Cotentin was ducal property. Wace has an unnamed knight at Henry's court speak up in favour of a formal separation of England from Normandy. The king knew that the crown should have gone to Robert 'according to justice and seniority of birth', and should leave Normandy in

---

199 WM, *GR*, I, pp. 706–7.
200 WM, *GR*, I, pp. 720–1. William of Mortain's relationship with Henry is explored in Strevett, 'The Anglo-Norman Aristocracy', pp. 164–81, where Dr Strevett comments, surely correctly, that the story of the cloak was no comic interlude, but a provocative symbol of a perceived injustice.
201 *OV*, VI, pp. 58–61.
202 *OV*, III, pp. 106–7.

peace. Henry was unwilling to grant the truce that the duke requested and so Robert prepared for war.

Robert issued a ducal edict confirming the separation of his own lordship from that of his brother. Henceforth, no man who held land from him in the duchy was to cross to England or remain with the king. They were not to become Henry's vassals or swear any oaths to him. In effect, Robert was acknowledging that condominium was unworkable when one of the parties was so obviously acting in bad faith. It was this hardening of Robert's position that led to war, as it left no room for many of the Norman nobility to continue their cross-Channel landholding. From then on, the barons had to calculate which of the brothers was the more likely win and side with him if possible.

Robert rebuilt castles and strengthened fortifications, mercenaries were recruited and their wages soon depleted the ducal revenues and any feudal aids he could call upon.[203] Wace's account, drawing on local knowledge and oral testimony, provides details about the fighting around Bayeux, Caen and the Cotentin. He presents Robert as a more active defender of his duchy and the struggle a more even contest. Orderic's account, by contrast, placed the advantage with the king as the dispute moved towards the decisive encounter outside Tinchebray.

'More like Saracens than Christians': The Sermon at Carentan, 1105

The actions of ducal supporters in the Bessin brought Henry to Normandy again in the spring of 1105.[204] Gunter of Aunay, castellan of Bayeux, Reginald de Warenne and other ducal retainers captured Henry's man, Robert fitz Hamo, and other members of the king's household. The king's men were imprisoned and ransomed, not merely for financial gain, but also as a demonstration of contempt for Henry. Orderic makes it clear that these men were breaking the peace established the year before and Henry's reaction was to prepare a fleet and invade Normandy.[205]

Henry's army landed at Barfleur in the last week of Lent, crossing the River Vire on Holy Saturday and halting at Carentan.[206] Although the timing of the invasion may simply have been due to the beginning of the campaigning season, it may also have been Henry's attempt to make political capital of the Paschal season in his propaganda battle with the duke. According to the *Worcester Chronicle*, 'almost all the Norman nobles abandoned their duke and

---

203 E.g. Robert's defensive trench at Caen could still be seen in Wace's day: *Roman de Rou*, lines 10893–8, pp. 328–9.

204 Green, *Henry I*, pp. 82–6.

205 *OV*, VI, pp. 60–1.

206 Easter 1105 was on 9 April.

lord and the fealty owed to him and rushed over to the gold and silver the king had brought with him.'[207]

Historians present the struggle between Robert and his brother as a civil war, assuming that Normandy and England formed, in effect, a single political entity, an Anglo-Norman *regnum* created by William the Conqueror in 1066.[208] This was not, however, how contemporaries understood matters. In 1087, the Conqueror had recognised the political separation of his duchy from the kingdom of England and, despite his best efforts, William Rufus had been forced to accept Robert's right to rule their ducal homeland. The Norman Conquest of England has been seen as a colonial enterprise, but the duchy and the kingdom remained separate political entities after 1066, albeit with certain connections.[209] Medieval rulers thought not in terms of integrating their lands and titles, but of adding them in series, as can be seen in the opening lines of many of their charters. William the Conqueror was *rex Anglorum et dux Normannorum* ('King of the English and duke of the Normans').[210]

Given Robert's status as the legitimate ruler of the duchy and the prestige of his participation in the Crusade, Henry had to justify his actions. The king was invading another Christian principality and seeking to depose its lawful ruler. For much of the rest of his reign, Henry and his supporters had to construct a plausible justification for what was done in Normandy.

At the beginning of his account of Henry's 1105 campaign, Orderic allowed Serlo, the exiled bishop of Sées, to speak for the king's party. Bishop Serlo, dressed in ecclesiastical vestments for celebrating the Easter mass, and 'sighing long and sadly' referred to the sufferings of the Church and people of Normandy:

> All Christians should mourn in their hearts to see the Church trodden underfoot and the wretched people destroyed. It is all too obvious in this church that the population of the Cotentin has been miserably uprooted; indeed that all Normandy, dominated by godless bandits, is without a true ruler. The church of God was once called a house of prayer; now you may see it shamefully crammed with worldly goods and the building which should be devoted exclusively to the Holy Sacraments has been turned into a communal storehouse for lack of a just protector.[211]

The liturgical setting for Bishop Serlo's speech also played a significant role in reinforcing the justice of the king's intervention. Easter was the greatest festival in the Christian calendar, redolent with images of redemption and renewal: what better time for the king to liberate Normandy from the ravages of war?

---

207 *JW*, III, *s.a.* 1105, pp. 106–9.
208 This is the central thesis of J. Le Patourel's *The Norman Empire* (Oxford, 1976).
209 D. Bates, 'Normandy and England after 1066', *EHR*, 104 (1989), pp. 851–80. On the colonial model, see F.J. West, 'The Colonial History of the Norman Conquest', *History*, 84 (1999), pp. 219–36; cf. J.C. Holt, 'Introduction' to his *Colonial England, 1066–1215* (London, 1997), xiii–xvii.
210 E.g. Bates, *Acta*, no. 199, pp. 632–3.
211 *OV*, VI, pp. 60–3.

Henry had to combat the prestige of Robert's participation in the expedition to Jerusalem. Ordinarily a successful pilgrimage to the Holy Land would have been seen as a significant achievement in itself, but participation in the liberation of the Holy City was a battle honour that eclipsed even the Conqueror's greatest achievement. It was difficult for Henry to argue that Robert had abandoned the Church unless he and his spokesmen could overturn his image as the great defender of Christendom and liberator of Jerusalem. It is no surprise, therefore, to find that Serlo's Easter diatribe against the duke emphasised his poor stewardship of the Church and called into question his status as a hero of Christendom.

Serlo was perhaps not the best man to deliver criticism about the stewardship of the church. In the face of Robert de Bellême's return to southern Normandy, Bishop Serlo of Sées had deserted his post and he was eager to recruit Henry as an ally.[212] Serlo of Sées' Easter sermon is worth examining in some detail, not only as a justificatory piece on behalf of the king, but also as medieval political theatre.

Serlo brought specific charges against Robert de Bellême, namely that he had burnt the church of Tournay in the diocese of Sées together with forty-five men and women inside it. The bishop mentioned such things to encourage the king to 'rise up boldly in the name of God, win the heritage of your fathers with the sword of justice and rescue your ancestral land and the people of God from the hands of reprobates'.[213] Serlo denied that Robert truly held Normandy, or governed as he should,

> ... instead, sunk in lethargy, he is dominated by William of Conversano and Hugh of Nonant, who is in command at Rouen, and Gunter his nephew and other men of little worth. Sad to relate he squanders the wealth of a great duchy on trifles and follies, while he himself often fasts until noon for lack of bread. Often he dares not rise from his bed, and cannot attend church, because he is naked and has no breeches, socks or shoes. Indeed the jesters and harlots who constantly keep company with him steal his clothes at night while he lies snoring in drunken sleep, and guffaw as they boast that they have robbed the duke.[214]

Serlo was reviving Robert's pre-Crusade *persona* in an effort to counter the prestige of participating in that expedition. Robert was paralysed by inactivity and dominated by his worthless favourites, upon whom he was squandering the wealth of the duchy. Serlo employed a well-known body metaphor to express the peril that Normandy was in: 'when the head is sick the whole body is afflicted; when the ruler is foolish the whole province is in danger and the wretched people suffer utter deprivation'.[215] Robert's rule was contrasted

---

212 *OV*, VI, pp. 60–1, tells us that Serlo was 'the first Norman to rush to offer his service to the king'.
213 *OV*, VI, pp. 60–1.
214 *OV*, VI, pp. 62–3. This allegation had been made earlier: *OV*, V, pp. 308–9.
215 *OV*, VI, pp. 62–3.

unfavourably with the active governance of his ancestors as duke. Serlo called upon Henry to become righteously angry and take up arms, not out of lust for earthly glory, but in order to defend his homeland.[216]

In Orderic's representation of the events at Carentan, Henry I took further counsel and then made a pledge:

> I will rise up to work for peace in the name of the Lord, and will devote my utmost endeavours to procure, with your help, the tranquillity of the Church of God.[217]

Henry's retinue led by the Count of Meulan urged him to defend the safety of *Neustria*, a rather archaic term by the twelfth century, but which referred to the Carolingian province out of which Normandy was carved, and allowed the link with Rollo, the first ruler of Normandy.

The rest of the sermon reprised an earlier theme employed when characterising the relationship between Duke Robert and his father. Serlo's homily was also a clerical critique of the habits and the very 'courtliness' of the royal court.[218] Serlo urged his congregation to obey divine law and then began to denigrate the hairstyles and sartorial fashions of Henry's men. 'All of you wear your hair in woman's fashion, which is not seemly for you who are made in the image of God and ought to use your strength like men.'[219] Serlo drew on contemporary ideas that outward appearance betrayed the condition of the soul:

> Long beards give them the look of he-goats, whose filthy viciousness is shamefully imitated by the degradations of fornicators and sodomites, and they are rightly abominated by decent men for the foulness of their vile lusts. By growing their hair long they make them seem like imitators of women and by womanly softness they lose their manly strength and are led to sin, and often fall wretchedly into hateful apostasy.[220]

Serlo continued in the same vein until he alluded to the Crusade which had given Robert the enhanced prestige he enjoyed in Normandy. In Serlo's opinion, these young men 'refrain from shaving their beards for fear that the short bristles should prick their mistresses when they kiss them, and in their hairiness *make themselves more like Saracens than Christians*'.[221] Orderic, through Serlo, did not only tar Henry's opponents with the sin of apostasy, but also identified them with the Saracens Robert had fought in the East.

---

216 *OV*, VI, pp. 62–5.
217 *OV*, VI, pp. 64–5.
218 *OV*, IV, pp. 188–90.
219 Cf. *OV*, V, p. 22, The Council of Rouen, 1096, decreed: 'no man shall grow his hair long; instead let him be shorn as befits a Christian, otherwise he shall be excluded from the threshold of the holy Mother Church, so that no priest shall perform any divine office for him or officiate at his burial'. On this theme, Stafford, 'The Meanings of Hair in the Anglo-Norman World', pp. 153–71.
220 *OV*, VI, pp. 64–7.
221 *OV*, VI, pp. 66–7.

It was an attempt to usurp Robert's crusader credentials as the struggle between the brothers reached its climax.[222] There is a detail in William of Malmesbury's account of Henry's invasion of Normandy which suggests that Robert's predisposition to piety had become more evident after 1100. Henry summoned his brother to England 'and remonstrated with him once gently by word of mouth, urging him "to play the duke and not the monk"; after that he went to Normandy and did the same more than once, far from gently, by armed force'.[223] Malmesbury was not the only one to remark on a certain detachment in Robert's behaviour since his return from Jerusalem.[224]

Serlo's sermon concluded with a ritual shaving of the king's men. Henry himself was the first to be shorn by the bishop, who just happened to have a pair of scissors handy. Henry's lead was followed by the Count of Meulan and 'most' of the magnates gathered around. The rest of the king's household also rushed to the episcopal barber and, once shorn, they trampled their severed tresses as so much refuse.[225] This was a theatrically staged piece of propaganda designed to distance the king's forces from those who remained loyal to Duke Robert. At the snip of a pair of scissors, the duke's reputation as a Christian hero was questioned and Henry's forces were re-branded as the 'army of Christ'. Serlo's intervention was timely as before Henry could confidently confront his brother he had to deal with renewed crusading enthusiasm in Northern France.

After Easter, Henry sent envoys to Philip I of France and summoned Count Geoffrey of Anjou to his aid. Philip's role in these struggles is unclear and he may initially have failed to support Robert. Despite the Carentan ritual, Henry's campaign achieved nothing decisive in 1105.[226] However, royal forces ended Robert's control of the most important towns in central Normandy. The *Worcester Chronicle* recorded that the king's men burnt Bayeux, and Caen also fell into the king's hands before he returned to England in the autumn.[227]

Such was the enormity of the destruction of the city and cathedral of Bayeux that it was commemorated in verse by Serlo, a ducal sympathiser associated with Bishop Odo. His *De capta Baiocensium civitate* ('On the capture of the city of Bayeux') describes Henry's assault with Manceaux, Breton, English and Norman troops.[228] Bayeux was defended by Gunter of Aunay and he

---

222   W.M. Aird, 'Le retour du Croisé: Robert Courteheuse, Duc de Normandie, et les conséquences de la Première Croisade' (forthcoming).
223   WM, *GR*, I, pp. 722–3.
224   Wace, *Roman de Rou*, lines 10923–30, pp. 328–9.
225   *OV*, VI, pp. 66–7.
226   *OV*, VI, pp. 68–9; *ASC*, E, s.a. 1105, pp. 113–14; Swanton, pp. 239–40; *HH*, pp. 452–3. Wace, *Roman de Rou*, says nothing of Serlo's Easter sermon.
227   *JW*, III s.a. 1105, pp. 106–7.
228   Serlo of Bayeux, 'De capta Baiocensium civitate', in *The Anglo-Latin Satirical Poets and Epigrammists of the Twelfth Century*, ed. T. Wright, Rolls Series (London, 1892), II, pp. 241–51. Cf. the studies by H. Böhmer, 'Der sogenannte Serlo von Bayeux und die ihm zugeschriebenen Gedichte', *Neues Archiv der Gesellschaft für ältere deutsche Geschichtskunde*, 22 (1897), pp. 701–38; Bates, 'Odo of Bayeux', pp. 13–17; and C.J. McDonough, 'Classical Latin Satire and the Poets of Northern France: Baudri of Bourgueil, Serlo of Bayeux, and Warner of Rouen', in *Latin Culture in*

attempted to win a respite by handing over Robert fitz Hamon, whom he had captured, but he refused to surrender the city to the king.[229] Wace's account presented Gunter's defence as effective and heroic. During the siege there was time enough for a joust outside Bayeux involving the king's mercenary, Brun, and the duke's man Robert of Argence. Robert killed Brun and after Henry took control of Normandy, he fled to Apulia fearing the king's hatred.[230]

The king was angered by his failure to take the town and put it to flames, capturing Gunter and his men. The town was then sacked with Count Helias and his troops from Maine profiting from the plunder.[231] William of Malmesbury's account suggests that the burning of Bayeux was popularly viewed as an act which threatened the king's soul and brought punishment for Robert fitz Hamon. Henry may have fired Bayeux to bring about a swift end to the campaign in central Normandy and it recalls his father's actions in the early 1050s at Domfront and Alençon, as well as the infamous Harrying of the North of England in the late 1060s. Bayeux's fate may influenced events at the nearby ducal city of Caen.

The men of Caen, 'hearing of the massacre of those at Bayeux and fearing they might suffer a similar fate, sent to the king, who was already hurrying towards them in fierce array, and made peace with him on his own terms'.[232] The city was held for Robert by the castellan Enguerrand, son of Ilbert, a tenant of the bishop of Bayeux.[233] The inhabitants of Caen, led by four prominent citizens, expelled Enguerrand and his men. The leaders of the royalist party were then rewarded by the king with property in England at 'Dalinton', which, Orderic says, was worth £80 *per annum*. Again Henry's campaign attracted criticism; even Orderic reported that Dalinton was henceforth known as *villa traditorum* or 'Traitors' Manor'.[234] There was obviously some unease at the king's tactics during the campaign of 1105 in Normandy. Wace provided further details of Henry's capture of Caen.

Wace knew the city well and preserved local traditions, despite writing some time afterwards. He described Robert's preparations to defend Caen:

the Eleventh Century. Proceedings of the Third International Conference on Medieval Latin Studies, Cambridge, September 9–12, 1998, ed. M.W. Herren, C.J. McDonough and R.G. Arthur, Publications of the Journal of Medieval Latin, 5, 2 vols. (Turnhout, 2002), II, pp. 102–15.

229 OV, VI, pp. 78–9; WM, GR, I, pp. 722–3. Robert fitz Hamon was wounded in the head and lost his reason. Malmesbury reports the rumour that Robert deserved his punishment because Henry had burnt Bayeux and its principal church in order to set him free. Henry rebuilt Bayeux and Robert made generous gifts to Tewkesbury Abbey to make amends. Cf. WM, GR, II, pp. 360–1. Cf. Wace, Roman de Rou, lines 11103–34, pp. 332–3, who suggests that Gunter raised funds for the defence of Bayeux by capturing those who had defected to the king. He also dramatically describes Robert's capture at Secqueville-en-Bessin (Roman de Rou, lines 11065–102).

230 Wace, Roman de Rou, lines 10945–11060, pp. 328–31.

231 OV, VI, pp. 78–9 and n. 3; cf. WM, GR, I, pp. 722–3; HH, pp. 452–3 says that Henry 'took Caen by means of money, Bayeux by arms, and with the aid of the count of Anjou'. Cf. ASC, E, s.a. 1105, pp. 113–14; Swanton, pp. 239–40; JW, III, s.a. 1105, pp. 106–7.

232 OV, VI, pp. 78–9.

233 Enguerrand witnessed several of Robert's charters: Haskins, Norman Institutions, p. 76.

234 OV, VI, pp. 78–9.

for example, a trench was dug from the Rue d'Esmeisine (now the Rue Saint-Jean) to Porte Milet on the banks of the Orne, and it could still be seen in Wace's day. The financial pressures of hiring mercenaries alienated Robert from the townsfolk, who provided the funds. Many burgesses committed their property and possessions to the care of monks and themselves fled to the abbeys. The duke drew criticism for allowing the burgesses to flee and, Wace says, he was deemed negligent, a trait that had been especially noticeable since his return from the Holy Land.[235]

Wace presented the loss of Caen as a grand conspiracy among the leading citizens who met in a garden next to the church of Saint-Martin. From the moment that they agreed to betray their lord, the garden remained barren. The duke, informed of the conspiracy against him, escaped through the Porte Milet, while his entourage was harassed and robbed by the gate-keeper.[236] It also gives the impression that the disloyalty of Caen's leading citizens was not viewed favourably by the inhabitants of Calvados. Wace's narrative suggests that Duke Robert still had popular support and that had the ordinary folk known of the conspiracy, the burgesses of Caen would have suffered.[237] Henry may have had some leverage with the burgesses of Caen as Robert fitz Hamo had captured powerful men from the town, including Thierry, the son of one of the leading citizens, Ralph fitz Ogier. Robert fitz Hamo was offered control of Caen, but his reputation was tarnished by his part in the duke's demise.[238]

After the capture of Bayeux and Caen, Henry's troops advanced on Falaise, but it was at this point that the king's coalition began to fragment. Robert's supporters may have been active in undermining the bonds between the king and his allies. Robert's men coined the nicknames 'Godric and Godiva' for the English king, making explicit Henry's connection with the Anglo-Saxon royal dynasty and underlining the fact that here, on Norman soil, was a foreign invading force.[239] Count Helias of Maine withdrew his men 'at the request of the Normans', surely a reference to Robert's supporters, although there were *Normanni* on both sides.[240] Helias's withdrawal was enough to prevent Henry storming Falaise, but there were skirmishes outside the town and a certain Roger of Gloucester was killed.[241]

Helias's decision to leave the assault on Falaise has been the subject of some speculation. He may have been swayed by the king's troubles with Archbishop Anselm or the advance towards Maine of the powerful Countess Adela of

---

[235] Wace, *Roman de Rou*, lines 11062–336, pp. 332–7.
[236] Wace, *Roman de Rou*, lines 11297–336, pp. 336–7.
[237] Wace, *Roman de Rou*, line 11280, pp. 336–7.
[238] Wace, *Roman de Rou*, lines 11163–242, pp. 334–5 and n. 341. On Robert fitz Hamo, *WJ*, II, pp. 248–9.
[239] WM, *GR*, I, pp. 716–17.
[240] *OV*, VI, pp. 78–9. Barton, 'Henry I, Count Helias of Maine', pp. 86–7.
[241] *OV*, VI, pp. 80–1 and n. 1. Roger was the son of Durand de Pistres, sheriff of Gloucester. Cf. WM, *GR*, I, pp. 722–3.

Blois-Chartres, Henry and Robert's sister.[242] The interests of Count Helias and Geoffrey Martel in the affairs of Anjou may also have been a factor in the withdrawal. The withdrawal at the request of the Normans may refer to peace negotiations between Robert and Henry in the late spring of 1105.

Robert and Henry met at Cintheaux near Falaise, at Pentecost (21–28 May) 1105 and tried to make peace. The negotiations failed due to unnamed 'seditious trouble-makers', but the failure suggests that there were some for whom a reconciliation between the brothers was a threat.[243] The failure of negotiations plunged Normandy into a round of burning and plundering from Pentecost to Michaelmas 1105. If Henry had indeed realised that the funds which were the bedrock of his campaign were running dangerously low, or that he had not gained overwhelming support in the duchy, he may have decided that until he could once again occupy the moral high ground after reconciliation with Archbishop Anselm, he would be well-advised to postpone the attempted conquest of Normandy.[244]

The Crusader and the Archbishop

Anselm of Canterbury and Bohemond of Antioch, men of very different character, inadvertently aided Robert's cause in 1105. Since 1103, Archbishop Anselm had been away from England because Henry I had refused to accept the archbishop's views on the Investiture Contest.[245] As his conflict with his brother intensified, Henry's exiled archbishop became a problem. Anselm's close relationship with Pope Paschal II meant that there was a very real danger that the king would have to conduct his campaign to seize Normandy as an excommunicate. A sentence of excommunication would absolve Henry's allies of their bonds to the king and, at the same time, highlighted the injustice of his invasion of an independent sovereign Christian country. Anselm's biographer, Eadmer, provides an eye-witness account of the proceedings of the summer and autumn of 1105. The English monk explained the significance of the rumours of the king's impending excommunication.

> Already in many places throughout England, France and Normandy a rumour had gone abroad that the King was on the point of being excommunicated by Anselm and accordingly for him, as for a sovereign not too well loved, many mischiefs were being prepared which it was thought would be brought to bear on him more effectually if he were excommunicated by a man of such eminence. The king himself

---

[242] Hollister, *Henry I*, pp. 189–90, and see Barton, 'Henry I, Count Helias and Tinchebray', pp. 86–8.

[243] *OV*, VI, pp. 80–1 and n. 2.

[244] The foregoing paragraph owes much to Barton's analysis in 'Henry I, Count Helias and Tinchebray', pp. 86–9.

[245] For Henry and Anselm, see R.W. Southern, *Saint Anselm. A Portrait in a Landscape* (Cambridge, 1990), pp. 277–307. For an introduction to issues of the Investiture Contest, e.g. Robinson, *The Papacy*, pp. 421–2, 433–4, 436–8.

was aware of this and accordingly it was a source of great satisfaction to him that Anselm's condemnation of him had been averted.[246]

In July 1105, Henry and Robert's sister, Adela, together with Ivo of Chartres, arranged a meeting between the king and the archbishop at Laigle on the Norman frontier. Eadmer suggests that the relationship between Adela and Anselm was especially close and that she had chosen the archbishop as 'the director and guardian of her life'.[247] Anselm had heard that the countess was seriously ill at Blois and he was anxious to see her. When the archbishop reached Blois he found Adela much recovered and remained with her for several days. Anselm informed Adela that he intended to excommunicate her brother Henry. Adela was distressed by this news and persuaded Anselm to accompany her to Chartres. Interestingly, Eadmer reports that Adela's other brother had all but lost his duchy. It was not, however, ineptitude or sloth which had produced this state of affairs. According to Eadmer:

> Now the king was at that time in Normandy and had conquered almost the whole of it. For the authority of Robert, Duke of Normandy, brother of King Henry, had at that time sunk so low in the general estimation that there was scarcely anyone who was willing to do for him any such service as among all nations it is usual to do for the sovereign of the country. Piety and an almost total absence of any desire for worldly wealth, both of which qualities were prominent in Robert's character, had produced this estimation of him.[248]

Eadmer's opinion of Robert supports other evidence that the duke had experienced a profound reaction to the Crusade. His predisposition to piety, enhanced by his pilgrimage to Jerusalem, produced in him a disengagement from the world.[249] If Robert was experiencing a reaction against the problems created for him by his brother's machinations, then he may have been willing to reach an agreement which left much of the duchy in the king's hands. After all, the pact with William Rufus in 1091 had allowed the king control of parts of Upper Normandy.

Henry contacted his sister and asked her to mediate with Anselm. The parties duly met at Laigle and the king affected joy at the arrival of the archbishop and promised to restore the revenues of the see of Canterbury.[250] Eadmer tells us that their former friendship was restored. There were still matters to resolve, most notably what was to be done with those clerics who had accepted investiture from the king, but a tentative settlement was reached on 22 July 1105 and messengers were despatched to Rome to have the agreement ratified.[251] Having bought time to repair his relationship with the arch-

---

246 *HN*, p. 166, trans. Bosanquet, p. 177.
247 *HN*, p. 164, trans. Bosanquet, p. 175.
248 *HN*, p. 165, trans. Bosanquet, p. 176.
249 Henry of Huntingdon specifically discusses Duke Robert's fate: *HH*, pp. 604–5.
250 Southern, *Saint Anselm*, p. 300.
251 *HN*, pp.165–6, trans. Bosanquet, p. 176.

bishop and raise more funds for the campaign against his brother, Henry returned to England in August 1105.

There was another reason for Henry to expedite his reconciliation with the archbishop. At the end of 1105 memories of the Crusade and consequently Robert's prominent role in the liberation of Jerusalem were being rekindled. It was one thing for the king and his supporters to put round rumours of an indolent and inept duke; it was quite another for them to combat the power of the public reputation of a pious and successful soldier of Christ.

The reason that the Crusade was in everyone's minds was that one of Robert's fellow crusaders was heading to France. In February 1106 a comet had appeared presaging 'many memorable events in many places'. In advance of his visit, the crusading 'star', Bohemond of Antioch, sent messengers to the princes of Northern France. He also wrote to Henry asking for his support for a new campaign in the East, probably to be directed against the Byzantine emperor, Alexios. Henry was reluctant to allow Bohemond to visit him fearing that he might lose men to an expedition to the East. Henry offered to meet him in Normandy before Easter 1106.[252]

The threat of losing men to Bohemond's venture made it necessary for Henry to emphasise the justice of his campaign against his brother Robert. The language used in Orderic's reconstruction of the king's campaigns suggests a 'crusade at home' along the lines of Helias of Maine's battle against Rufus.[253] Although Bohemond visited Rouen in late April 1106, there is no record of Robert meeting him. Perhaps the events at Antioch had soured their relationship. Bohemond did, however, encounter Archbishop Anselm. In Bohemond's party was a knight, Ilgyrus, who presented Anselm with some hairs of the Blessed Virgin that she had torn from her head as she witnessed Christ's crucifixion. He also presented these prestigious relics to the cathedrals at Rouen and Chartres, and the abbeys of Saint-Ouen and Bec.[254]

Bohemond was very popular and wherever he went he was fêted as a hero and encouraged to recount his adventures. Many nobles brought him their children and he willingly stood as godfather to them. Orderic tells us that the name 'Bohemond', previously unknown in the West, became so popular that it was adopted by thousands in 'the three continents of the globe'.[255] Bohemond also succeeded in persuading the ageing Philip I of France to allow him to marry his daughter Constance. A wedding feast was provided at Chartres by Adela, countess of Blois. Adela seems to have been working on Henry's behalf rather than Robert's.[256] As a finale to the wedding Bohemond gave a stirring

---

[252] OV, VI, pp. 68–9 and n. 6.

[253] OV, V, pp. 228–33.

[254] HN, pp. 179–80, trans. Bosanquet, pp. 192–3. Eadmer felt that the relics were genuine: HN, p. 181.

[255] OV, VI, pp. 70–1; WM, GR, I, pp. 692–3.

[256] Kimberley Lo Prete, 'The Anglo-Norman Card of Adela of Blois', Albion, 22 (1990), pp. 569–89; eadem, 'Adela of Blois: Familial Alliances and Female Lordship', in Aristocratic Women in Medieval France, ed. T. Evergates (Philadelphia, 1999), pp. 7–43.

account of his exploits in the East from the pulpit and ended with a call to arms.[257] By the time of Bohemond's marriage, Henry had been partly reconciled with Archbishop Anselm. At a meeting at the Norman frontier town of Laigle on 21 July 1105, Henry agreed to relinquish the right of investing clerics, but retained the right to expect them to perform homage to him. As Henry's relationship with the Church improved, his brother's deteriorated.

The Campaigns of 1106

In February 1106, Robert crossed to England and visited his brother at Northampton.[258] The visit may have been suggested by Archbishop Anselm and prepared by Robert de Bellême, who came to Henry's Christmas court in 1105. The *Anglo-Saxon Chronicle* reported that Bellême left only discord and his mission may have been an attempt to recover his English lands, rather than on behalf of the duke.[259] That Robert was willing to trust his brother's guarantee of safe-conduct again suggests that he wanted to reach an amicable settlement. Henry of Huntingdon wrote that Robert sought the 'free restoration of what had been taken away from his paternal inheritance'. The king rejected Robert's request and he returned angrily to Normandy.[260] However, Henry reported to Anselm that Robert had parted in 'a friendly manner', perhaps to disguise the fact that a meeting sponsored by the archbishop had faltered due to his own refusal to negotiate.[261] Huntingdon attributed the failure of the negotiations to divine providence, which suggests that he could see no other reason for the renewal of hostilities. There was, perhaps, more than a little sympathy for Robert's efforts to make peace. Time and again in his dealings with his brothers, Robert had shown willingness to reach agreement: Henry, on the other hand, was determined to conquer Normandy.

After the failure of Robert's mission and before August 1106, the king again invaded Normandy.[262] However, Henry's expedition nearly began disastrously, as the duke had concocted a scheme to kidnap him. Robert's collaborator was Abbot Robert of Saint-Pierre-sur-Dives, described by Orderic as 'a contemptible little man'.[263] The appointment of Abbot Robert created a scandal which the duke could ill-afford at this time. It was alleged that Robert had paid 140 marks of silver for the abbacy. Orderic denounced Abbot Robert as a simoniac and accused him of converting his abbey into a fortress, paying

---

257 *OV*, VI, pp. 70–1.
258 Henry was at Northampton in February, *Regesta* II, no. 737, p. 51.
259 *ASC*, E, *s.a.* 1106, p. 114; Swanton, p. 240. Green, *Henry I*, p. 86.
260 *HH*, pp. 452–3. *JW*, III, *s.a.* 1106, pp. 108–9; *ASC*, E, *s.a.* 1106, p. 114; Swanton, p. 240.
261 Anselm, *Ep.* 396, Schmitt, *Opera*, V, p. 340; Fröhlich, *Letters*, pp. 156–7. Henry also informed Anselm that he intended to invade Normandy again on Ascension Day, 3 May 1106.
262 *ASC*, E, *s.a.* 1106, p. 114; Swanton, p. 240.
263 *OV*, VI, pp. 72–3. Robert was a monk of Saint-Denis.

his troops with the possessions of the church.[264] The scandal of the abbacy of Saint-Pierre-sur-Dives may have prompted Bishop Ivo of Chartres' letter of complaint to Pope Paschal II about the condition of the Norman church under Duke Robert. Paschal's letter in reply accused Robert of treating the Church like a 'slave-girl' rather than the 'Bride of Christ'.[265]

Abbot Robert made an agreement with the duke and his magnates at Falaise, promising to deliver the king into their custody. The abbot went to Caen and met the king as if he were his friend and offered to hand over his castle. In order to separate Henry from his army, Abbot Robert suggested that the king should bring a small force so as not to alert the castle garrison. Nonetheless, the king rode all night with a force of seven hundred knights and arrived at the castle at dawn. Reginald de Warenne and Robert de Stuteville had occupied the castle and as the king approached they shouted abuse. The intention was that many knights were on their way from Falaise and other castles intending to attack the king. Greatly angered, the king ordered his men to attack the castle and they set fire to it and the nearby abbey. Reginald and Robert were captured with many others and some, who had fled to the church, were burned in its tower. The conflagration alarmed the ducal forces coming from Falaise and they retreated. Orderic ends his account by pointing out that those who had made the abbey and church of Saint-Pierre a stronghold had rightly perished. The captured abbot was flung over the back of a horse and taken to the king. Henry is reported to have sent him into exile, stating that only respect for the man's ecclesiastical status prevented him from being torn limb from limb on the spot.[266]

The Battle of Tinchebray, 1106

The autumn of 1106 was stormy, with thunderstorms, rains and war. Robert still had formidable allies in Robert de Bellême and William of Mortain and it is difficult to judge the accuracy of statements such as Henry of Huntingdon's that the king was supported by 'all the nobility of Normandy and the flower of England, Anjou and Brittany'.[267] King Henry visited the abbey of Bec on the Feast of the Assumption of the Virgin (15 August 1106) and attended a mass celebrated by Anselm. According to Eadmer, the final concord was reached between the archbishop and the king. Anselm was then encouraged to return to England as Henry prepared to confront his brother.

Having decided to target Count William of Mortain's lands in the south of the duchy, Henry built a siege castle at Tinchebray and entrusted it to Thomas

---

[264] OV, VI, pp. 74–5. Orderic associated the events of this year with a bout of influenza he suffered.
[265] See above, p. 2.
[266] OV, VI, pp. 80–3.
[267] HH, pp. 452–5; cf. JW, III, s.a. 1106, pp. 108–9; ASC, E, s.a. 1106, p. 114; Swanton, p. 240.

of Saint-Jean.[268] William of Mortain managed to bring supplies to his garrison despite the presence of the king's men. Count William's defence of Tinchebray was effective and the royal besiegers were confined to their fortification.[269] Henry was frustrated by this resistance and led an army in person to push matters further. Orderic wrote admiringly of the measures taken by the count to protect his castle.[270]

William then appealed to Duke Robert, Robert of Bellême and others for help. Fulfilling his obligation as a lord to defend his vassal in time of need, the duke summoned an army and issued a formal warning to his brother to raise the siege or risk a formal declaration of war. This is an interesting detail which suggests that up until that point, and despite the failure of negotiations at Northampton, Duke Robert, at least, considered that a state of peace existed between them. That said, Henry was once again in Normandy and unless he was formally invited into his brother's duchy – which is unlikely – this invasion might have been construed as an act of war. It is difficult to believe that Robert thought that his brother's intentions were anything but hostile.

The king 'hardened his heart, persisted in the siege and embarked on a more than civil war for the sake of future peace.'[271] The reference to the 'more than civil war' was derived from the Roman writer Lucan's *Pharsalia*, an account of the war between Pompey and Caesar:

> Of war I sing, war worse than civil … and of legality conferred on crime; I tell how an imperial people turned their victorious right hands against their own vitals; how kindred fought against kindred; how, when the compact of tyranny was shattered all the forces of the shaken world contended to make mankind guilty.[272]

Orderic's characterisation of the struggle for Normandy captures the fratricidal nature of the war, of '[b]rothers and kinsfolk … in arms on different sides', but his use of *bellum ciuile* has tended to obscure the fact that Henry had invaded the territory of another sovereign Christian state. That said, the reference to Lucan's work suggests a certain unease: illegal acts were given the appearance of legality.[273]

Henry's forces included Helias of Maine, William of Évreux, Robert of Meulan, William de Warenne, Ralph of Bayeux, Ralph of Conches, Robert de

---

268 Thomas of Saint-Jean became sheriff of Oxfordshire: Judith A. Green, *English Sheriffs to 1154* (London, 1990), p. 69.
269 The most detailed accounts for the battle fought outside Tinchebray are to be found in *OV*, VI, pp. 88–91, *HH*, pp. 452–5 and in a letter by a priest of Fécamp, printed by H.W.C. Davis, 'A Contemporary Account of the Battle of Tinchebrai', *EHR*, 24 (1909), pp. 728–9 and idem, 'The Battle of Tinchebrai: A Correction', *EHR*, 25 (1910), pp. 295–6. The letter is translated in D.C. Douglas and G.W. Greenway, *English Historical Documents, II, 1042–1189*, 2nd ed. (London, 1981), no. 9, pp. 329–30. See David, *Curthose*, Appendix F: 'The Battle of Tinchebray', pp. 245–8.
270 *OV*, VI, pp. 84–5.
271 *OV*, VI, pp. 84–5 and n. 3.
272 Lucan, *The Civil War* ('Pharsalia'), trans. J.D. Duff (Cambridge, MA, 1928), pp. 2–3.
273 *OV*, VI, pp. 84–7.

Montfort and Robert of Grandmesnil and many others with their troops. Duke Robert's ranks included his cousin William of Mortain, Robert de Bellême, Robert de Stuteville the elder, William de Ferrières and many others.[274] Robert had fewer mounted soldiers than Henry, but more infantry. There were kinsfolk on either side and this compelled some to withdraw rather than fight.

There were attempts by several churchmen to mediate. Prominent among them was Vitalis the hermit, founder of the Savignac monastic order and one of the many hermits who seem to have inhabited the forests and wastes on the borders of Brittany, Maine and Normandy.[275] He may have been among the ducal ranks, given that William of Mortain's father, Robert, had been his patron: he may also have been a protégé of Odo of Bayeux.[276]

Vitalis's intervention may have prompted a message from Henry to his brother, reported by Orderic. The king claimed that he had not invaded Normandy out of greed for any worldly lordship, nor did he aim to deprive his brother of the rights of the duchy. He was, he asserted, responding to the tearful petitions of the powerless asking for help for the Church of God, 'which like a pilot-less ship in a stormy sea is in peril'. Henry's message continued:

> You are a duke in name alone, openly mocked by your own servants, incapable of avenging the insult implicit in their scorn. Therefore cruel sons of iniquity oppress the Christian people living under your shadow, and have almost wholly depopulated many parishes in Normandy. Seeing these things, I am fired by the zeal of God, who governs us, and ask only to lay down my life for the safety of my brothers and the people of my beloved country.[277]

If Robert would hand over all of Normandy's castles, together with the duchy's judicial and administrative business and half of the duchy, he would be allowed to keep the rest 'without toil or responsibility'. He would also receive an annual sum, drawn from the English treasury, equivalent to the value of the other half. Henry offered his brother what was, in effect, a comfortable retirement:

> You can then enjoy feasts and games and all kinds of amusement in comfort. I for my part will undertake all the labours necessary to preserve peace, and will faithfully keep my promises while you rest, and with God's help will lawfully hold in check the brutality of would-be oppressors, so that they cannot trample his people underfoot.[278]

---

274 *OV*, VI, pp. 84–5 and nn. 8–9.
275 *OV*, VI, pp. 86–7; cf. *OV*, III, pp. 100–1 and IV, pp. 122–3.
276 *OV*, VI, p. 86, n. 1; cf. *OV*, IV, pp. 330–2. Vitalis had been Count Robert's chaplain and a canon of the church of Saint-Évroul at Mortain. See also, B. Golding, 'The Religious Patronage of Robert and William of Mortain', in *Belief and Culture in the Middle Ages. Studies presented to Henry Mayr-Harting*, ed. R. Gameson and Henrietta Leyser (Oxford, 2001), pp. 211–30 at 220–1.
277 *OV*, VI, pp. 86–7.
278 *OV*, VI, pp. 86–7.

Robert took counsel with his men and the king's proposal was rejected 'at once with scorn'. When Robert's reply was reported, Henry commended himself to God and asked for His protection in the coming battle.[279] Unfortunately, it is not known why Robert decided on this occasion not to try to reach an agreement with his brother.

Orderic's account has the tone of royalist propaganda and perhaps reflects a carefully prepared campaign to justify the annexation of Normandy.[280] On 28 September 1106, the king summoned the leaders of the *familia regis* and drew up his order of battle.[281] Henry released Reginald de Warenne and others captured during the attack on Saint-Pierre-sur-Dives, and, in an attempt to ward off divine retribution for his burning of the abbey church, Henry vowed to restore it.[282] Ralph of Bayeux commanded the first contingent of the king's army, Robert of Meulan the second and William of Warenne the third. William de Warenne's presence suggests a reason for the release of his brother. The English and Normans were kept near the king and command of the Manceaux and Bretons was given to Count Helias, stationed some distance away.

Duke Robert's vanguard was commanded by William of Mortain, on whose estates the battle was being fought; he may have demanded this place of honour for this reason. Robert of Bellême was given command of the rearguard. The duke's old friend, Edgar the Ætheling, also stood with him in the battle.[283] Both the royal and ducal forces fought on foot. Henry of Huntingdon suggested that this was so that they could fight more steadily, perhaps a reference to the heavily undulating terrain near Tinchebray, unsuitable for prolonged cavalry manoeuvres. The fact that the troops on both sides were dismounted might also have been intended as a statement of intent, in that it would be more difficult to flee on foot.[284] According to Orderic, the troops were so densely packed together that, when Count William's men came together with Ralph of Bayeux's contingent, there was no room to swing weapons for effective strikes. Henry of Huntingdon added that, although Robert and his troops were fewer in number, they were 'experienced in the Jerusalem wars' and he was able

---

279   *OV*, VI, pp. 88–9.
280   *OV*, VI, p. 88, n. 1.
281   WM, *GR*, I, pp. 722–3; *ASC*, E, *s.a.* 1106, p. 114; Swanton, p. 241; *JW*, III, *s.a.* 1106, pp. 108–11. Other sources give the date as 27 September (*WJ*, II, pp. 222–3) or 29 (Priest of Fécamp, in Davis, 'A Contemporary Account', p. 296).
282   *OV*, VI, pp. 88–9; cf. *Regesta*, II, no. 905, pp. 84–5.
283   *ASC*, E, *s.a.* 1106, pp. 114–15; Swanton, p. 241.
284   Strickland, *War and Chivalry*, pp. 140–1 and nn. 42–3, and J. Bradbury, 'Battles in England and Normandy, 1066–1154', *ANS*, 6 (1984), pp. 1–12, reprinted in Strickland, *Anglo-Norman Warfare*, pp. 182–93 (the version used here), at 187 and n. 29. Strickland (*op.cit.*, pp. 23, 169) makes the point that fighting on foot was not unusual, especially in the battles fought during Henry I's reign. Cf. M. Bennett, 'The Myth of the Military Supremacy of Knightly Cavalry', in *Armies, Chivalry and Warfare in Medieval Britain and France*, ed. M. Strickland (Stamford, 1998), pp. 304–16; S. Morillo, 'The "Age of Cavalry" Revisited', in Kagay, ed., *Circle of War*, pp. 45–58.

to repulse the royal forces in a brave and awe-inspiring manner.[285] Robert's crusade experience gave him an advantage and despite their numerical superiority, Henry's forces could not make inroads into the ducal lines. William of Mortain's men successfully harassed the king's troops at various points. Henry's ally, Count Helias of Maine, possibly in combination with the Breton cavalry, launched an attack on the duke's infantry from the flanks and cut down 225 in the first onslaught. Such was the impact of Helias's manoeuvre that Robert de Bellême took flight and abandoned the duke to his fate. Wace's account of the battle is perfunctory and there is a sense that he felt that the duke had been let down by those he trusted.[286]

Bellême's flight was probably decisive and Duke Robert of Normandy was captured by Henry's chancellor, Waldric. Orderic reported that Waldric later became bishop of Laon 'and greatly oppressed his subjects' to the extent that he was murdered by them in a 'pleasure-garden'. There may be a hint of disapproval here, a result of the cleric's participation in the battle at Tinchebray and his capture of the duke.[287] The Bretons seized Count William of Mortain and were reluctant to hand him over to the king. Robert de Stuteville, William de Ferrières and many others were taken prisoner. Henry pardoned and released many of those taken, but some were kept in fetters until the day they died, 'as their crimes deserved'.[288]

Orderic reported a speech made by Duke Robert in the aftermath of his defeat:

> Treacherous Normans deceived me by their lies and persuaded me to reject your counsels, my brother, which would have been my salvation if only I had followed them. I bound the defenders of Falaise by an oath, when I left them, that they would never surrender the castle of Falaise to anyone except me or William of Ferrières, whom I have found faithful in all things. So now, my brother make haste and send William to receive the fortress, for fear that Robert of Bellême may outwit you by some trick and, by occupying this almost impregnable castle before you do, hold out against you for a considerable time.[289]

Henry took his brother 'in a friendly and prudent fashion' to Falaise to secure its surrender. William de Ferrières had gone ahead to take possession of the castle and when the party arrived at Falaise, the duke ordered the burgesses to surrender the town and give the king their fealty. Robert's infant son, William, was brought to his uncle. Henry looked at the boy who was trembling with fear 'and comforted him with kind promises, for he had suffered too many

---

285   *HH*, pp. 454–5.
286   *OV*, VI, pp. 88–91; cf. *HH*, pp. 454–5; Wace, *Roman de Rou*, lines 11361–80, pp. 336–9.
287   Green, *Henry I*, p. 92, suggests that Robert was humiliated by being captured not by a knight but by a cleric. Cf. H.W.C. Davis, 'Waldric the Chancellor of Henry I', *EHR*, 26 (1911), pp. 84–9. Waldric was murdered on 25 April 1112. Guibert of Nogent provides an account of Waldric and his demise: see Benton, *Self and Society*, pp. 151–7.
288   *OV*, VI, pp. 90–1.
289   *OV*, VI, pp. 90–1.

disasters at a tender age'. Aware that there might be adverse public opinion if any harm came to the boy while he was in his custody, Henry handed him over to Helias of Saint-Saëns, Robert's loyal supporter.[290]

Ever mindful of public opinion, especially after the recent reconciliation with the archbishop of Canterbury, Henry despatched a letter to Anselm, probably within a few days of victory, as he made his way from Falaise to Rouen.[291] The letter was recorded by Eadmer:

> We inform your paternity and holiness that on an appointed and fixed day Robert, Duke of Normandy, with all the forces of knights and foot soldiers which by begging or buying he was able to bring together, fought with me furiously outside Tinchebray, and in the end, by the mercy of God, we were victorious without any great slaughter of our own men. Why should I say more? Divine mercy delivered into our hands the duke of Normandy, the count of Mortain, William Crispin, William of Ferrers, the aged Robert of Stuteville and others to the number of 400 knights and 10,000 foot soldiers, and Normandy itself. Of those slain by the sword there is no reckoning. I attribute the victory not to my own excellence and pride nor to my own strength but to the gift of divine providence. Therefore, venerable father, humbly and devoutly prostrate at the knees of your holiness, I beseech you to beseech the heavenly judge, by whose decision this victory, so glorious and so advantageous, has come to me, that it may not turn out to my loss or detriment but may lead to the initiation of good works and the service of God and to the preserving and strengthening of the position of God's holy Church in tranquillity and peace so that henceforth it may live at liberty and not be shaken by any storms of war. Witnessed by Waldric, the chancellor at Elbeuf.[292]

Henry's victory brought joy to 'all pious men' including Archbishop Anselm, but evil-doers and outlaws were compelled to cease their operations and flee in all directions.[293] Robert accompanied Henry to Rouen, where they were welcomed by the citizens. The king confirmed his father's laws and restored the ancient privileges of the city.[294] Another of the duke's close allies, Hugh de Nonant, surrendered the citadel of Rouen 'at the duke's command' and was rewarded by recovering his honour, taken by Robert de Bellême. The duke released all the other castellans of Normandy from the obligations of their fealty to him and they surrendered their castles 'with his consent' and were reconciled to Henry.

Robert had a large part to play in ending the hostilities in Normandy. He had accepted that the battle of Tinchebray was decisive and would not allow his men to continue resistance on his behalf. By releasing his men from their

290   *OV*, VI, pp. 92–3; cf. *OV*, IV, pp. 182–3.
291   *HN*, p. 184, trans. Bosanquet, p. 197.
292   *HN*, p. 184, trans. Bosanquet, p. 197; Anselm, *Ep.* 401, Schmitt, *Opera*, V, p. 345; Fröhlich, *Letters*, pp. 164–5. William Crispin, brother of Gilbert Crispin, Abbot of Westminster, was later pardoned, *OV*, VI, pp. 180–1. William was the son of Henry of Ferrers, *OV*, VI, pp. 84–5, cf. II, pp. 264–5, and IV, pp. 232–3. Elbeuf lies 18 kilometres south of Rouen.
293   Anselm, *Ep.* 402, Schmitt, *Opera*, V, p. 346; Fröhlich, *Letters*, pp. 166–7.
294   *OV*, VI, pp. 92–3 and n. 3.

fealty to him, Robert allowed them to surrender with honour, an important prerequisite if Henry was to rule Normandy with any measure of security. It also suggests that the duke's vassals believed that their lord was in no mortal danger at the hands of his brother, for their sense of honour would surely have compelled them to attempt to secure his release. The actions by Robert and Henry in the aftermath of the short battle at Tinchebray marked the formal cessation of hostilities and the end of Robert's independent rule of his father's duchy.

As William of Malmesbury pointed out, the battle of Tinchebray occurred forty years after William the Conqueror landed in England, but it was not in any sense England's belated revenge for Hastings.[295] Although there were Englishmen at Tinchebray, it was essentially a battle between Normans. It marked the reconstitution of the Conqueror's cross-Channel *regnum* and the end of Robert's attempt to rule independently of his brothers. For twelfth-century commentators, Tinchebray was God's judgement on Robert's rule and they constructed their accounts of his career with the events of 28 September 1106 in mind. Robert had at least been allowed to fight for his principality. In defeat the duke retained his honour, unlike those who, according to Wace, had deserted their lord:

> The duke was captured and the count [of Mortain] was captured; neither of them was rescued by their own men. Many men who held fiefs from them and who should have been with them abandoned their lord at this time of need; as a result of their shameful actions, they received rewards from the king, for which they were severely reproached.[296]

---

[295] WM, *GR*, I, pp. 722–3.
[296] Wace, *Roman de Rou*, lines 11373–80, pp. 338–9.

CHAPTER SEVEN

THE CAPTIVE

AFTER the defeat at Tinchebray, Robert was a prisoner of his brother, but he was still duke of Normandy. Henry I summoned all the magnates of Normandy to a council at Lisieux in the middle of October 1106. At Lisieux Henry firmly established peace throughout Normandy 'by his royal authority' and all robbery and plundering was to cease. Henry also announced that all churches were to hold their possessions as they had held them in 1087 and that all lawful heirs should hold their inheritances. The king took into his own hands all his father's demesnes and 'by judgement of wise counsellors decreed that all the gifts his brother had foolishly made to ungrateful men, and all the concessions he had made through weakness, should be null and void'.[1] By making 1087, specifically the day his father William the Conqueror had died, the reference point, Henry was, in effect, consigning Robert's rule in Normandy to oblivion. Henry's statement at Lisieux had the potential to set in train as many grievances over lands and other possessions as it was designed to settle. It resembles statements made by his father as he established his regime in the months after the battle of Hastings, when references to his predecessor as king, Edward the Confessor, effectively wrote King Harold II out of official memory.[2]

Robert had a significant role to play in the surrender of the remaining ducal strongholds in Normandy to his brother. There is a sense in which Robert recognised the hopelessness of continuing the struggle, although concern for the well-being of his young son, William, may have made the duke apprehensive. Robert had fought to keep his duchy, but it was unlikely that he could withstand a determined campaign by his brother backed by the overwhelming financial resources of the kingdom of England.

Robert was sent into captivity in England at the end of 1106. There may have been protests because Henry made repeated attempts to justify his actions in subsequent years. Orderic hinted at the disquiet that Robert's defeat and capture caused when he described Robert de Bellême's attempt to secure the

---

[1] *OV*, VI, pp. 92–5.
[2] E.g. Bates, *Acta*, no. 180.

aid of Count Helias of Maine in order to continue the war against Henry.[3] Robert de Bellême appealed to Helias saying that he needed his help:

> because the world is upside down. A younger brother has rebelled against an elder, a servant has conquered his master in war and thrown him into chains. Moreover he had robbed him of his ancestral inheritance and, as a perjured vassal, has taken his lord's rights into his own hand. But I have preserved my fealty to my natural lord, and as I obeyed the father faithfully, so I will obey the son to the end of my life. As long as I live I will never allow the man who has bound and imprisoned my lord and, what is more, his own, to rule Normandy in peace.

Bellême noted that he still held thirty-four strong castles and asked Helias to help his captive lord and 'restore him or his heir to the Norman duchy'.[4]

Through Robert de Bellême, a man for whom he usually had nothing but contempt, Orderic voiced the complaint of ducal supporters against the king's actions. Helias's reply, on the other hand, seemed to be a warning to Bellême to examine whether the restoration of Duke Robert was a sensible course of action. Helias counselled Bellême not to start anything he could or should not carry through:

> He ought also to make his business not to raise anyone higher than he deserves or allow any man who does not know how to rule himself to have authority over others. As a common proverb runs, 'he who seeks to elevate a fool presumes to defy God.'[5]

Orderic allowed Helias to voice a justification for Henry's actions. The king was driven to fight against his elder brother and lord, 'by most urgent necessity' and did so in response to the prayers of churchmen wretchedly oppressed by reprobates. It was acknowledged that, in the normal scheme of things, fighting against an elder brother or lord might be seen as wrong, for another proverb was trotted out: 'wrong must be done to put an end to a worse wrong'. Helias then outlined the problems Normandy had faced ever since Robert's return from Jerusalem.

Helias claimed that ever since his return from the Holy Land, Robert had succumbed to 'sloth and idleness'. The Latin word *torpor* can also be rendered by the more neutral term 'listlessness', rather than the loaded word 'sloth'. Similarly, *ignavia* might just as well be translated as 'inactivity'. If Robert had suffered debilitating effects from his arduous pilgrimage to Jerusalem, it would not be surprising to find him unwilling, perhaps because he was physically unable, to act as vigorously as he might have done earlier as duke. Nevertheless, Helias claimed, the duke's inactivity had encouraged lawless men to take advantage and embark on every kind of evil-doing. The Church had been oppressed for six years by plunder and arson. Poor people had been forced

---

3   *OV*, VI, pp. 94–5. Barton, 'Henry I, Count Helias and Tinchebray', p. 81.
4   *OV*, VI, pp. 94–5.
5   *OV*, VI, pp. 94–5.

into exile and monasteries had been robbed of possessions given to them in former times. It was claimed that such was the level of lawlessness that the celebration of mass had all but ceased. In support of his claims, Helias drew attention to the churches burned down in many parts of Normandy, and the depopulated parishes everywhere in a state of disorder. Bellême himself was accused of being one of the main perpetrators of these evil deeds. Finally, it was by the judgement of God that victory had been given to a 'friend of peace and justice.' Helias offered to intercede with Henry on Robert de Bellême's part if he would agree to abandon his evil machinations.[6] Orderic noted that because the friendship between Henry and Helias was strong, the reconciliation was effected. Bellême surrendered Argentan and all that he had obtained from the ducal demesne, but secured the *vicomté* of Falaise and everything that had belonged to his father. So, despite his vow to harass the king until he restored Duke Robert to his lordship, Robert de Bellême once again looked after his own interests first. Fickle self-interest was a common trait amongst the Norman aristocracy.

The Captive Duke

Robert was sent into captivity in England. Orderic tells us that this was to avoid the possibility that his supporters might stir up trouble in Normandy in their attempts to aid him.[7] The duke was being sent as a political prisoner into exile in his brother's kingdom.[8] Given that public outcry against his imprisonment could be engineered by Duke Robert's supporters, the king seems to have hoped that making his brother more inaccessible might dissuade potential ducal partisans. In addition, Henry may have felt more able to control access to the duke and prevent or control messages from Normandy reaching him. Nevertheless, even as a captive Robert remained a potential focus for rebellion against the king's control of Normandy.

It is unlikely that Robert was maltreated while a prisoner, or led away in chains. This would have been a provocative act, undermining his status as duke and inciting renewed opposition to the king.[9] It is difficult to distinguish a political prisoner from a hostage, or, indeed, a hostage from an honoured, if carefully watched, guest. Robert, as the king's brother and the duke of Normandy, not to mention a Crusade hero, enjoyed considerable status in the early twelfth century. To have maltreated him would have been counterproductive. It is probably better to imagine Robert held in a state of 'honourable captivity'. Nonetheless, Henry may have derived some satisfaction from

---

6 *OV*, VI, pp. 96–7.
7 *OV*, VI, pp. 98–9.
8 On political prisoners, see Jean Dunbabin, *Captivity and Imprisonment in Medieval Europe, 1000–1300* (Basingstoke, 2002), pp. 28–9.
9 See Dunbabin, 'Conditions of Captivity', in *Captivity*, pp. 114–29.

restricting his brother's movements and contacts beyond the purely pragmatic concern of preventing further rebellion. The king had, after all, been imprisoned by his elder brothers and Henry certainly emerges from the medieval sources as an individual likely to have borne a grudge. Henry's motive for keeping his brother under close supervision must also have provided an element of legitimacy for his actions in Normandy. The king was, in effect, ruling on behalf of his brother and with his brother's legitimacy. Initially, at least, Henry refrained from using the ducal title, perhaps in deference to this idea. He may also have considered that Robert deserved to be punished and that his captivity was a legitimate sentence for his misrule in Normandy.

It is difficult to discover much about Robert's period of captivity. Orderic wrote that the duke was incarcerated for twenty-seven years, which confirms that he was confined from 1106/7 until his death in 1134.[10] The length of Duke Robert's custody distinguishes his treatment from the more temporary confinement of other opponents captured in battle and then ransomed. Henry's father had imprisoned political opponents, including his brother Odo of Bayeux, for longer periods, although nowhere near as long as twenty-seven years.[11]

Initially, Robert was briefly confined at the royal castle in Wareham, Dorset, perhaps shortly after arriving in England.[12] Although the sources refer to 'Wareham' castle, Robert may have been incarcerated at Corfe in the Isle of Purbeck. The village of Corfe – although not the castle, which is post-Conquest – was the site of the murder of the Anglo-Saxon king Edward 'the Martyr', by elements acting on behalf of his half-brother Æthelred Unræd.[13] At this time it would not have been unusual to enter the south of England via Poole Harbour and Wareham, but perhaps Henry's choice of Wareham was intended as a reminder to his brother that there was a worse fate that imprisonment.

King Henry then entrusted his brother to his chancellor Bishop Roger of Salisbury, who accommodated the duke in his castle at Devizes in Wiltshire.[14] Bishop Roger had been recruited by Henry before 1100 when he was serving as a poor parish priest in the suburbs of Caen. The trait that recommended Roger to the future king was his ability to say the mass at some speed, making

---

10 OV, VI, pp. 98–9.

11 On this point, see Dunbabin, *Captivity*, p. 101.

12 'Annals of Winchester', in *Ann. Mon.*, II, p. 42.

13 Ann Williams, *Æthelred the Unready. The Ill-Counselled King* (London, 2003), pp. 1–17. There are other parallels with Robert's case. Ann Williams notes, *Æthelred*, p. 9, that, although he was the elder brother, opponents of Edward's succession pointed out that his mother was not a crowned queen when he was born, whereas Æthelred's mother had royal status at his birth. The 'porphyrogeniture' argument, as Ann Williams notes, was deployed by Henry I's supporters in the early twelfth century. Cf. Hollister, *Henry I*, p. 105, and Green, *Henry I*, pp. 20–41.

14 WM, *GR*, I, pp. 736–9. Cf. *JW*, III, *s.a.* 1113, pp. 134–5. In July 1113 another prisoner arrived at Wareham, Robert de Bellême, and it is possible that Duke Robert was moved to Devizes to avoid the possibility that these former allies might conspire together. That said, given Robert de Bellême's conduct at Tinchebray, the duke might not have been especially keen to rekindle their relationship.

him an ideal priest for military men.[15] A castle at Devizes, probably built by Bishop Roger's predecessor Osmund, burned down in 1113. This was almost certainly a wooden motte and bailey fortification, but Bishop Roger decided to rebuild in stone and by 1121 it was sufficiently completed for Roger to hold an ordination there.[16] Robert's place of imprisonment was an impressive edifice and Henry of Huntingdon claimed that 'there was none more splendid in the whole of Europe'.[17] Although castles of the twelfth century were designed as defensible fortifications, they were also lordly residences and offered a standard of accommodation which reflected the status of society's elite.[18] Duke Robert may thus have been living in some style as a political prisoner of his brother.

It is not clear whether Robert spent all his time in captivity under Roger's supervision in Devizes, or whether he accompanied his gaoler as the bishop fulfilled his episcopal and governmental duties. It is possible that captive and gaoler developed an understanding, especially if, as we are told, Robert was indeed a man of easy conversation.

In the later twelfth century, Geoffrey of Vigeois reported that Robert was freed by his brother, but was confined once again after raising an army.[19] This story was reiterated in the thirteenth century, when it was reported that Duke Robert had tried to escape in 1109. According to this account he was recaptured and blinded, but although this story influenced later opinion, it cannot be substantiated from the twelfth-century sources.[20]

The *Anglo-Saxon Chronicle* noted for the year 1126 that 'the king had his brother taken from the bishop Roger of Salisbury, and committed him to his son Robert earl of Gloucester, and had him led to Bristol and there put in the castle'.[21] The *Anglo-Saxon Chronicle* suggested that this was done on the advice of the king's daughter and through her uncle, King David of Scotland. It is not clear why the Empress Matilda had advised her father to remove Robert from Bishop Roger's custody. Henry I had just returned from Normandy and his daughter may have feared that, when it came to the succession, Bishop Roger may have had some sympathy for the aged duke, now in his mid-seventies or,

15 William of Newburgh, *The History of English Affairs*, ed. and trans. P.G. Walsh and M.J. Kennedy (Warminster, 1988), I, pp. 56–7. It should be noted that there is no other support for this story. Cf. E.J. Kealey, *Roger of Salisbury, Viceroy of England* (Berkeley and London, 1972), pp. 3–4.

16 'Annals of Winchester', in *Ann. Mon.*, II, p. 44. For the skill of Roger of Salisbury's stone-masons in buildings erected by the bishop at Salisbury and Malmesbury, see the comment by WM, *GR*, I, pp. 738–9.

17 *HH*, pp. 720–1. See *VCH, Wilts.*, x, pp. 237–8. Kealey, *Roger of Salisbury*, pp. 89–90.

18 C. Coulson, *Castles in Medieval Society. Fortresses in England, France, and Ireland in the Central Middle Ages* (Oxford, 2003).

19 Geoffrey of Vigeois, 'Chronica', in *RHF*, xii, p. 432.

20 Roger of Wendover, *Chronica sive Flores Historiarum*, ed. H.O. Coxe, 4 vols. (London, 1841–2), II, p. 39; Matthew Paris, *Historia Anglorum sive, ut vulgo dicitur, historia minor. Item, ejusdem abbreviatio chronicorum Angliae*, ed. F. Madden, 3 vols., Rolls Series (London, 1866–9), I, pp. 212–13. Cf. Green, *Henry I*, p. 216.

21 *ASC*, E, *s.a.* 1126, p. 127; Swanton, p. 256. *OV*, VI, pp. 380–1, reported that Robert was in prison at Devizes, when he had a dream that his son William Clito was killed on 27 July 1128.

more probably, Robert's son, William Clito.[22] Although undoubtedly loyal to his father, Robert of Gloucester himself may have requested custody of his uncle, perhaps out of curiosity and a desire to hear at first hand tales from the Crusade. Given the uncertainty over the succession, Henry I demonstrated considerable trust in his illegitimate son by transferring Duke Robert into his custody. At some date before 1134, the duke was moved from Bristol to Cardiff, still in Earl Robert's lordship.

Robert was probably kept in 'free custody' (*libera custodia*), the 'honourable captivity' mentioned above where his movements and contacts were monitored.[23] In Orderic's account of Henry I's meeting with Pope Calixtus II at Gisors on 23 or 24 November 1119, the king described the conditions of his brother's captivity:

> I have not kept my brother in fetters like a captured enemy, but have placed him as a noble pilgrim, worn out with many hardships, in a royal castle, and have kept him well supplied with abundance of food and other comforts and furnishings of all kinds.[24]

This might be seen as special pleading by the king, perhaps a response to criticism for the treatment of his brother. William of Malmesbury, writing about the same meeting, suggests that the pope 'had come with hostile intent, to lodge an emphatic protest at his [Henry's] holding in captivity his own brother, who was also a pilgrim of the Holy Sepulchre'.[25] The pope's predecessor, Paschal II, had ordered that the property of returning crusaders should be restored and Henry's seizure of the duchy might have been seen as against the spirit of this principle.[26] Henry portrayed his brother as a man exhausted by his pilgrimage, now deserving of rest amid the finer things of life.[27] The circumstances surrounding Calixtus's meeting with Henry may have also prompted the pope to bring up the subject of the king's brother.

The conference at Gisors was designed to bring about a settlement between Henry and Louis VI of France and Calixtus may have wanted to place Henry under a moral obligation to defend his actions in order to make him more amenable to a reconciliation with Louis. William of Malmesbury's account makes it clear that Henry won over the pope with an array of lavish gifts: 'eloquence is sure of a hearing when spiced with rich gifts'.[28]

William of Malmesbury agreed with Orderic that Robert's confinement was comfortable:

22 Chibnall, *Empress Matilda*, p. 53.
23 *WJ*, II, pp. 220–3. Cf. Dunbabin, *Captivity*, p. 115.
24 *OV*, VI, pp. 286–7.
25 WM, *GR*, I, pp. 734–5.
26 WM, *GR*, II, pp. 368–9.
27 Cf. WM, *GR*, I, pp. 734–7.
28 WM, *GR*, I, pp. 734–5.

He was captured and remains in open confinement (*libera custodia*) until the present time, having to thank his brother's praiseworthy sense of duty that he has nothing worse to suffer than solitude, if solitude can be called when he enjoys the continual attention of his guards, and plenty of amusement and good eating. He is held, then, surviving all the companions of his journey, and it is uncertain whether he will ever be allowed free again.[29]

William of Malmesbury, who was closely associated with Earl Robert of Gloucester, the duke's gaoler from 1126 onwards, makes it clear that Duke Robert's captivity was congenial. In his brief character sketch of Robert, Malmesbury also suggests that the duke may have been good company: 'He was a good speaker in his native tongue and no one was better company.'[30] It was not unusual for prisoners to eat and drink with their guards, although it might lead to escape attempts. For example, in February 1101, Ranulf Flambard, bishop of Durham, imprisoned by Henry I shortly after his succession, escaped from the Tower of London by exploiting the liberal conditions of his confinement.[31] He managed to have a length of rope hidden in a flagon of wine. The bishop then made merry with his guards and, when they had succumbed to the effects of the drink, he made his escape using the rope, which burned his gloveless hands.[32]

There is no evidence to suggest how Robert reacted to his twenty-eight years of confinement. If his experiences on the Crusade had led to a sense of disengagement from the world, then he may have viewed imprisonment as a fitting opportunity to leave behind the cares that came with his duties as duke in favour of a more introspective life. In his mid-fifties when he was captured, Robert may have welcomed a peaceful retirement of the kind others of his class sought by joining monasteries *ad succurendum*, that is, provided with accommodation and medical care if necessary, in return for a donation to the monastic house concerned.

There is very little evidence about the conditions in which Robert was kept. However, from the one surviving *Pipe Roll* for the reign of Henry I, there are references to the expenditure incurred in maintaining Robert in captivity.[33] The *Pipe Roll* recorded sums of money accounted for at the meeting of the Exchequer. In one entry the sum of £23 10 shillings was paid out for clothes ('in pannis') for the duke and in another note £12 was paid for 'furnish-

---

29 WM, *GR*, I, pp. 706–7. The passage was written before 1126 and was later revised after February 1134 to note that Robert was kept in prison until his death.

30 WM, *GR*, I, pp. 706–7.

31 WM, *GR*, I, pp. 558–9.

32 *OV*, V, pp. 310–13.

33 'Et in lib[er]at[ione] Archiep[iscop]i Rothomag[ensis], et in pannis Com[itis] Norman[norum] .xxiii. li[bras] et .x. s[olidos] nu[mero]; Et in Soltis. p[er] br[eve] R[egis] Fulcher[o] fil[io] Walt[heri] .xii. li[bras] p[ro] estruct[ura] Com[itis] Norman[norum]': *Magnus Rotulus Pipae de Anno Tricesimo-Primo Regni Henrici Primi*, ed. Joseph Hunter for the Record Commission (London, 1833), pp. 144, 148.

ings' ('estructura') provided for Robert.[34] These are substantial sums and they suggest that Henry was providing for his brother's comfortable old age. The sum of £12 was paid out to a certain Fulcher fitz Walter, who is addressed in a writ in favour of Ramsey Abbey from Henry I.[35] Fulcher appears to have been an official of some standing in London as he is addressed before Eustace the sheriff.[36] Fulcher's role in London might indicate that Duke Robert was brought to his brother's court at Westminster and therefore did not necessarily spend all of his time in Devizes, Bristol or Cardiff. Alternatively, Fulcher might simply have been charged with purchasing suitable clothes for Robert from London's drapers and was reclaiming his expenses.

William Clito

Robert's son, William Clito, did not share his father's prison after the defeat at Tinchebray.[37] William was probably only just over four years old when his father was captured.[38] He was not with his father on campaign and was being looked after at Falaise. When Robert and Henry arrived, William was brought before his uncle and 'trembled with fear' as he awaited the decision as to what was to be done with him. Henry comforted his nephew and his conciliatory attitude may have been part of a settlement with Robert in return for the surrender of the remaining ducal strongholds.[39] As Henry may also have feared for the consequences if any harm came to the boy, he decided not to keep him in his own court. As William's guardian he chose Helias of Saint-Saëns, a firm supporter of the duke.

Helias had married Robert's illegitimate daughter and had been given the county of Arques, which 'raised him to the highest rank in Normandy'.[40] Orderic characterised the relationship between the duke and Helias in the following way:

> Helias undertook with courage the duty imposed upon him, and always remained
> faithful to Duke Robert and his son William, for whom he endured much under the

---

[34] £23 10 shillings seems a large amount if *in pannis* is translated as 'for bread'. The Latin *panis* is indeed 'bread', but the word here is probably *pannus* meaning 'cloth' and thus 'clothes'; see Latham, *Revised Medieval Latin Word-List*, s.v. '2 pann/us', p. 330.

[35] *Regesta*, II, no. 1610a.

[36] Fulk fitz Walter has been identified as sheriff of London: Green, *English Sheriffs to 1154*, p. 58. Green cites the writ in favour of Ramsey Abbey.

[37] 'Clito' was the Medieval Latin equivalent of the Old English 'æðeling/ætheling' meaning 'prince'; cf. Latham, *Revised Medieval Latin Word-list*, s.v. 'clit/o', p. 92. It may be connected with Latin *inclutus* (*inclitus*), meaning 'famous' or 'celebrated'.

[38] *OV*, V, pp. 278–9. William Clito was born at Rouen, 25 October 1102: Hollister, 'The Anglo-Norman Civil War: 1101', p. 330 and n. 6 (in *Monarchy, Magnates and Institutions*, p. 92 and n. 6).

[39] *OV*, VI, pp. 92–3.

[40] *OV*, VI, pp. 92–3.

two kings, William and Henry; for he suffered labours and the evil of disinheritance, exile and many dangers.[41]

Henry's decision to surrender William into the hands of a known ducal supporter seems foolhardy unless he was acting according to an agreement with Robert. It is possible that Henry may have had some feeling of kinship with the boy named after his own father, but these putative affective bonds are not stated explicitly.[42] Henry may have underestimated the damage that a four-year-old disinherited son could do. He reasoned, perhaps, that until William came of age, his fate rested in the hands of his guardians, whom the king expected to be able to control. However, Henry had not reckoned with Helias of Saint-Saëns' astute understanding of the propaganda value of the sight of a pathetic child driven from his home by a wicked uncle.

Thus it is likely that Henry handed over his nephew to Helias of Saint-Saëns as a *quid pro quo* for Robert's co-operation in the pacification of Normandy. Once the duke was safely imprisoned across the Channel in England, Henry and his counsellors decided that it was dangerous to leave William Clito at large. It may even have been as early as the end of 1106 that Henry ordered the arrest of his nephew. Without warning, he sent Robert of Beauchamp, *vicomte* of Arques to the castle of Saint-Saëns to seize the boy.[43] Although Helias himself was absent, kinsfolk snatched William from his bed and saved him from his pursuers and the fate of his father.

When informed of the incident, Helias quickly found the boy and took him into exile. Orderic repeatedly noted Helias's loyalty to William Clito and seems to have admired his willingness to devote himself to the boy's welfare. Robert de Beauchamp took Helias's castle into the king's hands and it was later given to William de Warenne.[44]

Helias brought William up as if he was his own child. It is unknown how much Duke Robert knew of his son's wanderings, but he would doubtless have been reassured by Helias's conspicuous display of loyalty. He was not only keeping William secure from Henry's agents, but also promoting his cause wherever he went.[45] Helias made the most of every opportunity to explain William's grievances against his uncle. His presentation of the boy's case engendered an emotional response and a sense of injustice. Those who heard the tale were brought to love the young man because Helias had 'inclined their hearts towards suffering his [William's] degradation along with him'.[46]

In allowing Helias to assume responsibility for the safety of his nephew in the immediate aftermath of the battle of Tinchebray, Henry I seems to

41 *OV*, IV, pp. 182–3.
42 WM, *GR*, I, pp. 704–5.
43 *OV*, VI, pp. 162–3.
44 *OV*, VI, pp. 162–5.
45 *OV*, VI, pp. 164–5.
46 Cf. Barbara H. Rosenwein, *Emotional Communities in the Early Middle Ages* (Ithaca and London, 2006), pp. 86–9.

have made a grave error. Many Normans were inclined to support William and wanted him as their lord. Where these Normans saw William or heard Helias's propaganda is not certain, but Henry faced a severe problem. Robert de Bellême, 'remembering his love and friendship for the duke' and hoping to recover the authority he had once enjoyed, now decided to throw his weight behind young William's cause.[47] Elaborate plans were made by Helias and Robert de Bellême and, in addition to maintaining frequent contact with each other, they repeatedly visited King Louis VI of France, William, duke of Poitou, and other potential supporters, driving home their appeals through letters and envoys.[48]

William Clito and the Struggle for Normandy

If Robert had any thoughts of regaining control of Normandy – and it is not certain that he continued to harbour such ambition – his hopes lay with the fortunes of his son William. It might have been a comfort simply to know that Henry was harassed by William's supporters, or a cause for concern that his son was putting himself in harm's way on his behalf. Father and son were bound together through ties of honour as well as affective bonds. There are hints that Robert's affection for his son was recognised. William of Malmesbury noted that after Robert's wife died 'One consolation there was to lighten this great misfortune, the son born to him by his wife.'[49] Robert's captivity certainly provided a focus for his son's efforts and Robert's release was William's priority. But William also had reasons of his own to attempt to free Normandy from his uncle's grasp. When his father was defeated at Tinchebray, William's future role was thrown into doubt as were the dynastic ambitions of the lineage of the Conqueror's eldest son. Questions of filial and familial honour might not have been uppermost in the mind of the trembling child who appeared before Henry at Falaise in late 1106, but later these issues were doubtless impressed upon him by Helias of Saint-Saëns. After all, Robert's career as wronged eldest son and imprisoned Crusade hero gave William's guardians plenty of emotive material to work with.

For almost twenty years Henry's priority was to counter the support for his nephew both within and beyond the borders of Normandy.[50] Among the first to offer the boy aid was his kinsman, Count Baldwin VII of Flanders. William arrived at Baldwin's court in 1112–13, when he was about ten years old, and was knighted by the count a few years later.[51] Once knighted William became

---

47 *OV*, VI, pp. 164–5.
48 *OV*, VI, pp. 164–5.
49 WM, *GR*, I, pp. 704–5.
50 Sandy Burton Hicks, 'The Impact of William Clito upon the Continental Policies of Henry I of England,' *Viator*, 10 (1979), pp. 1–21.
51 Herman of Tournai, 'Liber de restauratione monasterii S. Martini Tornacensis,' in *MGH, Scriptores*, xiv, pp. 284–9. Cf. *OV*, VI, pp. 166–7, n. 2; Orderic's chronology is erroneous.

a more credible military figurehead for those opposed to Henry I. He soon gained a considerable reputation as a skilful and fearless warrior.[52]

On 4 November 1112 one of William Clito's most prominent Norman allies, Robert de Bellême, was captured by Henry I. The king charged Robert with failing to come to his court after being summoned three times; not rendering account as the king's *vicomte* and officer for the royal revenues for the *vicomtés* of Argentan, Exmes and Falaise; and committing other unspecified misdeeds.[53] Orderic assures us that a just judgement was reached in the royal court and Robert de Bellême was sentenced to close confinement in ankle chains. He was taken to Cherbourg before being transferred to Wareham when the king returned to England in July 1113.[54] Unlike the duke, Robert de Bellême was kept in chains and in the very closest confinement.[55]

Despite the removal of Robert de Bellême, Henry still faced major opposition to his control of the duchy.[56] There were concerted diplomatic efforts between Henry and those outside Normandy who opposed him. In the first week of Lent 1113, after spending Candlemas at Orderic's monastery of Saint-Évroul, the king met Count Fulk of Anjou in the *pagus* of Alençon at a local landmark known as the Petra Peculata.[57] The king's visit to Saint-Évroul demonstrated Henry's presence in a region that had until recently been dominated by the Bellême family. It also made an impression on Orderic and influenced his history of the king's reign.[58]

As a result of the negotiations Fulk of Anjou swore fealty to Henry and received the county of Maine from him as his vassal. To seal the deal, a marriage was contracted between Fulk's daughter and Henry's son, William. Also associated with the negotiations was the rehabilitation of Count William of Évreux, in exile in Anjou since November or December 1111, and the pardoning of Amaury de Montfort and William Crispin.[59] Louis VI of France also came

52 E.g. *HH*, pp. 482–3, description of William leading his forces at the Battle of Axpoele, 21 June 1128. Cf. the poet Walo's epitaph on William, at *HH*, Appendix 3, 'Walo's Epitaph on William Clito', pp. 836–8.

53 *OV*, VI, pp. 178–9.

54 *JW*, III, *s.a.* 1112, pp. 132–3; *s.a.* 1113, pp. 134–5.

55 *JW*, III, *s.a.* 1113, pp. 134–5. Cf. *HH*, pp. 458–9; *ASC*, E, *s.a.* 1113, p. 117; Swanton, pp. 243–4. WM, *GR*, I, pp. 724–5. Robert de Bellême was still alive at Wareham in 1130, but the date of his death is unknown, although his obit was celebrated at St Martin of Sées on May 8; see Kathleen Thompson, 'Orderic Vitalis and Robert of Bellême', *JMH*, 20 (1994), pp. 133–41; *eadem*, 'Bellême, Robert de, Earl of Shrewsbury and Count of Ponthieu (bap. c.1057, d. in or after 1130), Magnate', *Oxford DNB*.

56 *OV*, VI, pp. 178–9.

57 *OV*, VI, pp. 180–1 and nn. 1–2; between 19 and 26 February 1113.

58 *OV*, VI, pp. 180–1, tells us that Henry's actions brought joy to the churches of Saint-Évroul, Sées and Troarn. The king also restored to Saint-Évroul possessions confirmed to the monks by Robert de Bellême's father, Earl Roger; see *OV*, III, pp. 138–42.

59 *OV*, VI, pp. 148–9, reserved particular opprobrium for William of Évreux and his wife and noted that the count's body 'putrifies' (*computrescit*) at Saint-Wandrille along with that of his father. William Crispin had been captured at Tinchebray and, according to *HH*, pp. 458–9, he was exiled with the count of Évreux in 1112. Amaury de Montfort had incited his nephew Fulk of Anjou to attack Henry I: *OV*, VI, pp. 176–7.

to terms with Henry, perhaps fearing the consequences of the English king's alliance with Anjou and also facing problems of his own nearer home. The meeting took place in the last week of March 1113 near Gisors. Louis invested Henry with the lordship of Bellême, the county of Maine and the whole of Brittany, whose duke had become Henry's vassal.[60] The final triumph for King Henry in this year was the capture and burning down of the fortress at Bellême itself. Together with allies from Blois, Anjou and Mortagne, the king's forces defeated the garrison at the beginning of May. For William Clito and the cause of his father, the agreements between Henry and his opponents marked a considerable setback.[61]

Renewed Hostilities

Despite the successes of his uncle, William Clito still had support even in the courts of those who had made peace with Henry.[62] Prominent among these was Count William II of Nevers, who was a cousin of Louis VI's father, Philip I, and father of Helwise, countess of Évreux.[63] Count William was imprisoned by Henry I's nephew, Count Theobald of Blois. Louis VI pressed for the release of his friend and ally and at Easter (2 April) 1116, Henry crossed over to Normandy to aid Theobald.[64] Perhaps to test Henry's defences, Count Baldwin VII, William Clito's patron, attacked eastern Normandy.[65]

In the following year, 1117, Henry I faced an alliance between Baldwin, Louis and Fulk of Anjou, who took an oath 'that they would wrest Normandy from King Henry and give it to William, son of Robert, the duke of the Normans'.[66] Baldwin's aim was to restore William Clito to his paternal inheritance.[67] Members of the Norman aristocracy also joined the alliance against Henry, while he called on Theobald of Blois and the Count of the Bretons. Louis VI and Baldwin VII of Flanders attacked Normandy, but retreated after only one night fearing the arrival of Henry and his allies.

There were severe setbacks for Henry I in 1118. As well as the strain that his campaigns in Normandy were putting on the financial resources of his kingdom, that year saw the deaths of Queen Matilda and the king's chief

---

60 *OV*, VI, pp. 180–1. Suger, *Vie de Louis*, pp. 170–3, trans. Cusimano and Moorhead, pp. 105, 194. Green, *Henry I*, pp. 126–7.
61 *OV*, VI, pp. 182–3 and n. 4. For Henry I's problems in Normandy, see Judith A. Green, 'King Henry I and the Aristocracy of Normandy', in *La France anglaise au Moyen Age. Actes du IIIe congrès national des sociétés savantes* (Paris, 1988), pp. 161–73.
62 For Henry's perspective, see Green, *Henry I*, pp. 138–67.
63 *OV*, VI, pp. 148–9 and n. 1.
64 *HH*, pp. 460–1. Cf. *ASC*, E, *s.a.* 1116, p. 118; Swanton, pp. 246–7.
65 *ASC*, E, *s.a.* 1117, p. 119; Swanton, p. 247. *OV*, VI, pp. 190–1, condenses several campaigns into a chronologically confused narrative.
66 *HH*, pp. 460–1.
67 *OV*, VI, pp. 190–1.

counsellor, Robert of Meulan.[68] Matilda was buried in Westminster Abbey and it is possible that her god-father, Duke Robert, was allowed to attend, although the most detailed account of the funeral does not mention his presence, unless he was among the *principes*.[69] It was also reported that 'many Normans renounced the fealty they had sworn to King Henry and went over, in defiance of true justice, to the enemies of their natural lord, the French king Louis and his magnates'.[70]

The fighting was renewed in 1118 and Count Baldwin pushed further into Normandy, advancing through Ponthieu as far as Arques. The county of Ponthieu was ruled by William Talvas, son of Robert de Bellême. Whether William was an active participant on these campaigns in Normandy is not clear, but they may have been the occasion for the knighting of William Clito by Count Baldwin.[71]

Henry responded by arresting suspected sympathisers in Upper Normandy, including Count Henry of Eu and Hugh de Gournay, whose castles were taken into royal hands.[72] The king was suspicious of the Normans and garrisoned his castle at Bures with Breton and English mercenaries.[73] Nevertheless, there was considerable devastation in Upper Normandy and Orderic tells us that eighteen castellans persisted in their support for the exiled William. There was a major setback for Clito's cause, however, when Count Baldwin of Flanders was wounded during the campaign. Instead of convalescing he overindulged in the pleasures of the flesh, bringing on a long, lingering decline from September 1118 until his death on 17 June 1119.[74] Perhaps Orderic had William Clito and his father in mind when he wrote about Count Baldwin's death: 'All who had set their hopes on him knew from that time that we should put our trust not in man but in the Lord.'[75] Baldwin's successor, Charles 'the Good', decided to make peace with Henry thereby substantially weakening the alliance supporting William Clito.

One of the rebels against Henry presented a problem for Orderic. Robert Giroie belonged to a family which was one of the major patrons of Saint-Évroul. Duke Robert had restored to the family the castle of Saint-Céneri, which Robert of Bellême had taken.[76] As well as holding Saint-Céneri against the king, Robert Giroie stormed Henry's castle at Motte-Gautier (-de-

---

68 *HH*, pp. 462–3 and Henry of Huntingdon, 'De contemptu mundi', cc. 7–8, in *HH*, pp. 596–601; Matilda's death given as 1 May by *ASC*, E, *s.a.* 1118, p. 119; Swanton, p. 248. *JW*, III, *s.a.* 1118, pp. 142–3. Crouch, *The Beaumont Twins*, pp. 3–4.

69 *Hyde Chron.*, pp. 312–13, and Huneycutt, *Matilda*, pp. 145–6.

70 *JW*, III, *s.a.* 1118, pp. 142–3.

71 *OV*, VI, pp. 190–1. For William Talvas as count of Ponthieu, see *OV*, VI, pp. 14–15 and n. 3.

72 *OV*, VI, pp. 190–5.

73 *OV*, VI, pp. 190–1. Cf. *Hyde Chron.*, p. 313. Hugh de Gournay was put in fetters until he surrendered his castles.

74 *OV*, VI, pp. 190–1, Baldwin was wounded at Bures; cf. *Hyde Chron.*, p. 315, the wound was received at Eu; Suger, *Vie de Louis*, pp. 194–5; *HH*, pp. 462–3; WM, *GR*, I, pp. 730–1, says Arques.

75 *OV*, VI, pp. 190–1.

76 *OV*, IV, pp. 154–6, 292–4.

Clinchamp), a former Bellême castle in Maine. In addition, Giroie encouraged Fulk of Anjou to join the attack and Henry's forces based at Alençon were unable to prevent the castle's fall. Henry raged at his men when they returned from the unsuccessful defence. Although feeling shame that they had failed, they defended themselves by pointing out that the king had delayed too long in sending help. Henry's reaction was to give the former Bellême possessions including Sées and Alençon to his nephew Count Theobald of Blois, who, in turn, granted them to his brother Stephen.[77]

Members of the Norman aristocracy attempted to exploit Henry's problems. The struggle for Normandy gave them a political advantage and they sought to make capital out of it. For example, Richer, the heir to the lordship of Laigle, claimed his father's lands in England, but Henry favoured Richer's brothers, Geoffrey and Engenulf, who were serving in his household. After repeated requests were finally met by the king's contemptuous refusal, Richer took his case to Louis of France, who promised to send troops. Boosted by this support, Richer tried his request once again with Henry. He was rebuffed, but his uncle Rotrou of Mortagne, count of the Perche, advised the king not to let sedition spread and grant Richer's request.[78] Meanwhile Louis VI was advancing on Laigle. Richer had to inform him of the changed relationship with Henry and that he would have to break his pact with the French monarch. Louis attacked and burned Laigle in September 1118. Henry's attempt to end the French occupation of Laigle was thwarted by rumours that Hugh de Gournay, Stephen of Aumâle and their men were near Rouen awaiting William Clito's arrival for an assault on the city. Fearing the loss of Rouen, Henry retreated from Laigle leaving its French garrison to capture men from Moulins-la-Marche.[79]

In describing Henry's campaigns against William Clito's allies, Orderic made it clear that the king's major problem was that, in the confusion that always goes with wars of this kind, he could not trust his own men.[80] This was especially the case in wars between kinsmen:

> Men who ate with him favoured the cause of his nephew and his other enemies and, by spying into his secrets, greatly helped these men. This was indeed a more than civil war, and ties of blood bound together brothers and friends and kinsmen who were fighting on both sides, so that neither wished to harm the other. Many in Normandy then imitated Achitophel and Shimei and other turncoats, and committed deeds like those of the men who, deserting the king divinely ordained by Samuel, joined Absalom the parricide. This is exactly what many men did when they deserted the peace-loving prince elected and blessed by the bishops and, breaking the fealty they had pledged him as their lord, voluntarily embraced the cause of the beardless count to do wrong, not because duty forced them to it, but of their own free will.[81]

---

[77] *OV*, VI, pp. 196–7.
[78] *OV*, VI, pp. 196–7.
[79] *OV*, VI, pp. 198–9.
[80] *OV*, VI, pp. 200–1.
[81] *OV*, VI, pp. 200–3.

This passage might well have been describing the problems faced by Duke Robert before 1106. The disputes among members of William the Conqueror's family handed the political advantage to the aristocracy.

Henry's situation in 1118 was serious, but he had the resources of the kingdom of England behind him. A church council assembled at Rouen on 7 October that year was a conspicuous attempt to associate the king with the Norman Church and reinforce Henry's status as its legitimate protector. The council was also addressed by the papal legate. One of those who could not attend was Audoin, bishop of Évreux, whose city was taken by William Clito's supporter, Amaury de Montfort.[82] The fall of Évreux was followed by a general insurrection in the Évrecin, which forced Bishop Audoin into exile. According to Orderic, the bishop refused to shave his beard as a sign of mourning for his oppressed church.[83]

In November 1118, Henry's helmet saved him from serious injury during operations at Laigle. Further south, the men of Alençon also rebelled against the bad lordship of Henry's nephew, Stephen, count of Mortain.[84] Stephen's actions provoked a sworn conspiracy among the townsfolk of Alençon and an approach to Arnulf of Montgomery, brother of Robert de Bellême, and through him to Fulk of Anjou. Fulk's troops occupied the town and besieged Henry's garrison in the castle. When Henry's forces approached Alençon in December, Fulk routed the advance guard. The garrison was forced to surrender but allowed to leave unharmed.[85] The fall of Alençon to the opponents of Henry I encouraged others to revolt and Orderic suggests that the winter of 1118/19 was one of widespread lawlessness. Orderic, often portrayed as a partisan of King Henry, thought that William Clito had a legitimate claim to succeed to Normandy after his father's death.[86]

The gales that swept through England and northern France in the winter of 1118–19 were interpreted as portending great disasters and changes among the powerful.[87] Whether rumour 'than which nothing on earth travels faster' brought news to Duke Robert of his son or of Henry's setbacks in 1118 is, unfortunately, not recorded.[88] What is certain, however, is that Henry's government of Normandy was far from stable and the seriousness of his difficulties there should not be underestimated. Nevertheless, with the death of Baldwin of Flanders, William Clito had lost one of his major supporters.

During 1119, by taking a more diplomatic and conciliatory approach with his opponents within and beyond Normandy, Henry began to recover

---

82 *OV*, VI, pp. 202–5.

83 *OV*, VI, pp. 204–5.

84 *OV*, VI, pp. 204–7; E. King, 'Stephen of Blois, Count of Mortain and Boulogne', *EHR*, 115 (2000), pp. 271–96 at 276–7.

85 *OV*, VI, pp. 206–9 and cf. 'Gesta consulum andegavorum', in *Chroniques des comtes d'Anjou et des seigneurs d'Amboise*, ed. L. Halphen and R. Poupardin (Paris, 1913), pp. 155–61.

86 *OV*, VI, pp. 208–9 and n. 3.

87 *ASC*, E, *s.a.* 1118, pp. 119–20; Swanton, pp. 247–8. *OV*, VI, pp. 208–9.

88 *OV*, VI, pp. 206–7: 'Quod fama qua nil in terra uelocius mouetur longe lateque diuulgauit.'

lost ground. At Lent, he made peace with a number of barons in the strategically important Norman Vexin. Eustace of Breteuil, Henry's son-in-law,
threatened to withdraw from the king unless his family's castle of Ivry was
restored to him. Henry managed to placate him by promising to consider his
request and by handing over the son of Ralph Harenc, the custodian of Ivry,
as a hostage.[89] In return, Henry took custody of Eustace's two daughters as
hostages. According to Orderic, weaving a tale of cruel intrigue, Amaury de
Montfort, hoping to foment trouble between the king and Eustace, advised
the latter to blind the son of Ralph Harenc and send him back to his father.
When this was done, Ralph was understandably angry and asked the king for
redress. Henry, equally affronted, handed over his grand-daughters and Ralph
blinded the girls and slit their nostrils.[90]

When Eustace was informed of the mutilation of his daughters, he fortified his castles against the king and sent his wife, Juliana, to defend Breteuil.
At the invitation of the burgesses of Breteuil, Henry hurried to the town and
besieged his own daughter in the castle. Juliana hatched a plan to assassinate
her father and at a meeting she fired a cross-bow bolt at him but missed.
When Henry forced his daughter to surrender the fortification, he would not
allow her to leave freely. Juliana was forced to leap from the castle walls and
she 'fell shamefully, with bare buttocks into the depths of the moat'. This
happened during Lent, in the third week of February, when the moat was full
of icy water. As a counterweight to Eustace, Henry invested Ralph de Gael
with the Breteuil honour apart from Pacy, which was still held by Eustace.[91]

Rumour also worked against Henry. The men of Courcy and other garrisons nearby decided to support William Clito, 'hearing that almost all the
Normans had deserted the king and taken up his nephew's cause'.[92] Reginald
of Bailleul, once sheriff of Shropshire and married to Roger of Montgomery's
niece, renounced his fealty to the king at Falaise. Reginald refused to hand
over his castle at Le Renouard, but was not arrested as Henry decided to
honour the peace which usually protected those who attended his court. The
king contented himself with ominous threats. Henry and his men set off in
pursuit of Reginald and forced him to surrender his castle. The swift action
taken against Le Renouard discouraged the men of Courcy, Grandmesnil and
Montpinçon from similarly defying Henry.[93]

Louis VI was still threatening the frontier and took possession of the castle
at Andely. The French had, therefore, gained an important foothold along the
valley of the Seine. In response Henry fortified a castle at Noyon-sur-Andelle,

---

[89] On hostages and hostage-taking, see Adam J. Kosto, 'Hostages in the Carolingian World (714–840)',
   EME, 11 (2002), pp. 123–47 and R. Lavelle, 'The Use and Abuse of Hostages in Later Anglo-Saxon
   England', *EME*, 14 (2006), pp. 269–96.
[90] *OV*, VI, pp. 210–13.
[91] *OV*, VI, pp. 214–15.
[92] *OV*, VI, pp. 214–15.
[93] *OV*, VI, pp. 214–17.

where Saint-Évroul had a priory, which suggests that Orderic is likely to have been very well-informed about events in this area.[94]

Others rebelled against Henry, including the aged Richard of Fresnel (La Ferté-Frênel), whose family also had connections with Saint-Évroul. During Lent 1119, Richard revolted in support of his lord, Eustace of Breteuil, demonstrating that the bonds articulating this society had the potential to spread rebellion as vassals loyally supported their immediate lords. Others who had rebelled decided to return to Henry, including Robert, son of Ascelin Goel. Robert's example was followed by others.[95]

Orderic's *Historia* provides numerous examples of individuals and families deciding either to support or resist Henry. At one point he names those who remained loyal to the king and lists the major towns and cities that remained in royal hands.[96] There is no doubt, however, that Henry faced a constant struggle to keep the rebels at bay and prevent his nephew from gaining widespread support in the duchy.

In May 1119, however, there was a major diplomatic coup for Henry. The king brought his only legitimate son, William Ætheling, over to Normandy. Henry had been secretly formulating a plan to detach Fulk, count of Anjou, from William Clito's cause by arranging a marriage alliance. Envoys were sent between Henry and Fulk and, in June, William married Fulk's daughter Matilda at Lisieux.[97] As part of the accompanying peace settlement, Henry restored Robert of Bellême's son, William Talvas, to favour, granting him all his father's lands including Alençon, Almenèches and Vignats. Henry kept control of the citadels in each of these towns, however, reinstating the policy of his father. Also pardoned was Robert Giroie of Saint-Céneri, who regained Montreuil and Échauffour.

In celebration of the strengthening of his position, Henry convened a great council of nobles and prelates at Lisieux. He announced the death of Count Baldwin of Flanders and ordered the clergy to ring the bells and 'pray for the repose and pardon of his soul'. The news of Baldwin's demise, combined with the marriage alliance with Anjou, 'was a cause of rejoicing for some and mourning for others in Normandy'. Those rejoicing were Henry and his supporters: those mourning were William Clito and his.[98]

---

94 *OV*, VI, pp. 218–19 and n. 5.
95 *OV*, VI, pp. 218–19 and cf. pp. 228–9; Ascelin Goel had supported Robert against William Rufus: *OV*, III, pp. 208–210.
96 *OV*, VI, pp. 222–3.
97 *OV*, VI, pp. 224–5. Cf. *ASC*, E, *s.a.* 1119, p. 120; Swanton, p. 248; 'Gesta consulum', p. 161.
98 *OV*, VI, pp. 224–5.

Brémule: 'The Battle of the Two Kings'[99]

Henry made a punitive expedition through Normandy and he burnt Pont-Saint-Pierre, one of Eustace of Breteuil's castles and other strongholds.[100] During an attack on Évreux, Henry asked its bishop, Audoin, for his advice on whether or not to use fire. Given Henry's ruthless use of fire at Bayeux, Pont-Saint-Pierre and elsewhere, this episode seems like an attempt to represent these incendiary tactics as in some way sanctioned by the Church. As it was a dry August, the flames had a devastating effect once they had been kindled and the nunnery of Saint-Sauveur, together with the church of the Virgin Mary, were destroyed. Henry and his magnates promised to make amends for the destruction.[101] Orderic's description of the pathetic fate of the inhabitants of Évreux wandering as refugees raises questions about the idea that his *Historia* is unequivocal in its support for the king.[102]

There were further military engagements as the king's men tried to dislodge the garrison from Évreux and Amaury de Montfort and his allies attacked Pacy. This was bloody warfare and many, including some of noble status, were killed on both sides.[103]

In July 1119, Louis of France attacked the castles of Dangu and Châteauneuf along the River Epte. The castellan of Dangu was force to burn his own fortification, but the royal garrison of Châteauneuf resisted more successfully. Louis and his allies returned in August and marched against Andely and Noyon-sur-Andelle.[104] The French and English forces eventually confronted each other on a plain called Brémule.[105] In the French army was William Clito, who had 'armed himself there so that he might free his father from his long imprisonment and recover his ancestral inheritance'.[106] A number of other Normans had also joined the French ranks so that Brémule, like Tinchebray, saw fellow countrymen fighting on both sides, a fact sometimes concealed by references to the armies as simply 'French' and 'English'.[107]

Brémule, again like Tinchebray, was another battle where knights fought on foot. Henry's son Richard and a hundred knights were kept mounted and

99   *OV*, VI, pp. 240–1.
100 *OV*, VI, pp. 226–7.
101 *OV*, VI, pp. 228–9.
102 *OV*, VI, pp. 230–1.
103 *OV*, VI, pp. 232–3.
104 *OV*, VI, pp. 234–5; cf. *Hyde Chron.*, pp. 316–17; *HH*, pp. 462–5; WM, *GR*, I, pp. 732–5; *ASC*, E, s.a. 1119, p. 120; Swanton, p. 248; *WJ*, II, pp. 234–5. Cf. Suger, *Vie de Louis*, pp. 196–7; Cusimano and Moorhead, p. 117.
105 *OV*, VI, pp. 236–7, specifically calls Henry's forces 'Angli' rather than Normans.
106 *OV*, VI, pp. 236–7: 'Ibi Guillelmus Clito Rodberti ducis Normannorum filius armatus est; ut patrem suum de longo carcere liberaret, et auitam sibi hereditatem uendicaret.'
107 *OV*, VI, pp. 236–7. Peter of Maule was at the battle and probably provided Orderic's information.

ready for battle, but the other troops dismounted and joined the king.[108] The Norman William Crispin led the French charge against Henry's lines, but his horse and those of his fellow knights were killed resulting in some of them being captured. This setback persuaded Louis to order a withdrawal which turned into a disorderly flight. Before he could be restrained, William Crispin caught sight of Henry and, enraged with hatred, he managed to deliver a fierce blow to the king's head with his sword. Henry was saved from serious injury by the collar of his mail hauberk. William Crispin was struck down, perhaps by Henry himself, and narrowly avoided being killed by the king's angry men.[109]

Casualties in the battle were minimal with only three knights losing their lives:

> As Christian soldiers they did not thirst for the blood of their brothers, but rejoiced in a just victory given by God, for the good of Holy Church and the peace of the faithful.[110]

There is little information about William Clito's conduct in the battle. According to Orderic, William lost a palfrey in the encounter, but his cousin, William Ætheling, sent back the horse along with other goods he might need for his continuing exile. This act of generosity was at his father's suggestion. Whether Henry was making a barbed comment about William Clito's personal fortunes is unclear, but it would not be inconsistent with Henry's character.[111]

Some of Henry's enemies were pardoned, others incarcerated, and at least one, Guy of Clermont, died in prison in Rouen. Medieval battles were an opportunity for members of the chivalric class to establish or enhance their reputations. Equally, they were occasions where dishonourable conduct might bring shame. Peter of Maule was one of a number of those fleeing the defeat at Brémule who threw away their *cognitiones,* so that they would not be recognized. These 'cognizances' perhaps took the form of distinctive designs on shields meant to identify individuals whose standard mail armour would otherwise make them indistinguishable from their fellows. Peter of Maule and his companions then joined the ranks of their pursuers, shouting the appropriate war cries and making favourable comments about King Henry.[112]

Louis led another expedition into Normandy directed at Breteuil and with the aim of 'restoring Eustace's (of Breteuil) lost possessions and bringing back others who were in exile out of loyalty to the exiled William to their

---

108 On the battle of Brémule, see Bradbury, 'Battles in England and Normandy', pp. 189–90.

109 *OV,* VI, pp. 238–9; cf. *Hyde Chron.,* pp. 317–18; *HH,* pp. 462–5. J. Armitage Robinson, *Gilbert Crispin, Abbot of Westminster. A Study of the Abbey under Norman Rule* (Cambridge, 1911), p. 16.

110 *OV,* VI, pp. 240–1.

111 *OV,* VI, pp. 240–1.

112 *OV,* VI, pp. 242–3 and n. 1. T. Woodcock and J.M. Robinson, *The Oxford Guide to Heraldry* (Oxford, 1988), pp. 1–13.

former honours'.[113] Once again, Henry forced the French to withdraw. Richer of Laigle was reconciled with Henry through the intercession of his uncle Rotrou of Mortagne.[114]

The Council of Rheims, 1119

Towards the end of 1119, King Henry was called upon to justify his continuing imprisonment of Duke Robert of Normandy. The occasion was Pope Calixtus II's council at Rheims held between 19 and 30 October 1119 and a subsequent meeting between the pope and Henry I at Gisors in November that year.[115]

Louis VI of France attended the council and 'eloquent in speech, tall in stature, pale and corpulent' made his accusations against Henry I.[116] Orderic reported Louis's speech in detail and, if he had not been present himself at the council, his vivid account was certainly based on that of an eye-witness.[117] The account sheds light on the struggles on behalf of Duke Robert of Normandy and indicates that, two of the most powerful kings of Northern Europe were willing to recognise the papal *curia* as a court of arbitration. Louis' accusations against Henry ran as follows:

> He has violently invaded Normandy, which is part of my realm, and has treated Robert, duke of Normandy, atrociously, without regard to justice or right. He has injured this vassal of mine, who is his brother and lord, in many ways, and finally after capturing him has kept him for many years in prison, up to this day. See, here is William, the duke's son, who accompanies me to your presence, and whom he utterly disinherited and drove into exile. I have sent bishops and earls and other persons to ask him to send back the captive duke to me, but I have never succeeded in getting any satisfaction from him in this matter.[118]

Louis added further charges relating to the imprisonment of Robert de Bellême, the revolt of Count Theobald of Blois, and the capture of William of Nevers. It was left to Geoffrey, archbishop of Rouen, to respond on behalf of Henry I, but his speech was drowned out by shouts of disagreement. Perhaps in a stage-managed attempt to move business on, Hildegarde, countess of Poitou, came forward and, in a high-pitched, clear voice, made her case against her husband who had committed adultery with Malberge, the wife of the *vicomte* of Châtellerault.[119]

The council's business continued with Bishop Audoin of Évreux accusing Amaury de Montfort of driving him from his see and burning his church.

---

113   *OV*, VI, pp. 246–7.
114   *OV*, VI, pp. 250–1.
115   *OV*, VI, pp. 252–77; cf. Symeon, 'Historia Regum', II, pp. 254–6.
116   *OV*, VI, pp. 256–7.
117   *OV*, VI, xix–xxi.
118   *OV*, VI, pp. 256–7.
119   *OV*, VI, pp. 258–9 and n. 2.

One of Amaury's chaplains replied that it was, in fact, Bishop Audoin and Henry I who had burned the town and its churches. This provoked another uproar, 'with everyone speaking at the same time', until order was restored and the pope attempted to bring about peace. There is an immediacy in the account of the council that reinforces the idea that Orderic was relying on eye-witnesses.

Proceedings were interrupted while the pope went to Mouzon to meet the Emperor Henry V.[120] Other issues were brought before the pope, but nothing further was recorded about Duke Robert or his son until Calixtus II met with Henry in November. In the meantime, Henry's operations against Évreux resulted in petitions for the king's pardon from several rebels including Amaury de Montfort, Eustace of Breteuil, Hugh de Gournay and Robert of Neubourg. Finally, Stephen of Aumâle, who had aided William Clito and Baldwin of Flanders by admitting them to his castles, recognised how isolated he now was and also submitted to Henry.[121] The supporters of William Clito and Helias of Saint-Saëns only abandoned them with great reluctance, but there was no other way to win Henry's favour.[122]

In November 1119, Pope Calixtus II met Henry I at Gisors.[123] Henry behaved with impeccable humility before the pope, receiving him honourably and, falling prostrate at his feet, the king formally acknowledged Calixtus as the pope and his kinsman.[124] Recognising the king's display of humility, Calixtus blessed him and gave him the kiss of peace.[125]

In a private meeting, Calixtus told Henry that the purpose of the council at Rheims had been to restore general peace and he called upon Henry to play his part.[126] Then Calixtus addressed Henry on the question of Duke Robert's captivity:

> The law of God, providently concerned with the welfare of all men, ordains that each one shall possess what is lawfully his own, but shall not covet the property of others, nor do to another what he does not wish to be done to himself. Therefore the synod of the faithful determines in general and, great king, humbly begs your majesty that you should release your brother Robert, whom you have kept in shackles for many years, and restore to him and his son the duchy of Normandy which you have taken from them.[127]

The pope referred to Robert being kept in chains, but this seems to contradict reports that the duke was kept in 'free custody'. Rumours about the conditions

---

120 22 to 26 October 1119: *OV*, VI, pp. 264–5 and n. 3.
121 *OV*, VI, pp. 278–81.
122 *OV*, VI, pp. 282–3.
123 *OV*, VI, pp. 282–91; *Hugh the Chantor*, pp. 76–80; WM, *GR*, I, pp. 734–7.
124 *OV*, VI, pp. 282–3 and n. 4. Adeliza, wife of Reginald I of Burgundy and grandmother of Calixtus, was the sister of Robert I of Normandy, grandfather of Robert Curthose and Henry I.
125 *OV*, VI, pp. 282–3.
126 *Hugh the Chantor*, p. 77.
127 *OV*, VI, pp. 284–5.

in which Robert was being kept may have reached the pope, but it may be that Calixtus exaggerated the plight of the duke in order to play upon the king's conscience, such as it was. Henry's protracted reply was a comprehensive defence of his actions with regard to his brother and the duchy of Normandy. Henry claimed that he did not deprive his brother of Normandy, but:

> laid legal claim by battle to the just inheritance of our father, which my brother and nephew did not really possess themselves, because villainous bandits and blasphemous scoundrels wasted it. No respect was shown to priests and other servants of God, but near-paganism was rampant all over Normandy. Monasteries which our ancestors founded for the good of their souls were destroyed, and the cloister monks were scattered for lack of food. Churches too were plundered and many were burnt and fugitives seeking sanctuary were dragged from them. The parishioners cruelly slaughtered each other, and the survivors, who had no protector, bewailed their fate in the midst of great devastation. This is the tribulation that afflicted Normandy for almost seven years, so that no one could enjoy any security either at home or abroad.[128]

Henry claimed that churchmen had begged him for the love of God to help and he felt duty-bound to cross to Normandy where he was received by loyal barons such as William of Évreux and Robert of Meulan. He had no other option but to turn to force of arms to bring help because his brother had protected evil-doers and, relying on their counsel, had become an object of scorn and contempt. Henry named Gunter of Aunay, Roger de Lacy and Robert de Bellême and others as the true masters of Normandy, 'ruling under the guise of ducal authority'. These were men whom Henry had expelled from his own kingdom because of their criminality.

The king also claimed to have sent repeated messages to his brother offering his counsel, 'but he scorned to listen and used men who had plotted against me to resist me'. The king argued that he had pledged himself to the service of the Church and to using his royal office for the general good. Henry gave an account of his campaigns in 1105 and 1106, the capture of Bayeux and Caen and siege of Tinchebray. 'In this way,' he told the pope, 'I recovered the inheritance of my father with his entire demesne, and strove to uphold my father's laws according to God's will for the peace of his people.' By invoking the figure of his father Henry linked his own rule in Normandy with that of the Conqueror, suggesting that Robert's (and Rufus's) possession of the duchy deserved to be forgotten.

When it came to the treatment of his brother and nephew, Henry defended himself by denying the rumours which had obviously informed the pope's accusations:

> I have not kept my brother in fetters like a captured enemy, but have placed him as a noble pilgrim, worn out with many hardships, in a royal castle, and have kept

---

[128] *OV*, VI, pp. 284–5.

him well supplied with abundance of food and other comforts and furnishings of all kinds. I entrusted his five-year-old son to the guardianship of Helias, the duke's son-in-law, hoping that by developing his judgement and all his moral qualities and talents I might make him equal in every way to my own son.[129]

Henry acknowledged his brother's status as a pilgrim and characterised him as worn out by his exertions on the Crusade. Robert now enjoyed a comfortable and secure retirement, rather than a miserable imprisonment in chains.

Henry's suggestion that he had handed William Clito over to Helias of Saint-Saëns in the hope that he would be educated and made fit to share the benefits of the kingdom of England with his own son, needs to be taken with a large pinch of salt. Helias is portrayed as the villain corrupting the boy, abandoning his honour of Saint-Saëns, and inciting the French, Burgundians and others to attack Henry. The king claimed to have repeatedly sent for William, offering safe-conduct to his court and even offering him three English counties 'so that he might govern them and grow up among the petitioners of my court, to learn how much he might be valued in the future for good judgement and fairness towards rich and poor, and how firmly he might preserve royal justice and knightly discipline'. Needless to say, according to Henry, William had rejected this generous offer 'choosing to live as a beggar in exile among foreign rogues [rather] than to enjoy comforts with me.'[130]

The pope was astonished by Henry's statements, evidently because it refuted the information Calixtus had been given by other interested parties. Henry was praised for his actions and Calixtus suspended further discussion of Duke Robert and his son, as the other causes of the hostility between Henry and Louis VI were more pressing matters. Henry undertook to obey the pope's recommendations for the restoration of peace and asked Calixtus to relay a repetition of the terms previously offered to William Clito, 'for I both desire to give you complete satisfaction and wish to further the general tranquillity of the people and the advancement of my nephew as if he were my own son'.[131] Henry's offer to bring his nephew into his own household rings hollow, especially in light of his policies after his meeting with Calixtus.

Over the course of the following year, Henry's terms were made known to Louis and, according to Orderic at least, there was general rejoicing at the restoration of peace.[132] Henry's son, William Atheling, performed homage to Louis VI for Normandy, a gesture which set aside William Clito's claims to the duchy and must have been a great blow to the hopes of the young man and his supporters.[133] So, on 25 November 1120, Henry, satisfied with the

---

[129] *OV*, VI, pp. 286–9.
[130] *OV*, VI, pp. 288–9.
[131] *OV*, VI, pp. 288–91.
[132] *OV*, VI, pp. 290–1.
[133] *ASC*, E, *s.a.* 1120, pp. 120–1; Swanton, p. 249; *Hugh the Chantor*, p. 97; *Hyde Chron.*, p. 319; WM, *GR*, I, pp. 734–5; Symeon, 'Historia Regum', II, p. 258.

neutralisation of his nephew's threat to his hold on Normandy, set sail for England after an absence of four and a half years.

The White Ship

It is not known how much Duke Robert knew about the struggles of his son in Northern France, but his prison walls were surely not wholly impervious to rumour. Robert's confinement probably drew closer whenever the situation in Normandy deteriorated from the king's point of view. Whether Robert had the opportunity to support his son through diplomatic means is to be doubted, although there is an intriguing entry in the chronicle of the abbey of Montecassino in central Italy for the year 1117.

According to this record, Robert 'king of the English' sent envoys to the monastery asking that the monks would prevail upon the Lord's mercy on behalf of himself and his kingdom. To win over the monks he sent a large golden chalice. Understandably, this statement has been doubted and seen as possibly a scribal error. What the monk of Montecassino perhaps intended to record was the visit of envoys from *Henricus rex Anglorum* but *Robbertus* was inserted in error. The error, which shows some knowledge of the succession to the English throne, was evidently plausible and remained uncorrected. It is just possible that there was an attempt to win wider support for Robert beyond the confines of France and that envoys despatched by Louis VI on behalf of William Clito were seeking to undermine Henry's position. Robert had links with Italy during his exile and when he visited Montecassino en route to Jerusalem.[134]

Despite the defeat at Brémule, William Clito still attempted to secure the release of his father. He met with Henry in October 1119. Now deserted by all those who had pledged to help, William begged his uncle for the release of his father and promised that they would make a pilgrimage to Jerusalem and abandon attempts to overthrow Henry. With his customary tact, Henry merely offered his nephew money. William angrily replied that he would never accept money and he would never make peace, preferring to await the mercy of the Lord's judgement. He withdrew with Helias de Saint-Saëns declaring that he could never reach an agreement with Henry. It is surprising that Henry did not take this opportunity to arrest his nephew.[135]

On 25 November 1120, King Henry and many of his barons embarked from Barfleur on a night crossing of the Channel. There was a favourable

---

[134] Petrus Diaconus, 'Chronica Monasterii Casinensis', *MGH, Scriptores*, vii, p. 791, noticed in David, *Curthose*, p. 186 and n. 61: 'His porro diebus Robbertus rex Anglorum legatos ad hoc monasterium direxit, petens ut pro se atque pro statu regni sui Domini clementiam exorarent, calicemque aureum quantitatis non modicae beato Benedicto per eos dirigere studuit.' It must be admitted, however, that while this interpretation is not wholly implausible, this single record lacks corroboration.

[135] *Hyde Chron.*, pp. 320–1.

southerly wind and at the first watch of the night, the royal fleet set sail. The next morning Henry landed in England safely, but news soon reached him of a disaster that brought despair to the king and hope to William Clito and his father. Before he had left Normandy, Henry agreed to grant a favour to a certain Thomas son of Stephen, who owned a fine vessel called the *White Ship*. Thomas reminded the king that his father Stephen, son of Airard, had carried Henry's father in his ship during the invasion of 1066, and offered the services of the *White Ship*.[136] Henry had already made arrangements for himself, but decided to allow Thomas and his ship to carry William Atheling, his half-brother Richard, and many other nobles.[137] The crew of the *White Ship* hoped to profit from their commission and were rewarded with copious quantities of wine. While the ship was still in port, there was drinking to such an excess that several passengers disembarked 'because they realized that there was too great a crowd of wild and headstrong young men aboard'.[138]

Sea travel was regarded as perilous and it was customary for those about to embark on voyages to receive a blessing from the clergy. However, when the priests appeared ready to bless the *White Ship*, the drunkards aboard drove them away with abusive comments and snorts of laughter.[139] Unfortunately for the passengers the master and crew were as inebriated as themselves and when Thomas was ordered to try to overtake the king's vessel which had already put to sea, disaster struck. Although the sea was calm, the night was pitch black and the helmsman was not paying attention. With a cracking and splintering of timbers, the port side of the *White Ship* struck a submerged rock. The ship was holed and capsized, but not before there was time for a boat to be launched carrying William Atheling. He might have succeeded in reaching safety had not the cries of his sister, Matilda, the countess of Perche, called him back to the sinking ship. William's boat was brought alongside the *White Ship* but was overwhelmed as survivors jumped aboard. There were only one or two to tell the tale the next morning.[140] William Atheling drowned together with many of his companions.[141]

Henry's reaction to the news of his son's death was dramatic and he collapsed. He had to be led away to private chambers where he could give vent to his grief out of the sight of courtiers. The king's dynastic hopes had been dashed by the wreck of the *White Ship*.[142] There was general mourning at Henry's court and the disaster was commemorated in poems.[143] The death of

---

136 Stephen, son of Airard, may therefore have been the master of the *Mora*, the ship given to the Conqueror by his wife, Matilda.
137 WM, *GR*, I, pp. 760–1, suggests that William Atheling ordered the ship for himself and his companions.
138 *OV*, VI, pp. 296–7.
139 *OV*, VI, pp. 296–7.
140 Cf. WM, *GR*, I, pp. 758–63; Symeon, 'Historia Regum', II, p. 259; *HN*, pp. 288–9; *HH*, pp. 466–7; *WJ*, II, pp. 216–17, 246–51, 274–7. Green, *Henry I*, pp. 164–7.
141 *OV*, VI, pp. 304–5, supplies a detailed list of the casualties.
142 *OV*, VI, pp. 300–3.
143 *OV*, VI, pp. 302–5 and *HH*, pp. 466–7.

his only legitimate son threatened to reopen Henry's problems in Normandy. The cause of William Clito was boosted by the disaster and William of Malmesbury suggested that almost immediately Henry's diplomatic edifice collapsed.

On his return from Jerusalem, Fulk of Anjou decided once more to take up the cause of William Clito.[144] Amaury de Montfort, count of Évreux, who had become disgruntled with the activities of Henry's officials in his county, decided to persuade his nephew, Fulk, to arrange a marriage for William Clito.[145] Although it could be seen as a pragmatic, if rather insensitively precipitate, response to Henry's misfortunes, Fulk's decision may also have been influenced by his visit to the Holy Land, where he had been reminded of Duke Robert's exploits on the Crusade. Fulk was also angry that Henry did not return his daughter-in-law's dowry.[146] In February or March 1123, William Clito was married to Fulk's other daughter, Sibyl 'whose integrity and beauty and noble demeanour fitted her for a crown'. As a marriage portion he was granted the county of Maine, the steps in his own career thus mirroring his father's. The marriage, together with Amaury's activity on behalf of William Clito, once more persuaded a number of Normans to defy Henry.

The marriage was opposed by Henry who eventually defeated the plan by alleging consanguinity.[147] The king expended an enormous quantity of gold to persuade the pope to annul the marriage. Despite the fact that exactly the same objections could have been raised to the earlier marriage of Henry's son to Fulk's other daughter, Calixtus II formally dissolved the marriage on 26 August 1124.[148]

Henry took other steps to ensure that his brother's line would not benefit from the death of William Atheling. In January 1121, the king married Adeliza, the daughter of Duke Godfrey VII of Louvain.[149] Nevertheless, the changed circumstances forced many to reconsider their attitude to William Clito and his claims. A group of barons with interests on Normandy's frontier hatched a plot against Henry. At the core of the sworn conspiracy were Waleran of Meulan and his brothers-in-law, Hugh de Montfort, Hugh of Châteauneuf-en-Thimerais and William Lovel, lord of Ivry.[150]

The conspiracy was ratified on oath by Amaury, Waleran and the others at La Croix-Saint-Leufroi in September 1123. Henry's response was to lead a large army and to set out from Rouen in October that year. The rebellion came to a head at the battle of Bourgthéroulde on 26 March 1124.[151] The

144 OV, VI, pp. 310–11.
145 OV, VI, pp. 332–3.
146 WM, GR, I, pp. 762–3. OV, VI, pp. 330–1; after ten years at Henry's court, Matilda became a nun at Fontevrault.
147 OV, VI, pp. 164–7; cf. WM, GR, I, pp. 762–3.
148 OV, VI, pp. 166–7.
149 OV, VI, pp. 308–9 and n. 1. ASC, E, s.a. 1121, p. 121; Swanton, p. 249.
150 OV, VI, pp. 332–3.
151 OV, VI, pp. 348–53; cf. HH, pp. 472–3; ASC, E, s.a. 1124, pp. 124–6; Swanton, pp. 253–5; WJ, II, pp. 234–6; JW, III, s.a. 1124, pp. 156–7.

battle ended in disaster for the rebels who were captured and brought to Rouen for judgement. Henry had several of the knights blinded until Count Charles of Flanders protested that this was contrary to usual custom. Henry defended his actions by pointing out that as vassals they should have done all that they could to preserve their faith.[152]

As William Clito's allies returned one by one to Henry, he and Helias were forced to wander from place to place hoping to avoid the king's agents. Orderic's description of William's plight has a degree of *pathos* about it:

> William was a boy born to suffering and was never free from it as long as he lived. He was courageous and proud, handsome and perniciously addicted to knightly adventures; misplaced hope commended him to the people more than his own merits. In the houses of monks and clergy where he was often entertained, his extravagance even in exile brought more burden than honour, and to his countless adherents he brought more suffering than aid. Many were mistaken in their opinion of him, as was later clearly demonstrated by heaven.[153]

Despite this portrait of false hope and unfulfilled ambition, there is no doubt that Henry's main preoccupation for most of the twenty years or so after Tinchebray was the thwarting of the plans of his nephew and his allies.

William Clito, Count of Flanders

At the beginning of March 1127, Charles 'the Good', count of Flanders, was brutally assassinated as he prostrated himself in prayer before the altar of the church of St Donatian in Bruges.[154] The count and his intimate counsellors were murdered by the Erembalds, who opposed Charles's attempts to curb their power. The assassination of the count profoundly shocked contemporaries and plunged Flanders into a political crisis. Several individuals staked a claim to the comital title and the confusion gave Louis VI of France the opportunity to intervene as overlord. At his Christmas court in 1127, the king encouraged his nobles to aid William 'the Norman'. Louis reminded them of William's misfortunes, the poisoning of his mother, the capture of his father at Tinchebray and the loss of Normandy to his uncle, Henry.[155]

William Clito's fortunes had improved in January 1127, when Queen Adela of France married him to her half-sister.[156] William was also given Pontoise, Chaumont, Mantes and 'all the Vexin' in an evident attempt to challenge

---

152 *OV*, VI, pp. 352–5.
153 *OV*, VI, pp. 358–9.
154 *Galbert of Bruges, The Murder of Charles the Good*, trans. and ed. J.B. Ross (New York, 1959; reprinted Medieval Academy of America, 1982), pp. 111–12. Ross's translation is of the text edited by Henri Pirenne in *Histoire du Meurtre de Charles le Bon, comte de Flandre (1127–1128) par Galbert de Bruges* (Paris, 1891). Cf. *OV*, VI, pp. 370–1.
155 *OV*, VI, pp. 368–9.
156 *OV*, VI, pp. 370–1 and n. 1.

Henry I's control over that contested frontier region. Louis recognised William Clito's capabilities and potential as a key ally of the French crown. It was a logical step to sponsor his protégé as Charles's successor in Flanders.[157]

The year following the assassination of Charles the Good saw a struggle for the succession to Flanders and the pursuit of the count's murderers. The detailed account left by the notary Galbert reflects the shifting nature of the political scene in Flanders. In particular, Galbert changed his opinion of William Clito. At first, he criticised his actions as ruler, but came to condemn the lack of fidelity shown by those who had sworn to accept him as count. Louis' intervention in Flanders disturbed Henry because a hostile Flanders was a considerable threat to Upper Normandy. Henry responded by actively supporting rival claimants to Flanders, namely William of Ypres and Thierry of Alsace. He also attacked its trade with England, the source of much of the county's wealth.

In March 1127, King Louis summoned the leading men of Flanders to a meeting at Arras.[158] There, 'on the order and advice' of Louis VI, the barons of France and the leading men of Flanders elected William Clito as count.[159] He was invested with the county by the king and recognised as the legitimate count. However, William's policies together with Henry's machinations gradually alienated a significant number of barons and urban communities in Flanders. Count William dealt with those who were suspected of involvement in the conspiracy to murder Charles. In a display of judicial brutality, he despatched a number of the conspirators by precipitating them from the battlements of Bruges castle.[160]

William Clito proved himself to be a tireless military campaigner, but, gradually, opposition from the barons and towns of Flanders mounted until, by the end of April 1128, he was a 'wanderer in his own land of Flanders'.[161] His situation improved with the capture of his rival William of Ypres in April 1127, but Thierry of Alsace, backed by Henry I of England, remained a threat.[162] Several Normans joined William in Flanders and there may have been an element of xenophobia in the growing opposition to his rule.[163] In June 1128, William Clito won a major battle at Axspoele forcing his rival Thierry of Alsace to retreat to Bruges. Galbert of Bruges wrote with considerable admiration for William's military prowess, and his account became more and more critical of those who opposed him.

Whether any news of his son's exploits reached Duke Robert is not recorded although such news could travel swiftly from Flanders to England. Rumours

---

157 *OV*, VI, pp. 370–1.
158 *Galbert*, c. 47, pp. 75–7; Ross, pp. 186–9.
159 *Galbert*, c. 52, pp. 81–4 at 82; Ross, pp. 194–8 at 196.
160 *Galbert*, c. 81, pp. 124–6; Ross, pp. 250–2. Ross, p. 47, n. 55, suggested that precipitation may have been a peculiarly Norman form of punishment for rebellion introduced by the new count.
161 *Galbert*, c. 108, p. 156; Ross, p. 289.
162 *Galbert*, c. 79, pp. 122–3; Ross, pp. 248–9.
163 *OV*, VI, pp. 372–3.

of Count Charles's death reached London within two days.[164] If Robert was in contact with his son's followers in Flanders, then news received from them at the end of July 1128 would have distressed the old duke, now in his seventies.[165] In alliance with Duke Godfrey of Lorraine, William had attacked his enemies in the town of Aalst. During an attack on the castle on 27 July, William was unhorsed and before he could defend himself he was wounded in the hand by a foot-soldier's lance. The wound was deep and before long the young man began to complain of pain in his heart. According to Orderic 'that which they call holy fire infected the wound and the whole of his arm to the elbow turned as black as coal'.[166] After five days, William seems to have recognised that his wound was mortal and, like so many of his class, he asked to be made a monk. Having made a confession and receiving the host, he died aged about twenty-five.[167] William's faithful mentor, Helias of Saint-Saëns, was with the count at the end and he and the other barons decided to conceal the count's death until they had captured Aalst. Once the town had fallen, Helias arranged for William's funeral in the abbey of Saint-Bertin at Saint-Omer.[168] Thierry of Alsace assumed control as Count of Flanders and married William's widow, Sibyl of Anjou.[169]

The Last Years of Robert Curthose

It is not recorded how Duke Robert reacted to the death of his only legitimate son. According to Orderic, Robert, while a prisoner in Devizes, had a premonitory dream about his son's death. In the dream, Robert saw William wounded in the right arm by a lance; subsequently his son lost the arm. The next morning, before messengers arrived to bring the news, the duke announced that his son was dead.[170] If Robert was in Devizes, he was still in the custody of Roger of Salisbury when news arrived from Flanders carried by John, the son of Odo bishop of Bayeux. John also carried sealed letters from William in which the dying count asked Henry's pardon and begged him to pardon his supporters. Some of Clito's men were readmitted to royal favour, but others preferred to make the pilgrimage to Jerusalem.[171]

It is unlikely that Henry would have allowed Robert to attend William's funeral at Saint-Omer, given the growing support that his son had managed to acquire towards the end of his reign as count of Flanders. William may have

---

164 *Galbert*, c. 12, p. 22; Ross, p. 114.
165 According to Henry of Huntingdon, there were some who expected William Clito to become king; *HH*, 'De contemptu mundi', pp. 594–5.
166 *OV*, VI, pp. 376–7; 'Holy' or 'St Anthony's' fire was a form of infection, probably gangrene.
167 *OV*, VI, pp. 376–7; *Galbert*, c. 119, pp. 170–2; Ross, pp. 307–8.
168 *Galbert*, c. 119, p. 172; Ross, p. 308. *OV*, VI, pp. 376–9, records William's epitaph. Cf. Walo's epitaph for William in *HH*, Appendix 3, pp. 836–8.
169 *OV*, VI, pp. 378–9.
170 *OV*, VI, pp. 380–1.
171 *OV*, VI, pp. 378–9.

intended to use Flanders as a base from which to reclaim Normandy and free his father. The effort which Henry I expended in trying to prevent his nephew from being in such a position demonstrates that he perceived the danger as serious. William Clito's death marked the end of the struggle against Henry for the rebels 'had no-one to lead them in their rash pride after they lost the young leader for whose sake they had ravaged the fields of Normandy with fire and sword'.[172] Henry was preoccupied with securing the succession to England for his daughter the Empress Matilda and it was probably thought that Duke Robert, approaching his eighties, no longer posed a threat.

Robert survived another six years after the death of his son. Before February 1134, he was moved from Robert of Gloucester's castle at Bristol to Cardiff. The medieval castle at Cardiff was constructed in the former Roman *castrum*. There is no information on how Duke Robert spent his time in custody, but it is just possible that in his last years he managed to learn enough Welsh to compose an *englyn* in that language. The story may have been another of the legends that became attached to the duke, but it is not wholly implausible.[173]

In the late eighteenth century, a letter was sent to the editor of the *Gentleman's Magazine* by Edward Williams. Williams claimed that in collecting materials for a 'History of the ancient British Bards and Druids' he had chanced upon a manuscript belonging to Thomas Truman of Pant Lliwydd near Cowbridge in the Vale of Glamorgan. This manuscript, written around 1500, contained 'An account of the Lords Marchers of Glamorgan from Robert fitz Hamon down to Jasper, Duke of Bedford' together with the following poem and its short historical preface:

Pan oedd Rhobert Tywysog Norddmanti yngharchar Ynghastell Caerdyf, gan Robert ap Amon, medru a wnaeth ar y iaith Gymraeg; ac o weled y Beirdd Cymreig yno ar y Gwyliau efe a'u ceris, ac a aeth yn Fardd; a llyma englynion a gant efe.

> *Dar a dyfwys ar y clawdd,*
> *Gwedi, gwaedffrau gwedi ffrawdd;*
> *Gwae! wrth win ymtrin ymtrawdd.*

> *Dar a dyfwys ar y glâs,*
> *Gwedi gwaedffrau gwyr a lâs;*
> *Gwae! wr wrth y bo ai câs.*

---

172 *OV*, VI, pp. 380–1.

173 No other example of the unusual metre of the poem, the *englyn milwr*, has survived from the twelfth century. The tone of the poem is reminiscent of earlier ninth- and tenth-century saga poetry such as the *Canu Llywarch Hen* or the *Canu Heledd*. 'Robert's poem' demonstrates a knowledge of the conventions of this corpus of material, but it should be treated with caution. See further, Nerys Ann Jones, 'Y Gogynfeirdd a'r Englyn', in B.F. Roberts and Morfydd E. Owen, eds., *Beirdd a Thywysogion* (Cardiff, 1996), pp. 290–1. I am very grateful to Ffion Mair Jones and Ann Parry Owen at the University of Wales, Aberystwyth for their assistance on the authenticity of this poem. My thanks also to my colleagues Professor Sioned Davies, and Dylan Foster-Evans in the School of Welsh at Cardiff University.

Dar a dyfwys ar y tonn,
Gwedi gwaedffrau a briw bronn;
Gwae! a gar gwydd amryson.

Dar a dyfwys ym meillion,
A chan a'I briw ni bi gronn;
Gwae! wr wrth ei gaseion.

Dar a dyfwys ar dir pen,
Gallt, ger ymdonn Mor Hafren
Gwae! wr na bai digon hên.

Dar a dyfwys ynggwynnau,
A thwrf a thrin a thrangau;
Gwae! a wyl na bo Angau.

Rhobert Tywysog Norddmanti ai Cant.

Edward Williams offered the following translation of the poem and its preface:

When Robert, Duke of Normandy, was held a prisoner in Cardiff castle by Robert fitz Hamon, he acquired a knowledge of the Welsh language; and seeing the Welsh bards there on the high festivals, he became a Bard; and was the author of the following stanzas:

Oak that hast grown up on the mound,
Since the blood-streaming, since the slaughter;
Woe! to the war of words at the wine.

Oak that hast grown up in the grass,
Since the blood-streaming of those that were slain;
Woe! to man when there are that hate him.

Oak that hast grown up on the green,
Since the streaming of blood and the rending of breasts,
Woe! to him that loves the presence of contention.

Oak that hast grown up amid the trefoil grass,
And, because of those that tore thee, hast not attained to rotundity;
Woe! to him that is in the power of his enemies.

Oak that hast grown up on the grounds
Of the woody promontory fronting the contending waves of the Severn sea;
Woe! to him that is not old enough [old enough to die].

Oak that hast grown up in the storms,
Amid dins, battles and death;
Woe! to him that beholds what is not Death.

The Author, Robert Duke of Normandy [*literally*, 'sang this'].[174]

---

174 David, *Curthose*, pp. 187–9 and nn. 64–7. It was originally published in *The Gentleman's Maga-*
zine, lxiv, 2, pp. 981–2 in 1794. The translation is an amended version of that offered by David,
Curthose, p. 188.

Edward Williams associated the sentiments of the poem with 'the distressful incidents of the unfortunate and greatly injured duke's stormy life'. He was convinced that the imprisoned duke could indeed have seen the 'Severn Sea' or Bristol Channel from Cardiff castle and that the oak addressed in the poem was growing in Penarth, a village on a promontory lying across Cardiff Bay. Williams also concluded that the poem was additional evidence that 'the eyes of the duke were not put out, though the Cardiff tradition asserts that they were. I hope for the honour of human nature, that this tradition asserts a falsehood. My Welsh MS. account says nothing of the duke's eyes having been put out.'[175]

Although there are records of a number of examples of eleventh- and twelfth-century princes composing verse, the provenance of the poem attributed to Duke Robert is, unfortunately, a cause for concern.[176] The correspondent of the *Gentleman's Magazine* who provided the text of the poem was Edward Williams (1747–1826), also known as 'Iolo Morgannwg', who was largely responsible for the revival of the bardic order. He is, unfortunately, associated with pastiches and the forgery of ancient texts.[177] In the form as we have it, the poem might well have had its origins in the medieval period, but there is no other attribution to Duke Robert independent of that given by Edward Williams. Nevertheless, there is something romantic about the image of the aged duke gazing out from the keep of Cardiff castle towards the River Severn and reflecting on the vicissitudes of his career.

A Hero's Funeral

In the surviving historical records, Duke Robert's eventful life ended quietly and, judging by the brevity of the notices of his demise, unremarkably. He had been, after all, the duke of Normandy, a king's son, a Jerusalem pilgrim, the father of the count of Flanders, and a nobleman of the first rank. That his death was treated with a measure of reticence by those historians writing during his life or in the decade or so after it might reflect a certain indifference or, perhaps, a measure of embarrassment at the treatment of a man whose rightful duchy had been usurped, and the commemoration of whose achievements on the greatest chivalric adventure of the age had been set aside as contrary to the interests of his ambitious younger brother.

Orderic Vitalis, who has the most to say about Duke Robert, reported his

---

175 *Gentleman's Magazine*, lxiv, p. 982. It is difficult to agree with David, *Curthose*, p. 186, that Cardiff castle in the 1130s was still 'a wild frontier stronghold'.

176 William IX, duke of Aquitaine (d. 1126), was known as 'the first troubadour' and a composer of courtly poetry; Bumke, *Courtly Culture*, pp. 407, 427. For examples of English translations of medieval Welsh verse, see T. Conran, *Welsh Verse*, 3rd ed. (Bridgend, 1992), pp. 136–55.

177 Prys Morgan, *Iolo Morgannwg* (Cardiff, 1975). For Iolo's work in context, see Prys Morgan, 'From a Death to a View: The Hunt for the Welsh Past in the Romantic Period', in *The Invention of Tradition*, ed. E. Hobsbawm and T. Ranger (Cambridge, 1983), pp. 43–100.

death briefly. Having related Robert's dream about William Clito's demise, Orderic wrote: 'Who [Robert] himself died six years later [1134] at Cardiff, and was then taken from his prison and buried at Gloucester.'[178] Later, Orderic added a paragraph in annalistic style:

> In the year of our Lord 1134, the twelfth indiction, Robert II duke of the Normans, in the twenty-eighth year after he had been captured at Tinchebray and detained in his brother's prison, died in the month of February at Cardiff in Britain [Wales], and rests buried in the monastery of St Peter the Apostle at Gloucester.[179]

As far as Orderic was concerned, that was all that needed to be said about the death of one of the major characters in his monumental history of the Normans.

John of Worcester, after noting that Robert, who had been captured in a battle near the castle of Tinchebray and imprisoned for some time, had died at Cardiff, added the detail that Robert 'was taken to Gloucester, where he was buried with great honour before the altar in the church's floor.'[180] This is an important addition for it tells us that, in death, Robert was accorded great honour and his inhumation before the altar in the abbey church at Gloucester demonstrated that, at least in death, his status was recognised and his life worth commemorating. These details of course prompt us to ask who decided to accord Robert such recognition of his worth.

The exact date of Robert's death is provided by Robert of Torigny, in his continuation of the *Gesta Normannorum ducum*. He noted that Duke Robert 'died in England at Bristol, the fortress of his nephew Robert, earl of Gloucester, to whom King Henry had entrusted the custody of the duke. He died on 10 February and was buried in the church of St Peter of Gloucester in the year of our Lord 1134.'[181] Local Gloucester tradition noted that Robert died on the 'third of the nones of February' at the castle in Cardiff, but was

---

178 *OV*, VI, pp. 380–1.
179 *OV*, VI, pp. 412–13. William of Malmesbury merely noted that Robert died in prison; *GR*, I, pp. 706–7. Robert's death was not recorded by the *Anglo-Saxon Chronicle*. Henry of Huntingdon, pp. 454–5, and 'De contemptu mundi', c. 12, pp. 604–5, merely noted Robert's imprisonment until death. By the thirteenth century, the compiler of the 'Annals of Winchester' (*Ann. Mon.*, II, p. 50) had accused Henry I of blinding his brother: 'MCXXXIII. Hoc anno Robertus, frater regis Henrici, dux Normanniæ, quem rex ignita ut fertur pelve cæcari, in vinculis cruciatus suos morte finivit apud Glouecestriam.' ('1133 [*sic: recte* 1134]'). In this year, Robert, duke of Normandy, brother of king Henry, whom it was said the king had blinded with a burning lamp [*literally* 'a fiery basin-shaped lamp'], ended his life, tortured in chains at Gloucester.') The accusation is repeated in the 'Annals of Worcester', *s.a.* 1134, in *Ann. Mon.*, IV, p. 378. Cf. 'Annals of Waverley', in *Ann. Mon.*, II, p. 224; 'Annals of Dunstable', in *Ann. Mon.*, III, p. 14; 'Annals of Bermondsey', in *Ann. Mon.*, III, pp. 434–35; 'Annals of Osney and Chronicle of Thomas Wykes', in *Ann. Mon.*, IV, p. 19; 'Annals of Margam', in *Ann. Mon.*, I, p. 13; 'Annals of Tewkesbury', in *Ann. Mon.*, I, p. 45. Hollister does not discuss the alleged blinding of Curthose in his 'Royal Acts of Mutilation: The Case against Henry I', *Albion*, 10 (1978), pp. 330–40, reprinted in *Monarchy, Magnates and Institutions*, pp. 291–301. In his *Henry I*, p. 205, n. 4, the accusation is dismissed as 'clearly false'.
180 *JW*, III, *s.a.* 1134, pp. 212–13.
181 *WJ*, II, pp. 232–3. Robert's death was recorded as 11 February in the Mont-Saint-Michel Martyrology-Necrology: *Cartulary of Mont-Saint-Michel*, p. 250.

buried with honour in front of the principal altar in the church of St Peter at Gloucester.[182]

No details are given about the cause of Robert's death, although his age – he was into his early eighties – must have been a factor. The fact that he reached such an impressive age suggests that, despite the rigours of the Crusade and the other campaigns in which he fought, Robert possessed a generally robust constitution, although the expedition to the East may have affected his health. If, as is likely, he was accorded a comfortable detention, then there is no reason to believe that the conditions of his imprisonment hastened his demise.

There is no known account of Robert's last hours and only the briefest of notices about his burial. Given the importance of death in a society dominated by thoughts of the afterlife, and Robert's reputation for piety demonstrated so dramatically through his participation on the Crusade, it is worth trying to reconstruct the end to Robert's remarkable career. At the approach of death, Robert's spiritual needs were catered for, either by a personal chaplain, or by a priest in the retinue of his gaoler. As in any culture, there was a right way to prepare for death in Norman society. It was important to atone as far as possible for the sins committed in life. Unlike his brothers and father, Robert had the advantage of the spiritual benefits that had accrued from his pilgrimage to Jerusalem and, as he had remained in prison for twenty-eight years, he may have had little to confess.[183]

The form that Robert's passing took was heavily influenced by the conventions of the time. There is the problem of disentangling the ideal from the reality in descriptions of medieval death. It has been recognised that the relationship between the event and the text that represents that event is complex. Medieval deaths may indeed be described in conventional terms, but those conventions might accurately represent what happened, for the actors in the unfolding drama may have consciously chosen to comport themselves in a conventional manner.[184] No description of Robert's last days written within a few years of his death survives. In the thirteenth century, Matthew Paris, the monk historian of St Albans, provided a fuller account of Robert's death, but his sources for this information are unknown. Matthew Paris suggested that Robert's death was self-inflicted in that he stopped eating and drinking when his brother's gift of a scarlet cloak brought home to him the hopelessness of his situation. It seems that the king had ripped the hood of the cloak in trying it on. Not wishing to keep damaged goods he sent it to his brother, who noticed that the garment had been repaired. The realisation that he was

---

182 *Historia et cartularium monasterii sancti Petri Gloucestriae*, ed. W.H. Hart, Rolls Series (London, 1863–7), I, p. 15.

183 For a formula for death-bed confession attributed to Archbishop Anselm, see the text in *Memorials of St Anselm*, ed. R.W. Southern and F.S. Schmitt, O.S.B., Auctores Britannici Medii Aevi, I, The British Academy (Oxford, 1969), pp. 352–4.

184 See D. Crouch, 'The Culture of Death in the Anglo-Norman World', in C. Warren Hollister, ed., *Anglo-Norman Political Culture and the Twelfth-century Renaissance* (Woodbridge, 1997), pp. 157–80.

wholly dependent upon the brother who had usurped his duchy, blinded and imprisoned him, brought Robert to utter despair and from that point on he refused food and water, eventually dying cursing the day he was born.[185]

Robert's place of burial in front of the high altar in the monastic church of St Peter, Gloucester, suggests that someone had decided that in death the duke might be accorded the spiritual benefits of a close association with the Benedictine community there. The burial within a church of a layman was an honour usually reserved for founders and patrons. Burial before the altar was especially significant in that the deceased would be a presence at each celebration of the mass. The attention of the monks of Gloucester was drawn to Robert's grave by a candle which was kept burning constantly in his honour. To provide the funds for this, Henry I donated his manor of Rodele (Rodley-beyond-Severn?) 'to provide for a light to burn continually before the high altar for the soul of his brother Robert Curthose buried in that place, in the time of Abbot William' (*recte* Walter).[186] Henry I had made other *pro anima* donations to Gloucester Abbey for members of his family, but perhaps the provision of the perpetual light on Robert's grave was an acknowledgement by the king that he had treated the duke in a less than brotherly fashion and that he needed to make amends.[187] Whether the decision to bring Robert to Gloucester for burial was the king's is uncertain. Perhaps Robert, earl of Gloucester, had come to admire his uncle and wished to honour the hero of the Crusade. Robert's own preferences for a place of burial were never stated, but it is doubtful that Henry would have risked transporting the body to Normandy and re-igniting opposition to his rule.

The monks of Gloucester obviously felt that the burial of the duke before the altar brought a measure of prestige to their abbey. Robert may have been admitted to the Benedictine order and then given a monastic burial. Death provided medieval historians with an opportunity to reflect upon the essential emptiness of worldly power. Medieval churchmen described death as the great leveller in a literary genre characterised by tracts such as Henry of Huntingdon's *De contemptu mundi* ('On Contempt for the World').[188] For Henry of Huntingdon, his old age was a time to reflect on the meaning of his life and acknowledge, and if possible atone for, the sins of his youth: 'with advancing age, what was once soothing becomes abrasive, what tasted sweet becomes bitter'.[189]

If Robert had been admitted to the monastic order, his funeral and burial

---

185 *Matthaei Parisiensis, monachi sancti Albani, Chronica Maiora*, ed. H.R. Luard, Rolls Series (London, 1874), II, pp. 159–61. David, *Curthose*, pp. 201–2 provides a partial translation of the passage.

186 *Historia et cartularium sancti Petri Gloucestriae*, I, pp. 111–12.

187 *Regesta*, II, no. 1041, pp. 113–14. The phrase 'less than brotherly fashion' was used in the later twelfth century by William of Newburgh to describe Henry's custody of Robert: *History of English Affairs*, I, pp. 46–7.

188 *HH*, pp. 584–619.

189 *HH*, pp. 586–7.

would have been conducted according to Benedictine conventions, probably following Archbishop Lanfranc's 'Monastic Constitutions'.[190] As he had died away from the abbey, the monks would have sent a hearse for him and a pall to cover the body. Robert would have been brought to the monastic infirmary, where the rituals surrounding the death of a monk began. Bells were tolled three times at short intervals and the cantor of the abbey sang the responsory *Subuenite sancti Dei,* after which the priest added the prayer 'Set forth, O Christian soul' followed by the commendation of the soul. The body, naked apart from a shift, was washed by monks of appropriate status, while the chamberlain, ready with needle and thread, stood by with monastic vestments with which to dress the deceased. After the ritual bathing the monastic cowl was brought over the head and the body was sewn securely into its robes ready for placing on the hearse and being covered with the pall.[191]

At a signal from the prior, the monks bowed down and said the *Pater noster* while a priest sprinkled holy water and perfumed the body with incense. Further prayers were followed by the collect, bell-ringing and a responsory. The monks then processed with the body to the church, those carrying the holy water, the cross, candlesticks and thurible containing the incense leading the way with the body following last of all, carried by those who had washed it. As the body reached its position in the church the tolling of the bells ceased. The cross and a candlestick would have been set up at Robert's head and another candlestick at his feet. The candles continued to burn until the body was taken for burial. Prayers including the *Pater noster* were repeated and those monks not needed for the inhumation returned to their tasks. A certain number of monks remained with the corpse and chanted psalms, 'for the corpse should never be left without psalmody, save when a common office is being celebrated in choir'.[192] The duke's body was never left alone and the monks continued to recite the Psalter and prayers for his soul.[193] The presence of the dead man modified behaviour in the abbey and the brethren were forbidden to speak in the cloister as long as the deceased remained unburied.

The dead man received absolution from the abbot or his deputy and it was ordered that thirty masses should be celebrated for him over thirty days. After the celebration of High Mass, the funeral took place. Presumably, in Robert's case, the body remained in the choir of the abbey church. The monks processed to the body singing the *Verba Mea* with the great bells tolling three times

---

190 *The Monastic Constitutions of Lanfranc,* edited and translated by Dom David Knowles, revised ed. Christopher L. Brooke (Oxford, 2002), pp. 178–95. For the origins of these rituals, see F.S. Paxton, *Christianizing Death. The Creation of a Ritual Process in Early Medieval Europe* (Ithaca and London, 1990).

191 *Monastic Constitutions,* pp. 182–5.

192 *Monastic Constitutions,* pp. 184–5.

193 Vespers, Vigils and Lauds of the dead and the *Verba Mea.* Monks were delegated to pray for the deceased's soul through the watches into which the night was divided. See *Monastic Constitutions,* pp. 184–5.

to summon the other members of the community. With the monks standing around holding tapers and candles, the priest and his assistants began the rite for the burial. Robert's body would have been sprinkled with holy water and the priest would have stood at his head. The liturgy for the deceased was intoned until it was time to carry the body to the grave. Once again the bells tolled continually until the body entered the ground. With the monks drawn up in rank order around the grave, the officiating priest sprinkled the grave with holy water after which an assistant climbed down into the grave to perfume it with incense. The pall was laid across the grave while the body was placed carefully into the ground. According to Archbishop Lanfranc's instructions a scroll recording the absolution given the deceased was placed on his chest while the monks read it out. Once the body was covered in the grave the monks extinguished the candles and the tolling bells fell silent.[194]

---

[194] *Monastic Constitutions*, pp. 190–3.

EPILOGUE

A T some time in the thirteenth century a painted wooden effigy of a recumbent knight wearing a coronet was made and presented to the abbey church at Gloucester. The effigy depicts the knight with his legs crossed and he appears to be in the act of drawing his sword.[1] Since the fourteenth century at least, the effigy has been identified as representing Robert Curthose, duke of Normandy. From the time of Abbot Froucester (1381–1412), it was believed that Duke Robert was buried in the presbytery before the principal altar. Whether Robert's bones do indeed lie in front of Gloucester cathedral's high altar has not been substantiated through excavation and other evidence suggests that he might have been laid to rest in the chapter house.[2]

By the time a drawing was made of the effigy in the late 1560s, it rested on a painted mortuary box. Around the box are shields depicting the heraldic arms of the Nine Worthies of the World, those of Godfrey of Bouillon and of England and France.[3] The monument impressed visitors until the English Civil War in the seventeenth century, when Cromwell's soldiers broke up the effigy. The pieces were preserved and reassembled after the Restoration.[4]

The effigy at Gloucester is impressive, but its elegant proportions bear no resemblance to the surviving written descriptions of Robert's physique. Both the major medieval sources for his life agree that he was short and stout, although not unpleasing to the eye.[5] His stature was to blame for his nickname, but it could also be an advantage in battle. William of Malmesbury wrote of the Turkish general Corbaguath paying with his life for underestimating Robert's prowess by taking 'his measure by his size alone'.[6] Robert was difficult to dislodge from the saddle and his low centre of gravity gave him a distinct advantage as his own father found out to his cost at Gerberoy. He was also a fine archer as well as a consummate horseman.[7] For Gaimar:

---

[1] The effigy was drawn by Robert Cook, Clarenceux, in 1569, College of Arms MS. CN. 1569, in T.D. Kendrick, *British Antiquity* (London, 1950), plate X, b. Cf. Judith Hurtig, *Armored Gisant before 1400* (New York, 1979); D. Welander, *The History, Art and Architecture of Gloucester Cathedral* (Stroud, 1991), pp. 80–2, 113–17.

[2] Welander, *Gloucester Cathedral*, pp. 80–2. The effigy has been moved to the south ambulatory.

[3] Welander, *Gloucester Cathedral*, p. 116.

[4] Welander, *Gloucester Cathedral*, p. 115.

[5] *OV*, II, pp. 356–7; WM, *GR*, I, pp. 700–3.

[6] WM, *GR*, I, pp. 702–3.

[7] *JW*, III, s.a. 1079, pp. 32–3. *OV*, II, pp. 356–7.

Under heaven there was no better lord.
He was duke of Normandy.
Over the Normans he had lordship
Much good and many deeds of valour,
Much marvellous service and much beautiful chivalry,
This duke of Normandy performed.[8]

No-one seems to have doubted Robert's skills as a soldier, but medieval and modern commentators agree that, as a ruler, he was inept.

There were elements of his personality that suggest that he was an attractive figure at court. He could inspire steadfast loyalty as is witnessed in the case of Helias of Saint-Saëns, who served the duke and his son for perhaps forty years. Men were willing to follow him into battle and accompany him to Jerusalem. Even in 1106, Robert had sufficient resolve to confront his brother's larger army at Tinchebray.

As well as being brave, Robert was eloquent and able to give good advice to others.[9] This made him an especially effective mediator, as he demonstrated on the expeditions to Scotland and in the manner in which he defused the numerous disputes among the barons of Normandy. Robert was always willing to try to negotiate, especially when it came to the conflicts with William Rufus and Henry. It was perhaps because he was a skilled soldier that he recognised that the bloodshed and uncertainty of battle were to be avoided if possible. That the negotiations ultimately failed was usually due to the bad faith shown by his brothers and, perhaps, some naïveté on Robert's part.

When it came to ruling Normandy, he was seen as being too gentle and forgiving. He is perceived as lacking the single-minded determination of his father and his brothers, who were willing to impose their will. This biography has challenged that view and has shown Robert acting with determination and, at times, even a certain ruthlessness. Men were willing to bring their disputes to his court for arbitration and he was able to call out the 'army of Normandy' to enforce his policies.

Robert probably did lack the deviousness required to manipulate the hopes and fears of those at court. He was criticised for his prodigality in distributing largesse, and promises were made so recklessly that no-one could believe them. As characterised by Orderic, Robert was wholly ineffectual as duke:

Being merciful to suppliants he was too weak and pliable to pass judgement on wrongdoers; unable to pursue any plan consistently he was far too affable and obliging in all his relationships, and so he earned the contempt of corrupt and foolish men.[10]

8   *Gaimar*, lines 5738–44, p. 182: 'Suz ciel n'aveit meillur barun,/ Celui fud duc de Normendie,/ Sur Normanz ot la seignurie;/ Mainte bunté e maint barnage/ E maint estrange vassalage/ Fist icest duc de Normendie/ E mainte bele chevalerie.'
9   WM, *GR*, I, pp. 702–3.
10 *OV*, IV, pp. 114–15.

William of Malmesbury agreed:

> He was, then, a man with no memory for the wrongs done to him, and forgave
> offences beyond what was right; to all who came to him he gave the answer they
> desired rather than send them away disappointed, and anything that he could not
> give he promised.[11]

Robert could not bring himself to inflict harsh punishments and was perceived
as far too gentle to dispense justice. Men despised rather than respected or
feared him and that, according to Orderic and William of Malmesbury, added
up to a Normandy torn apart by the violence of powerful men.[12]

Robert's reputation has undoubtedly suffered in comparison with those
of his father and youngest brother. Historians from the nineteenth century
onwards, heavily influenced by the opinions of the twelfth-century writers,
have been critical of Robert. The voice of Orderic's account is clear in Edward
A. Freeman's estimation of Robert:

> Robert, it must always be noticed, is never charged with cruelty or oppression of any
> kind in his own person. His fault was exactly of the opposite kind. He was so mild
> and good-natured, so ready to listen to every suppliant, to give to every petitioner,
> to show mercy to every offender, that he utterly neglected the discharge of the first
> duty of his office, that which the men of his time called doing justice.[13]

Yet even Freeman had reservations about condemning the duke completely.
H.W.C. Davis commented on Robert's 'incapacity for sustained effort' and
David Douglas thought the duke 'devoid of statesmanship and sagacity' and
'suitably fashioned to be a tool in the hands of men less frank and more
astute than himself'.[14] Charles David, writing his biography of Robert in 1920
under the watchful eye of his doctoral supervisor, Charles Haskins, produced
a rather downbeat portrait of the duke.[15] Haskins himself, despite his significant contribution to the study of the government of Normandy under Robert,
interpreted the documents as evidence substantiating a negative assessment
of the duke's abilities. The dearth of charters was proof that the history of
Normandy under Robert was a 'dreary tale of private war, murder and pillage,
of perjury, disloyalty and revolt.'[16]

More recent assessments have been more positive, but Robert remains
a puzzling figure.[17] Freeman recognised long ago that there was a seeming
contradiction in Robert's character: 'Neither the warrior of the crusade nor

---

11 WM, *GR*, I, pp. 704–5. The similarities between Malmesbury's account and Orderic's criticisms
perhaps suggest that Henry I's propaganda lies behind their portraits of Robert.
12 *OV*, IV, pp. 114–15; WM, *GR*, I, pp. 704–5.
13 Freeman, *Reign of William Rufus*, I, p. 190.
14 H.W.C. Davis, *England under the Normans and Angevins, 1066–1272*, 7th ed. (London, 1921), p. 80;
Douglas, *William the Conqueror*, p. 237.
15 C.W. David, *Robert Curthose, Duke of Normandy* (Cambridge MA, 1920).
16 Haskins, *Norman Institutions*, pp. 62–78 at 62.
17 Green, 'Robert Curthose Reassessed', p. 116; Crouch, *The Normans*, pp. 214–15.

the negotiator with the Scot seems to be the same man as the Duke who could not be trusted to defend his own palace.'[18] But the successful crusader and skilful negotiator *was* the same man perceived to be a failure in Normandy.

For the Elizabethan poet Michael Drayton (1563–1631), Robert was a romantically tragic figure. In 'The Legend of Robert, Duke of Normandie' (first printed 1596; revised 1619), Drayton imagined Robert, old and blind, as the plaything of personifications of Fortune and Fame. For Drayton, Robert's piety was a key motif and it was this quality that finally freed him from Fortune's grasp.

> So farre it was from his religious mind,
> To mixe vile things, with those of heav'nly kind.[19]

The appeal of the story for Drayton was that the treatment Robert received was an indictment of monarchy and the scramble for court patronage. For Drayton, there was something unsavoury about kings and courts.[20]

In 1087, Robert had to deal with a baronial reaction to the death of William the Conqueror. The problems he confronted were perhaps more serious than has been appreciated and he did not have the resources of England to support a more robust response to baronial demands. Robert survived by seeking consensus, relying on bonds of fidelity and friendship, rather than more violent displays of coercive power. Even Orderic admitted that Normandy's problems stemmed from the actions of malevolent noblemen, rather than tyrannical oppressions perpetrated by Robert himself. The duke was berated for failing to curb the ambitions of men like Robert de Bellême, operating in the frontier regions of the duchy.

Robert's brothers viewed Normandy as a threat to their regimes. The duke provided a focus for those who were uneasy about the succession in 1087 and 1100. William and Henry were loathe to consider condominium and aimed to reconstitute the Conqueror's cross-channel *regnum*. In order to do this, they had to subvert the bonds of fidelity that articulated fundamental lord-vassal relationships. In 1104, William, count of Évreux complained that he was 'given away like a horse or ox'.[21] Henry's supporters claimed that the king was defending the Church in Normandy, but there is little to indicate that Robert neglected his duties there or that he was out of step with the ecclesiastical policies of his father and brothers. The evidence suggests that the problems in Normandy were greatly exacerbated, if not created, by royal policy between 1087 and 1106.

---

[18] Freeman, *Reign of William Rufus*, II, p. 298.

[19] Michael Drayton, 'The Legend of Robert, Duke of Normandie', in *Poems of Michael Drayton*, ed. J. Buxton, 2 vols. (London, 1953), II, pp. 495–524 at 521, lines 1580–1. Drayton's idea of Robert in competition with Fortune echoes William of Malmesbury, *GR*, I, pp. 706–7.

[20] Jean R. Brink, *Michael Drayton Revisited* (Boston, MA, 1990); Anne Lake Prescott, 'Michael Drayton (1563–1631), Poet', *Oxford DNB*.

[21] *OV*, VI, pp. 58–9.

Robert's participation in the Crusade seems to have had an effect on his personality. Before 1096, he had successfully countered threats to his rule in the duchy, whereas he seems less active after 1100. Henry exploited his brother's willingness to negotiate until he was ready to invade and conquer Normandy. One by one, Robert's allies deserted – Robert de Bellême on the field at Tinchebray. Robert's brothers and the barons of Normandy and England emerge from this story with little honour. William of Malmesbury recognised that Robert's personality was unsuited to his role:

> By this gentleness of character, a man who ought to have been praised for it, and to have won the affection of his subjects, goaded the Normans into such contempt that they thought him of no account at all.[22]

This study has focused on an individual life in an attempt to throw light on Norman society in the eleventh and twelfth centuries. Robert's struggles as ruler of Normandy have also highlighted the qualities needed by those in positions of power.[23] Effective lordship required more than military skill, eloquence, affability and the ability to deliver astute counsel. Adherence to notions of fidelity, honour and trust were handicaps if strong princely government was the aim. For earlier writers, less enamoured with 'great' kings, Robert Curthose was a tragic hero. His career is a commentary on the dangers of dynastic systems of public power. Personal courage and his simple faith were not enough to rule successfully. Robert Curthose's career is also a critique on medieval kingship. If many of the qualities demanded of individuals who wielded – *and wield* – power seem unattractive, this should come as no great surprise for, long ago, Henry of Huntingdon recognised that:

Regia res scelus est.[24]

---

22 WM, *GR*, I, pp. 704–5.
23 P. Wormald, 'Germanic Power Structures: the Early English Experience', in L. Scales and O. Zimmer, eds., *Power and the Nation in European History* (Cambridge, 2005), pp. 105–24.
24 'Royal business is wickedness [*or* a sin].' *HH*, pp. 604–5. It's no wonder Henry I had nightmares; see the illustrations from Oxford, Corpus Christi College 157, pp. 382–3 in *JW*, III, plates 1–4.

BIBLIOGRAPHY

Printed Primary Sources

The Abbey of Bec and the Anglo-Norman State 1034–1136, ed. Sally N. Vaughn (Woodbridge, 1981).

Les actes de Guillaume le Conquérant et de la reine Mathilde pour les Abbayes Caennaises, ed. L. Musset, Mémoires de la Société des Antiquaires de Normandie, vol. 37 (Caen, 1967).

Actus Pontificum Cenomannis in Urbe Degentium, ed. G. Bussonand and A. Ledru, Société des Archives Historiques du Maine (Le Mans, 1901).

Aelred of Rievaulx: The Historical Works, trans. Jane P. Freeland, ed. Marsha L. Dutton (Kalamazoo, MI, 2005).

Albert of Aachen, Historia Ierosolimitana. *History of the Journey to Jerusalem*, ed. and trans. Susan B. Edgington (Oxford, 2007).

The Anglo-Saxon Chronicle, A Collaborative Edition, Volume 6, MS. D, ed. G.P. Cubbin (Cambridge, 1996). *The Anglo-Saxon Chronicle, A Collaborative Edition, Volume 7, MS. E*, ed. Susan Irvine (Cambridge, 2004).

The Anglo-Saxon Chronicle, trans. and ed. M. Swanton (London, 1996).

Anna Comnena, The Alexiad, trans. E.R.A. Sewter (Harmondsworth, 1969).

Annales Monastici, ed. H.R. Luard, 5 vols., Rolls Series (London, 1864–9).

'Annals of Winchester', *Ann. Mon.*, II, pp. 3–112.

'Anselme de Saint-Remy, *Histoire de la Dédicace de Saint-Remy*', ed. Dom J. Hourlier, in *Contribution a l'annee Saint Benoît (480–1980). La Champagne Benedictine*, Travaux de l'Académie de Reims, 160 (Reims, 1981), pp. 179–297.

Antiquus cartularius ecclesiæ Baiocensis ou Livre Noir, ed. V. Bourienne, Société de l'Histoire de Normandie, 2 vols. (Rouen, 1907–8).

'Baldrici episcopi Dolensis Historia Jerosolymitana', in *RHC Occ.*, IV, pp. 1–111.

Bates, D., 'A Neglected English Charter of Robert Curthose, Duke of Normandy', *BIHR*, 59 (1986), pp. 122–4.

'Baudri of Bourgueil, "To Countess Adela"', trans. Monika Otter, *Journal of Medieval Latin*, 11 (2001), pp. 60–141.

The Bayeux Tapestry, L. Musset, trans. R. Rex (Woodbridge, 2005).

Benton, J.F., *Self and Society in Medieval France* (New York, 1970; revised ed. (Toronto, 1984).

Bouvris, J-M., 'Une version inédite de la confirmation par le duc Robert Courte-Heuse d'une donation faite en 1087 par Guillaume le Conquérant à l'abbaye de Saint-Etienne de Caen', *Revue de l'Avranchin et du pays de Granville*, 64, no. 331 (1987), pp. 82–85.

'The *Brevis Relatio de Guillelmo nobilissimo comite Normannorum*, written by a Monk of Battle Abbey', ed. Elisabeth M.C. van Houts, in *Chronology, Conquest and Conflict in Medieval England: Camden Miscellany*, Camden Fifth Series, 10 (Cambridge, 1997), pp. 1–48.

'The *Brevis Relatio de Guillelmo nobilissimo comite Normannorum*, written by a Monk of Battle Abbey', ed. and trans. Elisabeth M.C. van Houts, in *eadem, History and Family Traditions in England and the Continent, 1000–1200* (Aldershot, 1999), no. VII.

Brut y Tywysogyon or The Chronicle of the Princes, Peniarth MS 20 Version, ed. T. Jones (Cardiff, 1952). *Brut y Tywysogyon or The Chronicle of the Princes, Red Book of Hergest Version*, ed. T. Jones (Cardiff, 1955).

The Carmen de Hastingæ Proelio *of Guy Bishop of Amiens*, ed. and trans. F. Barlow (Oxford, 1999).

Cartulaire de l'abbaye de la Sainte-Trinité du Mont de Rouen, ed. A. Deville, in *Collection de cartulaires de France* (Paris, 1840).

Cartulaire de l'abbaye Saint-Vincent du Mans (572–1184), ed. l'abbé R. Charles and S. Menjot d'Elbenne (Mamers and Le Mans, 1886), vol. I.

The Cartulary of the abbey of Mont-Saint-Michel, ed. Katherine S.B. Keats-Rohan (Donington, 2006).

Charters and Custumals of the Abbey of Holy Trinity, Caen. Part 2. The French Estates, ed. J. Walmsley, Records of Social and Economic History, n.s. 22 (Oxford, 1994).

Charters of the Redvers Family and the Earldom of Devon, 1090–1217, ed. R. Bearman, Devon and Cornwall Record Society, 37 (1994).

The Chronicle of John of Worcester. Volume III, The Annals from 1067 to 1140 with the Gloucester Interpolations and the Continuation to 1141, ed. P. McGurk (Oxford, 1998)

Chronique de Robert de Torigni, ed. L. Delisle, 2 vols., Société de l'Histoire de Normandie (Rouen and Paris, 1872–3).

Chroniques des comtes d'Anjou et des seigneurs d'Amboise, ed. L. Halphen and R. Poupardin (Paris, 1913).

Benoît de Sainte-Maure, *Chronique des ducs de Normandie*, ed. Carin Fahlin, Bibliotheca Ekmaniania, 56 and 60 (Uppsala, 1951–54).

The Councils of Urban II, i. Decreta Claromontensia, ed. R. Sommerville, Annuarium Historiæ Conciliorum, Suppl., I (Amsterdam, 1972).

Davis, H.W.C., 'A Contemporary Account of the Battle of Tinchebrai', *EHR*, 24 (1909), pp. 728–9.

Davis, H.W.C., 'The Battle of Tinchebrai: A Correction', *EHR*, 25 (1910), pp. 295–6.

'De libertate Beccensis Monasterii', in J. Mabillon, ed., *Annales Ordinis Sancti Benedicti* (Paris, 1745), V, pp. 601–5.

The Deeds of Count Roger of Calabria and Sicily and of his Brother Duke Robert Guiscard, by Geoffrey Malaterra, trans. K.B. Wolf (Ann Arbor, MI, 2005).

The Deeds of God through the Franks. A Translation of Guibert de Nogent's Gesta Dei per Francos, trans. R. Levine (Woodbridge, 1997).

Delisle, L., 'Une lettre de Paschal II à Robert Courte-Heuse, duc de Normandie', *Bibliothèque de l'École des Chartes*, 71, pp. 465–6.

De Moribus et actis primorum Normannie ducum, ed. J. Lair, Mémoires de la Société des Antiquaires de Normandie (Caen 1865).

'De Obitu Willelmi', in *WJ*, II, pp. 184–91.

De Rebus Gestis Rogerii Calabriae et Siciliae Comitis auctore Gaufredo Malaterra, ed. E. Pontieri, Rerum Italicarum Scriptores, 2nd ed. (Bologna, 1927–8).

'Des Miracles advenus en L'Église de Fécamp', ed. M. l'Abbé Sauvage in *Mélanges, Documents*, 2e série, Société de l'Histoire de Normandie (Rouen, 1893), pp. 9–49.

Die Urkunden und Briefe der Markgräfin Mathilde von Tuszien, ed. Elke Goez and Werner Goez, MGH Diplomata Laienfürsten, 2 (Hanover, 1998).

Diplomatic Documents Preserved in the Public Record Office, I, 1101–1272, ed. P. Chaplais (London, 1964).

Donizone, 'Vita Mathildis Comitissae', ed. L. Bethmann, *MGH Scriptores*, 12 (Hanover, 1856), pp. 348–409.

Dudo of St Quentin. History of the Normans, trans. E. Christiansen (Woodbridge, 1998).

Eadmeri Historia Novorum in Anglia, ed. M. Rule, Rolls Series (London, 1884).

Eadmer's History of Recent Events in England. Historia Novorum in Anglia, trans. G. Bosanquet (London, 1964) [a translation of Books I–IV].

Early Yorkshire Charters, i–iii, ed. W. Farrer (Edinburgh, 1914–16); iv–xii, ed. C.T. Clay, Yorkshire Archaeological Society, Record Series, Extra Series, 1–3, 5–10 (1935–65).

The Ecclesiastical History of Orderic Vitalis, ed. Marjorie Chibnall, 6 vols. (Oxford, 1969–80).

English Historical Documents, II, 1042–1189, ed. D.C. Douglas and G.W. Greenway, 2nd ed. (London, 1981).

English Lawsuits from William I to Richard I, Vol. I, William I to Stephen, ed. R.C. van Caenegem, Selden Society, 106 (London, 1990).

L'Estoire des Engles, ed. T. Duffus Hardy and C.T. Martin, 2 vols., Rolls Series (London, 1888–9).

L'Estoire des Engleis by Geffrei Gaimar, ed. A. Bell (Oxford, 1960).

The First Crusade: The Accounts of Eye-Witnesses and Participants, ed. A.C. Krey (Princeton, PA, 1921).

The First Crusade. The Chronicle of Fulcher of Chartres and Other Source Materials, ed. E. Peters (Philadelphia, PA, 1971).

Fulcher of Chartres, Historia Hierosolymitana, ed. H. Hagenmeyer (Heidelberg, 1913).

Fulcher of Chartres, A History of the Expedition to Jerusalem, 1095–1127, trans. Frances R. Ryan (Knoxville, 1969).

Gabrieli, F., *Arab Historians of the Crusades*, trans. E.J. Costello (London, 1969).

Galbert of Bruges, The Murder of Charles the Good, trans. and ed. J.B. Ross (New York, 1959; reprinted 1982).

Geoffrey of Vigeois, 'Chronica' in *RHF*, XII.

'Gesta consulum andegavorum' in *Chroniques des comtes d'Anjou et des seigneurs d'Amboise*, ed. L. Halphen and R. Poupardin (Paris, 1913).

Gesta Francorum et Aliorum Hierosolimitanorum, ed. Rosalind Hill (London, 1962).

The Gesta Guillelmi of William of Poitiers, ed. and trans. R.H.C. Davis (†) and Marjorie Chibnall (Oxford, 1998).

The Gesta Normannorum Ducum of William of Jumièges, Orderic Vitalis and Robert of Torigni, ed. and trans. Elisabeth M.C. van Houts, 2 vols. (Oxford, 1992, 1995).

The Gesta Tancredi *of Ralph of Caen. A History of the Normans on the First Crusade*, trans. B.S. Bachrach and D.S. Bachrach (Aldershot, 2005).

'Gesta Tancredi in expeditione Hierosolymitana auctore Radulfo Cadomensi', in *RHC Occ.*, III, pp. 587–716.

Giraldus Cambrensis, 'De rebus a se gestis', in *Giraldus Cambrensis, Opera*, ed. J.S. Brewer, J.F. Dimock and G.F. Warner, 8 vols., Rolls Series (London, 1861–91), I, pp. 3–122.

Butler, H.E., ed. and trans., *The Autobiography of Gerald of Wales* (London, 1937; reprinted Woodbridge, 2005).

Guibertus abbas S. Mariae Nogenti, Dei Gesta per Francos, ed. R.B.C. Huygens, CCCM, 127A (Turnhout, 1996).

Hagenmeyer, H., *Die Kreuzzugsbriefe aus den Jahren, 1088–1100* (Innsbruck, 1901).

Henry of Huntingdon, Historia Anglorum. *The History of the English People*, ed. and trans. Diana Greenway (Oxford, 1996).

Herman, 'De Miraculis Sancti Eadmundi', in *Memorials of St Edmunds Abbey*, ed. T. Arnold, 3 vols., Rolls Series (London, 1890–6), I.

Herman of Tournai, 'Liber de restauratione monasterii S. Martini Tornacensis', in *MGH, Scriptores*, XIV.

Histoire du Meutre de Charles le Bon, comte de Flandre (1127–1128) par Galbert de Bruges, ed. H. Pirenne (Paris, 1891).

Historia Ecclesie Abbendonensis. The History of the Church of Abingdon, ed. and trans. J. Hudson (Oxford, 2002).

The Historia Vie Hierosolimitane *of Gilo of Paris*, ed. C.W. Grocock and J.E. Siberry (Oxford, 1997).

Hugh of Flavigny, 'Chronicon', ed. G.H. Pertz, in *MGH, Scriptores*, VIII, pp. 280–503.

Hugh the Chantor, The History of the Church of York, 1066–1127, trans. C. Johnson (London, 1961); revised ed. by M. Brett, C.N.L. Brooke and M. Winterbottom (Oxford, 1990).

Letters and Charters of Gilbert Foliot, ed. A. Morey and C.N.L. Brooke (Cambridge, 1967).

The Letters and Poems of Fulbert of Chartres, ed. and trans. F. Behrends (Oxford, 1976).

The Letters of Abelard and Heloise, trans. Betty Radice (Harmondsworth, 1974).

Letters of the Crusaders, ed. D.C. Munro (Philadelphia, PA, 1896).

The Letters of Saint Anselm of Canterbury, trans. W. Fröhlich, 3 vols., Cistercian Publications (Kalamazoo, MI, 1990, 1993 and 1994).

Le 'Liber' de Raymond d'Aguilers, ed. J.H. and L. Laurita Hill (Paris, 1969).

Liber Monasterii de Hyda, ed. E. Edwards, Rolls Series (London, 1866).

The Life of Christina of Markyate, a Twelfth-century Recluse, ed. and trans. H. Talbot (Oxford, 1959).

The Life of King Edward who Rests at Westminster Attributed to a Monk of Saint-Bertin, ed. and trans. F. Barlow, 2nd ed. (Oxford, 1992).

The Life of St Anselm, Archbishop of Canterbury, by Eadmer, ed. and trans. R.W. Southern (Oxford, 1972).

Lucan, *The Civil War* ['Pharsalia'], trans. J.D. Duff (Cambridge, MA, 1928).

Materials for the History of Thomas Becket, Archbishop of Canterbury, ed. J.C. Robertson, 7 vols., Rolls Series (London, 1875–85).

Matthew Paris, *Historia Anglorum sive, ut vulgo dicitur, historia minor. Item, ejusdem abbreviatio chronicorum Angliae*, ed. F. Madden, 3 vols., Rolls Series (London, 1866–9).

Memorials of St Anselm, ed. R.W. Southern and F.S. Schmitt, O.S.B., Auctores Britannici Medii Aevi, I, The British Academy (Oxford, 1969).

The Monastic Constitutions of Lanfranc, ed. and trans. D. Knowles and C.N.L. Brooke (Oxford, 2002).

The Normans in Europe, trans. and ed. Elisabeth M.C. van Houts (Manchester, 2000).

The Papal Reform of the Eleventh Century. Lives of Pope Leo IX and Pope Gregory VII, trans. I.S. Robinson (Manchester, 2004).

Peter Tudebode: Historia de Hierosolymitana Itinere, trans. J.H. and Laurita L. Hill (Philadelphia, PA, 1974).

Petrus Diaconus, 'Chronica Monasterii Casinensis', in *MGH, Scriptores*, VII.

Petrus Tudebodus: Historia de Hierosolymitana Itinere, ed. J.H. and Laurita L. Hill (Paris, 1977).

Raymond d'Aguilers. Historia Francorum qui ceperunt Iherusalem, trans. J.H. Hill and Laurita L. Hill (Philadelphia, PA, 1968).

Recueil des actes des ducs de Normandie (911–1066), ed. Marie Fauroux, Mémoires de la Société des Antiquaires de Normandie, 36 (Caen, 1961).

Regesta Regum Anglo-Normannorum 1066–1154, vol. i *Regesta Willelmi Conquestoris et Willelmi Rufi, 1066–1100*, ed. H.W.C. Davis (Oxford, 1913); vol. ii, *Regesta Henrici Primi 1100–1135*, ed. C. Johnson and H.A. Cronne (Oxford, 1956).

Regesta Regum Anglo-Normannorum. The Acta of William I (1066–1087), ed. D.R. Bates (Oxford, 1998).

The Register of Pope Gregory VII, 1073–1085, ed. H.E.J. Cowdrey (Oxford, 2002).

Robert the Monk's History of the First Crusade. Historia Iherosolimitana, trans. Carole Sweetenham (Aldershot, 2005).

'Roberti Monachi historia Iherosolimitana', *RHC Occ.*, III, pp. 717–882.

Roger of Wendover, *Chronica sive Flores Historiarum*, ed. H.O. Coxe, 4 vols. (London, 1841–2).

The Rule of St Benedict, trans. Justin McCann (London, 1976).

Sancti Anselmi Cantuariensis archiepiscopi Opera Omnia, ed. F.S. Schmitt, 6 vols. (Stuttgart-Bad Canstatt, 1963–68).

Serlo of Bayeux, 'De capta Baiocensium civitate', in *The Anglo-Latin Satirical Poets and Epigrammists of the Twelfth Century*, ed. T. Wright, Rolls Series (London, 1892), II, pp. 241–51.

Statius, *Thebaid, Books 1–7*, and *Thebaid, Books 8–12. Achilleid*, both ed. and trans. D.R. Shackleton Bailey (Cambridge, MA, 2003).

Suger, The Deeds of Louis the Fat, trans. R. Cusimano and J. Moorhead (Washington DC, 1992).

Suger, Vie de Louis VI le Gros, ed. H. Waquet (Paris, 1929).

Symeon of Durham, 'Historia Regum Anglorum', in *Symeonis monachi opera omnia*, ed. T. Arnold, 2 vols., Rolls Series (London, 1882–5), II, pp. 3–283.

Symeon of Durham, Libellus de Exordio atque procursu istius, hoc est Dunhelmensis Ecclesie. *Tract on the Origins and Progress of this the Church of Durham*, ed. and trans. D. Rollason (Oxford, 2000).

The Trotula. An English Translation of the Medieval Compendium of Women's Medicine, ed. and trans. Monica H. Green (Philadelphia, PA, 2001).

Vegetius: Epitome of Military Science, trans. N.P. Milner, 2nd revised ed. (Liverpool, 1996).

'Vita Beati Simonis comitis Crespeiensis auctore synchrono', in *PL*, 156, cols. 1211–1224.

Wace, *The Roman de Rou*, trans. G.S. Burgess (St Helier, 2002).

Walter Map, De Nugis Curialium. *Courtiers' Trifles*, ed. and trans. M.R. James, revised C.N.L. Brooke and R.A.B. Mynors (Oxford, 1983).

Welsh Verse, trans. T. Conran, 3rd ed. (Bridgend, 1992).

William of Malmesbury, Gesta Regum Anglorum. *The History of the English Kings*, Vol. I, ed. and trans. R.A.B. Mynors (†), completed by R.M. Thomson and M. Winterbottom (Oxford, 1998).

William of Malmesbury, Gesta Regum Anglorum. *The History of the English Kings*, Vol. II, 'General Introduction and Commentary', by R.M. Thomson in collaboration with M. Winterbottom (Oxford, 1999).

William of Newburgh, *The History of English Affairs*, ed. and trans. P.G. Walsh and M.J. Kennedy (Warminster, 1988), vol. I .

William of Tyre, A History of the Deeds Done Beyond the Sea, trans. E.A. Babcock and A.C. Krey, 2 vols. (New York, 1943).

William of Tyre, Chronicon, ed. R.B.C. Huygens, 1 vol. in 2, CCCM, 63/63A (Turnhout, 1986).

Secondary Sources

Abels, R.P. and B.S. Bachrach, *The Normans and their Adversaries at War. Essays in Memory of C. Warren Hollister* (Woodbridge, 2001).

Aird, W.M., 'An Absent Friend: The Career of Bishop William of St-Calais, 1080–1096', in D. Rollason, M. Harvey and M. Prestwich, eds., *Anglo-Norman Durham* (1994), pp. 283–97.

Aird, W.M., 'Frustrated Masculinity: The Relationship between William the Conqueror and his Eldest Son', in Dawn M. Hadley, ed., *Masculinity in Medieval Europe* (Harlow, 1999), pp. 39–55.

Aird, W.M., 'Le retour du Croisé: Robert Courteheuse, Duc de Normandie, et les conséquences de la Première Croisade' (forthcoming).

Aird, W.M., *St Cuthbert and the Normans. The Church of Durham, 1071–1153* (Woodbridge, 1998).

Airlie, S., 'The History of Emotions and Emotional History', *EME*, 10 (2) (2001), pp. 235–41.

Albu, Emily, *The Normans and their Histories. Propaganda, Myth and Subversion* (Woodbridge, 2001).

Albu, Emily, 'Probing the Passions of a Norman on Crusade: the *Gesta Francorum et aliorum Hierosolimitanorum*', *ANS*, 27 (2005), pp. 1–15.

Althoff, G., *Family, Friends and Followers. Political and Social Bonds in Early Medieval Europe* (Cambridge, 2004).

Althoff, G., 'Friendship and Political Order', in *Friendship in Medieval Europe*, ed. J. Haseldine (Stroud, 1999), pp. 91–105.

Althoff, G., '*Ira Regis*: Prolegomena to a History of Royal Anger', in Rosenwein, *Anger's Past*, pp. 59–74.

Althoff, G., 'Satisfaction: Peculiarities of the Amicable Settlement of Conflicts in the Middle Ages', in B. Jussen, ed., *Ordering Medieval Society. Perspectives on Intellectual and Practical Modes of Shaping Social Relations* (Philadelphia, PA, 2001), pp. 270–84.

Althoff, G., *Spielregeln der Politik im Mittelalter* (Darmstadt, 1997).

Ambrosius, L.E., ed., *Writing Biography. Historians and their Craft* (Lincoln, NB, 2004).

Ariès, P., *L'enfant at la vie famille sous l'ancien régime* (Paris, 1960), trans. R. Baldick, *Centuries of Childhood. A Social History of Family Life* (London, 1962).

Arnold, J.C., 'Arcadia becomes Jerusalem: Angelic Caverns and Shrine Conversion at Monte Gargano', *Speculum*, 75 (2000), pp. 567–88.

Asbridge, T., *The First Crusade. A New History* (London, 2004).

Atkinson, Clarissa W., *The Oldest Vocation. Christian Motherhood in the Middle Ages* (Ithaca, NY, 1991).

Bachrach, B.S., 'Crusader Logistics: from Victory at Nicaea to Resupply at Dorylaion', in *Logistics of Warfare in the Age of the Crusades*, ed. J.H. Pryor (London, 2006), pp. 43–62.

Bachrach, B.S., *Fulk Nerra, the neo-Roman Consul, 987–1040. A Political Biography of the Angevin Count* (Berkeley, CA, 1993).

Bachrach, B.S., 'William Rufus' Plan for the Invasion of Aquitaine', in R.P. Abels and B.S. Bachrach, eds., *The Normans and their Adversaries at War. Essays in memory of C. Warren Hollister* (Woodbridge, 2001), pp. 31–63.

Baldwin, M.W., ed., *A History of the Crusades, Volume I, The First Hundred Years* (Madison, Milwaukee and London, 1969).

Barlow, F., *Edward the Confessor* (London, 1970).

Barlow, F., *William Rufus* (London, 1983).

Barthélemy, D., 'Modern Mythologies of Medieval Chivalry', in *The Medieval World*, ed. Janet L. Nelson and P. Linehan (London, 2001), pp. 214–228.

Bartlett, R., *England under the Norman and Angevin Kings, 1075–1225* (Oxford, 2000).

Bartlett, R., *Gerald of Wales. A Voice of the Middle Ages* (Stroud, 2006).

Bartlett, R., *The Making of Europe. Conquest, Colonization and Cultural Change, 950–1350* (Harmondsworth, 1993).

Bartlett, R., *Trial by Fire and Water. The Medieval Judicial Ordeal* (Oxford, 1986).

Barton, R., 'Lordship in Maine: Transformation, Service and Anger', *ANS*, 17 (1994), pp. 41–63.

Barton, R., 'Henry I, Count Helias of Maine, and the Battle of Tinchebray', in D.F. Fleming and Janet M. Pope, *Henry I and the Anglo-Norman World. Studies in*

Memory of C. Warren Hollister, HSJ Special Volume 17, 2006 (Woodbridge, 2007), pp. 63–90.

Barton, R., *Lordship in the County of Maine, c.890–1160* (Woodbridge, 2004).

Barton, R., '"Zealous Anger" and the Renegotiation of Aristocratic Relationships in Eleventh- and Twelfth-century France', in Rosenwein, *Anger's Past*, pp. 153–70.

Bates, D.R., 'The Character and Career of Odo Bishop of Bayeux', *Speculum*, l (1975), pp. 1–20.

Bates, D.R., 'Charters and Historians of Britain and Ireland: Problems and Possibilities', in *Charters and Charter Scholarship in Britain and Ireland*, ed. Marie Therese Flanagan and Judith A. Green (London, 2005), pp. 1–14.

Bates, D.R., 'The Conqueror's Adolescence', *ANS*, 25 (2002), pp. 1–18.

Bates, D.R., 'The Conqueror's Earliest Historians and the Writing of his Biography', in *Writing Medieval Biography 750–1250. Essays in Honour of Professor Frank Barlow*, ed. D. Bates, Julia Crick and Sarah Hamilton (Woodbridge, 2006), pp. 129–41.

Bates, D.R., 'The Forged Charters of William the Conqueror and Bishop William of St Calais', in *Anglo-Norman Durham 1093–1193*, ed. D. Rollason, Margaret Harvey and M. Prestwich (Woodbridge, 1994), pp. 111–24.

Bates, D.R., 'Normandy and England after 1066', *EHR*, 104 (1989), pp. 851–80.

Bates, D.R., *Normandy before 1066* (London, 1982).

Bates, D., 'The Prosopographical Study of Anglo-Norman Royal Charters', in *Family Trees and the Roots of Politics*, ed. Katherine S.B. Keats-Rohan (Woodbridge, 1997), pp. 89–102.

Bates, D.R., 'Rouen from 900–1204: From Scandinavian Settlement to Angevin "Capital"', in J. Stratford, ed., *Medieval Art, Architecture and Archaeology at Rouen*, British Archaeological Association Conference Transactions (1993), pp. 1–11.

Bates, D.R., 'Writing a New Biography of William the Conqueror', in *State and Empire in British History*, ed. K. Kondo (Kyoto, 2003), pp. 9–20.

Bauduin, P., *La première Normandie (Xe–XIe siècles). Sur les frontières de la haute Normandie: identité et construction d'une principauté* (Caen, 2004).

Bauduin, P., 'Les sources de l'histoire du duché. Publications et inventaires récents', *Tabularia 'Études'*, 3 (2003), pp. 29–55.

Bennett, M., 'The Myth of the Military Supremacy of Knightly Cavalry', in *Armies, Chivalry and Warfare in Medieval Britain and France*, ed. M. Strickland (Stamford, 1998), pp. 304–16.

Bennett, M., 'Poetry as History? The *Roman de Rou* of Wace as a Source for the Norman Conquest', *ANS*, 5 (1983), pp. 21–39.

Bennett, M., 'Violence in Eleventh-century Normandy: Feud, Warfare and Politics', in G. Halsall, ed., *Violence and Society in the Early Medieval West* (Woodbridge, 1998), pp. 126–40.

Biddle, M., 'Seasonal Festivals and Residence: Winchester, Westminster, and Gloucester in the Tenth to Twelfth Centuries', *ANS*, 8 (1985), pp. 51–72.

Biddle, M., *The Tomb of Christ* (Stroud, 1999).

Blacker, Jean, *The Faces of Time. Portrayal of the Past in Old French and Latin Historical Narrative of the Anglo-Norman* Regnum (Austin, TX, 1994).

Bloch, M., *Feudal Society*, trans. L.A. Manyon, 2 vols., 2nd ed. (London, 1962).

Boas, A.J., *Jerusalem at the Time of the Crusades* (London, 2001).

Böhmer, H., *Kirche und Staat in England und in der Normandie im XI. und XII. Jahrhundert* (Leipzig, 1899).

Böhmer, H., 'Der sogenannte Serlo von Bayeux und die ihm zugeschreibenen Gedichte', *Neues Archiv der Gesellschaft für altere deutsche Geschichtskunde*, 22 (1897), pp. 701–38.

Boüard, M. de, *Guillaume le Conquérant* (Paris, 1984).

Bouchard, Constance Brittain, 'Consanguinity and Noble Marriages in the Tenth and Eleventh Centuries', *Speculum*, 56 (1981), pp. 268–87.

Bouchard, Constance Brittain, *Strong of Body, Brave and Noble. Chivalry and Society in Medieval France* (Ithaca, NY, and London, 1998).

Bouet, P., 'La *Revelatio ecclesiae sancti Michaelis* et son auteur', *Tabularia 'Études'*, no. 4 (2004), pp. 105–19.

Bouet, P. and Monique Dosdat, 'Les évêques normands de 985 à 1150', in P. Bouet and F. Neveux, eds., *Les évêques normands du XIe siècle* (Caen, 1995), pp. 19–37.

Bouet, P., Levy, B. and Neveux, F., eds., *The Bayeux Tapestry: Embroidering the Facts of History* (Caen, 2004).

Boussard, J., 'La seigneurie de Bellême aux Xe et XIe siècles', *Mélanges Louis Halphen* (Paris, 1951), pp. 43–54.

Bradbury, J., 'Battles in England and Normandy, 1066–1154,' in *ANS*, 6 (1984), pp. 1–12; reprinted in Strickland, *Anglo-Norman Warfare*, pp. 182–93.

Brett, M., 'John of Worcester and his Contemporaries', in *The Writing of History in the Middle Ages. Essays presented to Richard William Southern*, ed. R.H.C. Davis and J.M. Wallace-Hadrill (Oxford, 1981), pp. 101–26.

Briggs, C.F., 'Literacy, Reading, and Writing in the Medieval West', *JMH*, 26 (2000), pp. 397–420.

Brooke, C.N.L., *The Medieval Idea of Marriage* (Oxford, 1989).

Brown, S.D.B., 'Leavetaking: Lordship and Mobility in England and Normandy in the Twelfth Century', *History*, 79 (1994), pp. 199–215.

Brundage, J.A., 'An Errant Crusader: Stephen of Blois', *Traditio*, 16 (1960), pp. 380–95.

Brundage, J.A., *Law, Sex and Christian Society in Medieval Europe* (Chicago and London, 1987).

Buc, P., *The Dangers of Ritual. Between Early Medieval Texts and Social Scientific Theory* (Princeton, NJ, and London, 2001).

Buc, P., 'Political Rituals and Political Imagination in the Medieval West from the Fourth Century to the Eleventh', in *The Medieval World*, ed. P. Linehan and Janet L. Nelson (London, 2001), pp. 189–213

Bull, M., *Knightly Piety and the Lay Response to the First Crusade: The Limousin and Gascony, c.970–c.1130* (Oxford, 1993).

Bumke, J., *Courtly Culture. Literature and Society in the High Middle Ages* (Woodstock, NY, 2000).

Burke, P., *History and Social Theory* (Oxford, 1992).

Bynum, Caroline W., 'Did the 12th Century Discover the Individual?' in *eadem, Jesus as Mother. Studies in the Spirituality of the High Middle Ages* (Berkeley, CA, 1982), pp. 82–109.

Bynum, Caroline W., 'Why all the Fuss about the Body? A Medievalist's Perspective', *Critical Inquiry*, 22 (1995), pp. 27–31.

Callahan, D.F., 'Jerusalem in the Monastic Imaginations of the Early Eleventh Century' *HSJ*, 6 (1994), pp. 119–27.

Camille, M., 'The Image and the Self: Unwriting Late Medieval Bodies', in Sarah Kay and Miri Rubin, eds., *Framing Medieval Bodies* (Manchester, 1994), pp. 62–99.

Carr, D., 'Place and Time: On the Interplay of Historical Points of View', *History and Theory*, 40 (2001), pp. 153–67.

Carruthers, Mary, *The Book of Memory. A Study of Memory in Medieval Culture* (Cambridge, 1990).

Chaplais, P., *English Diplomatic Practice in the Middle Ages* (London, 2003).

Chibnall, Marjorie, 'Charter and Chronicle: The Use of Archive Sources by Norman Historians', in *Church and Government in the Middle Ages*, ed. C.N.L. Brooke, D.E. Luscombe, G.H. Martin and Dorothy M. Owen (Cambridge, 1976), pp.1–17.

Chibnall, Marjorie, *The Empress Matilda. Queen Consort, Queen Mother and Lady of the English* (Oxford, 1991).

Chibnall, Marjorie, 'Forgery in Narrative Charters', *Fälschungen im Mittelalter, Teil IV, Diplomatische Fälschungen (II)*, MGH Scriptores, 33, iv (Hanover, 1988), pp. 331–46.

Chibnall, Marjorie, 'Mercenaries and the *Familia Regis* under Henry I', *History*, 62 (1977), pp. 15–23.

Chibnall, Marjorie, 'Robert of Bellême and the Castle Tickhill', *Droit Privé et Institutions Régionales. Études historioques offertes à Jean Yver*, ed. R. Carabie, A. Guillot and L. Musset (Paris, 1976), pp. 151–6.

Chibnall, Marjorie, 'Women in Orderic Vitalis', *HSJ*, 2 (1990), pp. 105–21.

Chibnall, Marjorie, *The World of Orderic Vitalis* (Oxford, 1984; reprinted Woodbridge, 1996).

Christelow, Stephanie Mooers, '"Backers and Stabbers": Problems of Loyalty in Robert Curthose's Entourage', *Journal of British Studies*, 21 (1981), pp. 1–17.

Church, S.D., 'Some Aspects of the Royal Itinerary in the Twelfth Century', in *Thirteenth Century England*, 11 (2007), pp. 31–45.

Clanchy, M.T., *Abelard. A Medieval Life* (Oxford, 1997).

Clanchy, M.T., 'Did Henry III have a Policy?' *History*, 53 (1968), pp. 203–16.

Clanchy, M.T., 'Documenting the Self: Abelard and the Individual in History', *Historical Research*, 76 (2003), pp. 293–309.

Constable, C., *Letters and Letter Collections*, Typologie des Sources du Moyen Âge Occidental, Fasc. 17 (Turnhout, 1976).

Constable, G., 'Medieval Charters as a Source for the History of the Crusades', in P.W. Edbury, ed., *Crusade and Settlement* (Cardiff, 1985), pp. 73–89.

Coss, P.R., *The Knight in Medieval England* (Stroud, 1993).

Coulson, C., *Castles in Medieval Society. Fortresses in England, France, and Ireland in the Central Middle Ages* (Oxford, 2003).

Cowdrey, H.E.J., 'Bishop Ermenfrid of Sion and the Penitential Ordinance Following the Battle of Hastings', *JEH*, 20 (1969), pp. 225–42.

Cowdrey, H.E.J., 'Count Simon of Crépy's Monastic Conversion', in *Papauté, monachisme et théories politiques. 1: Le pouvoir et l'institution ecclésiale. Études d'histoire médiévale offertes à Michel Pacaut* (Lyons, 1994), pp. 253–266, reprinted in *idem, The Crusades and Latin Monasticism, 11th–12th Centuries* (Aldershot, 1999), no. XI.

Cowdrey, H.E.J., 'Death-bed Testaments', in *MGH Scriptores*, 33, iv (1988), pp. 703–24.

Cowdrey, H.E.J., *Lanfranc, Scholar, Monk and Archbishop* (Oxford, 2003).

Cowdrey, H.E.J., 'The Peace and Truce of God in the Eleventh Century', *P&P*, 46 (1970), pp. 42–67.

Cowdrey, H.E.J., *Pope Gregory VII, 1073–1085* (Oxford, 1998).

Cowdrey, H.E.J., 'Pope Gregory VII's "Crusading" Plan of 1074', in *Outremer*, ed. B.Z. Kedar, H.E. Mayer and R.C. Smail (1982), pp. 27–40.

Craster, H.H.E., 'The Red Book of Durham', *EHR*, 40 (1925), pp. 504–32.

Crouch, D., 'Beaumont, Robert de, Count of Meulan and First Earl of Leicester (d.1118), Magnate' *New Oxford DNB* (Oxford, 2004).

Crouch, D., *The Beaumont Twins. The Roots and Branches of Power in the Twelfth Century* (Cambridge, 1986).

Crouch, D., *The Birth of the Nobility. Constructing Aristocracy in England and France 900–1300* (Harlow, 2005).

Crouch, D., 'The Culture of Death in the Anglo-Norman World', in *Anglo-Norman Political Culture and the Twelfth-Century Renaissance*, ed. C. Warren Hollister (Woodbridge, 1997), pp. 157–80.

Crouch, D., 'A Norman *conventio* and Bonds of Lordship in the Middle Ages', in G. Garnett and J. Hudson, eds., *Law and Government in Medieval England and Normandy: Essays in Honour of Sir James Holt* (Cambridge, 1994), pp. 299–324.

Crouch, D., *The Normans. The History of a Dynasty* (London, 2002).

Crouch, D., 'Normans and Anglo-Normans: A Divided Aristocracy?' in D. Bates and Anne Curry, eds., *England and Normandy in the Middle Ages* (London, 1994), pp. 51–67.

Crouch, D., 'Robert de Beaumont, Count of Meulan and Leicester: His Lands, his Acts, and his Self-Image', in Fleming and Pope, eds., *Henry I and the Anglo-Norman World*, pp. 91–116.

Crouch, D., *Tournament* (London, 2005).

Dalton, P., 'Churchmen and the Promotion of Peace in King Stephen's Reign', *Viator*, 31 (2000), pp. 79–119.

Damian-Grint, P., *The New Historians of the Twelfth-Century Renaissance. Inventing Vernacular Authority* (Woodbridge, 1999).

David, C.W., *Robert Curthose, Duke of Normandy* (Cambridge, MA, 1920).

Davis, H.W.C., 'Waldric the Chancellor of Henry I', *EHR*, 26 (1911), pp. 84–9.

Davis, R.H.C., 'William of Jumièges, Robert Curthose and the Norman Succession', *EHR*, 95 (1980), pp. 597–606.

Declercq, G., 'Originals and Cartularies: The Organization of Archival Memory (Ninth–Eleventh Centuries)', in *Charters and the Use of the Written Word in Medieval Society*, ed. K. Heidecker (Turnhout, 2000), pp. 147–70.

Dibble, V.K., 'Four Types of Inference from Documents to Events', *History and Theory*, 3 (1963), pp. 203–21.

Dondi, Cristina, *The Liturgy of the Canons Regular of the Holy Sepulchre of Jerusalem. A Study and a Catalogue of the Manuscript Sources* (Turnhout, 2004).

Douglas, D.C., *William the Conqueror. The Norman Impact upon England* (London, 1964).

Duby, G., 'The Culture of the Knightly Class. Audience and Patronage', in R.L. Benson and G. Constable, eds., *Renaissance and Renewal in the Twelfth Century* (Oxford, 1982), pp. 248–62.

Duby, G., *The Knight, the Lady and the Priest. The Making of Modern Marriage in Medieval France*, trans. Barbara Bray (London, 1984).

Duby, G., 'Youth in Aristocratic Society. Northwestern France in the Twelfth Century', in *idem*, *The Chivalrous Society* (London, 1977), pp. 112–22.

Duff, Nora, *Matilda of Tuscany. La Gran Donna d'Italia* (London, 1909).

Duncan, A.A.M., 'The Foundation of St Andrews Cathedral Priory, 1140', *SHR*, 84 (2005), pp. 1–37.

Duncan, A.A.M., *The Kingship of the Scots, 842–1292* (Edinburgh, 2002).

Early, R., 'Le Château de Mayenne: les temoins archéologiques de l'évolution d'un centre de pouvoir entre le Xe et le XIIe siècle', *Château Gaillard*, 20 (2002), pp. 247–262.

Edbury, P.W. and J.G. Rowe, *William of Tyre: Historian of the Latin East* (Cambridge, 1988).

Edel, L., *Writing Lives. Principia Biographica* (New York, 1984).

Edgington, Susan B., 'The First Crusade: Reviewing the Evidence', in *The First Crusade. Origins and Impact*, ed. J. Phillips (Manchester, 1997), pp. 55–77.

Edgington, Susan B., 'Pagan Peverel: An Anglo-Norman Crusader', in *Crusade and Settlement*, ed. P.W. Edbury (Cardiff, 1985), pp. 93–7.

Eisenstadt, S.N., ed., *Max Weber, On Charisma and Institution Building. Selected Papers* (Chicago and London, 1968).

English, Barbara, 'William the Conqueror and the Anglo-Norman Succession', *Historical Research*, 64 (1991), pp. 221–36.

Evans, D., *Emotion. A Very Short Introduction* (Oxford, 2001).

Fanous, S. and Henrietta Leyser, eds., *Christina of Markyate. A Twelfth-century Holy Woman* (London, 2005).

Fenster, Thelma and D.L. Smail, eds., *Fama. The Politics of Talk and Reputation in Medieval Europe* (Ithaca, NY, 2003).

Fichtenau, H., *Living in the Tenth Century: Mentalities and Social Orders*, trans. P.J. Geary (Chicago, 1991).

Fliche, A., *Le Règne de Philippe Ier, roi de France (1060–1108)* (Paris, 1912).

Flori, J., *L'Essor de la Chevalerie, XIe–XIIe siècles* (Geneva, 1986).

Flori, J., 'Ideology and Motivations in the First Crusade', in Helen J. Nicholson, ed., *The Crusades* (Basingstoke, 2005), pp. 15–36.

Foley, M.P., 'Betrothals: Their Past, Present and Future', *Studia Liturgica*, 33.1 (2003), pp. 37–61.

Foreville, Raymonde, 'Un Chef de la première croisade: Arnoul Malecouronne', *Bulletin philologique et historique du comité des travaux historiques et scientifiques* (1953–4), pp. 377–90.

Foreville, Raymonde, 'The Synod of the Province of Rouen in the Eleventh and Twelfth

Centuries', in *Church and Government in the Middle Ages. Essays presented to C.R. Cheney on his 70th birthday*, ed. C.N.L. Brooke, D.E. Luscombe, G.H. Martin and Dorothy Owen (Cambridge, 1976), pp. 19–39.

France, J., 'Crusading Warfare', in *The Crusades*, ed. Helen J. Nicholson (Basingstoke, 2005), pp. 58–80.

France, J., 'The Election and Title of Godfrey de Bouillon', *Canadian Journal of History*, 18 (1983), pp. 321–9.

France, J., 'The Normans and Crusading', in R. Abels and B.S. Bachrach, eds., *The Normans and their Adversaries at War. Essays in memory of C. Warren Hollister* (Woodbridge, 2001), pp. 87–101.

France, J., *Victory in the East. A Military History of the First Crusade* (Cambridge, 1994).

France, J., *Western Warfare in the Age of the Crusades, 1000–1300* (London, 1999).

France, P. and W. St Clair, eds., *Mapping Lives. The Uses of Biography* (Oxford, 2002).

Freeman, E.A., *The Reign of William Rufus*, 2 vols. (Oxford, 1882).

Galbraith, V.H., 'The Literacy of the Medieval English Kings', *PBA*, 21 (1935), pp. 201–38.

Ganshof, F.-L., *La Flandre sous les premiers comtes* (Brussels, 1943).

Garnett, G., *Conquered England. Kingship, Succession and Tenure 1066–1166* (Oxford, 2007).

Garnett, G., 'Ducal Succession in Early Normandy', in *Law and Government in Medieval England*, ed. G. Garnett and J. Hudson (Cambridge, 1994), pp. 80–110.

Gathagan, Laura L., 'The Trappings of Power: the Coronation of Mathilda of Flanders', *HSJ*, 13 (1999), pp. 21–39.

Gauthiez, B., 'Hypothèses sur la fortification de Rouen au onzième siècle. Le donjon, la tour de Richard II et l'enceinte de Guillaume', *ANS*, 14 (1992), pp. 61–76.

Gauthiez, B., 'Paris, un Rouen capétien? (Développements comparés de Rouen et Paris sous les règnes de Henri II et Philippe Auguste)', *ANS* 16 (1994), pp. 117–36.

Gay, P., *Freud for Historians* (New York, 1985).

Gibson, Margaret, *Lanfranc of Bec* (Oxford, 1978).

Gillingham, J., '1066 and the Introduction of Chivalry into England', in G. Garnett and J. Hudson, eds., *Law and Government in Medieval England and Normandy. Essays in honour of Sir James Holt* (Cambridge, 1994), pp. 31–55.

Gillingham, J., 'Kingship, Chivalry and Love. Political and Cultural Values in the Earliest History Written in French: Geoffrey Gaimar's *Estoire des Engleis*', in *Anglo-Norman Political Culture and the Twelfth-century Renaissance*, ed. C. Warren Hollister (Woodbridge, 1997), pp. 33–58; reprinted in *The English in the Twelfth Century. Imperialism, National Identity and Political Values* (Woodbridge, 2000), pp. 233–58.

Gillingham, J., 'William the Bastard at War', in *Studies in Medieval History presented to R. Allen Brown*, ed. C. Harper-Bill and Janet L. Nelson (Woodbridge, 1989), pp. 141–58, reprinted in M. Strickland, ed., *Anglo-Norman Warfare* (Woodbridge, 1992), pp. 143–60.

Gillingham, J. and J.C. Holt, eds., *War and Government in the Middle Ages. Essays in honour of J.O. Prestwich* (Woodbridge, 1984).

Gittings, R., *The Nature of Biography* (Seattle, 1978).

Golding, B., 'The Religious Patronage of Robert and William of Mortain', in *Belief and Culture in the Middle Ages. Studies presented to Henry Mayr-Harting*, ed. R. Gameson and Henrietta Leyser (Oxford, 2001), pp. 211–30.

Golding, B., 'Robert of Mortain', *ANS*, 13 (1991), pp. 119–44.

Goody, J., *The Development of the Family and Marriage in Europe* (Cambridge, 1983).

Grabois, A., 'The Description of Jerusalem by William of Malmesbury: a Mirror of the Holy Land's Place in the Anglo-Norman Mind', *ANS*, 13 (1991), pp. 145–56.

Gransden, Antonia, *Historical Writing in England c.550 to c.1307* (London, 1974).

Green, Judith A., *The Aristocracy of Norman England* (Cambridge, 1997).

Green, Judith A., 'Fécamp et les rois anglo-normands', *Tabularia 'Études'*, 2 (2002), pp. 9–18.

Green, Judith A., *Henry I, King of England and Duke of Normandy* (Cambrudge, 2006).

Green, Judith A., 'Lords of the Norman Vexin', in Gillingham and Holt, eds., *War and Government*, pp. 46–63.

Green, Judith A., 'Robert Curthose Reassessed', *ANS*, 22 (1999), pp. 95–116.

Green, Judith A., 'Unity and Disunity in the Anglo-Norman State', *Historical Research*, 62 (1989), pp. 114–34.

Greenway, Diana, 'Authority, Convention and Observation in Henry of Huntingdon's *Historia Anglorum*', *ANS*, 18 (1995), pp. 105–21.

Greenway, Diana, 'Henry of Huntingdon and the Manuscripts of his *Historia Anglorum*', *ANS*, 9 (1986), pp. 103–26.

Gross, D.M., *The Secret History of Emotion. From Aristotle's Rhetoric to Modern Brain Science* (Chicago, 2006).

Guillot, O., *Le Comte d'Anjou et son entourage au XIe siècle*, 2 vols. (Paris, 1972).

Gurevich, A., *The Origins of European Individualism* (Oxford, 1995).

Hagenmeyer, H., *Chronologie de la Première Croisade, 1094–1100* (Paris, 1902; reprinted Hildesheim and New York, 1973).

Hagger, M., 'Kinship and Identity in Eleventh-century Normandy: the Case of Hugh de Grandmesnil, c. 1040–1098', *JMH*, 32 (2006), pp. 212–30.

Hamilton, B., 'The Impact of Crusader Jerusalem on Western Christendom', *Catholic Historical Review*, 80 (1994), pp. 695–713.

Hamilton, B., *The Latin Church in the Crusader States. The Secular Church* (London, 1980).

Hamilton, B., *Religion in the Medieval West* (London, 1986).

Hamilton, N., *Biography. A Brief History* (Cambridge, MA, 2007).

Hamilton, Sarah, 'Review Article: Early Medieval Rulers and their Modern Biographers', *EME*, 9 (2000), pp. 247–60.

Hanawalt, Barbara, 'Medievalists and the Study of Childhood', *Speculum*, 77 (2002), pp. 440–60.

Hanawalt, E. Albu, 'Dudo of St Quentin: the Heroic Past Imagined', *HSJ*, 6 (1994), pp. 111–18.

Harper-Bill, C., 'The Piety of the Anglo-Norman Knightly Class', *ANS*, 2 (1980), pp. 63–77, 173–76.

Haskins, C.H., *Norman Institutions* (New York, 1918).

Head, T., 'The Marriages of Christina of Markyate', *Viator*, 21 (1990), pp. 75–101.

Head, T. and R. Landes, eds., *The Peace of God. Social Violence and Religious Response in France around the Year 1000* (Ithaca and London, 1992).

Hemming, Jessica, '*Sellam Gestare*: Saddle-Bearing Punishments and the Case of Rhiannon', *Viator*, 28 (1997), pp. 45–64.

Herlihy, D., 'The Generation in Medieval History', *Viator*, 5 (1974), pp. 347–64.

Hicks, Sandy Burton, 'The Impact of William Clito upon the Continental Policies of Henry I of England', *Viator*, 10 (1979), pp. 1–21.

Hill, J.H., *Raymond IV of Saint-Gilles 1041 or 1042–1105* (Syracuse, 1962).

Hockey, F., 'The House of Redvers and its Monastic Foundations', *ANS*, 5 (1982), pp. 146–52.

Holdsworth, C.J., 'Peacemaking in the Twelfth Century', *ANS*, 19 (1997), pp. 1–17.

Hollister, C. Warren, 'The Anglo-Norman Civil War: 1101', *EHR*, 88 (1973), pp. 315–34; reprinted in *idem, Monarchy, Magnates and Institutions in the Anglo-Norman World* (London, 1986), pp. 77–96.

Hollister, C. Warren, 'The Campaign of 1102 against Robert of Bellême', in *Studies in Medieval History presented to R. Allen Brown*, ed. C. Harper-Bill, C.J. Holdsworth and Janet L. Nelson (Woodbridge, 1989), pp. 193–202.

Hollister, C.W., 'Courtly Culture and Courtly Style in the Anglo-Norman World', *Albion*, 20 (1988), pp. 1–18.

Hollister, C. Warren, *Henry I* (New Haven and London, 2001).

Hollister, 'Magnates and "Curiales" in Early Norman England', *Viator*, 4 (1973), pp. 115–22; reprinted in *idem, Monarchy, Magnates and Institutions in the Anglo-Norman World* (London, 1986), pp. 97–115.

Hollister, C. Warren, 'Normandy, France and the Anglo-Norman *regnum*', *Speculum*, 51 (1976), pp. 202–42, reprinted in *idem, Monarchy, Magnates and Institutions in the Anglo-Norman World* (London, 1986), pp. 17–57.

Hollister, C. Warren, 'The Rouen Riot and Conan's Leap', *Peritia*, 10 (1996), pp. 341–50.

Hollister, C. Warren, 'The Strange Death of William Rufus', *Speculum*, 48 (1973), pp. 637–53, reprinted in *idem, Monarchy, Magnates and Institutions in the Anglo-Norman World* (London, 1986), pp. 59–75.

Hollister, C. Warren, 'The Taming of a Turbulent Earl: Henry I and William of Warenne', *Réflexions Historiques*, 3 (1976), pp. 83–91, reprinted in *idem, Monarchy, Magnates and Institutions in the Anglo-Norman World* (London, 1986), pp. 137–44.

Hollister, C. Warren, 'William Clito', in *New Oxford DNB* (Oxford, 2004).

Hollister, C.W., and J.W. Baldwin, 'The Rise of Administrative Kingship: Henry I and Philip Augustus', *AHR*, 83 (1978), pp. 867–905.

Holt, J.C., *Colonial England, 1066–1215* (London, 1997).

Holt, J.C., 'Politics and Property in Early Medieval England', *P&P*, 57 (1972), pp. 3–52; 65 (1974), pp. 130–2, reprinted in *idem, Colonial England, 1066–1215* (London, 1997), pp. 113–59, at appendix 2, pp. 149–51.

Hooper, N., 'Edgar the Aetheling: Anglo-Saxon Prince, Rebel and Crusader', *ASE*, 14 (1985), pp. 197–214.

Housely, N., *Contesting the Crusades* (Oxford, 2006).

Houts, Elisabeth M.C. van, 'The Anglo-Flemish Treaty of 1101', *ANS*, 21 (1998), pp. 167–74.

Houts, Elisabeth M.C. van, 'L'exil dans l'espace anglo-normand', in P. Bouet and Véronique Gazeau, eds., *La Normandie et l'Angleterre au Moyen Âge* (Caen, 2003), pp. 117–27.

Houts, Elisabeth M.C. van, 'Historical Writing', in *A Companion to the Anglo-Norman World*, ed. C. Harper-Bill and Elisabeth van Houts (Woodbridge, 2003), pp. 103–34.

Houts, Elisabeth M.C. van, 'Historiography and Hagiography at Saint-Wandrille: the *Inventio et Miracula sancti Vulfranni*', *ANS*, 12 (1990), pp. 233–51.

Houts, Elisabeth M.C. van, 'Latin Poetry and the Anglo-Norman Court 1066–1135: the *Carmen de Hastingæ proelio*', *JMH*, 15 (1989), pp. 39–62.

Houts, Elisabeth M.C. van, *Local and Regional Chronicles*, Typologie des Sources du Moyen Âge Occidental, Fasc.74 (Turnhout, 1995).

Houts, Elisabeth M.C. van, *Memory and Gender in Medieval Europe, 900–1200* (London, 1999).

Houts, Elisabeth M.C. van, 'The Norman Conquest through European Eyes', *EHR*, 110 (1995), pp. 832–53.

Houts, Elisabeth M.C. van, 'Normandy and Byzantium in the Eleventh Century', *Byzantion*, 55 (1985), pp. 544–59.

Houts, Elisabeth M.C. van, trans. and ed., *The Normans in Europe* (Manchester, 2000).

Houts, Elisabeth M.C. van, 'The Origins of Herleva, Mother of William the Conqueror', *EHR*, 101 (1986), pp. 399–404.

Houts, Elisabeth M.C. van, 'Robert of Torigni as Genealogist', in *Studies in Medieval History presented to R. Allen Brown*, ed. C. Harper-Bill, C.J. Holdsworth, Janet Nelson (Woodbridge, 1989), pp. 215–33.

Houts, Elisabeth M.C. van, 'The Vocabulary of Exile and Outlawry in the North Sea Area around the First Millennium', in Laura Napran and Elisabeth M.C. van Houts, eds., *Exile in the Middles Ages* (Turnhout, 2004), pp. 13–28.

Houts, Elisabeth M.C. van, 'Wace as Historian', in *Family Trees and the Roots of Politics*, ed. Katherine S.B. Keats-Rohan (Woodbridge, 1997), pp. 103–32, reprinted in *The History of the Norman People. Wace's Roman de Rou*, trans. G.S. Burgess (Woodbridge, 2004), xxxv–lxii.

Houts, Elisabeth M.C. van, 'The Warenne View of the Past 1066–1203', *ANS*, 26 (2004), pp. 103–21.

Hudson, J., 'Henry I and Counsel', in *The Medieval State. Essays presented to James Campbell*, ed. J.R. Maddicott and D.M. Palliser (London, 2000), pp. 109–26.

Huneycutt, Lois L., *Matilda of Scotland. A Study in Medieval Queenship* (Woodbridge, 2003).

Isaac, S., 'The Problem with Mercenaries', in *The Circle of War in the Middle Ages. Essays on Medieval Military and Naval History*, ed. D.J. Kagay and L.J.A. Villalon (Woodbridge, 1999), pp. 101–10.

Itnyre, Cathy Jorgensen, 'The Emotional Universe of Medieval Icelandic Fathers and Sons', in *eadem.*, ed., *Medieval Family Roles* (New York and London, 1996), pp. 173–96.

Itnyre, Cathy Jorgensen, ed., *Medieval Family Roles* (New York and London, 1996).

Jaeger, C.S., *The Origins of Courtliness. Civilising Trends and the Formation of Courtly Ideals, 939–1210* (Philadelphia, PA, 1985).

Jahn, W., *Untersuchungen zur normannischer Herrschaft in Süditalien (1040–1100)* (Frankfurt-am-Main and New York, 1989).

Johnson, E., 'The Process of Norman Exile into Southern Italy', in Laura Napran and Elisabeth van Houts, eds., *Exile in the Middles Ages* (Turnhout, 2004), pp. 29–38.

Jolliffe, J.E.A., *Angevin Kingship*, 2nd ed. (London, 1963).

Jussen, B., *Spiritual Kinship as Social Practice. Godparenthood and Adoption in the Early Middle Ages*, trans. Pamela Selwyn (Cranbury, NJ, and London, 2000).

Kealey, E.J., *Roger of Salisbury, Viceroy of England* (Berkeley and London, 1972).

Keen, M., *Chivalry* (New Haven and London, 1984).

King, E.J., 'Dispute Settlement in Anglo-Norman England', *ANS*, 14 (1992), pp. 115–30.

King, E.J., 'Stephen of Blois, Count of Mortain and Boulogne', *EHR*, 115 (2000), pp. 271–96 at 276–7.

Knappen, M.M., 'Robert II of Flanders in the First Crusade', in L.J. Paetow, ed., *The Crusades and Other Historical Essays presented to Dana C. Munro by his former students* (New York, 1928), pp. 79–100.

Kosto, A.J., 'Hostages in the Carolingian World (714–840)', *EME*, 11 (2002), pp. 123–47.

Koziol, G., *Begging Pardon and Favour. Ritual and Political Order in Early Medieval France* (Ithaca, NY, 1992).

Koziol, G., 'Political Culture', in M. Bull, ed., *France in the Central Middle Ages* (Oxford, 2002), pp. 43–76.

Kupper, J.-L., 'L'oncle maternel et le neveu dans la société du Moyen Age', in *Académie royale de Belgique. Bulletin de la classe des lettres et des sciences morales et politiques*, ser. 6, 15:7–12, (2004), pp. 247–62.

Latouche, R., 'Essai de critique sur la continuation des *Actus Pontificum Cenomannis in urbe degentium*', *Le Moyen Age*, 11 (1907), pp. 225–75.

Latouche, R., *Histoire du Comté du Maine pendant le Xe et le XIe siècle* (Paris, 1910).

Lavelle, R., 'The Use and Abuse of Hostages in Later Anglo-Saxon England', *EME*, 14 (2006), pp. 269–96.

Lawson, M.K., *The Batlle of Hastings 1066* (Stroud, 2002).

Le Goff, J., 'The Symbolic Ritual of Vassalage', in *idem, Time, Work and Culture in the Middle Ages*, trans. A. Goldhammer (Chicago, 1980), pp. 237–87.

Le Goff, J., *My Quest for the Middle Ages*, trans. R. Veasey (Edinburgh, 2003); trans. from J. Le Goff, *A la recherche du Moyen Age*, with the collaboration of J.-M. de Montremy (Paris, 2003).

Le Hardy, G., 'Le dernier des ducs normands: Étude de critique historique sur Robert Courte-Heuse', *Bulletin de la Société des Antiquaires de Normandie*, 10 (Caen, 1882), pp. 3–184.

Le Patourel, J., 'Geoffrey of Montbray, Bishop of Coutances, 1049–93', *EHR*, 59 (1944), pp. 129–61.

Le Patourel, J., *The Norman Empire* (Oxford, 1976).

Le Patourel, J., 'The Norman Succession, 996–1135', *EHR*, 86 (1971), pp. 225–50.

Le Patourel, J., *Normandy and England, 1066–1144*, Stenton Lecture 1970 (Reading, 1971), reprinted in *idem, Feudal Empires Norman and Plantagenet* (London, 1984), no. VII.

Lemesle, B., *La société aristocratique dans le Haut-Maine (XIe–XIIe siècles)* (Rennes, 1999).

Lewis, C.P., 'Warenne, William (I) de, First Earl of Surrey (d.1088)', *Oxford DNB* (Oxford, 2004).

Leyser, K., 'Money and Supplies on the First Crusade', in *idem, Communications and Power in Medieval Europe. The Gregorian Revolution and Beyond*, ed. T. Reuter (London and Rio Grande, 1994), pp. 77–95.

Lindholm, C., *Charisma* (Oxford, 1990).

Lo Prete, Kimberly A., 'Adela of Blois and Ivo of Chartres', *ANS*, 14 (1992), pp. 131–52.

Lo Prete, Kimberly A., 'Adela of Blois as Mother and Countess', in *Medieval Mothering*, ed. J.C. Parsons and Bonnie Wheeler (New York, 1996), pp. 313–33.

Lo Prete, Kimberly A., *Adela of Blois. Countess and Lord (c.1067–1137)* (Dublin, 2007).

Lo Prete, Kimberly A., 'Adela of Blois: Familial Alliances and Female Lordship', in *Aristocratic Women in Medieval France*, ed. T. Evergates (Philadelphia, PA, 1999), pp. 7–43, 180–200.

Lo Prete, Kimberly A., 'The Anglo-Norman Card of Adela of Blois', *Albion* 22 (1990), pp. 569–89.

Loud, G.A., *The Age of Robert Guiscard. Southern Italy and the Norman Conquest* (Harlow, 2000).

Loud, G.A., 'Norman Italy and the Holy Land', in *The Horns of Hattin*, ed. B.Z. Kedar (Jerusalem, 1992), pp. 49–62.

Loyd, L.C., *The Origins of Some Anglo-Norman Families*, ed. C.T. Clay and D.C. Douglas, Harleian Society, 103 (1951).

Lynch, J.H., *Christianizing Kinship. Ritual Sponsorship in Anglo-Saxon England* (Ithaca, NY, 1998).

Macdonald, A.J., *Lanfranc. A Study of his Life, Work and Writing*, 2nd ed. (London, 1944).

MacLean, S., *Kingship and Politics in the Late Ninth Century. Charles the Fat and the End of the Carolingian Empire* (Cambridge, 2003).

MacMullen, R., *Feelings in History, Ancient and Modern* (New Haven, CT, 2003).

Maguire, H., ed., *Byzantine Court Culture from 829 to 1204* (Washington DC, 1997).

Maillefer, J.-M., 'Une famille aristocratique aux confins de la Normandie: Les Géré au XIe siècle', in *Autour du pouvoir ducal normand Xe–XIIe siècles*, ed. L. Musset, J.-M. Bouvris and J.-M. Maillefer (Caen, 1985), pp. 175–206.

Markowski, M., '*Crucesignatus*: Its Origins and Early Usage', *JMH*, 10 (1984), pp. 157–65.

Martindale, Jane, 'Secular Propaganda and Aristocratic Values: The Autobiographies of Count Fulk le Réchin of Anjou and Count William of Poitou, Duke of Aquitaine', in *Writing Medieval Biography 750–1250*, ed. David Bates, Julia Crick and Sarah Hamilton (Woodbridge, 2006), pp. 143–59.

Mason, Emma, *The House of Godwine. The History of a Dynasty* (London, 2004).

Mason, Emma, *St Wulfstan of Worcester, c.1008–1095* (Oxford, 1990).

Mason, Emma, *William II. Rufus, the Red King* (Stroud, 2005).

McCrank, L.J., 'Norman Crusaders in the Catalan Reconquest: Robert Burdet and the Principality of Tarragona', *JMH*, 7 (1981), pp. 67–82.

McDonough, C.J., 'Classical Latin Satire and the Poets of Northern France: Baudri of Bourgueil, Serlo of Bayeux, and Warner of Rouen', in *Latin Culture in the Eleventh Century: Proceedings of the Third International Conference on Medieval Latin Studies, Cambridge, September 9–12, 1998*, ed. M.W. Herren, C.J. McDonough and R.G. Arthur, Publications of the Journal of Medieval Latin, 5, 2 vols. (Turnhout, 2002), II, pp. 102–15.

McGurk, P., 'Worcester, John of (fl.1095–1140)', *Oxford DNB* (Oxford, 2004).

McQueen, W.B., 'Relations between the Normans and Byzantium, 1071–1112', *Byzantion*, 56 (1986), pp. 427–76.

Mooers, Stephanie L., '"Backers and Stabbers": Problems of Loyalty in Robert Curthose's Entourage', *Journal of British Studies*, 21 (1981), pp. 1–17.

Moore, R.I., *The First European Revolution, c. 975–1215* (Oxford, 2000).

Morgan, Prys, *Iolo Morgannwg* (Cardiff, 1975).

Morgan, Prys, 'From a Death to a View: The Hunt for the Welsh Past in the Romantic Period', in *The Invention of Tradition*, ed. E. Hobsbawm and T. Ranger (Cambridge, 1983), pp. 43–100.

Morillo, S., ed., *The Battle of Hastings* (Woodbridge, 1996).

Morris, C., 'The *Gesta Francorum* as Narrative History', *Reading Medieval Studies*, 19 (1993), pp. 55–71.

Morris, C., 'Policy and Visions: The Case of the Holy Lance at Antioch', in Gillingham and Holt, eds., *War and Government*, pp. 33–45.

Morrison, K., *Marx, Durkheim, Weber. Formations of Modern Social Thought* (London, 1995).

Moss, V., 'Normandy and England: the Pipe Roll Evidence', in *England and Normandy in the Middle Ages*, ed. D. Bates and Anne Curry (London, 1994), pp. 185–95.

Muldoon, J., 'Crusading and Canon Law', in Helen J. Nicholson, ed., *The Crusades* (Basingstoke, 2005), pp. 37–57.

Munro, D.C., 'A Crusader', *Speculum*, 7 (1932), pp. 321–35.

Murray, A.V., 'The Army of Godfrey of Bouillon, 1096–1099: Structure and Dynamics of a Contingent on the First Crusade', *Revue belge de philologie et d'histoire*, 70 (1992), pp. 301–29.

Murray, A.V., 'Money and Logistics in the Forces of the First Crusade: Coinage, Bullion, Service and Supply, 1096–99', in *Logistics of Warfare in the Age of the Crusades*, ed. J.H. Pryor (London, 2006), pp. 229–49.

Murray, A.V., 'Prosopography', in Helen J. Nicholson, ed., *The Crusades* (Basingstoke, 2005), pp. 109–29.

Murray, A.V., 'The Title of Godfrey of Bouillon as Ruler of Jerusalem', *Collegium Médiévale: Interdisciplinary Journal of Medieval Research*, 3 (1990), pp. 163–78.

Musset, L., 'Aux origines d'une classe dirigeante: les Tosny, grands barons normands du Xe au XIIe siècles', *Francia*, 5 (1978), pp. 45–80.

Musset, L., 'Recherches sur les pèlerins et les pèlerinages en Normandie jusqu'à la première Croisade', *AN*, 12 (1962), pp. 127–50.

Nadel, Ira B., *Biography. Fiction, Fact and Form* (London, 1984).

Napran, Laura, 'Exile in Context', in Laura Napran and Elisabeth van Houts, eds., *Exile in the Middles Ages* (Turnhout, 2004), pp. 1–9.

Nelson, Janet L., *Charles the Bald* (London, 1992).

Nelson, Janet L., 'Family, Gender and Sexuality in the Middle Ages', in M. Bentley, ed., *Companion to Historiography* (London, 1997), pp. 153–76.

Nelson, Janet L., 'The Problematic in the Private', *Social History*, 15 (1990), pp. 355–64.

Nelson, Janet L., 'Writing Early Medieval Biography', *History Workshop Journal*, 50 (2000), pp. 129–36.

Nicholas, D., *Medieval Flanders* (London, 1992).

Nicholas, Karen S., 'Countesses as Rulers in Flanders', in *Aristocratic Women in Medieval France*, ed. T. Evergates (Philadelphia, PA, 1999), pp. 111–37.

Nicholson, R.L., *Tancred: A Study of his Career and Work in Relation to the First Crusade and the Establishment of the Latin States in Syria and Palestine* (Chicago, 1940).

Nicolle, N., *Medieval Warfare Source Book, Volume I: Warfare in Western Christendom* (London, 1995).

Nip, R., 'The Political Relations between England and Flanders (1066–1128)', *ANS*, 21 (1998), pp. 145–67.

Offler, H.S., 'The Tractate *De iniusta vexacione Willelmi episcopi primi*', *EHR*, 66 (1951), pp. 321–41 reprinted in *idem, North of the Tees. Studies in Medieval British History*, ed. A.J. Piper and A.I. Doyle (Aldershot, 1996), VI.

Offler, H.S., 'William of St Calais, First Norman Bishop of Durham', *TAASDN*, 10 (1950), pp. 258–79.

Orme, N., *From Childhood to Chivalry. The Education of the English Kings and Aristocracy 1066–1530* (London, 1984).

Orme, N., *Medieval Children* (New Haven and London, 2001).

Painter, S., *William Marshal, Knight-Errant, Baron, and Regent of England* (Baltimore, MD, 1933).

Paris, G., 'Robert Courte-Heuse à la première croisade', *Comptes-rendus des séances de l'Académie des inscriptions et belles-lettres*, 34 (1890), pp. 207–12.

Parke, Catherine N., *Biography. Writing Lives* (New York and London, 2002).

Parkes, M.B., 'The Literacy of the Laity', in *idem, Scribes, Scripts and Readers. Studies in the Communication, Presentation and Dissemination of Medieval Texts* (London, 1991), pp. 275–97.

Parsons, J. Carmi and Wheeler, Bonnie, eds., *Medieval Mothering* (New York and London, 1996).

Partner, Nancy F., 'The Family Romance of Guibert of Nogent: His Story/Her Story', in Parsons and Wheeler, *Medieval Mothering*, pp. 359–79.

Partner, Nancy F., 'The Hidden Self: Psychoanalysis and the Textual Unconscious', in *eadem*, ed., *Writing Medieval History* (London, 2005), pp. 42–64.

Partner, Nancy, *Serious Entertainments: The Writing of History in Twelfth-Century England* (Chicago, 1977).

Paxton, F.S., *Christianizing Death. The Creation of a Ritual Process in Early Medieval Europe* (Ithaca and London, 1990).

Peirce, I., 'The Knight, his Arms and Armour in the Eleventh and Twelfth Centuries', in *The Ideals and Practice of Medieval Knighthood I*, eds. C. Harper-Bill and Ruth Harvey (Woodbridge, 1986), pp.152–64.

Piponnier, Françoise and Perrine Mane, *Dress in the Middle Ages* (New Haven and London, 1997).

Porges, W., 'The Clergy, the Poor and the Non-combatants on the First Crusade', *Speculum*, 21 (1946), pp. 1–23.

Power, D., *The Norman Frontier in the Twelfth and Early Thirteenth Centuries* (Cambridge, 2004).

Power, Eileen, *Medieval People* (London, 1924).

Prawer, J., 'The Jerusalem the Crusaders Captured: Contribution to the Medieval Topography of the City', in Edbury, *Crusade and Settlement*, pp. 1–16.

Pryor, J.H., 'Introduction: Modelling Bohemond's March to Thessalonike', in *idem*, *Logistics of Warfare in the Age of the Crusades* (London, 2006), pp. 1–24.

Pryor, J.H., 'The Oaths of the Leaders of the First Crusade to the Emperor Alexius I Comnenus. Fealty, Homage – Pistis, Douleia', *Parergon*, n.s. 2 (1984), pp. 111–32.

Purdie, Rhiannon, 'Dice-games and the Blasphemy of Prediction', in *Medieval Futures. Attitudes to the Future in the Middle Ages*, ed. J.A. Burrow and I.P. Wei (Woodbridge, 2000), pp. 167–84.

Raby, F.J.E., *A History of Secular Latin Poetry in the Middle Ages*, 2nd ed., 2 vols. (Oxford, 1957).

Ray, R.D., 'Orderic Vitalis and his Readers', *Studia Monastica*, 14 (1972), pp. 17–33.

Reddy, W.M., *The Navigation of Feeling. A Framework for the History of Emotions* (Cambridge, 2001).

Renoux, Annie, 'Château et pouvoir dans le comté du Maine: Mayenne du dernier tiers du IXe au début du XIIe siècle (c.870–1120)' *Château Gaillard*, 20 (2002), pp. 235–45.

Reuter, T., 'Assembly Politics in Western Europe from the Eighth Century to the Twelfth', in P. Linehan and Janet L. Nelson, eds., *The Medieval World* (London, 2001), pp. 432–50.

Rigg, A.G., *History of Anglo-Latin Literature 1066–1422* (Cambridge, 1992).

Riley-Smith, J., *The First Crusade and the Idea of Crusading* (London, 1993).

Riley-Smith, J., *The First Crusaders, 1095–1131* (Cambridge, 1997).

Riley-Smith, J., 'The State of Mind of Crusaders to the East' in *idem*, ed., *Oxford History of the Crusades* (Oxford, 1997), pp. 66–90.

Riley-Smith, J., 'The Title of Godfrey of Bouillon', *BIHR*, 52 (1979), pp. 83–6.

Ritchie, R.L.G., *The Normans in England before Edward the Confessor. An Inaugural Lecture* (Exeter, 1948).

Roberts, B., *Biographical Research* (Buckingham, 2002).

Robinson, I.S., *The Papacy, 1073–1198* (Cambridge, 1990).

Robinson, J. Armitage, *Gilbert Crispin, Abbot of Westminster. A Study of the Abbey under Norman Rule* (Cambridge, 1911).

Rosenthal, J.T., 'The Education of the Early Capetians', *Traditio*, 25 (1969), pp. 366–76.

Rosenwein, Barbara, ed., *Anger's Past. The Social Uses of an Emotion in the Middle Ages* (Ithaca, NY, and London, 1998).

Rosenwein, Barbara, 'Controlling Paradigms', in *eadem*, ed., *Anger's Past*, pp. 233–47.

Rosenwein, Barbara H., *Emotional Communities in the Early Middle Ages* (Ithaca, NY, and London, 2006).

Rosenwein, Barbara, 'Writing without Fear about Early Medeival Emotions', *EME* 10 (2) (2001), pp. 229–34.

Rowe, J.G., 'Paschal II and the Relation between the Spiritual and Temporal Powers in the Kingdom of Jerusalem', *Speculum*, 32 (1957), pp. 470–501.

Rubenstein, J., 'Biography and Autobiography in the Middle Ages', in *Writing Medieval History*, ed. Nancy Partner (London, 2005), pp. 22–41.

Sanders, I.J., *English Baronies: A Study of their Origin and Descent (1086–1327)* (Oxford, 1960).

Scott, F.S., 'Earl Waltheof of Northumbria', *Archaeologia Aeliana*, 4th ser., 30 (1952), pp. 149–213.

Searle, Eleanor, 'Fact and Pattern in Heroic History: Dudo of St Quentin', *Viator*, 15 (1984), pp. 75–85.

Shahar, Shulamith, *Childhood in the Middle Ages* (London, 1990).

Sharpe, R., '1088 – William II and the Rebels', *ANS*, 24 (2004), pp. 139–57.

Shepard, J., 'Byzantine Diplomacy, A.D. 800–1205: Means and Ends', in *Byzantine Diplomacy*, ed. J. Shepard and S. Franklin (Aldershot, 1992), pp. 41–71.

Shepard, J., 'The Uses of the Franks in Eleventh-century Byzantium', *ANS*, 15 (1993), pp. 275–305.

Shopkow, Leah, 'The Carolingian World of Dudo of St Quentin', *JMH*, 15 (1989), pp. 19–37.

Shopkow, Leah, *History and Community. Norman Historical Writing in the Eleventh and Twelfth Centuries* (Washington DC, 1997).

Short, I., 'Gaimar, Geffrei (fl.1136–1137)', *Oxford DNB* (Oxford, 2004).

Simek, R., *Heaven and Earth in the Middle Ages*, trans. Angela Hall (Woodbridge, 1996).

Skidelsky, R., 'Only Connect: Biography and Truth', in *The Troubled Face of Biography*, ed. E. Homberger and J. Charmley (London, 1988), pp. 1–16.

Skinner, Patricia, 'Gender and Memory in Medieval Italy', in Elisabeth van Houts, ed., *Medieval Memories. Men, Women and the Past, 700–1300* (Harlow, 2001), pp. 36–52.

Skinner, Patricia, *Health and Medicine in Early Medieval Southern Italy*, The Medieval Mediterranean, II (Leiden, 1997).

Skinner, Patricia, *Women in Medieval Italian Society* (Harlow, 2001).

Smail, R.C., *Crusading Warfare, 1097–1193*, 2nd ed. (Cambridge, 1997).

Southern, R.W., 'Aspects of the European Tradition of Historical Writing, 4: The Sense of the Past', *TRHS*, 5th ser., 23 (1973), pp. 243–63.

Southern, R.W., *Saint Anselm. A Portrait in a Landscape* (Cambridge, 1990).

Spear, D.S., *The Personnel of the Norman Cathedrals during the Ducal Period, 911–1204* (London, 2006).

Spear, D.S., 'William Bona Anima, Abbot of St Stephen's Caen (1070–79)', *HSJ*, 1 (1989), pp. 51–60.

Stafford, Pauline, 'The Meanings of Hair in the Anglo-Norman World: Masculinity, Reform, and National Identity', in Mathilde van Dijk and Renée Nip, eds., *Saints, Scholars, and Politicians. Gender as a Tool in Medieval Studies. Festschrift in honour of Anneke Mulder-Bakker on the occasion of her sixty-fifth birthday*, Medieval Church Studies, 15 (Turnhout, 2005), pp. 153–71.

Stafford, Pauline, *Queen Emma and Queen Edith. Queenship and Women's Power in Eleventh-century England* (Oxford, 1997).

Stafford, Pauline, *Queens, Concubines and Dowagers. The King's Wife in the Early Middle Ages* (Leicester, 1998).

Stafford, Pauline, 'Review article: Parents and Children in the Early Middle Ages', *EME*, 10 (2001), pp. 257–71.

Stearns, P.N. and Stearns, Carol Z., 'Emotionology: Clarifying the History of Emotions and Emotional Standards', *AHR*, 90 (1985), pp. 813–36.

Stewart, F.H., *Honor* (Chicago, 1994).

Stock, B., *The Implications of Literacy. Written Language and Models of Interpretation in the Eleventh and Twelfth Centuries* (Princeton, NJ, 1983).

Stone, L., *The Family, Sex and Marriage in England 1500–1800* (London, 1977; abridged and revised 1979).

Strevett, N., 'The Anglo-Norman Civil War of 1101 Reconsidered', *ANS*, 26 (2004), pp. 159–75.

Strickland, M., 'Réconcilation ou humiliation? La suppression de la rébellion aristocratique dans les royaumes anglo-normand et angevin', in Catherine Bougy and Sophie Poirey, eds., *Images de la contestation du pouvoir dans le monde normand (Xe–XVIIIe siècle)* (Caen, 2007), pp. 65–78.

Strickland, M., *War and Chivalry. The Conduct and Perception of War in England and Normandy, 1066–1217* (Cambridge, 1996).

Tabuteau, Emily Zack, 'The Family of Moulins-la-Marche', *Medieval Prosopography*, 13.1 (1992), pp. 29–65.

Tabuteau, Emily Z., 'Punishments in Eleventh-century Normandy', in W.C. Brown and P. Górecki, eds., *Conflict in Medieval Europe. Changing Perspectives on Society and Culture* (London, 2003), pp. 131–49.

Tabuteau, Emily Z., *Transfers of Property in Eleventh-century Norman Law* (Chapel Hill and London, 1988).

Tanner, Heather J., *Families, Friends and Allies. Boulogne and Politics in Northern France and England, c.879–1160* (Leiden, 2004).

Thomas, Hugh M., *The English and the Normans. Ethnic Hostility, Assimilation, and Identity 1066–c.1220* (Oxford, 2003).

Thompson, J.W., *The Literacy of the Laity in the Middle Ages* (Berkeley, CA, 1939; reprinted New York, 1963).

Thompson, Kathleen, 'Affairs of State: The Illegitimate Children of Henry I', *JMH*, 29 (2003), pp. 129–51.

Thompson, Kathleen, 'Bellême, Robert de, Earl of Shrewsbury and Count of Ponthieu (bap. c.1057, d. in or after 1130), Magnate', *Oxford DNB* (Oxford, 2004).

Thompson, Kathleen, 'Family and Influence to the South of Normandy in the Eleventh Century', *JMH*, 11 (1985), pp. 215–226.

Thompson, Kathleen, 'The Lords of Laigle: Ambition and Insecurity on the Borders of Normandy', *ANS*, 18 (1995), pp. 177–99.

Thompson, Kathleen, 'Orderic Vitalis and Robert of Bellême', *JMH*, 20 (1994), pp. 133–41.

Thompson, Kathleen, *Power and Border Lordship in Medieval France. The County of the Perche, 1000–1226* (Woodbridge, 2002).

Thompson, Kathleen, 'Robert [called Robert Curthose], Duke of Normandy (b. in or after 1050, d. 1134), Prince and Crusader', *Oxford DNB* (Oxford, 2004).

Thompson, Kathleen, 'Robert of Bellême Reconsidered', *ANS*, 13 (1990), pp. 263–86.

Thomson, R.M., *William of Malmesbury*, revised ed. (Woodbridge, 2003).

Truax, Jean A., 'Anglo-Norman Women at War: Valiant Soldiers, Prudent Strategists or Charismatic Leaders?' in *The Circle of War in the Middle Ages. Essays on Medieval Military and Naval History*, ed. D.J. Kagay and L.J.A. Villalon (Woodbridge, 1999), pp. 111–25.

Turner, R.V., 'The Children of Anglo-Norman Royalty and their Upbringing', *Medieval Prosopography*, 11 (1990), pp. 17–52.

Tyerman, C.J., *England and the Crusades 1095–1588* (Chicago and London, 1988).

Ullmann, W., *The Individual and Society in the Middle Ages* (London, 1967).

Verlinden, C., *Robert I le Frison* (Antwerp and Paris, 1935).

Walker, Garthine, 'Psychoanalysis and History', in *Writing History. Theory and Practice*, ed. S. Berger, H. Feldner and K. Passmore (London, 2003), pp. 141–60.

Walmsley, J., 'The Early Abbesses, Nuns and Female Tenants of the Abbey of Holy Trinity, Caen', *JEH*, 48:3 (1997), pp. 425–44.

Warner, D.A., 'Ritual and Memory in the Ottonian Reich: The Ceremony of Adventus', *Speculum*, 76 (2001), pp. 255–83.

Warren, W.L., 'Biography and the Medieval Historian', in *Medieval Historical Writing in the Christian and Islamic Worlds*, ed. D.O. Morgan (London, 1982), pp. 5–18.

Warren, W.L., *Henry II* (London, 1973).

Webber, N., *The Evolution of Norman Identity, 911–1154* (Woodbridge, 2005).

Weidemann, Magarete, *Geschichte des Bistums Le Mans von der Spätantike bis zur Karolingerzeit: Actus Pontificum Cenomannis in Urbe Degentium und Gesta Aldrici*, 3 vols. (Mainz, 2002).

West, F.J., 'The Colonial History of the Norman Conquest', *History*, 84 (1999), pp. 219–36.

White, G.H., 'The First House of Bellême', *TRHS*, 22 (1940), pp. 67–99.

Wightman, W.E., *The Lacy Family in England and Normandy 1066–1194* (Oxford, 1966).

Williams, Ann, *Æthelred the Unready. The Ill-Counselled King* (London, 2003).

Williams, Ann, *The English and the Norman Conquest* (Woodbridge, 1995).

Williams, Ann, 'The King's Nephew: the Family, Career and Connections of Ralph, Earl of Hereford', in *Studies in Medieval History presented to R. Allen Brown*, ed. C. Harper-Bill, C. Holdsworth and Janet L. Nelson (Woodbridge, 1989), pp. 327–43.

Williams, G.H., *The Norman Anonymous of 1100 A.D.* (Cambridge, MA, 1951).

Williams, S., *Emotion and Social Theory* (London, 2001).

Wolf, K.B., 'Crusade and Narrative: Bohemond and the *Gesta Francorum*', *JMH*, 17 (1991), pp. 207–16.

Woodcock, T. and J.M. Robinson, *The Oxford Guide to Heraldry* (Oxford, 1988), pp. 1–13.

Yewdale, R., *Bohemond I, Prince of Antioch* (Princeton, 1917).

Yver, J., 'Autour de l'absence d'avouerie en Normandie', *BSAN*, liii (1957 for 1955–6), pp. 188–283.

Yver, J., 'Les châteaux-forts en Normandie jusqu'au milieu du XIIe siècle', *BSAN*, 53 (1955–6), pp. 28–115.

Unpublished Dissertations

Gathagan, Laura L., 'Embodying Power: Gender and Authority in the Queenship of Mathilda of Flanders', unpublished Ph.D. dissertation, City University of New York, 2002.

Paul, Nicholas, 'Crusade and Family Memory before 1225', unpublished Ph.D. dissertation, Cambridge University, 2005.

Strevett, N., 'The Anglo-Norman Aristocracy under Divided Lordship: A Social and Political Study', unpublished Ph.D. dissertation, University of Glasgow, 2005.

INDEX

Place-names in Normandy are followed by *département*, those in England are followed by county.

Printed and bound by CPI Group (UK) Ltd, Croydon, CR0 4YY

13/04/2025

14656520-0004